12/29/14

13th Edition

Every Landlord's Legal Guide

Marcia Stewart, Ralph Warner J.D.,
& Attorney Janet Portman

NOLO
LAW for ALL

THIRTEENTH EDITION	MAY 2016
Cover & Book Design	TERRI HEARSH
Proofreading	IRENE BARNARD
Index	UNGER INDEXING
Printing	BANG PRINTING

Names: Stewart, Marcia, author. | Warner, Ralph E., author. | Portman, Janet, author.

Title: Every landlord's legal guide / Marcia Stewart, Ralph Warner, Janet Portman.

Description: Thirteenth edition. | Berkeley, CA : Nolo, 2016. | Includes bibliographical references and index.

Identifiers: LCCN 2015041879| ISBN 9781413322835 (pbk.) | ISBN 9781413322842 (epub ebook)

Subjects: LCSH: Landlord and tenant--United States--Popular works. | Landlords--United States--Handbooks, manuals, etc.

Classification: LCC KF590.Z9 S74 2016 | DDC 346.7304/34--dc23

LC record available at http://lccn.loc.gov/2015041879

This book covers only United States law, unless it specifically states otherwise.

Please note

We believe accurate, plain-English legal information should help you solve many of your own legal problems. But this text is not a substitute for personalized advice from a knowledgeable lawyer. If you want the help of a trained professional—and we'll always point out situations in which we think that's a good idea—consult an attorney licensed to practice in your state.

About the Authors

Marcia Stewart is the coauthor of *Every Tenant's Legal Guide, Renters' Rights, Leases & Rental Agreements, First-Time Landlord,* and *Nolo's Essential Guide to Buying Your First Home.* Marcia received a Master's degree in Public Policy from the University of California at Berkeley.

Ralph Warner is Nolo's Cofounder. He has dedicated his professional life to making plain-English legal information accessible and affordable to all Americans. Ralph is the author of a number of self-help law titles, including *Everybody's Guide to Small Claims Court, Save Your Small Business, Get a Life,* and many landlord-tenant and real estate publications. He holds a law degree from Boalt Hall School of Law at the University of California at Berkeley.

Janet Portman, an attorney and Nolo's Executive Editor, received undergraduate and graduate degrees from Stanford and a law degree from Santa Clara University. She is an expert on landlord-tenant law and the coauthor of *Every Tenant's Legal Guide, Every Landlord's Guide to Finding Great Tenants, First-Time Landlord, Renters' Rights, The California Landlord's Law Book: Rights and Responsibilities, California Tenant's Rights, Leases & Rental Agreements,* and *Negotiate the Best Lease for Your Business.* As a practicing attorney, she specialized in criminal defense before joining Nolo.

Table of Contents

16 Problems With Tenants: How to Resolve Disputes Without a Lawyer 351

17 Late Rent, Terminations, and Evictions 363

18 Lawyers and Legal Research 379

Appendixes

Introduction: Your Landlord Companion

Whether you own one rental property or a hundred, you want to run a profitable business, protect your investment, and avoid legal hassles. Your success depends heavily on knowing and complying with dozens of state, federal, and local laws that affect you. Fortunately, you don't need a law degree—just this book.

We'll take you step by step through all your important tasks, from accepting rental applications to returning security deposits when a tenant moves out and everything between, including preparing a lease, handling repairs, and dealing with tenants who pay rent late, make too much noise, or cause other problems. We cover straightforward procedures (such as how to legally reject a prospect) as well as more tricky situations (like what to do when a tenant threatens to withhold rent until you make certain repairs). Here's how we can help you:

State-specific legal info. This book includes all kinds of important state-specific information. Want to know about security deposit laws in your state? You can look up the deposit limit, find out whether you need to keep the deposit in a separate account or pay interest on it, and whether you're exempt from the rules based on the number of rental properties you own.

Legal forms and letters. This book includes dozens of forms, letters, notices, checklists, and agreements. From the most complicated (your lease or rental agreement) to the simplest (a time estimate for repair), we've got you covered, including forms for the collection, itemization, and return of deposits, and a landlord-tenant checklist to record the condition of the rental unit at the start and end of the tenancy. Each form is easy to customize and has complete instructions. There are filled-in samples in the text, and you'll find the forms on the companion page for this book on the Nolo website (see below for details).

Getting Expert Help

Throughout this book, we'll alert you to situations in which it's wise to get expert help beyond this book, including:

- **Preparing eviction papers.** We explain how to terminate a tenancy, but if you need to pursue an eviction lawsuit, get more help. Evictions are governed by very specific state and local laws and procedures.
- **Rentals in mobile home parks and marinas.** In most states, completely different sets of laws govern these rentals.
- **Renting out a condo or town house.** Many owners will find this book helpful, but additional rules will apply to your rental situation, courtesy of your homeowners' association's CC&Rs (covenants, conditions, and restrictions). Sometimes CC&Rs clash with, or may go beyond, federal, state, or local laws, and it's often difficult to predict, let alone determine, which approach a court would uphold.
- **Live-work units.** If you're renting out these units, you'll find this book helpful, but be aware that zoning regulations may apply.
- **Section 8 housing.** If you participate in the Section 8 rent-assistance program, you'll find most of the day-to-day recommendations of this book usable, but you'll need to use the lease addendum supplied by the housing authority that administers the program.

Time-tested and timely. This book, which first appeared in 1996, has been updated many times since to keep up with the constantly changing world of residential landlording. Ours is the only book on the shelf that combines current, comprehensive legal information and practical advice usable by landlords in every state. It now covers emerging issues such as how to restrict tenant use of short-term rental services such as Airbnb. And in case important laws change during the life of this edition, you'll find updates on this book's companion page (described below).

Our approach to running a residential rental business rests on recognizing that tenants are your best asset and the key element in your financial success. Our approach will guard your legal and financial interests and, at the same time, make your customers—your tenants—feel that your practices are fair and reasonable.

In a nutshell: Choose tenants carefully; keep good tenants happy; teach mediocre tenants how to improve; get rid of bad tenants by applying policies that are strict, fair, and legal; and back up everything with good records and paperwork. Follow that simple philosophy, and you can run a business that's both satisfying and profitable.

Get Updates, Forms, and More on This Book's Companion Page on Nolo.com

You can download any of the forms and worksheets in this book at:

www.nolo.com/back-of-book/ELLI.html

When there are important changes to the information in this book, we'll post updates on this same dedicated page (what we call the book's companion page). You'll find other useful information on this page, too, such as blogs, podcasts, and videos. See Appendix A for a list of forms available on Nolo.com.

Other Helpful Nolo Books and Resources for Landlords

Nolo publishes a comprehensive library of books for landlords and property managers. Besides *Every Landlord's Legal Guide,* Nolo offers:

- *Every Landlord's Guide to Finding Great Tenants,* by Janet Portman. Focuses solely on advertising and showing your rental, evaluating prospects, and choosing and rejecting tenants, with over 40 forms, including a credit report evaluation, marketing worksheets, and departing tenant's questionnaire. Especially useful for landlords who own multiunit properties or have a lot of tenant turnover.

- *Every Landlord's Guide to Managing Property,* by Michael Boyer. Provides practical and legal compliance advice for small-time landlords who manage property and tenants on the side (while holding down a day job). Includes do-it-yourself advice on handling day-to-day issues, such as nitty-gritty maintenance and conflicts with tenants regarding late rent, pets, and unauthorized occupants. Explains how to manage and grow a successful rental property business with minimal hassle and cost.

- *Every Landlord's Tax Deduction Guide,* by Stephen Fishman. Includes all the information you need to take advantage of tax deductions and write-offs available to landlords, such as depreciation, legal services, travel, and insurance. Includes instructions on filling out Schedule E.

- *Leases & Rental Agreements,* by Marcia Stewart, Ralph Warner, and Janet Portman. Includes a lease, rental agreement, and several other basic forms. If you own *Every Landlord's Legal Guide,* you don't need *Leases and Rental Agreements.*

- *The California Landlord's Law Book: Rights & Responsibilities,* by David Brown, Janet Portman, and Ralph Warner, and *The California Landlord's Law Book: Evictions,* by David Brown. Contain all the information California landlords need to run their business and handle an eviction in court by themselves. *Every Landlord's Legal Guide* covers residential landlord-tenant law in all 50 states, including California, but these books provide more details, including rent control rules in California cities and step-by-step instructions on how to file and handle an eviction lawsuit.

- *First-Time Landlord: Your Guide to Renting Out a Single-Family Home,* by Janet Portman, Ilona Bray, and Marcia Stewart. Covers the basics that first-time or "accidental" landlords need to rent and manage a single-family home or condo, including how to determine if a property will turn a profit, renting out a room in a house when owners are still living in it, and how to use a lease-option-to-buy contract.

You can order these books from Nolo's website (www.nolo.com) or by phone (800-728-3555). You can also find Nolo books at public libraries and bookstores.

In addition to these books, Nolo offers many single-copy interactive online forms of interest to landlords, such as state-specific leases and rental agreements.

The Nolo website includes other useful resources, including legal updates on this book's companion page (described above) and a legal research section to help you find federal, state, and local laws that affect your rental property. Be sure to check out the Landlords section of Nolo.com for a wide variety of articles of interest to landlords, including state eviction rules.

Screening Tenants: Your Most Important Decision

FORMS IN THIS CHAPTER

Chapter 1 includes instructions for and samples of the following forms:

- Rental Application
- Consent to Contact References and Perform Credit Check
- Tenant References
- Notice of Denial Based on Credit Report or Other Information
- Notice of Conditional Acceptance Based on Credit Report or Other Information
- Receipt and Holding Deposit Agreement

The Nolo website includes downloadable copies of these forms. See Appendix B for the link to the forms in this book.

Choosing tenants is the most important decision any landlord makes, and to do it well you need a reliable system. Follow the steps in this chapter to maximize your chances of selecting tenants who will pay their rent on time, keep their units in good condition, and not cause you any legal or practical problems later.

How Landlord's Associations Can Help

All the rules and procedures for choosing tenants may seem overwhelming the first time around. This chapter provides all the legal and practical information and forms you need to do the job right. You can also get a lot of advice from talking with other landlords. You may want to check out local or state rental property associations, which range from small, volunteer-run groups of landlords to substantial organizations with paid staff and lobbyists, that offer a wide variety of support and services to their members. Here are some services that may be available from your landlords' association:

- legal information and updates through newsletters, publications, seminars, and other means
- tenant screening and credit check services
- training and practical advice on compliance with legal responsibilities, and
- a place to meet other rental property owners and exchange information and ideas.

If you can't find an association of rental property owners in your phone book, ask other landlords for references. You can also contact the National Apartment Association (NAA), a national organization whose members include many individual state associations (www.naahq.org), and the National Multifamily Housing Council (www.nmhc.org), which provides useful networking opportunities and research.

If you're a first-time landlord renting out a single-family home or condo, check out the Nolo book *First-Time Landlord*, by Janet Portman, Marcia Stewart, and Ilona Bray.

RELATED TOPIC

Before you advertise your property for rent, make a number of basic decisions—including how much rent to charge, whether to offer a fixed-term lease or a month-to-month rental agreement, how many tenants can occupy each rental unit, how big a security deposit to require, and whether you'll allow pets. Making these important decisions should dovetail with writing your lease or rental agreement (see Chapter 2.)

Avoiding Fair Housing Complaints and Lawsuits

Federal and state antidiscrimination laws limit what you can say and do in the tenant selection process. Because the topic of discrimination is so important we devote a whole chapter to it later in the book (Chapter 5), including legal reasons for refusing to rent to a tenant and how to avoid discrimination in your tenant selection process. You should read Chapter 5 before you run an ad or interview prospective tenants. For now, keep in mind four important points:

1. **You are legally free to choose among prospective tenants as long as your decisions are based on legitimate business criteria.** You are entitled to reject applicants with bad credit histories, income that you reasonably regard as insufficient to pay the rent, or past behavior—such as property damage or consistent late rent payments—that makes someone a bad risk. A valid occupancy limit that is clearly tied to health and safety or legitimate business needs can also be a legal basis for refusing tenants. It goes without saying that you may legally refuse to rent to someone who can't come up with the security deposit or meet some other condition of the tenancy.

2. **Fair housing laws specify clearly illegal reasons to refuse to rent to a tenant.** Federal law prohibits discrimination on the basis of race, religion, national origin, gender, age, familial status, or physical or mental disability (including recovering alcoholics and people with a past drug addiction). Many states and cities also prohibit discrimination based on marital status or sexual orientation.

3. **Anybody who deals with prospective tenants must follow fair housing laws.** This includes owners, landlords, managers, and real estate brokers, and all of their employees. As the property owner, you may be held legally responsible for your employees' discriminatory statements or conduct, including sexual harassment. "Your Liability for a Manager's Acts," in Chapter 6, explains how to protect yourself from your employee's illegal acts.

4. **Consistency is crucial when dealing with prospective tenants.** If you don't treat all tenants more or less equally—for example, if you arbitrarily set tougher standards for renting to a member of a racial minority—you are violating federal laws and opening yourself up to lawsuits.

How to Advertise Rental Property

You can advertise rental property in many ways:

- posting a notice on Craigslist (see "Craigslist and Online Apartment Listing Services," below, for details)
- putting an "Apartment for Rent" sign in front of the building or in one of the windows
- taking out ads in a local newspaper
- posting flyers on neighborhood bulletin boards, such as the local laundromat or coffee shop
- listing with a local real estate broker that handles rentals
- hiring a property management company that will advertise your rentals as part of the management fee
- posting a notice with a university, alumni, or corporate housing office, or
- buying ads in apartment rental guides or magazines.

The kind of advertising that will work best depends on a number of factors, including the characteristics of the particular property (such as rent, size, amenities), its location, your budget, and whether you are in a hurry to rent. Many smaller landlords find that instead of advertising widely and having to screen many potential tenants in an effort to sort the good from the bad, it makes better sense to market their rentals through word of mouth—telling friends, colleagues, neighbors, and current tenants, and by posting on Facebook and other social media.

Craigslist and Online Apartment Listing Services

Dozens of online services now make it easy to reach potential tenants, whether they already live in your community or are moving from out of state.

Craigslist and other online community posting boards allow you to list your rentals at no or low charge and are a good place to start. Craigslist, the most established community board, has local sites for every major metropolitan area. Check out www.craigslist.org for details.

National apartment listing services are also available, with the largest ones representing millions of apartment units in the United States. Some of the most established are:

- www.apartments.com
- www.rentals.com
- www.rent.com
- www.apartmentsearch.com
- www.apartmentguide.com,
- www.forrent.com, and
- www.zumper.com.

These national sites offer a wide range of services, from simple text-only ads that provide basic information on your rental (such as the number of bedrooms) to full-scale virtual tours and floor plans of the rental property. Services typically include mobile apps, too. Prices vary widely depending on the type of ad, how long you want it to run, and any services you purchase (some websites provide tenant-screening services).

Before you use any online apartment rental service, make sure it's reputable. Find out how long the company has been in business and how they handle problems with apartment listings. Check for any consumer complaints, and avoid paying any hefty fee without thoroughly checking out a company and its services.

To stay out of legal hot water when you advertise, just follow these simple rules.

Describe the rental unit accurately. As a practical matter, you should avoid abbreviations and real estate jargon in your ad. Include basic details, such as:

- rent and deposit
- size—particularly number of bedrooms and baths
- location—either the general neighborhood or street address
- move-in date and term—lease or month-to-month rental agreement
- special features—such as fenced-in yard, view, washer/dryer, fireplace, remodeled kitchen, furnished, garage parking, doorman, hardwood floors, or wall-to-wall carpeting
- pets (whether you allow or not and any restrictions, such as dog breeds your insurance prohibits)
- your nonparticipation in the Section 8 program (assuming you have the choice—see Chapter 5 for details)
- phone number, website, and/or email for more details (unless you're going to show the unit only at an open house and don't want to take calls), and
- date and time of any open house.

If you have any important rules (legal and non-discriminatory), such as no smoking, put them in your ad. Letting prospective tenants know about your important policies can save you or your manager from talking to a lot of unsuitable people. For example, your ad might say you require credit checks in order to discourage applicants who have a history of paying rent late.

Be sure your ad can't be construed as discriminatory. The best way to do this is to focus only on the rental property—not on any particular type of tenant. Specifically, ads should never mention sex, race, religion, disability, or age (unless yours is really legally recognized senior citizens housing). And ads should never imply through words, photographs, or illustrations that you prefer to rent to people because of their age, sex, or race. For

example, an ad in a church newsletter that contains a drawing of a recognizably white (or black or Asian) couple with no children might open you to an accusation of discrimination based on race, age, and familial status (prohibiting children).

Quote an honest price in your ad. If a tenant who is otherwise acceptable (has a good credit history and impeccable references and meets all the criteria explained below) shows up promptly and agrees to all the terms set out in your ad, you may violate false advertising laws if you arbitrarily raise the price. This doesn't mean you are always legally required to rent at your advertised price, however. If a tenant asks for more services or different lease terms that you feel require more rent, it's fine to bargain and raise your price, as long as your proposed increase doesn't violate local rent control laws.

Don't advertise something you don't have. Some large landlords, management companies, and rental services have advertised units that weren't really available in order to produce a large number of prospective tenants who could then be directed to higher-priced or inferior units. Such bait-and-switch advertising is clearly illegal under consumer fraud laws, and many property owners have been prosecuted for such practices. So if you advertise a sunny two-bedroom apartment next to a rose garden for $800 a month, make sure that the second bedroom isn't a closet, the rose garden isn't a beetle-infested bush, and the $800 isn't the first week's rent.

Keep in mind that even if you aren't prosecuted for breaking fraud laws, your advertising promises can still come back to haunt you. A tenant who is robbed or attacked in what you advertised as a "high-security building" may sue you for medical bills, lost earnings, and pain and suffering.

Renting Property That's Still Occupied

Often, you can wait until the old tenant moves out to show a rental unit to prospective tenants. This gives you the chance to refurbish the unit and avoids problems such as promising the place to a new tenant, only to have the existing tenant not move out on time or leave the place a mess.

To eliminate any gap in rent, however, you may want to show a rental unit while its current tenants are still there. This can create a conflict; in most states, you have a right to show the still-occupied property to prospective tenants, but your current tenants are still entitled to their privacy.

To minimize disturbing your current tenant, follow these guidelines:

- Before implementing your plans to find a new tenant, discuss them with the outgoing tenant, so you can be as accommodating as possible.
- Give the current tenant as much notice as possible before entering and showing a rental unit to prospective tenants. State law usually requires at least one or two days. (See Chapter 13 for details.)
- Try to limit the number of times you show the unit in a given week, and make sure your current tenant agrees to any evening and weekend visits.
- Consider reducing the rent slightly for the existing tenant if showing the unit really will be an imposition.
- If possible, avoid putting a sign on the rental property itself, since this almost guarantees that your existing tenant will be bothered by strangers. Or, if you can't avoid putting up a sign, make sure any sign clearly warns against disturbing the occupant and includes a telephone number for information. Something on the order of "For Rent: Shown by Appointment Only. Call 555-1700. DO NOT DISTURB OCCUPANTS" should work fine.

If, despite your best efforts to protect their privacy, the current tenants are uncooperative or hostile, wait until they leave before showing the unit. Also, if the current tenants are complete slobs or have damaged the place, you'll be far better off to apply paint and elbow grease before trying to rerent it.

Dealing With Prospective Tenants and Accepting Rental Applications

It's good business, as well as a sound way to protect yourself from future legal problems, to carefully screen prospective tenants.

Tell Prospective Tenants Your Basic Requirements and Rules

Whether prospective tenants call about the rental, or just show up at an open house, it's best to describe all your general requirements—rent, deposits, pet policy, move-in date, maximum number of occupants, and the like—and any special rules and regulations up front. This helps you avoid wasting time showing the unit to someone who simply can't qualify—for example, someone who can't come up with the security deposit. Describing your general requirements and rules up front can also help avoid charges of discrimination, which can occur when a member of a racial minority or a single parent is told key facts so late in the process that she jumps to the conclusion that you've made up new requirements just to keep her out.

Also be sure to tell prospective tenants about the kind of personal information they'll be expected to supply on an application, including phone numbers of previous landlords and credit and employment references.

CAUTION

Show the property to and accept applications from everyone who's interested. Even if, after talking to someone on the phone, you doubt that a particular tenant can qualify, it's best to politely take all applications. Refusing to take an application may unnecessarily anger a prospective tenant, and may make the applicant more likely to look into the possibility of filing a discrimination complaint. And discriminating against someone simply because you don't like the sound of his or her voice on the phone (called linguistic profiling) is also illegal and may result in a discrimination claim. Show the property to and accept applications from anyone who's interested and make decisions about who will rent the property later. Be sure to keep copies of all applications. (See discussion of record keeping below.)

Getting a Unit Ready for Prospective Tenants

It goes without saying that a clean rental unit in good repair will rent more easily than a rundown hovel. And, in the long run, it pays to keep your rental competitive. Before showing a rental unit, make sure the basics are covered:

- Clean all rooms and furnishings, floors, walls, and ceilings—it's especially important that the bathroom and kitchen are spotless.
- Remove all clutter from closets, cupboards, and surfaces.
- Take care of any insect or rodent infestations.
- Make sure that the appliances and fixtures work. Repair leaky faucets and frayed cords, replace burnt-out lights, and check the unit for anything that might cause injury or violate health and safety codes. (Chapter 9 discusses state and local health and safety laws.)
- Cut the grass, trim shrubbery, and remove all trash and debris on the grounds.
- Update old fixtures and appliances, and repaint the walls and replace the carpets if necessary.

Nolo's *Every Landlord's Guide to Managing Property* includes extensive advice on preparing your rental units for new tenants, including detailed cleaning, painting, and repair routines, how to get rid of pet odors, and other specific turnaround tasks.

If the previous tenant left the place in good shape, you may not need to do much cleaning before showing it to prospective tenants. To make this more likely, be sure to send outgoing tenants a move-out letter describing your specific cleaning requirements and conditions for returning the tenant's security deposit. (Chapter 15 discusses move-out letters.)

Ask Interested Tenants to Complete a Rental Application

To avoid legal problems and choose the best tenant, ask all prospective tenants to fill out a written rental application that includes information on the applicant's employment, income, and credit; Social Security and driver's license numbers or other identifying information; past evictions or bankruptcies; and references.

A sample Rental Application is shown below and the Nolo website includes a downloadable copy. See Appendix B for the link to the forms in this book.

Before giving prospective tenants a Rental Application, complete the box at the top, filling in the property address, rental term, first month's rent, and any deposit or credit check fee tenants must pay before moving in. Here are some basic rules for accepting rental applications:

Give an application to all adult applicants. Each prospective tenant—everyone age 18 or older who wants to live in your rental property—should completely fill out a written application. This is true whether you're renting to a married couple or to unrelated roommates, a complete stranger, or the cousin of your current tenant.

Insist on a completed application. Always make sure that prospective tenants complete the entire Rental Application, including Social Security number (SSN) or Individual Taxpayer Identification Number (ITIN), explained below, driver's license number, or other identifying information (such as a passport number); current employment; and emergency contacts. You may need this information later to track down a tenant who skips town leaving unpaid rent or abandoned property. Also, you may need the Social Security number or other identifying information, such as a passport, to request an applicant's credit report.

> **CAUTION**
> **Don't ask for an applicant's date of birth.** This rental application does not ask applicants for their dates of birth (DOB). Many fair housing experts believe that doing so is risky, should a disappointed applicant attempt to challenge your rejection as an instance of age discrimination—having the date on the application at least establishes that you knew of the applicant's age. Some landlords still ask for the DOB, responding to credit reporting companies' requests for this information. You should be able to order a credit report and a screening report using the applicant's Social Security number; if vendors balk, you may want to ask for the DOB.

Rental Application

Separate application required from each applicant age 18 or older.

Date and time received by landlord _____

Credit check fee __$38_____ Received _____

THIS SECTION TO BE COMPLETED BY LANDLORD

Address of Property to Be Rented: __178 West 81st St., Apt. 4F_____

Rental Term: ☐ month-to-month ☑ lease from __March 1, 20xx__ to __February 28, 20xx__

Amounts Due Prior to Occupancy

First month's rent .... $ __3,000__

Security deposit .... $ __3,000__

Other (specify): __Broker's fee_____ $ __3,000__

TOTAL... $ __9,000__

Applicant

Full Name—include all names you use(d): __Hannah Silver_____

Home Phone: __609-555-3789__ Work Phone: __609-555-4567__ Cell Phone: __609-987-6543__

Email: __hannah@coldmail.com_____ Fax*:_____

Social Security Number: __123-00-4567__ Driver's License Number/State: __D123456/New Jersey__

Other Identifying Information: _____

Vehicle Make: __Toyota_____ Model: __Corolla__ Color: __White__ Year: __2012__

License Plate Number/State: __NJ1234567/New Jersey_____

Additional Occupants

List everyone, including minor children, who will live with you:

Full Name	Relationship to Applicant
Dennis Olson	Husband

Rental History

FIRST-TIME RENTERS: ATTACH A DESCRIPTION OF YOUR HOUSING SITUATION FOR THE PAST FIVE YEARS.

Current Address: __39 Maple St., Princeton, NJ 08540_____

Dates Lived at Address: __May 2008-date_____ Rent $ __2,000__ Security Deposit $ __4,000__

Landlord/Manager: __Jane Tucker_____ Landlord/Manager's Phone: __609-555-7523__

Reason for Leaving: __New job in NYC_____

* By providing this fax number I agree to receive facsimile advertisements from the landlord or management company.

Previous Address: _1215 Middlebrook Lane, Princeton, NJ 08540_

Dates Lived at Address: _June 2003-May 2008_ Rent $ _1,800_ Security Deposit $ _1,000_

Landlord/Manager: _Ed Palermo_ Landlord/Manager's Phone: _609-555-3711_

Reason for Leaving: _Better apartment_

Previous Address: _____

Dates Lived at Address: _____ Rent $ _____ Security Deposit $ _____

Landlord/Manager: _____ Landlord/Manager's Phone: _____

Reason for Leaving: _____

Employment History

SELF-EMPLOYED APPLICANTS: ATTACH TAX RETURNS FOR THE PAST TWO YEARS

Name and Address of Current Employer: _Argonworks, 54 Nassau St., Princeton, NJ_

_____ Phone: _609-555-2333_

Name of Supervisor: _Tom Schmidt_ Supervisor's Phone: _609-555-2333_

Dates Employed at This Job: _2000 - date_ Position or Title: _Marketing Director_

Name and Address of Previous Employer: _Princeton Times_

13 Junction Rd., Princeton, NJ Phone: _609-555-1111_

Name of Supervisor: _Dory Krossber_ Supervisor's Phone: _609-555-2366_

Dates Employed at This Job: _June 1996 - Feb. 2000_ Position or Title: _Marketing Associate_

ATTACH PAY STUBS FOR THE PAST TWO YEARS, FROM THIS EMPLOYER OR PRIOR EMPLOYERS.

Income

1. Your gross monthly employment income (before deductions): $ _8,000_
2. Average monthly amounts of other income (specify sources): $ _____
   Note: This does not include my husband's income. $ _____
   See his application. $ _____

TOTAL: $ _8,000_

Bank/Financial Accounts

	Account Number	Bank/Institution	Branch
Savings Account:	1222345	N.J. Federal	Trenton, NJ
Checking Account:	789101	Princeton S&L	Princeton, NJ
Money Market or Similar Account:	234789	City Bank	Princeton, NJ

Credit Card Accounts

Major Credit Card: ☑VISA ☐MC ☐Discover Card ☐Am Ex ☐Other: _____

Issuer: _City Bank_____ Account No. _1234 5555 6666 7777_

Balance $_1,000_____ Average Monthly Payment: $ _1,000_____

Major Credit Card: ☐VISA ☐MC ☐Discover Card ☐Am Ex ☑Other: _Dept. Store_

Issuer: _City Bank_____ Account No. _2345 0000 9999 8888_

Balance $ _2,000_____ Average Monthly Payment: $ _500_____

Loans

Type of Loan (mortgage, car, student loan, etc.)	Name of Creditor	Account Number	Amount Owed	Monthly Payment

Other Major Obligations

Type	Payee		Amount Owed	Monthly Payment

Miscellaneous

Describe the number and type of pets you want to have in the rental property: _None now, but we_ _might want to get a cat some time_

Describe water-filled furniture you want to have in the rental property: _None_____

Do you smoke?   ☐ yes ☑ no

Have you ever:

Filed for bankruptcy?	☐yes ☑no	How many times _____
Been sued?	☐yes ☑no	How many times _____
Sued someone else?	☐yes ☑no	How many times _____
Been evicted?	☐yes ☑no	How many times _____
Been convicted of a crime?	☐yes ☑no	How many times _____

Explain any "yes" listed above: _____

_____

_____

_____

_____

References and Emergency Contact

Personal Reference: _Joan Stanley_ Relationship: _Friend, coworker_

Address: _785 Spruce St., Princeton, NJ 08540_

_____ Phone: _609-555-4578_

Personal Reference: _Marnie Swatt_ Relationship: _Friend_

Address: _82 East 59th St., #12B, NYC_

_____ Phone: _212-555-8765_

Contact in Emergency: _Connie & Martin Silver_ Relationship: _Parents_

Address: _7852 Pierce St., Somerset, NJ 08321_

_____ Phone: _609-555-7878_

Source

Where did you learn of this vacancy? _Ryan Cowell, Broker_

I certify that all the information given above is true and correct and understand that my lease or rental agreement may be terminated if I have made any material false or incomplete statements in this application. I authorize verification of the information provided in this application from my credit sources, credit bureaus, current and previous landlords and employers, and personal references. This permission will survive the expiration of my tenancy.

Hannah Silver _February 15, 20xx_
Applicant Date

Notes (Landlord/Manager): _____

_____

_____

_____

_____

_____

_____

_____

_____

_____

_____

_____

_____

_____

_____

_____

Consent to Contact References and Perform Credit Check

I authorize ___Jan Gold_____ to
obtain information about me from my credit sources, current and previous landlords, employers, and personal
references, to enable ___Jan Gold_____ to evaluate my rental application.

I give permission for the landlord or its agent to obtain a consumer report about me for the purpose of this
application, to ensure that I continue to meet the terms of the tenancy, for the collection and recovery of any
financial obligations relating to my tenancy, or for any other permissible purpose.

*Michael Clark*_____
Applicant signature

Michael Clark_____
Printed name

123 State Street, Chicago, Illinois_____
Address

312-555-9876_____
Phone Number

February 2, 20xx_____
Date

You may encounter an applicant who does not have an SSN (only citizens or immigrants authorized to work in the United States can obtain one). For example, someone with a student visa will not normally have an SSN. If you categorically refuse to rent to applicants without SSNs, and these applicants happen to be foreign students, you're courting a fair housing complaint.

Fortunately, nonimmigrant aliens (such as people lawfully in the U.S. who don't intend to stay here permanently, and even those who are here illegally) can obtain an alternate piece of identification that will suit your needs as well as an SSN. It's called an Individual Taxpayer Identification Number (ITIN), and is issued by the IRS to people who expect to pay taxes. Most people who are here long enough to apply for an apartment will also be earning income while in the U.S. and will therefore have an ITIN. Consumer reporting agencies and tenant screening companies can use an ITIN to find the information they need to effectively screen an applicant. On the Rental Application, use the line "Other Identifying Information" for an applicant's ITIN.

> **CAUTION**
> **Do not consider an ITIN number as proof of legal status in the U.S.** The IRS does not research the taxpayer's immigration status before handing out the number.

Check for a signature and consider getting a separate credit check authorization. Be sure all potential tenants sign the Rental Application, authorizing you to verify the information and references and to run a credit report. (Some employers and others require written authorization before they will talk to you.) You may also want to prepare a separate authorization, signed and dated by the applicant, so that you don't need to copy the entire application and email or fax it every time a bank or employer wants proof that the tenant authorized you to verify the information. A sample Consent to Contact References and Perform Credit Check is shown above, and the Nolo website includes a downloadable copy. See Appendix B for the link to the forms in this book.

When you talk to prospective tenants, stick to questions on the application. Avoid asking questions that may discriminate, specifically any inquiries as to the person's birthplace, age, religion, marital status or children, physical or mental condition, or arrests that did not result in conviction. (See Chapter 5 for details on antidiscrimination laws.)

Request Proof of Identity and Immigration Status

In these security-sensitive times, many landlords ask prospective tenants to show their driver's license or other photo identification as a way to verify that the applicant is using his real name.

Except in California (Cal. Civ. Code § 1940.3), and New York City (N.Y.C. Admin. Code § 8-107(5)(a)), you may also ask applicants for proof of identity and eligibility to work under U.S. immigration laws, such as a work permit, a U.S. passport, or a naturalization certificate. Do so using Form I-9 (*Employment Eligibility Verification*) from the U.S. Citizenship and Immigration Services, or USCIS (a bureau of the U.S. Department of Homeland Security). This form (and instructions for completing it) are available at www.uscis.gov/i-9, or by phone at 800-375-5283. Remember that an Individual Taxpayer Identification Number (ITIN) is not proof of legal status in the U.S.—it is merely a way for the IRS to identify a taxpayer.

Some people who have the right to be in the United States, such as some students and other temporary visa holders, may not have the right to work, which is the focus of the I-9 form. To confirm their right to be in the U.S., ask for their I-94 or other document describing their status.

Under federal fair housing laws, you may not selectively ask for such immigration information— that is, you must ask all prospective tenants, not just those you suspect may be in the country illegally. It is illegal to discriminate on the basis of national origin, although you may reject someone on the basis of immigration status, as discussed in Chapter 5.

RELATED TOPIC
For a related discussion on security issues regarding suspected terrorists, see "Cooperating With Law Enforcement in Terrorism Investigations" in Chapter 13.

CAUTION
Take your time to evaluate applications. Landlords are often faced with anxious, sometimes desperate people who need a place to live immediately. On a weekend or holiday, especially when it's impossible to check references, a prospective tenant may tell you a terrific hard-luck story as to why normal credit- and reference-checking rules should be ignored in their case and why they should be allowed to move right in. Don't believe it. People who have planned so poorly that they will literally have to sleep in the street if they don't rent your place that day are likely to come up with similar emergencies when it comes time to pay the rent. Taking the time to screen out bad tenants will save you lots of problems later on.

Never, never let anyone stay in your property on a temporary basis. Even if you haven't signed a rental agreement or accepted rent, you give someone the legally protected status of a tenant by giving that person a key or allowing him or her to move in as much as a toothbrush. Then, if the person won't leave voluntarily, you will have to file an eviction lawsuit. Chapter 8 discusses the legal rights of occupants you haven't approved.

Checking References, Credit History, and More

If an application looks good, your next step is to follow up thoroughly. The time and money you spend are some of the most cost-effective expenditures you'll ever make.

CAUTION
Be consistent in your screening. You risk a charge of illegal discrimination if you screen certain categories of applicants more stringently than others. Make it your policy, for example, to always require credit reports; don't just get a credit report for a single parent or older applicants.

Here are six steps of a very thorough screening process. You should always go through at least the first three to check out the applicant's previous landlords, income, and employment, and run a credit check.

Check With Previous Landlords and Other References

Always call current and previous landlords or managers for references—even if you have a written letter of reference from a previous landlord. (A prior landlord may be a better source of information than a current one, since a past landlord has no motive to give a falsely glowing report on a troublemaker.) Also call employers and personal references listed on the application.

To organize the information you gather from these calls, use the Tenant References form, which lists key questions to ask previous landlords, managers, and other references. A sample is shown below and the Nolo website includes a downloadable copy. See Appendix B for the link to the forms in this book.

TIP
Check out pets, too. If the prospective tenant has a dog or cat, be sure to ask previous landlords if the pet caused any damage or problems for other tenants or neighbors. It's also a good idea to meet the dog or cat, so you can make sure that it's well-groomed and well-behaved, before you make a final decision. You must, however, accommodate a mentally or physically disabled applicant whose pet serves as a support animal—no matter how mangy-looking the pet might be. For more information on renting to tenants with pets, see Chapter 2, Clause 14.

Be sure to take notes of all your conversations and keep them on file. You may note your reasons for refusing an individual on the Tenant References form—for example, negative credit information, insufficient income, or your inability to verify information. You'll want to record this information so that you can survive a fair housing challenge if a disappointed applicant files a discrimination complaint against you.

Tenant References

Name of Applicant: _____Michael Clark_____

Address of Rental Unit: _____123 State Street, Chicago, Illinois_____

Previous Landlord or Manager

Contact (name, property owner or manager, address of rental unit): _Kate Steiner, 345 Mercer St.,_

___Chicago, Illinois; (312) 555-5432_____

Date: _____February 4, 20xx_____

Questions

When did tenant rent from you (move-in and move-out dates)? ____December 2008 to date___

What was the monthly rent? _____$1,250_____   Did tenant pay rent on time?   ☐ Yes   ☑ No

If rent was not paid on time, did you have to give tenant a legal notice demanding the rent?   ☐ Yes   ☑ No

If rent was not paid on time, provide details _____He paid rent a week late a few times_____

_____

Did you give tenant notice of any lease violation for other than nonpayment of rent?   ☐ Yes   ☑ No

If you gave a lease violation notice, what was the outcome? _____

Was tenant considerate of neighbors—that is, no loud parties and fair, careful use of common areas?

_____Yes, considerate_____

_____

Did tenant have any pets?   ☑ Yes   ☐ No   If so, were there any problems? _He had a cat, contrary_

_____to rental agreement_____

Did tenant make any unreasonable demands or complaints?   ☐ Yes   ☑ No   If so, explain: _____

_____

Why did tenant leave? _____He wants to live someplace that allows pets_____

_____

Did tenant give the proper amount of notice before leaving?   ☑ Yes   ☐ No

Did tenant leave the place in good condition? Did you need to use the security deposit to cover damage?

_____No problems_____

Any particular problems you'd like to mention? _____No_____

_____

Would you rent to this person again? _____Yes, but without pets_____

_____

Other comments: _____

_____

_____

Employment Verification

Contact (name, company, position): ___Brett Field, Manager, Chicago Car Company___

Date: ___February 5, 20xx___ Salary: $ ___80,000 + bonus___

Dates of Employment: ___March 2007 to date___

Comments: ___No problems. Fine employee. Michael is responsible and hard-working.___

Personal Reference

Contact (name and relationship to applicant): ___Sandy Cameron, friend___

Date: ___February 5, 20xx___ How long have you known the applicant? ___Five years___

Would you recommend this person as a prospective tenant? ___Yes___

Comments: ___Michael is very neat and responsible. He's reliable and will be a great tenant.___

Credit and Financial Information

___Mostly fine—see attached credit report___

Notes, Including Reasons for Rejecting Applicant

___Applicant had a history of late rent payments and kept a cat, contrary to the rental agreement.___

Occasionally, you may encounter a former landlord who is unwilling to provide key information. This reluctance may have nothing to do with the prospective tenant, but instead reflects an exaggerated fear of lawsuits. Landlords fear that their negative remarks about former tenants can be disclosed to rejected applicants if they request it, though under federal law, these conversations need not be disclosed when the landlord or landlord's employee is the one doing the calling (see "Choosing—And Rejecting—an Applicant," below). Still, most landlords do not understand this fine point of law, and many will be reluctant to be candid. But if a former landlord seems hesitant to talk, an approach that often works is to try to keep the person on the line long enough to verify the dates of the applicant's tenancy. If you get minimal cooperation, you might say something like this: "I assume your reluctance to talk about Julie has to do with one or more negative things that occurred while she was your tenant." If the former landlord doesn't say anything, you have all the answer you need. If she says instead, "No, I don't talk about any former tenants—actually, Julie was fairly decent," you have broken the ice and can probably follow up with a few general questions.

Verify Income and Employment

Obviously, you want to make sure that all tenants have the income to pay the rent each month. Call the prospective tenant's employer to verify income and length of employment. Make notes on the Tenant References form, discussed above.

Before providing this information, some employers require written authorization from the employee. You will need to mail or fax them a signed copy of the release included at the bottom of the Rental Application form or the separate Consent to Contact References and Perform Credit Check form shown above. If for any reason you question the income information you get by telephone—for example, you suspect a buddy of the applicant is exaggerating on his behalf—

you may also ask applicants for copies of recent paycheck stubs.

It's also reasonable to require documentation of other sources of income, such as Social Security, disability, workers' compensation, public assistance, child support, or alimony. To evaluate the financial resources of a self-employed person or someone who's not employed, ask for copies of recent tax returns or bank statements.

TIP

How much income is enough? Think twice before renting to someone if the rent will take more than one-third of their income, especially if they have a lot of debts.

Obtain a Credit Report

Private credit reporting agencies collect and sell credit files and other information about consumers. Many landlords find it essential to check a prospective tenant's credit history with at least one credit reporting agency to see how responsible the person is managing money. Jot your findings down on the Tenant References form.

TIP

Get the tenant's consent to run a credit report. Because many people think that you must have their written consent before pulling a credit report to evaluate a prospective tenant, we have included it in our consent forms (at the end of the Rental Application and in the separate Consent to Contact References and Perform Credit Check form). But there's another reason for doing this: A written consent will help you if, later, when the applicant is a tenant (or an ex-tenant), you decide that you need an updated credit report. For example, you may want to consult a current report in order to help you decide whether to sue a tenant who has skipped out and owes rent. Without a broadly written consent, your use of a credit report at that time might be illegal (see the FTC "Long" Opinion Letter, July 7, 2000, available on www.ftc.gov).

California Law on Application Screening Fees and Credit Reports

California state law limits credit check or application screening fees you can charge prospective tenants and specifies what you must do when accepting these types of fees. (Cal. Civ. Code § 1950.6.) Here are key provisions of the law:

- You may charge a screening fee whose maximum is regulated by law (Cal. Civ. Code § 1950.6); up to $45.99 through 2015. To learn the current allowable charge, go to the city of Berkeley's Rent Stabilization website (www.ci.berkeley.ca.us) and type "tenant application screening fee" in the search box. You'll get a list of articles, one of which will give the current allowable fee for all of California. (The notification is contained in the Berkeley Municipal Code § 13.78.010, Notification of state law limitation on tenant screening fees.)
- This screening fee may be used for "actual out-of-pocket costs" of obtaining a credit report, plus "the reasonable value of time spent" by a landlord in obtaining a consumer credit report or checking personal references and background information on a rental applicant.
- If you use the screening fee to obtain the applicant's credit report, you must give the applicant a copy of the report upon his or her request.

- If you spend less (for the credit report and your time) than the screening fee you collected, you must refund the difference. If you never get a credit report or check references on an applicant, you must refund the entire screening fee.
- Unless the applicant agrees in writing, you may not charge a screening fee if no rental unit is available. However, if a unit will be available within a reasonable period of time, you may charge the fee without obtaining the applicant's written permission.
- You must provide an itemized receipt when you collect an application screening fee. A sample receipt is shown below.

Landlords in California should also be aware that consumers may place a "freeze" on their credit reports, preventing anyone but specified parties (such as law enforcement) from getting their credit report. (Cal. Civ. Code §§ 1785.11.2 and following.) However, consumers can arrange for certain persons—such as a landlord or management company—to access their report; or the freeze itself can be suspended for a specified period of time. If an applicant has placed a freeze on his or her credit report, you'll need access so that you can receive a copy of their report. An applicant who fails to lift a freeze will have an incomplete application, which is grounds for rejecting that application. (Cal. Civ. Code § 1785.11.2(h).)

Sample California Application Screening Fee Receipt

This will acknowledge receipt of the sum of $ _____ by _____

_____ [Property Owner/Manager] from _____

[Applicant] as part of his/her application for the rental property at _____

_____ [Rental Property Address].

As provided under California Civil Code Section 1950.6, here is an itemization of how this $ _____ screening fee will be used:

☐ Actual costs of obtaining Applicant's credit/screening report $_____

☐ Administrative costs of obtaining credit/screening report and checking Applicant's references and background information $_____

☐ Total screening fee charged $_____

_____   _____
Applicant   Date

_____   _____
Owner/Manager   Date

How to Get a Credit Report

A credit report contains a gold mine of information for a prospective landlord. You can find out, for example, if a particular person has ever filed for bankruptcy or has been:

- late or delinquent in paying rent or bills, including student or car loans
- convicted of a crime, or, in many states, even arrested
- evicted (your legal right to get information on evictions, however, may vary among states)
- involved in another type of lawsuit such as a personal injury claim, or
- financially active enough to establish a credit history.

Depending on the type of report you order (the offerings vary according to the agency you deal with), you may also get an applicant's credit score, the most popular being the "FICO" score. This number, ranging from 300 to 850, purports to indicate the risk that an individual will default on payments. High credit scores indicate less risk. Generally, any score above 650 is considered a medium risk or less. Don't put too much value in a high credit score, since this number does not reflect the many other good-tenant characteristics (such as ability to get along with neighbors and take good care of your property) that are very important.

Information covers the past seven to ten years. To run a credit check, you'll need a prospective tenant's name, address, and Social Security number or ITIN (Individual Taxpayer Identification Number.) Three credit bureaus have cornered the market on credit reports:

- Equifax (www.equifax.com)
- TransUnion (www.transunion.com), and
- Experian (www.experian.com).

You cannot order a credit report directly from the big three bureaus. Instead, you'll need to work through a credit reporting agency or tenant screening service (type "tenant screening" into your browser's search box). Look for a company that operates in your area, has been in business for a while, and provides you with a sample report that's clear and informative. You can also find tenant screening companies in the yellow pages under "Credit Reporting Agencies." Your state or local apartment association may also offer credit reporting services. With credit reporting agencies, you can often obtain a credit report the same day it's requested. Fees depend on how many reports you order each month.

If you do not rent to someone because of negative information in a credit report, or you charge someone a higher rent because of such information, you must give the prospective tenant the name and address of the agency that reported the negative information. This is a requirement of the federal Fair Credit Reporting Act. (15 U.S. Code §§ 1681 and following.) You must also tell the person that he has a right to obtain a copy of the file from the agency that reported the negative information, by requesting it within 60 days of being told that your rejection was based on the individual's credit report.

Tenants who are applying for more than one rental are understandably dismayed at the prospect of paying each landlord to pull the same credit report. They may obtain their own report, make copies, and ask you to accept their copy. Federal law does not require you to accept an applicant's copy—that is, you may require applicants to pay a credit check fee for you to run a new report. Wisconsin is an exception: State law in Wisconsin forbids landlords from charging for a credit report if, before the landlord asks for a report, the applicant offers one from a consumer reporting agency and the report is less than 30 days old. (Wis. Adm. Code ATCP 134.05(4)(b).)

Credit Check Fees

It's legal in most states to charge prospective tenants a fee for the cost of the credit report itself and your time and trouble. Any credit check fee should be reasonably related to the cost of the credit check —$30 to $50 is common. California sets a maximum screening fee and requires landlords to provide an itemized receipt when accepting a credit check fee. See "California Law on Application Screening Fees and Credit Reports," above, for details.

Some landlords don't charge credit check fees, preferring to absorb the cost as they would any other cost of business. For low-end units, charging an extra fee can be a barrier to getting tenants in the first place, and a tenant who pays such a fee but is later rejected is likely to be annoyed and possibly more apt to try to concoct a discriminatory reason for the denial.

The Rental Application form in this book informs prospective tenants of your credit check fee. Be sure prospective tenants know the purpose of a credit check fee and understand that this fee is not a holding deposit and does not guarantee the rental unit. (We discuss holding deposits below.)

Also, if you expect a large number of applicants, you'd be wise not to accept fees from everyone. Instead, read over the applications first and do a credit check only on those who are genuine contenders (for example, exclude and reject those whose income doesn't reach your minimum rent-to-income ratio). That way, you won't waste your time (and prospective tenants' money) collecting fees from unqualified applicants.

CAUTION
It is illegal to charge a credit check fee if you do not use it for the stated purpose and pocket it instead. Return any credit check fees you don't use for that purpose.

Investigative or Background Reports

Some credit reporting companies and "tenant screening companies" also gather and sell background reports about a person's character, general reputation, personal characteristics, or mode of living. If you order a background check on a prospective tenant, it will be considered an "investigative consumer report" under federal law (the Fair Credit Reporting Act, 15 U.S. Code §§ 1681 and following, as amended by the Fair and Accurate Credit Transactions Act of 2003) and

you must tell the applicant, within three days of requesting the report, that the report may be made and that it will concern his character, reputation, personal characteristics, and criminal history. You must also tell the applicant that more information about the nature and scope of the report will be provided upon request; and, if asked, you must provide this information within five days.

If you turn down the applicant based wholly or in part on information in the report, you must tell the applicant that the application was denied based on information in the report, and give the applicant the credit or tenant screening agency's name and address.

What You're Looking For

In general, be leery of applicants with lots of debts —so that their monthly payments plus the rent obligation exceed 40% of their income. Also, look at the person's bill-paying habits, and, of course, pay attention to lawsuits and evictions.

Sometimes, your only choice is to rent to someone with poor or fair credit. If that's your situation, you might have the following requirements:

- good references from previous landlords and employers
- a creditworthy cosigner to cosign the lease (Chapter 2 includes a cosigner agreement)
- a good-sized deposit, as much as you can collect under state law (see Chapter 4), and
- proof of steps taken to improve credit—for example, enrollment in a debt counseling group.

If the person has no credit history—for example, a student or recent graduate—you may reject them or consider requiring a cosigner before agreeing to rent to them.

CAUTION
Handle credit reports carefully. Federal law requires you to keep only needed information, and to discard the rest. See "How to Handle Credit Reports," in Chapter 7 for precise information.

Verify Bank Account Information

If an individual's credit history raises questions about financial stability, you may want to double-check the bank accounts listed on the rental application. If so, you'll probably need an authorization form such as the one included at the bottom of the Rental Application, or the separate Consent to Contact References and Perform Credit Check (discussed above). Banks differ as to the type of information they will provide over the phone. Generally, banks will at most only confirm that an individual has an account there and that it is in good standing.

> **CAUTION**
> **Be wary of an applicant who has no checking or savings account.** Tenants who offer to pay cash or with a money order should be viewed with extreme caution. Perhaps the individual bounced so many checks that the bank dropped the account or the income comes from an illegitimate source—such as drug dealing.

Visiting the Homes of Prospective Tenants

Some landlords like to visit prospective tenants at their home to see how well they maintain a place. If you find this a valuable part of your screening process, and have the time and energy to do it, be sure you get the prospective tenants' permission first. Don't just drop by unexpectedly. Some landlords fabricate a reason for the visit ("I forgot to have you sign something"), but it's better to be honest regarding the purpose of your visit.

Review Court Records

If your prospective tenant has lived in the area, you may want to review local court records to see if collection or eviction lawsuits have ever been filed against them. Checking court records may seem like overkill, since some of this information may be available on credit reports, but it's an invaluable tool and is not a violation of antidiscrimination

laws as long as you check the records of every applicant who reaches this stage of your screening process. Because court records are kept for many years, this kind of information can supplement references from recent landlords. Call the local court that handles eviction cases for details, including the cost of checking court records.

Use Megan's Law to Check State Databases of Sexual Offenders

Not surprisingly, most landlords do not want tenants with criminal records, particularly convictions for violent crimes or crimes against children. Checking a prospective tenant's credit report, as we recommend above, is one way to find out about a person's criminal history. Self-reporting is another: Rental applications, such as the one in this book, typically ask whether the prospective tenant has ever been convicted of a crime, and, if so, to provide details.

"Megan's Law" may be able to assist you in confirming that some of the information provided in the rental application and revealed in the credit report is complete and correct (but see "Restricting Your Use of Megan's Law," below). Named after a young girl who was killed by a convicted child molester who lived in her neighborhood, this 1996 federal crime prevention law charged the FBI with keeping a nationwide database of persons convicted of sexual offenses against minors and violent sexual offenses against anyone. (42 U.S. Code §§ 16901 and following.) Every state has its own version of Megan's Law. These laws typically require certain convicted sexual offenders to register with local law enforcement officials, who keep a database on their whereabouts.

How Megan's Law Works

Unfortunately, the states are not consistent when it comes to using and distributing the database information. Notification procedures and the public's access rights vary widely:

- **Widespread notification/easy access.** A few states are "wide open"—they permit local law enforcement to automatically notify neighbors of the presence of sexual offenders on the database, by way of either letters, flyers, or notices published in local newspapers. Alternately, some states make the information available to anyone who chooses to access the database.

- **Selected notification/limited access.** Other states take a more restrictive approach, allowing law enforcement to release the information only if they deem it necessary. Or, states permit public access only to persons who demonstrate a legitimate need to know the names of convicted sexual offenders.
- **Restricted notification/narrow access.** Finally, many states are quite restrictive, permitting notification only to certain individuals or officials, and allowing access only to them.

For information on your state's Megan's Law and restrictions on your use of information derived from a Megan's Law database, contact your local law enforcement agency. To find out how to access your state's sex offender registry, you can also contact the Parents for Megan's Law (PFML) Hotline at 888-ASK-PFML or check www. parentsformeganslaw.org.

The Limitations of Megan's Law Searching

The early promise of Megan's Law databases was ambitious. Landlords expected that they could quickly find accurate information on any person, and freely use it to reject an applicant with an unsavory past. Several years' experience with the databases, and legal challenges to their use, have resulted in landlords' taking a much more cautious approach to running a Megan's Law search. Here are the issues:

- **Accuracy.** Megan's Law databases are notoriously inaccurate, the result of incomplete or old data or entries that mistake one person for another. You can't assume your search will be worth much.
- **Relevance.** The criminal offense you discover on the database may not be relevant to

whether this applicant is likely to be a threat to you, your tenants, or your property. For example, in some states consensual intercourse between minors (statutory rape) is an offense for which a person must register.
- **Misleading negatives.** Many convictions result from plea bargains. For example, someone charged with a registerable offense may end up with an assault conviction—perhaps because the prosecutor couldn't prove the charge, or because a chief witness disappeared. You'll never know whether the assault conviction was originally charged as such, or began as a far more serious charge and ended up less so because the defendant lucked out. In other words, a relatively harmless-looking conviction that would not bother you may in fact mask a more serious incident.

Tenants Will Be Checking You Out, Too

While you're checking out a potential tenant (asking for references and getting a credit report), don't be surprised if the tenant is checking you out, too. Savvy applicants will ask your current tenants what it's like to rent from you (including how quickly you handle repairs) and the pluses and minuses of living in the building.

There are also several websites that provide tenants background information about you and your property. One of the major ones is www. apartmentratings.com. This comprehensive website has over two million reviews of individual apartments and property managers nationwide. It includes other information useful to new tenants, such as the average prices of rentals in the neighborhood and proximity of registered sex offenders.

- **Expectations you create in other tenants.** If you do a database check, you should let applicants know that you're doing so (this will allow applicants to opt out of the application process, and may spare you a charge of invading their privacy). Residents will assume that you have not rented to anyone on a Megan's Law list.

They may relax their guard—for example, a family may assume it's okay for their children to be home alone after school. Suppose you've rented to someone who should have been on the list but mistakenly wasn't, and he assaults one of the children. The family could argue in court that they relied on your implied promise that the building was safe, and that you bear some of the responsibility since you rented to someone who posed a risk of harm.

- **Loss of other tenants.** Ironically, if you decide that a past offense was not relevant, and rent to this applicant, you may have to disclose his past (to save you from the fate described just above). Other tenants won't share your complacency, and will leave. Before you know it, your only tenant will be the one you least want.

- **Lawsuit waiting to happen.** Finally, you may be the unlucky landlord who's targeted by a lawyer armed with many legal theories of why the Megan's Law registration and search structure is unconstitutional. These arguments (due process, equal protection, privacy, and the like) are not far-fetched. They've been made already, and at some point, a judge is going to agree with one of these legal theories.

- **Illegal in some states.** Finally, in some states and cities you simply cannot use information derived from a Megan's Law database to discriminate. These laws provide for stiff penalties if you do. See "Restricting Your Use of Megan's Law," below.

Many landlord associations and landlords' lawyers have concluded that the problems associated with Megan's Law searches are simply not worth the questionable results you'll get when you run them. Their advice is to stick to the tried-and-true methods of thoroughly checking references and examining the applicant's credit report for unexplained gaps (which may be due to time in prison).

If your state does not provide an accessible database that you can use when you screen, or if

you decide not to screen, you may not learn of a person's past conviction for sexual offenses until after he registers his new address (yours) with the state's data collection agency. When he does so, you may get the flyer or phone call, but he'll already be a tenant. The fallout from angry neighbors and the negative publicity for your business can be dreadful. See "Criminal Convictions," in Chapter 17 for suggestions on what to do if you find out one of your current tenants is a convicted sexual offender.

Restricting Your Use of Megan's Law

The following states limit landlords' use of Megan's Law database information.

State	Rule
California	Database users may not access the information to deny housing.
Massachusetts	Database users cannot use the database to illegally discriminate—though past offenders are not clearly protected by state antidiscrimination laws.
Nevada	The state's website says that users cannot utilize the information to discriminate.
New Jersey	Users can't use sex offender information to deny housing unless the denial promotes public safety.

Choosing—And Rejecting—An Applicant

After you've collected applications and done some screening, you can start sifting through the applicants. Start by eliminating the worst risks: people with negative references from previous landlords, a history of nonpayment of rent, or poor credit or recent and numerous evictions.

Notice of Denial Based on Credit Report or Other Information

To: _Ryan Paige_
Applicant

1 Mariner Square
Street Address

Seattle, Washington 98101
City, State, and Zip Code

Your rights under the Fair Credit Reporting Act and Fair and Accurate Credit Transactions (FACT) Act of 2003. (15 U.S.C. §§ 1681 and following.)

THIS NOTICE is to inform you that your application to rent the property at _75 Starbucks Lane, Seattle, WA 98108_

has been denied because of [*check all that apply*]:

☑ Insufficient information in the credit report provided by:

Credit reporting agency: _ABC Credit Bureau_

Address, phone number, URL: _310 Griffey Way, Seattle, WA 98140; Phone: 206-555-1212; www.abccredit.com_

☐ Negative information in the credit report provided by:

Credit reporting agency: _____

Address, phone number, URL: _____

_____

☑ The credit score supplied on the credit report, _511_, was used in whole or in part when making the decision.

☑ The consumer credit reporting agency noted above did not make the decision not to offer you this rental. It only provided information about your credit history. You have the right to obtain a free copy of your credit report from the consumer credit reporting agency named above, if your request is made within 60 days of this notice or if you have not requested a free copy within the past year. You also have the right to dispute the accuracy or completeness of your credit report. The agency must reinvestigate within a reasonable time, free of charge, and remove or modify inaccurate information. If the reinvestigation does not resolve the dispute to your satisfaction, you may add your own "consumer statement" (up to 100 words) to the report, which must be included (or a clear summary) in future reports.

☐ Information supplied by a third party other than a credit reporting agency or you and gathered by someone other than myself or any employee. You have the right to learn of the nature of the information if you ask me in writing within 60 days of the date of this notice. This information was gathered by someone other than myself or any employee.

Jason McGuire
Landlord/Manager

_10-01-20xx_
Date

Chapter 5 discusses legal reasons for refusing to rent to a tenant, including convictions for criminal offenses. You'll want to arrange and preserve your information for two reasons: so that you can survive a fair housing challenge, if a disappointed applicant files a complaint; and so that you can comply with your legal duties to divulge your reasons for rejecting an applicant.

What Information Should You Keep on Rejected Applicants?

Be sure to note your reasons for rejection—such as poor credit history, pets (if you don't accept pets), or a negative reference from a previous landlord—on the Tenant References form or other paper so that you have a paper trail if an applicant accuses you of illegal discrimination. You want to be able to back up your reason for rejecting the person. Keep organized files of applications, credit reports, and other materials and notes on prospective tenants for at least three years after you rent a particular unit. Keep in mind that if a rejected applicant files a complaint with a fair housing agency or files a lawsuit, your file will be made available to the applicant's lawyers. Knowing that, choose your words carefully, avoiding the obvious (slurs and exaggerations) and being scrupulously truthful.

CAUTION

Be careful handling credit reports. Under the federal "Disposal Rule" of the Fair and Accurate Credit Transactions Act of 2003, you must take care that credit reports are stored in a secure place where only those who "need to know" have access. For advice on handling credit reports and other personal information on applicants, see "How to Handle Credit Reports" in Chapter 7.

How to Reject an Applicant

The Fair Credit Reporting Act, as amended by the Fair and Accurate Credit Transactions Act of 2003, requires you to give certain information to applicants whom you reject as the result of a report from a credit reporting agency (credit bureau) or from a tenant screening or reference service. (15 U.S. Code §§ 1681 and following.) These notices are known as "adverse action reports." The federal requirements do not apply if your decision is based on information that the applicant furnished or that you or an employee learned on your own.

If you do not rent to someone because of negative information contained in the credit report or their credit score (even if other factors also played a part in your decision) or due to an insufficient credit report, you must give the applicant the name and address of the agency that provided the credit report. Tell applicants they have a right to obtain a copy of the file from the agency that reported the negative information, by requesting it within the next 60 days or by asking within one year of having asked for their last free report. You must also tell rejected applicants that the credit reporting agency did not make the decision to reject them and cannot explain the reason for the rejection. Finally, tell applicants that they can dispute the accuracy of their credit report and add their own consumer statement to their report.

Use the Notice of Denial Based on Credit Report or Other Information form for this purpose. A sample is shown above and the Nolo website includes a downloadable copy. See Appendix B for the link to the forms in this book.

Assuming you choose the best-qualified candidate (based on income, credit history, and references), you have no legal problem. But what if you have a number of more or less equally qualified applicants? The best response is to use an objective tie-breaker: Give the nod to the person who applied first. If you cannot determine who applied first, strive to find some aspect of one applicant's credit history or references that objectively establishes that person as the best applicant. Be extra careful not to always select a person of the same age, sex, or ethnicity. For example, if you are a larger landlord who is frequently faced with tough choices and who always avoids an equally qualified minority or disabled applicant, you are exposing yourself to charges of discrimination.

Notice of Conditional Acceptance Based on Credit Report or Other Information

To: _William McGee_
Applicant
1257 Bay Avenue
Street Address
Anytown, FL 12345
City, State, and Zip Code

Your application to rent the property at _37 Ocean View Drive, #10-H, Anytown, FL 12345_

_____ [rental property address] has been accepted, conditioned on

your willingness and ability to: _Supply a cosigner that is acceptable to the landlord_

_____

Your rights under the Fair Credit Reporting Act and Fair and Accurate Credit Transactions (FACT) Act of 2003. (15 U.S.C. §§ 1681 and following.)

Source of information prompting conditional acceptance

My decision to conditionally accept your application was prompted in whole or in part by:

☑ Insufficient information in the credit report provided by:

Credit reporting agency: _____Mountain Credit Bureau_____

Address, phone number, URL: _75 Baywood Drive, Anytown, FL 12345. 800-123-4567._
www.mountaincredit.com

☐ Negative information in the credit report provided by:

Credit reporting agency: _____

Address, phone number, URL: _____

☑ The consumer credit reporting agency noted above did not make the decision to offer you this conditional acceptance. It only provided information about your credit history. You have the right to obtain a free copy of your credit report from the consumer credit reporting agency named above, if your request is made within 60 days of this notice or if you have not requested a free copy within the past year. You also have the right to dispute the accuracy or completeness of your credit report. The agency must reinvestigate within a reasonable time, free of charge, and remove or modify inaccurate information. If the reinvestigation does not resolve the dispute to your satisfaction, you may add your own "consumer statement" (up to 100 words) to the report, which must be included (or a clear summary) in future reports.

☐ Information supplied by a third party other than a credit reporting agency or you and gathered by someone other than myself or any employee. You have the right to learn of the nature of the information if you ask me in writing within 60 days of the date of this notice.

Jane Thomas _____   _May 15, 20xx_ _____
Landlord/Manager   Date

Conditional Acceptances

You may want to make an offer to an applicant but condition that offer on the applicant paying more rent or a higher security deposit (one that's within any legal limits, of course, as explained in Chapter 4), supplying a cosigner, or agreeing to a different rental term than you originally advertised. If your decision to impose the condition resulted from information you gained from a credit report or a report from a tenant screening service, you have to accompany the offer with an adverse action letter (described above). Use the Notice of Conditional Acceptance Based on Credit Report or Other Information, shown above. The Nolo website includes a downloadable copy. See Appendix B for the link to the forms in this book.

Finder's Fees and Holding Deposits

Almost every landlord requires tenants to give a substantial security deposit. The laws concerning how much can be charged and when deposits must be returned are discussed in Chapters 4 and 15. Here we discuss some other fees and deposits.

Finder's Fees

You may legitimately charge a prospective tenant for the cost of performing a credit check. Less legitimate, however, is the practice of some landlords, especially in cities with a tight rental market, of collecting a nonrefundable "finder's fee" or "move-in fee" just for renting the place to a tenant. Whether it's a flat fee or a percentage of the rent, we recommend against finder's fees. First, a finder's fee may be illegal in some cities and states (particularly those with rent control). Second, it's just a way of squeezing a little more money out of the tenant—and tenants will resent it. If you think the unit is worth more, raise the price.

Holding Deposits

If you make a deal with a tenant but don't actually sign a lease or rental agreement, you may want a cash deposit to hold the rental unit while you do a credit check or call the tenant's references. Or, if the tenant needs to borrow money (or wait for a paycheck) to cover the rent and security deposit, you might want a few hundred dollars cash to hold the place. And some tenants may want to reserve a unit while continuing to look for a better one.

Is this a wise course? Accepting a deposit to hold a rental unit open for someone is legal in some states but almost always unwise. Holding deposits do you little or no good from a business point of view, and all too often result in misunderstandings or even legal fights.

Rating Applicants on a Numerical Scale

To substantiate your claim that you are fair to all applicants, you may be tempted to devise a numerical rating system—for example, ten points for an excellent credit report, 20 points for an excellent past landlord reference, and the like. While this type of rating system may simplify your task, it has two significant drawbacks:

- Every landlord is entitled to rely on gut feelings regarding a potential tenant (as long as these are not illegally discriminatory—see Chapter 5). You can decline to rent to an applicant you feel, instinctively, is a creep. You can decline to rent to him in spite of stellar recommendations or a solid financial report. Use of a numerical rating system should not limit your exercise of good sense.
- If a rejected tenant sues you, you will have to hand over your rating sheet. It will be easier to explain your decision by referring to the whole picture, rather than defending every "point" allocated in your system. You do want to be able to point to the many specific background checks you performed and used to arrive at your decision, but you do not want to lock yourself into a numerical straitjacket that you will be asked to defend.

Receipt and Holding Deposit Agreement

This will acknowledge receipt of the sum of $ _____500_____ by _____Jim Chow_____

_____ "Landlord" from _____Hannah Silver_____

_____ "Applicant" as a holding deposit to hold vacant

the rental property at _178 West 81st St., #4F, New York City_____

_____ ,

until _____February 20, 20xx_____ at _____5 P.M._____ . The property will be rented to Applicant

on a _____one-year_____ basis at a rent of $ ____3,000____ per month, if Applicant signs

Landlord's written _____lease_____ and pays Landlord the first month's rent and a

$ _____3,000_____ security deposit on or before that date, in which event the holding deposit will be

applied to the first month's rent.

Applicant's rental of the rental property depends upon Landlord receiving a satisfactory report of Applicant's

references and credit history. Landlord and Applicant agree that if Applicant fails to sign the lease or rental

agreement and pay the remaining rent and security deposit, Landlord may retain of this holding deposit a sum

equal to the prorated daily rent of $ _____100_____ per day plus a $ _____50_____ charge to compensate

Landlord for time and labor.

_Hannah Silver_____   _February 16, 20xx_____
Applicant   Date

_Jim Chow_____   _February 16, 20xx_____
Landlord/Manager   Date

EXAMPLE: A landlord, Jim, takes a deposit of several hundred dollars from a prospective tenant, Michael. What exactly is Jim promising Michael in return? To rent him the apartment? To rent Michael the apartment only if his credit checks out to Jim's satisfaction? To rent to Michael only if he comes up with the rest of the money before Jim rents to someone who offers the first month's rent and deposit? If Jim and Michael disagree about the answers to any of these questions, it can lead to needless anger and bitterness and result in a small claims court lawsuit alleging breach of contract.

Another prime reason to avoid holding deposits is that the laws of most states are unclear as to what portion of a holding deposit you can keep if a would-be tenant decides not to rent or doesn't come up with the remaining rent and deposit money, or if the tenant's credit doesn't check out to your satisfaction.

In California, for example, the basic rule is that a landlord can keep an amount that bears a "reasonable" relation to the landlord's costs—for example, for more advertising and for prorated rent during the time the property was held vacant. A landlord who keeps a larger amount may be sued for breach of contract. A few states require landlords to provide a receipt for any holding deposit and a written statement of the conditions under which it is refundable.

If, contrary to our advice, you decide to take a holding deposit, it is essential that both you and your prospective tenant have a clear understanding in writing, including:

- the amount of the holding deposit
- your name and that of the applicant
- the address of the rental property
- the dates you will hold the rental property vacant
- the term of the rental agreement or lease
- conditions for renting the applicant the available unit—for example, satisfactory references and credit history and full payment of first month's rent and security deposit

- what happens to the holding deposit if the applicant signs the rental agreement or lease—usually, it will be applied to the first month's rent, and
- the amount of the holding deposit you will keep if the applicant doesn't sign a rental agreement or lease—for example, an amount equal to the prorated daily rent for each day the rental unit was off the market plus a small charge to cover your inconvenience.

A sample Receipt and Holding Deposit Agreement that covers each of these items is shown above and the Nolo website includes a downloadable copy. See Appendix B for the link to the forms in this book.

What to Do If Your Apartment Is Hard to Rent

If you have a problem filling vacancies, resist the temptation to loosen up on your screening requirements. In the long run, a tenant who constantly pays rent late, disturbs other neighbors, or damages your property is not worth the price of having your rental occupied. Instead of taking a chance on a risky applicant, consider whether the rent is too high as compared to similar properties. If so, lower it. Also, make sure the condition of the rental isn't affecting its desirability. A new paint job or carpeting may make a big difference. Some landlords have great success with resident referral programs in which you pay a premium to a tenant who refers someone to you whom you approve and sign up as a tenant. If all else fails, consider incentives such as a free month's rent or free satellite or cable TV service.

If you do provide incentives, be sure to offer them in a consistent and fair way to all eligible tenants in order to avoid charges of discrimination. Also, to avoid problems, be clear as to the terms of the freebies you're providing. For example, when exactly may the tenant use the "free" month's rent—after six months or beyond? How long will free satellite service last? How long must a referred tenant stay for you to award a premium?

Preparing Leases and Rental Agreements

FORMS IN THIS CHAPTER
Chapter 2 includes instructions for and samples of the following forms.
- Month-to-Month Residential Rental Agreement
- Month-to-Month Residential Rental Agreement (Spanish Version) (companion page only)
- Fixed-Term Residential Lease (companion page only)
- Fixed-Term Residential Lease (Spanish Version) (companion page only)
- Cosigner Agreement

The Nolo website includes downloadable copies of these forms. See Appendix B for the link to the forms in this book.

Interactive Online Lease Forms

The rental forms described here, which you can download from the book's companion page on the Nolo website, are good in all 50 states. To tailor them to your state's laws, use the charts included in this book's appendix.

If you prefer an interactive lease or rental agreement form, you can purchase one at Nolo.com. A 50-state form, as well as state-specific forms for many states, are available. And there's a special discount for purchasers of this book: just use coupon code **ELLIBOB13**.

The rental agreement or lease that you and your tenant sign forms the contractual basis of your relationship. Taken together with the laws of your state—and, in a few areas, local and federal laws—it sets out almost all the legal rules you and your tenant must follow.

Your rental agreement or lease is also an immensely practical document, full of crucial business details, such as how long the tenant can occupy your property and the amount of the rent.

Given their importance, there's no question that you need to create effective and legal agreements with your tenants. This chapter shows you how to prepare clearly written, fair, and effective lease and rental agreements, and provides clear explanations of each clause.

Why use our lease or rental agreement, when you probably already use a printed form that seems adequate? There are several good reasons:

- Our agreements are based on careful research of every state's landlord-tenant laws. Many preprinted forms ignore state-by-state differences. In particular, cheap online forms are riddled with errors, typically written by attorneys who practice in one state but assume the laws are similar in all. This doesn't stop websites that offer landlord forms from advertising state-specific leases. We don't use the illegal or unenforceable clauses that pepper many preprinted agreements. Some forms still include clauses that courts threw out years ago or are so one-sided as to be unenforceable.
- Our agreements are clearly written in plain English and easy for you and your tenants to understand. We believe strongly that it's to everyone's advantage to have a written agreement that clearly informs tenants of their responsibilities and rights.
- Our lease and rental agreements are available for download on the Nolo website (see Appendix B for the link to the forms in this book). You can easily tailor them to fit your own situation. Throughout the chapter, we suggest ways to modify clauses in certain

circumstances. We also caution you about changes likely to get you into legal hot water.

RESOURCE

Looking for an interactive state-specific lease form? The rental documents described in this chapter and included on the book's companion page on the Nolo website are good in all 50 states. You simply need to tailor the document to your state using the charts included in this book. If you prefer a digital lease or rental agreement form, check www.nolo.com.

CAUTION

Don't use our forms if the rent is subsidized by the government. You may need to use a special government lease if you rent subsidized housing, such as Section 8.

Which Is Better, a Lease or a Rental Agreement?

One of the key decisions you need to make is whether to use a lease or a rental agreement. To decide which is better for you, read what follows and carefully evaluate your own situation.

Month-to-Month Rental Agreement

A written rental agreement provides for a tenancy for a short period of time. The law refers to these agreements as periodic, or month-to-month, although it is often legally possible to base them on other time periods—for example, if the rent were due every two weeks.

A month-to-month tenancy is automatically renewed each month unless you or your tenant gives the other the proper amount of written notice (typically 30 days) to terminate the agreement. The rental agreements in this book are month to month, although you can change them to a different interval.

Month-to-month rental agreements give landlords more flexibility than leases. You may increase the rent or change other terms of the tenancy on relatively short notice (subject to any restrictions of local rent control ordinances). You may also end the tenancy at any time (again, subject to any rent control restrictions), as long as you give the required amount of advance warning. Not surprisingly, many landlords prefer to rent from month to month, particularly in urban areas with tight rental markets where new tenants can often be found in a few days and rents are trending upward.

On the flip side, a month-to-month tenancy probably means more tenant turnover. Tenants who may legally move out with only 30 days' notice may be more inclined to do so than tenants who make a longer commitment. Some landlords base their rental business strategy on painstakingly seeking high-quality long-term renters. If you're one of those, or if you live in an area where it's difficult to fill vacancies, you will probably want tenants to commit for a longer period, such as a year. But, as discussed below, although a fixed-term lease may encourage tenants to stay longer, it is no guarantee against turnover.

Fixed-Term Lease

A lease is a contract that obligates both you and the tenant for a set period of time—usually a year. With a fixed-term lease, you can't raise the rent or change other terms of the tenancy until the lease runs out, unless the lease itself allows future changes or the tenant agrees in writing.

In addition, you usually can't ask a tenant to move out or prevail in an eviction lawsuit before the lease term expires unless the tenant fails to pay the rent or violates another significant term of the lease or the law, such as repeatedly making too much noise, damaging the rental unit, or selling drugs on your property. This restriction can sometimes be problematic if you end up with a tenant you would like to be rid of but don't have sufficient cause to evict.

To take but one example, if you wish to sell the property halfway into the lease, the existence of long-term tenants—especially if they are paying less than the market rate—may be a negative factor. The new owner usually purchases all the obligations of the previous owner, including the obligation to honor existing leases. Of course, the opposite can also be true—if you have good, long-term tenants paying a fair rent, it may be very attractive to potential new owners.

At the end of the lease term, you have several options. You can:

- decline to renew the lease, except in the few areas where rent control requirements prohibit it
- sign a new lease for a set period, or
- do nothing—which means, under the law of most states, your lease will usually turn into a month-to-month tenancy if you continue to accept monthly rent from the tenant.

Chapter 14 discusses in detail how fixed-term leases end.

Although leases restrict your flexibility, there's often a big plus to having long-term tenants. Some tenants make a serious personal commitment when they enter into a long-term lease, in part because they think they'll be liable for several months' rent if they leave early. And people who plan to be with you over the long term are often more likely to respect your property and the rights of other tenants, making the management of your rental units far easier and more pleasant.

! CAUTION

A lease guarantees less income security than you think. As experienced landlords know well, it's usually not hard for a determined tenant to break a lease and avoid paying all of the money theoretically owed for the unused portion of the lease term. A few states allow tenants to break a lease without penalty in specific circumstances, such as the need to move to a nursing home. In addition, tenants who enter military service are entitled to break a lease. And many states require landlords to "mitigate" (minimize) the loss they suffer as a result of a broken lease—meaning that if a tenant moves out early, you must try to find another suitable tenant at the same or a greater rent. If you rerent the unit immediately (or if a judge believes it could have been rerented with a reasonable effort), the lease-breaking tenant is off the hook—except, perhaps, for a small obligation to pay for the few days or weeks the unit was vacant plus (sometimes) any costs you incurred in rerenting it.

You'll probably prefer to use leases in areas where there is a high vacancy rate or it is difficult to find tenants for one season of the year. For example, if you are renting near a college that is in session for only nine months a year, or in a vacation area that is deserted for months, you are far better off with a year's lease. This is especially true if you have the market clout to charge a large deposit, so that a tenant who wants to leave early has an incentive to find someone to take over the tenancy.

TIP

Always put your agreement in writing. Oral leases or rental agreements are perfectly legal for month-to-month tenancies and, in most states, for leases of a year or less. If you have an oral lease for a term exceeding one year, it becomes an oral month-to-month agreement after the first year is up. While oral agreements are easy and informal, it is never wise to use one. As time passes, people's memories (even yours) have a funny habit of becoming unreliable. You can almost count on tenants claiming that you made, but didn't keep, certain oral promises—for example, to repaint their kitchen or not increase their rent. Tenants may also forget key agreements, such as no subletting. And other issues, like how deposits may be used, probably aren't covered at all. Oral leases are especially dangerous, because they require that both parties accurately remember one important term—the length of the lease—over a considerable time. If something goes wrong with an oral rental agreement or lease, you and your tenants are all too likely to end up in court, arguing over who said what to whom, when, and in what context.

Leases and Rental Agreements in a Nutshell

Leases	Rental Agreements
You can't raise the rent or change other terms of the tenancy until the lease ends.	You may increase rent or change other terms of the tenancy on relatively short notice (subject to any restrictions of local rent control ordinances).
You usually can't end the tenancy before the term expires, unless the tenant doesn't pay rent or violates another term of the lease.	You or the tenant may end the tenancy at any time (subject to any rent control restrictions), by giving the required amount of written notice, typically 30 days.

Clause-by-Clause Instructions for Completing the Lease or Rental Agreement Form

This section explains each clause in the lease and rental agreement forms provided in this book. The instructions explain how to fill in the blanks and also refer you to the chapter that discusses important issues that relate to your choices. Before you complete any clause for the first time, read the detailed discussion about it in the appropriate chapter. For example, before you complete Clause 5, which covers rent, be sure to read Chapter 3.

Except for the important difference in the term of the tenancy (see Clause 4 in the forms), leases and written rental agreements are so similar that they are sometimes hard to tell apart. Both cover the basic terms of the tenancy (such as amount of rent and date due). Except where indicated below, the clauses are identical for the lease and rental agreement.

A filled-in sample rental agreement is included at the end of this chapter. This book's companion page includes copies of the Month-to-Month Residential Rental Agreement and the Fixed-Term Residential Rental Lease. Both are in English and Spanish.

Tips for Landlords Taking Over Rental Property

If you've recently bought (or inherited) property, you will likely be inheriting tenants with existing rental agreements or leases. Be sure the last owner gives you copies of all tenant and property files, including leases and rental agreements, details on deposits (location and amounts), house rules, maintenance and repair records, and all other paperwork and records relevant to the property. If you want to change any of the terms of the lease or rental agreement, follow our advice in the first part of Chapter 14.

How to Modify the Lease or Rental Agreement Form

You may want to modify our lease and rental agreement forms in some situations. The instructions suggest possible modifications for some of the clauses. If you make extensive changes on your own, however, you may wish to have your work reviewed by an experienced landlords' lawyer.

Don't be tempted to try to cram too many details into the lease or rental agreement. Instead, send new tenants a "move-in letter" that dovetails with the lease or rental agreement and highlights important terms of the tenancy—for example, how and where to report maintenance problems. You may also use a move-in letter to cover issues not included in the lease or rental agreement—for example, rules for use of a pool or laundry room or procedures for returning security deposits. Chapter 7 covers move-in letters.

RENT CONTROL

You may need to modify the forms if required by local ordinance. Local rent control ordinances may require that your lease or rental agreement include specific information—for example, the address of the local rent control board. Check your local ordinance for more information, and modify our forms accordingly.

Clause 1. Identification of Landlord and Tenant

This Agreement is entered into between _____ _____ [Tenant] and _____ [Landlord]. Each Tenant is jointly and severally liable for the payment of rent and performance of all other terms of this Agreement.

Every lease or rental agreement must identify the tenant and the landlord or the property owner—often called the "parties" to the agreement. The term "Agreement" (a synonym for contract) refers to either the lease or rental agreement.

Any competent adult—at least 18 years of age—may be a party to a lease or rental agreement. A teenager who is slightly under age 18 may also be a party to a lease in most states if he or she has achieved legal adult status through a court order (called emancipation), military service, or marriage.

The last sentence of Clause 1 states that if you have more than one tenant, they (the cotenants) are all "jointly and severally" liable for paying rent and abiding by the terms of the agreement. This essential bit of legalese simply means that each tenant is legally responsible for the whole rent and complying with the agreement. You can legally seek full compensation from any one of the tenants should the others skip out or be unable to pay, or evict all of the tenants even if just one has broken the terms of the lease—for example, by seriously damaging the property. Chapter 8 provides more detail on the concept of joint and several liability and discusses the legal obligations of cotenants.

How to Fill in Clause 1:

Fill in the names of all tenants—adults who will live in the premises, including both members of a couple. Doing this makes everyone who signs responsible for all terms, including the full amount of the rent. Chapter 8 discusses why it's crucial that everyone who lives in your rental unit sign the lease or rental agreement. Also, make sure the tenant's name matches his or her legal documents, such as a driver's license. You may set a reasonable limit on the number of people per rental unit as discussed in "Valid Occupancy Limits," in Chapter 5.

In the last blank, list the names of all landlords or property owners—that is, the names of every person who will be signing the lease or rental agreement. If you are using a business name, enter your name followed by your business name.

Clause 2. Identification of Premises

Subject to the terms and conditions in this Agreement, Landlord rents to Tenant, and Tenant rents from Landlord, for residential purposes only, the premises located at _____

_____ [the premises],

together with the following furnishings and appliances:

_____ . Rental of the premises also includes

_____ .

Clause 2 identifies the address of the property being rented ("the premises") and provides details on furnishings and extras such as a parking space. The words "for residential purposes only" are to prevent a tenant from using the property for conducting a business that might affect your insurance or violate zoning laws, or that might burden other tenants or neighbors.

How to Fill in Clause 2:

Fill in the street address of the unit or house you are renting. If there is an apartment or building number, specify that as well as the city and state.

Add as much detail as necessary to clarify what's included in the rental premises, such as kitchen appliances. If the unit has only a few basic furnishings, list them here. If the rental unit is fully furnished, state that here and provide detailed information on the Landlord-Tenant Checklist included in Chapter 7 or in a separate room-by-room list.

In some circumstances, you may want to elaborate on exactly what the premises do or do not include. For example, if the rental unit includes a parking space, storage in the garage or basement, or other use of the property, such as a gardening shed in the backyard or the use of a barn in rural areas, specifically include this information in your description of the premises.

Possible Modifications to Clause 2:

If a particular part of the rental property that might be assumed to be included is *not* being rented, such as a garage or storage shed you wish

to use yourself or rent to someone else, explicitly exclude it from your description of the premises.

Clause 3. Limits on Use and Occupancy

The premises are to be used only as a private residence for Tenant(s) listed in Clause 1 of this Agreement, and their minor children. Occupancy by guests for more than

_____

is prohibited without Landlord's written consent and will be considered a breach of this Agreement.

Clause 3 states that the rental unit is the residence of the tenants and their minor children only. It lets the tenants know they may not move anyone else in as a permanent resident without your consent. The value of this clause is that a tenant who tries to move in a relative or friend for a longer period has clearly violated a defined standard, which gives you grounds for eviction. (New York landlords, however, are subject to the "Roommate Law," RPL § 235-f, which allows tenants to move in relatives and other qualified individuals. The number of total occupants is still restricted, however, by any local statutes governing overcrowding.)

Clause 3 also allows you to set a time limit for guest stays. Even if you do not plan to strictly enforce restrictions on guests, this provision will be very handy if a tenant tries to move in a friend or relative for a month or two, calling that person a guest. It will give you the leverage you need to ask the guest to leave, request that the guest apply to become a tenant with an appropriate increase in rent, or, if necessary, evict the tenant for violating this lease provision. To avoid discrimination charges, don't make restrictions on guests that are based on the age or sex of the occupant or guest. Chapter 8 discusses guests in more detail.

How to Fill in Clause 3:

Fill in the number of days you allow guests to stay over a given time period without your consent. We suggest you allow up to ten consecutive days in any six-month period, but, of course, you may want to modify this based on your own preferences.

Investigate Before Letting a Tenant Run a Home Business

Millions of Americans run a business from their house or apartment. If a tenant asks you to modify Clause 2 to allow him to operate a business, you have some checking to do—even if you are inclined to say yes.

For one, you'll need to check local zoning laws for restrictions on home-based businesses, including the type of businesses allowed (if any), the amount of car and truck traffic the business can generate, outside signs, on-street parking, the number of employees, and the percentage of floor space devoted to the business. In Los Angeles, for example, dentists, physicians (except for psychiatrists), and unlicensed massage therapists, as well as many others, may not operate home offices. In addition, photo labs and recording studios are banned. (L.A. Muni. Code Ch. 1, Art. 2, § 12.05.A.16.) And if your rental unit is in a planned unit or a condominium development, check the CC&Rs of the homeowners' association.

You'll also want to consult your insurance company as to whether you'll need a different policy to cover potential liability of a tenant's employees or guests. In many situations, a home office for occasional use will not be a problem. But if the tenant wants to operate a business, especially one with people and deliveries coming and going, such as a therapy practice, jewelry importer, or small business consulting firm, you should seriously consider whether to expand or add coverage.

You may also want to require that the tenant maintain certain types of liability insurance, so that you won't wind up paying if someone gets hurt on the rental property—for example, a business customer who trips and falls on the front steps.

Finally, be aware that if you allow a residence to be used as a commercial site, your property may need to meet the accessibility requirements of the federal Americans with Disabilities Act (ADA). For more information on the ADA contact the U.S. Department of Justice, 950 Pennsylvania Ave., NW, Civil Rights Division, Disability Rights Section, Washington, DC 20530, call 800-514-0301 (800-514-0383 TTY), or check the ADA website at www.ada.gov.

> **CAUTION**
> **You may not be able to restrict a child care home business.** A tenant who wants to do child care in the rental may be entitled to do so, despite your general prohibition against businesses. In California and New York, for example, legislators and courts have declared a strong public policy in favor of home-based child care and have limited a landlord's ability to say no. (Cal. Health & Safety Code § 1597.40; *Haberman v. Gotbaum*, 698 N.Y.S.2d 406 (N.Y. City Civ. Ct. 1999).) If you're concerned, check with your state's office of consumer protection for information on laws that cover in-home child care in residential properties.

If you allow a tenant to run a business from your rental property, you may want to provide details in Clause 22 (Additional Provisions) of your lease or rental agreement.

> **CAUTION**
> **Don't discriminate against families with children.** You can legally establish reasonable space-to-people ratios, but you cannot use overcrowding as an excuse for refusing to rent to tenants with children. Space rules are available in your local or state housing code. Discrimination against families with children is illegal, except in housing reserved for senior citizens only. Just as important as adopting a reasonable people-to-square-foot standard in the first place is the maintenance of a consistent occupancy policy. If you allow three adults to live in a two-bedroom apartment, you had better let a couple with a child live in the same type of unit, or you are leaving yourself open to charges that you are illegally discriminating. Chapter 5 covers discrimination and occupancy standards.

Clause 4. Term of the Tenancy (Lease)

The term of the rental will begin on _____ ,
and end on _____ .

This clause sets out the key difference between a lease and a rental agreement: how long a rent-paying tenant is entitled to stay.

The lease form sets a definite date for the beginning and expiration of the lease and obligates both you and the tenant for a specific term.

Most leases run for one year. This makes sense, because it allows you to raise the rent at reasonably frequent intervals if market conditions allow. Leases may be shorter (six months) or longer (24 months)—this, of course, is up to you and the tenants. A long period—two, three, or even five years—can be appropriate, for example, if you're renting out your own house because you're taking a two-year sabbatical or if the tenant plans to make major repairs or remodel your property.

Chapter 14 discusses a tenant's liability for breaking a lease, what exactly happens at the end of a lease, monetary consequences if a tenant "holds over" or fails to leave after the lease ends, termination of fixed-term leases, and your duty to mitigate damages. It also covers notice requirements. You may want to specify some of these issues in the lease or rental agreement or in a move-in letter you send new tenants (see Chapter 7).

How to Fill in Clause 4 (Lease):

In the blanks, fill in the starting date and the expiration date. The starting date is the date the tenant has the right to move in, such as the first of the month. This date does not have to be the date that you and the tenant sign the lease. The lease signing date is simply the date that you're both bound to the terms of the lease. If the tenant moves in before the regular rental period—such as the middle of the month and you want rent due on the first of every month—you will need to prorate

the rent for the first partial month as explained in Clause 5 (Payment of Rent).

Possible Modifications to Clause 4 (Lease):

If you want to provide for a periodic rent increase, perhaps tied to a consumer price index or your operating expenses, you'll need to add language to this effect. Without this type of built-in increase, you can't increase the rent until the lease ends.

 CAUTION

Avoid liquidated damages provisions.
Some preprinted forms (not ours) include what lawyers quaintly call a "liquidated damages" clause. This means that if a tenant moves out before the lease expires, he is supposed to pay you a predetermined amount of money (damages) caused by his early departure. Unless the amount of liquidated damages is close to the damages a landlord actually suffers, this approach is likely to be illegal. Under the laws of most states, a tenant who moves out before the lease expires is legally responsible to pay only for the actual losses he caused (such as rent lost). If a suitable new tenant moves in immediately, this may be little or nothing. And, in most states, you are legally obligated to minimize your losses by trying to find a new tenant as soon as possible. Chapter 14 provides details on your responsibility to mitigate damages.

Clause 4. Term of the Tenancy (Rental Agreement)

The rental will begin on _____ , and continue on a month-to-month basis. Landlord may terminate the tenancy or modify the terms of this Agreement by giving the Tenant _____ days' written notice. Tenant may terminate the tenancy by giving the Landlord _____ days' written notice.

The rental agreement provides for a month-to-month tenancy and specifies how much written notice you must give a tenant to change or end a tenancy, and how much notice the tenant must provide you before moving out. Chapter 14 discusses changing or ending a month-to-month tenancy.

How to Fill in Clause 4 (Rental Agreement):

In the first blank, fill in the date the tenancy will begin. The date the tenancy will begin is the date the tenant has the right to move in, such as the first of the month. This date does not have to be the date that you and the tenant sign the rental agreement. The agreement signing date is simply the date that you're both bound to the terms of the rental agreement. If the tenant moves in before the regular rental period—such as the middle of the month and you want rent due on the first of every month—you will need to prorate the rent for the first partial month as explained in Clause 5 (Payment of Rent).

In the next two blanks, fill in the amount of written notice you'll need to give tenants to end or change a tenancy, and the amount of notice tenants must provide to end a tenancy. In most cases, to comply with the law of your state, this will be 30 days for both landlord and tenant in a month-to-month tenancy. See "State Rules on Notice Required to Change or Terminate a Month-to-Month Tenancy" in Appendix A for details.

Possible Modifications to Clause 4 (Rental Agreement):

This rental agreement is month to month, although you can change it to a different interval as long as you don't go below the minimum notice period required by your state's law. If you do, be aware that notice requirements to change or end a tenancy may also need to differ from those required for standard month-to-month rental agreements, since state law often requires that all key notice periods be the same.

RENT CONTROL
Your right to terminate or change the terms of a tenancy, even one from month to month, can be limited by a rent control ordinance. Such ordinances not only limit rent and other terms of tenancies, but also require the landlord to have a good reason to terminate a tenancy.

Clause 5. Payment of Rent

Regular monthly rent.

Tenant will pay to Landlord a monthly rent of $_____, payable in advance on the first day of each month, except when that day falls on a weekend or legal holiday, in which case rent is due on the next business day. Rent will be paid in the following manner unless Landlord designates otherwise:

Delivery of payment.

Rent will be paid:

☐ by mail, to _____

☐ in person, at _____

Form of payment.

Landlord will accept payment in these forms:

☐ cash

☐ personal check made payable to _____

☐ certified funds or money orders

☐ credit card

☐ bank debits

☐ electronic funds transfer _____

Prorated first month's rent.

For the period from Tenant's move-in date, _____, through the end of the month, Tenant will pay to Landlord the prorated monthly rent of $_____. This amount will be paid on or before the date the Tenant moves in.

This clause provides details on the amount of rent and when, where, and how it's paid. It requires the tenant to pay rent monthly on the first day of the month, unless the first day falls on a weekend or a legal holiday, in which case rent is due on the next business day. (Extending the rent due date for holidays is legally required in some states and is a general rule in most.)

We discuss how to set a legal rent and where and how rent is due in Chapter 3. Before you fill in the blanks, please read that chapter.

How to Fill in Clause 5:

Regular monthly rent. In the first blank, state the amount of monthly rent. Unless your premises are subject to a local rent control ordinance, you can legally charge as much rent as you want (or, more practically speaking, as much as a tenant will pay).

Delivery of payment. Next, specify to whom and where the rent is to be paid—by mail (most common) or in person (if so, specify the address, such as your office or to your manager at the rental unit). Be sure to specify the hours that rent can be paid in person, such as 9 a.m. to 5 p.m. weekdays and 9 a.m. to noon on Saturdays.

Form of payment. Note all the forms of payment you'll accept.

- Cash is an option, though generally not a good one; checks are safer.
- You can also provide for certified funds (such as a cashier's check) or money orders.
- For credit card payments, follow the instructions issued by the card's issuer.
- If you choose bank debits, give tenants the information they need to set this up.
- Finally, you may want to consider electronic funds transfers. An electronic funds transfer is the computer-based exchange of money from one account to another, either within a single financial institution or across multiple institutions. The parties involved decide whether the transfers will be automatic or manual.

Electronic funds transfers require little effort when all is going well, are not that difficult to set up, and are easy to monitor online. However, there are pros and cons with every payment method, so you should consider what is best for your situation. Examples include: direct deposit, wire transfer, and PayPal.

Describe any electronic means of payment you will accept and list any specific information that the tenant will need from you in order to successfully transfer the funds.

(Note that in California, you cannot insist on only cash or electronic funds transfer.)

Prorated first month's rent. If the tenant moves in before the regular rental period—let's say in the middle of the month, and you want rent due on the first of every month—you can specify the prorated amount due for the first partial month. To figure out prorated rent, divide the monthly rent by 30 days and multiply by the number of days in the first (partial) rental period. That will avoid confusion about what you expect to be paid. Enter the move-in date, such as "June 21, 20xx," and the amount of prorated monthly rent.

> **EXAMPLE:** Meg rents an apartment for $1,800 per month with rent due on the first of the month. She moves in on June 21, so she should pay ten days' prorated rent of $600 when she moves in. ($1,800 ÷ 30 = $60 × 10 days = $600.) Beginning with July 1, Meg's full $1,800 rent check is due.

If the tenant is moving in on the first of the month or the same day rent is due, write in "N/A" or "Not Applicable" in the section on prorated rent, or delete this section of the clause.

Possible Modifications to Clause 5:

Here are a few common ways to modify Clause 5:

Rent due date. You can establish a rent due date different from the first of the month, such as the day of the month on which the tenant moves in. For example, if the tenant moved in on July 10, rent would be due on the tenth of each month, a system that of course saves the trouble of prorating the first month's rent.

Frequency of rent payments. You are not legally required to have your tenant pay rent on a monthly basis. You can modify the clause and require that the rent be paid twice a month, each week, or by whatever schedule suits you.

Clause 6. Late Charges

> If Tenant fails to pay the rent in full before the end of the _____ day after it's due, Tenant will pay Landlord a late charge as follows: _____ .
> Landlord does not waive the right to insist on payment of the rent in full on the date it is due.

It is your legal right in most states to charge a late fee if rent is not paid on time. This clause spells out details on your policy on late fees. Charging a late fee does not mean that you give up your right to insist that rent be paid on the due date. To bring this point home, Clause 6 states that you do not waive the right to insist on full payment of the rent on the date it is due. A late fee is simply one way to motivate tenants to pay on time. A few states have statutes that put precise limits on the amount of late fees or when they can be collected. For advice on setting a late charge policy, see Chapter 3.

How to Fill in Clause 6:

In the first blank, specify when you will start charging a late fee. You can charge a late fee the first day rent is late, but many landlords don't charge a late fee until the rent is two or three days late.

Next, fill in details on your late rent fee, such as the daily charge and any maximum fee.

Possible Modifications to Clause 6:

If you decide not to charge a late fee (something we consider highly unwise), you may simply delete this clause. If you delete this clause, you'll need to renumber the remaining clauses.

Clause 7. Returned Check and Other Bank Charges

If any check offered by Tenant to Landlord in payment of rent or any other amount due under this Agreement is returned for lack of sufficient funds, a "stop payment," or any other reason, Tenant will pay Landlord a returned check charge of $_____ .

As with late charges, any bounced-check charges you require must be reasonable. Some states regulate the amount you can charge; in the absence of such regulation, you should charge no more than the amount your bank charges you for a returned check, probably $25 to $35 per returned item, plus a few dollars for your trouble. Some states regulate the maximum amount you can charge.

Chapter 3 covers returned check charges.

How to Fill in Clause 7:

In the blank, fill in the amount of the returned check charge.

Possible Modifications to Clause 7:

If you won't accept checks, or you are not charging a returned check fee (something we consider unwise), you may delete this clause from your lease or rental agreement (in which case, you'll need to renumber the remaining clauses).

Clause 8. Security Deposit

On signing this Agreement, Tenant will pay to Landlord the sum of $_____ as a security deposit. Tenant may not, without Landlord's prior written consent, apply this security deposit to the last month's rent or to any other sum due under this Agreement. Within _____ after Tenant has vacated the premises, returned keys, and provided Landlord with a forwarding address, Landlord will return the deposit in full or give Tenant an itemized written statement of the reasons for, and the dollar amount of, any of the security deposit retained by Landlord, along with a check for any deposit balance.

The use and return of security deposits is a frequent source of disputes between landlords and tenants. To avoid confusion and legal hassles, this clause is clear on the subject, including:
- the dollar amount of the deposit
- the fact that the deposit may not be used for the last month's rent without your prior written approval, and
- when the deposit will be returned, along with an itemized statement of deductions.

Chapters 4 and 15 (and the chart "State Security Deposit Rules" in Appendix A) cover the basic information you need to complete Clause 8, including state rules on how large a deposit you can require, when you must return it, and the type of itemization you must provide a tenant when deductions are made.

How to Fill in Clause 8:

Once you decide how much security deposit you can charge, fill in the amount in the first blank. Unless there's a lower limit, we suggest about two months as your rent deposit, assuming your potential tenants can afford that much. In no case is it wise to charge much less than one month's rent.

Next, fill in the time period when you will return the deposit. If there is no statutory deadline for returning the deposit, we recommend three to four weeks as a reasonable time to return a tenant's deposit. Establishing a fairly short period (even if the law of your state allows more time) will discourage anxious tenants from repeatedly bugging you or your manager for their deposit refund.

Possible Modifications to Clause 8:

The laws of several states require you to give tenants written information on various aspects of the security deposit, including where the security deposit is being held, interest payments, and the terms of and conditions under which the security deposit may be withheld. The "State Security Deposit Rules" chart in Appendix A gives you information on disclosures you may need to add to Clause 8. This chart also includes a list of states that require separate accounts for deposits or interest payments on deposits.

Nonrefundable Fees

We don't recommend nonrefundable fees—for one thing, they are illegal in many states. If you do collect a nonrefundable fee—for example, for cleaning or pets—be sure your lease or rental agreement is clear on the subject.

Even if it's not required, you may want to provide additional details on security deposits in your lease or rental agreement. Here are optional clauses you may add to the end of Clause 8.

The security deposit will be held at: (*name and address of financial institution*).

Landlord will pay Tenant interest on all security deposits at the prevailing bank rate.

Landlord may withhold only that portion of Tenant's security deposit necessary to: (1) remedy any default by Tenant in the payment of rent; (2) repair damage to the premises, except for ordinary wear and tear caused by Tenant; (3) clean the premises if necessary; and (4) compensate Landlord for any other losses as allowed by state law.

Clause 9. Utilities

Tenant will pay all utility charges, except for the following, which will be paid by Landlord: _____
_____
_____.

This clause helps prevent misunderstandings as to who's responsible for paying utilities. Normally, landlords pay for garbage (and sometimes water, if there is a yard) to help make sure that the premises are well maintained. Tenants usually pay for other services, such as phone, gas, electricity, Internet access, and cable TV.

How to Fill in Clause 9:

In the blank, fill in the utilities you—not the tenants—will be responsible for paying. If you will not be paying for any utilities, simply delete the last part of the clause ("except … Landlord:").

Disclose Shared Utility Arrangements

If there are not separate gas and electric meters for each unit, or a tenant's meter measures gas or electricity used in areas outside his unit (such as a water heater that serves several apartments or lighting in a common area), you should disclose this in your lease or rental agreement. Simply add details to Clause 20, Disclosures. This type of disclosure is required by law in some states (see "Required Landlord Disclosures," in Appendix A), and is only fair in any case. The best solution is to put in a separate meter for the areas served outside the tenant's unit. If you don't do that, you should:

- pay for the utilities for the tenant's meter yourself by placing that utility in your name
- reduce the tenant's rent to compensate for payment of utility usage outside of their unit (this will probably cost you more in the long run than if you either added a new meter or simply paid for the utilities yourself), or
- sign a separate written agreement with the tenant, under which the tenant specifically agrees to pay for others' utilities, too.

Consider Water Submetering

Making tenants pay for their water usage has become a popular way for landlords to recoup their water costs and increase their profits (studies have also shown that when tenants are billed directly, a property's overall water usage drops considerably). There are three ways to go about this. The best method is to have the water company install meters for each unit, so that each household pays the utility directly. Secondly, you can contract with a submetering company to install submeters, which transmit a unit's water usage directly to the company via digital signals (no need for a meter-reader to physically check the meter). The company bills each household directly, and the landlord pays an administrative fee. Finally, you can estimate each unit's usage by using the "RUBS" method (Ratio Utility Billing System), in which you estimate each unit's usage and share of the total bill based on the unit's square footage or number of occupants. The landlord pays the utility directly, then bills each household for its share.

All of these approaches have their limitations, however. Having the water company install individual meters is feasible in new construction, but usually not practical as a retrofit. Using a submetering company involves an initial expense (installing the submeters), though you may find an aggressive company willing to front the cost. And don't count on being able to pass through this cost (or the ongoing administrative costs) to your tenants, because some states or localities forbid it. As for RUBS, many tenants will object, arguing that whatever formula you use cannot take into account individuals' habits (the careful family of three might use less water than the wasteful couple next door, for example).

Be sure to do your homework before proceeding further. Your state might disallow submetering altogether, and your local laws might have something to say, too. Start by talking with your local water company. For more information on the issue of submetering, check out the website of the Utility Management & Conservation Association, at www.utilitymca.org., a trade association promoting agency energy conservation. If you decide to use a submetering company, shop around and look for a company with a solid reputation for customer service and accurate billing.

Clause 10. Prohibition of Assignment and Subletting

> Tenant will not sublet any part of the premises or assign this Agreement without the prior written consent of Landlord. Neither shall Tenants sublet or rent any part of the premises for short-term stays of any duration, including but not limited to vacation rentals. Violating this clause is grounds for terminating the tenancy.

Clause 10 is an antisubletting clause, breach of which is grounds for eviction. It prevents a tenant from subleasing during a vacation—letting someone stay in his place and pay rent while he's gone for an extended period of time—or renting out a room to someone unless you specifically agree.

Clause 10 is also designed to prevent assignments, a legal term that means your tenant transfers her entire tenancy to someone else. Practically, you need this clause to prevent your tenant from leaving in the middle of the month or lease term and moving in a replacement—maybe someone you wouldn't choose to rent to—without your consent.

By including Clause 10 in your lease or rental agreement, you have the option not to accept the person your tenant proposes to take over the lease. Under the law of most states, however, you should realize that if a tenant who wishes to leave early provides you with another suitable tenant, you can't both unreasonably refuse to rent to this person and hold the tenant financially liable for breaking the lease.

Chapter 8 discusses sublets and assignments in detail. Chapter 14 discusses what happens when a tenant breaks a lease.

CAUTION

If you want to restrict tenants from hosting guests via Airbnb, be sure your lease is clear on this. In recent years, online businesses such as Airbnb have acted as clearinghouses for short-term (less than 30-day) vacation rentals. Especially in vacation-destination cities, tenants have taken advantage of such services, essentially turning their rentals into short-term hotels and pocketing the money (at the same time, increasing wear and tear on the premises). As we discuss in Chapter 8, the law is unclear on whether

Renters' Insurance

Landlords often require tenants to obtain renters' insurance, especially in high-end rentals. This covers losses to the tenant's belongings as a result of fire or theft, as well as injury to other people or property damage caused by the tenant's negligence. Besides protecting the tenant from personal liability, renters' insurance benefits you, too: If damage caused by the tenant could be covered by either the tenant's insurance policy or yours, a claim made on the tenant's policy will affect the tenant's premiums, not yours. Renters' insurance will not cover intentional damage by the tenant.

Be advised that it may not be legal for you to require your tenants to carry renters' insurance (in particular, liability insurance). Judges in some states (including Oklahoma) have held that your tenants are by implication coinsureds under your own property policy, because their rent helps pay your premiums. Making tenants buy additional insurance that will cover any destruction they might cause to your property duplicates the insurance that you (and they) already carry and shouldn't be allowed, the theory goes. But unfortunately it's very hard to get a good handle on which states adopt this approach. Only Virginia has clear, statutory law on the subject: Virginia allows a landlord to require a tenant to pay for renters' insurance that's obtained by the landlord. However, if the landlord also requires a security deposit, the combined cost of the insurance premiums and the security deposit cannot exceed two months' rent. (Va. Code Ann. §§ 55-248.2 to -248.9.) Oregon also regulates landlords' requirements for renters' insurance (Ore. Rev. Stat. § 90.222.)

Landlords subject to rent control may not be able to require renters' insurance, because a court might consider the premiums as a rent overcharge. Clearly, before requiring tenants to carry renters' insurance, you'll need to check with your agent or lawyer on the legality of such a requirement in your state or locality.

If you decide to require insurance, insert a clause like the following under Clause 22, Additional Provisions. This will help assure that the tenant carries renters' insurance throughout his tenancy. The average cost of renters' insurance is typically less than $20 or $30 per month, depending on the location and size of the rental unit and the value of the policyholder's possessions. Some carriers offer discounts if tenants already have another type of insurance with their companies, and additional discounts for tenants who do not smoke (smoking is a major cause of house fires) and who can demonstrate they have risk-reduction measures such as smoke alarms, safes, alarm systems, or double-bolt locks.

Renters' Insurance

Within ten days of the signing of this Agreement, Tenant will obtain renters' insurance, and provide proof of purchase to Landlord. Tenant further agrees to maintain the policy throughout the duration of the tenancy, and to furnish proof of insurance on a ☐ yearly ☐ semiannual basis.

---

generic no-sublet clauses apply so as to forbid the practice of tenants hosting guests via Airbnb and similar services. For this reason, we have included the following sentence at the end of Clause 10 in our lease or rental agreement clause prohibiting subletting: "Neither shall Tenants sublet or rent any part of the premises for short-term stays of any duration, including but not limited to vacation rentals."

How to Fill in Clause 10:

You don't need to add anything to this clause in most situations. There may be local laws, however, that do apply, as discussed in Chapter 8.

Clause 11. Tenant's Maintenance Responsibilities

Tenant will: (1) keep the premises clean, sanitary, and in good condition and, upon termination of the tenancy, return the premises to Landlord in a condition identical to that which existed when Tenant took occupancy, except for ordinary wear and tear; (2) immediately notify Landlord of any defects or dangerous conditions in and about the premises of which Tenant becomes aware; and (3) reimburse Landlord, on demand by Landlord, for the cost of any repairs to the premises damaged by Tenant or Tenant's guests or business invitees through misuse or neglect.

Tenant has examined the premises, including appliances, fixtures, carpets, drapes, and paint, and has found them to be in good, safe, and clean condition and repair, except as noted in the Landlord-Tenant Checklist.

Clause 11 makes the tenant responsible for keeping the rental premises clean and sanitary. This clause also makes it clear that if the tenant damages the premises (for example, by breaking a window or scratching hardwood floors), it's his responsibility for the damage.

It is the law in some states (and wise in all) to notify tenants in writing of procedures for making complaints and repair requests. Clause 11 requires the tenant to alert you to defective or dangerous conditions.

Clause 11 also states that the tenant has examined the rental premises, including appliances, carpets, and paint, and found them to be safe and clean, except as noted in a separate form (the Landlord-Tenant Checklist, described in Chapter 7). Before the tenant moves in, you and the tenant should inspect the rental unit and fill out the Landlord-Tenant Checklist in Chapter 7, describing what is in the unit and noting any problems. Doing so will help you avoid disputes over security deposit deductions when the tenant moves out.

Chapter 9 provides details on landlords' and tenants' repair and maintenance responsibilities, recommends a system for tenants to request repairs, and offers practical advice on maintaining your rental property. Chapter 9 also covers tenant options (such as rent withholding) should you fail to maintain your property and keep it in good repair.

How to Fill in Clause 11:

You do not need to add anything to this clause.

> **CAUTION**
> **Don't fail to maintain the property.** In most states, language you stick in a lease or rental agreement saying a tenant gives up his right to habitable housing won't be effective. By law, you have to provide habitable housing,

no matter what the agreement says. If your tenants or their guests suffer injury or property damage as a result of poorly maintained property, you may be held responsible for paying for the loss. See Chapters 10, 11, and 12 for liability-related issues.

Clause 12. Repairs and Alterations by Tenant

a. Except as provided by law, or as authorized by the prior written consent of Landlord, Tenant will not make any repairs or alterations to the premises, including nailing holes in the walls or painting the rental unit.

b. Tenant will not, without Landlord's prior written consent, alter, rekey, or install any locks to the premises or install or alter any security alarm system. Tenant will provide Landlord with a key or keys capable of unlocking all such rekeyed or new locks as well as instructions on how to disarm any altered or new security alarm system.

Clause 12 makes it clear that the tenant may not make alterations and repairs without your consent, including painting the unit or nailing holes in the walls.

And to make sure you can take advantage of your legal right of entry in an emergency situation, Clause 12 specifically forbids the tenant from rekeying the locks or installing a security alarm system without your consent. If you do grant permission, make sure your tenant gives you duplicate keys or the name and phone number of the alarm company or instructions on how to disarm the security system so that you can enter in case of emergency. See Chapter 12 for more information on your responsibility to provide secure premises, and Chapter 13 for information on your right to enter rental property in an emergency.

The "except as provided by law" language in Clause 12 is a reference to the fact that, in certain situations and in certain states, tenants have a narrowly defined right to alter or repair the premises, regardless of what you've said in the lease or rental agreement. Examples include:

- **Alterations by a person with a disability, such as lowering countertops for a wheelchair-bound tenant.**

Under the federal Fair Housing Acts, a person with a disability may modify her living space to the extent necessary to make the space safe and comfortable, as long as the modifications will not make the unit unacceptable to the next tenant, or if the tenant with a disability agrees to undo the modification when she leaves. See Chapter 5 for details.

- **Use of the "repair and deduct" procedure.** In most states, tenants have the right to repair defects or damage that make the premises uninhabitable or substantially interfere with the tenant's safe use or enjoyment of the premises. Usually, the tenant must first notify you of the problem and give you a reasonable amount of time to fix it. (See Chapter 9 for more on this topic.)
- **Installation of satellite dishes and antennas.** Federal law gives tenants limited rights to install wireless antennas and small satellite dishes. See Chapter 9 for details.
- **Specific alterations allowed by state statutes.** In Connecticut, for example, tenants may install removable interior storm windows or other energy conservation measures without the landlord's prior consent. (Conn. Gen. Stat. Ann. § 47a-13a.) In Virginia (Va. Code Ann. § 55-248.18(D)) and Texas (Tex. Prop. Code Ann. §§ 92.151 and following), tenants may install burglary prevention devices. California tenants may install statutorily required door and window locks if the landlord has refused to do so. (Cal. Civ. Code § 1941.3.) Texas also gives tenants this right. (Tex. Prop. Code § 92.164.) Check your state statutes or call your local rental property association for more information on these types of laws.

How to Fill in Clause 12:

If you do not want the tenant to make any repairs without your permission, you do not need to add anything to this clause.

You may, however, want to go further and specifically prohibit certain repairs or alterations by adding details in Clause 12. For example, you may want to make it clear that any "fixtures"—a legal term that describes any addition that is attached to the structure, such as bolted-on bookcases or built-in dishwashers—are your property and may not be removed by the tenant without your permission.

If you do authorize the tenant to make any repairs, provide enough detail so that the tenant knows exactly what is expected, how much repairs can cost, and who will pay. For example, if you decide to allow the tenant to take over the repair of any broken windows, routine plumbing jobs, or landscaping, give specific descriptions and limits to the tasks. Chapter 9 includes a detailed discussion of delegating repair and maintenance responsibilities, a sample agreement form regarding tenant alterations and improvements, and an overview of legal issues regarding fixtures.

> CAUTION
> **If you want the tenant to perform maintenance work for you in exchange for reduced rent, don't write it into the lease or rental agreement.** Instead, use a separate employment agreement and pay the tenant for her services. That way, if she doesn't perform, you still have the full rent, and you can simply cancel the employment contract.

Clause 13. Prohibition Against Violating Laws and Causing Disturbances

Tenant is entitled to quiet enjoyment of the premises. Tenant and guests or invitees will not use the premises or adjacent areas in such a way as to: (1) violate any law or ordinance, including laws prohibiting the use, possession, or sale of illegal drugs; (2) commit waste (severe property damage); or (3) create a nuisance by annoying, disturbing, inconveniencing, or interfering with the quiet enjoyment and peace and quiet of any other tenant or nearby resident.

This type of clause is found in most form leases and rental agreements. It prohibits tenants (and their guests) from violating the law, damaging your property, or disturbing other tenants or nearby residents. Although this clause contains some legal jargon, it's probably best to leave it as is, since courts have much experience in working with terms like waste and nuisance (defined below).

This clause also refers to tenants' right to "quiet enjoyment" of the premises. As courts define it, the "covenant of quiet enjoyment" amounts to an implied promise that you will not act (or fail to act) in a way that seriously interferes with or destroys the ability of the tenant to use the rented premises—for example, by allowing garbage to pile up, tolerating a major rodent infestation, or failing to control a tenant whose constant loud music makes it impossible for other tenants to sleep.

If you want more specific rules—for example, no loud music played after midnight—add them to Clause 18: Tenant Rules and Regulations, or to Clause 22: Additional Provisions.

Chapter 16 includes a detailed discussion of how to deal with noisy tenants.

Waste and Nuisance: What Are They?

In legalese, committing **waste** means causing severe damage to real estate, including a house or an apartment unit—damage that goes way beyond ordinary wear and tear. Punching holes in walls, pulling out sinks and fixtures, and knocking down doors are examples of waste.

Nuisance means behavior that prevents tenants and neighbors from fully enjoying the use of their homes and results in a substantial danger to their health and safety. Continuous loud noise and foul odors are examples of legal nuisances that may disturb nearby neighbors and affect their "quiet enjoyment" of the premises. So, too, are selling drugs or engaging in other illegal activities that greatly disturb neighbors.

How to Fill in Clause 13:

You do not need to add anything to this clause.

Clause 14. Pets

No animal may be kept on the premises, without Landlord's prior written consent, except animals needed by tenants who have a disability, as that term is understood by law, and _____ under the following conditions: _____
_____
_____ .

This clause prevents tenants from keeping pets without your written permission. If you want, you can have a flat "no pets" rule, though many landlords report that pet-owning tenants are more appreciative, stable, and responsible than the norm. But it does provide you with a legal mechanism that will keep your premises from being waist-deep in Irish wolfhounds. Without this sort of provision, particularly in a fixed-term lease that can't be terminated early save for a clear violation of one of its provisions, there's little to prevent your tenant from keeping multiple, dangerous, or nonhousebroken pets, except for city ordinances prohibiting tigers and animal cruelty laws.

With the exception of trained dogs and some other animals used by people who have a mental or physical disability, you have the right to prohibit all pets, or to restrict the types of pets or dog breeds you allow. Your pet policy should cover not only pets the tenant may have, but also pets of guests. When setting your pet policy, be sure to check any insurance or homeowners' association restrictions as to breeds of dog, weight, number of pets, and species allowed.

How to Fill in Clause 14:

If you do not allow pets, simply delete the words "and _____ under the following conditions:".

If you allow pets, be sure to identify the type and number of pets in the first blank—for example, "one cat" or "one dog under 20 pounds." It's also wise to spell out your pet rules in the second blank, or in an attachment—for example, you may want to specify that the tenants will keep the grounds and street free of all animal waste, and that cats and dogs be spayed or neutered, licensed, and up-to-date on vaccinations. Your Tenant Rules and Regulations may be another place to do this. See Clause 18.

Should You Require a Separate Security Deposit for Pets?

Some landlords allow pets but require the tenant to pay a separate deposit to cover any damages caused by the pet. The laws of a few states specifically allow separate, nonrefundable pet deposits. Hawaii allows a separate pet deposit, not to exceed one month's rent, and not to apply to assistance animals. (Haw. Rev. Stat. § 521-44.) In other states, charging a designated pet deposit is legal only if the total amount you charge for deposits does not exceed the state maximum for all deposits. (See Chapter 4 for details on security deposits.)

Even where allowed, separate pet deposits can often be a bad idea because they limit how you can use that part of the security deposit. For example, if the pet is well-behaved, but the tenant trashes your unit, you can't use the pet portion of the deposit to clean up after the human. If you want to protect your property from damage done by a pet, you are probably better off charging a slightly higher rent or security deposit to start with (assuming you are not restricted by rent control or the upper security deposit limits).

It is illegal to charge an extra pet deposit for people with trained service or companion animals.

It is important to educate tenants from the start that you will not tolerate dangerous or even apparently dangerous pets; and that as soon as you learn of a worrisome situation, you have the option of insisting that the tenant get rid of the pet (or move). You may want to advise tenants that their pets must be well-trained and nonthreatening in the second blank of Clause 14; or you could set out your policy in your Rules and Regulations (if any). Your policy might look something like this:

Tenant's pet(s) will be well-behaved and under Tenant's control at all times and will not pose a threat or apparent threat to the safety of other tenants, their guests, or other people on or near the rental premises. If, in the opinion of Landlord, tenant's pet(s) pose such a threat, Landlord will serve Tenant with the appropriate notice to terminate the tenancy.

A policy against dangerous pets is only effective if it's enforced. To limit your liability if a tenant's pet injures someone on or even near your property, be sure that you or your manager follow through with your policy—by keeping an eye on your tenants' pets and by listening to and acting on any complaints from other tenants or neighbors. For more on landlord liability for dog bites and other animal attacks, see Chapter 10.

> ⊘ **CAUTION**
>
> **Enforce no-pets clauses.** When faced with tenants who violate no-pets clauses, landlords often ignore the situation for a long time, then try to enforce it later if friction develops over some other matter. This could backfire. In general, if you know a tenant has breached the lease or rental agreement (for example, by keeping a pet) and do nothing about it for a long time, you risk having legally waived your right to object. Better to adopt a policy you plan to stick to and then preserve your right to object, by promptly giving any offending tenant an informal written notice to get rid of the animal—see the warning letter in Chapter 16 for an example. Then follow through with a termination notice, subject to any rent control law requirements.

Renting to Pet Owners

The San Francisco Society for the Prevention of Cruelty to Animals (SPCA), one of several humane societies across the country that offers animal guidelines for landlords and tenants, including sample documents, such as a pet agreement. For more information, search their website at www.sfspca.org for "Tenants & Landlords" under the Resources section. For additional information, see the national Humane Society's website at www.humanesociety.org, and search "renting with pets."

Also, see *Every Dog's Legal Guide*, by Mary Randolph (Nolo), for more information on renting to pet owners.

Clause 15. Landlord's Right to Access

> Landlord or Landlord's agents may enter the premises in the event of an emergency, to make repairs or improvements, or to show the premises to prospective buyers or tenants. Landlord may also enter the premises to conduct an annual inspection to check for safety or maintenance problems. Except in cases of emergency, Tenant's abandonment of the premises, court order, or where it is impractical to do so, Landlord shall give Tenant _____ notice before entering.

Clause 15 makes it clear to the tenant that you have a legal right of access to the property to make repairs or to show the premises for sale or rental, provided you give the tenant reasonable notice. In most states, 24 hours is presumed to be a reasonable amount of notice. A few states require a longer notice period. Chapter 13 provides details on landlord's right to enter rental property and notice requirements.

How to Fill in Clause 15:

In the blank, indicate the amount of notice you will provide the tenant before entering, at least the minimum required in your state. If your state law simply requires "reasonable" notice or has no notice requirement, we suggest you provide at least 24 hours' notice.

Clause 16. Extended Absences by Tenant

> Tenant will notify Landlord in advance if Tenant will be away from the premises for _____ or more consecutive days. During such absence, Landlord may enter the premises at times reasonably necessary to maintain the property and inspect for damage and needed repairs.

This clause requires that the tenants notify you when leaving your property for an extended time. It gives you the authority to enter the rental unit during the tenant's absence to maintain the property as necessary and to inspect for damage and needed repairs. Chapter 13 discusses your legal right to enter during a tenant's extended absence.

How to Fill in Clause 16:

In the blank, fill in the minimum amount of time the tenant will be gone that will require the tenant to notify you of an extended absence. Ten or 14 days is common.

Clause 17. Possession of the Premises

> a. *Tenant's failure to take possession.*
>
>   If, after signing this Agreement, Tenant fails to take possession of the premises, Tenant will still be responsible for paying rent and complying with all other terms of this Agreement.
>
> b. *Landlord's failure to deliver possession.*
>
>   If Landlord is unable to deliver possession of the premises to Tenant for any reason not within Landlord's control, including, but not limited to, partial or complete destruction of the premises, Tenant will have the right to terminate this Agreement upon proper notice as required by law. In such event, Landlord's liability to Tenant will be limited to the return of all sums previously paid by Tenant to Landlord.

The first part of this clause (part a) explains that a tenant who chooses not to move in (take possession) after signing the lease or rental agreement will still be required to pay rent and satisfy other conditions of the agreement. This does not mean, however, that you can sit back and expect to collect rent for the entire lease or rental agreement term. As we explain in Chapter 14, you generally must take reasonably prompt steps to rerent the premises, and you must credit the rent you collect against the first tenant's rent obligation.

The second part of the clause (part b) protects you if you're unable, for reasons beyond your control, to turn over possession after having signed the agreement or lease—for example, if a fire spreads from next door and destroys the premises or contracted repairs aren't done on time. It limits your financial liability to the new tenant to the return of any prepaid rent and security deposits (the "sums previously paid" in the language of the clause).

CAUTION

Clause 17 may not limit your liability if you cannot deliver possession because the old tenant is still on the premises—even if he or she is the subject of an eviction which you ultimately win. When a holdover tenant prevents the new tenant from moving in, landlords are often sued by the new tenant for not only the return of any prepaid rent and security deposits, but also the costs of temporary housing, storage costs, and other losses. In some states, an attempt in the lease to limit the new tenant's recovery to the return of prepaid sums alone would not hold up in court. To protect yourself, you will want to shift some of the financial liability to the holdover tenant. You'll have a stronger chance of doing this if the old tenant has given written notice of his or her intent to move out. (See Clause 4, above, which requires written notice.)

How to Fill in Clause 17:

You do not need to add anything to this clause.

TIP

Don't rerent until you are positive that the unit will be available. If you have any reason to suspect that your current tenant will not vacate when the lease or rental agreement is up, think twice before signing a new lease or agreement or even promising the rental unit to the next tenant. If the current occupant is leaving of her own will or appears to have another dwelling lined up (perhaps you have received a query from the new landlord), chances are that she will leave as planned. On the other hand, if you declined to renew the lease or rental agreement and there are bad feelings between you, or you suspect that the tenant has fallen on hard times and has not obtained replacement housing—and certainly if she is the subject of an eviction—you are asking for trouble if you promise the unit to someone else.

Clause 18. Tenant Rules and Regulations

☐ Tenant acknowledges receipt of, and has read a copy of, tenant rules and regulations, which are attached to and incorporated into this Agreement by this reference. Tenant understands that serious or repeated violations of the rules may be grounds for termination. Landlord may change the rules and regulations without notice.

What's Covered in Tenant Rules and Regulations

Tenant rules and regulations typically cover issues such as:
- elevator use
- pool rules, including policies on guest use
- garbage and recycling pickups
- vehicles and parking regulations—for examples, restrictions of repairs on the premises, or types of vehicles (such as no RVs), or where guests can park
- lock-out and lost key charges
- pet rules
- security system use
- no smoking—either in common areas in multiunit building, including the hallways, lobby, garage, or walkways, or even in individual units (see Chapter 9 for more on no-smoking policies)
- specific details on what's considered excessive noise and rules to limit noise—for example, carpets or rugs required on hardwood floors (which usually aren't soundproof)
- dangerous materials—nothing flammable or explosive should be on the premises
- storage of bikes, baby strollers, and other equipment in halls, stairways, and other common areas
- specific landlord and tenant maintenance responsibilities (such as stopped-up toilets or garbage disposals, broken windows, rodent and pest control, lawn and yard maintenance)
- use of the grounds
- maintenance of balconies and decks—for instance, no drying clothes on balconies
- display of signs in windows
- laundry room rules, and
- waterbeds.

Many landlords don't worry about detailed rules and regulations, especially when they rent single-family homes or duplexes. However, in large multitenant buildings, rules are usually important to control the use of common areas and equipment—both for the convenience, safety, and welfare of the tenants and as a way to protect your property from damage. Rules and regulations also help avoid confusion and misunderstandings about day-to-day issues such as garbage disposal, use of recreation areas, and lost key charges.

Not every minor rule needs to be incorporated in your lease or rental agreement. But it is a good idea to specifically incorporate important ones (especially those that are likely to be ignored by some tenants), such as no smoking in individual units or common areas. Doing so gives you the authority to evict a tenant who persists in seriously violating your code of tenant rules and regulations. Also, to avoid charges of illegal discrimination, rules and regulations should apply equally to all tenants in your rental property. And make sure your tenants know that these rules apply to guests as well.

Because tenant rules and regulations are often lengthy and may be revised occasionally, we suggest you prepare a separate attachment. Be sure the rules and regulations (including any revisions) are dated on each page and signed by both you and the tenant.

You can usually change your rules and regulations without waiting until the end of the rental (for leases) or without giving proper notice (for rental agreements)—but only if the change is minor and not apt to affect the tenant's use and enjoyment of his tenancy. Shortening the pool hours in the winter months is an example of a minor change. Closing all laundry facilities in an attempt to save on water and electrical bills is a major change that should be the subject of a proper notice (for month-to-month tenants); this may be a step that you can't take at all if your building has tenants with leases. You'll have to wait until the longest lease is up for renewal.

How to Fill in Clause 18:

If you have a set of tenant rules and regulations, check the box. Do the same if your rental is in a community with homeowners' association or condo rules. If you do not have a separate set of tenant rules and regulations, simply delete this clause (in which case you will need to renumber the remaining clauses).

Clause 19. Payment of Court Costs and Attorney Fees in a Lawsuit

In any action or legal proceeding to enforce any part of this Agreement, the prevailing party ☐ shall not / ☐ shall recover reasonable attorney fees and court costs.

Many landlords assume that if they sue a tenant and win (or prevail, in legalese), the court will order the losing tenant to pay the landlord's court costs (filing fees, service of process charges, deposition costs, and so on) and attorney fees. In some states and under certain conditions, this is true. For example, an Arizona landlord who wins an eviction lawsuit is eligible to receive costs and fees even if the lease does not have a "costs and fees" clause in it. (Ariz. Rev. Stat. §§ 33-1315, 12-341.01.) But in most states, a court will order the losing tenant to pay your attorney fees and court costs only if a written agreement specifically provides for it.

If, however, you have an "attorney fees" clause in your lease, all this changes. If you hire a lawyer to bring a lawsuit concerning the lease and win, the judge will order your tenant to pay your court costs and attorney fees. (In rare instances, a court will order the loser to pay costs and fees even though there's no "attorney fees" clause in the lease, if it finds that the behavior of the losing party was particularly outrageous—for example, filing a totally frivolous lawsuit.)

But there's another important issue you may need to know about. By law in many states, an attorney fees clause in a lease or rental agreement works both ways, even if you haven't written it that way. That is, if the lease only states that you are entitled to attorney fees if you win a lawsuit, your tenants will be entitled to collect their attorney fees from you if they prevail. The amount you would be ordered to pay would be whatever the judge decides is reasonable.

So, especially if you live in a state that will read a "one-way" attorney fees clause as a two-way street, give some thought to whether you want to bind both of you to paying for the winner's costs and fees. Remember, if you can't actually collect a judgment containing attorney fees from an evicted tenant (which often happens), the clause will not help you. But if the tenant prevails, you will be stuck paying the tenant's court costs and attorney fees. In addition, the presence of a two-way clause will make it easier for a tenant to secure a willing lawyer for even a doubtful claim, because the source of the lawyer's fee (you, if you lose) will often appear more financially solid than if the client were paying the bill himself or herself.

Especially if you intend to do all or most of your own legal work in any potential eviction or other lawsuit, you will almost surely be better off not to allow for attorney fees. Why? Because if the tenant wins, you will have to pay the tenant's fees; but if you win, the tenant will owe you nothing, since you didn't hire an attorney. You can't even recover for the long hours you spent preparing for and handling the case.

How to Fill in Clause 19:

If you don't want to allow for attorney fees, check the first box before the words "shall not" and delete the word "shall."

If you want to be entitled to attorney fees and costs if you win—and you're willing to pay them if you lose—check the second box before the words "shall recover" and delete the words "shall not."

> ! CAUTION
> **If your rental property is in Ohio, do not include the attorney fees clause**—it's prohibited by law in Ohio. (Oh. Rev. Code Ann. § 5321.13(c).)

> ! CAUTION
> **Attorney fees clauses don't cover all legal disputes.** They cover fees only for lawsuits that concern the meaning or implementation of a rental agreement or lease—for example, a dispute about rent, security deposits, or your right to access (assuming that the rental document includes these subjects). An attorney fees clause would not apply in a personal injury or discrimination lawsuit.

Clause 20. Disclosures

Tenant acknowledges that Landlord has made the following disclosures regarding the premises:

☐ Disclosure of Information on Lead-Based Paint and/or Lead-Based Paint Hazards

☐ Other disclosures: _____

_____

Under federal law, you must disclose any known lead-based paint hazards in rental premises constructed prior to 1978. (Chapter 11 provides complete details on disclosing environmental health hazards such as lead, including the specific form you must use.)

State and local laws may require you to make other disclosures before a new tenant signs a lease or rental agreement or moves in. Some disclosures that may be required include:

- the name of the owner and the person authorized to receive legal papers, such as a property manager (see Clause 21)
- details on installation and maintenance of smoke detectors and alarms (this is included on the Landlord-Tenant Checklist in Chapter 7)
- hidden (not obvious) aspects of the rental property that could cause injury or substantially interfere with tenants' safe enjoyment and use of the dwelling—for example, a warning that the building walls contain asbestos insulation, which could become dangerous if disturbed (Chapters 10, 11, and 12 discuss landlord's liability for dangerous conditions)
- planned condominium conversions (discussed in Chapter 14), and
- the presence of a methamphetamine laboratory at the rental prior to the tenant's occupancy. Even if your state does not have a specific statutory disclosure requirement, you may need to disclose the information pursuant to your duty to notify tenants of nonobvious aspects of the rental that could cause injury. See Chapter 12 for information on dealing with the remains of a meth lab.

See "Required Landlord Disclosures," in Appendix A, for disclosures required by some states.

> $ RENT CONTROL
> **Rent control ordinances typically include additional disclosures,** such as the name and address of the government agency or elected board that administers the ordinance. (Chapter 3 discusses rent control.)

How to Fill in Clause 20:

If your rental property was built before 1978, you must meet federal lead disclosure requirements, so check the first box and follow the advice in Chapter 11.

If you are legally required to make other disclosures as described above, check the second box and provide details in the blank space, adding additional details or pages as necessary.

> **! CAUTION**
>
> **Some problems need to be fixed, not merely disclosed.** Warning your tenants about a hidden defect does not absolve you of legal responsibility if the condition makes the dwelling uninhabitable or unreasonably dangerous. For example, you are courting liability if you rent an apartment with a gas heater that you know might blow up, even if you warn the tenant that the heater is faulty. Nor can you simply warn your tenants about prior crime on the premises and then fail to do anything (like installing deadbolts or an alarm system) to promote safety. Chapters 10, 11, and 12 discuss problems that are proper subjects of warnings and those that ought to be fixed.

Clause 21. Authority to Receive Legal Papers

> The Landlord, any person managing the premises, and anyone designated by the Landlord are authorized to accept service of process and receive other notices and demands, which may be delivered to:
>
> The Landlord, at the following address: _____
> _____
>
> The manager, at the following address: _____
> _____
>
> The following person, at the following address: _____
> _____

It's the law in many states, and a good idea in all, to give your tenants information about everyone whom you have authorized to receive notices and legal papers, such as a tenant's notice that he or she is ending the tenancy or a tenant's court documents as part of an eviction defense. Of course, you may want to handle all of this yourself or delegate it to a manager or management company. Make sure the person you designate to receive legal papers is almost always available to receive tenant notices and legal papers. In some states, any nonresident owner must designate an agent who is a resident of or has a business office in the state.

Be sure to keep your tenants up to date on any changes in this information.

How to Fill in Clause 21:

Provide your name and street address or the name and address of someone else you authorize to receive notices and legal papers on your behalf, such as a property manager.

> **! CAUTION**
>
> **Do you trust your manager?** It's unwise to have a manager you wouldn't trust to receive legal papers on your behalf. You don't, for example, want a careless apartment manager to throw away notice of a lawsuit against you without informing you. That could result in a judgment against you and a lien against your property in a lawsuit you didn't even know about. For more information on using property managers, see Chapter 6.

Clause 22. Additional Provisions

> Additional provisions are as follows: _____
> _____
> _____
> _____.

In this clause, you may list any additional provisions or agreements that are unique to you and the particular tenant signing the lease or rental agreement, such as a provision that prohibits smoking in the tenant's apartment or in the common areas. For more information on restrictions on smoking, see Chapter 9.

If you don't have a separate Tenant Rules and Regulations clause (see Clause 18, above), you may spell out a few rules under this clause—for example, regarding lost key charges or use of a pool on the property.

How to Fill in Clause 22:

List additional provisions or rules here or in an attachment. If there are no additional provisions, delete this clause and remember to renumber the other clauses accordingly.

> **TIP**
> **There is no legal or practical imperative to put every small detail you want to communicate to the tenant into your lease or rental agreement.** Instead, prepare a welcoming, but no-nonsense, "move-in letter" that dovetails with the lease or rental agreement and highlights important terms of the tenancy—for example, how and where to report maintenance problems. You may also use a move-in letter to cover issues not included in the lease or rental agreement—for example, rules for use of a laundry room. Chapter 7 covers move-in letters.

> **CAUTION**
> **Do not include exculpatory clauses or hold-harmless clauses.** Many form leases include provisions that attempt to absolve you in advance from responsibility for all damages, injuries, or losses, including those caused by your legal misdeeds. These clauses come in two varieties:
> - Exculpatory: "If there's a problem, you won't hold me responsible," and
> - Hold-harmless: "If there's a problem traceable to me, you're responsible."
>
> Many exculpatory clauses are blatantly illegal and will not be upheld in court (Chapter 10 discusses exculpatory clauses). If a tenant is injured because of a dangerous condition you failed to fix for several months, no boilerplate lease language will protect you from civil and possibly even criminal charges.

Clause 23. Validity of Each Part

> If any portion of this Agreement is held to be invalid, its invalidity will not affect the validity or enforceability of any other provision of this Agreement.

This clause is known as a "savings" clause, and it is commonly used in contracts. It means that, in the unlikely event that one of the other clauses in this lease or rental agreement is found to be invalid by a court, the remainder of the agreement will remain in force.

How to Fill in Clause 23:

You do not need to add anything to this clause.

Clause 24. Grounds for Termination of Tenancy

> The failure of Tenant or Tenant's guests or invitees to comply with any term of this Agreement, or the misrepresentation of any material fact on Tenant's rental application, is grounds for termination of the tenancy, with appropriate notice to Tenant and procedures as required by law.

This clause states that any violation of the lease or rental agreement by the tenant, or by the tenant's business or social guests, is grounds for terminating the tenancy, according to the procedures established by your state or local laws. Making the tenant responsible for the actions of his guests can be extremely important—for example, if you discover that the tenant's family or friends are dealing illegal drugs on the premises, have damaged the property, or have brought a dog to visit a no-pets apartment. Chapter 17 discusses terminations and evictions for tenant violation of a lease or rental agreement.

This clause also tells the tenant that if he has made false statements on the rental application concerning an important fact—such as his prior criminal history—you may terminate the tenancy and evict if necessary.

How to Fill in Clause 24:

You do not need to add anything to this clause.

Clause 25. Entire Agreement

> This document constitutes the entire Agreement between the parties, and no promises or representations, other than those contained here and those implied by law, have been made by Landlord or Tenant. Any modifications to this Agreement must be in writing signed by Landlord and Tenant.

Month-to-Month Residential Rental Agreement

Clause 1. Identification of Landlord and Tenant

This Agreement is entered into between ___Marty Nelson_____

_____ [Tenant] and

___Alex Stevens_____ [Landlord].

Each Tenant is jointly and severally liable for the payment of rent and performance of all other terms of this Agreement.

Clause 2. Identification of Premises

Subject to the terms and conditions in this Agreement, Landlord rents to Tenant, and Tenant rents from Landlord, for residential purposes only, the premises located at ___137 Howell St., Philadelphia,___

___Pennsylvania_____ [the premises],

together with the following furnishings and appliances: _____

_____ .

Rental of the premises also includes _____

_____ .

Clause 3. Limits on Use and Occupancy

The premises are to be used only as a private residence for Tenant(s) listed in Clause 1 of this Agreement, and their minor children. Occupancy by guests for more than ___ten days every six months___

is prohibited without Landlord's written consent and will be considered a breach of this Agreement.

Clause 4. Term of the Tenancy

The rental will begin on ___September 15, 20xx_____ , and continue on a month-to-month basis. Landlord may terminate the tenancy or modify the terms of this Agreement by giving the Tenant

_____30_____ days' written notice. Tenant may terminate the tenancy by giving the Landlord

_____30_____ days' written notice.

Clause 5. Payment of Rent

Regular monthly rent.

Tenant will pay to Landlord a monthly rent of $___900_____ , payable in advance on the first day of each month, except when that day falls on a weekend or legal holiday, in which case rent is due on the next business day. Rent will be paid in the following manner unless Landlord designates otherwise:

Delivery of payment.

Rent will be paid:

☑ by mail, to ___Alex Stevens, 28 Franklin St., Philadelphia, Pennsylvania 19120_____

☐ in person, at _____

Form of payment.

Landlord will accept payment in the following forms:

☐ cash

☑ personal check made payable to Alex Stevens

☑ certified funds or money orders

☐ credit card

☑ bank debits

☐ electronic funds transfer

Prorated first month's rent.

For the period from Tenant's move-in date, ___September 15, 20xx___, through the end of the

month, Tenant will pay to Landlord the prorated monthly rent of $ __450__ . This amount

will be paid on or before the date the Tenant moves in.

Clause 6. Late Charges

If Tenant fails to pay the rent in full before the end of the ___third___ day after it's due, Tenant will

pay Landlord a late charge as follows: __$10, plus $5 for each additional day that the rent__

__remains unpaid. The total late charge for any one month will not exceed $45.__

Landlord does not waive the right to insist on payment of the rent in full on the date it is due.

Clause 7. Returned Check and Other Bank Charges

If any check offered by Tenant to Landlord in payment of rent or any other amount due under this

Agreement is returned for lack of sufficient funds, a "stop payment," or any other reason, Tenant will pay

Landlord a returned check charge of $ __15__ .

Clause 8. Security Deposit

On signing this Agreement, Tenant will pay to Landlord the sum of $ __1,800__ as a security

deposit. Tenant may not, without Landlord's prior written consent, apply this security deposit to the last

month's rent or to any other sum due under this Agreement. Within __30 days__

after Tenant has vacated the premises, returned keys, and provided Landlord with a forwarding address,

Landlord will return the deposit in full or give Tenant an itemized written statement of the reasons for,

and the dollar amount of, any of the security deposit retained by Landlord, along with a check for any

deposit balance.

[optional clauses here, if any]

The security deposit of $1,800 will be held at:

Federal Bank

1 Federal Street

Philadelphia, PA 19120

Clause 9. Utilities

Tenant will pay all utility charges, except for the following, which will be paid by Landlord:

garbage and water

.

Clause 10. Prohibition of Assignment and Subletting

Tenant will not sublet any part of the premises or assign this Agreement without the prior written consent of Landlord. Neither shall Tenants sublet or rent any part of the premises for short-term stays of any duration, including but not limited to vacation rentals. Violating this clause is grounds for terminating the tenancy.

Clause 11. Tenant's Maintenance Responsibilities

Tenant will: (1) keep the premises clean, sanitary, and in good condition and, upon termination of the tenancy, return the premises to Landlord in a condition identical to that which existed when Tenant took occupancy, except for ordinary wear and tear; (2) immediately notify Landlord of any defects or dangerous conditions in and about the premises of which Tenant becomes aware; and (3) reimburse Landlord, on demand by Landlord, for the cost of any repairs to the premises damaged by Tenant or Tenant's guests or business invitees through misuse or neglect.

Tenant has examined the premises, including appliances, fixtures, carpets, drapes, and paint, and has found them to be in good, safe, and clean condition and repair, except as noted in the Landlord-Tenant Checklist.

Clause 12. Repairs and Alterations by Tenant

a. Except as provided by law, or as authorized by the prior written consent of Landlord, Tenant will not make any repairs or alterations to the premises, including nailing holes in the walls or painting the rental unit.

b. Tenant will not, without Landlord's prior written consent, alter, rekey, or install any locks to the premises or install or alter any security alarm system. Tenant will provide Landlord with a key or keys capable of unlocking all such rekeyed or new locks as well as instructions on how to disarm any altered or new security alarm system.

Clause 13. Violating Laws and Causing Disturbances

Tenant is entitled to quiet enjoyment of the premises. Tenant and guests or invitees will not use the premises or adjacent areas in such a way as to: (1) violate any law or ordinance, including laws prohibiting the use, possession, or sale of illegal drugs; (2) commit waste (severe property damage); or (3) create a nuisance by annoying, disturbing, inconveniencing, or interfering with the quiet enjoyment and peace and quiet of any other tenant or nearby resident.

Clause 14. Pets

No animal may be kept on the premises without Landlord's prior written consent, except animals needed by tenants who have a disability, as that is a term is understood by law, and one dog under 20 pounds under the following conditions: _Tenant complies with Pet Rules set out in separate attachment to this Agreement._

_____

_____ .

Clause 15. Landlord's Right to Access

Landlord or Landlord's agents may enter the premises in the event of an emergency, to make repairs or improvements, or to show the premises to prospective buyers or tenants. Landlord may also enter the premises to conduct an annual inspection to check for safety or maintenance problems. Except in cases of emergency, Tenant's abandonment of the premises, court order, or where it is impractical to do so, Landlord shall give Tenant _____ 24 hours' _____ notice before entering.

Clause 16. Extended Absences by Tenant

Tenant will notify Landlord in advance if Tenant will be away from the premises for _____ seven _____ or more consecutive days. During such absence, Landlord may enter the premises at times reasonably necessary to maintain the property and inspect for damage and needed repairs.

Clause 17. Possession of the Premises

a. *Tenant's failure to take possession.*

If, after signing this Agreement, Tenant fails to take possession of the premises, Tenant will still be responsible for paying rent and complying with all other terms of this Agreement.

b. *Landlord's failure to deliver possession.*

If Landlord is unable to deliver possession of the premises to Tenant for any reason not within Landlord's control, including, but not limited to, partial or complete destruction of the premises, Tenant will have the right to terminate this Agreement upon proper notice as required by law. In such event, Landlord's liability to Tenant will be limited to the return of all sums previously paid by Tenant to Landlord.

Clause 18. Tenant Rules and Regulations

☑ Tenant acknowledges receipt of, and has read a copy of, tenant rules and regulations, which are attached to and incorporated into this Agreement by this reference. Tenant understands that serious or repeated violations of the rules may be grounds for termination. Landlord may change the rules and regulations without notice.

Clause 19. Payment of Court Costs and Attorney Fees in a Lawsuit

In any action or legal proceeding to enforce any part of this Agreement, the prevailing party
☐ shall not / ☑ shall recover reasonable attorney fees and court costs.

Clause 20. Disclosures

Tenant acknowledges that Landlord has made the following disclosures regarding the premises:

☑ Disclosure of Information on Lead-Based Paint and/or Lead-Based Paint Hazards

☐ Other disclosures: _____

_____

_____

_____ .

Clause 21. Authority to Receive Legal Papers

The Landlord, any person managing the premises, and anyone designated by the Landlord are authorized to accept service of process and receive other notices and demands, which may be delivered to:

☑ The Landlord, at the following address: _____ 28 Franklin St., Philadelphia, Pennsylvania 19120

_____ .

☐ The manager, at the following address: _____

_____ .

☐ The following person, at the following address: _____

_____ .

Clause 22. Additional Provisions

Additional provisions are as follows: _____

_____

_____

_____

_____

_____

_____

_____

Clause 23. Validity of Each Part

If any portion of this Agreement is held to be invalid, its invalidity will not affect the validity or enforceability of any other provision of this Agreement.

Clause 24. Grounds for Termination of Tenancy

The failure of Tenant or Tenant's guests or invitees to comply with any term of this Agreement, or the misrepresentation of any material fact on Tenant's rental application, is grounds for termination of the tenancy, with appropriate notice to Tenant and procedures as required by law.

Clause 25. Entire Agreement

This document constitutes the entire Agreement between the parties, and no promises or representations, other than those contained here and those implied by law, have been made by Landlord or Tenant. Any modifications to this Agreement must be in writing signed by Landlord and Tenant.

Sept. 1, 20xx	*Alex Stevens*	Landlord		
Date	Landlord or Landlord's Agent	Title		
28 Franklin Street				
Street Address				
Philadelphia	Pennsylvania		19120	215-555-1578
City	State	Zip Code	Phone	Email
Sept. 1, 20xx	*Marty Nelson*		215-555-8751	
Date	Tenant		Phone	
Date	Tenant		Phone	
Date	Tenant		Phone	

This clause establishes that the lease or rental agreement and any attachments (such as rules and regulations) constitute the entire agreement between you and your tenant. It means that oral promises (by you or the tenant) to do something different with respect to any aspect of the rental are not binding. Any changes or additions must be in writing. Chapter 14 discusses how to modify signed rental agreements and leases.

How to Fill in Clause 25:

You do not need to add anything to this clause.

Signing the Lease or Rental Agreement

Prepare two identical copies of the lease or rental agreement to sign, including all attachments. You and each tenant should sign both copies. At the end of the lease or rental agreement, there's space to include your signature, street address, phone number, and email, or that of the person you authorize as your agent, such as a property manager. There's also space for the tenants' signatures and phone numbers. Again, as stressed in Clause 1, make sure all adults living in the rental unit, including both members of a couple, sign the lease or rental agreement. And check that the tenant's name and signature match his or her driver's license or other legal document.

If the tenant has a cosigner, you'll need to add a line for the cosigner's signature or use a separate form. Cosigners are discussed below.

If you alter our form by writing or typing in changes, be sure that you and all tenants initial the changes when you sign the document, so as to forestall any possibility that a tenant will claim you unilaterally inserted changes after he or she signed.

Give one copy of the signed lease or rental agreement to the tenant(s) and keep the other one for your files. If you are renting to more than one tenant, you don't need to prepare a separate agreement for each cotenant. After the agreement is signed, cotenants may make their own copies of the signed document.

> **CAUTION**
> **Don't sign a lease until all terms are final and the tenant understands what's expected.** All of your expectations should be written into the lease or rental agreement (or any attachments, such as Tenant Rules and Regulations) before you and the tenant sign the document. Never sign an incomplete document assuming last-minute changes can be made later. And be sure your tenant clearly understands the lease or rental agreement before signing (this may mean you'll need to review it clause by clause). Chapter 7 discusses how to get your new tenancy off to the right start.
>
> If English is not the tenant's first language, give the tenant a written translation. (We include Spanish versions of our lease and rental agreement forms on Nolo's website. See Appendix B for the link to the forms in this book.) Some states require this; California, for example, requires landlords who discuss the lease primarily in Spanish, Chinese, Tagalog, Vietnamese, or Korean, to give the applicant an unsigned, translated version of the lease before asking the applicant to sign (doesn't apply when the tenant supplies his own translator, someone who is not a minor and can fluently read and speak both languages). (Cal. Civil Code § 1632.) But even if it's not legally required, you want your tenants to know and follow the rules.

About Cosigners

Some landlords require cosigners (sometimes known as guarantors) on rental agreements and leases, especially when renting to students who depend on parents for much of their income. The cosigner signs a separate agreement or the rental agreement or lease, under which she agrees to be jointly and severally liable with the tenant for the tenant's obligations—that is, to cover any rent or damage-repair costs the tenant fails to pay (Clause 1 discusses the concept of joint and several liability). The cosigner retains responsibility regardless of whether the tenant sublets or assigns his agreement. Clause 11 discusses sublets and assignments, and Chapter 8 covers these issues in detail.

In practice, a cosigner's promise to guarantee the tenant's rent obligation may have less value than at first you might think. This is because the threat of eviction is the primary factor that motivates a

Cosigner Agreement

1. This Cosigner Agreement [Agreement] is entered into on ___September 1___ , ___20xx___ , between
   ___Marty Nelson_____ [Tenant],
   ___Alex Stevens_____ [Landlord],
   and ___Sandy Cole_____ [Cosigner].

2. Tenant has leased from Landlord the premises located at ___137 Howell Street, Philadelphia, PA___
   _____[Premises].

   Landlord and Tenant signed a lease or rental agreement specifying the terms and conditions of this rental

   on ___September 1_____ , ___20xx___ . A copy of the lease or rental agreement is attached to

   this Agreement.

3. Cosigner agrees to be jointly and severally liable with Tenant for Tenant's obligations arising out of the
   lease or rental agreement described in Paragraph 2, including but not limited to unpaid rent, property
   damage, and cleaning and repair costs. Cosigner further agrees that Landlord will have no obligation to
   give notice to Cosigner should Tenant fail to abide by the terms of the lease or rental agreement. Landlord
   may demand that Cosigner perform as promised under this Agreement without first using Tenant's
   security deposit.

4. If Tenant assigns or subleases the Premises, Cosigner will remain liable under the terms of this Agreement
   for the performance of the assignee or sublessee, unless Landlord relieves Cosigner by written termination
   of this Agreement.

5. Cosigner appoints Tenant as his or her agent for service of process in the event of any lawsuit arising out
   of this Agreement.

6. If Landlord and Cosigner are involved in any legal proceeding arising out of this Agreement, the prevailing
   party will recover reasonable attorney fees, court costs, and any costs reasonably necessary to collect a
   judgment.

___Alex Stevens_____   ___September 1, 20xx___
Landlord/Manager   Date

___Marty Nelson_____   ___September 1, 20xx___
Tenant   Date

___Sandy Cole_____   ___September 1, 20xx___
Cosigner   Date

tenant to pay the rent, and obviously you cannot evict a cosigner. Also, since the cosigner must be sued separately in either a regular civil lawsuit or in small claims court, actually doing so—for example, if a tenant stiffs you for a month's rent—may be more trouble than it's worth.

Clause 5 of the cosigner agreement designates the tenant as the cosigner's "agent for service of process." This bit of legal jargon will save you some time and aggravation if you decide to sue the cosigner—it means that you won't have to find the cosigner and serve him personally with notification of your lawsuit. Instead, you can serve the legal papers meant for the cosigner on the tenant (who will be easier to locate). It's then up to the tenant to get in touch with the cosigner. If the cosigner fails to show up, you will be able to win by default. Of course, you still have to collect, and that may involve hiring a lawyer (particularly if the cosigner lives in another state). You can always assign the judgment to a collection agency and resign yourself to giving the agency a cut of any recovery.

In sum, the benefits of having a lease or rental agreement cosigned by someone who won't be living on the property are largely psychological. But these benefits may still be worth something: A tenant who thinks you can (and will) sue the cosigner—who is usually a relative or close friend—may be less likely to default on the rent. Similarly, a cosigner asked to pay the tenant's debts may persuade the tenant to pay. In addition, the cosigner agreement cautions the tenant and cosigner that you can go directly to the cosigner without having to give the cosigner notice, or warning, that the tenant has failed to perform a financial obligation; and you can make this demand without first dipping into the tenant's security deposit.

Because of the practical difficulties associated with cosigners, many landlords refuse to consider them, which is legal in every situation but one: If a tenant with a disability who has insufficient income (but is otherwise suitable) asks you to accept a cosigner who will cover the rent if needed, you must relax your blanket rule at least to the extent of investigating the suitability of the proposed cosigner. If that person is solvent and stable, federal law requires you to accommodate the applicant by accepting the cosigner, in spite of your general policy. (*Giebeler v. M & B Associates*, 343 F.3d 1143 (9th Cir. 2003).)

If you decide to accept a cosigner, you may want to have that person fill out a separate rental application and agree to a credit check—after all, a cosigner who has no resources or connection to the tenant will be completely useless. Should the tenant and her prospective cosigner object to these inquiries and costs, you may wonder how serious they are about the guarantor's willingness to stand behind the tenant. Once you are satisfied that the cosigner can genuinely back up the tenant, add a line at the end of the lease for the dated signature, phone, and address of the cosigner, or use the cosigner agreement form we provide here.

A sample Cosigner Agreement is shown above, and the Nolo website includes a downloadable copy. See Appendix B for the link to the forms in this book. Simply fill in your name and your tenant's and cosigner's names, the address of the rental unit, and the date you signed the agreement with the tenant.

CAUTION

If you later amend the rental agreement or lease (a topic discussed in Chapter 14), have the cosigner sign the new version. Generally speaking, a cosigner is bound only to the terms of the exact lease or rental agreement he cosigns.

Basic Rent Rules

 FORMS IN THIS CHAPTER

    Chapter 3 includes instructions for and a sample of the following form:

• Agreement for Delayed or Partial Rent Payments

    The Nolo website includes a downloadable copy of this form. See Appendix B for the link to the forms in this book.

O ne of your foremost concerns as a landlord is receiving your rent—on time and without hassle. It follows that you need a good grasp of the legal rules governing rent. This chapter outlines basic state and local rent laws affecting how much you can charge, as well as where, when, and how rent is due. It also covers rules regarding grace periods, late rent, returned check charges, and rent increases.

Avoiding Rent Disputes

Here are three guidelines that can help you and your tenants have a smooth relationship when it comes to an area of utmost interest to both of you: rent.

- Clearly spell out rent rules in your lease or rental agreement as well as in a move-in letter to new tenants.
- Be fair and consistent about enforcing your rent rules.
- If rent isn't paid on time, follow through with a legal notice telling the tenant to pay or move— the first legal step in a possible eviction—as soon as possible.

RELATED TOPIC
Related topics covered in this book include:

- Lease and rental agreement provisions relating to rent: Chapter 2
- Collecting deposits and potential problems with calling a deposit "last month's rent": Chapter 4
- Compensating a manager with reduced rent: Chapter 6
- Highlighting rent rules in a move-in letter to new tenants and collecting the first month's rent: Chapter 7
- Cotenants' obligations for rent: Chapter 8
- Rent withholding and other tenant options when a landlord fails to maintain the premises in good condition: Chapter 9
- Tenants' obligation to pay rent when breaking a lease: Chapter 14
- Accepting rent after a 30-day notice is given: Chapter 14
- Evicting a tenant for nonpayment of rent: Chapter 17
- State rent rules: Appendix A.

How Much Can You Charge?

In most states, the law doesn't limit how much rent you can charge; you are free to charge what the market will bear. However, in some cities and counties, rent control ordinances do closely govern how much rent a landlord can legally charge. (Rent control is discussed below.) And in Connecticut, which does not have rent control, tenants may challenge a rent that they believe is excessive. (Conn. Gen. Stat. Ann. §§ 7-148B and following.)

If you aren't subject to rent control, it's up to you to determine how much your rental unit is worth. To do this, check rents of comparable properties in your area, and visit a few places that sound similar to yours. Local property management companies, real estate offices that handle rental property, and Craigslist can also provide useful information. In addition, local apartment associations—or other landlords you meet at association functions—are a good source of pricing information.

Many wise landlords choose to charge just slightly less than the going rate as part of a policy designed to find and keep excellent tenants. As with any business arrangement, it usually pays in the long run to have your tenants feel they are getting a good deal. In exchange, you hope the tenants will be responsive to your business needs. This doesn't always work, of course, but tenants who feel their rent is fair are less likely to complain over trifling matters and more likely to stay for an extended period.

Rent Control

SKIP AHEAD
Unless you own property in California; the District of Columbia; Takoma Park, Maryland; Newark, New Jersey; or New York, you aren't affected by rent control and you can skip this section.

Communities in only five states—California, the District of Columbia, Maryland, New Jersey, and

New York—have laws that limit the amount of rent landlords may charge. Typically, only a few cities or counties in each state have enacted local rent control ordinances (also called rent stabilization, maximum rent regulation, or a similar term), but often these are some of the state's largest cities— for example, San Francisco, Los Angeles, New York City, and Newark all have some form of rent control.

RESOURCE
California rent control. California landlords should consult *The California Landlord's Law Book: Rights & Responsibilities*, by David Brown, Ralph Warner, and Janet Portman; and *The California Landlord's Law Book: Evictions*, by David Brown. These books are published by Nolo and are available at bookstores and public libraries. They may also be ordered directly from Nolo's website, www.nolo.com, or by calling 800-728-3555.

The Rent Control Board

In most cities, rent control rests in the hands of a rent control board of five to ten people. Board members often decide annual rent increases, fines, and other important issues. (In many areas, the law itself limits how and when the rent may be raised.)

The actual rent control ordinance is a product of the city council or county board of supervisors. But the rent control board is in charge of interpreting the provisions of the law, which can give the board significant power over landlords and tenants.

Rent control laws commonly regulate much more than rent. For example, owners of rent-controlled properties must follow specific eviction procedures. Because local ordinances are often quite complicated and vary widely, this book cannot provide details on each city's program. Instead, we provide a general description of what rent control ordinances cover.

If you own rental property in a city that has rent control, you should always have a current copy of the ordinance and any regulations interpreting it. And be sure to keep up to date; cities change their rent control laws frequently, and court decisions also affect them. It's a good idea to subscribe to publications of the local property owners' association, and pay attention to local politics to keep abreast of changes in your rent control ordinance and court decisions that may affect you.

CAUTION
Know the law or pay the price. Local governments typically levy fines—sometimes heavy ones—for rent control violations. Violation of a rent control law may also give a tenant a legal ground on which to win an eviction lawsuit. Depending on the circumstances, tenants may also be able to sue you.

Property Subject to Rent Control

Not all rental housing within a rent-controlled city is subject to rent control. Generally, new buildings as well as owner-occupied buildings with two (or sometimes even three or four) units or fewer are exempt from rent control ordinances. Some cities also exempt rentals in single-family houses and luxury units that rent for more than a certain amount.

Limits on Rent

Rent control ordinances typically set a base rent for each rental unit that takes into account several different factors, including the rent that was charged before rent control took effect, operation and upkeep expenses, inflation, and housing supply and demand. The ordinances allow the base rent to be increased under certain circumstances or at certain times.

Rent Increases for Existing Tenants

Most local ordinances build in some mechanism for rent increases. Here are just a few common examples:

Annual increases. Some ordinances automatically allow a specific percentage rent increase each year. The amount of the increase may be set by the rent control board or may be a fixed percentage or a percentage tied to a local or national consumer price index.

Increased expenses. Some rent control boards have the power to adjust rents of individual units based on certain cost factors, such as increased taxes or maintenance or capital improvements. The landlord may need to request permission from the rent control board before upping the rent.

The tenant's consent. In some cities, landlords may increase rent under certain circumstances only if the tenants voluntarily agree to the increase—or don't protest it.

A word of caution: Even if you are otherwise entitled to raise the rent under the terms of your rent control ordinance, the rent board may be able to deny you permission if you haven't adequately repaired and maintained your rental units.

Where to Get Information About Rent Control

- **Your city rent control board.** It can supply you with a copy of the current local ordinance, and possibly also with a brochure explaining the ordinance.
- **Your state or local apartment owners' association.** Virtually every city with a rent control ordinance has an active property owners' association. The New York City Rent Stabilization Association, for example, gives members information and help on rent matters and offers mediation for tenant complaints.
- **Local attorneys who specialize in landlord-tenant law.** Check the yellow pages, search online, or ask another landlord. Chapter 18 discusses how to find and work with a lawyer.

Rent Increases When a Tenant Moves

In most rent control areas, landlords may raise rent—either as much as they want or by a specified percentage—when a tenant moves out (and a new one moves in) or when a tenant renews a lease. This feature, called "vacancy decontrol," "vacancy rent ceiling adjustment," or a similar term, is built into many local ordinances.

In practice, it means that rent control applies to a particular rental unit only as long as a particular tenant (or tenants) stays there. If that tenant voluntarily leaves or, in some cities, is evicted for a legal or "just" cause (discussed below), the rental unit is subject to rent control again after the new (and presumably higher) rent is established.

> **EXAMPLE:** Marla has lived in Edward's apartment building for seven years. During that time, Edward has been allowed to raise the rent only by the modest amount authorized by the local rent board each year. Meanwhile, the market value of the apartment has gone up significantly. When Marla finally moves out, Edward is free to charge the next tenant the market rate. But once set, that tenant's rent will also be subject to the rent control rules, and Edward will again be limited to small annual increases as approved by the rent control board.

In some cities, no rent increase is allowed at all, even when a tenant moves out. Check your ordinance.

Legal or "Just Cause" Evictions

For rent control to work—especially if the ordinance allows rents to rise when a tenant leaves—it must place some restrictions on tenancy terminations. Otherwise, landlords who wanted to create a vacancy so they could raise the rent would be free to throw out tenants, undermining the whole system. Recognizing this, many local ordinances require landlords to have a legal or just cause—that is, a good reason—to terminate and, if the tenant doesn't leave on his own, evict.

Just cause is usually limited to a few reasons provided in the ordinance. If you really need to evict a tenant, you should have no problem finding your reason on the approved list. Here are a few typical examples of a legal or just cause to evict a tenant:

- The tenant violates a significant term of the lease or rental agreement—for example, by failing to pay rent or causing substantial damage to the premises. However, in many situations, you're legally required to first give the tenant a chance to correct the problem.

- The landlord wants to move into the rental unit or give it to an immediate family member.
- The landlord wants to substantially remodel the property, which requires the tenant to move out.
- The tenant creates a nuisance—for example, by repeatedly disturbing other tenants or engaging in illegal activity, such as drug dealing, on the premises.

Rent control ordinances often affect renewals as well as terminations midway through the rental term. Unless you can point to a just cause for tossing a tenant out, you may need to renew a lease or rental agreement under the same terms and conditions.

Your Right to Go Out of Business

It's not uncommon for landlords in rent-controlled cities to decide to get out of the residential rental business entirely. To do so, however, they must evict tenants, who will protest that the eviction violates the rent control ordinance.

No rent control ordinance can force you to continue with your business against your will. However, if you withdraw rental units from the market, you must typically meet strict standards regarding the necessity of doing so. Rent control boards do not want landlords to use going out of business as a ruse for evicting long-term tenants, only to start up again with a fresh batch of tenants whose rents will invariably be substantially higher.

If you decide to go out of business and must evict tenants, check your ordinance carefully. It may require you to give tenants a lengthy notice period or offer tenants relocation assistance, and may impose a minimum time period during which you may not resume business. If you own multiple units, the rent control ordinance may prohibit you from withdrawing more than a specified number of units; and if the premises are torn down and new units constructed, the ordinance may insist that you offer former tenants a right of first refusal. State law may also address these issues. Contact your local landlords' association or rent control board for details on the specifics.

Registration of Rental Units

Some rent control ordinances require landlords to register their properties with the local rent control agency. This allows the rent board to keep track of the city's rental units, and the registration fees provide operating funds.

Deposits and Notice Requirements

Rent control ordinances may impose rules regarding security deposits or interest payments and the type of notice you must give tenants when you want to raise the rent or terminate a tenancy. The requirements of these local ordinances are in addition to any state law requirements. For example, state law may require a 30-day notice for a rent increase. A local rent control law might also require the notice to tell the tenant that the rent control board can verify that the new rental amount is legal under the ordinance.

When Rent Is Due

Most leases and rental agreements, including the ones in this book, call for rent to be paid monthly, in advance, on the first day of the month. See Clause 5 of the form agreements in Chapter 2.

First Day, Last Day, or In-Between?

The first of the month is a customary and convenient due date for rent, at least in part because many tenants get their paychecks on the last workday of the month. Also, the approach of a new month can, in itself, help remind people to pay monthly bills due on the first.

It is perfectly legal to require rent to be paid on a different day of the month, and may make sense if the tenant is paid at odd times. Some landlords make the rent payable each month on the date the tenant first moved in. Generally, it's easier to prorate rent for a short first month and then require that rent be paid on the first of the next month. But if you have only a few tenants, and don't mind having tenants paying you on different days of the month, it makes no legal difference.

Special rules for tenants who receive public assistance. Some states make special provisions for rent due dates for public assistance recipients. Public assistance recipients in Hawaii, for example, tenants who receive public assistance may change the rent due date to within three business days (excluding Saturdays, Sundays and holidays) after the mailing date of public assistance checks. They need to make a onetime prorated payment to cover the period between the original due date in the rental agreement and a newly established due date.

Whatever rent due date you choose, be sure to put it in your lease or rental agreement. If you don't, state law may do it for you. In several states, for month-to-month rental agreements, rent is due in equal monthly installments at the beginning of each month, unless otherwise agreed.

In a few states, however, rent is not due until the end of the term unless the lease or rental agreement says otherwise. You would probably never deliberately allow a tenant who moved in on the first day of the month to wait to pay rent until the 31st. Nor would you want tenants to continue to pay at the end of the month. By specifying that rent is due on the first of the month in your lease or rental agreement, you won't have to worry.

Collecting Rent More Than Once a Month

If you wish, you and the tenant can agree that the rent be paid twice a month, each week, or on whatever schedule suits you. The most common variation on the standard monthly payment arrangement is having rent paid twice a month. This is a particularly good idea if you have tenants who have relatively low-paying jobs and get paid twice a month, because they may have difficulty saving the needed portion of their midmonth check until the first of the month.

When the Due Date Falls on a Weekend or Holiday

The lease and rental agreements in this book state that when the rent due date falls on a weekend day or legal holiday, the tenant must pay it by the next business day. See Clause 5 of the form agreements in Chapter 2.

This is legally required in some states; it is the general rule in most. If you want to insist that the tenant always get the rent check to you on the first, no matter what, you'll have to check the law in your state to make sure it's allowed. It's probably not worth the trouble.

Grace Periods for Late Rent

Lots of tenants are absolutely convinced that if rent is due on the first, but they pay by the fifth (or sometimes the seventh or even the tenth) of the month, they have legally paid their rent on time because they are within a legal grace period. This is simply not true. It is your legal right to insist that rent be paid on the day it is due, and you should use your lease or rental agreement and move-in letter to disabuse tenants of this bogus notion.

In practice, many landlords do not get upset about late rent or charge a late fee (discussed below) until the rent is a few days past due. And your state law may require you to give tenants a few days to come up with the rent before you can send a termination notice. Even so, your best approach is to consistently stress to tenants that rent must be paid on the due date.

> **CAUTION**
> **If you wait more than three or five days to collect your rent, you are running your business unwisely, and just extending the time a nonpaying tenant can stay.** Be firm, but fair. Any other policy will get you into a morass of special cases and exceptions and will cost you a bundle in the long run. If you allow exceptions only in extreme circumstances, tenants will learn not to try and sell you sob stories.

Evictions for Nonpayment of Rent

Failure to pay rent on time is by far the most common reason landlords go to court and evict tenants. First, however, a landlord must give the tenant a written notice, demanding that the tenant either pay within a few days or move out. How long the tenant is allowed to stay depends on state law; in most places, it's about three to five days.

In most instances, the tenant who receives this kind of notice pays up, and that's the end of it. But if the tenant doesn't pay the rent (or move), you can file an eviction lawsuit. Chapter 17 explains the kinds of termination notices that landlords must use when tenants are behind on the rent, and includes a brief summary of evictions. Appendix A includes details on state laws on termination for nonpayment of rent.

If you find yourself delivering too many pay-the-rent-or-leave notices to a particular tenant, you may want to end the tenancy—even if the tenant always comes up with the rent at the last minute.

Where and How Rent Is Due

You should specify in your lease or rental agreement where the tenant should pay the rent and how you want it paid—for example, by check or money order only. See Clause 5 of the form agreements in Chapter 2.

CAUTION

California landlords should take special care to inform tenants of where and how rent is paid. State law (Cal. Civ. Code §§ 1962 and 1962.5) requires landlords to notify tenants (either in a separate writing or in a written rental agreement or lease) of the name and street address of the owner or manager responsible for collection of rent, how rent is to be paid, and who is available for services of notices. A landlord may not evict for nonpayment of any rent that came due during any period that the landlord was not in compliance with this requirement.

Where Rent Must Be Paid

You have several options for where the tenant pays you rent.

By mail. Allowing tenants to mail you the rent check is the most common method of payment, by a long shot. It's pretty convenient for everyone, and you can make it even easier by giving tenants pre-addressed (and stamped, if you're feeling generous) envelopes.

At home. You can send someone to each unit, every month, to pick up the rent. But this more old-fashioned way of collecting the rent isn't well-suited to modern life, when most people aren't at home during the day.

At your office. Requiring the rent to be paid personally at your place of business or manager's office is feasible (and, in some states, legal) only if you have an on-site office. Asking tenants to drive across town is both unreasonable and counter-productive, because inevitably some of them just won't get around to it. This approach does have certain advantages. It makes the tenant responsible for getting the rent to you at a certain time or place, and avoids issues such as whether or not a rent check was lost or delayed in the mail. It also guarantees at least a bit of personal contact with your tenants, and a chance to air little problems before they become big ones.

If your lease or rental agreement doesn't specify where you want tenants to pay you rent, state law may decide. Under statutes in several states rent is payable at the dwelling unit unless otherwise agreed. This is yet another reason to specify in your rental agreement or lease that your tenant may pay by check or at your on-site office.

Form of Rent Payment

You should also specify in your lease or rental agreement how rent must be paid: by cash, check, credit card, or money order. See Clause 5 of the form agreements in Chapter 2.

For most landlords, rental checks are routine. You can eliminate the time spent mailing or walking a check to the bank by sending it right to the bank electronically. If a tenant doesn't have a checking account or has bounced too many checks, you may want to require a certified check or money order.

You should never accept postdated checks. The most obvious reason is that the check may never be good. You have absolutely no assurance that necessary funds will ever be deposited in the account. In addition, a postdated check may, legally, be considered a "note" promising to pay on a certain date. In some states, if you accept such a note (check), you have no right to bring an eviction action while the note is pending. Far better to tell the tenant that rent must be paid in full on time and to give the tenant a late notice if it isn't.

Easy Ways to Pay the Rent

More and more owners, especially those with large numbers of rental units, are looking for ways to ensure that rent payments are quick and reliable. Here are two common methods.

Online banking. Tenants with bank accounts that they trust will always have enough money on deposit to be able to handle the rent, may be willing to set up an automatic transfer. On the day they specify, the rent funds are electronically transferred to your account. Every major bank offers this service, some for a small fee.

Credit card. If you have enough tenants to make it worthwhile, explore the option of accepting credit cards. You must pay a fee—a percentage of the amount charged—for the privilege, but the cost may be justified if it results in more on-time payments and less hassle for you and your tenants. Keep in mind that you'll need to have someone in your on-site office to process the credit card payments and give tenants receipts. And if your tenant population is affluent enough, consider requiring automatic credit card debits.

CAUTION

Don't accept cash unless you have no choice. You are a likely target for robbery if word gets out that you are taking in large amounts of cash once or twice a month. And if you accept cash knowing that the tenant earned it from an illegal act, such as drug dealing, the government could seize it from you under federal and state forfeiture laws. If you do accept cash, be sure to provide a written, dated receipt stating the tenant's name and rental unit and the amount of rent and time period for which rent is paid. Such a receipt is required by law in a few states, and it's a good idea everywhere.

Changing Where and How Rent Is Due

If you've been burned by bounced checks from a particular tenant, you may want to decree that, from now on, you'll accept nothing less than a certified check or money order, and that rent may be paid only during certain hours at the manager's office.

Be careful. It may be illegal to suddenly change your terms for payment of rent without proper notice to the tenant—unless you are simply enforcing an existing term. For example, if your rental agreement states that you accept only money orders, you are on solid ground when you tell a check-bouncing tenant that you'll no longer accept her checks, and that your previous practice of doing so was merely an accommodation not required under the rental agreement.

If, however, your lease or rental agreement doesn't say where and how rent is to be paid, your past practice may legally control how rent is paid until you properly notify the tenant of a change. If you want to require tenants to pay rent at your office, for example, you must formally change a month-to-month rental agreement, typically with a written 30-day notice. If you rent under a lease, you will have to wait until the lease runs out.

Service Fees for Bounced Checks

Many states allow recipients of bounced checks to collect a service fee, which would apply even if your lease doesn't specify any consequences for a dishonored check. For example:

Arizona	Landlord may charge no more than $25, plus the amount charged by landlord's bank for processing the check. (Ariz. Rev. Stat. § 44-6852.)
California	Landlord may charge $25 for the first bounced check, and $35 for each additional bounced check. (Cal. Civ. Code § 1719.)
Florida	Landlord may collect damages by sending the following notice: "You are hereby notified that a check or electronic funds transfer, numbered _____, in the face amount of _____, issued or initiated by you on (date), drawn upon (name of bank), and payable to _____, has been dishonored. Pursuant to Florida law, you have 15 days following the date of this notice to tender payment of the full amount of such check or electronic funds transfer plus a service charge of $25, if the face value does not exceed $50; $30, if the face value exceeds $50 but does not exceed $300; $40, if the face value exceeds $300; or an amount of up to 5 percent of the face amount of the check, whichever is greater, the total amount due being _____ and _____ cents. Unless this amount is paid in full within the time specified above, the holder of such check or electronic funds transfer may turn over the dishonored check or electronic funds transfer and all other available information relating to this incident to the state attorney for criminal prosecution. You may be additionally liable in a civil action for triple the amount of the check or electronic funds transfer, but in no case less than $50, together with the amount of the check or electronic funds transfer, a service charge, court costs, reasonable attorney's fees, and incurred bank fees, as provided in s. 68.065, Florida Statutes." (Fla. Stat. Ann. § 832.062.)
Georgia	Landlord may charge no more than $30 or 5% of the face amount of the dishonored check (whichever is greater). If landlord's bank charges a fee for processing the bounced check, landlord may add that amount to the fee. (Ga. Code Ann. § 16-9-20.)
Illinois	Landlord may demand additional costs and expenses (maximum $25) incurred when trying to collect on the check, including interest as regulated by law, but only if the landlord makes a written demand, delivered by certified mail, that the check be made good, giving the tenant 30 days to comply and warning that such additional costs will be incurred. (810 Ill. Comp. Stat. § 5/3-806.)
Minnesota	A service charge, not to exceed $30, may be imposed immediately on any dishonored check. Notice of service charge must be conspicuously displayed. Tenant must have notice that civil penalties may be imposed for nonpayment. (Minn. Stat. Ann. § 604.113.)
Nevada	A seller, or his or her agent, may collect a fee of not more than $25 for each check that was accepted by the seller as payment for goods or services and, upon presentment to the drawee, was not honored because the drawer stopped payment on the check, the drawer does not have an account with the drawee, or the drawer does not have sufficient funds in his or her account or credit with the drawee to cover the amount of the check. (Nev. Rev. Stat. Ann. § 597.960.)
Oregon	If a check is dishonored, the payee may collect from the maker a fee not to exceed $35. (Ore. Rev. Stat. § 30.701.)
Virginia	Landlord may not charge more than the sum of $50 plus the amount charged by landlord's bank for processing the check. (Va. Code Ann. § 55-248.4 & § 248-31.)
Washington	Landlord may charge 12% interest plus the cost of collection (not to exceed $40 or the face amount of the check, whichever is less). Landlord must first send tenant a notice of dishonor, and wait 15 days, before imposing the fee. (Wash. Rev. Code Ann. § 62A.3-515.)

Your state's consumer protection office should be able to tell you whether your state has a similar law. For a list of state consumer protection agencies, see www.usa.gov/stateconsumer.

Late Charges and Discounts for Early Payments

If you're faced with a tenant who hasn't paid rent on the due date, you probably don't want to immediately hand out a formal notice telling the tenant to pay the rent or leave. After all, it's not going to do anything positive for your relationship with the tenant, who may have just forgotten to drop the check in a mailbox. But how else can you motivate tenants to pay rent on time?

A fairly common and sensible practice is to charge a reasonable late fee and highlight your late fee policy in your lease or rental agreement and move-in letter to new tenants. See Clause 6 of the form agreements in Chapter 2.

Some states have statutes that put precise limits on late fees (see the "Late Fees" column in the "State Rent Rules" chart in Appendix A). But even if your state doesn't have specific rules, you are still bound by general legal principles that prohibit unreasonably high fees. Courts in some states have ruled that contracts that provide for unreasonably high late charges are not enforceable—which means that if a tenant fights you in court (either in an eviction lawsuit or a separate case brought by the tenant), you could lose. And, obviously, excessive late fees generate tenant hostility, anyway.

RENT CONTROL

Some rent control ordinances also regulate late fees. Check any rent control ordinances applicable to your properties.

Unless your state imposes more specific statutory rules on late fees, you should be on safe ground if you adhere to these principles.

The late fee should not apply until at least three to five days after the due date. Imposing a stiff late charge if the rent is only one or two days late may not be upheld in court.

The total late charge should not exceed 4%–5% of the rent. That's $30 to $38 on a $750-per-month rental. State law in Maine sets a 4% limit, and Maryland and North Carolina both set 5% limits on late charges. Even in states with no statutory limits, a higher late charge, such as 10%, might not be upheld in court.

If the late fee increases each day the rent is late, it should be moderate and have an upper limit. A late charge that increases without limit each day could be considered interest charged at an illegal ("usurious") rate. State laws set the maximum allowable rate of interest, typically less than 10%, that may be charged for a debt. (Ten dollars a day on a $1,000-per-month rent is 3,650% annual interest.) A more acceptable late charge would be $10 for the first day rent is late, plus $5 for each additional day, up to a maximum of 5% of the rental amount.

Don't try to disguise excessive late charges by giving a "discount" for early payment. For one thing, this kind of "discount" is illegal in some states. One landlord we know concluded he couldn't get away with charging a $100 late charge on an $850 rent payment, so, instead, he designed a rental agreement calling for a rent of $950 with a $100 discount if the rent was not more than three days late. Ingenious as this ploy sounds, it is unlikely to stand up in court, unless the discount for timely payment is very modest. Giving a relatively large discount is in effect the same as charging an excessive late fee, and a judge is likely to see it as such.

Anyway, fooling around with late charges is wasted energy. If you want more rent for your unit, raise the rent (unless you live in a rent control area). If you are concerned about tenants paying on time—and who isn't?—put your energy into choosing responsible tenants.

If you have a tenant with a month-to-month tenancy who drives you nuts with late rent payments, and a reasonable late charge doesn't resolve the situation, terminate the tenancy with the appropriate notice.

Returned Check Charges

It's legal to charge the tenant an extra fee if a rent check bounces (see Clause 7 of the form agreements in Chapter 2). If you're having a lot of trouble with bounced checks, you may want to change your policy to accept only money orders for rent.

Like late charges, bounced check charges must be reasonable. You should charge no more than the amount your bank charges you for a returned check charge, probably $10 to $20 per returned item, plus a few dollars for your trouble.

It is a poor idea to let your bank redeposit rent checks that bounce. Instead, tell the bank to return bad checks to you immediately. Getting a bounced check back quickly alerts you to the fact that the rent is unpaid much sooner than if the check is resubmitted and returned for nonpayment a second time. You can use this time to ask the tenant to make the check good immediately. If the tenant doesn't come through, you can promptly serve the necessary paperwork to end the tenancy.

If a tenant habitually gives you bad checks, give the tenant a notice demanding that he pay the rent or move. If the tenant doesn't make the check good by the deadline, you can start eviction proceedings.

Partial or Delayed Rent Payments

On occasion, a tenant suffering a temporary financial setback will offer something less than the full month's rent, with a promise to catch up as the month proceeds, or at the first of the next month. Although generally this is a bad business practice, you may nevertheless wish to make an exception where the tenant's financial problems truly appear to be temporary and you have known the person for a long time.

If you do give a tenant a little more time to pay some or all of the rent, establish a schedule, in writing, for when the rent will be paid. Then monitor the situation carefully. Otherwise, the tenant may try to delay payment indefinitely, or make such small and infrequent payments that the account is never brought current. A signed agreement—say for a one-week extension—lets both you and the tenant know what's expected. If you give the tenant two weeks to catch up and she doesn't, the written agreement precludes

any argument that you had really said "two to three weeks." A sample Agreement for Delayed or Partial Rent Payments is shown below and the Nolo website includes a downloadable copy. See Appendix B for the link to the forms in this book.

If the tenant does not pay the rest of the rent when promised, you can, and should, follow through with the appropriate steps to terminate the tenancy.

Raising the Rent

Except in cities with rent control, your freedom to raise rent depends primarily on whether the tenant has a lease or a month-to-month rental agreement.

When You Can Raise Rent

For the most part, a lease fixes the terms of tenancy for the length of the lease. You can't change the terms of the lease until the end of the lease period unless the lease itself allows it or the tenant agrees. When the lease expires, you can present the tenant with a new lease that has a higher rent or other changed terms. It's always safest to give tenants at least a month or two notice of any rent increase before negotiating a new lease.

In contrast, you can raise the rent in a periodic tenancy just by giving the tenant proper written notice, typically 30 days for a month-to-month tenancy. (If you collect rent every 15 days, you probably have to give your tenant only 15 days' notice.) State law may override these general rules, however. In a few states, landlords must provide 45 or 60 days' notice to raise the rent for a month-to-month tenancy. See "State Rules on Notice Required to Change or Terminate a Month-to-Month Tenancy" in Appendix A and the Chapter 14 discussion of changing terms during the tenancy. You'll need to consult your state statutes for the specific information you must provide in a rent increase notice, how you must deliver it to the tenant, and any rights tenants have to dispute rent increases.

Agreement for Delayed or Partial Rent Payments

This Agreement is made between ___Betty Wong_____

_____[Tenant(s)]

and ___John Lewis_____ , [Landlord/Manager].

1. ___Betty Wong_____

   _____[Tenant(s)]

   has/have paid ___one-half of her $1,000 rent for apartment #2 at 111 Billy St.,___

   ___Phoenix, Arizona_____

   on _____March 1, 20xx_____. The rent due date is ___March 1, 20xx_____ .

2. ___John Lewis_____[Landlord/Manager]

   agrees to accept all the remainder of the rent on or before _____March 15, 20xx_____ ,

   and to hold off on any legal proceeding to evict _____Betty Wong_____

   _____[Tenant(s)] until that date.

___John Lewis_____   ___March 2, 20xx_____
Landlord/Manager   Date

___Betty Wong_____   ___March 2, 20xx_____
Tenant   Date

_____   _____
Tenant   Date

_____   _____
Tenant   Date

How Much Can You Raise the Rent?

In areas without rent control, there is no limit on the amount you can increase the rent of a month-to-month or other periodic tenant. Also, as noted in "How Much Can You Charge?" above, tenants in Connecticut can challenge rent increases they feel are excessive. Similarly, there is no restriction on the period of time between rent increases. You can legally raise the rent as much and as often as good business dictates. Of course, common sense should tell you that if your tenants think your increases are unfair, you may end up with vacant units or a hostile group of tenants looking for ways to make you miserable. As a courtesy, you may wish to tell your tenants of the rent increase personally, perhaps explaining the reasons—although reasons aren't legally necessary, except in areas covered by rent control.

Avoiding Tenant Charges of Retaliation or Discrimination

You can't legally raise a tenant's rent as retaliation—for example, in response to a legitimate complaint or rent-withholding action—or in a discriminatory manner. The laws in many states actually presume retaliation if you increase rent soon—typically, within three to six months—after a tenant's complaint of defective conditions. See the Chapter 16 discussion of general ways to avoid tenant charges of retaliation. "State Laws Prohibiting Landlord Retaliation" in Appendix A lists state-by-state details.

One way to protect yourself from charges that ordinary rent increases are retaliatory or discriminatory is to adopt a sensible rent increase policy and stick to it.

For example, many landlords raise rent once a year in an amount that more or less reflects the increase in the Consumer Price Index. Other landlords use a more complicated formula that takes into account other rents in the area, as well as such factors as increased costs of maintenance or rehabilitation. They make sure to inform their tenants about the rent increase in advance and apply the increase uniformly to all their tenants. Usually, this protects the landlord against any claim of a retaliatory rent increase by a tenant who has coincidentally made a legitimate complaint about the condition of the premises.

> **EXAMPLE:** Lois owns two multiunit complexes. In one of them, she raises rents uniformly, at the same time, for all tenants. In the other apartment building, where she fears tenants hit with rent increases all at once will organize and generate unrest, Lois does things differently: She raises each tenant's rent in accordance with the Consumer Price Index on the yearly anniversary of the date each tenant moved in. Either way, Lois is safe from being judged to have retaliatorily increased rents, even if a rent increase to a particular tenant follows on the heels of a complaint.

Of course, any rent increase given to a tenant who has made a complaint should be reasonable—in relation to the previous rent, what you charge other similarly situated tenants, and rents for comparable property in the area—or you are asking for legal trouble.

> **EXAMPLE:** Lonnie has no organized plan for increasing rents in his 20-unit building, but simply raises them when he needs money. On November 1, he raises the rent for one of his tenants, Teresa, without remembering her recent complaint about her heater. Teresa is the only one to receive a rent increase in November. She has a strong retaliatory rent increase case against Lonnie, simply because an increase that seemed to single her out coincided with her exercise of a legal right. If the increase made her rent higher than those for comparable units in the building, she will have an even better case.

Security Deposits

Most landlords quite sensibly ask for a security deposit before entrusting hundreds of thousands of dollars' worth of real estate to a tenant. But it's easy to get into legal trouble over deposits, because they are strictly regulated by state law, and sometimes also by city ordinance.

The law of most states dictates how large a deposit you can require, how you can use it, when you must return it, and more. Many states require you to put deposits in a separate account and pay interest on them. You cannot escape these requirements by putting different terms in a lease or rental agreement. You may face substantial financial penalties for violating state laws on security deposits.

This chapter explains how to set up a clear, fair system of setting, collecting, and holding deposits. It may exceed the minimum legal requirements affecting your property, but it will ultimately work to your advantage, resulting in easier turnovers, better tenant relations, and fewer legal hassles.

Where to Get More Information on Security Deposits

Start by referring to "State Security Deposit Rules" in Appendix A. If you have any questions of what's allowed in your state, you should get a current copy of your state's security deposit law (statute) or an up-to-date summary from a landlords' association.

In addition, be sure to check local ordinances in all areas where you own property. Cities, particularly those with rent control, may add their own rules on security deposits, such as a limit on the amount you can charge or a requirement that you pay interest on deposits.

> **CAUTION**
>
> **This discussion is limited to security deposit statutes.** Some states do not have statutes on every aspect of security deposits. That doesn't mean that there is no law on the subject. Court decisions (what lawyers call "case law") in your state may set out quite specific requirements

for refundability of deposits, whether they should be held in interest-bearing accounts, and the like. This book doesn't cover all this case law, but you may need to check it out yourself. To find out whether courts in your state have made decisions you need to be aware of, contact your state or local property owners' association or do some legal research on your own.

> **RELATED TOPIC**
>
> **Related topics covered in this book include:**
> - Charging prospective tenants' credit check fees, finder's fees, or holding deposits: Chapter 1
> - Writing clear lease and rental agreement provisions on security deposits: Chapter 2
> - Highlighting security deposit rules and procedures in move-in and move-out letters to the tenant: Chapters 7 and 15
> - Returning deposits and deducting for cleaning, damage, and unpaid rent; how to handle legal disputes involving deposits: Chapter 15
> - State Security Deposit Rules: Appendix A.

Purpose and Use of Security Deposits

All states allow you to collect a security deposit when a tenant moves in and hold it until the tenant leaves. The general purpose of a security deposit is to assure that a tenant pays rent when due and keeps the rental unit in good condition. Rent you collect in advance for the first month is not considered part of the security deposit.

State laws typically control the amount you can charge and how and when you must return security deposits. When a tenant moves out, you will have a set amount of time (usually from 14 to 30 days, depending on the state) to either return the tenant's entire deposit or provide an itemized statement of deductions and refund any deposit balance.

Although state laws vary, you can generally withhold all or part of the deposit to pay for:

- unpaid rent
- repairing damage to the premises (except for "ordinary wear and tear") caused by the tenant, a family member, or a guest

- cleaning necessary to restore the rental unit to its level of cleanliness at the beginning of the tenancy (taking into consideration "ordinary wear and tear"), or
- restoring or replacing rental unit property taken by the tenant.

States typically also allow you to use a deposit to cover the tenant's obligations under the lease or rental agreement, which may include payment of utility charges.

You don't necessarily need to wait until a tenant moves out to tap into their security deposit. You may, for example, use some of the tenant's security deposit during the tenancy—for example, because the tenant broke something and didn't fix it or pay for it. In this case, you should require the tenant to replenish the security deposit.

> **EXAMPLE:** Millie pays her landlord Maury a $1,000 security deposit when she moves in. Six months later, Millie goes on vacation, leaving the water running. By the time Maury is notified, the overflow has damaged the paint on the ceiling below. Maury repaints the ceiling at a cost of $250, taking the money out of Millie's security deposit. Maury is entitled to ask Millie to replace that money, so that her deposit remains $1,000.

To protect yourself and avoid misunderstandings with tenants, make sure your lease or rental agreement is clear on the use of security deposits and the tenant's obligations. See Clause 8 of the form agreements in Chapter 2.

> **TIP**
> **A few states exempt some landlords from security deposit rules.** For details, see the "State Security Deposit Rules" chart in Appendix A.

Dollar Limits on Deposits

Many states limit the amount you can collect as a deposit to an amount equal to one or two months of rent. And the limit within each state sometimes varies depending on various factors such as:

- age of the tenant (senior citizens may have a lower deposit ceiling)
- whether the rental unit is furnished
- whether you have a month-to-month rental agreement or a long-term lease, and
- whether the tenant has a pet or waterbed.

For details, see "State Security Deposit Rules," in Appendix A.

In some states, the rent you collect in advance for the last month is not considered part of the security deposit limit, while in others it is.

> **CAUTION**
> **An inconsistent security deposit policy is an invitation to a lawsuit.** Even if your motives are good—for example, you require a smaller deposit from a student tenant—you risk a charge of illegal discrimination by other tenants who did not get the same break.

How Much Deposit Should You Charge?

Normally, the best advice is to charge as much as the market will bear, within any legal limits. The more the tenant has at stake, the better the chance your property will be respected. And, the larger the deposit, the more financial protection you will have if a tenant leaves owing you rent.

The market, however, often keeps the practical limit on deposits lower than the maximum allowed by law. Your common sense and your business sense need to work together in setting security deposits. Here are a number of considerations to keep in mind:

- **Charge the full limit in high-risk situations—** for example, where there's a lot of tenant turnover, if the tenant has a pet and you're concerned about damage, or if the tenant's credit is shaky and you're worried about unpaid rent.
- **Consider the psychological advantage of a higher rent rather than a high deposit.** Many tenants would rather pay a slightly higher rent than an enormous deposit. Also, many acceptable,

solvent tenants have a hard time coming up with a hefty deposit, especially if they are still in a rental and are awaiting the return of a previous security deposit. And remember, unlike the security deposit, the extra rent is not refundable.

> **EXAMPLE:** Lenora rents out a three-bedroom furnished house in San Francisco for $6,000 a month. Because total deposits on furnished property in California can legally be three times the monthly rent, Lenora could charge up to $18,000. This is in addition to the first month's rent of $6,000 that Lenora can (and should) insist on before turning the property over to a tenant. But, realistically, Lenora would probably have difficulty finding a tenant if she insisted on receiving an $18,000 deposit plus the first month's rent, for a total of $24,000. So she decides to charge only one month's rent for the deposit but to increase the monthly rent. That gives Lenora the protection she feels she needs without imposing an enormous initial financial burden on her tenants.

- **Single-family homes call for a bigger deposit.** Unlike multiunit residences, where close-by neighbors or a manager can spot, report, and quickly stop any destruction of the premises, the single-family home is somewhat of an island. The condition of the interior and even the exterior may be hard to assess. And, of course, the cost of repairing damage to a house is likely to be higher than for an apartment. Unless you live next door or can frequently check the condition of a single-family rental, a substantial security deposit is a good idea.

- **Gain a marketing advantage by allowing a deposit to be paid in installments.** If rentals are plentiful in your area, with comparable units renting at about the same price, you might give yourself a competitive edge by allowing the tenant to pay the deposit in several installments over a few months, rather than one lump sum.

 TIP

If allowed under state law, require renters' insurance as an alternative to a high security deposit. If you're worried about damage but don't think you can raise the deposit any higher, require renters' insurance. Chapter 2 contains an optional clause that you add to your lease or rental agreement requiring the tenant to maintain renters' insurance, and explains the legal limitations that may apply in your state or locality. While you're at it, evaluate your own insurance policy to make sure it is adequate. If the tenant's security deposit is inadequate to cover any damage and there is no renters' insurance (or it won't cover the loss), you may be able to collect from your own carrier.

Last Month's Rent

It's a common—but often unwise—practice to collect a sum of money called "last month's rent" from a tenant who's moving in. Landlords tend to treat this money as just another security deposit, and use it to cover not only the last month's rent but also other expenses such as repairs or cleaning.

Problems can arise when:

- you try to use the last month's rent to cover repairs or cleaning, or
- the rent has gone up during the tenancy— and you want to top off the last month's rent.

We'll look at these situations below.

Applying Last Month's Rent to Damage or Cleaning

If you collect a sum of money labeled last month's rent and your tenant is leaving (voluntarily or involuntarily), chances are that he will not write a rent check for the last month. After all, he's already paid for that last month, right? Surprisingly, many tenants do pay for the last month anyway, often forgetting that they have prepaid. What happens to that last month's rent?

Ideally, the tenant will leave the place clean and in good repair, enabling you to refund the entire last month's rent and all or most of the tenant's security deposit. But if the tenant leaves the place a mess, most states allow you to treat "last month's rent" as part of the security deposit and use all or part of it for cleaning or to repair or replace damaged items.

> **EXAMPLE:** Katie required her tenant Joe to pay a security deposit of one month's rent, plus last month's rent. Her state law allowed a landlord to use all advance deposits to cover a tenant's unpaid rent or damage, regardless of what the landlord called the deposit. When Joe moved out, he didn't owe any back rent, but he left his apartment a shambles. Katie was entitled to use the entire deposit, including that labeled last month's rent, to cover the damage.

A few states, such as Massachusetts (M.G.L.A. 186 § 15B) and New York (GOL § 7-103(1)), restrict the use of money labeled as "last month's rent" to its stated purpose: the rent for the last month of your occupancy. In these states, if you use any of the last month's rent to repair the cabinet the tenant broke, you're violating the law.

> **EXAMPLE:** Mike collected a security deposit of one month's rent, plus last month's rent, from his tenant Amy. Mike's state required that landlords use money collected for the last month as last month's rent only, not for cleaning or repairs. When Amy moved out, she didn't owe any rent but she, too, left her apartment a mess. Mike had to refund Amy's last month's rent and, when the remaining security deposit proved too little to cover the damage Amy had caused, Mike had to sue Amy in small claims court for the excess.

In general, it's a bad idea to call any part of the deposit "last month's rent." Why? Because if your state restricts your use of the money, you've unnecessarily hobbled yourself. And if your state considers last month's rent part of the security deposit, you haven't gained anything. You may have even put yourself at a disadvantage, because you've given the tenant the impression that the last month's rent is taken care of. You would be better off if the tenant paid the last month's rent when it came due, leaving the entire security deposit available to cover cleaning and repairs.

> **EXAMPLE 1:** Fernando rents out a $600-per-month apartment in a state where the security deposit limit is two months' rent. Fernando charged his tenant, Liz, a total deposit of $1,200, calling $600 a security deposit and $600 last month's rent. Liz used this last month's rent for the last month when she gave her notice to Fernando. This left Fernando with the $600 security deposit. Unfortunately, when Liz moved out, she left $700 worth of damages, sticking Fernando with a $100 loss.

> **EXAMPLE 2:** Learning something from this unhappy experience, Fernando charged his next tenant a simple $1,200 security deposit, not limiting any part of it to last month's rent. This time, when the tenant moved out, after paying his last month's rent as legally required, the whole $1,200 was available to cover the cost of any repairs or cleaning.

How a Rent Increase Affects Last Month's Rent

Avoiding the term "last month's rent" also keeps things simpler if you raise the rent, but not the deposit, before the tenant's last month of occupancy. If you have collected the last month's rent in advance, and the rent at the end of your tenancy is the same as when your tenant moved in, your tenant is paid up. However, if the rent has increased, but you have not asked your tenant to top off the last month's rent, questions arise. Does the tenant owe you for the difference? If so, can you take money from the tenant's security deposit to make it up?

Unfortunately, there are no clear answers. But because landlords in every state are allowed to ask tenants to top off the last month's rent at the time they increase the rent, judges would probably allow you to go after it at the end of the tenancy, too. Whether you get the difference from your security deposit or sue the tenant in small claims court is somewhat academic.

> **EXAMPLE:** When Rose moved in, the rent was $800 a month, and she paid this much in advance as last month's rent, plus an additional $800 security deposit. Over the years the landlord, Artie, has raised the rent

to $1,000. Rose does not pay any rent during the last month of her tenancy, figuring that the $800 she paid up front will cover it. Artie, however, thinks that Rose should pay the $200 difference. Artie and Rose may end up in small claims court fighting over who owes what. They could have avoided the problem by discussing the issue of last month's rent when Rose's tenancy began.

How to Avoid Problems With Last Month's Rent

To minimize confusion and disputes, avoid labeling any part of the security deposit last month's rent and get issues involving last month's rent straight with your tenant at the outset.

Clause 8 of the form agreements in Chapter 2 makes it clear that the tenant may not apply the security deposit to the last month's rent. Even with this type of clause, a tenant who's leaving may ask to use the security deposit for the last month's rent. Chapter 15 discusses how to handle these types of requests.

Interest and Accounts on Deposits

In most states, you don't have to pay tenants interest on deposits or put them in a separate bank account. In other words, you can simply put the money in your personal bank account and use it, as long as you have it available when the tenant moves out.

See "State Security Deposit Rules," in Appendix A, for details on which states have rules regarding interest on and separate accounts for deposits.

Separate Accounts

Several states require you to put security deposits in a separate account, sometimes called a "trust" account, rather than mixing the funds with your personal or business accounts. Some states require landlords to give tenants information on the location of this separate trust account at the start of the tenancy, usually as part of the lease or rental agreement. The idea is that by isolating these funds, it is more likely that you will have the money available whenever the tenant moves out and becomes entitled to it. In addition, separating these deposits makes it easier to trace them if a tenant claims that they were not handled properly. You are not required to set up separate accounts for every tenant. If you keep one account, be sure to maintain careful records of each tenant's contribution.

Interest

Several states require landlords to pay tenants interest on security deposits. Of course, you may find that it helps your relationship with your tenants to pay interest on deposits even if this is not a legal requirement. It's up to you.

Even among the states that require interest, there are many variations. A few states, such as Illinois, don't require small landlords to pay interest on deposits (only landlords who rent 25 or more units, in either a single building or a complex located on contiguous properties, must pay interest on deposits held for more than six months. (765 Ill. Comp. Stat. § 715/1.) Others, such as Iowa, allow landlords to keep any interest earned during the early period of tenancy (in Iowa, interest earned during the first five years of the tenancy belongs to the landlord (Iowa Code § 562A.12)).

State laws typically establish detailed requirements, including:

- **The interest rate to be paid.** Usually it's a little lower than the bank actually pays, so the landlord's costs and trouble of setting up the account are covered.
- **When interest payments must be made.** The most common laws require payments to be made annually, and also at termination of tenancy.
- **Notification landlords must give tenants as to where and how the security deposit is being held and the rate of interest.** See Clause 8 of the form agreements in Chapter 2 for details on states that require this type of notification.

Chicago, Los Angeles, and several other cities (typically those with rent control) require landlords to pay or credit tenants with interest on security deposits, even if the state law does not impose this duty. A few cities require that the funds be kept in separate interest-bearing accounts.

Nonrefundable Deposits and Fees

In general, state laws are often muddled on the subject of nonrefundable deposits and fees. A few states, such as California, Hawaii, Montana, and Oregon, specifically prohibit landlords from charging any fee or deposit that is not refundable. Some states specifically allow landlords to collect a fee that is not refundable—such as for pets or cleaning (see "States That Allow Nonrefundable Fees," below). While most of these states don't require terms to be spelled out in the lease or rental agreement, it's still a good idea to do so, in order to avoid disputes with your tenant.

Generally, it's best to avoid the legal uncertainties and not try to collect any nonrefundable fees from tenants. It's much simpler just to consider the expenses these fees cover as part of your overhead, and figure them into the rent. By avoiding non-refundable fees, you'll prevent a lot of time-consuming disputes with tenants.

If you have a specific concern about a particular tenant—for example, you're afraid a tenant's pet will damage the carpets or furniture—just ask for a higher security deposit. That way, you're covered if the pet causes damage, and, if it doesn't, the tenant won't have to shell out unnecessarily.

Charging a set fee can actually backfire. If you collect $100 for cleaning, for example, but when the tenant moves out the unit needs $200 worth of cleaning, you're stuck. You've already charged for cleaning, and the tenant could make a good argument that you're not entitled to take anything more out of the security deposit for cleaning.

If, despite our advice, you want to charge a nonrefundable fee, check your state's law to find what (if any) kinds of nonrefundable fees are allowed. Then, make sure your lease or rental agreement is clear on the subject.

! **CAUTION**
Don't charge a "redecoration fee" if you're already collecting the maximum allowed security deposit. A judge is likely to view the redecoration fee as an additional, and illegal, security deposit.

States That Allow Nonrefundable Fees

The following states have statutes that permit at least certain types of nonrefundable fees, such as for cleaning or pets:

Arizona	Nevada	Washington
Florida (by custom)	North Carolina	West Virginia
Georgia	Utah	Wyoming

Citations to these statutes are in "State Security Deposit Rules" in Appendix A.

In addition, most states allow landlords to charge prospective tenants a nonrefundable fee for the cost of a credit report and related screening expenses.

In states that have no statute on the subject, the legality of nonrefundable fees and deposits is determined in court. For example, courts in Texas and Michigan have ruled that a landlord and tenant may agree that certain fees will be nonrefundable. (*Holmes v. Canlen Management Corp.*, 542 S.W.2d 199 (1976); *Stutelberg v. Practical Management Co.*, 245 N.W.2d 737 (1976).)

How to Increase Deposits

Especially if you rent to a tenant for many years, you may want to increase the amount of the security deposit. The legality of doing this depends on the situation:

- **Leases.** If you have a fixed-term lease, you may not raise the security deposit during the term of the lease, unless the lease allows it. Security deposits may be increased, however, when the lease is renewed or becomes a month-to-month tenancy.

- **Written rental agreements.** With a month-to-month tenancy, you can increase a security deposit the same way you raise the rent, typically by giving the tenant a written notice 30 days in advance of the change. Of course, you can increase the security deposit without also increasing the rent as long as you don't exceed the maximum legal amount.

EXAMPLE: Jules rents out an apartment for $750 a month in a state that limits security deposits to one month's rent. If he raises the rent to $1,000, the maximum deposit he may collect goes up to $1,000. But the deposit does not go up automatically. To raise the deposit amount, Jules must give the tenant the required notice.

 RENT CONTROL
Local rent control ordinances typically restrict your right to raise deposits as well as to raise rents.

Handling Deposits When You Buy or Sell Rental Property

When you sell rental property, what should you do with the deposits you've already collected? After all, when the tenant moves out, she'll be entitled to her deposit back. Who owes her the money? In most states, whoever happens to be the landlord at the time a tenancy ends is legally responsible for complying with state laws requiring the return of security deposits. That means that you may need to hand over the deposits to the new owner. Read your state's statutes carefully as to how this transfer is handled, including any requirements that tenants be notified of the new owner's name, address, and phone number.

If you buy rental property, make sure you know the total dollar amount of security deposits. For a multiunit building, it could be tens of thousands of dollars.

Discrimination

FORMS IN THIS CHAPTER

Chapter 5 includes instructions for and a sample of the following form:

• Verification of Disabled Status

The Nolo website includes a downloadable copy of this form. See Appendix B for the link to the forms in this book.

So that all Americans would have the right to live where they chose, Congress and state legislatures passed laws prohibiting housing discrimination. Most notable of these are the federal Fair Housing Acts, which outlaw discrimination based on race or color, national origin, religion, sex, familial status, or disability. Many states and cities have laws making it illegal to discriminate based on additional factors, such as marital status or sexual orientation. Courts play a role, too, by interpreting and applying antidiscrimination laws. It is safe to say that unless you have a legitimate business reason to reject a prospective tenant (for example, poor credit history), you risk a fair housing complaint and a potentially costly lawsuit.

The discussion in this chapter is intended not only to explain the law, but to steer you away from hidden discrimination traps. It explains:

- legal reasons to turn down prospective tenants, such as a bad credit history or too many people for the size of the rental unit
- protected categories (such as race and religion) identified by federal and state laws prohibiting housing discrimination
- precautions to ensure that managers don't violate housing discrimination laws
- legal penalties for housing discrimination, including tenant lawsuits in state and federal courts, and
- whether your insurance policy is likely to cover the cost of defending a discrimination claim, and the cost of the judgment if you lose the case.

RELATED TOPIC

Chapter 1 also discusses how to avoid discrimination in advertising your property, accepting applications, and screening potential tenants, as well as how to document why you chose—or rejected—a particular tenant.

Legal Reasons for Rejecting a Rental Applicant

The most important decision you make, save possibly for deciding whether to purchase rental property in the first place, is your choice of tenants. Chapter 1 recommends a system for carefully screening potential tenants in order to select people who will pay rent on time, maintain your property, and not cause you any problems. Here we focus more closely on making sure that your screening process does not precipitate a costly charge of discrimination.

Remember that only certain kinds of discrimination in rental housing are illegal, such as selecting tenants on the basis of religion or race. You are legally free to choose among prospective tenants as long as your decisions are based on valid and objective business criteria, such as the applicant's ability to pay the rent and properly maintain the property. For example, you may legally refuse to rent to prospective tenants with bad credit histories, unsteady employment histories, or even low incomes that you reasonably regard as insufficient to pay the rent. Why? Because these criteria for tenant selection are reasonably related to your right to run your business in a competent, profitable manner (sometimes called your "legitimate business interests"). And if a person who fits one or more obvious "bad tenant risk" criteria happens to be a member of a minority group, you are still on safe legal ground as long as:

- You are consistent in your screening and treat all tenants more or less equally—for example, you always require a credit report for prospective tenants.
- You are not applying a generalization about people of a certain group to an individual.
- You can document your legal reasons for not renting to a prospective tenant.

But pay attention to the fact that judges, tenants' lawyers, and government agencies that administer and enforce fair housing laws know full well that some landlords try to make up and document legal reasons to discriminate, when the real reason is that they just don't like people with a particular racial, ethnic, or religious background. So, if you refuse to rent to a person who happens to be African-American, has children, or speaks only Spanish, be sure you document your legitimate business reason specific to that individual (such as insufficient income or a history of eviction for nonpayment of rent). Be prepared to show that your tenant advertising, screening, and selection processes have been based on objective criteria and that a more qualified applicant has always gotten the rental unit.

This section discusses some of the common legal reasons you may use to choose or reject applicants based on your business interests. A valid occupancy limitation (such as overcrowding) can also be a legal basis for a refusal, but since this issue is fairly complicated, we have devoted a separate section to the subject.

Objective Tenant Selection Criteria—What Do They Look Like?

"Objective criteria" are tenancy requirements that are established before the applicant even walks in the door, and are unaffected by the personal value judgments of the person asking the question. For example, a requirement that an applicant must never have been evicted for nonpayment of rent is "objective," because it is a matter of history and can be satisfied by a clear "yes" or "no." "Subjective criteria," on the other hand, have no preestablished correct answers, and the results of the questions will vary depending on the person who poses the question—for example, a requirement that the applicant present "a good appearance" has no predetermined "right" answer and will be answered differently by each person who asks the question. Subjective criteria are always suspicious in a housing context because their very looseness allows them to mask deliberate illegal discrimination.

So much for theory. Here are a few examples of allowable, objective criteria for choosing tenants:

- no prior bankruptcies
- two positive references from previous landlords
- sufficient income to pay the rent—for example, an income that is at least three times the rent
- signed waiver allowing you to investigate applicant's credit history, and
- satisfactory credit report.

TIP

To protect yourself in advance, always note your reasons for rejecting a tenant on the application. An applicant you properly reject may nevertheless file a discrimination complaint with a fair housing agency. Recognizing this, you want to be able to prove that you had a valid business reason for refusing to rent to the particular person, such as negative references from a previous landlord. This means you need to routinely document your good reasons for rejecting all potential tenants before anyone files a discrimination claim.

Poor Credit Record or Income

You can legitimately refuse to rent to a prospective tenant who has a history of nonpayment of rent or you reasonably believe would be unable to pay rent in the future.

Here's some advice on how to avoid charges of discrimination when choosing tenants on the basis of income or credit history.

Do a credit check on every prospective tenant, and base your selection on the results of that credit check. Accepting or rejecting tenants based on objective criteria tied to a credit report is the best way to protect yourself against an accusation that you're using a bad credit history as an excuse to illegally discriminate against certain prospective tenants. For example, if you establish rules saying you won't rent to someone with bad credit or who is evicted by a previous landlord for nonpayment of rent (information commonly found in credit reports), be sure you apply this policy to all tenants. Chapter 1 shows you how to check a prospective tenant's credit history and find out whether an applicant has ever been evicted, gone through bankruptcy, or been convicted of a crime.

Avoid rigid point systems that rank prospective tenants on the basis of financial stability and other factors. Some landlords evaluate prospective tenants by giving each one a certain number of points at the outset, with deductions for bad credit and negative references and additional points for extremely good ones. Points are also awarded based on length of employment and income. The person with the highest score gets the nod. Point systems give the illusion of objectivity, but because the weight you give each factor is, after all, subjective, they can still leave you open to charges of discrimination.

Don't discriminate against married or unmarried couples by counting only one spouse's or partner's income. Always consider the income of persons living together, married or unmarried, in order to avoid the accusation of marital status discrimination or sex discrimination.

If your state prohibits discrimination based on personal characteristics or traits, don't give too much weight to years spent at the same job, which can arguably discriminate against certain occupations. For example, software designers and programmers commonly move from one employer to another.

Negative References From Previous Landlords

You can legally refuse to rent to someone based on what a previous landlord or manager has to say—for example, that the tenant was consistently late paying rent, broke the lease, or left the place a shambles.

Evictions and Civil Lawsuits Involving a Tenant

Credit reports typically indicate whether the applicant has been involved in civil lawsuits, such as an eviction or breach of contract suit. For many landlords, an eviction lawsuit is a red flag. Can you reject a tenant on this basis? It depends.

If a former landlord has filed—and won—an eviction lawsuit against the applicant, you have solid grounds to reject this person. Be careful, however, if the credit report indicates that the applicant, not the former landlord, won the eviction suit: A tenant who has been vindicated in a court of law has not done anything wrong, even though you may suspect that the person is a troublemaker who just got lucky. If you reject someone simply because an eviction lawsuit was

filed against them, and if you live in a state that prohibits discrimination on the basis of someone's personal characteristic or trait, you are risking a charge that you are discriminating. In most situations, however, if the applicant is truly a poor prospect, the information you get from prior landlords and employers will confirm your suspicions, and you can reject the applicant on these more solid grounds (negative references).

The credit report may also indicate that the applicant is now, or has been, involved in another type of civil lawsuit—for example, a custody fight, a personal injury claim, or a dispute with an auto repair shop. If the legal matter has nothing to do with the applicant's rental history, ability to pay the rent, or satisfy your other tenancy requirements, you may be on shaky ground if you base a rejection solely on that basis.

Criminal Records

Understandably, many landlords wish to check an applicant's criminal history, and credit reports will often include this information. Can you reject an applicant because of a conviction for drunk driving, or murder or drug use? What if there was an arrest but no conviction?

Convictions. If an applicant has been convicted for criminal offenses, you are probably entitled to reject him on that basis. After all, a conviction indicates that the applicant was not, at least in that instance, a law-abiding individual, which is a legitimate criterion for prospective tenants or managers. For example, you may reject someone with convictions for crimes against children.

There is one exception, however, and this involves convictions for past drug use: As explained below, past drug addiction is considered a disability under the Fair Housing Amendments Act, and you may not refuse to rent to someone on that basis—even if the addiction resulted in a conviction. People with convictions for the sale or manufacture of drugs or current drug users are not, however, protected under federal law.

Arrests. A more difficult problem is posed by the person who has an arrest record but no conviction. Under our legal system, a person is presumed not guilty until the prosecution proves its case or the arrestee pleads guilty. So, is it illegal to deny housing to someone whose arrest did not result in a conviction? Because "arrestees" are not, unlike members of a race or religion, protected under federal or state law, you could probably reject an applicant with an arrest history without too much fear of legal consequences. But there is an easy way to avoid even the slightest risk: Chances are that a previously arrested applicant who is *truly* a bad risk will have plenty of other facts in his or her background (like poor credit or negative references) that will clearly justify your rejection. In short, if you do a thorough check on each applicant, you'll get enough information on which to base your decision.

Incomplete or Inaccurate Rental Application

A carefully designed rental application form is a key tool in choosing tenants, and we include a rental application in Chapter 1. This (or any other) application will do its job only if the applicant provides you with all the necessary information. Obviously, if you can reject applicants on the basis of negative references or a bad credit history, you can reject them for failing to allow you to check their background, or if you catch them in a lie.

Inability to Meet Legal Terms of Lease or Rental Agreement

It goes without saying that you may legally refuse to rent to someone who can't come up with the security deposit or meet some other valid condition of the tenancy, such as the length of the lease.

Pets

You can legally refuse to rent to people with pets, and you can restrict the types or size of pets you accept. In fact, your insurance may prohibit renting to tenants with certain breeds of dogs (and if the rental is part of a homeowners' association, additional pet restrictions may apply). You can also, strictly speaking, let some tenants keep a pet and say no to others—because pet owners, unlike members of a religion or race, are not as a group protected by antidiscrimination laws. However, from a practical point of view, an inconsistent pet policy is a bad idea, because it can only result in angry, resentful tenants. Also, if the pet owner you reject is someone in a protected category and you have let someone outside of that category rent with a pet, you are courting a discrimination lawsuit.

Keep in mind that you cannot refuse to rent to someone with an animal if that animal is a service or companion animal—for example, a properly trained dog for a person with disability. (42 U.S. Code § 3604(f)(3)(B).) Clause 14 of the form lease and rental agreements in Chapter 2 discusses pet policies and legal issues.

Sources of Antidiscrimination Laws

This section reviews the sources of antidiscrimination laws: the federal Fair Housing Act of 1968 and the federal Fair Housing Amendments Act of 1988 (throughout this chapter, we refer to these laws as the federal Acts), the 1866 Civil Rights Act, and state and local antidiscrimination laws. "Types of Illegal Discrimination," which follows, discusses specific types of discrimination that will almost surely get you into trouble with a federal, state, or local housing agency.

The Federal Fair Housing Acts

The Fair Housing Act and Fair Housing Amendments Act (42 U.S. Code §§ 3601–3619, 3631), which are enforced by the U.S. Department of Housing and Urban Development (HUD), address many types of housing discrimination. They apply to all aspects of the landlord-tenant relationship throughout the U.S.

How Fair Housing Groups Uncover Discrimination

Landlords who turn away prospective tenants on the basis of race, ethnic background, or other group characteristics obviously never come out and admit what they're doing. Commonly, a landlord falsely tells a person who's a member of a racial minority that no rentals are available, or that the prospective tenant's income and credit history aren't good enough. From a legal point of view, this can be a dangerous—and potentially expensive—tactic. Here's why: Both HUD and private fair housing groups are adept at uncovering this discriminatory practice by having "testers" apply to landlords for vacant housing. Typically, a tester who is African-American or Hispanic will fill out a rental application, listing certain occupational, income, and credit information. Then, a white tester will apply for the same housing, listing information very similar to—or sometimes not as good as—that given by the minority applicant.

A landlord who offers to rent to a white tester, and rejects—without valid reason—a minority applicant who has the same (or better) qualifications, is very likely to be found to be guilty of discrimination. Such incidents have resulted in many hefty lawsuit settlements. Fortunately, it's possible to avoid the morass of legal liability for discrimination by adopting tenant screening policies that don't discriminate, and applying them evenhandedly.

Types of Discrimination Prohibited

The Fair Housing Act prohibits discrimination on the following grounds (called protected categories):

- race or color or religion
- national origin
- familial status—includes families with children under the age of 18 and pregnant women and elderly persons
- disability or handicap, and
- sex, including sexual harassment.

Although the federal Acts use certain words to describe illegal discrimination (such as "national origin"), the Department of Housing and Urban Development and the courts are not limited to the precise language of the Acts. For instance, sexual harassment is a violation of law because it qualifies as discrimination on the basis of sex—even though the term "sexual harassment" is not used in the text of the law itself.

Aspects of Landlord-Tenant Relationship Covered

The federal Acts essentially prohibit landlords from taking any of the following actions based on race, color, religion, national origin, familial status, disability, or sex:

- advertising or making any statement that indicates a limitation or preference based on race, religion, or any other protected category
- falsely denying that a rental unit is available
- setting more restrictive standards for selecting tenants
- refusing to rent to members of certain groups
- before or during the tenancy, setting different terms, conditions, or privileges for rental of a dwelling unit, such as requiring larger deposits of some tenants, or adopting an inconsistent policy of responding to late rent payments
- during the tenancy, providing different housing services or facilities, such as making a community center or other common area available only to selected tenants, or
- terminating a tenancy for a discriminatory reason.

An individual who suspects discrimination may file a complaint with HUD or a state or local fair housing agency, or sue you in federal or state court. Guests of tenants may also sue landlords for housing discrimination under the federal Acts. (*Lane v. Cole*, 88 F.Supp.2d 402 (E.D. Pa., 2000).) Landlords may always, however, impose reasonable restrictions on guest stays.

> CAUTION
> **Failure to stop a tenant from making discriminatory or harassing comments to another tenant may also get you into legal trouble.** If one tenant reports that another is making ethnic or racial slurs or threatening violence because of their race, religion, ethnicity, or other characteristic that is considered a protected category, act promptly. A simple oral warning may stop the problem, but if not, a warning letter may be in order (see Chapter 16 for advice on writing warning letters). Depending on the situation, an eviction for tenant violation of the lease clause on quiet enjoyment of the premises may be warranted. If violence is involved, you'll need to act quickly and call the police. As with all tenant complaints, keep good records of conversations to protect yourself from tenant complaints that you acted illegally by failing to stop discrimination or harassment or that an eviction was illegal.

Seniors' Housing

If you have a multifamily property and decide you'd like to rent exclusively to seniors, you can do so as long as you follow federal guidelines. You have two options:

- **80% of your residents must be 55 or older.** You must make it known to the public, through your advertising, that you offer senior housing, and must verify applicants' ages. Once you've reached the 80% mark, you can set any other age restriction as long as it does not violate any state or local bans on age discrimination. For example, you could require the remaining 20% of tenants to be over 18 years of age, as long as no state or local law forbids such a policy.
- **Housing for tenants 62 and older.** All of your residents must be 62 or older. This includes spouses and adult children, but excludes caregivers and on-site employees.

Exempt Property

The following types of property are exempt from the federal ban against discrimination in housing, as long as their rental is accomplished without the use of discriminatory advertising (42 U.S.C.A. § 3603(b) & § 3607):

- owner-occupied buildings with four or fewer units (this is called the "Mrs. Murphy" exemption)
- single-family housing, as long as the owner owns no more than three such houses at any one time
- certain types of housing operated by religious organizations and private clubs that limit occupancy to their own members, and
- with respect to age discrimination only, housing geared toward seniors. See "Seniors' Housing," above.

> CAUTION
> **State and local laws may cover federally exempt units.** Even though your property may be exempt under federal law, similar state or local anti-housing-discrimination laws may nevertheless cover your rental units. For example, owner-occupied buildings with four or fewer units are exempt under federal law, but not under California law.

More Information From HUD and State Agencies

For more information about the Fair Housing Act, free copies of federal fair housing posters, and technical assistance on accessibility requirements, contact one of HUD's many local offices. You'll find a list of state and local offices on the HUD website at www.hud.gov (click the tab "State Info"). You can also call the agency's Housing Discrimination Hotline at 800-669-9777 (or 800-927-9275 TTY).

For information on state and local housing discrimination laws, contact your state fair housing agency. You'll find a list of state and local agencies, with contact information, on the HUD website, as well as at www.nationalfairhousing.org, a website maintained by the National Fair Housing Alliance.

The 1866 Civil Rights Act

Passed at the end of the Civil War, the 1866 Civil Rights Act also bans discrimination in housing.

(42 U.S.C.A. § 1981.) Its prohibition of "racial discrimination" covers African-Americans, Hispanics, and all dark-skinned persons. Importantly, unlike the federal Fair Housing Acts, the Civil Rights Act does not exempt the "Mrs. Murphy" situation, in which the owner lives on premises that consist of four or fewer units. This means that all landlords, no matter the size of their properties or whether they live in them, may not lawfully discriminate against African-Americans, Hispanics, or other dark-skinned persons.

Display Fair Housing Posters in Rental Office

Federal regulations require you to put up special fair housing posters wherever you normally conduct housing-related business. You must display a HUD-approved poster saying that you rent apartments in accordance with federal fair housing law (24 Code of Federal Regulations (CFR) §§ 110 and following). Many state laws have similar requirements.

Hang the fair housing posters in a prominent spot in the office or area where you greet prospective tenants and take applications. If you have a model apartment, it's a smart idea to hang a poster there, too. To get free posters, available in English and Spanish, contact the U.S. Department of Housing and Urban Development.

State and Local Antidiscrimination Laws

Most state and local laws prohibiting housing discrimination echo federal antidiscrimination law in that they outlaw discrimination based on race or color, national origin, religion, familial status, disability, and sex. (If your state law doesn't track federal law group by group, it makes little difference—you're still bound by the more-inclusive federal law.) But state and local laws often go in the other direction—they may provide more detail and may also forbid some kinds of discrimination—such as discrimination based on marital status—that aren't covered by federal law. For example, in states that prohibit discrimination based on marital status, it would be illegal to refuse to rent to divorced people. And some cities have very specific rules. For example, New York City landlords may not reject prospective tenants because of their chosen occupation (as long as it's a lawful occupation), and may not discriminate against registered domestic partners (either same-sex or heterosexual).

Types of Illegal Discrimination

In the sections that follow, we'll look at each of the categories of illegal discrimination and explore their obvious and not-so-obvious meaning.

Race, Color, or Religion

Fortunately, the amount of overt racial and religious discrimination has lessened over the last several decades. This is not to say, however, that discrimination doesn't exist, especially in subtle forms. And, unfortunately, HUD may see "discrimination" where your intent was completely well intentioned. Below, we'll look at some of the common examples of both intentional (but subtle) discrimination and unintended discrimination.

Intentional, Subtle Discrimination

It goes without saying that you should not overtly treat tenants differently because of their race or religion—for example, renting only to members of your own religion or race is obviously illegal. Deliberate discrimination should not be cavalierly dismissed, however, as a thing of the past practiced by insensitive oafs. Unexpected situations can test your willingness to comply with equal treatment laws and can reveal subtle forms of intentional discrimination that are just as illegal as blatant discrimination. Consider the following scenario.

EXAMPLE: Several tenants in Creekside Apartments reserved the common room for a religious occasion. Creekside management learned that the tenants were members of a white supremacist religion that believes in the inferiority of all nonwhites and non-Christians. Creekside was appalled at the thought of these ideas being discussed on its premises, and denied the group the use of the common room. The tenants who were members of this group filed a discrimination complaint with HUD on the basis of freedom of religion. HUD supported the religious group and forced Creekside to make the common room available. Creekside wisely sent all tenants a memo stating that making the common room available reflects management's intent to comply with fair housing laws and not their endorsement of the principles urged by any group that uses the room.

As the above example illustrates, religions that are outside the mainstream are protected under the federal Acts.

> ! CAUTION
> **Don't discriminate on the basis of how applicants sound over the phone.** Academic studies have shown that people can often identify a person's ethnic background based on short phone conversations. Researchers have tested this theory on unsuspecting landlords, some of whom rejected large numbers of African-American applicants compared to equally qualified white callers. Fair housing advocacy groups, described in "How Fair Housing Groups Uncover Discrimination," above, can be expected to use this tactic as a way to build a case against landlords whom they suspect of regular, illegal discrimination.

Unintended Discrimination

In Chapter 1, we discussed the unintended discriminatory messages that are conveyed when advertisements feature statements such as "safe Christian community" or "Sunday quiet times enforced." (Both ads may be understood as suggesting that only Christians are welcome as tenants.) The same considerations apply to your dealings with your tenants after they have moved in. Conscientious landlords should carefully review tenant rules, signs, newsletters, and all communications to make

sure that they cannot be construed in any way to benefit, support, or discriminate against any racial or religious group. The examples and advice we give below may seem "politically correct" in the extreme, but take our word for it, they are based on actual fair housing complaints and deserve to be taken seriously.

- The apartment complex newsletter invites everyone to a "Christmas party" held by the management. Non-Christian tenants might feel that this event is not intended for them and therefore that they have been discriminated against. A better approach: Call it a "Holiday Party" and invite everyone.
- Management extends the use of the common room to tenants for "birthday parties, anniversaries, and Christmas and Easter parties." A better idea: Invite your tenants to use the common room for special celebrations, rather than list specific Christian holidays.
- In an effort to accommodate your Spanish-speaking tenants, you translate your move-in letter and house rules into Spanish. Regarding the use of alcohol in the common areas, the Spanish version begins, "Unlike Mexico, where drinking is practiced in public places, alcoholic beverages may not be consumed in common areas … ." Because to many people this phrase implies an ethnic generalization, it may well become the basis for a fair housing complaint.
- The metropolitan area where you own residential rental property contains large numbers of both Spanish-speaking and Cantonese-speaking people. Advertising in only Spanish, or translating your lease into only Cantonese, will likely constitute a fair housing violation because it suggests that members of the other group are not welcome. Of course, if you advertise only in English, you are not violating fair housing laws.

National Origin

Like discrimination based on race or religion, discrimination based on national origin is illegal, whether it's practiced openly and deliberately or unintentionally.

Even if you are motivated by a valid business concern, but choose tenants in a way that singles out people of a particular nationality, it's still illegal. Say, for instance, that two Hispanic tenants recently skipped out on you, owing you unpaid rent. So you decide to make it a practice to conduct credit checks only on Hispanics. An Hispanic applicant may interpret your actions as sending a negative message to Hispanics in general: Hispanics are not welcome because you assume all of them skip out on debts. A fair housing agency or a court of law would probably agree that this sort of selective policy is illegal discrimination.

On the other hand, if you require all prospective tenants to consent to a credit check (as well as meeting other objective criteria as discussed above), you will get the needed information, but in a nondiscriminatory way.

Discriminatory comments as well as policies can get you in trouble, too, as one New York owner learned the hard way. The landlord told a Honduran applicant that she couldn't rent an apartment because "Spanish people … like to have loud music." The applicant sued the landlord for the discriminatory statement. A federal court ordered the landlord to pay $24,847 in damages: $7,000 to compensate her for her losses; $9,736 for attorney fees; $2,111 for court costs; and $6,000 to penalize the landlord for making the discriminatory comment. (*Gonzales v. Rakkas*, 1995 WL 451034 (E.D. N.Y., 1995).)

TIP

If you ask one person a question, ask everyone. It cannot be emphasized enough that questions on a prospective tenant's legal status must be put to all applicants, not just the ones who you suspect are illegal, and not just the ones who are applying to live in one of your buildings in a certain part of town.

Discrimination on the Basis of Immigration Status

Landlords often ask whether they may legally require that all tenants be in the United States legally—in other words, that they be citizens, permanent residents, visa holders, or have some other right to be here. There may be legitimate and legal business reasons why some landlords impose this requirement. For example, they may believe that people without legal status may be more likely to break their leases than others who have no need to live somewhat in the shadows. However, another motivating factor may be distrust of some renters simply because they are from other countries. Not surprisingly, landlords who are in the second camp typically require documentation of only those applicants who they suspect may be here illegally—those whose skin color, accents, or other characteristics suggest that they're "not from here." And therein lies the problem.

HUD has addressed this issue with great care. Because "immigration status" is not a protected category under the federal fair housing laws, it is not illegal to require that all applicants provide "identity documents" that establish that they meet rental criteria (which, presumably, can include legal residency). However, HUD hastily adds that "a person's ability to pay rent or fitness as a tenant is not necessarily connected to his or her immigration status." ("Immigration Status and Housing Discrimination Frequently Asked Questions," found on www.NLIHC.org (search for it by name).) And HUD makes it very clear that if landlords intend to ask for residence verification, they must ask all applicants, not only those whom they suspect may be here without legal status. Requiring verification from only some applicants is almost always an instance of race, color, or national origin discrimination.

Note that in New York City and in California, however, landlords are specifically prohibited from asking applicants for immigration status.

Familial Status

Discrimination on the basis of familial status includes not only openly refusing to rent to families with children or to pregnant women, but also trying to accomplish the same goal by setting overly restrictive space requirements (limiting the maximum number of people permitted to occupy a rental unit), thereby preventing families with children from occupying smaller units.

We discuss how to establish reasonable occupancy standards later in this chapter. The fact that you can legally adopt occupancy standards, however, doesn't mean you can use "overcrowding" as a euphemism for refusing to rent to tenants with children, if you would rent to the same number of adults. A few landlords have adopted criteria that for all practical purposes forbid children under the guise of preventing overcrowding—for example, allowing only one person per bedroom, with a couple counting as one person. Under these criteria, a landlord would rent a two-bedroom unit to a husband and wife and their one child, but would not rent the same unit to a mother with two children. This practice, which has the effect of keeping all (or most) children out of a landlord's property, would surely be found illegal in court and would result in monetary penalties.

It would also be illegal to allow children to occupy ground floor units only, or to designate certain apartments or buildings within an apartment community as "family" units.

It is essential to maintain a consistent occupancy policy. If you allow three adults to live in a two-bedroom apartment, you had better let a couple with a child (or a single mother with two children) live in the same type of unit, or you leave yourself open to charges that you are illegally discriminating.

> **EXAMPLE:** Jackson owned and managed two identical one-bedroom units in a duplex, one of which he rented out to three flight attendants who were rarely there at the same time. When the other unit became vacant, Jackson advertised it as a one-bedroom, two-person apartment. Harry and Sue Jones and their teenage daughter were turned away because they exceeded Jackson's occupancy limit of two people. The Jones family, learning that the companion unit was rented to three people, filed a complaint with HUD, whose investigator questioned Jackson regarding the inconsistency of his occupancy policy. Jackson was convinced that he was in the wrong, and agreed to rent to the Jones family and to compensate them for the humiliation they had suffered as a result of being refused.

Finally, do not inquire as to the age and sex of any children who will be sharing the same bedroom. This is their parents' business, not yours.

Disability

The Fair Housing Amendments Act prohibits discrimination against people who:

- have a physical or mental disability that substantially limits one or more major life activities—including, but not limited to, hearing, mobility and visual impairments, chronic alcoholism (but only if it is being addressed through a recovery program), mental illness, HIV positive, AIDS, AIDS-Related Complex, and mental retardation
- have a history or record of such a disability, or
- are regarded by others as though they have such a disability.

The law also protects those who are "associated with" someone who has a disability, such as a family member, cotenant, or caregiver who lives with the tenant or makes house visits.

You may be shocked to see what is—and what is not—considered a disability. Although it may seem odd, alcoholism is classed as a protected disability. Does this mean that you must rent to a drunk? What about past, and current, drug addiction? Let's look at each of these issues.

Recovering Alcoholics

You may encounter an applicant, let's call him Ted, who passes all your criteria for selecting tenants but whose personal history includes a disquieting note:

Employers and past landlords let you know that Ted has a serious drinking problem that he is dealing with by attending AA meetings. As far as you can tell, Ted has not lost a job or a place to live due to his drinking problem. Can you refuse to rent to Ted for fear that he will drink away the rent, exhibit loud or inappropriate behavior, or damage your property? No, you cannot, unless you can point to specific acts of misbehavior or financial shakiness that would sink any applicant, regardless of the underlying cause. Your fear alone that this might happen (however well-founded) will not legally support your refusal to rent to Ted.

In a nutshell, you may not refuse to rent to what HUD calls a "recovering alcoholic" simply because of his status as an alcoholic—you must be able to point to specific facts other than his status as an alcoholic in recovery that render him unfit as a tenant.

> **EXAMPLE:** Patsy applied for an apartment one morning and spoke with Carol, the manager. Patsy said she would have to return that afternoon to complete the application form because she was due at her regular Alcoholics Anonymous meeting. Carol decided on the spot that she did not want Patsy for a tenant, and she told Patsy that the unit "had just been rented," which was a lie. (Patsy continued to see the newspaper ad for the unit.) Patsy filed a complaint with HUD, alleging that she was an alcoholic who had been discriminated against. Because Carol could not point to any reason for turning Patsy away other than her assumption that Patsy, as a recovering alcoholic, would be a bad tenant, the judge awarded Patsy several thousand dollars in damages.

Unfortunately, HUD has not been very helpful in explaining what steps an alcoholic must take in order to qualify as "recovering." Regular attendance at AA meetings and counseling probably qualify, but an alcoholic who is less conscientious may not make the grade. In any event, you as the landlord are hardly in a position to investigate and verify an applicant's personal habits and medical history. So how can you choose tenants without risking a violation of law?

The answer lies in putting your energies into thorough reference checking that will yield information that can unquestionably support a rejection at the rental office. If the applicant, recovering or not, is truly a bad risk, you'll discover facts (like job firings, bad credit, or past rental property damage) independent of the thorny problem of whether the person has entered the "recovery" stage of his alcoholism. And if you have a current tenant whom you suspect of alcoholism, use the same approach —focus on his behavior as a tenant, regardless of his status as an alcoholic. If the tenant damages your property or interferes with your other tenants' ability to quietly enjoy their property, he is a candidate for eviction regardless of whether he is in or out of recovery, just as would be any tenant who exhibited this behavior. Consider the following scenario, which is what Carol should have done.

> **EXAMPLE:** Same facts as above, except that Carol went ahead and took an application from Patsy later that day and checked her references. Patsy's former landlord told Carol that Patsy had refused to pay for damage from a fire she had negligently caused; Patsy's employment history showed a pattern of short-lived jobs and decreasing wages. Carol noted this information on Patsy's application form and, as she would have done for any applicant with a similar background, Carol rejected Patsy. Patsy filed a complaint with HUD, again claiming discrimination on the basis of her alcoholism. When the HUD investigator asked to see Patsy's application and questioned Carol about her application criteria for all applicants, he concluded that the rejection had been based on legally sound business reasons and was not, therefore, a fair housing violation.

Drug Users

Under the Fair Housing Amendments Act, a person who has a past drug addiction is classed as someone who has a record of a disability and, as such, is protected under the fair housing law. You may not refuse to rent to someone solely because he is an ex-addict, even if that person has felony convictions for drug use. Put another way, your fear that the person will resume his illegal drug use is not sufficient grounds to reject the applicant. If you do a thorough background check, however, and discover a rental or employment history that would defeat any applicant, you may reject the person as long as it is clear that the rejection is based on these legal reasons.

On the other hand, someone who currently and illegally uses drugs is breaking the law, and you may certainly refuse to rent to him—particularly if you reasonably suspect the person is dealing drugs. Also, if the applicant has felony convictions for dealing or manufacturing illegal drugs, as distinct from convictions for possession of drugs for personal use, you may use that history as a basis of refusal.

Mental or Emotional Impairments

Like alcoholics or past drug users, applicants and tenants who had, or have (or appear to have) mental or emotional impairments must be evaluated and treated by the landlord and manager on the basis of their financial stability and histories as tenants, not on the basis of their mental health status. Unless you can point to specific instances of past behavior that would make a prospective tenant dangerous to others, such as assaults on tenants or destruction of property, or you have other valid business criteria for rejecting the person, a refusal to rent or a special requirement such as cosigner on the lease could result in a fair housing complaint.

No "Approved List" of Disabilities

The physical and mental disabilities that are covered by the Fair Housing Acts range from the obvious (wheelchair use and sensory disabilities) to those that may not be so apparent. The law reaches to past drug users and to those who are HIV positive.

The list of groups protected by the law is not, however, set in stone. What may seem to you like an individual's hypochondria or personal quirk may become a legally accepted disability if tested in court. For example, tenants with hypertension (which may lead to more serious medical problems) have been known to ask for protection under the fair housing laws, as have tenants suffering from "building material sensitivity" (sensitivities to vapors emitted from paint, upholstery, and rugs). Similarly, tenants who have a sensitivity or problem that is widespread throughout the population, such as asthma or allergies, may also win coverage under the fair housing laws. Contact your local HUD office to find out whether the courts have extended fair housing protections in these situations.

Questions and Actions That May Be Considered to Discriminate Against the Disabled

You may not ask an applicant or tenant if she has a disability or illness, and may not ask to see medical records, inquire about the type of medication the person takes, or ask about their ability to live independently. If it is obvious that someone has a disability—for example, the person is in a wheelchair or wears a hearing aid—it is illegal to inquire how severely he is disabled. We describe how to verify a claimed disability below.

Unfortunately, even the most innocuous, well-meaning question or remark can get you into trouble, especially if you decide not to rent to the person. What you might consider polite conversation may be taken as a probing question designed to discourage an applicant.

> **EXAMPLE:** Sam, a Vietnam veteran, was the owner of Belleview Apartments. Jim, who appeared to be the same age as Sam and who used a wheelchair, applied for an apartment. Thinking that Jim might have been injured in the Vietnam War, Sam questioned Jim about the circumstances of his disability, intending only to pass the time and put Jim at ease. When Jim was not offered the apartment—he did not meet the financial criteria that Sam applied to all applicants—he filed a complaint with HUD, alleging discrimination based on his disability. Sam was unable to convince the HUD investigator that his questions were not intended to be discriminatory, and, on the advice of his attorney, Sam settled the case for several thousand dollars.

Your well-intentioned actions, as well as your words, can become the basis of a fair housing complaint. You are not allowed to "steer" applicants to units that you, however innocently, think would be more appropriate. For example, if you have two units for rent—one on the ground floor and one three stories up—do not fail to offer to show both units to the applicant who is movement-impaired, however reasonable you think it would be for the person to consider only the ground floor unit.

The Rights of Tenants With Disabilities to Enter and Live in an Accessible Place

Your legal obligations toward applicants and tenants with disabilities extend beyond the questions you may ask or conversations you may have. The physical layout of your leasing office and other areas open to the public (where applicants will go to inquire about vacancies, for example) must be wheelchair-accessible.

You must also concern yourself with the fair housing laws after you have rented a home to a person with a disability. The Fair Housing Amendments Act requires that landlords:

- **accommodate** the needs of tenants with disabilities, at the landlord's own expense (42 U.S. Code § 3604(f)(3)(B)), and
- allow tenants with disabilities to make reasonable **modifications** of their living unit or common areas at their expense if that is what is needed for the person to comfortably and safely live in the unit. (42 U.S. Code § 3604(f)(3)(A).)

We'll look briefly at each of these requirements.

Accommodations. You are expected to adjust your rules, procedures, or services in order to give a person with a disability an equal opportunity to use and enjoy a dwelling unit or a common space. Accommodations include such things as:

- parking—if you provide parking in the first place, providing a close-in, spacious parking space for a tenant who uses a wheelchair
- service or companion animals—allowing a guide dog, hearing dog, or service dog in a residence that otherwise disallows pets

- rent payment—allowing a special rent payment plan for a tenant whose finances are managed by someone else or by a government agency
- reading problems—arranging to read all communications from management to a blind tenant, and
- phobias—for example, providing a tub and clothesline for a tenant whose anxiety about machines makes her unable to use the washer and dryer.

Does your duty to accommodate tenants with disabilities mean that you must bend every rule and change every procedure at the tenant's request? Generally speaking, the answer is no. You are expected to accommodate "reasonable" requests, but need not undertake changes that would seriously impair your ability to run your business. For example, if an applicant uses a wheelchair prefers the third-story apartment in a walk-up building constructed in 1926 to the one on the ground floor, you do not have to rip the building apart to install an elevator.

Modifications. Where your duty to accommodate the needs of tenants with disabilities ends, your obligation to allow the tenant to modify living space may begin. A person with disabilities has the right to modify his living space to the extent necessary to make it safe and comfortable, as long as the modifications will not make the unit unacceptable to the next tenant, or the tenant with a disability agrees to undo the modification when he leaves. Examples of modifications undertaken by a tenant with a disability include:

- lowering countertops for a wheelchair-bound tenant
- installing special faucets or door handles for persons with limited hand use
- modifying kitchen appliances to accommodate a blind tenant, and
- installing a ramp to allow a wheelchair-bound tenant to negotiate two steps up to a raised lobby or corridor.

Do You Need to Accommodate Tenants With Disabilities Who Are Dangerous?

You do not have to accommodate a tenant with a disability who poses a direct threat to others' safety, or who is likely to commit serious property damage. You must rely on objective evidence, such as current conduct or a recent history of disruptive behavior, before concluding that someone poses a threat. In particular, consider the following:

- The nature, severity, and duration of the risk of injury. For example, someone whose behavior is merely annoying is not as worrisome as someone who is prone to physical confrontations.
- The probability that injury will actually occur. Here, you must take into account to what extent the person is likely to follow through with worrisome acts.
- Whether there are any reasonable accommodations that will eliminate the direct threat. For example, if you can diffuse a situation by changing a rule or procedure, you may need to.

Applying the three criteria mentioned above can be challenging. For example, suppose residents tell you about a tenant who has threatened them with a baseball bat on several occasions. In keeping with your policy to enforce your "no threats" policy, you terminate the tenant's lease. The tenant's lawyer contacts you and suggests that as soon as his client resumes appropriate medication, the behavior will stop. Must you give this a try?

The answer is yes, though you can ask for satisfactory assurance that the tenant will receive appropriate counseling and periodic medication monitoring so that he will no longer pose a direct threat. To be sure, receiving such assurances, such as periodic letters from counselors or therapists, puts you uncomfortably in the thick of your tenant's personal problems, but there is no other way to meet your obligations to other tenants (to maintain a safe environment). You'd be on solid ground to continue with the termination if the tenant refused to work with you in this way.

You are not obliged to allow a tenant with a disability to modify his unit at will, without prior approval. You are entitled to ask for a reasonable description of the proposed modifications, proof that they will be done in a workmanlike manner, and evidence that the tenant is obtaining any necessary building permits.

Unless the property is located in Massachusetts, or it is federally financed, tenants must pay for their modifications. (But if your building opened for occupancy on or after March 13, 1991, and the modification is needed because the building doesn't comply with HUD's accessibility requirements (see "New Buildings and Tenants With Disabilities," below), you must pay for the modification.) If a tenant proposes to modify the unit in such a way that will require restoration when the tenant leaves (such as the repositioning of lowered kitchen counters), you may require that the tenant pay into an interest-bearing escrow account the amount estimated for the restoration. (The interest belongs to the tenant.)

> **CAUTION**
> **Your duty to evaluate any request begins when you learn of it,** even if it's oral or communicated through a third party, such as an applicant's friend or family member.

Verification of Disabled Status

When a tenant or applicant asks for a modification or accommodation, it may be obvious that the person falls within the legal definition of a disabled person, and that the request addresses that disability. In those cases—think of a blind applicant who asks to keep a seeing eye dog—it would be pointless for you to demand proof that the person has a disability and needs the accommodation. (Indeed, doing so might result in a harassment lawsuit.) However, many times the claimed disability, and the appropriateness of the request, are not so clear. You're entitled to ask for verification that the tenant has a disability and needs the specific modification requested, but you must do so carefully.

New Buildings and Tenants With Disabilities

The Fair Housing Amendments Act (42 U.S. Code §§ 3604(f)(3)(C) and 3604(f)(7)) imposes requirements on new buildings of four or more units that were first occupied after March 13, 1991. All ground floor units and every unit in an elevator building must be designed or constructed so that:

- there is an accessible route from the public right of way outside the building (such as the sidewalk) to all units and common areas
- the "primary entrance" of each rental unit is accessible
- any stair landing shared by more than one rental unit is handicapped accessible (*U.S. v. Edward Rose & Sons*, 384 F.3d 258 (6th Cir. 2004))
- the public and common areas are "readily accessible to and usable by" people with disabilities, including parking areas (a good rule of thumb is to reserve 2% of the spaces)
- entryway doorways have 36" of free space *plus* shoulder and elbow room; and interior doorways are at least 32" wide
- interior living spaces have wheelchair-accessible routes throughout, with changes in floor height of no more than ¼"
- light switches, outlets, thermostats, and other environmental controls are within the legal "reach range" (15" to 48" from the ground)
- bathroom walls are sufficiently reinforced to allow the safe installation of "grab bars," and
- kitchens and bathrooms are large enough to allow a wheelchair to maneuver within the room (40" turning radius minimum) and have sinks and appliances positioned to allow side or front use.

For more information on accessibility requirements, see HUD's informative website, www.hud.gov (search "fair housing accessibility guidelines").

For years, landlords asked for a doctor's letter. Now, according to a HUD and Department of Justice guidance memo, you must be willing to listen to less formal sources. (*Reasonable Accommodations Under the Fair Housing Act*, Joint Statement of the Department of Housing and Urban Development and the Department of Justice, March 5, 2008.) Sources of reliable information include:

- **The individual himself.** A person can prove that he has met the requirement for having a legal disability (and that a modification or accommodation addresses that disability) by giving you a "credible statement." Unfortunately, the guidance memo does not define this term.
- **Documents.** A person who is under 65 years of age and receives Supplemental Security Income or Social Security Disability Insurance benefits is legally disabled. Someone could establish disability by showing you relevant identification cards. Likewise, license plates showing the universal accessibility logo, or a driver's license reflecting the existence of a disability, are sufficient proof.
- **Doctors or other medical professionals, peer support groups, nonmedical service agencies.** Information from these sources might come through letters, phone calls, or personal visits.
- **Reliable third parties.** This wide-open source of information could include friends, associates, and roommates, though some fair housing experts interpret this phrase as meaning any "third-party professional who is familiar with the disability." We don't know whether this definition will become the standard used by courts.

Many prospects and tenants will turn to a third party, usually a professional, when you ask for verification. Although you can certainly leave it up to that party to provide the written documentation, you can also give the "Verification of Disabled Status" form to your tenants, asking them to give it to their doctors or other professionals. Using this form is a convenient and safe way to elicit the information you need (and keep unwanted details out of the picture). Specifically, this form:

- **Evidences your willingness to entertain the tenant's request.** When you give the form to your tenant, make a note in the prospect's or

Verification of Disabled Status

Marion Welby, MD
Third-party professional's name
31 Circle Drive, Suite 2
Address
Centerville, VA 12345

555-123-4567
Phone number
September 5, 20xx
Date

Dear _____ Mr. Greene _____ (Landlord or manager's name),

I am a _____ medical doctor licensed to practice in Virginia _____

_____ (describe third-party professional's work or occupation).

I am familiar with _____ Al Blake _____ (Tenant), who is under my care or supervision.

In my opinion, _____ Al Blake _____ (Tenant) is *legally disabled*, as that term is defined by federal law (Fair Housing Amendments Act, 42 United States Code section 3602(h)):

A disabled person is someone who

(1) has a physical or mental impairment that substantially limits one or more of such person's major life activities, or

(2) has a record of having such an impairment, or

(3) is regarded as having such an impairment.

_____ Al Blake _____ (Tenant) has requested the following accommodation or modification to the rental premises at 1530 Park Drive, #7, Centerville, VA _____ (address of rental property): lower countertops in kitchen, lower light switches in hall, kitchen, bathroom, and bedroom _____ (describe proposed accommodation or modification).

In my opinion, this proposed accommodation or modification is needed in order for _____ Al Blake _____

_____ (Tenant) to live safely and comfortably at the rental premises.

I am willing to testify under oath or sign a sworn declaration consistent with my representations in this letter, should the need arise.

Marion Welby, MD   September 5, 20xx
Signature   Date

Marion Welby, MD
Print name

tenant's file. This note may come in handy should you later be accused of discouraging (or even outright denying) the tenant's request.

- **Educates the third party as to the legal standard for being considered to have a disability.** By placing the federal definition of "disabled" right on the form, you're reminding the signer that this is the standard he or she must keep in mind when verifying status.

- **Identifies the precise modification or accommodation.** When you give the form to your tenant, fill in the accommodation or modification that's been requested. If you leave it blank, you risk the insertion of irrelevant or extra requests that you and the tenant have not discussed. Of course, it's possible that the third party may have additional suggestions, and if so, there's room for those suggestions (which will be subject to the same "reasonableness" standard as are all modification and accommodation requests, as explained in "How to Respond to Unreasonable Requests for Accommodations or Modifications," below).

- **Eliminates the chance that the third party will give you details of the tenant's disability.** You don't need these details, and you don't want to know them, either (you never want to give a tenant the ability to accuse you of misusing this information). A third party may nevertheless think you require the full picture and may include it in a letter. There's no place on this form for these details.

- **Cautions the third party that this is a serious matter.** You'll see that the form ends with the signer's statement that he or she will be willing to testify under oath or sign a sworn declaration consistent with his or her representations on the form. A reputable professional who is truly familiar with your tenant should not be deterred by this cautionary ending. In the unlikely event that your tenant is using someone to fraudulently verify the tenant's status, that person might think twice when seeing this concluding sentence.

A sample Verification of Disabled Status form is shown above and the Nolo website includes a downloadable copy. See Appendix B for the link to the forms in this book.

How to Respond to Unreasonable Requests for Accommodations or Modifications

The law requires you to agree to "reasonable" requests for accommodations or modifications. You don't have to go along with unreasonable ones, but you can't simply say "No" and shut the door. You must engage in what HUD calls an "interactive process" with the disabled person. In essence, this means you have to get together and try to reach an acceptable compromise. For example, suppose you require tenants to pay rent in person at the manager's office. A tenant with a disability asks that the manager collect the rent at her apartment. Since this would leave the office unstaffed, you suggest instead that the tenant mail the rent check. This may be a reasonable compromise.

Sex and Sexual Harassment

You may not refuse to rent to a person on the basis of gender—for example, you cannot refuse to rent to a single woman solely because she is female. Neither may you impose special rules on someone because of their gender—for example, limiting upper-story apartments to single females.

Illegal sex discrimination also includes sexual harassment—refusing to rent to a person who resists your sexual advances, or making life difficult for a tenant who has resisted such advances.

What is sexual harassment in a rental housing context? Courts have defined it as:

- a pattern of persistent, unwanted attention of a sexual nature, including the making of sexual remarks and physical advances, or a single instance of highly egregious behavior. A manager's persistent requests for social contact, or constant remarks concerning a tenant's appearance or behavior, could constitute sexual harassment, as could a single extraordinarily offensive remark, or

- a situation in which a tenant's rights are conditioned upon the acceptance of the owner's or manager's attentions. For example, a manager who refuses to fix the plumbing until the tenant agrees to a date is guilty of sexual harassment. This type of harassment may be established on the basis of only one incident.

EXAMPLE: Oscar, the resident manager of Northside Apartments, was attracted to Martha, his tenant, and asked her repeatedly for a date. Martha always turned Oscar down and asked that he leave her alone. Oscar didn't back off, and began hanging around the pool whenever Martha used it. Oscar watched Martha intently and made suggestive remarks about her to the other tenants. Martha stopped using the pool and filed a sexual harassment complaint with HUD, claiming that Oscar's unwanted attentions made it impossible for her to use and enjoy the pool and even to comfortably live at Northside. Oscar refused to consider a settlement when the HUD investigator spoke to him and Martha about his actions. As a result, HUD pursued the case in court, where a federal judge ordered Oscar to leave Martha alone and awarded several thousand dollars in damages to Martha.

CAUTION

Sexual harassment awards under the Civil Rights Act have no limits. Owners and managers who engage in sexual harassment risk being found liable under either the Fair Housing Act or Title VII of the 1964 Civil Rights Act, which also prohibits sexual discrimination. The Fair Housing Act limits the dollar amount of damages that can be levied against the defendant, but there are no limits to the amount of punitive damages that can be awarded in Title VII actions. Punitive damages are generally not covered by insurance, and it is far from clear whether even actual damages in a discrimination case (that is, nonpunitive damages such as pain and suffering) will be covered, either.

Age

The federal fair housing law does not expressly use the word "age," but, nevertheless, discrimination on the basis of age is definitely included within the ban against discrimination on the basis of familial status. Many states and localities, however, have laws that directly address the issue of age.

Can you, as the landlord, refuse to rent to an older person solely because you fear that her frailty or dimming memory will pose a threat to the health or safety of the rest of your tenants? Or, can you favor younger tenants over equally qualified elderly tenants because you would like your property to have a youthful appearance?

The answer to these questions is no. You may feel that your worry about elderly tenants is well-founded, but unless you can point to an actual incident or to facts that will substantiate your concern, you cannot reject an elderly applicant on the basis of your fears alone. For example, you could turn away an older applicant if you learned from a prior landlord or employer that the person regularly forgot to lock the doors, failed to manage his income so that he was often late in paying rent, or demonstrated an inability to undertake basic housekeeping chores. In other words, if the applicant has demonstrated that he or she is unable to live alone, your regular and thorough background check should supply you with those facts, which are legally defensible reasons to refuse to rent. As for your stylistic preference for youthful tenants, this is age discrimination in its purest form, and it will never survive a fair housing complaint.

EXAMPLE: Nora's 80-year-old mother Ethel decided that it was time to find a smaller place and move closer to her daughter. Ethel sold her home and applied for a one-bedroom apartment at Coral Shores. Ethel had impeccable references from neighbors and employers and an outstanding credit history. Nonetheless, Mike, the manager of Coral Shores, was concerned about Ethel's age. Fearful that Ethel might forget to turn off the stove, lose her key, or do any number of other dangerous things, Mike decided on the spot not to rent to her. Ethel filed a fair housing complaint, which she won on the basis of age discrimination.

Learning from his experience with Ethel, Mike, the manager at Coral Shores, became more conscientious in screening tenants. The following example shows how he avoided another lawsuit on age discrimination.

> **EXAMPLE:** William was an elderly gentleman who decided to sell the family home and rent an apartment after his wife passed away. He applied for an apartment at Coral Shores. Since William had no "prior rental history," Mike, the manager, drove to William's old neighborhood and spoke with several of his former neighbors. Mike also called William's personal references. From these sources, Mike learned that William had been unable to take care of himself the last few years, having been completely dependent on his wife. Mike also learned that, since his wife's death, William had made several desperate calls to neighbors and family when he had been unable to extinguish a negligently started kitchen fire, find his keys, and maintain basic levels of cleanliness in his house. Mike noted these findings on William's application and declined to rent to him on the basis of these specific facts.

Renting to Minors

You may wonder whether the prohibition against age discrimination applies to minors (in most states, people under age 18). A minor applicant who is legally "emancipated"—is legally married, or has a court order of emancipation or is in the military—has the same status as an adult. This means you will need to treat the applicant like any other adult. In short, if the applicant satisfies the rental criteria that you apply to everyone, a refusal to rent to a minor could form the basis of a fair housing complaint. On the other hand, if the applicant is not emancipated, she lacks the legal capacity to enter into a legally binding rental agreement with you.

The issue of age discrimination may also arise during a well-established tenancy. You may have a tenant who has lived alone competently for years but who, with advancing age, appears to be gradually losing the ability to live safely by himself. Determining the point when the tenant should no longer live alone is a judgment call that will vary with every situation, and we cannot provide a checklist of "failings" that will suffice for everyone. There is, however, one universal ground rule that will, by now, sound pretty familiar: You cannot take action merely on the basis of the person's age or because you fear what that person might do. You must be able to point to real, serious violations of the criteria that apply to all tenants before you can evict or take action against an elderly tenant.

> **CAUTION**
> **Elderly tenants may also qualify as disabled tenants, who are entitled to accommodation under the law.** An elderly tenant who, because of her age, cannot meet one of your policies may be entitled to special treatment because she also qualifies as a disabled person. In other words, you may not be able to use an elderly tenant's inability to abide by one of the terms of the tenancy as the basis of an eviction—instead, you may be expected to adjust your policy in order to accommodate her disability. For example, an elderly tenant who is chronically late with the rent because of her sporadic disorientation might be entitled to a grace period, or a friendly reminder when the rent is due; whereas a nondisabled tenant who is chronically late with the rent is not entitled to such special treatment. And if an elderly tenant can't negotiate the stairs, the legal solution is a ramp (assuming the cost is not unreasonable), not an eviction notice.

Marital Status

Federal law does not prohibit discrimination on the basis of marital status (oddly, being married isn't included within the federal concept of "familial status"). Consequently, in most states you may legally refuse to rent to applicants on the grounds that they are (or are not) married. The issue comes up when a landlord chooses a married couple over a single applicant, or when an unmarried couple applies for a rental (or a current tenant wants to move in a special friend).

Some states have addressed these situations. About 20 states plus the District of Columbia ban discrimination on the basis of marital status, but most of these extend protection to married couples only. In these states, landlords cannot legally prefer single, platonic roommates (or one-person tenancies) over married couples. What about the reverse—preferring married couples over single roommates or a single tenant? Courts in Maryland, Minnesota, New York, and Wisconsin have ruled that the term "marital status" only protects married people from being treated differently from single people, not vice versa.

Now then, what about the remaining possibility—an unmarried couple? In only a few states—Alaska, California, Massachusetts, and New Jersey—does the term "marital status" include unmarried couples. If you own rental property in these four states, can you reject unmarried couples solely because they aren't married? It depends on your reasons. If you refuse to rent to unmarried couples on the grounds that cohabitation violates your religious beliefs and you live in California, Massachusetts, Michigan, or New Jersey, the answer is no.

TIP

Unmarried tenants may be protected by a city or county ordinance prohibiting discrimination on the basis of sexual orientation. Although usually passed to protect the housing rights of gay and lesbian tenants, most local laws forbidding discrimination based on sexual orientation also protect unmarried heterosexual couples as well. In addition, unmarried people may be able to challenge a landlord's refusal to rent to them on the basis of sex discrimination, which is covered by the federal Acts.

Sexual Orientation and Gender Identity

Housing discrimination based on sexual orientation and gender identity is prohibited in 19 states plus the District of Columbia: California, Colorado, Connecticut, Delaware, the District of Columbia, Hawaii, Illinois, Iowa, Maine, Maryland, Massachusetts, Minnesota, New Jersey, Nevada, New Mexico, Oregon, Rhode Island, Vermont, and Washington. In addition, four states prohibit housing discrimination based on sexual orientation: New Hampshire, New York, and Wisconsin. In addition, many cities prohibit discrimination on the basis of sexual orientation and gender identity, including Atlanta, Chicago, Detroit, Miami, New York, Pittsburgh, and Seattle. For more information on state or local laws, contact the National LGBTQ Task Force, 202-393-5177, or check its website at www.thetaskforce.org.

Source of Income

In several states, including California, Connecticut, the District of Columbia, Maine, Massachusetts, Minnesota, New Jersey, North Dakota, Oklahoma, Oregon, Utah, Vermont, and Wisconsin, you may not refuse to rent to a person simply because he is receiving public assistance (many localities in other states have similar law). You may, however, refuse to rent to persons whose available incomes fall below a certain level, as long as you apply that standard across the board.

Understand that the prohibition against discriminating on the basis of source of income does not necessarily mean that you must participate in the Section 8 program. In the states that ban discrimination based on the source of income, tenants' lawyers have argued that the ban supports their theory that landlords should not be free to decline to participate in government-subsidized programs; but these cases have not been universally successful. As noted in "Section 8 and Low-Income Housing Programs," below, if you don't want to participate in a Section 8 program, seek legal counsel.

Arbitrary Discrimination

After reading the above material outlining the types of illegal discrimination, you may be tempted to assume that it is legal to discriminate for any reason not mentioned by name in a state or federal law. For example, because none of the civil rights

Section 8 and Low-Income Housing Programs

Many tenants with low incomes qualify for federally sub-sidized housing assistance, the most common being the tenant-based Section 8 program of the federal Department of Housing and Urban Development (HUD). ("Section 8" refers to Section 8 of the United States Housing Act of 1937, 42 U.S. Code § 1437f.) That program pays part of the rent directly to you. The local public housing agency, you, and the tenant enter into a one-year agreement, which includes a written lease addendum supplied by the local public housing agency. The tenant pays a percentage of his monthly income to you, and the housing agency pays you the difference between the tenant's contribution and what it determines is the market rent each month.

The Pros and Cons of Section 8 Participation

Section 8 is a mixed bag for landlords. It offers several advantages:

- The housing agency pays the larger part of the rent on time every month, and the tenant's portion is low enough that he shouldn't have too much trouble paying on time, either.
- If the tenant doesn't pay the rent and you have to evict him, the housing agency guarantees the tenant's unpaid portion, and also guarantees payment for damage to the property by the tenant, up to a certain limit.
- You'll have a full house if your neighborhood or area is populated by low-income tenants.

Section 8's disadvantages are legion, however. They include:

- The housing agency's determination of what is market rent is often low, and the program caps the security deposit (which may be lower than your state's maximum).
- You are locked into a tenancy agreement for one year, and can't terminate the tenancy except for nonpayment of rent or other serious breach of the lease. (Evictions based on grounds other than nonpayment of rent or other serious breaches are difficult.)
- When HUD experiences a budget crunch, it cuts the public housing agencies' budgets. As a result, the housing agencies are likely to lower the landlords' allotments. Though this practice is legally iffy, it's done anyway.

- New Section 8 landlords must often wait up to a month or longer for a qualifying, mandatory inspection—during which they see no rent. These inspections often reveal picky, minor violations that state inspectors wouldn't cite for.

Call your local public housing agency if you wish to participate in the Section 8 program. They will refer eligible applicants to you, arrange for an inspection of the rental property, and prepare the necessary documents (including the lease addendum) if you decide to rent to an eligible applicant. Be sure to get a copy from HUD of the Section 8 rules and procedures that all participating landlords must use. Often, they vary significantly from your state or local law.

Must Landlords Participate in Section 8?

Landlords have traditionally been able to choose not to participate in the Section 8 program without fear of violating the federal fair housing laws. However, as the federal government's ability to provide sufficient low-income housing diminishes, this is changing in some localities. In New Jersey, for example, if an existing tenant becomes eligible for Section 8 assistance, you may not refuse to accept the vouchers—you must participate in the program as to this tenant, at least. (*Franklin Tower One v. N.M.*, 157 N.J. 602; 725 A.2d 1104 (1999).) In Connecticut, Maryland, and Massachusetts, landlords may not refuse to rent to existing or new tenants who will be paying with Section 8 vouchers. (*Commission on Human Rights and Opportunities v. Sullivan Associates*, 250 Conn. 763; 739 A.2d 238 (1999); Mass. Gen. Laws ch. 151B, § 4(10); *Montgomery County v. Glenmont Hills Associates Privacy*, 936 A.2d 325 (2007).)

Some states have required landlord participation in Section 8 by way of their ban on discrimination on the basis of source of income ("SOI"). These states make Section 8 vouchers one of the protected sources, and include Connecticut, Maine, Massachusetts, Minnesota, New Jersey, North Dakota, Oklahoma, Oregon, Utah, Vermont, Wisconsin, and the District of Columbia. However, localities in other states may pass laws that include Section 8 as a protected SOI (some cities in California and New York City, for example) even though there is no state-wide protection in those states.

laws specifically prohibit discrimination against men with beards or long hair, you might conclude that such discrimination is permissible. This is not always true.

For example, even though California's Unruh Civil Rights Act (Cal. Civ. Code §§ 51–53.7, 54.1–54.8) contains only the phrases "sex, race, color, religion, ancestry, national origin, disability, medical condition, genetic information, marital status, gender identity, citizenship, primary language, or sexual orientation" to describe types of discrimination that are illegal, the courts have ruled that these categories are just examples of illegal discrimination. The courts in California have construed the Unruh Act to forbid all discrimination on the basis of one's personal characteristic or trait.

Even if you live in a state that does not specifically outlaw arbitrary discrimination, there is a very strong practical reason why you should not engage in arbitrary discrimination—for example, based on obesity, occupation, or style of dress. Because fair housing law includes numerous protected categories —race, sex, religion, and so on—chances are that a disappointed applicant can fit himself or herself into at least one of the protected categories and file a discrimination claim. Even if the applicant does not ultimately win his or her claim, the time, aggravation, and expense caused by his attempt will be costly to the landlord.

> **EXAMPLE:** Jane, a lawyer, applied for an apartment and returned her application to Lee, the landlord. Lee had spent the better part of the last year fighting a frivolous lawsuit brought by a former tenant (who was also a lawyer), and the thought of renting to another lawyer was more than Lee could bear. Jane's credit, rental, and personal references were excellent, but she was turned away.
>
> One of Lee's tenants told Jane that Lee had refused her solely because she was a lawyer. This made Jane angry, and she decided to get even. Although her state did not have a law prohibiting arbitrary discrimination, that didn't stop Jane. She filed a fair housing complaint alleging that she had been turned away because she was single, female, and Jewish. The complaint was ultimately dismissed, but not before it had cost Lee a bundle of time and energy to defend.

Valid Occupancy Limits

Your ability to limit the number of people per rental unit is one of the most hotly debated issues in the rental housing industry. Like most controversial topics, it has two sides, each with a valid point. No one disputes the wisdom of enforcing building codes that specify minimum square footage per occupant for reasons of health and safety. But it is another matter altogether when even relatively small families—especially those with children—are excluded from a large segment of the rental market because landlords arbitrarily set unreasonable occupancy policies.

The law allows you to establish an occupancy policy that is truly tied to health and safety needs. In addition, you can adopt standards that are driven by a legitimate business reason or necessity, such as the capacities of your plumbing or electrical systems. Your personal preferences (such as an exaggerated desire to reduce wear and tear by limiting the number of occupants, or to ensure a quiet uncrowded environment for upscale older tenants), however, do not constitute a legitimate business reason.

If your occupancy policy limits the number of tenants for any reason other than health, safety, and legitimate business needs, you risk charges of discrimination against families, known in legalese as "familial status" discrimination. Occupancy policies that cross over the line into discrimination toward families are discussed above.

The federal government has taken the lead in establishing occupancy standards through passage of the Fair Housing Amendments Act. But states and localities may also set their own occupancy standards, and many have. And this is where things get tricky: Ordinarily, when the federal government legislates on a particular subject, states and localities are free to pass laws on the subject, too, as long as they're equally (or more) protective of the targeted group. But the federal government's guidance (a mere memo to regional HUD directors) specifically reminded its readers that Congress didn't intend to develop "a national occupancy code." ("Fair Housing Enforcement—Occupancy Standards Notice of Statement of Policy," CFR Vol. 63, No. 243, Dec. 18, 1998.) The memo practically invited states and localities to set their own occupancy standards, and didn't make it clear whether those standards had to be at least as generous (to tenants) as the federal guidance. As a result, some states developed occupancy standards that, when applied, resulted in fewer people allowed in the rental. Landlords were perplexed: Which standard did they need to follow? Their policy might be legal when examined in a state court, using state occupancy standards, but illegal when tested in a federal court, using the HUD guidance. And some states, like California, developed standards that resulted in more occupants than the federal guidance.

The way out of this morass is, fortunately, rather commonsense. To avoid lawsuits, you need to adopt an occupancy policy that is at least as generous as the federal standard, which is explained just below. And just in case your state or locality has legislated more generous standards, you'll have to follow them. If they're less generous, don't take a chance, because you can be sure that a tenant's lawyer will choose to sue you using the federal standard.

Finding out whether your occupancy policy is legal is not always a simple matter. You must answer three questions for each rental situation:

- How many people must you allow in that particular unit under the federal standard?
- How many people must you allow in that unit under the state standard?
- How many people must you allow in that unit under the local standard?

Once you know the answers to each of these questions, the rest is easy: To avoid a federal, state, or local fair housing complaint, simply apply the occupancy standard that is the least restrictive— that is, the one that allows the most people. If you don't follow the least restrictive standard, be prepared to show that your policy (allowing fewer people) is motivated by reasons of health or safety or a legitimate business reason.

Unfortunately, getting the answers to the three questions is often difficult. This section will attempt to guide you through the process. It covers:

- federal occupancy standards
- common state occupancy standards and local laws on the subject
- how to calculate the number of occupants that must be allowed for each rental unit, and
- "legitimate business reasons" that might support a more restrictive policy than the law allows.

Minimum and Maximum Numbers of Occupants

Two kinds of laws affect your occupancy standards:

- **Minimum occupancy standards.** Federal, state, and local occupancy standards establish the minimum number of occupants you must allow in a particular unit. If you set a lower occupancy limit, you may be accused of violating a fair housing law.
- **Maximum occupancy limits.** State and local health and safety codes may set maximum limits on the number of tenants, based purely on the size of the unit and number of bedrooms and bathrooms.

The Federal Occupancy Standard

Federal law allows you to establish "reasonable" restrictions on the number of persons per dwelling. These restrictions must be motivated by legitimate business reasons or the need to preserve the health and safety of the occupants.

The Department of Housing and Urban Development, or HUD, interprets federal law by means of memos, guidelines, and regulations. Unfortunately, HUD has never been very helpful when it comes to explaining what a "reasonable" restriction on persons per dwelling might be. HUD has simply said that a policy of two persons per bedroom will, as a general rule, be considered reasonable, but that other factors will also be considered when determining whether a landlord was illegally discriminating by limiting the number of people in a rental unit. Because the number of bedrooms is not the only factor, the federal test has become known as the "two-per-bedroom-plus" standard. These other factors include:

- the size of the bedrooms and rental unit—if the unit or the bedrooms are small, you may take that into account
- age of the children—babies do not have the same space requirements as teenagers, and you may take that into account
- configuration of the rental unit—if a room could serve as a bedroom, but there is no access to a bathroom except through another bedroom, you might be able to designate that room a "nonbedroom" and limit the number of occupants accordingly
- physical limitations of the building—for example, limitation of the sewerage or electrical system
- state and local building codes that impose their own set of minimum space requirements per occupant, and
- prior discrimination complaints against the landlord—if you must respond to a fair housing complaint, you will be at a disadvantage if you are known to repeatedly violate antidiscrimination laws.

The flexibility of the federal standard helps landlords because it lets them take into account all the particulars of a given situation. But it also means that you cannot set an occupancy limit for a unit and know for certain that it will pass the federal test. The legal occupancy maximum cannot be determined until you analyze every applicant. For example, if you decide that the family with a newborn needs less space than one with a teenager, the occupancy limit for the same unit will be different for each family.

As you might imagine, a federal "standard" that changes according to the makeup of every applicant has proven very difficult and confusing to apply, but you must do your best to apply it conscientiously.

Begin by multiplying the number of bedrooms times two, and then think about the factors listed above. For example, is one of the bedrooms so small as to be unsuitable for two people? On the other hand, could a room that you might think of as a den be usable as another bedroom? Could a couple with a baby in a bassinet comfortably occupy a bedroom that would be unsuitable for three adults? As you can see, use of the two-per-bedroom-plus standard may result in an occupancy limit that might be below or above twice the number of bedrooms.

> **EXAMPLE:** Murray owned a large, old house that had been remodeled into two apartments. The upstairs unit had large rooms, two bedrooms, and two bathrooms. The lower apartment was considerably smaller, with one bedroom and one bath.
>
> *The Upstairs.* Murray was approached by a family of five: three young children and two adults. He realized that the large bedroom could safely sleep three children, so he figured that the five people in this family came within the federal standards.
>
> *The Downstairs.* The first applicants for the lower apartment were three adults. Murray told them that the occupancy limit was two. Later, a couple with a newborn applied for the apartment. Realizing that a bassinet could easily fit into the bedroom, Murray adjusted his occupancy limit and rented to the couple.

Common State and Local Occupancy Standards

Even if you are okay under the federal standard, you can't relax just yet. Remember, states and localities can set their own occupancy standards, as long as they are more generous than the federal government. You must comply with any state or local standard or (if a complaint is filed) risk prosecution by the state or local agency that administers the standard.

It is crucial to check whether any state or local standard applies to you. Contact your local and state housing authority for information, or the U.S. Department of Housing and Urban Development (HUD) office.

New York landlords, for example, must comply with the "Unlawful Restrictions on Occupancy" law, commonly known as the "Roommate Law." (N.Y. RPL § 235-f.) The Roommate Law prohibits New York landlords from limiting occupancy of a rental unit to just the tenant named on the lease or rental agreement. It permits tenants to share their rental units with their immediate family members, and, in many cases, with unrelated, nontenant occupants, too, so long as a tenant (or tenant's spouse) occupies the unit as a primary residence. The number of total occupants is still restricted, however, by local laws governing overcrowding.

> (!) CAUTION
> **Remember, you must apply the most generous standard—federal, state, or local—in determining how many people may occupy a particular rental unit.** If you are unsure of the result, it is always safer to err on the side of more, rather than fewer, occupants.

Legitimate Reasons for a More Restrictive Occupancy Policy

What if you decide that your particular rental unit ought to be occupied by fewer than the most generous number you got when you calculated the occupancy under the federal, state, and local laws? If you set an occupancy limit that is lower than the legal standard, you must be prepared to defend it with a legitimate business reason. This term is impossible to describe in the abstract, since its meaning will vary with the circumstances of every rental property. Here are some examples of legitimate business reasons that have been advanced by landlords who have established occupancy limits lower than the government standard:

- **Limitations of the infrastructure.** The plumbing or electrical systems cannot accommodate more than a certain amount of use. (*U.S. v. Weiss*, 847 F.Supp 819 (1994).)
- **Limitations of the facilities.** Common areas and facilities (such as laundry rooms and hallways) would be overcrowded if more occupants were allowed.
- **Dilapidation that common sense tells you would result from more people living in the structure.** The house is so small that allowing more occupants would result in unreasonable wear and tear. (*Pfaff v. U.S. Department of Housing and Urban Development*, 88 F.3d 739 (1996).)

If your occupancy policy is lower than the most generous applicable legal standard, be prepared for an uphill fight. It is very difficult to establish a "winning" legitimate business reason that justifies a lower occupancy standard. You'd be wise to hire a neutral professional, such as an engineer, to evaluate and report on the limiting factor in light of your community's needs (for example, you'll want a report that measures your boilers' limited hot water delivery against the number of residents who you think should reasonably live there). Get that report *before* imposing a restrictive occupancy policy, and make sure it really justifies your decision to use more restrictive occupancy standards.

You will need to carefully assess whether it's worth your time and money to fight a fair housing complaint. In order to establish that your lower occupancy policy is based upon legitimate business reasons and is therefore legal, you'll need to convince a fair housing judge that:

- changing the limiting factor (such as rewiring the rental unit's electrical system to accommodate more use) is impractical from a business perspective, or
- common sense, your business experience, and the practice of landlords in your area support your lower number, or
- limiting the number of occupants is the only practical way to address the limiting factor.

Here are some examples of situations in which landlords have argued that their occupancy policy, which was lower than that allowed by the most generous applicable law, should nonetheless survive a fair housing challenge. In both cases, the landlord argued that the limitations of the septic system justified a more restrictive occupancy standard. In the first example, the landlord prevailed. In the second example, the landlord failed to establish that his occupancy policy was based upon legitimate business reasons.

EXAMPLE 1: John and Mary Evans advertised the small two-bedroom cottage on their property as suitable for two people only. Their occupancy limit was based on the limitations of the septic system, which could legally accommodate no more than four people (the Evanses and two tenants in the cottage). John and Mary declined to rent to a family of four, who then filed a fair housing complaint. At the conciliation meeting arranged by the housing authority, John and Mary presented an engineer's report on the limitations of the septic system. The report estimated that it would cost many thousands of dollars to expand the septic system to accommodate more than four people on the property. The hearing officer accepted the Evanses' explanation and decided not to take the complaint further.

EXAMPLE 2: The occupancy policy for all the units at Westside Terrace was three persons per apartment, even for the two-bedroom units. A family of four applied for one of the two-bedrooms and was turned down. When the family filed a complaint with HUD, the owner of Westside Terrace justified the policy on the grounds that the building's infrastructure—its sewage capacities, pipes, and common areas—could not support as many people as would result from allowing four persons in the two-bedroom apartment units. Westside also presented evidence that it would be prohibitively expensive to upgrade these facilities. The judge heard evidence from structural and sanitary engineers which indicated that these facilities were capable of handling that number of people and had done so many times in the past. HUD decided that Westside's restrictive occupancy policy was not based on legitimate business needs, and ruled against it.

Managers and Discrimination

If you hire a manager, particularly one who selects tenants, make certain that he fully understands and abides by laws against housing discrimination. On the other hand, if you use an independent management company (which is a true independent contractor, rather than an employee such as a resident manager), the possibility that you will be liable for their discriminatory acts is greatly decreased. (See Chapter 6 on landlord liability for a manager's conduct and strategies for avoiding problems in this area.)

You should always let your tenants know that you, as well as your manager, intend to abide by the law, and that you want to know about and will address any fair housing problems that may arise. While this will not shield you from liability if you are sued due to your manager's conduct, it might (if you are lucky) result in the tenant's initial complaint being made to you, not a fair housing agency. If you hear about a manager's discriminatory act and can resolve a complaint before it gets into "official channels," you will have saved yourself a lot of time, trouble, and money.

One way to alert your tenants and prospective tenants to your commitment to the fair housing laws is to write all ads, applications, and other material given to prospective tenants to include a section containing your antidiscrimination stance. Prepare a written policy statement as to the law and your intention to abide by it. See the sample statement below.

Also, be sure to display fair housing posters on the premises, as described earlier in the chapter.

If, despite your best efforts, you even suspect your manager may use unlawful discriminatory practices to select or deal with tenants—whether on purpose or inadvertently—you should immediately resume control of the situation yourself. Alternatively, this may be the time to shield yourself from potential liability and engage the services of an independent management company, which in most cases will be responsible for its employees' actions.

**Sample Statement on
Equal Opportunity in Housing**

FROM: Shady Dell Apartments

TO: All Tenants and Applicants

It is the policy of the owner and manager of Shady Dell Apartments to rent our units without regard to a tenant's race, ethnic background, sex, age, religion, marital or family status, physical disability, gender identity, or sexual orientation. As part of our commitment to provide equal opportunity in housing, we comply with all federal, state, and local laws prohibiting discrimination. If you have any questions or complaints regarding our rental policy, call the owner at (phone number).

CAUTION
Never give managers or rental agents the authority to offer their own rent concessions or "deals" to selected tenants or applicants. If you want to offer inducements—a discount for signing an extended lease or one free month for tenants who begin renting in the month of March—do so on a consistent basis. Make sure offers are available to all tenants who meet the requirements of the special deal. Otherwise, a tenant who gets a worse deal from your manager than his identically situated neighbor is sure to complain—and if he is a member of a group protected by fair housing laws, he's got the makings of a case against you.

Unlawful Discrimination Complaints

A landlord accused of unlawfully discriminating against a prospective or current tenant may end up before a state, federal, or local housing agency, or in state or federal court. According to HUD, the number of fair housing complaints (most involving rentals) has declined in the last few years, from around 10,000 complaints in fiscal year 2010, to a little more than 8,000 in fiscal year 2013. According to the most recent HUD data (covering fiscal year 2013), 53% involved claims concerning disability discrimination,

and 28% were claims involving race (this is a notable difference from earlier years, when disability and race used to account for nearly the same percentage of complaints). ("HUD Annual Report on Fair Housing, FY 2013.") This section gives you a brief description of the legal process involved in each arena and the consequences of discrimination charges.

SEE AN EXPERT
Get expert help to defend a housing discrimination lawsuit. With the exception of a suit brought in small claims court, you should see an attorney if a tenant sues you or files an administrative complaint against you for discrimination. For advice on finding and working with an attorney or doing your own legal research, see Chapter 18.

When a Tenant Complains to a Fair Housing Agency

A prospective or current tenant may file a discrimination complaint with either HUD (by phone, mail, or online) or the state or local agency charged with overseeing fair housing complaints. A federal HUD complaint must be filed within one year of the alleged violation, but state statutes or local ordinances may set shorter time periods. If the complaint is filed with HUD, the agency should (but doesn't always) conduct an investigation within 180 days. (Time periods for state housing agencies vary.)

After HUD investigates the complaint (and this is true of most state agencies as well), it will either dismiss the complaint or attempt to reach a conciliation agreement (compromise) between you and the person filing the complaint. For example, a tenant might agree to drop his complaint in exchange for a sum of money or your written promise to rent him an apartment or, if he's a current tenant, to stop discriminatory practices.

If conciliation is unsuccessful, the fair housing agency will hold an administrative hearing (a trial before a judge but without a jury) to determine whether discrimination has occurred. If the administrative law judge decides that a fair housing violation occurred, he or she will direct that the violation be corrected in the ways described below.

HUD litigation is typically long and laborious. It is not unusual for cases to take up to ten years before they are concluded.

When a Tenant Sues in Federal or State Court

A tenant may also file suit in federal court or state court. This can be done even after filing an administrative complaint (as long as he has not signed a conciliation agreement or a HUD administrative hearing has not started). If the tenant goes to federal court, he must do so within two years of the alleged violation.

In a typical federal lawsuit, the aggrieved tenant (or would-be tenant) has gone to a private lawyer immediately after the alleged discriminatory incident. The attorney prepares a complaint and also asks the court for an expedited hearing, hoping to get an order from the court directing the landlord to cease the discriminatory practice. These orders are called "temporary restraining orders," and they are granted if the plaintiff (the tenant) can convince the judge that he has a good chance of winning and will suffer irreparable harm if immediate relief isn't granted. The order remains in place until a more formal hearing is held. Open-and-shut cases of discrimination often settle at the temporary restraining order stage.

Penalties for Discrimination

If a state or federal court or housing agency finds that discrimination has taken place, it may order you to do one or more of the following:

- rent a particular unit to the person who was discriminated against
- pay the tenant for "actual" or "compensating" damages, including any additional rent the tenant had to pay elsewhere as a result of being turned down, and damages for humiliation or emotional distress
- pay the tenant punitive damages (extra money as punishment for especially outrageous discrimination) and the tenant's attorney fees

- in the case of a disability violation, retrofit your property or set up an escrow fund to be used for retrofitting in the future, and
- pay a civil penalty to the federal government. The maximum penalty under the federal Fair Housing Acts is $16,000 for a first violation, and $70,000 for a third violation within seven years. (24 C.F.R. § 180.671.) Many states have comparable penalties.

Even if you are ultimately vindicated, the costs of defending a discrimination claim can be devastating. Your insurance policy may cover the dollar costs, but it cannot compensate you for lost time and aggravation. Careful attention to the discrimination rules described in this chapter and Chapter 1 will, we hope, save you from this fate.

> ## CAUTION
> **If you are the subject of a fair housing complaint, do not take the matter "into your own hands."** It is illegal to retaliate against, threaten, coerce, intimidate, or interfere with anyone who either files a complaint with HUD, cooperates in the investigation of such a complaint, or exercises a fair housing right.

Insurance Coverage in Discrimination Claims

Even the most conscientious landlords may find themselves facing a fair housing claim or a discrimination lawsuit. If this happens to you, will your insurance policy cover the cost of defending the claim and, if you lose, the cost of the settlement or judgment? The answers to these questions depend entirely on two highly variable factors: the wording of your insurance policy and the decisions of the courts in your state in similar cases. In short, there are no answers that will apply to everyone, but we can alert you to the issues that arise in every situation. At the very least, knowing how insurance companies are likely to approve or deny defense and judgment costs in discrimination claims should help you as you evaluate your own policy.

RELATED TOPIC

Chapter 10 discusses broad types of liability insurance, coverage for managers and other employees, and coverage for injuries suffered as a result of defective conditions on the property. The advice in that chapter on choosing property insurance is also relevant to choosing liability coverage for discrimination claims.

The Insurance Company's Duty to Defend: Broader Than the Duty to Cover

When you purchase liability insurance, you buy two things: the promise of the insurance company to defend you if you are sued for an act that arguably falls within the coverage of the policy, and its promise to pay the settlement or damage award if you lose. But sometimes (as is the case in fair housing claims) it is unclear whether, assuming you lose the case, your policy covers the conduct that gave rise to the claim. When this happens, your insurance company will usually defend you, but it may reserve the right to argue about whether it is obligated to pay the damages if the case is lost. Before you purchase insurance, find out exactly what's covered, including punitive damages in discrimination cases.

Most owners of residential rental property carry a comprehensive liability insurance policy, which typically includes business liability coverage. With this type of coverage, the insurance company agrees to pay on your behalf all sums that you are legally obligated to pay as damages "for bodily injury, property damage, or personal injury caused by an occurrence to which this insurance applies." The policy will generally define the three key terms "bodily injury," "occurrence," and "personal injury." The definitions will determine whether the insurance company will help you with a discrimination claim.

CAUTION

Find out if your policy covers administrative claims (complaints to fair housing agencies such as HUD). Insurance companies in several states have successfully argued that their duties to defend and cover you extend only to lawsuits, not fair housing agency claims. Ask your agent.

Definition of "Bodily Injury"

Discrimination complaints rarely include a claim that the victim suffered a physical injury at the hands of the landlord or manager. It is far more likely that the tenant or applicant will sue for the emotional distress caused by the humiliation of the discriminatory act.

"Bodily injury" does not usually include emotional distress. Courts in a few states, however, have held that bodily injury does include emotional distress. If your state does not include emotional distress in the concept of bodily injury, an insurance company may be able to successfully argue that a discrimination complaint is not covered by the policy.

Definition of "Personal Injury"

Insurance policies also typically provide coverage for "personal injury," or an injury that arises out of the conduct of your business. Personal injuries typically include false arrest, libel, slander, and violation of privacy rights; they also include "wrongful entry or eviction or other invasions of the right of private occupancy." As you can see from this definition, personal injuries include items that are neither bodily injuries nor accidental. And the definition includes some offenses, like libel, that seem somewhat similar to discrimination.

Nevertheless, an insurance company may argue that a discrimination claim isn't covered under a policy's definition of "personal injury."

Very few courts have addressed this question, let alone answered it, but in those that have, the answers have been quite mixed. For example, coverage has been denied on the grounds that "discrimination" is a specific wrong and, had the insurance company intended to cover discrimination, it would have specifically mentioned it. Coverage for discrimination claims by prospective tenants (such as applicants who have been turned away) has been denied on the theory that "the right of private occupancy" is a right enjoyed only by current, not would-be, tenants. Still other courts, realizing that the language in the policy is far from clear, have been willing to resolve the question in favor of the insured, and have ordered the insurance company to at least defend the lawsuit.

A Policy Specifically for Discrimination Claims and Lawsuits

As you've just learned, if you're sued for discrimination, it may be difficult or impossible to get coverage under your commercial general liability (CGL) policy. Another type of policy will offer you narrow, but certain coverage. This coverage is called "Tenant Discrimination Insurance," and it works a bit differently than your CGL policy. A CGL policy supplies the defense attorney and all resources to defend against the claim, as well as any judgment, up to the limits of your policy. When using Discrimination insurance, however, you find your own lawyer and, once a lawsuit or claim is filed (with HUD or any state or local fair housing agency), you get reimbursed for legal costs from that point on, and the amount of any judgment.

The Discrimination policy does not present any of the thorny issues encountered with a CGL policy—even intentional, blatant acts of discrimination will be covered. The policy will exclude class actions, suits by employees, any legal work and settlement that occurred without the other side having filed a lawsuit or a claim; and it may exclude punitive damages or fines, depending on state law. One definite drawback is that you must initiate the request for reimbursement, and if the carrier balks, you have to take action (with your CGL, the insurance company in most instances will step up on notice of the claim and defend you at least).

Discrimination insurance is not well known. It is relatively inexpensive (starting with a yearly premium of just over $2,000 for coverage of up to $1 million, with a $5,000 deductible). If you are interested, contact your insurance agent or broker and ask for information. You may have to supply the source: "NAS Insurance Services" is the underwriter. For more information, see www.nasinsurance.com.

In sum, there are at least three ways that insurance companies can deny coverage, if not also the defense of a fair housing claim and award: They can claim that the discriminatory act resulted in emotional distress, which is not a type of bodily injury; they can argue that an act of discrimination was intentional, and thus not an accidental occurrence to which the policy applies; and they can argue that discrimination is not one of the personal injuries that are covered by the policy. We suggest that you give the matter some thought when choosing a broker and negotiating your policy—but by far the best use of your energy is to make sure that your business practices do not expose you to these claims in the first place.

Discrimination and Public Policy

An insurance company will occasionally argue that it should not have to cover a landlord's intentional acts of discrimination because discrimination is an evil act that someone should not be able to insure against. While this argument has some persuasive aspects—discrimination is, indeed, contrary to public policy—it falls apart when you acknowledge that all sorts of other intentional bad acts (like libel and slander) are perfectly insurable. Courts have not been persuaded by the "public policy" argument. Be sure to check with your insurance broker whether your policy covers intentional acts of discrimination.

Definition of "Occurrence"

Your insurance company will defend and pay out on a claim if it is caused by an occurrence to which the policy applies. An "occurrence" is typically defined as an accident, whose results are neither expected nor intended from the standpoint of the insured (the property owner).

It doesn't take much brainwork to see how an insurance company can argue that an act of discrimination—like turning away a minority applicant—cannot be considered an "occurrence," because it is by definition intentional, not accidental. Courts in a few states, including Louisiana, Oregon, and South Dakota, have ruled in favor of insurance companies on this issue, and courts in other states have ruled similarly when the question has come up in employment discrimination cases.

Property Managers

FORMS IN THIS CHAPTER

Chapter 6 includes instructions for and a sample of the following form:

- Property Manager Agreement

The Nolo website includes a downloadable copy of this form. See Appendix B for the link to the forms in this book.

Many landlords hire a resident manager to handle all the day-to-day details of running an apartment building, including fielding tenants' routine repair requests and collecting the rent. Landlords who own several rental properties (large or small) may contract with a property management firm in addition to, or in place of, a resident manager. Hiring a manager can free you from many of the time-consuming (and tiresome) aspects of being a residential landlord. But it can also create some headaches of its own: lots of paperwork for the IRS; worries about liability for a manager's acts; and the responsibility of finding, hiring, and supervising an employee. This chapter explains how to weigh all these factors and how to minimize complications if you do decide to get some management help.

In some states, you may not have a choice—you may be required, by law, to hire a manager. California, for example, requires a resident manager on the premises of any apartment complex with 16 or more units. (Cal. Code of Regulations, Title 25, § 42.) New York City has similar requirements for buildings with nine or more units. Check with your state or local rental property owners' association to see if your state requires resident managers, or do your own research on the subject.

RESOURCE

Several other Nolo books provide useful information on hiring, managing, and firing employees:

- *The Employer's Legal Handbook*, by Fred S. Steingold, is a complete guide to the latest workplace laws and regulations. It covers everything you need to know about hiring and firing employees, drug tests of employees, personnel policies, employee benefits, discrimination, and other laws affecting small business practices.
- *The Manager's Legal Handbook*, Lisa Guerin and Sachi Barreiro, has excellent information about hiring employees.

- *The Essential Guide to Federal Employment Laws*, by Lisa Guerin and Sachi Barreiro, has extensive discussions on relevant federal laws, including the Fair Labor Standards Act, Americans with Disabilities Act, Equal Pay Act, Immigration Reform and Control Act, Fair Credit Reporting Act, and Occupational Safety and Health Act, as well as state and federal employment discrimination laws.
- *Dealing With Problem Employees: A Legal Guide*, by Lisa Guerin and Amy DelPo, includes chapters on hiring, evaluating, disciplining, and firing employees.
- *The Essential Guide to Workplace Investigations*, by Lisa Guerin, gives employers practical information on how to investigate and resolve workplace problems.

These Nolo books are available at bookstores and public libraries. They may also be ordered directly from Nolo's website, www.nolo.com, or by calling 800-728-3555.

For free general information on employment law, from discrimination to workers' compensation, see Nolo's articles in the Employment Law Center at www.nolo.com.

Property Managers and Building Supers

The focus in this chapter is on property managers, not supers (which are more common in places like New York City). While there aren't any hard and fast rules, here's the difference between a building superintendent (super) and a manager.

Property managers usually have more tenant-relations responsibilities than supers do, such as taking apartment applications, accepting rent, and responding to tenant problems and complaints. You might also authorize a trusted manager to purchase building supplies and hire outside contractors for specialized repairs—up to an agreed-upon spending limit, of course.

Building supers, on the other hand, usually concentrate on building repairs and maintenance tasks. They often possess special skills and are experienced at running complicated heating plants and air conditioning systems. Customarily, supers don't collect rent or take rental applications.

The legal issues as to hiring and compensating managers and supers are generally the same.

Hiring Your Own Resident Manager

If you put some thought into writing a job description, and some effort into recruiting and hiring a good manager, you'll avoid problems down the road. Don't hurry the process, or jump into an informal arrangement with a tenant who offers to help out if you'll take a little off the rent—you'll almost surely regret it.

Decide the Manager's Duties, Hours, and Pay

Why do you want to hire a manager? You need to answer this question in some detail as your first step in the hiring process. Here are the key issues you need to decide.

What are the manager's responsibilities? The Property Manager Agreement included in this book includes a list of duties you may want to delegate, such as selecting tenants, collecting rents, and hiring and paying repair people. Finding an on-site manager who can handle all these aspects of the job, however, is a tall order—so tall that many owners restrict the on-site manager's job to handling routine repairs and maintenance chores. Listing the job duties and skills you're looking for in a manager will make the hiring process more objective and will give you ready standards to measure which applicants are most qualified.

Is the job full or part time? How many hours do you anticipate the manager working? What hours do you expect the manager to be on the rental property or available (for example, by pager or cell phone)?

Will the manager live on the rental property or off? If you just want someone to collect the rent and handle minor repairs, they don't necessarily need to live in. Obviously, you need a vacant apartment for a resident manager.

How much do you plan to pay the manager? You may pay an hourly wage, generally ranging from $15 to $25 per hour, or a flat salary. How much you pay depends on the manager's responsibilities, the number of hours, time of day and regularity of the schedule, benefits, and the going rate in your community. You can get an idea how much managers are paid by asking other landlords or checking want ads for managers. Offering slightly above the going rate in your area should allow you to hire the best, most experienced candidates. If you do this, you might want to try and tap into the local grapevine of experienced managers to see if maybe you can snag someone who wants to move up.

Illegal Discrimination in Hiring

Federal, state, and local laws prohibit many kinds of discrimination in hiring. The Equal Pay Act applies to every employer, regardless of size; the Immigration Reform and Control Act of 1986 (IRCA) applies to employers with four or more employees. Title VII of the Civil Rights Act and the Americans with Disabilities Act apply only if you employ 15 or more people. Some state laws apply even if you have only one employee, such as California's prohibition on worker harassment.

Pay attention to these laws even if they do not specifically bind your business. Doing so will not hinder you from making a decision based on sound business reasons: skills, experience, references. The laws only forbid making a decision based on a factor that isn't reasonably related to the applicant's ability to do the job. Following them will protect you from accusations of discrimination.

Here are some of the factors on which these laws make it illegal to discriminate: race, color, gender, religious beliefs, national origin, age (if the person is 40 or older), and disability. Several states and cities also prohibit discrimination based on marital status, sexual orientation, or other factors. Contact your state fair employment office for details.

Much of the advice in Chapter 5, which deals with illegal discrimination against tenants, will also be of help when you're hiring a manager.

Should you give the manager reduced rent? Some landlords prefer giving a resident manager reduced rent in exchange for management services, rather than paying a separate salary. This isn't a good idea—for one thing, reduced rent alone won't work for a full-time manager. Reduced rent in exchange for being a manager can be a particular problem in rent control areas, since you may not be able to adjust rent easily. If you later have to fire a manager who is compensated by reduced rent, you may run into problems when you insist that the ex-manager go back to paying the full rent. But if the tenant-manager pays the full rent and receives a separate salary, there will be no question that he is still obligated to pay the full rent, as he has done all along.

Your obligations as an employer are the same whether you compensate the manager with reduced rent or a paycheck—for example, you must still pay Social Security and payroll taxes, as discussed below. However, paying the manager by reducing rent can create problems under wages and hours and overtime laws.

Advertise the Job

Some landlords find great managers via word of mouth by talking to tenants, friends, and relatives, or getting the word out through Facebook or other social media. Others run a Craigslist ad, use an employment agency, or advertise elsewhere. What will work best depends on your particular property and needs. In writing an ad, stick to the job skills needed and the basic responsibilities—for example, "Fifty-unit apartment complex seeks full-time resident manager with experience in selecting tenants, collecting rent, and apartment maintenance."

Screen Potential Managers Over the Phone

When people call about the manager's job, be ready to describe the responsibilities, pay, and hours. Then ask some questions yourself—you'll be able to quickly eliminate unlikely candidates and avoid wasting time interviewing inappropriate people. Use the phone call to get information on potential employees, including their:

- experience and qualifications
- interest in the position and type of work
- current employment, and
- ability to work at the proposed pay and schedule.

Jot notes of your conversation so you can follow up later in a personal interview.

Interview Strong Candidates

Limit your interviews to people you're really interested in hiring as manager. There's no point meeting with someone who's unqualified or unsuitable for the job. When setting interviews, ask potential managers to bring a résumé with relevant experience and names and phone numbers of four or five references.

A face-to-face meeting provides the opportunity to get in-depth information about a person's background, work experience, and ability to handle the manager's job, and allows you to assess an individual's personality and style.

Before you begin interviewing, write down questions focusing on the job duties and the applicant's skills and experience. To avoid potential charges of discrimination, ask everyone the same questions, and don't ask questions that are not clearly job-related—for example, the applicant's medical condition, religion, or plans for having children.

Here are some examples of questions that are appropriate to ask potential managers:

- "Tell me about your previous jobs managing rental properties."
- "How much experience do you have collecting rents? Doing general repairs? Keeping records of tenants' complaints of repair problems?"
- "What have you liked most about previous manager jobs? What have you liked least?"
- "What kinds of problems have you encountered as a property manager? How did you solve them?"
- "Why do you want this job?"

You might also ask some more direct questions, like:

- "What would you do if a tenant who had paid rent on time for six months asked for a ten-day extension because money was short as a result of a family problem?"
- "What would you do if a tenant called you at 11 p.m. with a complaint about a clogged sink?"

Get a Completed Application

If your manager will also be a tenant, make sure he or she (like all other tenants) completes a rental application (as discussed in Chapter 1) and that you check references and other information carefully. Be sure the applicant signs a form authorizing you to check credit history and references, such as the Consent to Contact References and Perform Credit Check form in Chapter 1.

If your manager is not also a tenant, prepare your own application (you can use the Rental Application in Chapter 1 and cross out what's not relevant) or ask prospective managers to bring a résumé with their employment and educational background.

! CAUTION

When you check a prospective manager's application or résumé, be sure to look for holes—dates when the person didn't indicate an employer. The applicant may be covering up a bad reference. Insist that the applicant explain any gaps in employment history.

Check References

No matter how wonderful someone appears in person or on paper, it's essential to contact former employers. Ideally, you should talk with at least two former employers or supervisors with whom the applicant held similar positions.

Before calling any references, make a list of key questions. Ask about the applicant's previous job responsibilities, character and personality traits, strengths and weaknesses, and reasons for leaving

the job. Review your interview notes for issues you want to explore more—for example, if you sense that the potential manager really doesn't seem organized enough to handle all the details of the manager's job, ask about it. Take your time and get all the information you need to determine whether the applicant is the best person for the job.

Character Traits of a Good Manager

Look for a person who is:

- **Honest and responsible.** This is especially important if the manager will be entitled to receive legal documents and papers on your behalf.
- **Patient.** Predictably, dealing with tenants, repair people, and guests will have its share of hassles. A person with a short fuse is a definite liability.
- **Financially responsible.** This should be demonstrated by a good credit history.
- **Personable yet professional.** Good communication skills are a must, both with you and your current and prospective tenants and any other workers the manager may supervise (for example, a cleaning crew).
- **Fastidious.** One of the manager's responsibilities will be to keep the building and common areas neat, clean, and secure.
- **Meticulous about maintaining records.** This is particularly important if collecting rent will be part of the job.
- **Fair and free of biases.** This is a must if the manager will be showing apartments, taking rental applications, or selecting tenants.
- **Unafraid of minor confrontations with tenants.** This is particularly important if the manager will be collecting overdue rents and delivering eviction notices, and handling disputes between tenants (for example, complaints over noise).

Employers are often reluctant to say anything negative about a former employee for fear of being hit by a lawsuit for defamation. Many may refuse to give any information other than the dates the person worked and the position held. It may be helpful to send the former employer a copy of the applicant's signed consent to disclosure of employment information. If a former employer is not forthcoming, you'll need to learn to read between the lines. If a former employer is neutral, offers only faint praise, or overpraises a person for one aspect of a job only—"always on time"—he may be hiding negative information. Ask former employers: "Would you hire this person back if you could?" The response may be telling. If a reference isn't glowing and doesn't cover all aspects of the job, check several other references—or hire someone else.

Check Credit History and Background

Checking an individual's credit history is especially important if you want a manager to handle money. Someone with large debts may be especially tempted to skim money from your business. And a prospective manager with sloppy personal finances is not a good choice for managing rental property. Before you order a credit report, be sure you get the applicant's consent.

You may also wish to ask a credit bureau or tenant screening company to do an investigative or background report, similar to the one some landlords run on tenants (see Chapter 1 for details).

CAUTION

Handle credit reports carefully. Federal law requires you to keep only needed information, and to discard the rest. See "How to Handle Credit Reports," in Chapter 7 for precise information.

Check Criminal and Driving Records

A property manager occupies a position of trust, often having access to tenants' apartments as well as to your money. Obviously, it's essential that the manager not present a danger to tenants. You may want to check an applicant's criminal history; credit reports often include this information. Depending on your state's laws concerning use of Megan's Law databases, you may want to use the database to check for registered sex offenders as explained in Chapter 1.

Another reason for thoroughness is your personal liability—if a manager commits a crime, you may be held responsible as discussed in "Protect Tenants From Your Employees" in Chapter 12.

Our best advice is check carefully and consider the type, seriousness, and dates of any prior convictions and how they relate to the job. *The Employer's Legal Handbook*, by Fred S. Steingold (Nolo), includes information on state laws on obtaining and using information on arrest and conviction records when making employment decisions.

If a manager will be driving your car or truck, be sure your insurance covers someone driving your vehicle as part of their employment.

Offer the Position and Put Your Agreement in Writing

Once you make your decision and offer someone the manager's job, you may need to do some negotiations. The potential employee may, for example, want a higher salary, different hours, more vacation, a different rental unit, or a later starting date than you offer. It may take some compromises to establish mutually agreeable work arrangements. When all terms and conditions of employment are mutually agreed upon, you and the manager should complete a Property Manager Agreement (discussed below) that covers manager responsibilities, hours, and pay that can be terminated at any time for any reason by either party.

We recommend that when you hire a tenant as a manager, you also sign a separate month-to-month rental agreement that can be terminated by either of you with the amount of written notice, typically 30 days, required under state law.

Why Do You Need a Written Agreement?

Landlords and resident managers often agree orally on the manager's responsibilities and compensation, never signing a written agreement.

Even though oral agreements are usually legal and binding, they are not advisable. Memories fade, and you and your employee may have different recollections of what you've agreed to. If a dispute arises between you and the manager, the exact terms of an oral agreement are difficult or impossible to prove if you end up arguing about them in court. It is a far better business practice to put your understanding in writing.

How to Reject Applicants for the Manager's Job

It used to be a matter of simple courtesy to inform unsuccessful applicants by sending a quick but civil rejection letter, which cut down on postinterview calls, too. You didn't owe them an explanation, however, and were usually better off saying as little as possible.

Is this approach still legal? It depends on why you have rejected the applicant. If your reasons come from information that the applicant has provided, or if the applicant doesn't have the qualifications for the job, you can still use the courteous-but-minimalist approach. For example, if the applicant tells you that she has never managed real estate property, or if the interview reveals that the applicant doesn't have the necessary "people skills," you can simply say that someone more qualified got the job.

However, if your rejection is based on information from a credit reporting agency that collects and sells credit files or other information about consumers, you must comply with the Fair Credit Reporting Act (15 U.S. Code §§ 1681 and following). See "How to Reject an Applicant" in Chapter 1 for more details, including a sample Notice of Denial Based on Credit Report or Other Information form.

CAUTION

Don't promise long-term job security. When you hire someone, don't give assurances that you may not be able to honor and that may give an applicant a false sense of security. Your best protection is to make sure your Property Manager Agreement emphasizes your right to fire an employee at will—and have the applicant acknowledge this in writing (see Clause 6 of the agreement shown below). This means you'll have the right to terminate the employment at any time for any reason that doesn't violate the law.

How to Prepare a Property Manager Agreement

Below is an example of a sound written agreement that spells out the manager's responsibilities, hourly wage or salary, hours, schedule, and other terms. The step-by-step instructions that follow take you through the process of completing your own agreement.

The Nolo website includes a downloadable copy of the Property Manager Agreement. See Appendix B for the link to the form in this book.

Clause 1. Parties

Here, you provide details about you and the manager and the location of the rental property, and state that the rental agreement is a separate document.

Clause 2. Beginning Date

Fill in the month, day, and year of the manager's first day of work.

Clause 3. Responsibilities

This form includes a broad checklist of managerial duties, such as rent collection, maintenance, and repair. Check all the boxes that apply to your situation. In the space provided, spell out what is required, with as much detail as possible, particularly regarding maintenance responsibilities.

To make sure your manager doesn't act illegally on the job, also prepare a more detailed set of instructions to give to the manager when he or she starts work. We show a sample below, which you can tailor to your particular situation and state laws (for example, on discrimination and notice of entry requirements).

Clause 4. Hours and Schedule

Before filling this section in, check with your state department of labor or employment for wage and hour laws that may affect the number of hours you can schedule a manager to work in a day or days in a week. Don't expect a manager to be on call 24 hours a day. In most circumstances, you must pay overtime after 40 hours per week.

Should You Pay Benefits?

No law requires you to provide paid vacation, paid holidays, or premium pay for weekend or holiday work (unless it's for overtime). While most states do not require paid sick leave either, a handful of states require employers to provide at least a few paid sick days each year. Fringe benefits are not required, although larger employers (those with 50 or more full-time employees) may need to provide health insurance under Obamacare. You may want to provide your manager with some of these extras if you can afford to do so.

Clause 5. Payment Terms

Here you state how much and when you pay your manager. Specify the interval and dates on which you will pay the manager. For example, if the payment is weekly, specify the day. If payment is once each month, state the date, such as "the first of the month." If the payment is twice each month, indicate the dates, such as *"the 15th and the 30th, or the last previous weekday if either date falls on a weekend."*

Clause 6. Ending the Manager's Employment

This clause gives you the right to fire a manager any time for any legal reason. It makes clear that you are not guaranteeing a year's, or even a month's, employment to your new hire. You can legally fire your manager any time for any or no reason—as long as it's not for an illegal reason. In return, your manager can quit at any time, for any reason—with or without notice.

Clause 7. Additional Agreements and Amendments

Here you provide details about any areas of the manager's employment that weren't covered elsewhere in the agreement, such as the number of vacation or sick days, or any paid holidays the manager is entitled to each year, or how you plan to reimburse managers for the cost of materials they purchase for repairs.

The last part of this section is fairly standard in written agreements. It states that this is your entire agreement about the manager's employment, and that any changes to the agreement must be in writing.

Together, these provisions prevent you or your manager from later claiming that additional oral or written promises were made, but just not included in the written agreement.

> **CAUTION**
> **Make changes in writing.** If you later change the terms of your agreement, write the new terms down and have each person sign.

Clause 8. Place of Execution

Here you specify the city and state in which you signed the agreement. If there's any legal problem with the agreement later, it may be resolved by the courts where it was signed. Be advised, however, that the laws where the work is to be performed may be applied instead. So if, for example, you sign the Property Manager Agreement at your office in Maryland, but your rental property and the manager's workplace is in nearby Washington, DC, the different laws of Washington, DC, may be applied by a court.

Your Legal Obligations as an Employer

Whether or not you compensate a manager with reduced rent or a regular salary, you have specific legal obligations as an employer, such as following laws governing minimum wage and overtime. If you don't pay Social Security and meet your other legal obligations as an employer, you may face substantial financial penalties.

Most Resident Managers Are Employees, Not Independent Contractors

A resident manager will probably be considered your employee by the IRS and other government agencies. Employees are guaranteed a number of workplace rights that are not guaranteed to people who work as independent contractors. To be considered an independent contractor, a person must offer services to the public at large and work under an arrangement in which he or she controls the means and methods of accomplishing a job. Most tenant-managers are legally considered to be employees because they work for only one property owner who hires them, sets the hours and responsibilities, and determines the particulars of the job. A manager might qualify for independent contractor status if he or she works for several different landlords and contrrols how the work is performed.

RESOURCE

Start out by getting IRS Publication 15 (Circular E), *Employer's Tax Guide,* **which provides details about your tax and record-keeping obligations.** Contact the IRS at 800-829-4933 or www.irs.gov to obtain a free copy of this and other IRS publications and forms. *Tax Savvy for Small Business,* by Frederick W. Daily and Jeffrey A. Quinn (Nolo), covers strategies that will help you minimize taxes and stay out of legal trouble, including how to deduct

business expenses, write off or depreciate long-term business assets, keep the kinds of records that will satisfy the IRS, get a tax break from business losses, and handle a small business audit.

Employer Identification Number

As an employer, you need a federal identification number for tax purposes. If you are a sole proprietor without employees, you can use your Social Security number. Otherwise, you need to get an "employer identification number" (EIN) from the IRS. To obtain an EIN, complete IRS Form SS-4, *Application for Employer Identification Number.* Use the IRS website to apply online (go to www.irs.gov, and search for "EIN."

Income Taxes

The IRS considers the manager's compensation as taxable income to the manager. For that reason, your manager must fill out IRS Form W-4, *Employee's Withholding Allowance Certificate,* when hired. You must deduct federal taxes from each paycheck (and state taxes if required), and turn over the withheld funds each quarter to the IRS and the appropriate state tax agency. You must provide the manager with IRS Form W-2, *Wage and Tax Statement,* for the previous year's earnings by January 31. The W-2 form lists the employee's gross wages and provides a breakdown of any taxes that you withheld.

Social Security and Medicare Taxes ("FICA")

Federal Insurance Contributions Act (FICA) taxes go toward the employee's future Social Security and Medicare benefits. Every employer must pay the IRS a "payroll tax," currently equal to 7.65% of the employee's gross compensation—that is, paycheck amount before deductions (6.2% goes to Social Security, 1.45% goes to Medicare). You must also deduct an additional 7.65% from the employee's wages and turn it over (with the payroll tax) to the IRS quarterly. For updated information

Property Manager Agreement

1. Parties

This Agreement is between ___Jacqueline Marsh_____,

Owner of residential real property at ___175 Donner Avenue, Brooklyn, New York_____,

_____,

and ___Bradley Finch_____,

Manager of the property. Manager will be renting unit ___Number 5___ of the property under a separate

written rental agreement that is in no way contingent upon or related to this Agreement.

2. Beginning Date

Manager will begin work on ___April 10, 20xx_____.

3. Responsibilities

Manager's duties are set forth below:

Renting Units

☑ answer phone inquiries about vacancies

☑ show vacant units

☑ accept rental applications

☐ select tenants

☑ accept initial rents and deposits

☐ other (specify) _____

☐ _____

☐ _____

Vacant Apartments

☑ inspect unit when tenant moves in and document condition of rental

☑ inspect unit when tenant moves out and document condition of rental

☐ clean unit after tenant moves out, including:

　☐ floors, carpets, and rugs

　☐ walls, baseboards, ceilings, lights, and built-in shelves

　☐ kitchen cabinets, countertops, sinks, stove, oven, and refrigerator

　☐ bathtubs, showers, toilets, and plumbing fixtures

　☐ doors, windows, window coverings, and miniblinds

　☑ other (specify) ___Hire and supervise cleaning service to clean rental unit when___

　☐ ___a tenant moves out.___

Rent Collection

☑ collect rents when due

☑ sign rent receipts

☑ maintain rent collection records

☑ collect late rents and charges

☑ inform Owner of late rents

☑ prepare late rent notices

☑ serve late rent notices on tenants

☑ serve rent increase and tenancy termination notices

☑ deposit rent collections in bank

☐ other (specify) _____

☐ _____

Maintenance

☑ vacuum and clean hallways and entryways

☑ replace lightbulbs in common areas

☑ drain water heaters

☑ clean stairs, decks, patios, facade, and sidewalks

☐ clean garage oils on pavement

☐ mow lawns

☐ rake leaves

☑ trim bushes

☑ clean up garbage and debris on grounds

☐ shovel snow from sidewalks and driveways or arrange for snow removal

☐ other (specify) _____

☐ _____

Repairs

☑ accept tenant complaints and repair requests

☑ inform Owner of maintenance and repair needs

☑ maintain written log of tenant complaints

☑ handle routine maintenance and repairs, including:

    ☑ plumbing stoppages

    ☑ garbage disposal stoppages/repairs

    ☑ faucet leaks/washer replacement

- ☑ toilet tank repairs
- ☑ toilet seat replacement
- ☑ stove burner repair/replacement
- ☑ stove hinges/knobs replacement
- ☑ dishwasher repair
- ☑ light switch and outlet repair/replacement
- ☐ heater thermostat repair
- ☐ window repair/replacement
- ☐ painting (interior)
- ☐ painting (exterior)
- ☑ replacement of keys
- ☐ other (specify) _____
- ☐ _____

Other Responsibilities

_____

_____

_____

_____

_____

_____

_____

4. Hours and Schedule

Manager will be available to tenants during the following days and times: _Monday through Friday,_
1 p.m. - 6 p.m (on the property) and by phone other times . If the hours required to carry
out any duties may reasonably be expected to exceed _____20_____ hours in any week, Manager shall
notify Owner and obtain Owner's consent before working such extra hours, except in the event of an
emergency. Extra hours worked due to an emergency must be reported to Owner within 24 hours.

5. Payment Terms

a. Manager will be paid:

- ☐ $ _____ per hour
- ☐ $ _____ per week
- ☑ $ _____1,800_____ per month
- ☐ Other: _____

b. Manager will be paid on the specified intervals and dates:

☐ Once a week on every _____

☐ Twice a month on _____

☑ Once a month on ___the first of the month___

☐ Other (specify) _____

6. Ending the Manager's Employment

Owner may terminate Manager's employment at any time, for any reason that isn't unlawful, with or without notice. Manager may quit at any time, for any reason, with or without notice.

7. Additional Agreements and Amendments

a. Owner and Manager additionally agree that: ___Manager will be available to consult with Owner's attorney as needed, and will provide sworn testimony if necessary.___

_____

_____

_____

_____

_____

_____

_____

b. All agreements between Owner and Manager relating to the work specified in this Agreement are incorporated in this Agreement. Any modification to the Agreement must be in writing and signed by both parties.

8. Place of Execution

Signed at ___Brooklyn___, ___New York___
City   State

___Jacqueline Marsh___   ___April 3, 20xx___
Owner   Date

___Bradley Finch___   ___April 3, 20xx___
Manager   Date

on payroll taxes, including additional Medicare taxes for employees who earn more than $200,000 in a calendar year, see the most current edition of Circular E (*IRS Employer's Tax Guide*).

If you compensate your manager with reduced rent, you must still pay the FICA payroll tax, unless you meet certain conditions, explained below. For example, an apartment owner who compensates a manager with a rent-free $500/month apartment must pay 7.65% of $500, or $38.25, in payroll taxes each month. The manager is responsible for paying another 7.65% ($38.25) to the IRS.

You do not have to pay FICA taxes on the value of the reduced rent if the following conditions are met:

- the manager's unit is on your rental property
- you provide the unit for your convenience (or to comply with state law, since some states require on-site managers for properties of a certain size)
- your manager must actually work as a manager, and
- the manager accepts the unit as a condition of employment—in other words, he must live in the unit in order to be your resident manager.

Help With Paperwork

Employers are responsible for a certain amount of paperwork and record keeping such as time and pay records. If you hate paperwork, your accountant or bookkeeper can probably handle it for you. Or, a reputable payroll tax service that offers a tax notification service will calculate the correct amount of Social Security, unemployment, workers' compensation, and other taxes due; produce the check to pay your manager; and calculate the taxes and notify you when the taxes are due.

Payroll services can be cost-effective even if you employ only one or two people. But when you look for one, it pays to shop around. To get cost quotes, check the Web or your yellow pages under Payroll Service or Bookkeeping Service. Avoid services that charge set-up fees—basically, a fee for putting your information into the computer—or extra fees to prepare W-2 forms or quarterly and annual tax returns.

CAUTION

Always pay payroll taxes on time. If you don't, the IRS will find you—and you could be forced out of business by the huge penalties and interest charges it will add to the delinquent bill. And unlike most other debts, you must pay back payroll taxes even if you go through bankruptcy.

Unemployment Taxes

A manager who is laid off, quits for good reason, or is fired for anything less than gross incompetence or dishonesty is probably entitled to unemployment benefits. These benefits are financed by unemployment taxes paid by employers. You must pay a federal unemployment tax (FUTA) at a rate of 6% of the first $7,000 of the employee's wages for the year. (The actual FUTA tax rate will be lower if you pay state unemployment taxes for your employee.) In addition to contributing to FUTA, you may also be responsible for contributing to an unemployment insurance fund in your state.

RESOURCE

Contact the IRS for information on Form 940 (used for tax returns), FUTA, and a local office of your state department of labor or employment or the government agency that oversees your state income tax program for state tax requirements.

Minimum Wage and Overtime

However you pay your manager—by the hour, with a regular salary, or by a rent reduction—you should monitor the number of hours worked to make sure you're complying with the federal Fair Labor Standards Act (FLSA; 29 U.S. Code §§ 201 and following) and any state minimum wage laws.

The federal minimum hourly wage is $7.25 an hour.

If your state's (or city's) minimum wage is higher than the federal rate, you must pay the higher rate.

If you compensate your manager by a rent reduction, you may not be able to count the full amount of the rent reduction in complying with minimum wage laws.

Federal wage and hour laws also require employers to pay time-and-a-half if an employee works more than 40 hours a week (with a few exceptions). Some states (most notably California) require you to pay overtime if an employee works more than eight hours in a day, even if the employee works less than 40 hours in a week.

> **RESOURCE**
> **For information on minimum wage laws, overtime rules, and record-keeping requirements,** see the U.S. Department of Labor's website at www.dol.gov. Also see IRS Publication 15-B, *Employer's Tax Guide to Fringe Benefits*, available at www.irs.gov. You can also contact the nearest office of the U.S. Labor Department's Wage and Hour Division or a local office of your state's department of labor or employment.

Equal Pay for Equal Work

You must provide equal pay and benefits to men and women who do the same job or jobs that require substantially equal skills, effort, and responsibility. This is required by the Equal Pay Act, an amendment to the FLSA.

Workers' Compensation Insurance

Workers' compensation provides some replacement income and pays medical expenses for employees who are injured or become ill as a result of their jobs. It's a no-fault system—an injured employee is entitled to receive benefits whether or not you provided a safe workplace and whether or not the manager's own carelessness contributed to the injury. (You are, of course, required by federal and state laws to provide a reasonably safe workplace.) But you, too, receive some protection, because the manager, in most cases, cannot sue you for damages. In addition, the manager is limited to

fixed types of compensation—basically, partial wage replacement and payment of medical bills. Employees may also receive compensation and vocational training, if they're left with a permanent impairment and unable to return to the same line of work. The manager can't get paid for pain and suffering or mental anguish.

To cover the costs of workers' compensation benefits for employees, you'll need to purchase a special insurance policy—either through a state fund or a private insurance company. Each state has its own workers' compensation statute. Many states require all employers to get coverage; however, some states set a minimum number of employees (generally between three and five) before coverage is required.

Most wise landlords obtain workers' compensation insurance, whether or not it's required. If you don't, and you're sued by a manager who is injured on the job—for example, by falling down the stairs while performing maintenance—or even by a violent tenant, you face the possibility of a lawsuit for a large amount of money.

> **CAUTION**
> **Workers' comp doesn't apply to intentional acts.** Workers' compensation typically won't cover you from employee lawsuits for injuries caused by your intentional or reckless behavior—for example, if you know of a dangerous condition but refuse to fix it, resulting in an injury.

> **RESOURCE**
> **Contact your state workers' compensation office for information on coverage and costs.**

Immigration Laws

When you hire someone, even someone who was born and raised in the city where your rental property is located, you must review documents such as a passport or birth certificate that prove the employee's identity and employment eligibility. You and each new employee are required to complete

USCIS Form I-9, *Employment Eligibility Verification.* These rules come from the Immigration Reform and Control Act (IRCA), a federal law that prohibits hiring undocumented workers. The law, enforced by the U.S. Citizenship and Immigration Services (USCIS), prohibits hiring workers who don't have government authorization to work in the U.S.

RESOURCE
For more information, contact the USCIS by phone at 800-375-5283, or check their website at www. uscis.gov.

New Hire Reporting Form

Within a short time after you hire someone—20 days or less—you must file a New Hire Reporting form with a designated state agency. The information on the form becomes part of the National Directory of New Hires, used primarily to locate parents so that child support orders can be enforced. Government agencies also use the data to prevent improper payment of workers' compensation and unemployment benefits or public assistance benefits. For more information, check out the website of the Federal Office of Child Support Enforcement, www. acf.hhs.gov/programs/css; click "Employers."

Management Companies

Property management companies are often used by owners of large apartment complexes and by absentee owners too far away from the property to be directly involved in everyday details. Property management companies generally take care of renting units, collecting rent, taking tenant complaints, arranging repairs and maintenance, and evicting troublesome tenants. Of course, some of these responsibilities may be shared with or delegated to resident managers who, in some instances, may work for the management company.

A variety of relationships between owners and management companies is possible, depending on your wishes and how the particular management company chooses to do business. For example, if you own one or more big buildings, the management company will probably recommend hiring a resident manager. But if your rental property has only a few units, or you own a number of small buildings spread over a good-sized geographical area, the management company will probably suggest simply responding to tenant requests and complaints from its central office.

Pros and Cons of Management Companies

One advantage of working with a management company is that you avoid all the legal hassles of being an employer: paying payroll taxes, buying workers' compensation insurance, withholding income tax. The management company is an independent contractor, not an employee. It hires and pays the people who do the work. Typically, you sign a contract spelling out the management company's duties and fees. Most companies charge a fixed percentage—about 5% to 10%—of the total rent collected. (The salary of any resident manager is additional.) This gives the company a good incentive to keep the building filled with rent-paying tenants.

Another advantage is that management companies are usually well-informed about the law, keep good records, and are adept at staying out of legal hot water in such areas as discrimination, invasion of privacy, and returning deposits.

The primary disadvantage of hiring a management company is the expense. For example, if you pay a management company 10% of the $14,000 you collect in rent each month from tenants in a 20-unit building, this amounts to $1,400 a month and $16,800 per year. While many companies charge less than 10%, it's still quite an expense. Also, if the management company works from a central office with no one on-site, tenants may feel that management is too distant and unconcerned with their day-to-day needs.

Management Company Contracts

Management companies have their own contracts, which you should read thoroughly and understand before signing. Be sure you understand how the company is paid and its exact responsibilities.

A management contract is not a take it or leave it deal. You should negotiate the company's fee, obviously, as well as any extra charges you can expect to pay during the length of the contract. You may also specify spending limits for ordinary repairs. And if you are picky about who works on your property, you may be able to specify that certain repairpersons or firms should be called before others are used.

Policies on screening tenants, maintenance and repairs, and letting contracts aren't usually part of the management contract itself, but should be clearly communicated, so that the management company knows what you expect.

Questions to Ask When You Hire a Management Company

- Who are its clients: owners of single-family houses, small apartments, or large apartment complexes? Look for a company with experience handling property like yours. Also ask for client references, and check to see whether other landlords are satisfied with the management company. (Don't forget to ask these landlords how their tenants feel about the service they get. Unhappy tenants are bad business.)
- What services are provided?
- What are the costs? What services cost extra?
- Will the management company take tenant calls 24 hours a day, seven days a week?
- Will there be an individual property manager assigned to your property? How frequently will the property manager visit and inspect your building?
- Is the company located fairly close to your property?
- Are employees trained in landlord-tenant law? Will the company consult an attorney qualified in landlord-tenant matters if problems arise, such as disputes over rent?
- If your property is under rent control, are company personnel familiar with the rent control law?
- Can you terminate the management agreement without cause on reasonable notice?

It's a good idea to write down these understandings and attach them to the contract as an addendum or attachment.

Special Issues Involving Leases and Insurance

The contract with your management company will usually address the issues of leases and insurance.

Leases

Many management companies will insist on using their own leases. Since they are the ones who will deal with problems, management companies often want to be the ones who will set the rules. You may find that the company's lease is acceptable—but you may also find that it is not. For example, it's common to see late-fee policies that exceed a fair and legal limit. No surprise—the more money collected by the management company, the more money it earns for itself.

If the management company uses a lease that is legally amiss, it's clearly a sign to look elsewhere. Now, what about other clauses in the company lease that are legal but not to your liking, such as a prohibition against pets? Again, no surprise—most management companies assume that pets equal more work, and they prefer not to have to deal with them. If the company will not negotiate with you over changing their "standard" lease, you may want to talk to other management companies that will be more flexible.

Insurance

All landlords need comprehensive liability insurance. Special issues arise when you hire a management company. Most important, both you and the management company need to show proof that you are each insured—and you each should be added to the other's policy as an "additional insured." Here's how it works.

You should require proof that the management company is insured under a comprehensive general liability policy, with extra coverage for "errors and omissions" and employee dishonesty. When you are added as an "additional insured," you get the benefit of that policy. If you are named in a lawsuit over something that the management company allegedly did or didn't do, you will be covered by the management company's insurer. They will defend you and pay out any settlement or verdict that results against you. Your insurance broker should be able to recommend how much insurance is adequate.

The management company will demand proof that you, too, carry adequate amounts of liability insurance, and they will also want to be named as an additional insured in your policy. If you don't currently have enough insurance coverage, the management company may refuse to take your business.

Fortunately, adding a landlord or a management company as an additional insured is not a big deal. Insurance companies do it all the time, generally at no additional cost. Simply contact your broker and ask that the management company be added. Ask the broker to send a certificate of insurance to the management company. And don't forget to demand the same of the management company—you, too, want a certificate of insurance safely in your files.

Your Liability for a Manager's Acts

Depending on the circumstances, you may be legally responsible for the acts of a manager or management company. For example, you could be sued and found liable if your manager or management company:

- refuses to rent to a qualified tenant (who is a member of a minority group or has children, for example) or otherwise violates antidiscrimination laws
- sexually harasses a tenant
- makes illegal deductions from the security deposit of a tenant who has moved out, or does not return the departing tenant's deposit within the time limit set by your state law
- ignores a dangerous condition, such as substandard wiring that results in an electrical fire, causing injury or damage to the tenant, or security problems that result in a criminal assault on a tenant

- invades a tenant's privacy by flagrant and damaging gossip or trespass, or
- commits a crime such as assaulting a tenant.

In short, a landlord who knows the law but has a manager (or management company) who doesn't could wind up in a lawsuit brought by prospective or former tenants.

Here's how to protect your tenants and yourself.

Choose your manager carefully. Legally, you have a duty to protect your tenants from injury caused by employees you know or should know pose a risk of harm to others. If someone gets hurt or has property stolen or damaged by a manager whose background you didn't check carefully, you could be sued, so it's crucial that you be especially vigilant when hiring a manager who will have easy access to rental units.

Make sure your manager is familiar with the basics of landlord-tenant law, especially if your manager will be selecting tenants or serving eviction notices. One approach is to give your manager a copy of this book to read and refer to. In addition, you'll want to provide detailed instructions that cover likely trouble areas, such as the legal rules prohibiting discrimination in tenant selection. Below is a sample set of instructions for a manager with fairly broad authority; you can tailor them to fit your situation. You'll also need to add any requirements that are imposed by the laws in your state—for example, stricter discrimination laws or notice requirements for entering rental property than are outlined in the sample instructions. Have the manager sign a copy of the instructions and give it to you.

Keep an eye on your manager, and listen to tenants' concerns and complaints. Encourage your tenants to report problems to you. If you hear about or suspect problems—for example, poor maintenance of the building or sexual harassment—do your own investigating. For example, when you have a vacancy, have someone you suspect the manager might discriminate against apply for a vacancy. How does your manager treat the applicant? Would you want to defend a lawsuit brought by

Sample Instructions to Manager

Dear New Manager:

Welcome to your new position as resident manager. Here are important instructions to guide you as you perform your duties under our management agreement. Please read them carefully and keep them for future reference.

1. Discrimination in rental housing on the basis of race, religion, sex, familial status, age, national or ethnic origin, or disability is illegal—whether you are accepting rental applications for vacant apartments or dealing with current residents. Your duties are to advertise and accept rental applications in a nondiscriminatory manner. This includes allowing all individuals to fill out applications and offering the unit on the same terms to all applicants. After you have collected all applications, please notify me at the phone number listed below. I will sort through the applications, set up interviews, and decide whom to accept.

2. Tenants have a right to feel comfortable and relaxed in and near their homes. To be sure all do, please avoid any comments, actions, or physical contact that could be considered offensive, even by those whom you might see as being overly sensitive on the issue. Remember, harassment is against the law and will not be tolerated.

3. Do not issue any rent increase or termination notices without my prior approval.

4. Treat all tenants who complain about defects, even trivial defects or ones you believe to be nonexistent, with respect. Enter all tenant complaints into the logbook I have supplied to you on the day they are made. Respond to tenant complaints about the building or apartment units immediately in emergencies or if the complaint involves security, and respond to other complaints within 24 hours. If you cannot correct (or arrange to correct) any problem or defect yourself, please telephone me immediately.

5. Except in serious life- or property-threatening emergencies, never enter (or allow anyone else to enter) a tenant's apartment without consent or in his or her absence, unless you have given written notice at least 24 hours in advance, either delivered personally or, if that's not possible, posted on the door. If you have given the tenant 24-hour written notice, you may enter in the tenant's absence during ordinary business hours to do repairs or maintenance work, unless the tenant objects. If the tenant objects, do not enter, but instead call me.

6. When a tenant moves in, and again when he or she moves out, inspect the unit. If possible, have the tenant accompany you. On each occasion, both you and the tenant should complete and sign a Landlord-Tenant Checklist form. Take digital pictures or make a video during both walkthroughs.

7. If you think a tenant has moved out and abandoned the apartment, do not enter it. Telephone me first.

8. Once a tenant has vacated an apartment and given you the key, keep track of all costs necessary to repair damages in excess of ordinary wear and tear. Give me a copy of this list, along with a notation of the amount of any back rent, the before

Sample Instructions to Manager (continued)

and after Landlord-Tenant Checklist forms, and the departing tenant's forwarding address. Please make sure I see this material within a week after the tenant moves out, preferably sooner. I will mail the itemization and any security deposit balance to the tenant.

9. If you have any other problems or questions, please do not hesitate to call me on my cell phone or at home. Leave a message on my voicemail if I am not available.

Sincerely,

Terry Herendeen

Terry Herendeen, Owner

1111 Maiden Lane, Omaha, Nebraska 54001

402-555-1234 (cell phone)

402-555-5678 (home)

I have received a copy of this memorandum and have read and understood it.

Dated: _____ April 7, 20xx _____

Barbara Louis

Barbara Louis, Manager

the prospective tenant? Try to resolve problems and get rid of a bad manager before problems accelerate and you end up with an expensive tenants' lawsuit.

Emergency Contacts and Procedures for Your Employees

It's an excellent idea to prepare a written set of emergency procedures for the manager, including:

- owner's name and emergency phone number, so your employee can contact you in case of emergency
- names and phone numbers of nearest hospital and poison control center
- ambulance, police and fire departments, and a local taxi company
- names and phone numbers of contractors who can respond to a building emergency on a 24-hour basis, including any licensed plumber, electrician, locksmith, boiler mechanic, elevator service company, and air conditioner maintenance company with whom you have set up an account, and
- procedures to follow in case of a fire, flood, hurricane, tornado, or other disaster, including how to safely shut down elevators, water, electricity, and gas.

Make sure your insurance covers illegal acts of your employees. No matter how thorough your precautions, you may still be liable for your manager's illegal acts—even if your manager commits an illegal act in direct violation of your instructions. To really protect yourself, purchase a good landlord's insurance policy.

Notifying Tenants of the Manager

In many states, you are legally required to give tenants the manager's name and address and tell them that the manager is authorized to accept legal documents on your behalf, such as termination of tenancy notices or court documents in an eviction lawsuit.

We recommend that you give tenants this information in writing, whether or not your state's law requires it. It is included in our lease and rental agreements (see Clause 21 in Chapter 2), but don't forget to notify tenants who moved in before you hired the manager.

Two sample disclosure notices are shown below. You should give each tenant a copy and post another in a prominent place in the building.

Be sure your Property Manager Agreement, discussed above, notes the manager's authority in this regard. You can put details in the last section, Additional Agreements and Amendments.

Sample Disclosure Notices as to Address of Manager and Owner

Notice: Address of Manager of Premises

Muhammad Azziz, 1234 Market Street, Apartment 1, Boston, Mass., is authorized to manage the residential premises at 1234 Market Street, Boston, Mass. If you have any complaints about the condition of your unit or common areas, please notify Mr. Azziz immediately at 555-1200. He is authorized to act for and on behalf of the owner of the premises for the purpose of receiving all notices and demands from you, including legal papers (process).

Notice: Address of Owner of Premises

Rebecca Epstein, 12345 Embarcadero Road, Boston, Mass., is the owner of the premises at 1234 Market Street, Boston, Mass.

Firing a Manager

Unless you have made a commitment (oral or written contract) to employ a manager for a specific period of time, you have the right to terminate her employment at any time. But you cannot do it for an illegal reason, such as:

- race, age, gender, or other prohibited forms of discrimination, or
- retaliation against the manager for calling your illegal acts to the attention of authorities.

EXAMPLE: You order your manager to dump 20 gallons of fuel oil at the back of your property. Instead, the manager complains to a local environmental regulatory agency, which fines you. If you now fire the manager, you will be vulnerable to a lawsuit for illegal termination.

The High Cost of a Bad Manager: Sexual Harassment in Housing

If tenants complain about illegal acts by a manager, pay attention. The owners of a Fairfield, California, apartment complex learned this lesson the hard way—by paying more than a million dollars to settle a tenants' lawsuit.

The tenants, mostly single mothers, were tormented by an apartment manager who spied on them, opened their mail, and sexually harassed them. They were afraid to complain, for fear of eviction. When they did complain to the building's owners, the owners refused to take any action—and the manager stepped up his harassment in retaliation.

Finally, tenants banded together and sued, and the details of the manager's outrageous and illegal conduct were exposed. The owners settled the case before trial for $1.6 million.

To head off the possibility of a wrongful termination lawsuit, be prepared to show a good business-related reason for the firing. It's almost essential to back up a firing with written records documenting your reasons. Reasons that may support a firing include:

- performing poorly on the job—for example, not depositing rent checks promptly, or

continually failing to respond to tenant complaints

- refusing to follow instructions—for example, allowing tenants to pay rent late, despite your instructions to the contrary
- possessing a weapon at work
- being dishonest or stealing money or property from you or your tenants
- endangering the health or safety of tenants
- engaging in criminal activity, such as drug dealing
- arguing or fighting with tenants
- behaving violently at work, or
- unlawfully discriminating against or harassing prospective or current tenants.

Ideally, a firing shouldn't come suddenly or as a surprise. Give your manager ongoing feedback about job performance and impose progressive discipline, such as an oral or written warning, before termination. Do a six-month performance review (and more often, if necessary) and keep copies. Solicit comments from tenants twice a year (as mentioned earlier) and, if comments are negative, keep copies.

Handling Requests for References

One of your biggest problems after a manager quits or has been fired may be what to tell other landlords or employers who inquire about the former manager. You may be tugged in several directions:

- You want to tell the truth—good, bad, or neutral—about the former manager.
- You want to help the former manager find another job for which he is better suited.
- You don't want to be sued for libel or slander because you say something negative.

Legally, you're better off saying as little as possible, rather than saying anything negative. Just say that it's your policy not to comment on former managers. Besides, if you politely say, "I would rather not discuss Mr. Jones," the caller will get the idea.

Evicting a Manager

If you fire a manager, you may often want the ex-
employee to move out of your property, particularly
if there is a special manager's unit or the firing
has generated (or resulted from) ill will. How easy
it will be to get the fired manager out depends
primarily on whether or not you have separate
management and rental agreements.

SEE AN EXPERT
**In many cases, you'll want the eviction lawsuit
to be handled by an attorney who specializes in landlord-
tenant law.** See Chapter 18 for advice on finding a qualified
lawyer.

If you and the tenant-manager signed separate
management and rental agreements, firing the
manager does not affect the tenancy. The ex-manager
will have to keep paying rent but will no longer work
as manager. Evicting the former manager is just
like evicting any other tenant. You will have to give
a normal termination notice, typically 30 days for
month-to-month tenancies, subject to any applicable
rent control restrictions. If the tenant has a separate
fixed-term lease, you cannot terminate the tenancy
until the lease expires.

If you are evicting the manager for not paying
rent or for violating a lease or rental agreement
term (for example, by damaging rental property),
you may be able to provide less notice. See Chapter
17 for details.

We do not recommend using a single management/
rental agreement. Among other reasons, it may be
difficult to evict the ex-manager in this situation.

Getting the Tenant Moved In

FORMS IN THIS CHAPTER

Chapter 7 includes instructions for and samples of the following forms:

- Landlord-Tenant Checklist
- Move-In Letter

The Nolo website includes downloadable copies of these forms. See Appendix B for the link to the forms in this book.

Legal disputes between landlords and tenants can be almost as emotional as divorce court battles. Many disputes are unnecessary and could be avoided if—right from the very beginning—tenants knew their legal rights and responsibilities. A clearly written lease or rental agreement, signed by all adult occupants, is the key to starting a tenancy. But there's more to establishing a positive attitude when new tenants move in. You should also:

- inspect the property, fill out a Landlord-Tenant Checklist with the tenant, and photograph the rental unit and
- prepare a move-in letter highlighting important terms of the tenancy and your expectations, such as how to report repair problems.

States That Require a Landlord-Tenant Checklist

Several states require landlords to give new tenants a written statement on the condition of the rental premises at move-in time, including a comprehensive list of existing damages. Tenants in these states often have the right to inspect the premises to verify the accuracy of the landlord's list and to note any problems.

The following are among the states that require initial inspections. Check the statutes for the exact requirements in your state, including the type of inspection required at the end of the tenancy. For citations, see "State Security Deposit Rules" in Appendix A.

Arizona	Massachusetts	North Dakota
Georgia	Michigan	Utah
Hawaii	Montana	Virginia
Kansas	Nevada	Washington
Kentucky	New Hampshire	Wisconsin
Maryland		

Inspect the Rental Unit

To eliminate the possibility of all sorts of future arguments, it is absolutely essential that you (or your representative) and prospective tenants (together, if possible) check the place over for damage and obvious wear and tear before the tenant moves in. The best way to document what you find is to jointly fill out a Landlord-Tenant Checklist form.

In some states, the law requires you to give new tenants a written statement on the condition of the premises at move-in time, including a comprehensive list of existing damage, see "States That Require a Landlord-Tenant Checklist," above. Tenants in many of these states have the right to inspect the premises as to the accuracy of the landlord's list, and to note any problems. But even if this procedure is not legally required, you should follow it to avert later problems.

Use a Landlord-Tenant Checklist

A Landlord-Tenant Checklist, inventorying the condition of the rental property at the beginning and end of the tenancy, is an excellent device to protect both you and your tenant when the tenant moves out and wants the security deposit returned. Without some record as to the condition of the unit, you and the tenant are all too likely to get into arguments about things like whether the kitchen linoleum was already stained, the garbage disposal was broken, the stove was filthy, or the bathroom mirror was already cracked when the tenant moved in.

The checklist provides good evidence as to why you withheld all or part of a security deposit. And, coupled with a system to regularly keep track of the rental property's condition, the checklist will also be extremely useful to you if a tenant withholds rent, breaks the lease and moves out, or sues you outright, claiming the unit needs substantial repairs. See Chapter 9 for instructions and forms that will let you stay updated on the condition of your rental properties.

Landlord-Tenant Checklist

GENERAL CONDITION OF RENTAL UNIT AND PREMISES

572 Fourth St.
_____
Street Address

Apt. 11 Washington, D.C.
_____
Unit No. City

	Condition on Arrival	Condition on Departure	Estimated Cost of Repair/ Replacement
Living Room			
Floors & Floor Coverings	OK		
Drapes & Window Coverings	Miniblinds discolored		
Walls & Ceilings	OK		
Light Fixtures	OK		
Windows, Screens, & Doors	Window rattles		
Front Door & Locks	OK		
Fireplace	OK		
Other	N/A		
Other			
Kitchen			
Floors & Floor Coverings	Cigarette burn hole		
Walls & Ceilings	OK		
Light Fixtures	OK		
Cabinets	OK		
Counters	Stained		
Stove/Oven	Burners filthy (grease)		
Refrigerator	OK		
Dishwasher	N/A		
Garbage Disposal	OK		
Sink & Plumbing	OK		
Smoke Detector	OK		
Windows, Screens, & Doors	OK		
Other			
Dining Room			
Floors & Floor Covering	OK		
Walls & Ceilings	Crack in ceiling		
Light Fixtures	OK		
Windows, Screens, & Doors	OK		
Smoke Detector	OK		
Other			

	Condition on Arrival		Condition on Departure		Estimated Cost of Repair/ Replacement
Bathroom(s)	Bath #1	Bath #2	Bath #1	Bath #2	
Floors & Floor Coverings	OK				
Walls & Ceilings	Wallpaper peeling				
Windows, Screens, & Doors	OK				
Light Fixtures	OK				
Bathtub/Shower	Tub chipped				
Sink & Counters	OK				
Toilet	Base of toilet very dirty				
Other					
Other					
Bedroom(s)	Bdrm #1	Bdrm #2	Bdrm #3	Bdrm #1	Bdrm #2	Bdrm #3	
Floors & Floor Coverings	OK	OK				
Windows, Screens, & Doors	OK	OK				
Walls & Ceilings	OK	OK				
Light Fixtures	Dented	OK				
Smoke Detector	OK	OK	OK			
Other	Water stains in closet					
Other						
Other						
Other Areas					
Heating System	OK				
Air Conditioning	OK				
Lawn/Garden	OK				
Stairs and Hallway	OK				
Patio, Terrace, Deck, etc.	N/A				
Basement	OK				
Parking Area					
Other					
Other					
Other					
Other					
Other					

☑ Tenants acknowledge that all smoke detectors and fire extinguishers were tested in their presence and found to be in working order, and that the testing procedure was explained to them. Tenants agree to test all detectors at least once a month and to report any problems to Landlord/Manager in writing. Tenants agree to replace all smoke detector batteries as necessary.

FURNISHED PROPERTY

	Condition on Arrival			Condition on Departure			Estimated Cost of Repair/ Replacement
Living Room							
Coffee Table	Two scratches on top						
End Tables	OK						
Lamps	OK						
Chairs	OK						
Sofa	OK						
Other							
Other							
Kitchen							
Broiler Pan	N/A						
Ice Trays	N/A						
Other							
Other							
Dining Room							
Chairs	OK						
Stools	N/A						
Table	Leg bent slightly						
Other							
Other							
Bathroom(s)	Bath #1		Bath #2	Bath #1		Bath #2	
Mirrors	OK						
Shower Curtain	Torn						
Hamper	N/A						
Other							
Bedroom(s)	Bdrm #1	Bdrm #2	Bdrm #3	Bdrm #1	Bdrm #2	Bdrm #3	
Beds (single)	OK	N/A					
Beds (double)	N/A	OK					
Chairs	OK	OK					
Chests	N/A	OK					
Dressing Tables	OK	OK					
Lamps	OK	OK					
Mirrors	OK	OK					
Night Tables	OK	N/A					
Other							

	Condition on Arrival	**Condition on Departure**	**Estimated Cost of Repair/ Replacement**
Other			
Other Areas			
Bookcases	N/A		
Desks	N/A		
Pictures	Hall picture frame chipped		
Other			
Other			

Use this space to provide any additional explanation:

_____

_____

_____

_____

_____

_____

_____

_____

_____

_____

_____

_____

Landlord-Tenant Checklist completed on moving in on _____ May 1, 20xx _____ and approved by:

Bernard Cohen and _Maria Crouse_
Landlord/Manager   Tenant

                                          Sandra Martino
                                          Tenant

                                          _____
                                          Tenant

Landlord-Tenant Checklist completed on moving out on _____ and approved by:

_____ and _____
Landlord/Manager   Tenant

                                          _____
                                          Tenant

                                          _____
                                          Tenant

A sample Landlord-Tenant Checklist is shown above, and the Nolo website includes a download-able copy. See Appendix B for the link to the forms in this book.

How to Fill Out the Checklist

You and the tenant should fill out the checklist together. If that's impossible, complete the form and then give it to the tenant to review. The tenant should note any disagreement and return it to you within a few days.

The checklist is in two parts. The first side covers the general condition of each room. The second side covers furnishings, such as a living room lamp or bathroom shower curtain.

You will be filling out the first column—*Condition on Arrival*—before the tenant moves in. The last two columns—*Condition on Departure* and *Estimated Cost of Repair/Replacement*—are for use when the tenant moves out and you inspect the unit again. At that time the checklist will document your need to make deductions from the security deposit for repairs or cleaning, or to replace missing items. See Chapter 15 for details on returning security deposits and using the checklist at move-out time.

When you look at the checklist included here, you'll see that we have filled out the first column (*Condition on Arrival*) with rooms and elements in these rooms. If you happen to be renting a one-bedroom, one-bath unit, our preprinted form will work just fine. However, chances are that your rental has a different number of rooms or elements in those rooms than those on the checklist form. Changes are no problem if you use the downloadable form. You can change the entries in the *Condition on Arrival* column of the checklist, and you can add or delete rows. For example, you may want to add a row for another bedroom or a service porch, or add room elements such as a trash compactor or fireplace. You may also delete items, such as a dishwasher.

The following sections explain how to complete the checklist—once you've tailored it to your particular rental.

General Condition of Rental Unit and Premises

In the *Condition on Arrival* column, make a note—as specific as possible—of items that are not working or are dirty, scratched, or simply in bad condition. For example, don't simply note that the refrigerator "needs fixing" if an ice maker doesn't work—it's just as easy to write "ice maker broken, should not be used." If the tenant uses the ice maker anyway and causes water damage, he cannot claim that you failed to tell him. Be sure to note any mildew, pest, or rodent problems. (Better yet, fix these before the new tenant moves in.)

Mark "OK" next to items that are in satisfactory condition—basically, clean, safe, sanitary, and in good working order.

CAUTION
Make repairs and clean thoroughly before showing a rental unit. To get the tenancy off to the best start and avoid all kinds of hassles over repairs, handle problems before the start of a new tenancy. You must fix certain defects—such as a broken heater or leaking roof—under state and local housing codes. You may often be able to cover your repair and cleaning costs by deducting expenses from the outgoing tenant's security deposit (assuming the tenant is responsible for the problem).

Furnishings

The second part of the checklist covers furnishings, such as lamps or shower curtains. Obviously, you can simply delete this section of the checklist if your unit is not furnished.

If your rental property has rooms or furnishings not listed on the checklist, edit the form as explained above. If you are renting out a large house or apartment or providing many furnishings, be sure to include this information.

Sign the Checklist

After you and your new tenant agree on all of the particulars of the rental unit, you each should sign and date every page of the checklist, including any attachments. Keep the original and give the tenant a copy. If the tenant filled out the checklist on his own, make sure you review his comments, note any disagreement, and return a copy to him. You should make the checklist part of your lease or rental agreement, as we recommend in Chapter 2, Clause 11.

Be sure the tenant also checks the box on the bottom of the second page of the checklist stating that the smoke detector and fire extinguisher—required for new occupancies in many states and cities—were tested in his presence and shown to be in working order. This section on the checklist also requires the tenant to test the smoke detector monthly and to replace the battery when necessary. By doing this, you'll limit your liability if the smoke detector fails and results in fire damage or injury.

Add testing of carbon monoxide detectors if your state, such as California, requires these.

TIP

Be sure to keep the checklist up-to-date if you repair, replace, add, or remove items or furnishings after the tenant moves in. Both you and the tenant should initial and date any changes.

Photograph the Rental Unit

Taking photos or videos of the unit before a new tenant moves in is another excellent way to avoid disputes over security deposit deductions. In addition to the checklist, you'll be able to compare "before" and "after" pictures when the tenant leaves. This should help refresh your tenant's memory, which may result in her being more reasonable. Certainly, if you end up in mediation or court for not returning the full security deposit, being able to document your point of view with photos or videos will be invaluable. In addition, photos or a video can also help if you have to sue a former tenant for cleaning and repair costs above the deposit amount.

Whether you take a photo with your phone or use a separate camera, make two sets of the photos as soon as possible. Give one set to your tenant. Each of you should date and sign both sets of photos. If you make a video, clearly state the time and date when the video was made.

You should repeat this process when the tenant leaves, as part of your standard move-out procedure. Chapter 15 discusses inspecting the unit when a tenant leaves.

Send New Tenants a Move-In Letter

A move-in letter should dovetail with the lease or rental agreement and provide basic information such as the manager's phone numbers (day and night) and office hours. You can also use a move-in letter to explain any procedures and rules that are too detailed or numerous to include in your lease or rental agreement—for example, how and where to report maintenance problems, details on garbage disposal/recycling, parking, mail, and laundry rooms. and building quiet hours. Consider including a brief list of maintenance dos and don'ts as part of the move-in letter—for example, how to avoid overloading circuits and proper use of the garbage disposal. Alternatively, large landlords may use a set of Rules and Regulations to cover some of these issues, see Clause 18 of the form agreements in Chapter 2.

A sample move-in letter is shown below, and the Nolo website includes a downloadable copy (see Appendix B for the link to the forms in this book). You should tailor this move-in letter to your particular needs—for example, alter it if you don't employ a resident manager or if your property is subject to rent control.

We recommend that you make a copy of each tenant's move-in letter for yourself and ask him to sign the last page, indicating that he has read it.

Move-In Letter

September 1, 20xx
_____
Date

Frank O'Hara
_____
Tenant

139 Porter Street
_____
Street Address

Madison, Wisconsin 53704
_____
City and State

Dear Frank ,
_____
        Tenant

Welcome to Apartment 45 B at Happy Hill Apartments

_____ (address of rental unit). We hope you will enjoy living here.

This letter is to explain what you can expect from the management and what we'll be looking for from you.

Rent: Rent is due on the first day of the month. There is no grace period for the payment of rent. (See Clauses 5 and 6 of your rental agreement for details, including late charges.) Also, we don't accept postdated checks.

New Roommates: If you want someone to move in as a roommate, please contact us first. If your rental unit is big enough to accommodate another person, we will arrange for the new person to fill out a rental application. If it's approved, all of you will need to sign a new rental agreement. Depending on the situation, there may be a rent increase to add a roommate.

Notice to End Tenancy: To terminate your month-to-month tenancy, you must give at least 28 days' written notice. We have a written form available for this purpose. We may also terminate the tenancy, or change its terms, on 28 days' written notice. If you give less than 28 days' notice, you will still be financially responsible for rent for the balance of the 28-day period.

Deposits: Your security deposit will be applied to costs of cleaning, damages, or unpaid rent after you move out. You may not apply any part of the deposit toward any part of your rent in the last month of your tenancy. (See Clause 8 of your rental agreement.)

Manager: Sophie Beauchamp (Apartment #15, phone 555-1234) is your resident manager. You should pay your rent to her and promptly let her know of any maintenance or repair problems (see below) and any other questions or problems. She's in her office every day from 8 a.m. to 10 a.m. and from 4 p.m. to 6 p.m. and can be reached by phone at other times.

Landlord-Tenant Checklist: By now, Sophie Beauchamp should have taken you on a walk-through of your apartment to check the condition of all walls, drapes, carpets, and appliances and to test the smoke alarms and fire extinguisher. These are all listed on the Landlord-Tenant Checklist, which you should have reviewed carefully and signed. When you move out, we will ask you to check each item against its original condition as described on the Checklist.

Maintenance/Repair Problems: We are determined to maintain a clean, safe building in which all systems are in good repair. To help us make repairs promptly, we will give you Maintenance/Repair Request forms to report to the manager any problems in your apartment, such as a broken garbage disposal, or on the building or grounds, such as a burned-out light in the garage. (Extra copies are available from the manager.) In an emergency, or when it's not convenient to use this form, please call the manager at 555-1234.

Semiannual Safety and Maintenance Update: To help us keep your unit and the common areas in excellent condition, we'll ask you to fill out a form every six months updating any problems on the premises or in your rental unit. This will allow you to report any potential safety hazards or other problems that otherwise might be overlooked.

Annual Safety Inspection: Once a year, we will ask to inspect the condition and furnishings of your rental unit and update the Landlord-Tenant Checklist. In keeping with state law, we will give you reasonable notice before the inspection, and you are encouraged to be present for it.

Insurance: We highly recommend that you purchase renters' insurance. The building property insurance policy will not cover the replacement of your personal belongings if they are lost due to fire, theft, or accident. In addition, you could be found liable if someone is injured on the premises you rent as a result of your negligence. If you damage the building itself—for example, if you start a fire in the kitchen and it spreads—you could be responsible for large repair bills.

Moving Out: It's a little early to bring up moving out, but please be aware that we have a list of items that should be cleaned before we conduct a move-out inspection. If you decide to move, please ask the manager for a copy of our Move-Out Letter, explaining our procedures for inspection and returning your deposit.

Telephone Number Changes: Please notify us if your home or work phone number changes, so we can reach you promptly in an emergency.

Please let us know if you have any questions.

Sincerely,

Tom Guiliano   *September 1, 20xx*
Landlord/Manager   Date

I have read and received a copy of this statement.

Frank O'Hara   *September 1, 20xx*
Tenant   Date

(As an extra precaution, ask him to initial each page.) Although this step may seem paranoid now, you won't think so if you get in a dispute with a tenant who claims you never told him something important (like the need to purchase renters' insurance).

Be sure to update the move-in letter from time to time as necessary.

Cash Rent and Security Deposit Checks

Every landlord's nightmare is a new tenant whose first rent or deposit check bounces and who must be dislodged with time-consuming and expensive legal proceedings.

To avoid this, never sign a rental agreement, or let a tenant move furniture into your property or take a key, until you have the tenant's cash, certified check, or money order for the first month's rent and security deposit. An alternative is to cash the tenant's check at the bank before the move-in date. (While you have the tenant's first check, photocopy it for your records. The information on it can be helpful if you ever need to sue to collect a judgment from the tenant.) Be sure to give the tenant a signed receipt for the deposit.

Clause 5 of the form lease and rental agreements in Chapter 2 requires tenants to pay rent on the first day of each month. If the move-in date is other than the first day of the month, rent is prorated between that day and the end of that month.

Organize Your Tenant Records

A good system to record all significant tenant complaints and repair requests will provide a valuable paper trail should disputes develop later—for example, regarding your right to enter a tenant's unit to make repairs or the time it took for you to fix a problem. Without good records, the outcome of a dispute may come down to your word against your tenant's—always a precarious situation.

How to Establish a Filing System

Set up a file folder on each property with individual files for each tenant. Include the following documents:

- tenant's rental application, references, credit report, and background information, including information about any cosigners
- a signed lease or rental agreement, plus any changes made along the way
- Landlord-Tenant Checklist and photos or video made at move-in, and
- signed move-in letter.

After a tenant moves in, add these documents to the individual's file:

- your written requests for entry
- rent increase notices
- records of repair requests, and details of how and when they were handled—if you keep repair records on the computer, you should regularly print out and save files from past months; if you have a master system to record all requests and complaints in one log, you would save that log separately, not necessarily put it in every tenant's file
- safety and maintenance updates and inspection reports, and
- correspondence and other relevant information, including copies of important emails. See "Using Email for Notices or Other Communications with Tenants," at the end of this chapter.

> CAUTION
> **Good records are especially important if you end up suing a tenant who breaks the lease.** Chapter 14 explains the kinds of records to keep, such as receipts for advertising the property.

There are several property management software programs that allow you to keep track of every aspect of your business, from the tracking of rents to the follow-up on repair requests. Especially if you own many rental properties, these programs are well worth the cost, or you can set up your own database for each tenant with spaces for the following information:

- address or unit number
- move-in date
- home phone number
- name, address, and phone number of employer
- credit information, including up-to-date information as to where tenant banks
- monthly rent amount and rent due date
- amount and purpose of deposits plus any information your state requires on location of deposit and interest payments
- vehicle make, model, color, year, and license plate number
- emergency contacts, and
- whatever else is important to you.

Once you enter the information into your database, you can sort the list by address or other variables and easily print labels for rent increases or other notices.

How to Handle Credit Reports

Under federal law, you must take special care that credit reports (and any information stored elsewhere that is derived from credit reports) are stored in a secure place where only those who "need to know" have access. ("Disposal Rule" of the Fair and Accurate Credit Transactions Act of 2003, known as the FACT Act, 69 Fed. Reg. 68690.) In addition, you must dispose of such records when you're done with them, by burning them or using a shredder. This portion of the FACT Act was passed in order to combat the increasing reports of identity theft. It applies to every landlord who pulls a credit report, no matter how small your operation. The Federal Trade Commission, which interprets the Act, encourages you to similarly safeguard and dispose of *any* record that contains a tenant's or applicant's personal or financial information. This would include the rental application itself, as well as any notes you make that include such information.

Implementing the Disposal Rule will require some effort and follow-through, though it need not be a burdensome chore. Follow these suggestions:

- **Maintain applicant, tenant, and employee files in a locked cabinet.** This is a good practice for many reasons. Only you and your manager should have access to these files.
- **Determine when you no longer have a legitimate business reason to keep an applicant's credit report.** The Act requires you to dispose of credit reports or any information taken from them when you no longer need them. Unfortunately, you may need these reports long after you've rejected or accepted an applicant—they may be essential in refuting a fair housing claim. Under federal law, such claims must be filed within two years of the claimed discrimination, but some states set longer periods. Keep the records at least two years, and longer if your state gives plaintiffs extra time.
- **Establish a system for purging old credit reports.** Don't rely on haphazard file purges to keep you legal when it comes to destroying old reports. Establish a purge date for every applicant for whom you pull a report and use a tickle system.
- **Choose an effective purging method.** The Disposal Rule requires you to choose a level of document destruction that is reasonable in the context of your business. For example, a landlord with a few rentals would do just fine with an inexpensive shredder, but a multi-property operation might want to contract with a shredding service.
- **Don't forget computer files.** Reports stored on your computer or phone, or information derived from them, must also be kept secure and deleted when no longer needed. Purchase a utility that will "wipe" the data completely—that is, a program that will delete not only the directory, but the text as well.

The Disposal Rule comes with teeth for those who willfully disregard it—that is, for those who know about the law and how to comply but who deliberately refuse to do so. You could be liable for a tenant's actual damages resulting from identity theft (say, the cost of covering a portion of a credit card's unauthorized use), or damages per violation of between $100 and $1,000, plus the tenant's attorney fees and costs of suit, plus punitive damages. The FTC and state counterparts can also enforce the Act and impose fines.

How to Respond to Security Breaches

Despite your best efforts, information about your tenants may become lost or stolen. If you lose a laptop, become prey to a computer hacker, or suffer the consequences of a dishonest employee, sensitive identifying information about residents and applicants may result in their identify theft.

Almost every state (excepting Alabama, New Mexico, and South Dakota) has laws on the books concerning security breaches. These laws cover who should comply, define the information that's at issue ("personal information"), define what constitutes a breach, provide notice requirements, and note any exemptions. To find the law in your state, go to the website of the National Conference of State Legislatures (www.ncsl.org) and enter "security breach notification laws" in the search box.

If you're in a state with no breach notification law, head to the Federal Trade Commission, which gives excellent guidance on how to alert applicants and residents if you experience a security breach. Go to www.business.ftc.gov, and look for the article, "Information Compromise and the Risk of Identity Theft" (or, just type that title into your browser's search box). You'll also find a model notification letter to send tenants. If your state has its own notification requirements, you'll need to comply with them, too. Contact your state's office of consumer affairs. You can find yours at www.consumeraction.gov.

Organize Income and Expenses for Schedule E

If you've been in the landlording business for any length of time, you will be used to reporting your income and expenses on Schedule E (assuming you file IRS Form 1040 to pay your taxes). The Schedule is relatively simple. For each address (which may include multiple rental units), you report the year's rent and list enumerated expenses (the first page of Schedule E is reproduced below). You can download a fillable version of Schedule E from www.irs.gov.

Many landlords find it easiest to use *QuickBooks* or another accounting software package to track their income and expenses. There are also programs designed specifically for completing Schedule E, notably *Quicken Rental Property Manager*, which allows you to track income, expenses, and tax deductions, and converts the information into a Schedule E at tax time. You can also design your own spreadsheet using *Excel* or a similar program to keep track of rental income and expenses. Finally, there's always the old-fashioned way of making your own paper ledger of income and expenses.

Of course, the system you use to track income and expenses is only as good as the information you enter. To maximize tax deductions, keep receipts and records of all rental-property-related expenses, such as interest payments on mortgage loans, property taxes, professional fees (your accountant, attorney, property management), insurance, repairs, advertising and tenant screening, and membership fees, plus all income from rent, late fees, and the like.

RESOURCE
For detailed information on completing Schedule E and valuable tax advice for landlords, see *Every Landlord's Tax Deduction Guide*, by Stephen Fishman (Nolo). For personalized advice, consult an accountant or tax professional (and remember, buying this book or consulting with a tax pro are both tax-deductible expenses).

SCHEDULE E
(Form 1040)

Department of the Treasury
Internal Revenue Service (99)

Supplemental Income and Loss

(From rental real estate, royalties, partnerships, S corporations, estates, trusts, REMICs, etc.)

▶ Attach to Form 1040, 1040NR, or Form 1041.

▶ Information about Schedule E and its separate instructions is at *www.irs.gov/schedulee.*

OMB No. 1545-0074

2015

Attachment
Sequence No. **13**

Name(s) shown on return

Your social security number

Part I	Income or Loss From Rental Real Estate and Royalties

Note: If you are in the business of renting personal property, use **Schedule C** or **C-EZ** (see instructions). If you are an individual, report farm rental income or loss from **Form 4835** on page 2, line 40.

A Did you make any payments in 2015 that would require you to file Form(s) 1099? (see instructions) ☐ Yes ☐ No

B If "Yes," did you or will you file required Forms 1099? ☐ Yes ☐ No

1a	Physical address of each property (street, city, state, ZIP code)
A	
B	
C	

1b Type of Property (from list below)	**2** For each rental real estate property listed above, report the number of fair rental and personal use days. Check the **QJV** box only if you meet the requirements to file as a qualified joint venture. See instructions.		Fair Rental Days	Personal Use Days	QJV
A		**A**			☐
B		**B**			☐
C		**C**			☐

Type of Property:

1 Single Family Residence 3 Vacation/Short-Term Rental 5 Land 7 Self-Rental
2 Multi-Family Residence 4 Commercial 6 Royalties 8 Other (describe)

Income:	Properties:		A	B	C
3 Rents received	**3**				
4 Royalties received	**4**				
Expenses:					
5 Advertising	**5**				
6 Auto and travel (see instructions)	**6**				
7 Cleaning and maintenance	**7**				
8 Commissions.	**8**				
9 Insurance	**9**				
10 Legal and other professional fees	**10**				
11 Management fees	**11**				
12 Mortgage interest paid to banks, etc. (see instructions)	**12**				
13 Other interest.	**13**				
14 Repairs.	**14**				
15 Supplies	**15**				
16 Taxes	**16**				
17 Utilities.	**17**				
18 Depreciation expense or depletion	**18**				
19 Other (list) ▶ _____	**19**				
20 Total expenses. Add lines 5 through 19	**20**				
21 Subtract line 20 from line 3 (rents) and/or 4 (royalties). If result is a (loss), see instructions to find out if you must file **Form 6198**	**21**				
22 Deductible rental real estate loss after limitation, if any, on **Form 8582** (see instructions)	**22**	( )	( )	( )	( )

23a	Total of all amounts reported on line 3 for all rental properties	**23a**		
b	Total of all amounts reported on line 4 for all royalty properties	**23b**		
c	Total of all amounts reported on line 12 for all properties	**23c**		
d	Total of all amounts reported on line 18 for all properties	**23d**		
e	Total of all amounts reported on line 20 for all properties	**23e**		
24	**Income.** Add positive amounts shown on line 21. **Do not** include any losses	**24**	
25	**Losses.** Add royalty losses from line 21 and rental real estate losses from line 22. Enter total losses here	**25**	( )
26	**Total rental real estate and royalty income or (loss).** Combine lines 24 and 25. Enter the result here. If Parts II, III, IV, and line 40 on page 2 do not apply to you, also enter this amount on Form 1040, line 17, or Form 1040NR, line 18. Otherwise, include this amount in the total on line 41 on page 2	**26**	

For Paperwork Reduction Act Notice, see the separate instructions.   Cat. No. 11344L   Schedule E (Form 1040) 2015

Using Email for Notices or Other Communications With Tenants

You and your tenant may often send each other messages by email rather than by post, or communicate via text messages. Will those communications serve you as well as a mailed letter, if you need evidence that the message was received at the other end?

Suppose, for example, that you want to give notice terminating a tenant's month-to-month rental agreement, and do so by sending an email that's 30 days (your state's notice period) in advance of the termination date. Or, say you need to send your tenant a request for entry so that you can show the unit to an electrician you've hired to upgrade the wiring. If you end up in a legal dispute and your tenant challenges you in court, saying that you never told him about your decision to terminate or alerted him to the electrician's visit, you'll need confirmation that the emails were received.

> CAUTION
> **Check your lease for notice instructions!**
> Often, the lease or rental agreement contains a clause that describes how landlords and tenants should deliver "notices and demands." Unfortunately, most of the time you'll see a generic requirement that they be delivered "in writing." But as email communications have become more and more common, some lawyers are drafting notice clauses that take email into account.

On the One Hand: Electronic Notice Is Acceptable in Most Situations

Two laws confirm the acceptability of electronic notices: "UETA" (the Uniform Electronic Transactions Act), adopted in some form by 47 states and the District of Columbia (not adopted in Illinois, New York, or Washington), and "ESIGN" (Electronic Signatures in Global and National Commerce Act), a federal law. Unless some other law prohibits it, UETA and ESIGN permit the use of electronic signatures and electronic notices. Put another way, under both of these laws, a legal notice cannot be denied admission in court simply because it is electronic (and not on paper).

On the Other Hand: Emails May Be Legal, But Demonstrating Their Receipt Is Not Cheap

While it may be legally acceptable to use email, proving the tenant received your email is another matter. While some sophisticated services such as RPost (www.rpost.com) allow you to send tamper-proof attachments and electronic signatures, they may be expensive, depending on volume.

The Bottom Line: Stick With a Traditional Mail or Delivery Service

Currently, there is no cost-efficient way for a landlord to obtain evidence of delivery of an email message. Text messages are even harder to track, and evidence of receipt isn't available short of complex searches through users' accounts. Rarely would a landlord/tenant dispute support the expense of such a search.

If you're worried about being able to prove the receipt of your email or text, you'd be best served to also print it and mail it return receipt requested … the old fashioned way.

Cotenants, Sublets, and Assignments

 FORMS IN THIS CHAPTER

Chapter 8 includes instructions for and samples of the following forms:

- Landlord-Tenant Agreement to Terminate Lease
- Consent to Assignment of Lease
- Letter to Original Tenant and New Cotenant

The Nolo website includes downloadable copies of these forms. See Appendix B for the link to the forms in this book.

Conscientious landlords go to a lot of trouble to screen prospective tenants. However, all your sensible precautions will be of little avail if unapproved tenants simply move in at the invitation of existing tenants. Not only is it possible that you'll have difficulty getting these tenants to pay rent or maintain the rental unit, but if they fail to do so, you may have an extra tough time evicting them.

This chapter helps you analyze your options when your tenant asks questions like these:

- "Can I sublet my apartment?"
- "May I get someone else to take over the rest of my lease?"
- "Is it okay if I move in a roommate?"

We also advise you on what to do when your tenant attempts to do any of the above *without* consulting you. Because, as with so many of life's problematic situations, the best defense is a good offense, we prepare you in advance for these situations by suggesting that you protect your interests from the outset by using lease clauses that limit occupants and require your permission for subleasing or assigning. In particular, this chapter explains:

- why everyone living in a rental unit should sign a lease or rental agreement
- the legal differences between sublets and assignments
- your right (and legal and practical limitations) to prohibit sublets and assignments
- how to add a tenant to an existing tenancy, and
- how to deal with repeated overnight guests.

RELATED TOPIC

Related topics covered in this book include:

- Limiting how long tenants' guests may stay: Chapter 2 (Clause 3)
- Requiring your written consent in advance for any sublet or assignment of the lease or rental agreement, or for any additional people to move in: Chapter 2 (Clauses 1, 3, and 10)
- Your duty to rerent the property if a tenant neither sublets nor assigns, but simply breaks the lease: Chapter 14

- Returning security deposits when one tenant leaves but the others stay: Chapter 15.

CAUTION

New York tenants have special rights. By virtue of New York's Roommate Law (RPL § 235-f), New York tenants have the right to bring in certain additional roommates without obtaining the landlord's prior approval and subject only to any applicable local laws on overcrowding. If you own rental property in New York, be sure you understand this law before setting restrictions on tenants and roommates.

Cotenants

When two or more people rent property together, and all sign the same rental agreement or lease—or enter into the same oral rental agreement and move in at the same time—they are cotenants. Each cotenant shares the same rights and responsibilities for the rent and other terms of the lease or rental agreement. In addition, each cotenant is legally responsible to the landlord to carry out all of the terms of the lease, including being obligated to pay the entire rent and 100% of any damages to the premises if the others fail to pay their share.

Obligation for Rent

Among themselves, cotenants may split the rent equally or unequally, depending on their own personal arrangement. However, any cotenant who signs a lease or rental agreement with you is independently liable for all of the rent. Landlords often remind cotenants of this obligation by inserting into the lease a chunk of legalese which says that the tenants are "jointly and severally" liable for paying rent and adhering to terms of the agreement (see "Joint and Several Liability," below). If one tenant can't pay his share a particular month or simply moves out, the other tenant(s) must still pay the full rent during the rental period.

Joint and Several Liability

"Joint and several" refers to the sharing of obligations and liabilities among two or more people—both as a group and as individuals. When two or more tenants are "jointly and severally liable," you can choose to hold all of them, or just one of them, responsible to pay rent and to abide by the rules of the tenancy.

That means you may demand the entire rent from just one tenant should the others skip out, or evict all of the tenants even if just one has broken the terms of the lease.

Clause 1 of the form lease and rental agreements in Chapter 2 makes cotenants jointly and severally liable. Cotenants are jointly and severally liable for rent and other obligations—even if your lease or rental agreement does not include this clause. Nonetheless, we recommend you include a "jointly and severally liable" clause to alert tenants to this responsibility.

EXAMPLE: James and Helen sign a month-to-month rental agreement for a $1,200 apartment rented by Blue Oak Properties. They agree between themselves to each pay half of the rent. After three months, James moves out without notifying Helen or Blue Oak. As one of two cotenants, Helen is still legally obligated to pay Blue Oak all the rent (although she might be able to recover James's share by suing him).

Blue Oak has four options if Helen can't pay the rent:

- Blue Oak can give Helen a written notice to pay up or leave (called a Notice to Pay Rent or Quit in most states), and follow through with an eviction lawsuit if Helen fails to pay the entire rent or move within the required amount of time (usually three to five days).
- If Helen offers to pay part of the rent, Blue Oak can legally accept it, but should make it clear that Helen is still responsible for the entire rent. It's important to make this clear, since it's common for one cotenant to offer only "my portion" of the rent, when in fact each cotenant (roommate) is liable for the entire rent.

- If Helen wants to stay and finds a new cotenant with a decent credit history, Blue Oak may not be able to withhold its approval of the new person and still hold Helen to her obligation to pay 100% of the rent. If Blue Oak accepts a new person, it should, however, have him become a cotenant by signing a rental agreement (as discussed below).
- If Helen wants to stay and proposes a cotenant who proves to be unacceptable to Blue Oak (because the applicant does not meet Blue Oak's usual credit or income specifications for every new tenant), Blue Oak may say "No" and evict Helen if Helen is unable to pay the entire rent.

Violations of the Lease or Rental Agreement

In addition to paying rent, each tenant is responsible for any cotenant's action that violates any term of the lease or rental agreement—for example, each cotenant is liable if one of them seriously damages the property or moves in an extra roommate or a dog contrary to the lease or rental agreement. This means you can hold all cotenants responsible and can terminate the entire tenancy with the appropriate notice, even though some of the cotenants objected to the dog or weren't consulted by the prime offender.

If you must evict a tenant for a breach other than for nonpayment of rent (in which case you would evict all the tenants), you must decide whether to evict only the offending cotenant or all of them. Your decision will depend on the circumstances. You have no legal obligation to evict a blameless cotenant (for example, one who has no control over a dog-owning cotenant). Practically, of course, you'll want to be sure the innocent tenant can still shoulder the rent after his problem roommate is gone. On the other hand, because cotenants are "jointly and severally liable," you also have the legal right to evict all cotenants (even those who claim not to have caused the difficulty) and start over.

Special Rules for Married Couples

We strongly recommend that everyone who lives in a rental unit—including both members of a married couple—be required to sign the lease or rental agreement. This underscores your expectation that each individual is responsible ("jointly and severally liable") for the rent and the proper use of the rental property.

If, however, you neglect to have either the husband or wife sign the lease, that person may still be directly responsible to you. That's because, in some states, a spouse is financially responsible for the necessities of life of the other, including rent.

But rather than counting on your state's law for protection, just put both names on the lease or rental agreement and make them each cotenants. And, if one of your tenants gets married during the lease term, prepare a new agreement and have both spouses sign it.

Disagreements Among Cotenants

Usually, cotenants make only an oral agreement among themselves concerning how they will split the rent, occupy bedrooms, and generally share their joint living space. For all sorts of reasons, roommate arrangements may go awry. If you have been a landlord for a while, you surely know all about cotenants who play the stereo too loud, are slobs, pay their share of the rent late, have too many overnight guests or create some other problem that their roommates can't abide. If the situation gets bad enough, the tenants may start arguing about who should leave, whether one cotenant can keep another out of the apartment, or who is responsible for what part of the rent.

The best advice we can give landlords who face serious disagreements among cotenants is this: Don't get involved in spats between cotenants, as a mediator or otherwise. The reasons for our advice are both practical and legal.

On the practical side, you probably do not have the time to get to the bottom of financial or personal disputes; and, even if you do, you have no ability to enforce any decisions among your tenants. (How could you enforce a ruling that one tenant must occupy the smaller of the two bedrooms?)

On the legal side, too, you are largely helpless. For example, you cannot threaten eviction if a tenant violates an agreement with the other tenant and occupies the larger bedroom, unless you put that particular "offense" into the lease as a ground for eviction. And since it's impossible to design a lease that will predict and list every possible roommate disagreement, attempting to use a legal solution will be of little help.

If one or more cotenants approach you about a dispute, explain that they must resolve any disagreements among themselves. Remind them that they are each legally obligated to pay the entire rent, and that you are not affected by any rent-sharing agreements they have made among themselves. If one cotenant asks you to change the locks to keep another cotenant out, tell the tenant that you cannot legally do that—unless a court has issued an order that the particular tenant stay out.

The wisdom of remaining aloof during tenants' squabbles stops at the point that you fear for the physical safety of one of your tenants. Call the police immediately if you hear or witness violence between tenants, or if a reliable source tells you about it. If you have any reasonable factual basis to believe that a tenant intends to harm another tenant, you may also have a legal duty to warn the intended victim (who probably already knows) and begin proceedings to evict the aggressor. Failure to sensibly intervene where violence is threatened might result in a finding of liability if the aggressor carries through with the threat. (The fact that the parties are cotenants instead of tenants in different rental units would be immaterial to a court when determining liability.)

In the meantime, if one tenant fears violence from a cotenant, consider taking the following steps:

- Suggest mediation if you think there is a potential for a reasoned resolution.

When Couples Separate

Landlords need to be alert to the special emotional and possibly legal situations presented by a couple who rent the premises together and undergo a nasty break-up. Whether they are married or not dealing with feuding lovers who are living together is never easy. Here are some issues to consider:

- Especially if the couple is married, one tenant may not have the legal right to deprive the other of a place to live without a court order. If violence—or even the threat of it—is involved, the fearful spouse (usually the woman) is entitled to get a quick court order restraining the other partner from coming near her, either as part of a divorce filing or, in some states, separately. To help facilitate this, you might check out how to get a restraining order (there is usually a nonlawyer procedure) and make this information available to affected tenants. For advice, call the police department, your local courthouse, a women's shelter, or an advocacy organization for women.
- If one married tenant changes the locks without your consent to keep the other out, you probably have no legal liability. (If your lease or rental agreement—like the one in this book—prohibits changing the locks without the landlord's permission, you probably have grounds for eviction.) But you should not normally participate in acts that will keep one member of a married couple out (say, by changing the locks yourself) without a court restraining order, which specifically bars the other member of the couple from coming near the remaining tenant.
- When it comes to unmarried couples, you should know if your state or municipality grants any legal status to long-term relationships between people who are not married (these can take the form of either common law marriages or domestic partner laws). If so, the law may treat people in these relationships similarly to married couples.
- When unmarried couples—whether of the same or opposite sex—separate, the law treats them as roommates. But in many states, a fearful member of an unmarried couple can qualify for a civil restraining order banning the other from the joint home, using a procedure similar to that available to married couples.

- Contact the local police department or court clerk's office on behalf of the intended victim for information on obtaining a temporary restraining order, and urge the victim to apply for one. If the judge decides that the situation merits it, he or she will issue an order forbidding the aggressor tenant from coming near the other.
- Evict the aggressor or all cotenants on the lease. If you choose to allow a blameless tenant to stay, keep in mind that the remaining tenant's ability to pay the rent may be severely curtailed by the absence of a paying cotenant.

EXAMPLE: Andy and his roommate Bill began their tenancy on friendly terms. Unfortunately, it soon became clear that their personal habits were completely at odds. Their arguments regarding housekeeping, guests, and their financial obligations to contribute to the rent escalated to a physical fight. As a result, they each asked their landlord, Anita, to evict the other.

After listening to Andy's and Bill's complaints, Anita referred them to a local mediation service, and they agreed to participate. The mediator's influence worked for a while, but Andy and Bill were soon back at loud, unpleasant shouting matches. Anita initiated eviction proceedings against both, on the grounds that their disruptive behavior interfered with the rights of the other tenants to the quiet enjoyment of their homes.

Domestic Violence Situations

States have begun to extend special protections to victims of domestic violence. If you are responding to a problematic rental situation that involves domestic violence, proceed cautiously and check first with local law enforcement or a battered women's shelter regarding special laws that may apply. Your state may have rules like the following (see "State Laws in Domestic Violence Situations," in Appendix A, for specific laws).

- **Antidiscrimination status and eviction protection.** Rhode Island has made it illegal to discriminate against someone who is a victim of domestic violence. (R.I. Gen. Laws § 34-37-2.4.) This means that landlords cannot refuse to rent (or terminate) solely because the person is a victim of domestic violence. (See Chapter 5 for complete information on discrimination.) In Virginia, landlords may not evict a tenant who is a victim of domestic violence occurring on the property when the tenant has secured a restraining order against the perpetrator or has asked the landlord not to admit that person. (Va. Code Ann. § 55-248.31(D).)

- **Early termination rights.** In Arizona, a tenant who is a victim of domestic violence can end a lease with 30 days' notice, upon showing the landlord proof (such as a protective order) of her status as a domestic violence victim. (Ariz. Rev. Stat. § 33-1318.) In Washington, tenant victims who have reported domestic violence, stalking, or sexual assaults (or who have protective orders) may terminate without giving the usual amount of notice. (Wash. Rev. Code Ann. § 59.18.575.) Similarly, in Texas a victim of domestic violence may terminate without notice and avoid liability for future rent if the victim shows the landlord a protective order or temporary injunction concerning the victim or any other occupant. (Tex. Prop. Code Ann. § 92.016(f).) In Oregon, they can terminate with 14 days' notice. (Ore. Rev. Stat. Ann. §§ 90.453 and following.) In North Carolina, landlords must change the locks to protect a resident tenant when shown a court order directing a perpetrator to stay away. (N.C. Gen. Stat. § 42-42.3.) Tenants in Illinois are entitled to new locks when they report a credible, imminent threat of violence from

someone who is not on the lease, and can terminate without future liability for rent if they provide the landlord with written evidence of a credible, imminent threat of violence (such as medical, court, or police evidence of the situation) prior to or within three days of vacating. (765 Ill. Comp. Stat. §§ 750/1 and following.)

Several other states, including California, Indiana, Maryland, Michigan, Minnesota, New York, Utah, and Wyoming, plus the District of Columbia, give domestic violence victims the right to terminate their lease early.

Limits on rental clauses. In Arizona, landlords cannot include clauses providing for termination in the event of a tenant's call for police help in a domestic violence situation, nor can landlords make tenants pay for the cost of such calls. (Ariz. Rev. Stat. § 33-1315.) Colorado also prohibits such clauses. (Col. Rev. Stat. § 38-12-402.)

- **Three-day notice exceptions.** Iowa gives victims who have secured a restraining order (or reported the violence) some relief from a three-day termination notice. (Iowa Code Ann. § 562A.27A(1).)

- **Section 8 tenants.** Normally, Section 8 tenants may move without jeopardizing their right to continued public assistance only if they notify their public housing authority ahead of time, terminate their lease according to the lease's provisions, and locate acceptable replacement housing. Domestic violence victims, however, may circumvent these requirements if they have otherwise complied with other Section 8 requirements, have moved in order to protect someone who is or has been a domestic violence victim, and "reasonably believed" that they were imminently threatened by harm from further violence. (Violence Against Women and Department of Justice Reauthorization Act of 2005, 42 U.S. Code § 1437f (r)(5).)

In the absence of a state law giving victims of domestic violence early termination rights or other domestic violence protections, don't automatically say "No" to an early termination or other related request. First, because your policy will usually affect female, not male, tenants, it can be attacked in court as indirectly discriminating on the basis of sex (several lawsuits brought in states without statutory protections have succeeded on this theory). Aside from your vulnerability to being sued, keep in mind that it may be essential to the safety of the victim to allow her to quickly move. Finally, even your bottom line may benefit from allowing the tenancy to end immediately—what you lose in rent may pale in comparison with what your repair costs may be if your property is damaged, not to speak of the fall-out from negative publicity if the situation escalates.

Although your state (and the federal law mentioned above) may give some special protections to domestic violence victims, these accommodations do not prohibit you from terminating, if necessary, for nonpayment of rent. Unfortunately, all too often the abuser will leave the property but the remaining victim struggles to pay the rent. You may legally terminate the tenancy of a domestic violence victim who falls behind in the rent, just as you would any tenant who hasn't paid.

When a Cotenant Leaves

When a cotenant leaves and someone is proposed as a substitute, you want three things to happen:

- The departing tenant should sign a Landlord-Tenant Agreement to Terminate Lease (shown below).
- You should investigate the proposed new tenant, beginning with the application process (like any new tenancy).
- The remaining tenant(s), including the replacement tenant, should sign a new lease or rental agreement.

These steps are all discussed below.

There are three reasons for formally "resetting the stage" this way: (1) to ensure that you continue to receive the entire rent, (2) to ensure that any new tenant meets your criteria for selecting tenants, and (3) to avoid the specter of the return—or attempted return—of the departed tenant who claims that he never *really* intended to leave.

Leases vs. Rental Agreements

Our discussion of subleasing and assigning assumes that there is an underlying lease for a term of one year or more. If there is a long amount of time remaining on a lease, both landlord and tenant will be very concerned about a number of issues, including a tenant's obligation for remaining rent and the landlord's duty to find a new tenant and limit (mitigate) his losses.

By contrast, a month-to-month tenancy lasts no more than 30 days. When a tenant wants to leave before the end of the 30 days (to sublet and return, say, on day 28, or to assign the rental agreement and not return at all), the short amount of time (and rent money) remaining on the rental agreement may make a landlord less willing to accept the substitute.

You should not be any less thorough in checking the background of a proposed subtenant or assignee of a rental agreement, however. In theory, the amount of money at stake may be less than that involved in a lease, since the tenancy usually can be terminated with 30 days' notice for any reason. In reality, however, other considerations (such as the health and safety of other tenants, or the possibility of accepting a tenacious bad apple who proves difficult and expensive to evict) suggest the need for the same background checking that is used in evaluating any new tenant.

The rent. Although the departing tenant will still be technically liable for the rent until you formally release him from the lease or rental agreement (except where he has given timely written notice), this may not be worth much if he has left for parts unknown. And, although the remaining tenants (individually and as a group) are liable for the rent, too, they may not be able (or willing) to pay the departing tenant's share. You are almost always better off signing a lease with a new tenant if he is acceptable.

Who is entitled to live in the rental unit. As an added advantage, formally terminating a cotenant's lease or rental agreement and preparing a new one, signed by the remaining tenant(s) and any replacement tenant, will make it clear that the outgoing tenant is no longer entitled to possession of the property. Although you do not want to become entangled in your tenants' personal lives, you also want to avoid being dragged into disputes regarding who is entitled to a key and the use of your rental property.

Common Terms

Prime Tenant. We use this term to refer to the original tenant—someone you chose from a pool of applicants and who has signed a lease or rental agreement. This is our shortcut term—it has no legal meaning.

Here are common terms that do have accepted legal meaning.

Tenant. Someone who has signed a lease or a rental contract, or who has gained the status of a tenant because the landlord has accepted his presence on the property or has accepted rent from him. A tenant has a legal relationship with the landlord that creates various rights and responsibilities for both parties.

Cotenants. Two or more tenants who rent the same property under the same lease or rental agreement. As far as the landlord is concerned, each is 100% responsible for carrying out the agreement (in legal slang, "jointly and severally liable"), including paying all the rent.

Subtenant. Someone who subleases (rents) all or part of the premises from a tenant (not from the landlord).

Assignment. The transfer by a tenant of all his rights of tenancy to another tenant (the "assignee"). Unlike a subtenant, an assignee rents directly from landlord.

Roommates. Two or more people, usually unrelated, living under the same roof and sharing rent and expenses. A roommate is usually a cotenant, but in some situations may be a subtenant.

But what happens if, despite your vigilance, a new tenant moves in without your permission who isn't acceptable to you? Assuming you see no reason to change your mind, you have a right to evict all cotenants under the terms of the clause in your lease or rental agreement that prohibits unauthorized sublets.

What to Do When a Tenant Wants to Sublet or Assign

Ideally, you want to rent to tenants who will stay a long time, or at least the entire term of the lease. But, despite your best efforts, you will encounter tenants who, for various reasons such as a job-related move, will want to leave before the expiration of their lease. Sometimes, of course, these tenants simply disappear. Other tenants, out of regard for their promise, or to recover as much as possible of their deposit, or maybe just out of concern that you will pursue them or damage their credit rating, will want to leave "legally" by supplying a stand-in for the balance of the term.

What should you do if a tenant approaches you with a request to move out, substituting another tenant in her place? Because our lease and rental agreements (Clause 10) prohibit sublets or assignments without your written consent, you have some flexibility. This section discusses your options.

Create a New Tenancy

In most situations, your best bet when confronted with a tenant who wants to sublease or assign is to simply insist that the tenancy terminate and a new one begin—with the proposed "subtenant" or "assignee" as the new prime tenant.

Suppose a tenant wants to sublet her apartment for six months while she is out of the area, or assign the last four months of her lease because she has to move for employment reasons. If the proposed new tenant passes your standard screening process, agree to take the tenant—on the condition that the proposed new tenant sign a new lease and become a prime tenant. This gives you the most direct legal relationship with the substitute. In other words, simply treat your tenant's wish to sublet or assign as a wish to get out from under the lease early, with a candidate for the next occupant at the ready.

The way to accomplish this is to first release your original tenant from her obligations under the lease (see the sample Landlord-Tenant Agreement to Terminate Lease, below). Then, begin the new tenancy with the substitute in the same way that you begin any tenancy: sign a lease, present a move-in letter, and so on.

Comparing Subleases and Assignments

	Sublease	Assignment
Rent	New tenant (sub-tenant) is liable to the prime tenant, not to the landlord. Prime tenant is liable to landlord.	New tenant (assignee) is liable to the landlord. Old tenant is liable if new tenant doesn't pay.
Damage to premises	Prime tenant is liable for damage caused by new tenant.	Absent an agreement to the contrary, prime tenant is not liable for damage caused by new tenant.
Violations of lease	Landlord can't sue new tenant for money losses caused by violating lease, because new tenant never signed lease. New tenant can't sue landlord for lease violations, either.	New tenant and landlord are bound by all terms in lease except those that were purely personal to the landlord or old tenant.
Eviction	Landlord can sue to evict new tenant for any reason old tenant could have been evicted. But to evict subtenant, landlord must also evict old tenant.	Landlord can sue to evict new tenant for any reason old tenant could have been evicted.

What are the pros and cons of this approach as compared to accepting a subtenancy or assignment? Here are a few:

- **Subtenancy.** If you allow a subtenancy, you have no direct legal relationship with the new tenant. Practically, this means that if you should need to sue her for damage to the property or failure to pay rent, you cannot do it directly; you must involve the original tenant.

- **Assignment.** If you allow the tenant to assign the lease, the new tenant (the assignee) steps into the original tenant's legal shoes and (unlike a subtenant) has a complete legal relationship with you. In short, you can take legal action directly against the assignee in any dispute. In addition, you get one significant advantage: If the new tenant fails to pay the rent, the old one is still legally responsible to do so. So why prefer a new tenancy? Simply because insisting on a regular tenancy will do away with any misunderstanding about who is liable. If disagreements later arise concerning liability for damages or rent, the new tenant knows exactly where she stands.

The sample Landlord-Tenant Agreement to Terminate Lease below will terminate the original tenancy so that you can rent the property to the new tenant. Then, if and when the first tenant wants to return and the second voluntarily leaves, you can again rent to the first, using a new lease. A copy of the Landlord-Tenant Agreement to Terminate Lease is available on the Nolo website. See Appendix B for the link to the forms in this book.

In most cases, tenants should be happy that you're letting them off the hook. But what if the original tenant really does want to return and is uneasy about having you rent to the new tenant directly, because he fears the second person may not honor her promise to leave? Your answer should normally be a polite version of "That's

Landlord-Tenant Agreement to Terminate Lease

_____Robert Chin_____ [Landlord]

and _____Carl Mosk_____ [Tenant]

agree that the lease they entered into on _____November 1, 20xx_____ , for premises at

__56 Alpine Terrace, Hamilton, Tennessee_____ ,

will terminate on ____January 5, 20xx_____ .

_____Robert Chin_____   _____December 28, 20xx_____
Landlord/Manager   Date

_____Carl Mosk_____   _____December 28, 20xx_____
Tenant   Date

your problem." Think of it this way: Your tenant is admitting that he doesn't completely trust the new tenant to move out on demand, even though he selected her. You don't want to be in the middle of this type of situation. It's better that the original tenant bear the brunt of any problem—if there is one—than you.

Allow a Sublet or Assignment

Although you are almost always better off starting a new, independent tenancy with a proposed stand-in tenant, there are situations in which you may want to agree to a subtenancy or assignment.

You might, for example, want to accommodate —and keep—an exceptional, long-term tenant who has every intention of returning and whose judgment and integrity you have always trusted. If the proposed stand-in meets your normal tenant criteria, you may decide that it is worth the risk of a subtenancy or assignment in order to keep the prime tenant.

Another good reason is a desire to have a sure source of funds in the background. This might come up if you have a prime tenant who is financially sound and trustworthy, but a proposed stand-in who is less secure but acceptable in every other respect. By agreeing to a sublet or assignment, you have someone in the background (the prime tenant) still responsible for the rent. The risk you incur by agreeing to set up a subtenancy or assignment and the hassle that comes with dealing with more than one person may be worth what you gain in keeping a sure and reliable source of funds on the hook.

> **EXAMPLE:** The Smith family rented a duplex for a term of two years but, after 18 months, the father's employer transferred him to another city. Mr. Smith asked Bob, the landlord, to agree to an assignment of the balance of the lease to Mr. Smith's 19-year-old son, who wanted to finish out his school year at the local college. Knowing that the son was a decent and conscientious young man, Bob agreed, but did not insist that Mr. Smith terminate his tenancy.

> Bob realized that keeping Dad in the picture was insurance against the unlikely but possible event that the son would not be able to keep up with the rental payments. Another way Bob could accomplish this same goal would be to end the old lease and create a new one with Mr. Smith's son, but require that Dad also sign it as a guarantor.

If you would prefer not to allow a subtenancy or assignment, but the original tenant presses you, don't reject a proposed subtenant or assignee unless you have a good business reason. In a few states, including California and Florida, you may not unreasonably withhold your consent when asked to allow a sublet or assignment, no matter what the lease or rental agreement says. In broad terms, this requirement means that you must use the same criteria in evaluating the proposed stand-in that you used when choosing the prime tenant.

You can stay out of trouble by evaluating the proposed tenant by exactly the same standards that you use in evaluating any other new tenant: financial stability, credit history, references, and other criteria described in Chapter 1. If the would-be subtenant or assignee passes your tests, great; rent to him or her. If he fails the test that you apply to all potential tenants, you will be legally justified in saying no.

Then, if the prime tenant goes ahead and breaks the lease, leaving you with lost rents and rerental expenses, you can sue. You should be able to show a judge that you fairly considered (but objectively rejected) the proposed new tenant as part of your duty to try to limit (mitigate) your losses. But if the prime tenant convinces the judge that you unreasonably turned down an acceptable substitute tenant, chances are you'll lose.

> **CAUTION**
> **Don't discriminate illegally.** If you turn down a proposed subtenant or assignee for an illegal reason (racial discrimination, for example), you are vulnerable to a lawsuit under federal laws and some state and local laws.

Cotenants Can Sublet and Assign, Too

The legal principles that apply to tenants who want to sublet or assign also apply to a cotenant who wants to do the same thing. For example, it is not unusual for one of several roommates to want to sublet for a period of time, or assign the remainder of the lease. If you followed our advice and insisted that all roommates be official cotenants on the lease, you are well-positioned to react to the cotenant's request, just as you would if the request came from a lone tenant.

Only Landlords Can Evict Tenants

A cotenant may not terminate another cotenant's tenancy. Termination and eviction are available only to landlords.

But a tenant who rents out part of his premises to another (called a subtenant) has considerably more power. If you allow this kind of subtenancy, realize that you have allowed your tenant to be a "landlord" as well (he's your tenant *and* the subtenant's landlord). And in his role as landlord to a subtenant, he *does* have the right to terminate and evict the subtenant.

Most owners want to control when and if the local police show up on their property to enforce eviction decrees. For this reason alone, you should prohibit "tenancies within tenancies" by insisting that every occupant become a full-fledged cotenant.

Sublets

A *subtenant* is someone who rents all or part of the property from a tenant and does not sign a rental agreement or lease with you. A subtenant either:

- rents (sublets) an entire dwelling from a tenant who moves out temporarily—for example, for the summer, or
- rents one or more rooms from the tenant, who continues to live in the unit.

The key to subtenant relationships is that the original tenant retains the primary relationship with you and continues to exercise some control over the rental property, either by occupying part of the unit or by reserving the right to retake possession at a later date. The prime tenant functions as the subtenant's landlord. The subtenant is responsible to the prime tenant for the rent, which is usually whatever figure they have agreed to between themselves. The prime tenant, in turn, is responsible to the landlord for the rent. The written or oral agreement by which a tenant rents to a subtenant is called a *sublease*, because it is under the primary lease.

Subtenancies are often a pain in the neck for landlords. Besides the obvious hassles of dealing with people coming and going, landlords in some states are limited by law to the kinds of lawsuits they can bring against subtenants—for example, you may be able to sue to correct behavior that is contrary to the lease, but not sue for money damages. This means, for instance, that a subtenant may go to court to force you to maintain habitable housing, but you could not sue that subtenant for money damages if he left the place a mess and the security deposit was insufficient to cover your loss (you would have to sue the original tenant). If you have an excellent long-term tenant who really wants to return after subleasing for a few months, you may want to risk it.

> CAUTION
> **Don't accept rent from a subtenant.** Repeatedly taking rent from a subtenant, plus taking other actions that indicate that you have basically forgotten about the prime tenant, might turn a subtenancy into a tenancy—and take the prime tenant off the hook for rent.

Assignments

From a landlord's point of view, assignments are usually preferable to subleases. With an assignment, you have more control over the tenant, because you have a direct legal relationship with the assignee.

An *assignee* is a person to whom the prime tenant has turned over the entire lease. In most

Consent to Assignment of Lease

Carolyn Friedman _____ [Landlord] and

Joel Oliver _____ [Tenant]

and Sam Parker _____ [Assignee]

agree as follows:

1. Tenant has leased the premises at ___5 Fulton, Indianapolis, Indiana___

    _____

    from Landlord.

2. The lease was signed on ___April 1, 20xx___ and will expire on ___March 31, 20xx___ .

3. Tenant is assigning the balance of Tenant's lease to Assignee, beginning on ___November 1, 20xx___ ,
    and ending on ___March 31, 20xx___ .

4. Tenant's financial responsibilities under the terms of the lease are not ended by virtue of this
    assignment. Specifically, Tenant understands that:

    a. If Assignee defaults and fails to pay the rent as provided in the lease, namely on ___the first of___
        ___the month___ , Tenant will be obligated to do so within ___three___ days of being notified by
        Landlord; and

    b. If Assignee damages the property beyond normal wear and tear and fails or refuses to pay for
        repairs or replacement, Tenant will be obligated to do so.

5. As of the effective date of the assignment, Tenant permanently gives up the right to occupy the
    premises.

6. Assignee is bound by every term and condition in the lease that is the subject of this assignment.

Carolyn Friedman _____   _October 1, 20xx_ _____
Landlord/Manager   Date

Joel Oliver _____   _October 1, 20xx_ _____
Tenant   Date

Sam Parker _____   _October 1, 20xx_ _____
Assignee   Date

states, this means simply that the prime tenant has moved out permanently. The assignee not only moves into the premises formerly occupied by the prime tenant, but into her legal shoes, as well. Unlike a subtenant, whose legal relationship is with the prime tenant, not you, the assignee rents directly from you. If things go wrong with respect to behavior or money matters under the lease, the assignee can sue or be sued by the landlord.

Assignment doesn't, however, completely sever the legal relationship between you and the original tenant. Oddly enough, the original tenant remains responsible for the rent if the assignee fails to pay. Absent an agreement to the contrary, however, the prime tenant is not liable for damage to the premises caused by the assignee. (The Consent to Assignment of Lease form, discussed above, protects you by incorporating this promise.)

How to Assign a Lease

Typically, to accomplish an assignment the landlord and the tenant write "Assigned to John Doe" on the lease at each place where the prime tenant's name appears. The new tenant, John Doe, then signs at each place where the original tenant signed. If this is all that's done, the prime tenant remains liable for the rent, but not for damage to the property.

We suggest that a formal "Consent to Assignment of Lease" document also be used, such as the sample shown above. The Nolo website includes a downloadable copy. See Appendix B for the link to the forms in this book. Using this Consent to Assignment of Lease form protects you in two additional respects:

- It educates the prime tenant to the fact that he will remain liable for the rent if the assignee defaults.
- It obligates the prime tenant to cover damages to the property beyond normal wear and tear if the assignee refuses or is unable to do so.

Generally, the landlord and assignee are bound by promises made in the lease signed by the original tenant. For example, the lease provision in which the landlord agreed to return the security deposit in a certain manner is still in effect; it now benefits the assignee. And the assignee must honor the previous tenant's promise to abide by the lease's noise rules and use restrictions. Only in very unusual situations, where a lease provision is purely personal, is it not transferred. For example, a promise by a tenant to do a landlord's housekeeping in exchange for a rent reduction would not automatically pass to an assignee.

> **CAUTION**
>
> **Liability for injuries remains the same.** If a subtenant or assignee is injured on your property, the question of whether you are liable will be the same as if the injured person were the original tenant.

When a Tenant Brings in a Roommate

Suppose now that love (or poverty) strikes your tenant and he wants to move in a roommate. Assuming your lease or rental agreement restricts the number of people who can occupy the unit (as ours does in Clause 3), the tenant must get your written permission for additional tenants.

Giving Permission for a New Roommate

Although you may be motivated to accommodate your tenant's friend, your decision to allow a new cotenant should be based principally on whether or not you believe the new person will be a decent tenant. After all, if the original tenant moves out at some later date (maybe even because the new person is so awful), you will remain stuck with this person. So, always have the proposed new tenant complete a rental application, and follow your normal screening procedures. If the new person meets your standards (a good credit record and references), and there is enough space in the unit, you will probably want to say yes.

Letter to Original Tenant and New Cotenant

Date July 22, 20xx

Dear Abby Rivas and
       New Cotenant

       Phoebe Viorst ,
       Original Tenant or Tenants

As the landlord of 239 Maple Street

_____ [address] , I am pleased that

       Abby [new cotenant]

has proved to be an acceptable applicant and will be joining Phoebe

_____ [original tenant or tenants] as a cotenant. Before

       Abby [new cotenant]

moves in, everyone must sign a new lease that will cover your rights and responsibilities. Please contact me at

the address or phone number below at your earliest convenience so that we can arrange a time for us to meet

and sign a new lease. Do not begin the process of moving in until we have signed a lease.

Sincerely yours,

Sam Stone
Landlord

       1234 Central Avenue
Street Address

       Sun City, Minnesota
City and State

       612-555-4567
Phone

CAUTION

Don't give spouses the third degree. The one exception to the rule of checking new tenants carefully has to do with spouses. If the new tenant is a spouse and there's no problem with overcrowding, be very careful before you say no. Refusal without a good, solid reason could be considered illegal discrimination based on marital status. In short, it's fine to check the person out, but say no only if you discover a real problem.

Preparing a New Rental Agreement or Lease

If you allow a new person to move in, make sure he becomes a full cotenant by preparing a new lease or rental agreement—possibly with some changed terms, such as the amount of rent—for signature by all tenants. (Chapter 14 discusses how.) Do this before the new person moves in to avoid the possibility of a legally confused situation.

We suggest that you send a letter to the original tenant and the new tenant as soon as you decide to allow the newcomer to move in. A sample Letter to Original Tenant and New Cotenant is shown above and the Nolo website includes a downloadable copy. See Appendix B for the link to the forms in this book.

Raising the Rent

When an additional tenant comes in, it is both reasonable and legal (in either a lease or a rental agreement situation) for you to raise the rent (and/or the security deposit), unless you live in an area covered by a rent control law that prohibits you from doing so. Obviously, from your point of view, more people living in a residence means more wear and tear and higher maintenance costs in the long run. Also, as long as your increase is reasonable, it should not be a big issue with existing occupants, who, after all, will now have someone else to pay part of the total rent.

Just as you may want to take this opportunity to raise the rent, you may also want to increase the amount of the security deposit. Again, however, if the property is subject to rent control, you may need to petition the local rent control board for permission to increase the rent based on an increased number of occupants.

TIP

Make rent policy clear in advance. To avoid making tenants feel that you invented a rent increase policy at the last minute to unfairly extract extra money, it's a good idea to establish in advance your rent policies for units occupied by more than one person. A move-in letter is a good place to do this. That way, your request for higher rent when an additional roommate moves in will simply be in line with what you charge everyone who occupies a unit of a certain size with a certain number of people.

Guests and New Occupants You Haven't Approved

Our form rental agreement and lease include a clause requiring your written consent for guests to stay overnight more than a reasonable amount of time. We recommend that you allow guests to stay up to ten days in any six-month period without your written permission (see Clause 3 of the form lease and rental agreements in Chapter 2). The value of this clause is that a tenant who tries to move someone in for a longer period has clearly violated a defined standard, which gives you grounds for eviction.

When deciding when and whether to enforce a clause restricting guest stays, you'll need to use a good amount of common sense. Obviously, the tenant whose boyfriend regularly spends two or three nights a week will quickly use up the ten-day allotment. However, it would be unrealistic to expect the boyfriend (assuming he has his own apartment) to become a cotenant, and you may not object to the arrangement at all. In short, you'll want to turn a blind eye.

At the same time, you may well want to keep your lease or rental agreement clause restricting guests, in the event that an occasional arrangement starts to become too permanent. But don't be surprised if a tenant claims that your prior willingness to disregard the clause limiting guests means you gave up the right to enforce it. The best way to counter this claim is to be as consistent as you can. (Don't let one tenant have a guest five nights a week and balk when another does so for two.) As long as you are reasonably consistent, a court will likely side with you if push comes to shove and you decide to evict a tenant who completely refuses to obey your rules.

Remind tenants that they are responsible for their guests' behavior and that guests must also comply with the lease or rental agreement provisions—for example, pet rules, noise limits, use of parking spaces, and the like. See Clause 24 of the form lease and rental agreements in Chapter 2.

> **CAUTION**
>
> **Avoid discrimination against guests.** In many states and cities, you cannot legally object to a tenant's frequent overnight guests based on your religious or moral views. For example, it is illegal to discriminate against unmarried couples, including gay or lesbian couples, in many states and cities. It is also illegal to discriminate against tenants' guests because of their race or other protected category.

If a tenant simply moves a roommate in on the sly—despite the fact that your lease or rental agreement prohibits it—or it appears that a "guest" has moved in clothing and furniture and begun to receive mail at your property, it's best to take decisive action right away. If you think your tenant is reasonable, send a letter telling the tenant that the new roommate or longtime guest must move out immediately. (You can use the Warning Letter for Lease or Rental Agreement Violation in Chapter 16 for this purpose.) But if you feel that the tenant will not respond to an informal notice, use a formal termination notice as explained in Chapter 17. If you allow the situation to continue, the danger is strong that the roommate will turn into a subtenant—one you obviously haven't screened or approved of. This can have significant negative consequences: While a subtenant doesn't have all the rights of a tenant, she is entitled, in an eviction proceeding, to the same legal protection as a tenant. And she may even turn into a de facto prime tenant if the original tenant suddenly moves out.

Again, your best choice is to insist that the roommate or guest fill out a formal application. Assuming he checks out, you may also increase the rent or the security deposit, unless that's prohibited by any applicable rent control ordinance.

If you do not want to rent to the guest or roommate, and if that person remains on the premises, make it immediately clear in writing that you will evict all occupants based on breach of the occupancy terms of the lease if the person doesn't leave immediately.

> **SEE AN EXPERT**
>
> **Get help to evict unwanted occupants.** If you want to get rid of an unacceptable new occupant, initiate legal proceedings quickly. The longer you wait, the easier it will be for unauthorized occupants to claim that—if only by inaction alone—you have consented to their presence, giving them the status of a tenant. Technically, these proceedings are not an eviction (only tenants can be evicted), but are instead either a criminal complaint for trespassing or a civil suit aimed at ridding the property of a squatter. If you are faced with this situation, contact the local police and ask for assistance. If they refuse to act (which is common, since they will be worried that the trespasser may have attained the status of a tenant), you will probably need to consult a lawyer for advice.

> **Housesitters Are Subtenants**
>
> Many tenants, particularly with pets, have housesitters (typically unpaid) stay in their apartment while they're away for a long vacation or business trip. Even if your tenant doesn't collect rent from a housesitter, that person is still legally a subtenant. Treat a housesitter the way you'd treat any proposed subtenant, and remind the tenant that your written consent is required.

Short-Term Rentals Like Airbnb

In recent years, online businesses such as Airbnb have acted as clearinghouses for short-term (less than 30-day) vacation rentals. Using residential property as a short-term rental raises concerns not only for landlords, but for city governments as a whole. Here's an overview of the key issues.

Landlords' Concerns

Especially in vacation-destination cities, tenants have begun listing their rented apartments and homes, essentially subletting their rentals, pocketing the money, and also increasing wear and tear on the premises. Landlords are universally against such use, but the issue is whether their rental agreements or leases clearly prohibit this practice.

This book is intended for landlords who engage in the traditional business of landlording—that is, renting to long-term tenants under month-to-month rental agreements or leases. Consequently, we do not address the problems faced by landlords whose traditional tenants begin to let out their homes to short-term occupants. Because of certain legal differences between regular and such short-term rentals, the law is unclear on whether standard no-sublet clauses apply so as to forbid this practice. For this reason, we advise using the following sentence at the end of a lease or rental agreement clause prohibiting subletting: "Neither shall Tenant(s) sublet or rent any part of the premises for short-term stays of any duration, including but not limited to vacation rentals." This language is included in Clause 10 of our own standard lease and month-to-month rental agreements.

Cities' Concerns

Many local governments point out that using single-family apartments and homes as hotels violates their laws that regulate hotels, which require permits, involve inspections, and include hotel taxes. Many other cities, counties, and other municipalities have legal restrictions on short-term home rentals, including New Orleans and New York City. Local rules vary greatly from place to place. The restrictions in some cities are quite severe and make most short-term rentals illegal. Other cities, such as Palm Desert, California, have much more liberal rules, allowing short-term rentals as long as the property owner registers with the city,

and/or obtains a license or permit, and pays all applicable fees and taxes.

Residential property owners who decide to forego traditional long-term renting, and instead use their property for a series of short-term rentals, should not use the forms in this book, and we do not offer any advice on whether this practice would be legal under a city's ordinance. Similarly, tenants who want to sublet their rentals to short-term occupants should not use this book or its forms.

> CAUTION
> **Be sure to check condo or homeowners' association restrictions.** If your rental property is a condominium or cooperative, or is part of a planned development, your use of your property is governed by deed-like restrictions commonly called covenants, conditions, and restrictions (CC&Rs), or by bylaws duly adopted by the governing board. These may bar short-term rentals entirely, or subject them to restrictions. Unlike zoning laws or local ordinances, CC&Rs and bylaws are enforced by the homeowners' association or coop board, which may impose fines on violators and place liens on the property to collect them.

How to Find Your Local Laws and Other Legal Restrictions on Short-Term Rentals

Airbnb's website (www.airbnb.com) has a summary of the legal requirements of about 50 cities, with links for more information (check "Responsible Hosting" under the "Hosting" section). If your city isn't listed here, the first place to check is your local municipal or administrative code, which may be available online at your local government's website. To find yours, check out www.statelocalgov.net or www.municode.com, or call your city's zoning board or local housing authority. You might also check out the Short Term Rental Advocacy Center (www.stradvocacy.org) created by Airbnb, HomeAway, Trip Advisor, and FlipKey, for information on restrictions on short-term rentals.

Landlord's Duty to Repair and Maintain the Premises

FORMS IN THIS CHAPTER

Chapter 9 includes instructions for and samples of the following forms:

- Resident's Maintenance/Repair Request
- Time Estimate for Repair
- Semiannual Safety and Maintenance Update
- Agreement Regarding Tenant Alterations to Rental Unit

The Nolo website includes downloadable copies of these forms. See Appendix B for the link to the forms in this book.

Landlords are required by law to provide rental property that meets basic structural, health, and safety standards. And if you don't meet your duties, tenants may have the legal right to:

- reduce or withhold rent
- pay for repairs themselves and deduct the cost from the rent
- sue you, or
- move out without notice and without responsibility for future rent.

Some states set more stringent requirements than others. But you will be better off in the long run if you go beyond satisfying the letter of the law. Here's why:

Happy tenants. Tenants are likely to be satisfied and easy to deal with. They will stay longer, resulting in fewer interruptions of your income stream.

Better negotiations with tenants. Knowing that your housing complies with state and local housing codes, you can respond from a position of strength if a disgruntled tenant complains without grounds about a repair or maintenance issue. You can negotiate a reasonable solution with the tenant because you know you are likely to win if the dispute ends up in court.

Lower risk of lawsuits. You will be far less likely to face the risk of tenant lawsuits based on habitability problems or injuries resulting from defective conditions.

Cheaper insurance. A good record (no lawsuits, no housing code violations) can mean lower insurance premiums.

RELATED TOPIC
Related topics covered in this book include:
- Writing clear lease and rental agreement provisions for repair and maintenance: Chapter 2
- Setting valid occupancy limits: Chapter 5
- Delegating maintenance and repair responsibilities to a manager: Chapter 6
- Highlighting repair and maintenance procedures in a move-in letter to new tenants and using a Landlord-

Tenant Checklist to keep track of the condition of the premises: Chapter 7
- Your liability for injuries caused by defective housing conditions: Chapter 10
- Your responsibility to clean up environmental hazards: Chapter 11
- Your responsibility for crime: Chapter 12
- Your right to enter rental premises for repairs and inspections: Chapter 13
- Inspecting the rental unit before the tenant moves out: Chapter 15
- How to negotiate with tenants over legal disputes such as rent withholding: Chapter 16
- How to research state laws, local ordinances, and court cases on repair and maintenance responsibilities: Chapter 18.

Your Duty to Keep the Premises Livable

You are legally required to keep rental premises livable. In most states, the legal doctrine requiring this is called the "implied warranty of habitability." In other words, when you rent out a unit, you give the tenant an unspoken guarantee that it will be in livable condition. Arkansas is the only state that doesn't follow this rule, but landlords' responsibility there is much the same, because local laws (particularly in urban areas) usually specify health and safety requirements that amount to requiring habitable housing.

The implied warranty of habitability comes from either:

- local building codes or state statutes that specify minimum requirements for heat, water, plumbing, and other essential services, or
- widely held notions of what constitutes decent housing, derived from court opinions.

Unfortunately, in many states it's not clear which source (building codes, state statutes, court decisions, or even a mix of all of them) is the basis for the implied warranty. Why does it matter? Because the source of the warranty determines your responsibilities and the legal remedies available to tenants.

Finally, a quaint-sounding but still very powerful legal rule, the "implied covenant of quiet enjoyment," also contributes to your duty to offer and maintain fit premises. This covenant or promise, which exists by law between you and your tenants, means that you will do nothing to disturb their right to peacefully and reasonably use their rented space—and conversely, that you'll act in a way that enables peaceful use. Examples of violations of the covenant of quiet enjoyment include:

- tolerating a nuisance, such as allowing garbage to pile up or a major rodent infestation
- failing to provide sufficient working electrical outlets, so that tenants cannot use appliances, and
- failing to fix a leaky roof, which deprives a tenant of the use of the rented space.

Although the covenant of quiet enjoyment is not as far-reaching as the implied warranty of habitability, the remedies available to tenants are substantially the same in both cases.

Local or State Housing Laws

In some states, (including the District of Columbia, Idaho, and West Virginia), if you comply with applicable state or local housing codes, you've satisfied the implied warranty of habitability. Landlords in these states enjoy the luxury of knowing that they can find out the exact details of their repair and maintenance responsibilities. Substantial compliance with the housing codes (rather than literal, 100% compliance) is generally sufficient.

These codes regulate structural aspects of buildings and usually set space and occupancy standards, such as the minimum size of sleeping rooms. They also establish minimum requirements for light and ventilation, sanitation and sewage disposal, heating, water supply (such as how hot the water must be), fire protection, and wiring (such as the number of electrical outlets per room). In addition, the codes typically make property owners responsible for keeping common areas (or parts of the premises which the owner controls) clean, sanitary, and safe.

Court Decisions

In many states, including California, Iowa, New York, and Vermont, the implied warranty of habitability is independent of any housing code. The standard is whether the premises are "fit for human occupation" or "fit and habitable." Usually, however, a substantial housing code violation is also a breach of the warranty of habitability. But even if you comply with housing codes, a court can require more of you.

Who Pays to Fix Habitability Problems?

In most situations, landlords are responsible for paying to keep rental property habitable, whether at the beginning of the tenancy or during it, if problems arise as a result of normal wear and tear or the actions of a third party, such as a vandal. But if a tenant does something to make the property unfit—for example, by negligently breaking the water main—the financial burden of fixing it falls on the tenant. You remain responsible for seeing that the work gets done and the property is returned to a habitable state, but you could rightly bill the tenant for the repair. (Clause 11 of the form lease and rental agreements in Chapter 2 alerts the tenant to this responsibility.)

What "Fit" and "Habitable" Mean

You must always:

- Keep common areas, such as hallways and stairways, safe and clean.
- Maintain electrical, plumbing, sanitary, heating, ventilating, air-conditioning, and other facilities and systems, including elevators.
- Supply water, hot water, and heat in reasonable amounts at reasonable times.
- Provide trash receptacles and arrange for trash removal.

Additional responsibilities can depend on your circumstances. Here are some other factors to consider.

The climate. In climates that experience severe winters, storm windows or shutters may be considered basic equipment. Housing in wet, rainy areas needs to be protected from the damp. In Oregon, for example, courts have specifically made landlords responsible for waterproofing. In areas prone to insect infestations, landlords may be required to provide extermination services. Florida landlords must exterminate bedbugs, mice, roaches, and ants.

The neighborhood. In a high-crime area, good locks, security personnel, exterior lighting, and secure common areas may be seen as a necessity, as important as water and heat. (See Chapter 12.)

The environment. Lead-based paint, mold, asbestos building materials, and other environmental hazards can pose significant health problems and may make buildings unfit for habitation. (See Chapter 11.)

How to Meet Your Legal Repair and Maintenance Responsibilities

A conscientious landlord can meet repair and maintenance responsibilities by following these steps.

Comply With State and Local Housing Codes

Checking out state law and local housing ordinances, and complying with all requirements, should adequately protect you from most tenant claims of uninhabitability. State laws generally require you to make all repairs and do whatever is necessary to put and keep the premises in a fit and habitable condition. Local housing codes are often more specific, and you need need to know what they call for in the way of structural requirements, facilities, and essential services such as plumbing and heat. Your local building or housing authority, and health or fire department, can provide this information.

Be sure to find out about all ordinances affecting your repair and maintenance responsibilities—for example, many cities require the installation of smoke detectors in residential units, or security items such as viewing devices in doors that open onto a hallway. Some cities also make owners responsible for the prevention of infestation and, if necessary, the extermination of insects, rodents, and other pests.

RESOURCE

Finding the laws. Appendix A includes citations for the major state laws affecting landlords. You can find these statutes online, or contact your state consumer protection agency for pamphlets or brochures that describe your repair and maintenance responsibilities in less legalistic terms. For a list of state consumer protection agencies, go to www.usa.gov/state-consumer. To find building codes for all 50 states and major cities, check out the Building Code State and Local Resource Center at www.cmdgroup.com/building-codes.

How Housing Code Requirements are Enforced

Local building, health, or fire department authorities may discover code violations through routine inspections or in response to a tenant complaint. When property changes hands or is used as collateral for a loan, there's usually an inspection.

Once a violation is found, you'll get a citation requiring you to remedy it within a certain amount of time, such as five business days. If you don't make the repairs within the time allowed, the city or county may sue you. Moreover, in many cities, continued failure to comply with cited violations of local housing laws is a criminal misdemeanor punishable by fines or even imprisonment. In some cases, local officials may require you to provide tenants with temporary alternative housing until the violation is corrected.

Tenants may also point out code violations if they do not pay the rent, or attempt to pay less, on the grounds that the premises are substandard. If you try to evict a tenant for not paying rent, the tenant may claim housing code violations as justification.

Get Rid of Dangers to Children

Local ordinances prohibit "attractive nuisances." These are conditions that tend to attract children, such as abandoned vehicles; wells and shafts; basements; abandoned equipment or appliances; excavations; and unsafe fences, structures, or foliage. If children are hurt while playing in or on an attractive nuisance, you may be held liable.

Don't Allow Nuisances, Such as Excessive Noise

Besides "attractive nuisances," local housing codes prohibit nuisances in general, broadly defined as whatever is dangerous to human life or detrimental to health, as determined by the public health officer—for example, overcrowding a room with occupants, providing insufficient ventilation or illumination or inadequate sewage or plumbing facilities, or allowing drug dealing on the premises. A landlord found to have created or tolerated a nuisance will be subject to the code's enforcement and penalty provisions.

Be especially vigilant when it comes to noise, which can be a major nuisance. Landlords often hear complaints about noisy tenants—for example, an upstairs neighbor who clumps about in work boots every day at five a.m. If you ignore such complaints, you can get hit with code violations, court-ordered rent reductions, and even punitive damages. In one case, a New York City tenant complained about loud noise from a neighboring apartment in the late night and early morning hours. Neither the owner nor manager took any effective steps to stop it. A court ruled that the continuous, excessive noise violated the warranty of habitability, and entitled the tenant to a 50% rent abatement. (*Nostrand Gardens Co-Op v. Howard*, 221 A.D.2d 637, 634 N.Y.S.2d 505 (2d Dept., 1995).) For more advice on dealing with noisy tenants, including how to write an effective warning letter, see "When Warning Notices Are Appropriate" in Chapter 16.

Clause 13 of our form lease and rental agreements in Chapter 2 prohibits tenants from causing disturbances or creating a nuisance—that is, behavior (such as excessive noise) that prevents neighbors from enjoying the use of their own homes.

Consider Smoking Restrictions

There's a considerable trend among rental owners to adopt no-smoking policies both in common areas, such as lobbies, and individual rental units. (The ill effects of secondhand smoke are well known, smoke damages furnishings and paint, and smoking is a fire danger.) Many owners have found that advertising a smoke-free environment gives them a distinct marketing advantage.

Several cities have also passed no-smoking laws for multifamily buildings. The city of San Rafael, California, for example, prohibits smoking in all duplex and multifamily residential units that share a common wall. For details see www.smokefreemarin.com/multi-unit-housing.html.

If you do allow smoking in units, you may face complaints from nonsmoking tenants bothered by fumes wafting up from outside balconies, through windows, under doorjambs, or through the ventilation and heating systems.

An increasing number of frustrated neighbors have advanced creative and successful arguments based on three legal theories:

- **Nuisance.** Tenants have argued that the presence of smoke, like any noxious fume or noise, constitutes a legal nuisance in that it exposes others to a serious health risk. When courts buy this argument, the fact that the smoker did not have a no-smoking clause in his lease or rental agreement is immaterial. (In Utah, secondhand smoke is by law a nuisance, giving affected tenants a right under specified circumstances to sue the landlord or the smoker, demanding that the smoking stop, and asking for damages. (Utah Code Ann. § 78b-6-1101.))
- **Covenant of quiet enjoyment.** Neighbors have also claimed that their ability to use and enjoy their homes has been significantly diminished by the presence of smoke.
- **Warranty of habitability.** Some neighbors have persuaded judges that the smoke is so pervasive and noxious that it renders their rental unfit. In many states, this allows affected neighbors to break their leases.

Also, tenants with certain disabilities are protected from secondhand smoke under the Americans with Disabilities Act and the federal Fair Housing Act, as well as state and local regulations.

You may also want to consider addressing tenants' use of e-cigarettes, which are electronic heating devices that heat and vaporize a solution that typically contains nicotine. Although there's no "secondhand smoke," there *is* "secondhand aerosol" (quaintly called "vapor" by manufacturers). This by-product is a visible soup that contains nicotine, ultrafine particles, and low levels of toxins that are known to cause cancer. For more information on the effects of secondhand aerosol, search for "Electronic Smoking Devices and Secondhand Aerosol" on the website noted just below.

TIP

Consider letting a tenant who complains about smoke break the lease. In view of the increasing success that nonsmoking tenants are enjoying when they take their complaints to court, you'll probably come out ahead.

RESOURCE

Current information on non-smoking policies and e-cigarettes. Check the Americans for Nonsmokers' Rights website (www. no-smoke.org) for lists of state and local laws restricting smoking (search "Smokefree Lists, Maps, and Data") and e-cigarettes.

Medical Marijuana Smoking

Many states have passed "compassionate use" laws, but federal law has not followed suit—the cultivation, possession, and use of marijuana is still illegal under federal law. For this reason, landlords are free to disallow marijuana possession, use, or growing on the premises, even where the tenant has state-sanctioned, medical approval to use it. Accordingly, even tenants who have a recognizable disability under federal law cannot expect landlords to vary a no-marijuana policy pursuant to an accommodation under the federal Americans with Disabilities Act (ADA).

In practical terms, marijuana smoking can have the same effect on tenants in a multi-family building as regular tobacco smoke. But practicalities may also solve the problem for a tenant who has a legitimate need for marijuana and medical permission to use it: As more and more states allow its use for medical conditions, producers are making drops, liquids, and solid foods that contain the necessary chemical ingredients of marijuana but omit the smoke. Tenants who purchase and responsibly consume such items should not pose a problem for landlords or other tenants.

Don't Try to Evade Your Legal Responsibilities

Some landlords have attempted to get around their responsibilities for keeping premises habitable. They have tenants sign a lease saying that they understand that the landlord isn't promising to keep the premises habitable, or they argue that a tenant who moved into or stayed in substandard housing waived the right to a habitable dwelling.

In a rare showing of unanimity, courts almost everywhere have rejected both these arguments. Except for a handful of states, including Maine and Texas (and even there, in limited circumstances), neither a tenant waiver (at the beginning of the tenancy or during its life) nor a disclaimer in the lease will relieve you of the responsibility to provide fit and habitable housing.

You may, however, legally delegate some repair and maintenance responsibilities to tenants. See "Delegating Landlord's Responsibilities to Tenants," below.

> **CAUTION**
> **Choose your lease or rental agreement carefully.** Preprinted leases available in office supply stores or online are usually not designed for the laws of each state and could include clauses that could be illegal in your state. To be on solid ground, consult your state and local laws and use the lease or rental agreement in this book or available on Nolo.com.

Make Sure You—And Your Tenant— Know the Tenant's Obligations

State and local housing laws generally require tenants to maintain their units. If a dwelling is rendered uninhabitable due to the tenant's actions, the tenant will have a difficult, if not impossible, time fighting eviction or avoiding responsibility for the repair bill. (If the tenant won't pay up, you can deduct the expense from the security deposit.) Your lease or rental agreement should spell out these basic tenant obligations, whether or not they are required by law in your state. See Clause 11 of the form agreements in Chapter 2.

Common Myths About Repairs and Maintenance

Many landlords (and tenants) are under the mistaken impression that every time a rental unit turns over, certain maintenance work is legally required. In fact, the actual condition of the unit determines what repairs and maintenance are necessary.

Paint. No state law requires you to repaint the interior every so often, but local ordinances might (New York City's does). So long as the paint isn't creating a habitability problem—for example, paint that's so thick around a window that the window can't be opened—it should comply with the law. Lead-based paint, however, may create all sorts of legal problems—for example, if a child becomes ill from eating lead-based paint chips, a court may find you liable because of your carelessness.

Drapes and carpets. So long as drapes and carpets are not sufficiently damp or mildewy to constitute a health hazard, and so long as carpets don't have dangerous holes that could cause someone to trip and fall, you aren't legally required to replace them.

Windows. A tenant who carelessly breaks a window is responsible for repairing it. If a burglar, vandal, or neighborhood child broke a window, however, you are responsible for fixing it.

Keys. Many tenants think that they're entitled to fresh locks upon move-in. In some states (such as Texas) and in some cities, this is true. But even if you're not legally required to rekey, you should do so in order to reduce the chance of break-ins.

Keep the rental unit as clean and safe as the condition of the premises permits. For example, if the kitchen has a rough, unfinished wooden floor that is hard to keep clean, you should not expect it to be shiny and spotless—but a tenant with a new tile floor would be expected to do a decent job. If you have to do a major clean-up when the tenant moves out, you may legitimately deduct its cost from the security deposit.

Keep plumbing fixtures as clean as their condition permits. For example, bathtub caulking that has sprouted mold and mildew will render the tub unusable (or at least disgusting). Because it could have been prevented by proper cleaning, the tenant is responsible. On the other hand, if the bathroom has no fan and the window has been painted shut, the bathroom will be hard to air out; resulting mildew might be your responsibility.

Dispose of garbage, rubbish, and other waste. For instance, if mice or ants invaded the kitchen because a tenant forgot to take out the garbage before leaving on a two-week vacation, the tenant would be responsible for paying any necessary extermination costs.

Use electrical, plumbing, sanitary, heating, ventilating, air-conditioning, and other facilities and other systems, including elevators, properly. Examples of abuse by tenants include overloading electrical outlets and flushing large objects down the toilet.

Fix things the tenant breaks or damages. A tenant who causes a serious habitability problem on your property—for example, carelessly breaking the heater—is responsible for it. You can insist that she pay for the repair. The tenant can't just decide to live without heat for a while to save money. If necessary, you can use the security deposit to pay for it and, if that isn't enough, sue the tenant (in small claims court, if possible) besides. You can't, however, charge a tenant for problems caused by normal wear and tear—for example, a carpet that has worn out from use.

Report problems. Some states require tenants to inform the landlord, as soon as practicable, of defective conditions that the tenant believes the landlord doesn't know about and has a duty to repair.

CAUTION

Be sure your lease or rental agreement makes the tenant financially responsible for repairing damage caused by the tenant's negligence or misuse. (See Clause 11 of the form agreements in Chapter 2.) That means that where the tenant or his friends or family cause damage— for example, a broken window, a toilet clogged with children's toys, or a freezer that no longer works because the tenant defrosted it with a carving knife—it's the tenant's responsibility to make the repairs or to reimburse

you for doing so. If a tenant refuses to repair or pay for the damage he caused, you can use the security deposit to cover the bill, then demand that the tenant bring the deposit up to its original level (if he refuses, he's a candidate for termination and eviction). Or you can sue, perhaps in small claims court, for the cost of the repairs.

Repair What You Provide or Promise

State and local housing laws typically deal with basic living conditions—heat, water, and plumbing, for example. They do not usually deal with amenities—features that are not essential but make living a little easier, such as drapes, washing machines, swimming pools, saunas, parking places, intercoms, and dishwashers. Although housing laws do not require you to furnish these things, if you do, you might be legally required to maintain or repair them. The law reasons that by providing amenities, you also promise to maintain them.

If the lease or rental agreement says that you will repair or maintain certain items, such as appliances, the promise is express. When you (or a manager or rental agent) say something that indicates that you will be responsible for repairing or maintaining an item or facility, the promise is implied. Implied promises are also found where you have, over time, repeatedly repaired or maintained certain aspects of the rental, establishing a practice of repair that the tenant can rely upon. Here are some typical examples of implied promises.

EXAMPLE 1: Tina sees Joel's ad for an apartment, which says "heated swimming pool." After Tina moves in, utility costs rise, and Joel stops heating the pool regularly. Joel has violated his implied promise to keep the pool heated. If he wants more flexibility, he should avoid ad language that commits him to such things.

EXAMPLE 2: When Joel's rental agent shows Tom around the building, she goes out of her way to show off the laundry room, saying, "Here's the terrific laundry room—it's for the use of all the tenants." Tom rents the apartment. Later, all the washing machines break down, but Joel won't fix them. Joel has violated his implied promise to maintain the laundry room appliances in working order.

EXAMPLE 3: Tina's apartment has a built-in dishwasher. When she rented the apartment, neither the lease nor the landlord said anything about the dishwasher or who was responsible for repairing it. The dishwasher has broken down a few times, and whenever Tina asked Joel to fix it, he did. By doing so, Joel has established a usage or practice that he—not the tenant—is responsible for repairing the dishwasher.

If you violate an express or implied promise relating to the condition of the premises, the tenant may sue you (usually in small claims court) for money damages for breach of contract, and may be able to pursue other legal remedies, discussed below.

Set Up a Responsive Maintenance System—And Stick to It

If you fail to maintain the premises, you'll face various financial losses and legal problems, both from tenants—who may withhold rent and pursue other legal remedies—and from government agencies that enforce housing codes. Your best bet to avoid problems in the first place is to design a maintenance program that meets housing laws *and* satisfies the question, "Is this building safe, sound, and fit for people to live in?" In doing so, you should be mindful of a larger goal: to attract and keep reliable tenants who will stay as long as possible.

Avoiding Problems With a Good Maintenance and Repair System

Your best defense against disputes with tenants is to establish and communicate a clear, easy-to-follow procedure for tenants to ask for repairs and to document all complaints, respond quickly when complaints are made, and schedule annual safety inspections. If you employ a manager or management company, make sure they follow your guidelines as well.

Recommended Repair and Maintenance System

Follow these steps to avoid maintenance and repair problems with tenants:

1. Provide tenants with a safe, well-maintained property—for example, by installing good outdoor lighting, trimming tree limbs away from the building, and having an effective snow removal plan in cold-winter climates.

2. Clearly set out the tenant's responsibilities for repair and maintenance in your lease or rental agreement. See Clauses 11, 12, and 13 of the form agreements in Chapter 2.

3. Use the written Landlord-Tenant Checklist form (Chapter 7) to check over the premises and fix any problems before new tenants move in.

4. Don't assume tenants know how to handle routine maintenance problems such as a clogged toilet or drain. Make it a point to explain the basics when a tenant moves in and include a brief list of maintenance dos and don'ts with your move-in materials. For example, explain:
   • how to avoid overloading circuits
   • proper use of garbage disposal
   • location and use of fire extinguisher, and
   • problems tenant should definitely not try to handle, such as electrical repairs.

5. Encourage tenants to immediately report plumbing, heating, weatherproofing, or other defects or safety or security problems—whether in the tenant's unit or in common areas such as hallways and parking garages. Use the Resident's Maintenance/Repair Request form discussed below.

6. Keep a written log (or have your property manager keep one) of all complaints, including those made orally. This should include a box to indicate your immediate and any follow-up responses (and subsequent tenant communications), as well as a space to enter the date and brief details of when the problem was fixed. The Resident's Maintenance/Repair Request form, below, can serve this purpose.

7. Keep a file for each rental unit with copies of all complaints and repair requests from tenants and your response. As a general rule, you should respond in writing to every tenant repair request (even if you also do so orally or by email). In Chapter 7, "Using Email for Notices and Other Communications to Tenants" explains why it's important to communicate with tenants in writing, rather than just use email.

8. Handle repairs as soon as possible, but definitely within the time any state law requires. Notify the tenant by phone and follow up in writing if repairs will take more than 48 hours, excluding weekends. Keep the tenant informed—for example, if you have problems scheduling a plumber, let your tenant know with a phone call, note, or email.

9. Twice a year, give your tenants a checklist on which to report any potential safety hazards or maintenance problems that might have been overlooked (see the Semiannual Safety and Maintenance Update, described in "Tenant Updates and Landlord's Regular Safety and Maintenance Inspections," below). Respond promptly and in writing to all requests, keeping copies in your file.

10. Once a year, inspect all rental units, using the Landlord-Tenant Checklist as a guide as discussed in "Tenant Updates and Landlord's Regular Safety and Maintenance Inspections," below. Keep copies of the filled-in checklist in your file.

11. Especially for multiunit projects, place conspicuous notices in several places around the property about your determination to operate a safe, well-maintained building, and list phone numbers for tenants to call with maintenance requests.

12. Remind tenants of your policies and procedures for keeping the building in good repair in every written communication by printing them at the bottom of all routine notices, rent increases, and other communications. Tenants will be more likely to keep you apprised of maintenance and repair problems if you remind them that you are truly interested. A notice regarding complaint procedures such as the one below will be helpful.

13. Take care when hiring and supervising contractors for projects involving specialized skills or major repairs. Check individual references and licenses and state rules before hiring any outside workers—whether a handyperson or skilled contractor.

Sample Notice to Tenants Regarding Complaint Procedure

Fair View Apartments wants to maintain all apartment units and common areas in excellent condition so that tenants enjoy safe and comfortable housing. If you have any questions, suggestions, or requests regarding your unit or the building, please direct them to the manager between 9 a.m. and 6 p.m., Monday through Saturday, either by calling 555-9876 or by dropping off a completed Maintenance/Repair Request form at the manager's office. In case of an emergency, please call 555-1234 at any time.

Benefits of Establishing a Repair and Maintenance System

In addition to a thorough system for responding to problems, you should establish a good, nonintrusive system of periodic maintenance inspections. It will give you several advantages:

- **Prevention.** The system we recommend lets you fix little problems before they grow into big ones. For example, you would want to replace the washer in the upstairs bathtub before the washer fails, the faucet can't be turned off, and the tub overflows, ruining the floor and the ceiling of the lower unit.

- **Good tenant relations.** Communication with tenants creates a climate of cooperation and trust that can work wonders in the long run. Keeping good tenants happy is an investment in your business.

- **Rent withholding defense.** A responsive communication system gives you an excellent defense if unreasonable tenants seek to withhold or reduce rent for no good reason.

Resident's Maintenance/Repair Request

Date: _August 29, 20xx_

Address: _392 Main St., #402, Houston, Texas 77002_

Resident's name: _Mary Griffin_

Phone (home): _555-4321_   Phone (work): _555-5679_

Problem (be as specific as possible): _Garbage disposal doesn't work_

_____

_____

_____

_____

_____

Best time to make repairs: _After 6 p.m. or Saturday morning_

Other comments: _____

_____

_____

_____

I authorize entry into my unit to perform the maintenance or repair requested above, in my absence, unless stated otherwise above.

Mary Griffin
Resident

· ·

FOR MANAGEMENT USE

Work done: _Fixed garbage disposal (removed spoon)_

Time spent: _1/2_ hours

Date completed: _August 30, 20xx_   By: _Paulie_

Unable to complete on: _____ , because: _____

_____

Notes and comments: _____

_____

Hal Ortiz   _August 30, 20xx_
Landlord/Manager   Date

You may still have to go to court to evict the tenant, but your carefully documented procedures will provide a paper trail. If you make it your normal business practice to save all repair requests from tenants, the absence of a request is evidence that the tenant didn't complain. And if you need to establish as part of an eviction procedure that a claimed problem is phony, you may want to have the repair person who looked at the supposed defect come to court to testify as to why it was phony.

- **Limit legal liability.** An aggressive repair policy backed up by an excellent record-keeping system can help reduce your potential liability to tenants who sue for injuries suffered as a result of defective conditions on your property. There are two reasons for this: First, it is less likely that there will be injuries in the first place if your property is well-maintained. Second, in many situations an injured person must prove that your negligence (carelessness) caused the problem. You may be able to defeat this claim by demonstrating that you actively sought out and quickly fixed all defects.

EXAMPLE: Geeta owns a 12-unit apartment complex and regularly encourages tenants to request repairs in writing on a form she's prepared. Several prominent signs, as well as reminders on all routine communications with tenants, urge tenants to report all problems. Most tenants do so. One month, Ravi simply doesn't pay his rent. After her phone calls are not answered, Geeta serves a Notice to Pay Rent or Quit. Still Ravi says nothing.

When Geeta files an eviction suit, Ravi claims he withheld rent because of a leaky roof and defective heater that Geeta refused to repair. At trial, Geeta testifies that she routinely saves all tenants' filled-out forms for at least a year, and that she has no record of ever receiving a complaint from Ravi, even though she gave him blank forms and sent notices twice a year asking to be informed of any problems. She also submits her complaint log, which has a space to record oral requests. The judge has reason to doubt Ravi ever complained, and rules in Geeta's favor.

Resident's Maintenance/Repair Request Form

One way to assure that defects in the premises will be reported by conscientious tenants—while helping to refute bogus tenant claims about lack of repairs—is to include a clause in your lease or rental agreement requiring that tenants notify you of repair and maintenance needs. Make the point again and describe your process for handling repairs in your move-in letter to new tenants.

Many tenants will find it easiest (and most practical) to call or email you or your manager with a repair problem or complaint, particularly in urgent cases. Make sure you have an answering machine, voicemail, or other service available at all times to accommodate tenant calls. Check your messages frequently when you're not available by phone.

We also suggest you provide all tenants with a Resident's Maintenance/Repair Request form. Give each tenant five or ten copies when they move in and explain how the form should be used to request specific repairs. (See the sample, above.) Be sure that tenants know to describe the problem in detail and to indicate the best time to make repairs. Email tenants a blank copy of the form, make sure tenants know how to get more copies. Your manager (if any) should keep an ample supply of the Resident's Maintenance/Repair Request form in her rental unit or office.

You (or your manager) should complete the entire Resident's Maintenance/Repair Request form or keep a separate log for every tenant complaint, including those made by phone. (See the discussion below.) Keep a copy of this form or your log in the tenant's file, along with any other written communication. Be sure to keep good records of how and when you handled tenant complaints, including reasons for any delays and notes on conversations with tenants. For a sample, see the bottom of the Resident's Maintenance/Repair Request form (labeled For Management Use, shown above). You might also jot down any other comments regarding repair or maintenance problems you observed while handling the tenant's

Time Estimate for Repair

Stately Manor Apartments

August 30, 20xx
Date

Mary Griffin
Tenant

392 Main St., #402
Street Address

Houston, Texas 77002
City and State

Dear Mary Griffin ,

　　　　　　　　　　Tenant

Thank you for promptly notifying us of the following problem with your unit: _____

Garbage disposal doesn't work

We expect to have the problem corrected on _____ September 3, 20xx _____ due to the following:

Garbage disposal part is out of stock locally, but has been ordered and will be

delivered in a day or two.

We regret any inconvenience this delay may cause. Please do not hesitate to point out any other problems that may arise.

Sincerely,

Hal Ortiz
Landlord/Manager

complaint. The Resident's Maintenance/Repair Request form can be downloaded from the Nolo website, see Appendix B for the link to the forms in this book.

Tracking Tenant Complaints

Most tenants will simply call or email you when they have a problem or complaint, rather than fill out a Resident's Maintenance/Repair Request form. For record-keeping purposes we suggest you always fill out this form, regardless of whether the tenant does. In addition, it's also a good idea to keep a separate chronological log or calendar with similar information on tenant complaints. A faithfully kept log will qualify as a "business record," admissible as evidence in court, that you can use to establish that you normally record tenant communications when they are made. By implication, the *absence* of an entry is evidence that a complaint was *not* made. This argument can be important if your tenant has reduced or withheld rent or broken the lease on the bogus claim that requests for maintenance or repairs went unanswered.

Responding to Tenant Complaints

You should respond almost immediately to all complaints about defective conditions by talking to the tenant and following up (preferably in writing). Explain when repairs can be made or, if you don't yet know, tell the tenant that you will be back in touch promptly. Use a form such as the Time Estimate for Repair; it is shown above. The Nolo website includes a downloadable copy. See Appendix B for the link to the forms in this book. This doesn't mean you have to jump through hoops to fix things that don't need fixing or to engage in heroic efforts to make routine repairs. It does mean you should take prompt action under the circumstances—for example, immediate action should normally be taken to cope with broken door locks or security problems. Similarly, a lack of heat or hot water (especially in winter in cold areas) and safety hazards such as broken steps or exposed electrical wires should be dealt with on an emergency basis.

One way to think about how to respond to repair problems is to classify them according to their consequences. Once you consider the results of *inaction,* your response time will be clear:

- **Personal security and safety problems = injured tenants = lawsuits.** Respond and get work done immediately if the potential for harm is very serious, even if this means calling a 24-hour repair service or having you or your manager get up in the middle of the night to put a piece of plywood over a broken ground floor window.
- **Major inconvenience to tenant = seriously unhappy tenant = tenant's self-help remedies (such as rent withholding) and vacancies.** Respond and attempt to get work done as soon as possible, or within 24 hours, if the problem is a major inconvenience to tenant, such as a plumbing or heating problem.
- **Minor problem = slightly annoyed tenant = bad feelings.** Respond in 48 hours (on business days) if not too serious.

Yes, these deadlines may seem tight and, occasionally, meeting them will cost you a few dollars extra, but, in the long run, you'll be way ahead.

If you're unable to take care of a repair right away, such as a dripping faucet, and if it isn't so serious that it requires immediate action, let the tenant know when the repair will be made. It's often best to do this orally (a message on the tenant's answering machine should serve), and follow up in writing by leaving a notice under the tenant's door. If there's a delay in handling the problem (maybe the part you need to fix the oven has to be ordered), explain why you won't be able to act immediately.

CAUTION

Respect tenant's privacy. To gain access to make repairs, the landlord can enter the rental premises only with the tenant's consent, or after having given

Semiannual Safety and Maintenance Update

Please complete the following checklist and note any safety or maintenance problems in your unit or on the premises.

Please describe the specific problems and the rooms or areas involved. Here are some examples of the types of things we want to know about: garage roof leaks, excessive mildew in rear bedroom closet, fuses blow out frequently, door lock sticks, water comes out too hot in shower, exhaust fan above stove doesn't work, smoke alarm malfunctions, peeling paint, and mice in basement. Please point out any potential safety and security problems in the neighborhood and anything you consider a serious nuisance.

Please indicate the approximate date when you first noticed the problem and list any other recommendations or suggestions for improvement.

Please return this form with this month's rent check. Thank you.

—The Management

Name: _____Mary Griffin_____

Address: _____392 Main St., #402_____

_____Houston, Texas_____

Please indicate (and explain below) problems with:

- ☐ Floors and floor coverings _____
- ☐ Walls and ceilings _____
- ☐ Windows, screens, and doors _____
- ☐ Window coverings (drapes, miniblinds, etc.) _____
- ☐ Electrical system and light fixtures _____
- ☑ Plumbing (sinks, bathtub, shower, or toilet) ___Water pressure low in shower___
- ☐ Heating or air conditioning system _____
- ☑ Major appliances (stove, oven, dishwasher, refrigerator) ___Exhaust fan above stove doesn't work___
- ☐ Basement or attic _____
- ☑ Locks or security system ___Front door lock sticks_____
- ☐ Smoke detector _____
- ☐ Fireplace _____
- ☐ Cupboards, cabinets, and closets _____
- ☐ Furnishings (table, bed, mirrors, chairs) _____
- ☐ Laundry facilities _____
- ☐ Elevator _____
- ☐ Stairs and handrails _____
- ☐ Hallway, lobby, and common areas _____
- ☐ Garage _____

☐ Patio, terrace, or deck _____

☑ Lawn, fences, and grounds _____ Shrubs near back stairway need pruning _____

☐ Pool and recreational facilities _____

☐ Roof, exterior walls, and other structural elements _____

☐ Driveway and sidewalks _____

☐ Neighborhood _____

☑ Nuisances _____ Tenant in #501 often plays stereo too loud _____

☐ Other _____
_____

Specifics of problems: _____
_____
_____
_____
_____
_____

Other comments: _____
_____
_____
_____
_____

_____Mary Griffin_____   _____February 1, 20xx_____
Tenant   Date

. . . .

FOR MANAGEMENT USE

Action/Response: _____ Fixed kitchen exhaust fan and sticking front door lock on _____
_____February 15, and adjusted water pressure in shower. Pruned shrubs on February 21._____
_____Spoke with tenant in #501 about keeping stereo low on February 2._____
_____
_____
_____
_____
_____

_____Hal Ortiz_____   _____February 22, 20xx_____
Landlord/Manager   Date

reasonable notice or the specific amount of notice required by state law, usually 24 hours. See Chapter 13 for rules and procedures for entering a tenant's home to make repairs and how to deal with tenants who make access inconvenient for you or your maintenance personnel.

TIP

If you can't attend to a repair right away, avoid possible rent withholding. Some landlords voluntarily offer a "rent rebate" if a problem can't be corrected in a timely fashion, especially if it's serious, such as a major heating or plumbing problem. A rebate builds goodwill and avoids rent withholding.

If, despite all your efforts to conscientiously find out about and make needed repairs on a timely basis, a tenant threatens to withhold rent, move out, or pursue another legal remedy discussed above, you should respond promptly in writing, telling him either:

- when the repair will be made and the reasons why it is being delayed—for example, a replacement part may have to be ordered to correct the running sound in a bathroom toilet, or
- why you do not feel there is a legitimate problem that justifies rent withholding or other tenant action—for example, point out that the running sound may be annoying, but the toilet still flushes and is usable.

At this point, if you feel the tenant is sincere, you might also consider suggesting that you and the tenant mediate the dispute. If you feel the tenant is trying to concoct a phony complaint to justify not paying the rent, take action to evict him.

Make Your Contractor's Insurance Policy Cover You, Too

As you go about maintaining your rental property, you'll be using outside workers to do everything from fixing minor problems to renovating entire rental units. If you hire a contractor to do extensive work, you should make sure that the contractor has insurance and that it covers you, too. Minor jobs, such as calling a plumber to install a new sink, don't require this level of attention.

Here's the problem you will avoid: Suppose your contractor does a poor job that results in an injury to a tenant or guest. The injured person may sue you, and unless your own insurance policy covers contractors' negligence, you won't be covered. Even if your policy will cover, you'll be better off if you can shift coverage onto the contractor (the fewer claims others make on your policy, the better). The way to do this is to require contractors to do the following:

- Before work begins (and ideally before you sign a contract with the contractor), have the contractor add you as an "additional insured" to the contractor's commercial general liability policy. As an additional insured, you will be covered in case someone makes a claim on the policy based on actions of the contractor at your work site.

- Require the contractor to give you a "certificate of insurance," which will prove that the contractor has the insurance and that you were added. Ask for an "ACORD 25" form, which the insurance company should supply.

- Get a copy of the policy and make sure that the work you're having the contractor do is covered by the policy. Be sure that the name on the policy is the same name the contractor is using on the work contract with you.

- In your written contract with the contractor, include a clause like the following: "Contractor will have a commercial general liability insurance policy of at least [dollar amount] per occurrence and [dollar amount] aggregate in effect as of the date contractor begins work. Contractor will maintain the policy throughout the duration of the job, and will promptly notify [owner's name] of any diminution in coverage or cancellation. In the event of any claim, this policy will apply as primary insurance. Contractor will provide additional insurance for any work that requires additional insurance. Contractor will not begin work until Contractor has given [owner's name] a satisfactory certificate of insurance."

Tenant Updates and Landlord's Regular Safety and Maintenance Inspections

In addition to a thorough and prompt system for responding to problems after they have been brought to your attention, you should establish a good, nonintrusive system of frequent and periodic maintenance inspections. In short, encouraging your tenants to promptly report problems as they occur should not be your *sole* means of handling your maintenance and repair responsibilities. Here's why: If the tenant is not conscientious, or if he simply doesn't notice that something needs to be fixed, the best reporting system will not do you much good. To back it up, you need to force the tenant (and yourself) to take stock at specified intervals. In the sections below, we'll explain the tenant update system and the landlord's annual safety inspection. Make sure your lease or rental agreement and move-in letter cover these updates and inspections as well.

Tenant's Semiannual Safety and Maintenance Update

You can (nicely) insist that your tenants think about and report needed repairs by giving them a Semiannual Safety and Maintenance Update on which to list any problems in the rental unit or on the premises—whether it's low water pressure in the shower, peeling paint, poor ventilation, or noisy neighbors. Asking tenants to return this Update twice a year should also help you in court if you are up against a tenant who is raising a false implied warranty of habitability defense, particularly if the tenant did not note any problems on his most recently completed Update. As with the Resident's Maintenance/Repair Request form, be sure to note how you handled the problem on the bottom of the form. A sample Semiannual Safety and Maintenance Update is shown above and the Nolo website includes a downloadable copy. See Appendix B for the link to the forms in this book.

Landlord's Annual Safety Inspection

Sometimes, even your pointed reminder (by use of the Semiannual Update) that safety and maintenance issues need to be brought to your attention will not do the trick: If your tenant can't recognize a problem even if it stares him in the face, you'll never hear about it, either. In the end, you must get into the unit and inspect for yourself.

You should perform an annual "safety and maintenance inspection" as part of your system for repairing and maintaining the property. For example, you might make sure that items listed on the Semiannual Safety and Maintenance Update—such as smoke detectors, heating and plumbing systems, and major appliances—are in fact safe and in working order. If a problem develops with one of these items, causing injury to a tenant, you may be able to defeat a claim that you were negligent by arguing that your periodic and recent inspection of the item was all that a landlord should reasonably be expected to do.

In many states, you have the right to enter a tenant's home for the purpose of a safety inspection. This does not mean, however, that you can just let yourself in unannounced. All states that allow for inspections require advance notice; some specify 24 hours, others simply state that the landlord must give "reasonable notice." To be on the safe side, check your state's statutes and, if all that is required is "reasonable notice," allow 24 hours at least.

What should you do if your tenant objects to your safety inspection? If your state allows landlords to enter for this purpose (and if you have given adequate notice and have not otherwise abused your right of entry by needlessly scheduling repeated inspections), the tenant's refusal is grounds for eviction. If your state does not allow the landlord to enter and inspect the dwelling against the tenant's will, you have a problem. Even if your own lease or rental agreement provision allows for inspections, the provision may be considered illegal and unenforceable. Also, evicting a tenant because she refused to allow such an inspection might constitute illegal retaliatory eviction.

There may be, however, a practical way around the uncooperative tenant who bars the door. Point out that you take your responsibility to maintain the property very seriously. Remind her that you'll be checking for plumbing, heating, electrical, and structural problems that she might not notice, which could develop into bigger problems later if you're not allowed to check them out. Most tenants will not object to yearly safety inspections if you're courteous about it—giving plenty of notice and trying to conduct the inspection at a time convenient for the tenant. (You might offer to inspect at a time when she is home, so that she can see for herself that you will not be nosing about her personal items.)

Tenant Responses to Unfit Premises: Paying Less Rent

If you fail to live up to your legal duty to maintain your property, your tenants may have a variety of legal responses, each one designed to pressure you into compliance. Hopefully, you will run your business in such a way that your tenants will have no reason to take legal action. But even the most conscientious landlord may encounter a tenant who attempts to avoid his responsibility to pay the rent by claiming that the premises are unfit. If you are a victim of a scam like this, you'll need to know how to defend yourself.

Your tenants' options will probably include one or more of what we call the "big sticks" in a tenant's self-help arsenal. These include:

- withholding the rent
- repairing the problem (or having it repaired by a professional) and deducting the cost from the rent
- calling state or local building or health inspectors
- moving out, or
- paying the rent and then suing you for the difference between the rent the tenant paid and the value of the defective premises.

If you haven't fixed a serious problem that truly makes the rental unit uninhabitable—rats in the kitchen, for example—you can expect that a savvy tenant will use one or more of these options. In this section, we'll explain the two options that involve paying less rent; we'll explain the others below.

Tenants cannot use these options unless three conditions are met:

- **The problem is serious, not just annoying, and imperils the tenant's health or safety.** Not every building code violation or annoying defect in a rental home (like the water heater's ability to reach only 107 degrees F, short of the code-specified 110 degrees) justifies use of a "big stick" against the landlord.
- **The tenant told you about the problem and gave you a reasonable opportunity to get it fixed, or the minimum amount of time required by state law, but you failed to fix it.** In some states, you are given a statutorily specified amount of time (ten days to three weeks is common); in others, you must respond within a reasonable time under the circumstances.
- **The tenant (or a guest) caused the problem, either deliberately or through carelessness or neglect.** If so, the tenant's use of one of the self-help options won't be upheld.

Rent Withholding

If you have not met the responsibility of keeping your property livable, your tenant may be able to stop paying rent until the repairs are made. Called rent withholding or rent escrowing, most states have established this option by statute or have authorized the same by court decision; some cities also have ordinances allowing it. See "State Laws on Rent Withholding and Repair and Deduct Remedies," in Appendix A. Rent withholding can be done *only* in states or cities that have specifically embraced it.

The term "withholding" is actually a bit misleading, since in some states and cities a tenant can't simply keep the rent money until you fix the problem. Instead, tenants often have to deposit the withheld rent with a court or a neutral third party or escrow account set up by a local court or housing agency until the repairs are accomplished.

Some states that allow rent withholding do so in a roundabout way, by giving tenants an "affirmative defense" to an eviction action if they have not paid the rent due to seriously substandard conditions and have been sued for eviction. In these states, tenants can defend against the eviction by arguing that the landlord's failure to maintain a fit and habitable rental excused them from the duty to pay rent. If the judge or jury sides with the tenant, they will defeat the landlord's lawsuit.

Before a tenant can properly withhold the rent, (by using a formal escrow procedure, or by not paying the rent and expecting to defend an eviction lawsuit by mounting an affirmative defense), three requirements must be met:

- The lack of maintenance or repair has made the dwelling unlivable.
- The problems were not caused by the tenant or his guest, either deliberately or through neglect.
- You've been told about the problem and haven't fixed it within a reasonable time or the minimum amount required by state law.

In addition, under most rent withholding laws, tenants cannot withhold rent if they are behind in the rent or in violation of an important lease clause. In short, tenants who use this drastic measure need to be squeaky clean.

Typical Rent Withholding Requirements

If rent withholding is allowed in your state or city, check the law to find out:

- what circumstances justify rent withholding (normally, only significant health and safety problems justify the use of the remedy, but statutes vary as to the particulars)
- whether the tenant must give you a certain amount of notice (ten to 30 days is typical) and time to fix the defect, or whether the notice and response time simply be "reasonable" under the circumstances

- whether the tenant must ask a local court for permission to withhold rent, provide compelling reasons why the rental is not livable, and follow specific procedures, and
- whether the tenant must place the unpaid rent in a separate bank account or deposit it with a court or local housing agency, and how this is done.

Illegal Lease Clauses: Don't Limit Your Tenant's Right to Withhold the Rent Under State Law

Some landlords insert clauses in their leases and rental agreements purporting to prohibit a tenant from withholding the rent, even if a property is uninhabitable. In many states, the rent withholding law itself makes this practice flatly illegal. But even where a state statute or court decision does not specifically disallow this side step, these clauses may be tossed out if a tenant nevertheless withholds rent and you attempt to evict him for nonpayment of rent. Why? Because a judge will approve a tenant's waiver of his right to withhold rent only if his "waiver" has been the subject of real negotiations between him and you, and not something you have insisted upon unilaterally. If you gave your tenant a preprinted lease (with a habitability waiver) and told him to take it or leave it, a judge is likely to decide that the so-called "waiver" was in fact imposed by you and, consequently, invalid. In short, your attempt to take away the right to use this option may be worthless.

What Happens to the Rent?

While repairs are being made, the tenant may continue to pay the entire rent to the court or housing authority or may be directed to pay some rent to you and the balance to the court or housing authority. If the rent money is being held by a court or housing authority, you can sometimes ask for release of some of the withheld rent to pay for repairs. When the dwelling is certified as fit by the local housing inspectors or the court, any money in the account is returned to you, minus court costs and inspection fees.

If your state's withholding law does not require the tenant to escrow the rent and a court has not been involved, the tenant may make his own arrangements as to what to do with the money. Careful tenants (who want to prove that they are not withholding rent simply because they do not have the money) will devise their own escrow set-up, by placing the rent in an attorney's trust account or a separate bank account dedicated solely for that purpose.

Rogue Rent Withholding: Without Legal Authority

In states that don't permit withholding by either statute or court decision, tenants may nevertheless attempt to reduce the rent on their own. For example, if the water heater is broken and you haven't fixed it despite repeated requests, your tenant may decide to pay a few hundred dollars less per month, figuring that a cold-water flat is only worth that much.

Can you terminate and evict a tenant who gives you a short rent check in a state that has not authorized rent withholding? In some states, the answer is yes. In others, however, a tenant's partial withholding may survive an eviction lawsuit, especially if the defects were significant and your failure to fix them flagrant and long-standing. The wise course is not to gamble—if you lose the eviction lawsuit, you may get hit with the tenant's court costs and attorney fees. Attend to maintenance problems before they escalate into rent wars.

Once you have made the repairs, you'll undoubtedly expect full payment of the withheld rent. But don't be surprised if your tenant argues that he should be compensated for having had to live in substandard conditions. He may want a retroactive reduction in rent, starting from the time that the premises became uninhabitable. (Some states limit tenants to a reduction starting from the time you were notified of the problem.)

Reducing the rent is also known in legalese as rent "abatement" or "recoupment."

Your tenant may press for a retroactive rent abatement through a court process or through negotiation with you. The following section describes how a judge will determine how much you should compensate your tenant for the inconvenience of having lived in a substandard rental unit. If a court is not involved, you and the tenant can use this same system in your own negotiations.

Determining the Value of a Defective Rental Unit

How does a judge determine the difference between the withheld rent and what a defective, unlivable unit was really worth? There are two widely used ways.

Figuring the market value. In some states, statutes or court cases say that if you've left the unit in a defective condition, all you're entitled to is the fair market value of the premises in that condition. For example, if an apartment with a heater normally rented for $1,200 per month, but was worth only $600 without operable heating, you would be entitled to only $600 a month from the escrowed funds. Of course, the difficulty with this approach—as with many things in law—is that it is staggeringly unrealistic. An apartment with no heat in winter has *no* market value, because no one would rent it. As you can see, how much a unit is worth in a defective condition is extremely hard to determine.

By percentage reduction. Another slightly more sensible approach is to start by asking what part of the unit is affected by the defect, and then to calculate the percentage of the rent attributable to that part. For example, if the roof leaked into the living room of a $1,500-a-month apartment, rendering the room unusable, a tenant might reduce the rent by the percentage of the rent attributable to the living room. If the living room were the main living space and the other rooms were too small to live in comfortably, the percentage of loss would be much greater than it would be in more spacious apartments. Obviously, this approach is far from an exact science, either.

EXAMPLE: When Henry and Sue moved into their apartment, it was neat and well-maintained. Soon after, the building was sold to an out-of-state owner, who hired an off-site manager to handle repairs and maintenance. Gradually, the premises began to deteriorate. At the beginning of May, 15 months into their two-year lease, Henry and Sue could count several violations of the building code, including the landlord's failure to maintain the common areas, remove the garbage promptly, and fix a broken water heater.

Henry and Sue sent numerous requests for repairs to their landlord over a two-month period, during which they gritted their teeth and put up with the situation. Finally they had enough and checked out their state's rent withholding law. They learned a tenant could pay rent into an escrow account set up by their local court. Henry and Sue went ahead and deposited their rent into this account.

During the time that they lived in these uninhabitable conditions, Henry and Sue were not required to pay full rent. Using the "market value" approach, the court decided that their defective rental was worth half its stated rent. Accordingly, since the landlord owed them a refund for portions of their rent for May and June, Henry and Sue would be paid this amount from the escrow account.

The balance of the rent in the account would be released to the landlord (less the costs of the escrow and the tenants' attorney fees), but only when the building inspector certified to the court that the building was up to code and fit for human habitation.

Henry and Sue could continue to pay 50% of the rent until needed repairs were made and certified by the building inspector.

Repair and Deduct

If you let your rental property fall below the fit and habitable standard, tenants in many states may be able to use a legal procedure called "repair and deduct." It works like this: Under certain conditions the tenant can, without your permission and without filing a lawsuit, have the defect repaired and subtract the cost of the repairs from the following month's rent. The repair and deduct remedy is available only if state or local law has authorized it.

Like the rent withholding option described above, the repair and deduct remedy cannot be invoked at whim. Instead, most states have established specific criteria a tenant must meet before legally qualifying to use the repair and deduct procedures: The defect must either be inexpensive, involve an essential service, or both (depending on the wording of the statute); and the subject of the repair must clearly be the landlord's responsibility. Let's look more closely at these requirements.

Repairs Must Qualify

A few states allow the repair and deduct remedy for minor repairs only, such as a leaky faucet or stopped-up sink. In most states there is a dollar limit or a specific percentage of the month's rent—for example, $300 or less than one-half the monthly rent, whichever is greater.

Most states allow tenants to use the repair and deduct remedy only for essential services, such as the procuring of heat and water or for conditions that materially affect the habitability of the premises, safety of the tenant, or terms of the lease. For example, in Massachusetts, a tenant can spend up to four months' rent, but only for health code violations certified by an inspector. (Mass. Gen. Laws ch. 111, § 127L.) Some states allow the remedy to be used in either situation.

> **EXAMPLE:** On a chilly November evening, the pilot light for Larry's heater failed. He called his building manager, who promised to fix it soon. After calling the manager several more times to no avail and suffering through three frigid days with no heat, Larry called a heater repair person, who came promptly and replaced the broken mechanism for $150. Since Larry lives in a state that allows the repair and deduct remedy, Larry deducted $150 from his next rent check and gave his manager the repair bill.

Repairs Must Be Your Responsibility

A tenant cannot use the rent deduction method to fix a defect or problem that was caused by the careless or intentional act of the tenant or a guest of the tenant. Thus, a tenant cannot use this remedy to replace a window he broke himself. Also, since in most states the tenant is required to keep the dwelling as clean and orderly as the premises permit, he cannot use the remedy if the problem is traceable to his carelessness or unreasonable use of the property.

You Must Be Notified of the Problem

Before using the repair and deduct remedy, the tenant must notify you of the problem. He need not, however, inform you that he intends to utilize the remedy if you fail to respond. Each state has its own procedures and timeline for notification. Generally, the tenant's notice must be in writing. However, in some states the law simply requires that the tenant give the landlord or manager "reasonable" notice of the problem (this could be orally or in writing).

You Must Be Given Time to Fix the Problem

Statutes often give you a specified amount of time to make needed repairs before a tenant can legally use the repair and deduct remedy. For nonemergency repairs, this is typically within ten to 14 days of being notified by the tenant in writing. In the case of an emergency (such as a hole in the roof or a defective heater in winter), you must respond promptly. However, in some states no time limits are given; instead, you must make the repairs in a reasonable time.

There's a Limit to How Much Rent the Tenant Can Deduct

In states that allow the repair and deduct remedy, the amount the tenant deducts is always limited to the actual and reasonable amount spent on the repair. In addition, many states impose a dollar limit on tenants' repairs. In Hawaii, for example, the tenant may withhold up to $500; in Arizona, the amount the tenant withholds must be less than $300 or an amount equal to one-half the periodic rent, whichever is greater. And in California, a

tenant is limited to deducting one month's rent to make repairs. In most states, tenants must present an itemized accounting for the work when using this remedy and presenting less than a full month's rent.

There's a Limit to Use of the Repair and Deduct Remedy

Many states limit how often tenants may pursue this option—for example, no more than once or twice in any 12-month period. Just because a tenant has used up his ability to utilize the remedy does not mean, however, that a landlord who has refused to fix a problem can ignore it. The tenant can still invoke any of the other remedies described in this chapter: rent withholding, filing a lawsuit in small claims court, or moving out.

There Are Other Negative Effects of Repair and Deduct

A tenant's use of the repair and deduct remedy can have unpleasant consequences. The tenant may not hire a skilled, reasonably priced repair person who does the job just as you would have done. Consequently, the chances for a needlessly expensive job or a shoddy one are great. Careful adherence to the high-quality maintenance system described below should help you avoid this fate.

> **EXAMPLE:** When Matt opened the cupboard underneath his bathroom sink, he saw that the flexible hose connecting the pipe nipple to the sink was leaking. He turned off the water and called his landlord, Lee, who promised to attend to the problem right away. After three days without a bathroom sink, Matt called a plumber, who replaced the hose for $100. Matt deducted this amount from his next rent check. Lee thought no more about this until he got a frantic call from the tenant in the apartment beneath Matt's. She described her ceiling as looking like a giant, dripping sponge. Lee called his regular plumber to check the problem out. His plumber told Lee that the repair on Matt's sink had been done negligently, resulting in a major leak into the walls. If Lee had called his own plumber, the job would have been done right in the first place, saving Lee lots of money and hassle.

Sample Letter Suggesting Compromise on Rent Withholding

May 3, 20xx

Tyrone McNab
Villa Arms, Apt. 4
123 Main Street
Cleveland, Ohio 44130

Dear Mr. McNab:

I am writing you in the hope that we can work out a fair compromise to the problems that led you to withhold rent. You have rented a unit at the Villa Arms for the last three years, and we have never had a problem before. Let's try to resolve it.

To review briefly, on May 1, Marvin, my resident manager at Villa Arms, told me that you were temporarily withholding your rent because of several defective conditions in your apartment. Marvin said you had asked him to correct these problems a week ago, but he hasn't as yet attended to them. Marvin states that you listed these defects as some peeling paint on the interior wall of your bedroom, a leaky kitchen water faucet, a running toilet, a small hole in the living room carpet, and a cracked kitchen window.

I have instructed Marvin to promptly arrange with you for a convenient time to allow him into your apartment to repair all these problems. I am sure these repairs would already have been accomplished by now except for the fact that Hank, our regular repair person, has been out sick for the last ten days.

I understand that these problems are annoying and significant to you, and I acknowledge that they should have been attended to more promptly. However, I do not believe that they justify rent withholding under state law. Rent withholding is allowed only when the defects make the premises unfit for habitation. I do not think, however, that in the long run either one of us would be well served by stubbornly standing on our rights or resorting to a court fight. My first wish is to come to an amicable understanding with you that we can live with and use to avoid problems like this in the future.

Because of the inconvenience you have suffered as a result of the problems in your apartment, I am prepared to offer you a prorated rebate on your rent for ten days, this being the estimated length of time it will have taken Marvin to remedy the problems from the day of your complaint. As your monthly rent is $900, equal to $30 per day, I am agreeable to your paying only $600 rent this month.

If this is not acceptable to you, please call me at 555-1234 during the day. If you would like to discuss any aspect of the situation in more detail, I would be pleased to meet with you at your convenience. I will expect to receive your check for $600, or a call from you, before May 10.

Sincerely,

Sandra Schmidt

Sandra Schmidt
Owner, Villa Arms

A tenant's use of repair and deduct will also complicate (or frustrate) your accounts. You should be tracking maintenance costs in order to itemize them on your Schedule E tax return. But when tenants use repair and deduct, you have no receipt (with your name on it), and no direct way to prove the expense (short of arguing that the lowered rent reflects that expense). Keep things straightforward by paying for repairs yourself.

Your Options If a Tenant Withholds, Reduces, or Repairs and Deducts Rent

When confronted with a tenant who does not pay all or part of the rent, many landlords almost reflexively turn to a lawyer to bring an eviction lawsuit. But even if you eventually get the tenant evicted (and you may not, if the judge finds the tenant's rent withholding was justified), it is usually only after considerable cost. This is appropriate in some circumstances, especially when the tenant is clearly wrong and simply throwing legal sand in the air in an effort to obscure the fact that he can't or won't pay rent. But it's important to realize that tenants can fall into at least two other categories:

- tenants who have some right on their side— that is, the needed repairs or maintenance should have been done more promptly, and
- tenants who sincerely thought they had the right to withhold or repair and deduct rent, but who overreacted to the problem or just did the wrong thing under the law.

How you react when a tenant reduces, repairs and deducts, or withholds rent should depend on which category the tenant fits into. The following sections look at your options depending on the three categories: obvious troublemakers, mistaken but sincere tenants who are worth salvaging, and tenants who had some justification for using the remedy they chose.

Obvious Troublemakers

If you keep your rental properties in good shape and properly handle repair and maintenance

problems, your best bet may be to promptly and legally terminate the tenancy of any tenant who pays you less or no rent.

If you're heading for court, you may need to consult a lawyer or do some legal research first on your state's laws on evictions. If you do end up in court, be prepared to prove the following:

- The claimed defect was nonexistent, and nothing justified the tenant's failure to pay the rent.
- The tenant caused the defect himself in order to avoid paying rent.
- The claimed defect was not really serious or substantial enough to give the tenant the right to pursue a particular remedy, such as rent withholding.
- Even if the defect was substantial, you were never given adequate notice and a chance to fix it. (At this point you should present a detailed complaint procedure to the court as we recommend above. You should show, if possible, that the tenant didn't follow your complaint procedure.)
- The tenant failed to comply with some other aspect of the rent withholding law. For example, in states that require the tenant to place the withheld rent in escrow with the court, a tenant's failure to do so may defeat her attempt to use the procedure at all. A tenant who repeatedly failed to use the escrow procedure might be a candidate for eviction.

! CAUTION
If in doubt, hold off on eviction. Sometimes it's hard to know if a tenant is truly a bad apple or just badly confused as to her legal rights. Until you are sure the tenant fits into the first category (had absolutely no good reason to reduce, withhold, or repair and deduct rent), don't try to evict the tenant. Under the law of virtually every state, retaliatory evictions are penalized, often severely—that is, you may not evict a tenant in retaliation for his asserting a particular right, such as the right to withhold rent or complain to governmental authorities about health or safety problems.

Mistaken But Sincere Tenants

If you think the tenant is wrong, but sincere—that is, she probably isn't trying to make up an excuse for not paying rent, but nevertheless is clearly not legally eligible to abate, withhold rent, or repair and deduct—your best course is usually to try and work things out with the tenant in a face-to-face meeting. If, for example, the tenant used the repair and deduct remedy, but you were never given adequate legal notice (and would have had the problem fixed for $50 less if you had been), it may make sense to accept the tenant's solution but make sure the tenant knows how to notify you of the problems in the future. It may be painful to make this sort of compromise, but it is not nearly as bad as trying to evict the tenant and risking that a judge might even agree with her course of action.

The chances for resolving a conflict will be greater if you have a compromise system in place when you need it. When you find yourself dealing with a tenant who is not an obvious candidate for eviction (and especially if the tenant has some right on her side, as discussed below), consider taking the following steps:

1. Meet with the tenant (or tenants) and negotiate. You should be interested in establishing a good solution to avoid problems in the future and not in determining who was "right."
2. If negotiation fails, suggest mediation by a neutral third party. Check out how this works in advance so you can move quickly should the need arise again.
3. Put your solution in writing.
4. If the process indicates a larger problem with tenant dissatisfaction, encourage the tenant or tenants to meet with you regularly to solve it.

In many cases, it may be possible for you and the tenant to come to a mutually acceptable agreement using this system. On your end, this might mean promptly having the necessary work done and better maintaining the unit in the future. You might also give the tenant a prorated reduction in rent for the period between the time the tenant notified you of the defect and the time it was corrected. In exchange, the tenant might promise to promptly notify you of problems before resorting to the same tactic in the future.

> **EXAMPLE:** A leaky roof during a rainy month deprives a tenant, Steve, of the use of one of his two bedrooms. If Steve gave his landlord, Joe, notice of the leak, and Joe did not take care of the problem quickly, Steve might be justified in deducting $300 from the $800 rent for that month. However, if Steve didn't tell Joe of the problem until the next month's rent was due, a compromise might be reached where Steve bears part of the responsibility, by agreeing to deduct only $100 from the rent.

The first step in working toward a compromise with the tenant who uses rent abatement, withholding, or repair and deduct is to call him. If you're reluctant to call, you might want to try a letter. See the sample letter above suggesting a compromise on rent withholding.

Tenants Who Are Partially Right

Sometimes, despite your best efforts to keep on top of repair and maintenance issues, a repair job falls through the cracks. It could happen while you are on vacation and your backup system doesn't work, or maybe you simply need a better manager. If, in all fairness, a tenant was justified in using rent withholding or repair and deduct, admit it and take steps to rectify the situation. For example, after getting the necessary work done, you might try to make use of the compromise procedure outlined above. Once the immediate problem is behind you, treat what happened as an opportunity to review, revise, and improve your maintenance and repair procedures:

- **Complaint procedure.** Do you have a complaint system that makes it easy for tenants to communicate their concerns? Are complaint forms readily available and easy to use?
- **Tenant education.** Do your tenants know that you intend to respond quickly to repair and maintenance problems? Do you need to remind all tenants, via a tenant notice or newsletter, of your complaint procedure?

- **Management response.** Does management respond reasonably quickly to a tenant's request for repairs?

Earlier in this chapter we provided detailed suggestions for how to set up and implement a maintenance program designed to identify repair needs before they become repair problems.

Tenant Responses to Unfit Premises: Calling Inspectors, Filing Lawsuits, and Moving Out

Tenants who are faced with unfit rentals are not limited to withholding rent or repairing the defects themselves. Other options that do not involve paying less rent include calling government inspectors, breaking the lease and moving out, and suing in small claims court.

Reporting Code Violations to Housing Inspectors

A tenant may complain to a local building, health, or fire department about problems such as inoperable plumbing, a leaky roof, or bad wiring. If an inspector comes out and discovers code violations, you will be given an order to correct the problem. Fines and penalties usually follow if you fail to comply within a certain amount of time (often five to 30 business days). If there's still no response, the city or county may sue you. In many cities, your failure to promptly fix cited violations of local housing laws is a misdemeanor (minor crime) punishable by hefty fines or even imprisonment. In rare cases, especially if tenants' health is imperiled, local officials may even require that the building be vacated.

In many areas, getting reported to a building inspector is a very big deal—an inspector who finds lots of problems can force you to clear them up immediately. But there is wide variation as to the effectiveness of building inspectors. In some cities, there are very few inspectors compared to the number of tenant complaints, and courts are

largely unable to follow up on the properties that are cited. But chances are that if the complaint procedure proves ineffective, your tenant will turn to a more effective option, such as filing a lawsuit or moving out.

Severe Code Violations Will Close Your Building

If a judge decides that a building's condition substantially endangers the health and safety of its tenants, and repairs are so extensive they can't be made while tenants inhabit the building, the result may be an order to vacate the building. You usually won't have a chance to come to the court hearing to object to this dire consequence—your tenants will simply be told to get out, sometimes within hours.

In some states, you must pay for comparable temporary housing nearby. Some statutes also make you cover moving expenses and utility connection charges and give the original tenant the first chance to move back in when the repairs are completed. To find out whether you'll be liable for relocation expenses, check your state statutes (listed in "State Landlord-Tenant Statutes" in Appendix A). Look in the index to your state's codes under "Landlord-Tenant" for subheadings such as "Relocation Assistance" or "Padlock Orders."

Lawsuits by the Tenant

A consumer who purchases a defective product—be it a car, a hair dryer, or a steak dinner—is justified in expecting a minimum level of quality, and is entitled to compensation if the product is seriously flawed. Tenants are consumers, too, and may remain in possession of the premises and still sue you for the following:

- partial or total refund of rent paid while the housing conditions were substandard
- the value, or repair costs, of property lost or damaged as a result of the defect—for example, furniture ruined by water leaking through the roof

- compensation for personal injuries—including pain and suffering—caused by the defect, and
- attorney fees.

In some states, tenants may also seek a court order—similar to a rent withholding scheme—directing you to repair the defects, with rent reduced until you show proof to the court that the defects have been remedied.

⊘ **CAUTION**

You may not retaliate against a tenant who files a lawsuit and stays on the property. (See Chapter 16 for a discussion of retaliatory eviction.) It may seem inconsistent for a tenant to take the extreme step of suing you and expecting to remain on the property. Nevertheless, a tenant who sues and stays is exercising a legal right. Retaliation, such as delivering a rent increase or a termination notice, is illegal and will give the tenant yet another ground on which to sue.

Moving Out

If a tenant's dwelling isn't habitable and you haven't fixed it, he also has the right to move out—either temporarily or permanently. These drastic measures are justified only when there are truly serious problems, such as the lack of essential services or the total or partial destruction of the premises. Tenants may also use these options if environmental health hazards such as lead paint dust make the unit uninhabitable.

Tenant's Right to Move Out When the Unit Is Uninhabitable

The 49 states (and the District of Columbia) that require you to provide habitable housing allow tenants to move out if you don't do your job. Depending on the circumstances, tenants may move out permanently, by terminating the lease or rental agreement, or temporarily. This approach is borrowed directly from consumer protection laws. Just as the purchaser of a seriously defective car may sue to undo the contract or return the car for a refund, tenants can consider the housing contract terminated and simply return the rental unit to you if the housing is unlivable.

The law, of course, has a convoluted phrase to describe this simple concept. It's called "constructive eviction," which means that, by supplying unlivable housing, you have for all practical purposes "evicted" the tenant. A tenant who has been constructively evicted (that is, he has a valid reason to move out) has no further responsibility for rent.

Your state statute may have specific details, such as the type of notice tenants must provide before moving out because of a major repair problem. You may have anywhere from five to 21 days to fix the problem, depending on the state and, sometimes, the seriousness of the situation. Check your state law for details.

Temporary moves. In many states, if you fail to provide heat or other essential services, tenants may procure reasonable substitute housing during the period of your noncompliance. They may recover the costs (as long as they're reasonable) of substitute housing up to an amount equal to the rent.

Permanent moves. A tenant who moves out permanently because of habitability problems may also be entitled to money from you to compensate them for out-of-pocket losses. For example, the tenant may be able to recover for moving expenses and the cost of a hotel for a few days until they find a new place. Also, if the conditions were substandard during prior months when the tenant did pay the full rent, you may be sued for the difference between the value of the defective dwelling and the rent paid. In addition, if the tenant is unable to find comparable housing for the same rent, and ends up paying more rent than they would have under the old lease, you may be on the hook for the difference.

> **EXAMPLE:** Susan signed a one-year lease for a beachfront apartment. She thought it was a great deal because the monthly rent of $700 was considerably less than similar properties in the neighborhood.

Susan's dream of an apartment began to turn into a nightmare when she discovered, soon after moving in, that the bedroom was full of mildew that attacked every surface and interfered with her breathing. After numerous complaints to the landlord, which were ignored, Susan moved out at the end of four months and rented a comparable apartment nearby for $800. She then sued the landlord for the following:

- **Compensation for the months she had endured the defective conditions.** Susan asked for the difference between the agreed-upon rent and the real value of the apartment (the apartment with its defects), times four (the number of months she paid rent).

- **The benefit of her bargain.** Susan pointed out that the rent for the first apartment was a real bargain, and that she had been unable to find a similar apartment for anything less than $800 per month. She asked for the added rent she will have to pay ($100) times eight, the number of months left on her original lease.

- **Moving costs.** Susan asked for the $250 cost of hiring a moving company to transport her belongings to her new home.

After hearing Susan's arguments and the landlord's feeble defense, the judge decided that Susan was entitled to:

- **Compensation for past problems.** The mildew problem, which had forced Susan to sleep in the living room, had essentially reduced the one-bedroom apartment to a studio apartment, which would have rented for $400 per month. Accordingly, Susan was entitled to a refund of $300 for each of the four months, or $1,200.

- **The benefit of her bargain.** The judge acknowledged that a similar apartment, such as the one she rented when she moved out, cost $100 more per month than the one she had originally rented, and awarded her that amount per month times eight, or $800.

- **Moving costs.** The judge ruled that Susan's moving costs of $250 were reasonable, and ordered the landlord to pay them.

Tenant's Right to Move Out When There Is Damage to the Premises

A tenant whose home is significantly damaged—either by natural disaster or any other reason beyond his responsibility or control—has the right to consider the lease at an end and to move out. Depending on the circumstances of the damage and the language in your lease or rental agreement, however, everyone may not be able to simply walk away from the lease or rental agreement with no financial consequences. A tenant may have the legal right to your assistance with substitute housing or living expenses. Obviously, the tenant whose rental unit is destroyed by a natural disaster has less reason to expect resettlement assistance from you than one whose home is destroyed by fire caused by your botching an electrical repair job. And the tenant whose home burns down because he left the stove on all night will probably find himself at the other end of a lawsuit.

Natural or third-party disasters. State laws vary on the extent of your responsibility depending on the cause of the damage. If a fire, flood, tornado, earthquake, or other natural disaster renders the dwelling unlivable, or if a third party is the cause of the destruction (for instance, a fire due to an arsonist), your best bet is to look to your insurance policy for help in repairing or rebuilding the unit. While waiting for the insurance coverage to kick in, give month-to-month tenants a termination notice (typically 30 days' notice is required). In some cases, you may be required by law to pay the tenant for substitute housing for 30 days. With tenants who have a lease, you may be obligated to pay for substitute housing for a longer period until the tenant finds a comparable replacement. To be prudent, raise the issue of tenant assistance with your insurance broker at the time the policy is purchased so that you know exactly where you stand if a disaster strikes.

Destruction that is traceable to the landlord. If it can be shown that you or your employees were even partially responsible for the damage, your legal responsibility to the tenant is likely to increase.

You may be expected to cover a longer period of temporary housing, and, if the substitute housing is more expensive, you may be stuck with paying the difference between the new rent and the old rent. The insurance issue will also take on a different cast: Some policies exclude coverage for natural disasters, but include (as is standard) coverage for the owner's negligent acts. The facts surrounding the property damage or destruction, applicable state law, and the wording of your insurance policy will determine how each situation is handled.

If a tenant moves out due to damage or destruction of the premises, for whatever cause, it will be important for you and the tenant to sign a written termination of the rental agreement or lease once the tenant is relocated, see the sample Landlord-Tenant Agreement to Terminate Lease in Chapter 8. This allows you to proceed with the repair or rebuilding without the pressure of tenants waiting to move in immediately. If you want to rerent to the same tenant, a new lease or rental agreement can be drawn up at that time.

Minor Repairs

You are much more likely to face tenants' minor complaints—such as leaky faucets, temperamental appliances, worn carpets, noisy heaters, hot water heaters that produce too little hot water—than major problems that make a unit unlivable. To avoid hassles with tenants over minor repairs, you may delegate responsibility to a tenant—particularly one who is especially reliable and handy. "Delegating Landlord's Responsibilities to Tenants," below, shows how to delegate minor repairs and maintenance.

You have different legal duties depending on whether a problem is major (affecting the habitability of the rental unit) or minor. Major jobs are yours, period. Minor repair and maintenance includes:

- small plumbing jobs, like replacing washers and cleaning drains
- system upkeep, like changing heating filters
- structural upkeep, like replacing excessively worn flooring

- small repair jobs, like fixing broken light fixtures or replacing the grout around bathtub tile, and
- routine repairs to and maintenance of common areas, such as pools, spas, and laundry rooms.

Most often, minor repairs are your job. But you are not required to keep the rental premises looking just like new—ordinary wear and tear does not have to be repaired during a tenancy. (When the tenant moves out, however, the cost of dealing with ordinary wear and tear will fall on you and cannot come out of the security deposit.) And if the tenant or one of his guests caused a minor repair problem, carelessly or intentionally, the tenant is responsible for repairing it—or, if your lease or rental agreement prohibits him from doing so, paying you to do it.

If the tenant had nothing to do with the repair problem, and it's not a cosmetic issue, chances go way up that you are responsible, for one of the following reasons:

- A state or local building code requires you to keep the damaged item (for example, a kitchen sink) in good repair.
- A state or local law specifically makes it your responsibility.
- Your lease or rental agreement provision or advertisement describes or lists particular items, such as hot tubs, trash compactors, and air conditioners; by implication, this makes you responsible for maintaining or repairing them.
- You made explicit promises when showing the unit—for example, regarding the security or air conditioning system.
- You made an implied promise to provide a particular feature, such as a whirlpool bathtub, because you have fixed or maintained it in the past.

Each of these reasons is discussed below. If you're not sure whether or not a minor repair or maintenance problem is your responsibility, scan the discussion to find out.

Building Codes

States (and sometimes cities) write building codes that cover structural requirements, such as roofs, flooring, and windows, and essential services, such as hot water and heat. If your tenant's repair request involves a violation of the building code, you may be facing a habitability problem, as discussed above. But building codes often cover other, less essential, details as well. For example, codes may specify a minimum number of electrical outlets per room; if a broken circuit breaker means that there are fewer working outlets, the consequence is probably not an unfit dwelling, but you are still legally required to fix the problem.

Landlord-Tenant Laws

Some state laws place responsibility for specific minor repairs and maintenance on the landlord. A common example is providing garbage receptacles and arranging for garbage pick-up. Many states have their own special rules. In Alaska, for example, the law makes landlords responsible for maintaining appliances supplied by them. (Alaska Stat. § 34.03.100.)

In many states, renters of single-family residences may agree to take on responsibilities that would otherwise belong to the landlord, such as disposing of garbage. For details, check your state's landlord-tenant codes under "State Landlord-Tenant Statutes," which are listed in Appendix A.

Promises in the Lease or Rental Agreement

When it comes to legal responsibility for repairs, your own lease or rental agreement is often just as important (or more so) than building codes or state laws. If your written agreement describes or lists items such as drapes, washing machines, swimming pools, saunas, parking places, intercoms, or dishwashers, you must provide them in decent repair. And the promise to provide them carries with it the implied promise to maintain them.

Promises in Ads

If an advertisement for your unit described or listed a feature, such as a cable TV hookup, especially if the feature is emphasized, you must follow through with these promises, even if your written rental agreement says nothing about the feature. Items such as dishwashers, clothes washers and dryers, garbage disposals, microwave ovens, security gates, and Jacuzzis must be repaired by you if they break through no fault of the tenant.

Promises Made Before You Rented the Unit

It's a rare landlord or manager who refrains from even the slightest bit of puffing when showing a rental to a prospective tenant. It's hard to refrain from announcing rosy plans for amenities or services that haven't yet materialized ("We plan to redo this kitchen—you'll love the snappy way that trash compactor will work!"). Whenever you make promises like these, even if they're not in writing, your tenant can legally hold you to them.

Implied Promises

Suppose your rental agreement doesn't mention a garbage disposal, and neither did any of your advertising. And you never pointed it out when showing the unit. But there is a garbage disposal, and it was working when the tenant moved in. Now the garbage disposal is broken—do you have to fix it? Many courts will hold you legally responsible for maintaining all significant aspects of the rental unit. If you offer a unit that *already has* certain features—light fixtures that work, doors that open and close smoothly, faucets that don't leak, tile that doesn't fall off the wall—many judges reason that you have made an implied contract to keep them in workable order throughout the tenancy.

The flip side of this principle is that when your tenant has paid for a hamburger, the waiter—you—doesn't have to deliver a steak. In other words, if the rental was shabby when the tenant moved in, and you never gave the tenant reason to believe that it would be spruced up, he has no legal right to demand improvements—unless, of course, he can point to health hazards or code violations. As when you offer secondhand goods "as is" for a low price, legally your buyer/tenant is stuck with the deal.

Another factor that is evidence of an implied contract is your past conduct. If you have consistently fixed or maintained a particular feature of a rental, such as a dishwasher, you have an implied obligation to continue doing so.

Tenant Options If Landlord Refuses to Make Minor Repairs

If you have determined that the repair problem is minor and falls fairly in your lap, it's wise to attend to it promptly. Although your tenant's health and safety may not be immediately imperiled (as is true with major repairs), you don't want to court disaster. For example, the repair may be minor now but have the potential to become major and expensive; there may be a potential for injury and liability; or the problem may affect other renters, presenting the unpleasant possibility of a cadre of disgruntled tenants.

If you refuse to fix a minor problem that is your responsibility, your tenant has several options. He may:

- fix it himself
- report you to the housing inspectors, if the problem involves a code violation
- attempt to use one of the legal options designed for habitability problems, such as rent withholding or repair and deduct
- break the lease and move out, or
- sue you, usually in small claims court.

Some of these responses are appropriate, and others may not be—we'll explain why below. But keep in mind that even if a tenant improperly responds, your being in the right may be an illusory victory. Legal disputes—in court or out—are expensive and time-consuming. Unless the tenant is a whining prima donna who demands constant, unnecessary repairs, it's usually wiser to fix the problem and nip the issue in the bud.

Fixing the Problem Themselves

Your exasperated tenant might strap on his tool belt and fix the minor problem himself. If he's handy and has used the proper procedures and materials, you may come out ahead. But you have no way of gauging his expertise, and there is always the possibility that the tenant will do a slipshod job, either negligently or through spite.

> **EXAMPLE:** Colin decided to replace a window that was broken by his son's basketball. He removed the shards of glass, fitted a new pane in place and caulked the circumference. He did not, however, paint the caulk; a year later it had cracked, allowing rainwater to seep onto the windowsill and down the wall. His landlord Sarina was furious when she realized that she would have to replace the sill and the drywall, simply because Colin had not done a workmanlike job. The cost of these repairs exceeded Colin's security deposit, and Sarina had to sue him in small claims court for the balance, which she had a hard time collecting.

Reporting Code Violations

If the minor repair problem constitutes a code violation, such as inadequate electrical outlets or low water pressure, your tenant may find an ally in the building or housing agency in charge of enforcing the code. Whether the tenant will get an effective response from the agency will depend on the seriousness of the violation, the workload of the agency, and its ability to enforce its compliance orders. Since by definition the problem is minor, it's unlikely to get much action, especially if code enforcement officials are already overworked. But his complaint will remain on file, which is a public record that may come back to haunt you.

EXAMPLE: Randall was a successful landlord who owned several properties. A rotten and poorly supported deck at one of his apartment houses collapsed, killing one tenant and injuring several others. Randall was sued by the injured tenants and the family of the deceased for intentionally violating building codes when constructing the deck. Local news coverage made much of the fact that he had been cited numerous times for minor code violations; this publicity made it extremely difficult for him to get a fair trial. The jury found in favor of the plaintiffs and awarded them several million dollars. Because this tragedy was not the result of Randall's negligence, but rather an expected consequence of deliberately ignoring proper building procedures, Randall's insurance company refused to cover the award. Randall was forced to declare bankruptcy.

Using Rent Withholding or Repair and Deduct

Tenants often make the mistake of using these powerful remedies, usually reserved for major habitability problems, for minor repairs. If your tenant has done so, you should be able to terminate and evict for nonpayment of rent. Be sure to read your state's statute or other authority carefully to make sure that there's no way your tenant can justify his action under your state's withholding or repair and deduct laws.

Breaking the Lease

A disgruntled tenant may decide it's not worth putting up with your unwillingness to handle minor repairs and may simply break the lease and move out. A defect that is truly minor does not justify this extreme step. But being in the right does you little good here—in most states, you'll have to take reasonable steps to rerent and credit the new rent to the departed tenant's responsibility for the balance of the rent. The fact that he left because he didn't like the squeaky closet door does not relieve you of this duty.

Suing in Small Claims Court

Be it ever so minor, your tenant is entitled to get what he paid for—and if he doesn't, he might decide to sue in small claims court. Small claims court judges usually won't order you to paint, fix the dishwasher, or repair the intercom. The judge may, however, order that the tenant be compensated in dollars for living in a rental unit with repair problems, on the theory that the tenant is not getting the benefit of what he's paying rent for—for example, a functioning dishwasher, presentable paint, or a working air conditioner. You may be ordered to pay the tenant an amount that reflects the difference between his rent and the value of the unit with repair problems. To calculate this amount, the judge will use one of the methods described above in "Tenant Responses to Unfit Premises."

How much of a threat is a small claims suit likely to be? A judge is not going to adjust the rent because a little grout is missing from the bathroom tile. But if the dishwasher is broken, three faucets leak noisily, and the bathroom door won't close, your tenant's chances of winning go way up.

Delegating Landlord's Responsibilities to Tenants

You may want to delegate some repair and maintenance responsibilities to the tenants themselves—perhaps you live at a distance and the tenant is particularly responsible and handy. Is this legal? Courts in each state have faced this question and have come to several different conclusions. While we cannot offer a countrywide analysis of each state's position, here are the basics.

Do Not Delegate Responsibility for Major Repairs and Maintenance to the Tenant

By law, housing must be habitable, because society has decided that it is unacceptable for landlords to offer substandard dwellings. For this reason, the implied warranty of habitability and the covenant of quiet enjoyment cannot be waived by a tenant in most states. In other words, even though the tenant may be willing to live in substandard housing, society has decided that it will not tolerate such conditions.

It is a small but logical step to the next question of whether you can delegate to the tenant the responsibility of keeping the premises fit for habitation. Many courts have held that you cannot, fearing that the tenant will rarely be in the position, either practically or financially, to do the kinds of repairs that are often needed to bring a structure up to par.

Even if you do have the legal right, it is always a mistake to try and delegate to a tenant your responsibility for major maintenance of essential services, such as heat, plumbing, or electricity, or repairs involving the roof or other parts of the building structure. And remember, even inexpensive jobs can have enormous repercussions if done poorly. For instance, replacing an electrical outlet seems simple, but the results of an improper job (fire or electrocution) can be devastating. Think twice before entrusting sensitive jobs to people who are not experts.

How to Delegate Minor Repairs and Maintenance to Tenants

Delegating minor repairs is usually a different issue. Under the law of some states, and as a matter of sensible practice in all states, you may delegate minor repairs and maintenance responsibilities to the tenant—such as mowing the lawn, trimming the bushes, and sweeping the lobby—without making the tenant responsible for keeping the structure habitable. Practically speaking, however, you must be willing to check to see if the work is done properly. If you wish to delegate responsibilities to a tenant, be advised that, as far as any *other* tenants are concerned (and probably with respect to the living space of the tenant-repairperson, too), your delegation of certain maintenance and repair duties to one tenant does not relieve you of the ultimate responsibility for meeting state and local health and safety laws.

Always remember that the implied warranty of habitability makes you responsible for maintenance of common areas—for example, cleaning hallways and mowing the lawn. If you transfer this duty to someone who fails to do it, the transfer will not shield you if you are hauled into court for failure to maintain the premises. On the other hand, if you monitor the manner in which the job is being done and step in and get it done right if the tenant does a poor job, there should be no practical problems.

Repair and maintenance arrangements between landlords and tenants often lead to dissatisfaction—typically, the landlord feels that the tenant has neglected certain tasks, or the tenant feels that there is too much work for the money. When a court is asked to step in, the validity of the arrangement will typically be judged along the following lines:

- **Was it in writing?** Any agreement as to repairs or maintenance should be written and signed, either as part of the lease or rental agreement (see Clause 12 of the form agreements in Chapter 2), or as a separate employment agreement (discussed below).

- **Was it a fair bargain?** You must adequately pay the tenant for the services provided. Often, this payment consists of a reduction in rent. A judge may look askance at a $50 reduction in monthly rent for 20 hours of work, which represents a pay scale well below the minimum wage.

- **Is it fair to other tenants?** Some courts will also inquire as to whether your agreement adversely affects your obligations to other tenants. For example, if your tenant-maintenance person does his job poorly or only now and then, the other tenants will have to live with his spotty performance.

- **Have you treated the delegation separately from your other duties as the landlord?** The agreement you have with your tenant has nothing to do with your other responsibilities. For example, if you and your tenant agree that she will do gardening work in exchange for a reduction in rent, and you feel that she is not doing a proper job, you may not respond by shutting off her water or retaliating in other ways. The proper recourse is to discuss the problem with the tenant and, if it persists, to cancel the arrangement.

① CAUTION

Be careful delegating repairs involving hazardous materials. The simplest repair may actually create an environmental health hazard, which may open you to liability on three fronts: You may be sued by the exposed tenant, sued by other tenants who might also be affected, and cited by the relevant regulating agency for allowing an untrained or uncertified person to work on toxic materials. For example, preparing a surface for a seemingly innocuous paint job may actually involve the creation of lead-based paint dust, and the quick installation of a smoke alarm could involve the disturbance of an asbestos-filled ceiling. Handling and disposal of toxic materials is highly regulated, and violations may subject you to significant fines.

Landlords May Be Able to Delegate More Repair Responsibilities to Single-Family Residences

In several states, the landlord and tenant of a single-family dwelling may agree in writing that the tenant is to perform some of the landlord's statutory duties—to arrange for garbage receptacles and garbage disposal, running water, hot water, and heat—in addition to making other specified repairs. States allowing this type of delegation typically require that the transaction be entered into in good faith—meaning that each side completely understands their rights and responsibilities, and neither pressures the other. In addition, the work must usually not be necessary to cure the landlord's failure to substantially comply with health and safety codes.

Although the possibility for delegation is greater in some single-family rental situations than it is in a multiunit context, we caution owners of single-family rental properties to think carefully before entering into an arrangement of this type. Unless you are very sure about the skill and integrity of your tenant, the possibilities for shoddy work and disagreements are as great as they are in any rental situation, and indeed the consequences (poor work done to an entire house) may be greater.

Compensating a Tenant for Repair and Maintenance Work

Paying an on-site tenant to do repair and maintenance tasks, such as keeping hallways, elevators, or a laundry room clean or maintaining the landscaping, is preferable to giving the tenant a reduction in rent for work performed. Why? Because if the job is not done right, you can simply cancel the employment arrangement, rather than having to amend the lease or rental agreement in order to reestablish the original rent. By paying the tenant separately, there will be no question that he is still obligated to pay the full rent as he has done all along.

You May Have to Pay Federal and State Tax on Your Tenant-Repairperson

Paying your handy tenant $100 per month, or reducing his rent by this amount, in exchange for maintenance and repair duties may have important tax consequences for you. That person may be considered your "employee" (as distinguished from an independent contractor). If you "pay" the person more than a certain amount per year, either in cash or in the form of a rent reduction, you may be obliged to pay Social Security and meet other legal obligations as an employer. These obligations are covered in the Chapter 6 discussion of compensating a tenant-manager.

Landlord Liability for Tenant Repair and Maintenance Work

The delegation of basic repair and maintenance work to a tenant may not relieve you of liability if the repair is done poorly and someone is injured or property is damaged as a result.

Of course, you could always try to recoup your losses by suing that tenant (called "seeking indemnity" in legalese), but your chances of recovery will be slim unless your tenant has sufficient monetary assets. On the other hand, a maintenance or repair service will generally carry its own insurance (you should confirm this before you engage their services).

The cruelest cut of all could be the ability of the tenant-repair person to sue you if he is injured performing the repair tasks. The tenant could argue that you had no business entrusting a dangerous job to someone whose expertise was not proven—and, in some courts and in front of some juries, he might prevail. A carefully written exculpatory clause might shield you from liability in some situations, but you can never be 100% sure that the clause will be upheld in court. Exculpatory clauses are explained in Chapter 10.

> **EXAMPLE:** Clem, the landlord, hired Tom, the teenage son of a longtime tenant, for yard work. Part of Tom's job consisted of mowing the two front lawns, which were separated by a gravel walkway. Tom cut the first lawn and, without turning off the mower, pushed it over the gravel to the second lawn. Pieces of gravel were picked up by the blades and fired to the side, where they struck and partially blinded a child playing in the next yard. Clem was sued and faced an uphill battle with his insurance company as to whether Tom's negligence was covered under Clem's policy.

Tenants' Alterations and Improvements

Your lease or rental agreement probably includes a clause prohibiting tenants from making any alterations or improvements without your express, written consent, see Clause 12 of our lease or rental agreement forms in Chapter 2. For good reason, you'll want to make sure tenants don't change the light fixtures, replace the window coverings, or install a built-in dishwasher unless you agree first.

But in spite of your wish that your tenants leave well enough alone, you're bound to encounter the tenant who goes ahead without your knowledge or consent. On the other hand, you may also hear from an upstanding tenant that she would, indeed, like your consent to her plan to install a bookshelf or closet system. To know how to deal with unauthorized alterations or straightforward requests, you'll need to understand some basic rules.

 RELATED TOPIC
Tenants with disabilities have rights to modify their living space that may override your ban against alterations without your consent. See Chapter 5 for details.

Improvements That Become Part of the Property (Fixtures)

Anything your tenant attaches to a building, fence, or deck or the ground itself (lawyers call such items "fixtures") belongs to you, absent an agreement saying it's the tenant's. This is an age-old legal principle, and, for good measure, it's wise to spell it out in your lease or rental agreement. This means when the tenant moves out, you are legally entitled to refuse her offer to remove the fixture and return the premises to its original state.

When a landlord and departing tenant haven't decided ahead of time as to who will own the fixture, the dispute often ends up in court. Judges use a variety of legal rules to determine whether an object—an appliance, flooring, shelving, or plumbing—is something that the tenant can take with her or is a permanent fixture belonging to you. Here are some of the questions judges ask when separating portable from nonportable additions:

- **Did your tenant get your permission?** If the tenant never asked you for permission to install a closet organizer, or she did and got no for an answer, a judge is likely to rule for you—particularly if your lease or rental agreement prohibits alterations or improvements.

- **Did the tenant make any structural changes that affect the use or appearance of the property?** If so, chances are that the item will be deemed yours, because removing it will often leave an unsightly area or alter use of part of the property. For example, if a tenant modifies the kitchen counter to accommodate a built-in dishwasher and then takes the dishwasher with her, you will have to install another dishwasher of the same dimensions or rebuild

Agreement Regarding Tenant Alterations to Rental Unit

_____Iona Lott_____ [Landlord]

and ____Doug Diep_____ [Tenant]

agree as follows:

1. Tenant may make the following alterations to the rental unit at: ____75A Cherry Street, Pleasantville,___

    ___North Dakota_____

    ___1. Plant three rose bushes along walkway at side of residence._____

    ___2. Install track lighting along west (ten-foot) kitchen wall._____

    _____

    _____

    _____

    _____

    _____.

2. Tenant will accomplish the work described in Paragraph 1 by using the following materials and procedures:

    ___1. Three bare-root roses, hybrid teas, purchased from Jackson-Perky and____

    _____planted in March._____

    ___2. "Wallbright" track lighting system purchased from "Lamps and More," plus____

    _____necessary attachment hardware._____

    _____

    _____

    _____.

3. Tenant will do only the work outlined in Paragraph 1 using only the materials and procedures outlined in Paragraph 2.

4. The alterations carried out by Tenant:

    ☒ will become Landlord's property and are not to be removed by Tenant during or at the end of the tenancy, or

    ☐ will be considered Tenant's personal property, and as such may be removed by Tenant at any time up to the end of the tenancy. Tenant promises to return the premises to their original condition upon removing the improvement.

5. Landlord will reimburse Tenant only for the costs checked below:

    ☒ the cost of materials listed in Paragraph 2

    ☒ labor costs at the rate of $ _____25_____ per hour for work done in a workmanlike manner acceptable to Landlord, up to _____10_____ hours.

6. After receiving appropriate documentation of the cost of materials and labor, Landlord shall make any payment called for under Paragraph 5 by:

   ☑ lump sum payment, within _____10_____ days of receiving documentation of costs, or

   ☐ by reducing Tenant's rent by $ _____ per month for the number of months necessary to cover the total amounts under the terms of this agreement.

7. If under Paragraph 4 of this contract the alterations are Tenant's personal property, Tenant must return the premises to their original condition upon removing the alterations. If Tenant fails to do this, Landlord will deduct the cost to restore the premises to their original condition from Tenant's security deposit. If the security deposit is insufficient to cover the costs of restoration, Landlord may take legal action, if necessary, to collect the balance.

8. If Tenant fails to remove an improvement that is his or her personal property on or before the end of the tenancy, it will be considered the property of Landlord, who may choose to keep the improvement (with no financial liability to Tenant), or remove it and charge Tenant for the costs of removal and restoration. Landlord may deduct any costs of removal and restoration from Tenant's security deposit. If the security deposit is insufficient to cover the costs of removal and restoration, Landlord may take legal action, if necessary, to collect the balance.

9. If Tenant removes an item that is Landlord's property, Tenant will owe Landlord the fair market value of the item removed plus any costs incurred by Landlord to restore the premises to their original condition.

10. If Landlord and Tenant are involved in any legal proceeding arising out of this agreement, the prevailing party shall recover reasonable attorney fees, court costs, and any costs reasonably necessary to collect a judgment.

Iona Lott _____   _February 10, 20xx_ _____
Landlord   Date

Doug Diep _____   _February 10, 20xx_ _____
Tenant   Date

the space. The law doesn't impose this extra work on landlords, nor does it force you to let tenants do the return-to-original work themselves.

- **Is the object firmly attached to the property?** In general, additions and improvements that are nailed, screwed, or cemented to the building are likely to be deemed "fixtures." For example, hollow-wall screws that anchor a bookcase might convert an otherwise free-standing unit belonging to the tenant to a fixture belonging to you. Similarly, closet rods bolted to the wall become part of the structure and would usually be counted as fixtures. On the other hand, shelving systems that are secured by isometric pressure (spring-loaded rods that press against the ceiling and floor) involve no actual attachment to the wall and, for that reason, are not likely to be classified as fixtures.

Improvements That Plug or Screw In

The act of plugging in an appliance doesn't make the appliance a part of the premises. The same is true for simple connectors or fittings that join an appliance to an electrical or water source. For example, a refrigerator or freestanding stove remains the property of the tenant. Similarly, portable dishwashers that connect to the kitchen faucet by means of a coupling may be removed.

- **What did you and the tenant intend?** Courts will look at statements made by you and the tenant to determine whether there was any understanding as to her right to remove an improvement. In some circumstances, courts will even infer an agreement from your actions—for instance, if you stopped by and gave permission for your tenant to install what you referred to as a portable air conditioner, or helped her lift it into place. By contrast, if the tenant removes light fixtures and, without your knowledge, installs

a custom-made fixture that could not be used in any other space, it is unlikely that the tenant could convince a judge that she reasonably expected to take it with her at the end of her tenancy.

Responding to Improvement and Alteration Requests

If a tenant approaches you with a request to alter your property or install a new feature, chances are that your impulse will be to say no. Don't be too hasty—as you'll see below, requests for telecommunications access (cable access, satellite dishes, and antennas) are governed by special rules. As for other types of requests, perhaps the question comes from an outstanding tenant whom you would like to accommodate and would hate to lose. Instead of adopting a rigid approach, consider these alternatives.

Option One. Is the improvement or alteration one that is easily undone? For example, if your tenant has a year's lease and you plan to repaint when she leaves, you can easily fill and paint any small holes left behind when she removes the bookshelf bolted to the wall (and you can bill her for the spackling costs, as explained below). Knocking out a wall to install a wine closet is a more permanent change and not one you're likely to agree to.

Option Two. Is the improvement or alteration an enhancement to your property? For example, a wine closet might actually add value to your property. If so, depending on the terms of the agreement you reach with your tenant, you may actually come out ahead.

Before you accommodate your tenant's requests, decide which option makes sense in the circumstances and which you prefer. For example, you may have no use for an air conditioner attached to the window frame, and your tenant may want to take it with her. You'll need to make sure that she understands that she is responsible for restoring the window frame to its original condition, and that if her restoration attempts are less than acceptable, you will be justified in deducting from her security deposit the amount of money necessary to do the job right. (And if the deposit is insufficient, you can sue her in small claims court for the excess.) On the other hand, a custom-made window insulation system may enhance your property (and justify a higher rent later on) and won't do your tenant any good if she takes it with her. Be prepared to hear your tenant ask you to pay for at least some of it.

If you and the tenant reach an understanding, put it in writing. As shown in the sample Agreement Regarding Tenant Alterations to Rental Unit, above (and included as a download on the Nolo website— see Appendix B for the link), you will want to carefully describe the project and materials, including:

- whether the improvement or alteration is permanent or portable
- the terms of the reimbursement, if any, and
- how and when you'll pay the tenant, if at all, for labor and materials.

Our agreement makes it clear that the tenant's failure to properly restore the premises, or removal of an alteration that was to be permanent, will result in deductions from her security deposit or further legal action if necessary.

Cable TV Access

If your building is already wired for cable, tenants who want to sign up need only call the cable provider to activate the existing cable line to their unit. But what if you do *not* have cable access available already? And what if you have a contract with one provider, but a tenant wants another?

Congress has decreed that all Americans should have as much access as possible to information that comes through a cable or through wireless transmissions. (Federal Telecommunications Act of 1996, 47 U.S. Code §§ 151 and following.) The Act makes it very difficult for state and local governments, zoning commissions, homeowners' associations, or landlords to restrict a person's ability to take advantage of these types of communications.

Previously Unwired Buildings

If your property does not have cable, you may continue to say no to tenants who ask you for access. But don't be surprised if, in response, your tenant mounts a satellite dish on the balcony, wall, or roof. We discuss your ability to regulate these devices below.

Exclusive Contracts With Cable Providers

The FCC has ruled that in every state, exclusive contracts that you may have with cable companies are unenforceable, and exclusive clauses in existing contracts will not be enforced. So any exclusive clauses you may now have in your contracts are unenforceable, and you may not enter into any new ones. You do *not*, however, have to let any cable company who asks into your building.

Hosting Competing Cable Companies in Multiunit Buildings

Several cable companies may now be competing for your tenants' business. Until recently, adding a cable provider meant letting that company run cable from the street all the way to each rental unit that signed up for the provider's service. The initial section of that cable run, a large cable called the riser, runs from the street to a ground-level utility closet and up to the utility closets on each floor. Adding this cable is not a big deal. But the second leg, called the "home run" portion, consists of wires that run from the riser through hallway ceilings on each floor and toward each individual apartment (the last 12 inches are called "home wires"). Adding a second set of home run wires is expensive and sometimes impossible.

Now, however, you may be able offer the home run part of existing cable to a different cable provider when a tenant asks to switch providers. A federal appellate case covering Colorado, Kansas, New Mexico, Oklahoma, Utah, and Wyoming has held that when a cable company no longer services a customer in a multiunit building, the building owner has the right to ask the provider to share the home run portion of their cable with a competitor, unless the owner's contract with the cable company gives the company the right to maintain unused cable. (*Time Warner Entertainment Co., L.P. v. Everest*, 381 F.3d 1039 (2004).) Courts in other states will probably follow this ruling, though they are not bound by it.

CAUTION

Don't confuse "forced access" with your rights as a landlord. Forced access refers to the technology that lets consumers choose from among several Internet Service Providers (ISPs) when they subscribe to a cable modem-based broadband service. The argument around forced access is between cable providers and ISPs. Many require cable companies to provide open access to ISPs.

If you have a contract with a cable provider and would like to invite competitors to service tenants who want alternate service, check the contract carefully for language covering maintenance of the cables the provider installed. Look for clauses that give the company the right to maintain and control cables irrespective of whether they're currently used. You may want to review the contract with your attorney. When you negotiate future contracts, keep these points in mind:

- Get rid of language that gives the provider the right to control or maintain inside wiring (including home run wiring) after the contract with you or any individual tenant expires.
- Be sure that you get control of unused home run wiring at the expiration of your contract or when a tenant decides to discontinue service. This will explicitly give you the right to offer it to a competitor. If the cable provider really wants your business, it may agree that unused home run wires will be deemed abandoned. Or, you may have to buy the wires from the provider.

TIP

Require telecom companies to label their cables when they bring them into your building. Under the National Electrical Code and FCC regulations, telecoms must remove, abandon, or sell their cables when their license with you is up. If they refuse to do so—or if they're bankrupt—you'll have to do it. To make sure you can identify the abandoned risers (the large cables that run from the street to utility closets) and don't mistakenly cut current risers, require companies to label them with permanent, weatherproof tags, and to give you an as-built diagram that will be amended if the company does any further work during the license term.

Satellite Dishes and Antennas

Wireless communications have the potential to reach more people with less hardware than any cable system. But there is one, essential piece of equipment: A satellite dish with wires connecting it to the television set or computer.

You may be familiar with the car-sized dishes often seen in backyards or on roofs of houses—the pink flamingo of the new age. Now, smaller and cheaper dishes, two feet or less in diameter, are available. Wires from the dishes can easily be run under a door or through an open window to an individual TV or computer. Predictably, tenants have bought dishes and attached them to roofs, windowsills, balconies, and railings. Landlords have reacted strongly, citing their unsightly looks and the potential for liability should a satellite dish fall and injure someone below.

Fortunately, the Federal Communications Commission (FCC) has provided considerable guidance on residential use of satellite dishes and antennas ("Over-the-Air Reception Devices Rule," 47 CFR § 1.4000, further explained in the FCC's Fact Sheet, "Over-the-Air Reception Devices Rule"). Basically, the FCC prohibits landlords from imposing restrictions that unreasonably impair your tenants' abilities to install, maintain, or use an antenna or dish that meet criteria described below. Here's a brief overview of the FCC rule.

RESOURCE

For details on the FCC's rule on satellite dishes and antennas, see www.fcc.gov/guides/installing-consumer-owned-antennas-and-satellite-dishes or call the FCC at 888-CALL-FCC (toll free; 888-TELL-FCC for TTY). The FCC's rule was upheld in *Building Owners and Managers Assn. v. FCC*, 254 F.3d 89 (D.C. Cir. 2001).

Devices Covered by the FCC Rule

The FCC's rule applies to video antennas, including direct-to-home satellite dishes that are less than one meter (39.37 inches) in diameter (or any size in Alaska); TV antennas; and wireless cable antennas. These pieces of equipment receive video programming signals from direct broadcast satellites, wireless cable providers, and television broadcast stations. Antennas up to 18 inches in diameter that transmit as well as receive fixed wireless telecom signals (not just video) are also included.

Exceptions: Antennas used for AM/FM radio, amateur ("ham") and Citizen's Band ("CB") radio, or Digital Audio Radio Services ("DARS") are excluded from the FCC's rule. You may restrict the installation of these types of antennas, in the same way that you can restrict any modification or alteration of rented space.

Permissible Installation of Satellite Dishes and Antennas

Tenants may place antennas or dishes only in their own, exclusive rented space, such as inside the rental unit or on a balcony, terrace, deck, or patio. The device must be wholly within the rented space (if it overhangs the balcony, you may prohibit that placement). Also, you may prohibit tenants from drilling through exterior walls, even if that wall is also part of their rented space.

Tenants *cannot* place their reception devices in common areas, such as roofs, hallways, walkways, or the exterior walls of the building. Exterior windows are no different from exterior walls—for this reason, placing a dish or antenna on a window by means of a series of suction cups is impermissible under the FCC rule (obviously, such an installation is also unsafe). Tenants who rent single-family homes, however, may install devices in the home itself or on patios, yards, gardens, or similar areas.

Restrictions on Satellite Installation Techniques

Landlords are free to set restrictions on how the devices are installed, as long as the restrictions are not unreasonably expensive, or if the restrictions are imposed for safety reasons or, if your property qualifies, to preserve historic aspects of the structure. You cannot insist that your maintenance personnel (or professional installers) do the work.

Expense

Landlords may not impose a flat fee or charge additional rent to tenants who want to erect an antenna or dish. On the other hand, you may be able to insist on certain installation techniques that will add expense—as long as the cost isn't excessive and reception will not be impaired. Examples of acceptable expenses include:

- insisting that an antenna be painted green in order to blend into the landscaping, or
- requiring the use of a universal bracket that future tenants could use, saving wear and tear on your building.

CAUTION

Be consistent in setting rules for tenant improvements. Rules for mounting satellite dishes or antennas shouldn't be more restrictive than those you establish for artwork, flags, clotheslines, or similar items. After all, attaching these telecommunications items is no more intrusive or invasive than bolting a sundial to the porch, screwing a thermometer to the wall, or nailing a rain gauge to a railing. For general guidance, see the discussion above, of "Tenants' Alterations and Improvements."

Safety Concerns

You can insist that tenants place and install devices in a way that will minimize the chances of accidents and will not violate safety or fire codes. For example, you may prohibit placement of a satellite dish on a fire escape, near a power plant, or near a walkway where passersby might accidentally hit their heads. You may also insist on proper installation techniques, such as those explained in the instructions that come with most devices. What if proper installation (attaching a dish to a wall) means that you will have to eventually patch and paint a wall? Can you use this as a reason for preventing installation? No—unless you have legitimate reasons for prohibiting the installation, such as a safety concern. You can, however, charge the tenant for the cost of repairing surfaces when the tenant moves out and removes the device.

> **TIP**
>
> **Require tenants who install antennas or dishes to carry renters' insurance.** If a device falls or otherwise causes personal injury, the policy will cover a claim. See "Renters' Insurance" in Chapter 2 for more information.

Preserving Your Building's Historical Integrity

It won't be easy to prevent installation on the grounds that doing so is needed to preserve the historical integrity of your property. You can use this argument only if your property is included in (or eligible for) the National Register of Historic Places, the nation's official list of buildings, structures, objects, sites, and districts worthy of preservation for their significance in American history, architecture, archaeology, and culture. For more information on how to qualify for the Register, see www.cr.nps.gov/nr.

Placement and Orientation of Antennas and Reception Devices

Tenants have the right to place an antenna where they'll receive an "acceptable quality" signal. As long as the tenant's chosen spot is within the exclusive rented space, not on an exterior wall or in a common area as discussed above, you may not set rules on placement—for example, you cannot require that an antenna be placed only in the rear of the rental property if this results in the tenant's receiving a "substantially degraded" signal or no signal at all.

Reception devices that need to maintain line-of-sight contact with a transmitter or view a satellite may not work if they're stuck behind a wall or below the roofline. In particular, a dish must be on a south wall, since satellites are in the southern hemisphere. Faced with a reception problem, a tenant may want to move the device to another location or mount it on a pole, so that it clears the obstructing roof or wall. Tenants who have no other workable exclusive space may want to mount their devices on a mast, in hopes of clearing the obstacle. They may do so, depending on the situation:

- **Single-family rentals.** Tenants may erect a mast that's 12 feet above the roofline or less without asking your permission first—and you must allow it if the mast is installed in a safe manner. If the mast is taller than 12 feet, you may require the tenant to obtain your permission before erecting it—but if the installation meets reasonable safety requirements, you should allow its use.
- **Multifamily rentals.** Tenants may use a mast as long as it does not extend beyond their exclusive rented space. For example, in a two-story rental a mast that is attached to the ground-floor patio and extends into the air space opposite the tenant's own second floor would be permissible. On the other hand, a mast attached to a top-story deck, which extends above the roofline or outward over the railing, would not be protected by the FCC's rule—a landlord could prohibit this installation because it extends beyond the tenant's exclusive rented space.

How to Set a Reasonable Policy on Satellite Dishes and Antennas

Although it's not entirely clear, the FCC appears to have ruled that tenants do not need your permission before installing their antennas or dishes—as long as they have placed them within their exclusive rented space and otherwise abided by the rules explained above. This means that you won't get to review a tenant's plans before the tenant installs a dish or antenna—though you can certainly react if you find that the FCC's standards have not been met.

The smart thing to do is to educate your tenants beforehand, in keeping with the FCC's guidelines, so that you don't end up ripping out an antenna or satellite dish that has been placed in the wrong spot or attached in an unsafe manner. In fact, the FCC directs landlords to give tenants written notice of safety restrictions, so that tenants will know in advance how to comply. We suggest that you include guidelines in your Rules and Regulations, or as an attachment to your lease or rental agreement. For guidance on developing sound policies, see the FCC's website at www.fcc. gov/guides/installing-consumer-owned-antennas-and-satellite-dishes.

Supplying a Central Antenna or Satellite Dish for All Tenants

Faced with the prospect of many dishes and antennas adorning an otherwise clean set of balconies, you may want to install a central antenna or dish for use by all.

You may install a central antenna, and may restrict the use of antennas by individual tenants, only if your device provides all of the following:

- **Equal access.** The tenant must be able to get the same programming or fixed wireless service that tenants could receive with their own antennas.
- **Equal quality.** The signal quality to and from the tenant's home via your antenna must be as good as or better than what they could get using their own devices.

- **Equal value.** The costs of using your device must be the same as or less than the cost of installing, maintaining, and using an individual antenna.
- **Equal readiness.** You can't prohibit individual devices if installation of a central antenna will unreasonably delay the tenant's ability to receive programming or fixed wireless services—for example, when your central antenna won't be available for months.

If you install a central antenna after tenants have installed their own, you may require removal of the individual antennas, as long as your device meets the above requirements. In addition, you must pay for the removal of the tenant's device and compensate the tenant for the value of the antenna.

How to Handle Disputes About Antennas and Satellite Dishes

In spite of the FCC's attempts to clarify tenants' rights to reception and landlords' rights to control what happens on their property, there are many possibilities for disagreements. For example, what exactly is "acceptable" reception? If you require antennas to be painted, at what point is the expense considered "unreasonable"?

Ideally, you can try to avoid disputes in the first place by setting reasonable policies. But, if all else fails, here are some tips to help you resolve the problem with a minimum of fuss and expense.

Discussion, Mediation, and Help From the FCC

First, approach the problem the way you would any dispute—talk it out and try to reach an acceptable conclusion. Follow our advice in Chapter 16 for settling disputes on your own—for example, through negotiation or mediation. You'll find the information on the FCC website very helpful. The direct broadcast satellite company, multichannel distribution service, TV broadcast station, or fixed wireless company may also be able to suggest alternatives that are safe and acceptable to both you and your tenant.

Get the FCC Involved

If your own attempts don't resolve the problem, you can call the FCC and ask for oral guidance. You may also formally ask the FCC for a written opinion, called a Declaratory Ruling. For information on obtaining oral or written guidance from the FCC, follow the directions as shown on the FCC website at www.fcc.gov/guides/installing-consumer-owned-antennas-and-satellite-dishes. Keep in mind that unless your objections concern safety or historic preservation, you must allow the device to remain pending the FCC's ruling.

Go to Court

When all else fails, you can head for court. If the antenna or satellite dish hasn't been installed yet and you and the tenant are arguing about the reasonableness of your policies or the tenant's plans, you can ask a court to rule on who's right (just as you would when seeking the FCC's opinion). You'll have to go to a regular trial court for a resolution of your dispute, where you'll ask for an order called a "Declaratory Judgment." Similarly, if the antenna or dish *has* been installed and you want a judge to order it removed, you'll have to go to a regular trial court and ask for such an order. (Unfortunately, the simpler option of small claims court will not usually be available in these situations, because most small courts handle only disputes that can be settled or decided with money, not court opinions about whether it's acceptable to do—or not do—a particular task.)

Needless to say, going to regular trial court means that the case will be drawn-out and expensive. You could handle it yourself, but be forewarned—you'll need to be adept at arguing about First Amendment law and Congressional intent and be willing to spend long hours in the library or online preparing your case. In the end, you may decide that it would have been cheaper to provide a building-wide dish (or good cable access) for all tenants to use.

Landlord's Liability for Tenant Injuries From Dangerous Conditions

As a property owner, you are responsible for keeping your premises safe for tenants and guests. If you don't meet that responsibility, you can be liable for injuries that are caused, for example, by a broken step or defective wiring. Injured tenants can seek financial compensation for medical bills, lost earnings, pain and other physical suffering, permanent physical disability and disfigurement, and emotional distress. Tenants can also look to you for the costs of property damage that results from faulty or unsafe conditions. In extreme cases, a single personal injury verdict against your business could wipe you out.

If a tenant is injured on your property, contact your insurance company the minute you hear about it (your policy probably requires it). Your agent will tell you what to do next—for example, you may need to write down details of the accident. The majority of claims against landlords are settled without trial, usually though negotiations with your insurance company. If your tenant does file a lawsuit, you'll need to hire a lawyer.

This chapter provides an overview of your liability for tenant injuries. Most important, it offers suggestions on how to avoid injuries and liability through preventive repair and maintenance.

RELATED TOPIC

Related topics covered in this book include:

- Lease and rental agreement provisions covering landlords' and tenants' responsibilities for repairs, damage to premises, and liability-related issues, such as disclosure of hidden defects: Chapter 2
- How to minimize your liability for your property manager's mistakes or illegal acts: Chapter 6
- How to comply with state and local housing laws and avoid safety and maintenance problems and potentially dangerous situations on your rental property: Chapter 9
- Your liability for environmental health hazards: Chapter 11
- Your liability for crime on the premises, including injuries or losses to tenants by strangers or other tenants, and liability for drug dealing on rental property: Chapter 12

- Your liability for nonphysical injuries caused by intentional discrimination (Chapter 5), invasion of privacy (Chapter 13), and retaliatory conduct against the tenant (Chapter 16)
- How to choose a lawyer and pay for legal services: Chapter 18.

When Landlords Have Been Held Liable for Tenant Injuries

Just a few examples of injuries for which tenants have recovered money damages due to the landlord's negligence:

- Tenant falls down a staircase due to a defective handrail.
- Tenant trips over a hole in the carpet on a common stairway not properly maintained by the landlord.
- Tenant injured and property damaged by fire resulting from an obviously defective heater or wiring.
- Tenant gets sick from pesticide sprayed in common areas and on exterior walls without notice.
- Tenant's child is scalded by water from a water heater with a broken thermostat.
- Tenant slips and falls on a puddle of oil-slicked rainwater in the garage.
- Tenant's guest slips on ultraslick floor wax applied by the landlord's cleaning service.
- Tenant receives electrical burns when attempting to insert a stove's damaged plug into a wall outlet.
- Tenant slips and falls on wet grass cuttings left on a common walkway.

How to Prevent Injuries

Preventing an injury is a lot better than arguing about whose fault it was later. Here are steps you can take to protect yourself from lawsuits and hefty insurance settlements—and at the same time make your tenants' lives safer and happier.

Although how to protect against some types of risks may be obvious to you, how to protect against many others won't be. Get help from people who are experienced in identifying and dealing with risks. One excellent resource is your insurance company's safety inspector; your insurance agent can tell you whom to contact. Another good approach is to ask your tenants to identify all safety risks, no matter how small.

Maintain the Property Well

Our first piece of advice is the most obvious, but like a lot of obvious steps, it's often overlooked: Regularly look for dangerous conditions on the property and fix them promptly. Keep an eye out for structural problems, environmental health hazards, and any other dangerous or unsafe conditions that could contribute to an injury. For example, you can head off many trip-and-fall accidents simply by providing good lighting in hallways, parking garages, and other common areas. Keep good records on the dates and details of your property inspections and any follow-up repairs done. Ask your tenants, manager, employees, and insurance company to help you spot problems. When you become aware of a repair problem with an obvious potential for injury, put it on the top of your to-do list. Call in professional inspectors when the potential for injury or damage is great—for example, consult a structural engineer, not your handyman or even your general contractor, if you're not sure about the soundness of your fireplace or chimney.

Comply With Building Codes

Local and state health, safety, and building codes may prescribe very specific requirements for you. For example, electrical codes specify how much of a load you may place on individual circuits; building codes tell you how sturdy your deck piers must be. Once you establish basic compliance with these rules, you can't just forget about them. Because they change occasionally, stay current by reviewing them at least once a year. If your structure and the way you maintain it are up to code, you should avoid most lawsuits based on your violation of a statute.

Warn of Dangers You Can't Fix

If there are problems that you cannot control and eliminate, such as the presence of environmental hazards, educate your tenants to the dangers and their need to follow safety procedures. You have a duty to warn tenants and others about naturally occurring dangers (such as loose soil) and man-made dangers (like low doorways or steep stairs) that may not be obvious but which you know (or should know) about. Disclose hidden defects in your lease or rental agreement (see Clause 20 of the agreements in Chapter 2), or include a section in a move-in letter (Chapter 7), so that it can never be claimed that a tenant was not warned of a dangerous condition. If appropriate, also post warning signs near the hazard.

> **EXAMPLE:** Towering eucalyptus trees lined the side and back yards of the duplex Jack and Edna owned. During windy weather, the trees often dropped big strips of bark and branches. Realizing this, Jack and Edna warned their tenants to steer clear of the trees during windy spells. As an extra precaution, they included a written warning to this effect in a move-in letter to new tenants and posted signs near the trees.

Solicit and Respond Quickly to Tenants' Safety Complaints

As explained in "Responding to Tenant Complaints" in Chapter 9, make sure tenants know that you are always receptive to a legitimate concern regarding building safety. Respond appropriately—a sticky front door lock that still works might merit having the locksmith come the next day; a broken lock deserves the 24-hour locksmith.

Back your policy up with a good record-keeping system. Doing so will help you should you be challenged later. For example, suppose a tenant notifies you of a loose step. As soon as possible, you should post warning tape and signs, and arrange to have it repaired soon. Writing in your records that the loose step will be fixed tomorrow by your handyman, and noting that you placed the tape and signs, and advised your tenant to take an alternate staircase, will show that you did all that was reasonably necessary. If the tenant disregards your advice and uses the stairs anyway, you'll be able to show that you acted prudently and should not be responsible for any injuries that he suffered as a result of his decisions.

Install and Maintain Basic Safety Features

Make sure your property is well-equipped with smoke detectors, fire extinguishers, good interior lighting, and ample outside lighting. Candidly appraise the security situation around your property, and improve protection if the conditions warrant it. Chapter 12 discusses liability for criminal acts on the property.

Don't Allow Dangerous Pets

It's not common, but you could be liable for the injuries caused by a tenant's pet, be it a common household companion or exotic animal.

An injured person would have to show that you:

1. actually knew (or, in view of the circumstances, must have known) of the animal's dangerous propensities, and
2. could have prevented the injury.

Fear of liability is not a reason to impose a blanket no-pets rule; cases against landlords are actually very rare. But just as you keep an eye on other dangerous conditions on the property, be aware of the potential for injury from pets. If a tenant does have a demonstrably dangerous pet, he has caused a legal nuisance, and you can require that the tenant get rid of the animal or face eviction. In Chapter 9, see "Don't Allow Nuisances."

> ! CAUTION
> **Don't let tenants keep wild animals.**
> Legally, keeping wild animals is generally considered an "ultrahazardous activity." You will be presumed to know of the dangerous aspects of a wild animal as soon as you learn that it's on the property. So if your tenant keeps a monkey and you know (or should know) about it, a court will assume

that you understood the danger, and you may be liable if the animal causes injury and you failed to take steps to prevent it.

Remove Dangers to Children

If children are drawn onto your property due to an irresistibly interesting (to children) but dangerous feature, such as a stack of building materials or an abandoned refrigerator or well (known in legal jargon as an "attractive nuisance"), you must exercise special care. If the danger can be cleaned up or removed (like a pile of junk or an abandoned refrigerator), do so. If not, place physical barriers that will keep children away from it. Warning signs aren't enough—young children can't read, and all children tend to ignore warnings.

Even if you don't create a dangerous situation yourself, but allow a tenant to do so, you may also be legally liable. For example, a tree house that your tenant builds in the backyard or a play structure that parents buy for their own children might attract other neighborhood children. If one of them falls from the tree or structure and is injured, you could be liable because you let the attractive nuisance remain on your property.

> **EXAMPLE:** An apartment building owner took great pride in the fishpond in the courtyard. The yard was accessible to the general public, and neighborhood children frequently came to watch the fish. When one child fell in and nearly drowned, the child's parents sued the landlord. The landlord was found liable for the child's accident on the grounds of negligence—the landlord should have known that the fishpond was dangerous and that unsupervised children could come onto the property and fall into the pond. The landlord should have gotten rid of the pond or fenced it off so that small children were kept out.

Laws sometimes regulate activities and conditions that are attractive and dangerous to children. For example, laws commonly require the removal of doors from unused refrigerators and the fencing or removal of abandoned cars or piles of junk.

Be sure to inform tenants of your concerns regarding anything that might be attractive and dangerous to children. For example, if the tenant of your single-family home has placed a trampoline on the property, make sure it's behind a sturdy fence so that neighborhood kids don't wander in and use it in a dangerous manner. If it can't be fenced, insist that it be removed.

Take Special Precautions With Swimming Pools

Swimming pools can mean deep trouble because they are so dangerous, and attractive, to children. Many places have laws that require fences around swimming pools and impose construction and height requirements on those fences. Landlords who fail to comply with such fencing requirements are often found liable for tragic drownings.

If your property includes a pool, you must of course comply with all safety laws. You should also take special care to make sure your tenants and their guests appreciate the dangers involved. Remind tenants that they are responsible for the proper supervision of their children. All the fencing in the world will not protect a young child who is left unattended inside a pool enclosure.

Rules requiring constant adult supervision of children and the need to walk carefully on wet, slippery surfaces should be part of any move-in letter and the rules and regulations that are part of your lease or rental agreement. The rules (including a reminder that there is no lifeguard on duty) should be repeated on signs posted near the pool. Pool supply stores are a good source of easy-to-read signs.

Supervise Contractors and Other Workers

If construction work is done on your property, make sure that the contractor and any workers (including your own) in charge of the work secure the site and remove or lock up dangerous tools or equipment whenever the site is left unattended. Remember, a pile of sand or a stack of sheet rock might look like work to an adult, but fun to a child. You might consider sending your tenants written notice of the intended project, suggesting that they take care during the construction period.

Using Exculpatory Clauses to Shield Yourself From Liability

Landlords used to be able to protect themselves from most lawsuits brought by tenants by using a lease clause that absolved the landlord of responsibility for injuries suffered by a tenant, even those caused by the landlord's negligence. Known as "exculpatory clauses," these blanket provisions are now rarely enforced by courts.

In unusual situations, you may want to include a narrowly worded "exculpatory clause" in your lease, to shield yourself from liability for injuries. For example, if you delegate appropriate repair and maintenance duties to a tenant (see Chapter 9 for tips on delegation of repairs), you might want to make it clear that the tenant is not to look to you if he injures himself in the course of his duties. An exculpatory clause, however, will *not* shield you from liability if your tenant injures a third party.

EXAMPLE: Sadie and Hal live in one half of their duplex and rent out the other. They offer Fred, their tenant, a rent reduction if he will be responsible for the upkeep of the lawn. As part of the bargain, Fred agrees to absolve Sadie and Hal of any liability if a defect in the lawn causes him an injury. Because this agreement is the result of good-faith negotiations on both sides, each party receives a benefit from the deal, and the delegated duties (gardening on a small piece of property affecting only the landlords and their one tenant) could safely and reasonably be performed by their tenant, the agreement would likely be upheld if either side challenged it later in court.

When Fred trips on a sprinkler and hurts his ankle, he is bound by the exculpatory clause and cannot sue Sadie and Hal for his injury. But when Mac, a delivery person, slips on wet grass cuttings that Fred carelessly leaves on the walkway, Fred, Sadie, and Hal find themselves at the other end of Mac's personal injury claim.

You can't use an exculpatory clause to shield yourself from all liability; if you're negligent, you're almost certainly going to be held responsible for any tenant injuries that result, no matter what your lease says.

Liability and Other Property Insurance

A well-designed insurance program can protect your rental property from losses caused by many types of perils, including damage to the property caused by fire, storms, burglary, and vandalism. A comprehensive policy will also include liability insurance, covering injuries or losses suffered by others as the result of defective conditions on the property. Equally important, liability insurance covers the cost of settling personal injury claims, including lawyers' bills for defending personal injury lawsuits.

 RELATED TOPIC
"How to Meet Your Legal Repair and Maintenance Responsibilities," in Chapter 9, explains how to make sure you're covered by the insurance policy of any contractor you work with.

Choosing Liability Insurance Coverage

All landlords should buy liability insurance. Advice on property insurance in general and working with an insurance agent are covered below.

Get Enough Coverage!

Liability policies are designed to cover you against lawsuit settlements and judgments up to the amount of the policy limit, including both what you pay the injured person and the lawyers hired to handle the lawsuit. They provide coverage for a host of common perils, such as tenants falling and getting injured on a defective staircase. Liability policies usually state a dollar limit per occurrence and an aggregate dollar limit for the policy year. For example, your policy may say that it will pay up to $300,000 per occurrence for personal injury and a total of $1 million in any one policy year.

Depending on the value of your property and the value of the assets you are seeking to protect, buying more coverage in the form of an "umbrella policy" is a very good idea, especially in large metropolitan areas, where personal injury damage awards can be very high. Umbrella policies are not expensive, because they are rarely called upon—so the premium may be a relatively cheap way to obtain peace of mind, at the very least.

Buy Commercial General Liability Coverage

Commercial General Liability coverage is the broadest type of liability coverage, described just above, that you can purchase. Make sure your liability policy covers not only physical injury but also libel, slander, discrimination, unlawful and retaliatory eviction, and invasion of privacy suffered by tenants and guests. This kind of coverage can be very important in discrimination claims, see Chapter 5.

Buy Non-Owned Auto Liability Insurance

Be sure to carry liability insurance not only on your own vehicles but also on your manager's car or truck if it will be used for business purposes. Non-owned auto insurance will protect you from liability for accidents and injuries caused by your manager or other employee while running errands for you in their own vehicle.

Terrorism Insurance

The huge losses of September 11, 2001 produced a predictable response from insurance companies: They began writing liability and property policies that specifically excluded coverage for losses due to acts of terrorism. Congress reacted by passing the Terrorism Risk Insurance Act (15 U.S. Code §§ 6701 and following) to help ensure that property owners have access to adequate, affordable terrorism insurance. The law requires insurance companies to offer coverage for losses due to acts of terrorism, and to void any clauses in existing policies that exclude coverage. If you want coverage under an existing policy, you are entitled to buy it.

What Liability Insurance Doesn't Cover

Punitive damages are extra monetary awards, above the amount needed to compensate an injured person. They are intended to punish willful or malicious behavior.

As you might expect, insurers would like to be able to exclude punitive damages from coverage, but the industry has never adopted a standard exclusion clause. (Insurance policies are typically made up of canned, commonly used clauses that are used by virtually every insurance company.) If a policy does not specifically state whether or not punitive damages are covered (and most do not), it will be up to the courts of the state where the policyholder lives to decide whether standard policy language covers punitive awards.

States have not been consistent in their treatment of this issue. Courts in some states have ruled that punitive damages are not covered by standard comprehensive liability policies, while others have reached the opposite conclusion. Your insurance agent should be able to tell you how the courts in your state have ruled.

It's clear, however, that intentional harm or violations of criminal statutes are not covered. But it is often a matter of debate as to whether a particular act was intended. While illegal discrimination, physical assaults, harassment, or retaliation (by you or your manager) are often treated by insurers as intentional acts not covered by the policy, most liability insurers will at least pay for the defense of such lawsuits.

Choosing Property Insurance

When you go to buy property coverage, there are four main questions to consider.

What Business Property Is Insured?

Be sure your insurance covers all the property you want protected. In addition to your basic property insurance, which insures the entire building, you may need additional policies to cover:

- additions under construction

- outdoor fixtures, such as pole lights
- washing machines and other appliances
- items used to maintain the building, such as gardening equipment and tools
- boilers and heavy equipment, or
- personal business property such as computers used in managing your rental business.

> **TIP**
> **Make sure tenants know that your insurance does not cover loss or damage (caused by theft or fire) to their personal property.** Tenants need to buy their own renters' insurance to cover their personal property. This does not mean, however, that you cannot be sued by a tenant (or his insurance company) if your negligence caused his loss. Your commercial general liability policy should cover you in this event.

What Perils Are Insured Against?

Be sure you know what kind of losses the property policy covers. Fire damage is covered in even the most basic policies, but damage from mud slides, windstorms, and the weight of snow may be excluded. Earthquake insurance and flood insurance are typically separate. They are often expensive and have a very high deductible, but they still are a good option if your building is highly susceptible to earthquake or flood damage. Whatever policy you decide on, read it carefully before you pay for it—not just when you've suffered a loss.

Check out "loss of rents" insurance, which covers you for the loss of rents from units that have been sidelined—for example, due to a fire or other calamity. This coverage will kick in even if you can move the tenant to another, vacant unit.

How Much Insurance Should You Buy?

Obviously, the higher the amount of coverage, the higher the premiums. You don't want to waste money on insurance, but you do want to carry enough so that a loss wouldn't jeopardize your business.

Be sure to carry enough insurance on the building to rebuild it. There's no need to insure the total value of your real property (land and structures), because land doesn't burn. Especially if you're in an area where land is very valuable, this is a big consideration. If you're in doubt as to how much it would cost you to rebuild, have an appraisal made so you know that your idea of value is realistic. (Be sure to get a rebuilding quote, not a quote on the sales value of the structure.) Because the cost of rebuilding may increase, it's wise to get a new appraisal every few years. Your insurance agent should be able to help you.

Should You Buy Coverage for Replacement Cost?

Basic fire insurance contracts cover the actual cash value of the structure, not its full replacement value. But policies are routinely available with replacement cost coverage. This is the coverage you want.

Plain "cost of replacement" coverage, however, won't be adequate if you need to bring an older building up to code after a fire or other damage. Legal requirements adopted since the building was constructed will probably require a stronger, safer, more fire-resistant building when you rebuild. Doing this can cost far more than simply replacing the old building. To cope with this possibility, you want a policy that will not only replace the building but pay for all legally required upgrades. This coverage is called "Ordinance of Law Coverage," and it is almost never included in standard policies. You must ask for it.

Working With an Insurance Agent

Here are some tips for choosing an insurance agent.

Find a knowledgeable agent who takes the time to analyze your business operations and come up with a sensible program for you. Get recommendations from people who own property similar to yours, or from real estate people with several years' experience—they will know who comes through and who doesn't. Working with an agent who knows your business is advantageous because that person is already a fair way along the learning curve when it comes to helping you select affordable and appropriate insurance.

Steer clear of an agent who whips out a package policy and claims it will solve your problems. While there are some excellent packages available, neither you nor your insurance agent will know for sure until the agent asks you a lot of questions and thoroughly understands your business. If the agent is unable or unwilling to tailor your coverage to your particular business, find someone else.

Be frank with your agent. Reveal all areas of unusual risk. If you fail to disclose all the facts, you may not get the coverage you need. Or, in some circumstances, the insurance company may later take the position that you misrepresented the nature of your operation and, for that reason, deny you coverage.

Make sure you know what your policy covers and what's excluded. Does the policy exclude damage from a leaking sprinkler system? From a boiler explosion? From an earthquake? If so, and these are risks you face, find out whether they can be covered by paying an extra premium.

Check out pet restrictions. Be sure to find out whether your insurance policy includes restrictions as to species, breeds of dog, or weight and number of pets allowed.

Insist on a highly rated carrier. Insurance companies are rated according to their financial condition and size. The most recognized rater is the A.M. Best Company, which assigns letter ratings according to financial stability (A++ is the highest) and Roman numeral ratings reflecting the size of a company's surplus (XV is the best). Given that 80% of American companies receive an A rating or higher, you don't want to choose a company rated less than that. As to surplus, you will be on solid ground to require an "X." Your local public library's business section or reference desk will likely have the *Best's Key Rating Guide.* For details, see www.ambest.com.

 RELATED TOPIC
If you have a manager or other employees, you may need workers' compensation insurance. See Chapter 6.

! CAUTION
Consider insuring the cost of rubble removal and engineering surveys. Ruined buildings don't just disappear. They have to be demolished, carted away, and disposed of, and you might have to hire an engineer to oversee the whole process. A standard policy won't cover these costs, which can be astonishing—for example, you might have to comply with special disposal procedures if there is lead paint or asbestos in the debris. You can buy an endorsement for a reasonable sum that will protect you.

Saving Money on Insurance

Few landlords can really afford to adequately insure themselves against every possible risk. You need to decide what types of insurance are really essential and how much coverage to buy. Many factors affect this decision, including the condition and location of the rental property. Here are some guidelines that should help.

Set Priorities

Beyond any required coverage for your business, ask these questions: What insurance do I really need? What types of property losses would threaten the viability of my business? What kinds of liability lawsuits might wipe me out? Use your answers to tailor your coverage to protect against these potentially disastrous losses. Get enough property and liability coverage to protect yourself from common claims. Buy insurance against serious risks where the insurance is reasonably priced.

Select High Deductibles

The difference between the cost of a policy with a $250 deductible (the amount of money you must pay out of pocket before insurance coverage kicks in) and one with a $500, $1,000, or even higher deductible is significant—particularly if you add up the premium savings for five or ten years. Consider using money saved with a higher deductible to buy other types of insurance you really need. For example, the amount you save by having a higher deductible might pay for "loss of rents" coverage.

Take Preventive Measures to Avoid Losses

Good safety and security measures, such as regular property inspections, special fire prevention measures, or requiring that tenants purchase renters' insurance may eliminate the need for some types of insurance or lead to lower insurance rates. (When tenants have renters' policies, accidents that they cause will be covered by their policies; without them, your policy may end up footing the bill. When the chances of a claim go down, rates should decrease, too.) Ask your insurance agent what you can do to get a better rate.

Comparison Shop

No two companies charge exactly the same rates; you may be able to save a significant amount by shopping around. But unusually low prices may be a sign of a shaky company. Or it may be that you're comparing policies that provide very different coverage. Make sure you know what you're buying, and review your coverage and rates periodically.

RESOURCE
For more information on choosing business insurance, see the Insurance Information Institute's website at www.iii.org.

Your Liability for Tenant Injuries

If a tenant is injured on your property, are you liable? It isn't always easy to determine. Basically, you may be liable for injuries resulting from your:

- negligence or unreasonably careless conduct
- violation of a health or safety law
- failure to make certain repairs
- failure to keep the premises habitable, or
- reckless or intentional acts.

In rare instances, state law may make you automatically liable for certain kinds of injuries, even if you weren't careless.

More than one of these legal theories may apply in your situation, and a tenant can use all of them when pressing a claim. The more plausible reasons a tenant can give for your liability, the better the tenant will do when negotiating with your insurance company or making a compelling case in court.

Negligence

A tenant who files a personal injury claim will most likely charge that you acted negligently—that is, acted carelessly, in a way that wasn't reasonable under the circumstances—and that the injury was caused by your carelessness.

Negligence is always determined in light of the unique facts of each situation. For example, if you don't put adequate lights in a dark, remote stairwell, and a tenant is hurt because she couldn't see the steps and fell, your failure to install the lights might be negligence. On the other hand, extra lights in a lobby that's already well-lit would not be a reasonable expectation.

Whether or not you were negligent and are likely to be held responsible for a tenant's injury depends on answers to six questions. Your insurance adjuster (or a judge or jury, if the case goes to court) will consider these same questions when evaluating a tenant's claim.

Question 1: Did you control the area where the tenant was hurt or the thing that hurt the tenant?

In most cases, you will be held responsible for an injury if you were legally obligated to maintain and repair the injury-causing factor. For example, you normally have control over a stairway in a common area, and if its disrepair causes a tenant to fall, you will likely be held liable. You also have control over the building's utility systems. If a malfunction causes injury (like boiling water in a tenant's sink because of a broken thermostat), you will likewise be held responsible. On the other hand, if a tenant is hurt when his own bookcase falls on him, you won't be held responsible, because you do not control how the bookcase was built, set up, or maintained.

Question 2: Was an accident foreseeable?

You may be responsible for an injury if a tenant can show that an accident was foreseeable. For

example, common sense tells anyone that loose handrails or stairs are likely to lead to accidents, but it would be unusual for injuries to result from peeling wallpaper or a thumbtack that's fallen from a bulletin board. If a freak accident does happen, chances are you will not be held liable.

Question 3: How difficult or expensive would it have been for you to reduce the risk of injury?

The chances that you will be held responsible for an accident are greater if a reasonably priced response could have averted it. If something as simple as warning signs, a bright light, or caution tape could have prevented people from tripping over an unexpected step leading to a patio, you should have taken the step. But if there is a great risk of very serious injury, you will be expected to spend more money to avert it. For example, a high-rise deck with rotten support beams must be repaired, regardless of the cost, because there is a great risk of collapse and dreadful injuries to anyone on the deck. If you knew about the condition of the deck and failed to repair it, you would surely be held liable if an accident did occur.

Question 4: Was a serious injury likely to result from the problem?

If a major injury was the likely result of a dangerous situation—the pool ladder was broken, making it likely a tenant would fall as he climbed out—you are expected to take the situation seriously and fix it fast.

The answers to these four questions should tell you whether or not there was a dangerous condition on your property that you had a legal duty to deal with. Lawyers call this having a "duty of due care."

> **EXAMPLE 1:** Mark broke his leg when he tripped on a loose step on the stairway from the lobby to the first floor. Because the step had been loose for several months, chances are his landlord's insurance company would settle a claim like this. Mark's position is strong because:

- Landlords are legally responsible for (in control of) the condition of the common stairways.
- It was highly foreseeable to any reasonable person that someone would slip on a loose step.
- Securing the step would have been simple and inexpensive.
- The probable result of leaving the stair loose— falling and injuring oneself on the stairs—is a serious matter.

EXAMPLE 2: Lee slipped on a marble that had been dropped on the public sidewalk outside his apartment by another tenant's child a few minutes earlier. Lee twisted his ankle and lost two weeks' work. Lee will have a tough time establishing that his landlord had a duty to protect him from this injury because:

- Landlords have little control over the public sidewalk.
- The likelihood of injury from something a tenant drops is fairly low.
- The burden on a landlord to eliminate all possible problems at all times by constantly inspecting or sweeping the sidewalk is unreasonable.
- Finally, the seriousness of any likely injury resulting from not checking constantly is open to great debate.

EXAMPLE 3: James suffered a concussion when he hit his head on a dull-colored overhead beam in the apartment garage. When the injury occurred, he was standing on a stool, loading items onto the roof rack of his SUV. Did his landlord have a duty to take precautions in this situation? Probably not, but it's not cut-and-dried:

- Landlords exercise control over the garage and have a responsibility to reasonably protect tenants from harm there.
- The likelihood of injury from a beam is fairly slim, because most people don't stand on stools in the garage, and those who do have the opportunity to see the beam and avoid it.
- As to eliminating the condition that led to the injury, it's highly unlikely anyone would expect a landlord to rebuild the garage. But it's possible that a judge might think it reasonable to paint the beams a bright color and post warning signs, especially if lots of people put trucks and other large vehicles in the garage.

- Injury from low beams is likely to be to the head, which is a serious matter.

In short, this situation is too close to call, but an insurance adjuster or jury might decide that James was partially at fault (for not watching out for the beams) and reduce any award accordingly.

If, based on these first four questions, you had a legal duty to deal with a condition on the premises that posed a danger to tenants, keep going. There are two more questions to consider.

Question 5: Did you fail to take reasonable steps to prevent an accident?

The law doesn't expect you to take Herculean measures to shield tenants from a condition that poses some risk. You are required to take only reasonable precautions. For example, if a stair was in a dangerous condition, was your failure to fix it unreasonable in the circumstances? Let's take the broken step that Mark (Example 1, above) tripped over. Obviously, leaving it broken for months is unreasonably careless—that is, negligent—under the circumstances.

But what if the step had torn loose only an hour earlier, when another tenant dragged a heavy footlocker up the staircase? Mark's landlord would probably concede that he had a duty to maintain the stairways, but would argue that the manager's daily sweeping and inspection of the stairs that same morning met that burden. In the absence of being notified of the problem, the landlord would probably claim that his inspection routine met his duty of keeping the stairs safe. If a jury agreed, Mark would not be able to establish that the landlord acted unreasonably under the circumstances.

Question 6: Did your failure to take reasonable steps to keep tenants safe cause an injury?

This question establishes the crucial link between your negligence and a tenant's injury. Not every dangerous situation results in an accident. A tenant has to prove that an injury was the result of your carelessness, and not some other reason. Sometimes this is self-evident: One minute a tenant is fine, and the next minute she's slipped on a freshly waxed floor and has a broken arm. But it's not always so simple. For example, in the case of the loose stair, the landlord might be able to show that the tenant barely lost his balance because of the loose stair and that he had really injured his ankle during a touch football game he'd just played.

Landlord Liability for Injuries to Guests and Trespassers

If you have acted negligently and a tenant's guest or even a trespasser is injured, will you be liable? The answer varies with each state. In a few states, you're liable no matter why the injured person was on your property. As a general rule, however, you have a reduced duty of care when it comes to nontenants, especially trespassers. For example, a tenant who is injured when falling from an unfenced porch will have a fairly strong case for charging you with negligence; a trespasser, even an innocent one who has come to the wrong address, who falls off the same porch might have a harder time recovering from you.

Here's a final example, applying all six questions to a tenant's injury.

> **EXAMPLE:** Scotty's apartment complex had a pool bordered by a concrete deck. On his way to the pool, Scotty slipped and fell, breaking his arm. The concrete where he fell was slick because the landlord had spilled cleaning solution on it.
> - Did the landlord control the pool area and the cleaning solution? Absolutely. The pool was part of a common area, and the landlord had done the cleaning.
> - Was an accident like Scotty's foreseeable? Certainly. It's likely that a barefoot person heading for the pool would slip on slick cement.
> - Could the landlord have eliminated the dangerous condition without much effort or money? Of course. All that was necessary was to hose the deck down.
> - How serious was the probable injury? Falling on cement presents a high likelihood of broken bones, a serious injury.

The answers to these four questions established that the landlord owed Scotty a duty of care.
- Had his landlord also breached this duty? A jury would probably answer yes—and conclude that leaving spilled cleaning solution on the deck was an unreasonable thing to do.
- Did the spilled cleaning solution cause Scotty's fall? This one is easy, because several people saw the accident and others could describe Scotty's robust fitness before the fall. Because Scotty himself hadn't been careless, he has a good case.

Violation of a Health or Safety Law

Many state and local laws require smoke detectors, sprinklers, inside-release security bars on windows, childproof fences around swimming pools, and so on. To put real teeth in these important laws, legislators (and sometimes the courts) have decided that a landlord who doesn't take reasonable steps to comply with certain health or safety statutes is legally considered negligent. If that negligence results in an injury, the landlord is liable for it. A tenant doesn't need to prove that an accident was foreseeable or likely to be serious; nor does a tenant have to show that complying with the law would have been relatively inexpensive. The legal term for this rule is "negligence per se."

> **EXAMPLE:** A local housing code specifies that all kitchens must have grounded power plugs. There are no grounded plugs in the kitchen of one of your rental units. As a result, a tenant is injured when using an appliance in an otherwise safe manner. In many states, your violation of the law would mean you were legally negligent. If a tenant can show that the ungrounded plug caused injury, you will be held liable.

Your violation of a health or safety law may also indirectly cause an injury. For example, if you let the furnace deteriorate in violation of local law, and a tenant is injured trying to repair it, you will probably be liable, unless the tenant's repair efforts are extremely careless.

EXAMPLE: The state housing code requires landlords to provide hot water. In the middle of the winter, a tenant's hot water heater has been broken for a week, despite his repeated complaints to the landlord. Finally, to give a sick child a hot bath, a tenant carries pots of steaming water from the stove to the bathtub. Doing this, he spills the hot water and burns himself seriously.

The tenant sues the landlord for failure to provide hot water as required by state law. Many people would probably conclude that the tenant's response to the lack of hot water was a foreseeable one, and, knowing this, the landlord's insurance company would probably be willing to offer a fair settlement.

Failure to Make Certain Repairs

For perfectly sensible reasons, many landlords do not want tenants to undertake even fairly simple tasks like painting, plastering, or unclogging a drain. Many leases and rental agreements (including the ones in this book) prohibit tenants from making any repairs or alterations without the landlord's consent, or limit what a tenant can do. If you do allow tenants to perform maintenance tasks, be sure to do so with a clear, written agreement, as explained in Chapter 9.

But in exchange for reserving the right to make all these repairs yourself, the law imposes a responsibility. If, after being told about a problem, you don't maintain or repair something a tenant is not to touch—for example, an electrical switch—and the tenant is injured as a result, you could be held liable. The legal reason is that you breached the contract (the lease) by not making the repairs. (You may be negligent, as well; remember, there is nothing to stop a tenant from presenting multiple reasons why you should be held liable.)

EXAMPLE: The sash cords in the living room window in Shanna's apartment break, making it necessary to support the entire weight of the window while raising or lowering it and securing it with a block of wood. Because Shanna's lease includes a clause forbidding repairs of any nature, she reports the problem to Len, the owner. Despite his promises to repair the window, Len never gets around to it. One hot summer evening

Shanna attempts to raise the heavy window, but her hands slip and the window crashes down on her arm, breaking it. Shanna threatens to sue Len, claiming that he negligently delayed the repair of the window, and further that the lease clause forbidding any repairs by the tenant contractually obligated Len to attend to the problem in a reasonably prompt manner. Mindful of the strength of Shanna's arguments, and fearful that a jury would side with Shanna and give her a large award, Len's insurance company settles the case for several thousand dollars.

Failure to Keep the Premises Habitable

One of your basic responsibilities is to keep the rental property in a "habitable" condition. Failure to maintain a habitable dwelling may make you liable for injuries caused by the substandard conditions. For example, a tenant who is bitten by a rat in a vermin-infested building may argue that your failure to maintain a rat-free building constituted a breach of your duty to keep the place habitable, which in turn led to the injury. The tenant must show that you knew of the defect and had a reasonable amount of time to fix it.

This theory applies only when the defect is so serious that the rental unit is unfit for human habitation. For example, a large, jagged broken picture window would make the premises unfit for habitation in North Dakota in winter, but a torn screen door in southern California obviously would not.

EXAMPLE: Jose notified his landlord about the mice that he had seen several times in his kitchen. Despite Jose's repeated complaints, the landlord did nothing to eliminate the problem. When Jose reached into his cupboard for a box of cereal, he was bitten by a mouse. Jose sued his landlord for the medical treatment he required, including extremely painful rabies shots. He alleged that the landlord's failure to eradicate the rodent problem constituted a breach of the implied warranty of habitability, and that this breach was responsible for his injury. The jury agreed and gave Jose a large monetary award.

(Jose might also claim that the landlord was negligent because he didn't get rid of the mice or violated a state or local statute concerning rodent control.)

Reckless or Intentional Acts

"Recklessness" usually means extreme carelessness regarding an obvious defect or problem. A landlord who is aware of a long-existing and obviously dangerous defect but neglects to correct it may be guilty of recklessness, not just ordinary carelessness.

If you or an employee acted recklessly, a tenant's monetary recovery could be significant. This is because a jury has the power to award not only actual damages (which include medical bills, loss of earnings, and pain and suffering) but also extra, "punitive" damages for outrageous or extremely careless behavior. Punitive damages, which are not covered by insurance, are awarded to punish recklessness and to send a message to others who might behave similarly. The size of the punitive award is likewise up to the jury and is often reduced later by a judge or appellate court.

> **EXAMPLE:** The handrail along the stairs in Jack's apartment house had been hanging loose for several months. Two or three times, Jack taped the supports to the wall, which did no good. One night when Hilda, one of Jack's tenants, reached for the railing, the entire thing came off in her hand, causing her to fall and break her hip.
>
> Hilda sued Jack for her injuries. In her lawsuit, she pointed to the ridiculously ineffective measures that Jack had taken to deal with a clearly dangerous situation, and charged that he had acted with reckless disregard for the safety of his tenants. (Hilda also argued that Jack was negligent because of his unreasonable behavior and because he had violated a local ordinance regarding maintenance of handrails.) The jury agreed with Hilda and awarded her punitive damages in addition to actual damages.

Intentional Harm

If you or your manager struck and injured a tenant during an argument, that would be an intentional act for which you would be liable. Less obvious, but no less serious, are emotional or psychological injuries which can also be inflicted intentionally. Intentional infliction of emotional distress may arise in these situations:

- **Sexual harassment.** Repeated, disturbing attentions of a sexual nature which leave a tenant fearful, humiliated, and upset can form the basis for a claim of intentional harm.

  EXAMPLE: Rita's landlord Mike took every opportunity to make suggestive comments about her looks and social life. When she asked him to stop, he replied that he was "just looking out for her" and stepped up his unwanted attentions. Rita finally had enough, broke the lease, and moved out. When Mike sued her for unpaid rent, she turned around and sued him for the emotional distress caused by his harassment. He was slapped with a multithousand-dollar judgment, including punitive damages.

- **Assault.** Threatening or menacing someone without actually touching them is an assault, which can be enormously frightening and lead to psychological damage.
- **Repeated invasions of privacy.** Deliberately invading a tenant's privacy—by unauthorized entries, for example—may cause extreme worry and distress.

The Law Makes You Liable

In rare circumstances, you may be responsible for a tenant's injury even though you did your best to create and maintain a safe environment and were not negligent. This legal principle is called "strict liability," or liability without fault.

In most states, strict liability is imposed only when a hidden defect poses an unreasonably dangerous risk of harm to a group of persons who can't detect or avoid it. For example, Massachusetts landlords are subject to strict liability if tenants are poisoned by lead-based paint.

If a Tenant Was at Fault, Too

If the tenant is partially to blame for an injury, your liability for the tenant's losses will be reduced accordingly.

Limiting Your Personal Liability With a Corporation or Limited Liability Company

You might want to organize your rental property business as a corporation or a limited liability company ("LLC"). Legally, it's a separate entity from the individuals who own or operate it. You may be the only owner and the only employee of your corporation or LLC, but—if you follow sensible organizational and operating procedures—you and your corporation or LLC are separate legal entities. This means that the corporation or LLC, not your personal bank account, is liable for any awards or settlements won by injured tenants. (If you are successfully sued for discrimination committed by one of your employees or managers, however, your status as a corporation or an LLC may not protect you from being personally liable.)

If you do not form an LLC or corporation, you can protect personal assets to a large degree by purchasing adequate insurance.

RESOURCE

LLC or Corporation? **by Anthony Mancuso (Nolo), helps you decide, based on your circumstances and the laws of your state, whether it's better to incorporate or form an LLC.**

Form Your Own Limited Liability Company by Anthony Mancuso (Nolo), explains LLCs and shows you how to form one in your state.

Nolo.com offers an online way to form a corporation or LLC that's valid in your state.

Tenant Carelessness

If a tenant is guilty of unreasonable carelessness—for example, he was drunk and didn't watch his step when he tripped on a loose tread on a poorly maintained stairway—he may not be able to collect damages from the landlord (or may not collect as much as he would have if he hadn't been careless). It depends on the state.

- In a number of states, tenants can collect according to the percent of blame attributed to the landlord, no matter how careless the tenant was, too. For example, a tenant can collect 75% of the damages if the landlord was 75% to blame.
- Some states allow tenants to recover a portion of their damages only if their carelessness was equal to or lower than the landlord's. In these states, for example, if the tenant and landlord were equally blameworthy, the tenant could collect only half of the damages. A tenant who was 51% at fault couldn't collect at all.
- In other states, tenants can recover a portion of their damages only if their carelessness was less than the landlord's. If the tenant and landlord were equally at fault, the tenant gets nothing; a tenant who was 25% at fault gets only 75% of his damages.
- A few states don't allow a tenant to collect a dime if he was at all careless, even 1% at fault.

Tenant Risk-Taking

If a tenant deliberately chose to act in a way that caused or worsened the injury, another doctrine may apply. Called "assumption of risk," it refers to a tenant who knows the danger of a certain action and takes the chance anyway.

> **EXAMPLE:** In a hurry to get to work, a tenant takes a shortcut to the garage by using a walkway that he knows has uneven, broken pavement. The tenant disregards the sign posted by his landlord: "Use Front Walkway Only." If the tenant trips and hurts his knee, he'll have a hard time pinning blame on his landlord, because he deliberately chose a known, dangerous route to the garage.

In some states, a tenant who is injured as a result of putting himself in harm's way cannot recover anything, even if your negligence contributed to the injury. In other states, a tenant's recovery is diminished according to the extent that he appreciated the danger involved.

How Much Money an Injured Tenant May Recover

A tenant who was injured on your property and has convinced an insurance adjuster or jury that you are responsible can ask for monetary compensation, called "compensatory damages." Given the often quirky nature of American juries, these costs can be enormous. Here are things a tenant can be compensated for:

Medical care and related expenses. This includes doctors' and physical therapists' bills, including future care.

Missed work time. A tenant can sue for lost wages and income while out of work and undergoing medical treatment for injuries. He can also recover for expected losses due to continuing care.

Pain and other physical suffering. The type of injury the tenant has suffered and its expected duration affect the amount awarded for pain and suffering. Insurance adjusters require objective corroboration of a tenant's level of discomfort, such as a doctor's prescription of strong pain medication. The longer a tenant's recovery period, the greater the pain and suffering.

Permanent physical disability or disfigurement. Long-lasting or permanent effects—such as scars, back or joint stiffness, or a significant reduction in mobility—increase the amount of damages.

Loss of family, social, career, and educational experiences or opportunities. A tenant who demonstrates that the injury prevented a promotion or better job can ask for compensation for the lost income.

Emotional damages resulting from any of the above. Emotional pain, including stress, embarrassment, depression, and strains on family relationships, may be compensated. Insurance adjusters require proof, such as evaluations from a therapist, physician, or counselor.

Punitive damages. Punitive damages are awarded if a judge or jury decides that you acted outrageously, either intentionally or recklessly. As a general rule, you won't be liable for punitive damages if you refrain from extreme neglect and intentional wrongs against tenants and others.

RESOURCE

For free information on legal issues regarding liability and insurance, see the articles and FAQs at www.nolo.com.

How to Win Your Personal Injury Claim, by Joseph Matthews, explains personal injury cases and how to work out a fair settlement without going to court.

Everybody's Guide to Small Claims Court, by Ralph Warner, provides detailed advice on small claims court, which, in most states, allows lawsuits for about $3,000 to $10,000.

Represent Yourself in Court, by Paul Bergman and Sara J. Berman, will help you prepare and present your case should you end up in court.

Mediate, Don't Litigate: Strategies for Successful Mediation, by Peter Lovenheim and Lisa Guerin, gives detailed information on the mediation process. (eBook version only, available at www.nolo.com.)

These Nolo books are available at bookstores and public libraries. You can also order or download them at www.nolo.com or by calling 800-728-3555.

Landlord's Liability for Environmental Health Hazards

FORMS IN THIS CHAPTER

Chapter 11 includes samples of the following forms:

- *Protect Your Family From Lead in Your Home Pamphlet*
- *Disclosure of Information on Lead-Based Paint and/or Lead-Based Paint Hazards*

The Nolo website includes downloadable copies of these forms (in both English and Spanish). See Appendix B for the link to the forms in this book.

In 1863, an English judge could write that "Fraud apart, there is no law against letting [leasing] a tumble-down house." But in 21st century America, it's no longer legal to be a slumlord. Landlords must exercise a duty of due care toward tenants and guests alike. As discussed in Chapter 9, this duty requires you to maintain the structural integrity of the rental property. If needed repairs are not made and, as a result of defective conditions, a tenant is injured, you may be found liable.

Here we focus on an additional responsibility that has been imposed on landlords in the last few decades: the duty to divulge and remedy environmental health hazards, including some not caused by you. Put bluntly, landlords are increasingly likely to be held liable for tenant health problems resulting from exposure to environmental hazards in the rental premises. This liability is based on many of the same legal theories discussed in Chapter 10, such as negligence and negligence per se (negligence that is automatic when a statute is broken).

This chapter provides an overview of the legal and practical issues involving landlord liability for environmental health hazards, specifically asbestos, lead, radon, carbon monoxide, mold, and bedbugs.

RELATED TOPIC
Related topics covered in this book include:
- How to make legally required disclosures of environmental hazards to tenants: Chapter 2
- Maintaining habitable property by complying with housing laws and avoiding safety problems: Chapter 9
- Your liability for tenant's injuries from defective housing conditions: Chapter 10.

Asbestos

Exposure to asbestos has long and definitively been linked to an increased risk of cancer, particularly for workers in the asbestos manufacturing industry or in construction jobs. More recently, the danger of asbestos in homes has also been acknowledged.

Houses built before the mid-1970s often contain asbestos insulation around heating systems, in ceilings, and in other areas. Until 1981, asbestos was also widely used in many other building materials, such as vinyl flooring and tiles. Asbestos that begins to break down and enter the air—for example, when it is disturbed during maintenance or renovation work—can become a significant health problem to tenants.

Until recently, however, private owners of residential rental property had no legal obligation to test for the presence of asbestos. A landlord whose tenant developed an asbestos-related disease could successfully defend himself if he could convince the judge or jury that he did not know of the presence of asbestos on his rental property.

Landlords' protection from liability for asbestos exposure all but evaporated in 1995, when the U.S. Occupational Safety and Health Administration (OSHA) issued a 200-page regulation setting strict workplace standards for the testing, maintenance, and disclosure of asbestos. Because your building will be a "workplace" for anyone working there on renovations or repairs, your building will be subject to OSHA's strict guidelines if it contains (or might contain) asbestos.

OSHA Regulations for Landlords

Regulations of the U.S. Occupational Safety and Health Administration (OSHA) require rental property owners to install warning labels, train staff, and notify people who work in areas that might contain asbestos. In certain situations, owners must actually test for asbestos.

These regulations apply to large landlords who employ maintenance staff (or managers who do maintenance work) and small-scale landlords who have no employees, but who do hire outside contractors for repair and maintenance jobs. OSHA regulations apply to any building constructed before 1981, even if you don't plan to remodel or otherwise disturb the structure. Unless you rule out the presence of asbestos by having a licensed inspector test the property, it is *presumed* that asbestos is present, and the regulations apply.

OSHA protections vary according to how much you're disturbing asbestos. For example, workers who are involved in removing asbestos receive maximum protection; those who merely perform superficial custodial tasks need less.

- **Custodial work.** Employees and contractors whose work involves direct contact with asbestos or materials that are presumed to include it—for example, certain types of floors and ceilings—or who clean in areas near asbestos are subject to OSHA regulations for "general industry." The cleaning service that washes asbestos tiles in the lobby of a pre-1981 building, or the handyman who installs smoke alarms that are embedded in acoustic-tile ceilings made with asbestos, would both fall within the custodial work category. Custodial workers must receive two hours of instruction (including appropriate cleaning techniques) and use special work procedures under the supervision of a trained superior. The general industry standard does not require testing for asbestos. Of course, if you know that high levels of asbestos are present, even custodial tasks must be performed with appropriate levels of protection, such as special masks and clothing.

- **Renovation or repairs.** Stricter procedures are triggered by removal, repair, or renovation of asbestos or asbestos-containing materials— for example, in heating systems or ceilings. At this level of activity, you must test for the presence of asbestos and assess exposure by monitoring the air. Workers must get 16 hours of training per year, oversight by a specially trained person, and respiratory protection in some situations. In addition, employers must conduct medical surveillance of certain employees and maintain specified records for many years. So, for example, your decision to replace that ugly, stained acoustic-tile ceiling would require, first, that the material be tested for asbestos, followed by worker training and protection measures that are appropriate to the level of exposure. If you hire a contractor to do the job, the contractor will take care of these requirements, and you'll see the work reflected in the contractor's invoice.

> ! CAUTION
> **There is no escaping OSHA's asbestos regulations under the theory that what you don't know about can't cause legal problems.** You might think that you can escape OSHA's asbestos regulations by personally doing minor repair and maintenance and hiring independent contractors to do the major jobs. This might work for a while, until you hire a law-abiding contractor who acknowledges the independent duty to protect employees and performs asbestos testing. The results of the tests will, of course, become known to you, because you'll see the report and pay the bill.

Key Aspects of OSHA Asbestos Regulations

Which buildings are affected. The regulations apply to pre-1981 structures and newer structures found to contain asbestos.

Where asbestos is likely to be found. The regulations cover two classes of materials: those that definitely contain asbestos (such as certain kinds of flooring and ceilings) and those that the law *presumes* to contain asbestos. The second class is extremely inclusive, describing, among other things, any surfacing material that is "sprayed, troweled on, or otherwise applied." This means virtually every dwelling built before 1981 must be suspected of containing asbestos.

What work is covered. The regulations apply to custodial work and to renovation and repair work.

How to Limit Your Liability for Asbestos

If asbestos is present on your property and can be shown to be the cause of a tenant's illness, you could be found liable if you didn't disclose it, or for other reasons. Some states may consider the presence of airborne asbestos to be a breach of the implied warranty of habitability, which (depending on the state) would give the tenant the right to break the lease and move out without notice, pay less rent, withhold the entire rent, or sue to force you to bring the dwelling up to a habitable level.

Limiting your liability for asbestos-related injuries (to tenants and workers alike) begins with understanding a fundamental point: Unless you perform detailed testing to rule out the presence of asbestos, every pre-1981 structure must be treated as if it does contain asbestos. Take these steps:

- Get a copy of the OSHA regulations or the guidelines that are based on them. (See "Asbestos resources," below.)

- Realize that almost any repair or maintenance work—no matter how small—may involve asbestos materials. Test for the presence of asbestos in advance for the benefit of workers and tenants.

- If you learn of the presence of asbestos, tell your tenants. For example, if there is asbestos in the walls but it is not a health problem, point out that it is not likely to pose a danger and that you will monitor the situation.

- If possible, don't disturb asbestos. Unless the asbestos has begun to break down and enter the air, it is usually best to leave it alone and monitor it. This means that it simply may not make economic sense to do certain types of remodeling jobs. Seek an expert's opinion before taking action.

- If you must disturb asbestos—for example, when stripping floor tiles in a lobby—warn all tenants before the work starts, giving them an opportunity to avoid the area. Use written notices and place cones and caution tape around the area. You might even consider temporarily relocating your tenants. The costs of a few days or weeks in alternate housing pales compared to the expense, monetary and human, of responding to a personal injury lawsuit by an exposed tenant.

- If you learn that asbestos material is airborne (or is about to be), seek an expert's advice on how to remedy the situation. When removal is necessary, hire trained asbestos removal specialists, and make sure the debris is legally disposed of in approved hazardous waste disposal sites.

- Make sure tenants don't disturb any spaces containing asbestos, such as walls and ceilings. You might need to prohibit tenants from hanging planters from the ceiling or otherwise making holes in the ceiling. See Clause 12 of the form lease and rental agreement in Chapter 2, which prohibits tenant repairs.

- Require tenants to report any deterioration to you—for example, in sprayed-on acoustical plaster ceilings.

- Monitor asbestos as part of regular safety and maintenance procedures, discussed in Chapter 9.

RESOURCE

Asbestos resources. For information on asbestos rules, inspections, and control, contact the nearest office of the U.S. Occupational Safety and Health Administration (OSHA), go to www.osha.gov, or call 800-321-OSHA. At the website, look for asbestos in the A to Z Index. You'll find the regulations, as well as informative materials that interpret and apply the regulations.

Be sure to check into free OSHA interactive software, called *Asbestos Advisor* (on the OSHA website), that will walk you through questions designed to help identify asbestos in your property and suggest the most sensible solution.

For additional information on asbestos, including negative health effects, see the EPA website at www.epa.gov/asbestos.

Lead

As we all know, exposure to lead-based paint or lead water pipes may lead to serious health problems, particularly in children. Brain damage, attention disorders, and hyperactivity have all been associated with lead poisoning. Landlords who are found responsible for lead poisoning (even if they did not know of the presence of the lead) may face liability for a child's lifelong disability. Jury awards and settlements for lead poisoning are typically enormous, because they cover remedial treatment and education of a child for the rest of his life, and include an award for the estimated loss of earning capacity caused by the injury.

Buildings constructed before 1978 are likely to contain some source of lead, be it lead-based paint, lead pipes, or lead-based solder used on copper pipes. (In 1978, the federal government required the reduction of lead in house paint; lead pipes are generally only found in homes built before 1930, and lead-based solder in home plumbing systems was banned in 1988.) Pre-1950 housing that has been allowed to deteriorate is by far the greatest source of lead-based paint poisoning.

A federal law, the Residential Lead-Based Paint Hazard Reduction Act (commonly referred to as Title X [Ten]) is aimed at evaluating the risk of poisoning in each housing situation and taking appropriate steps to reduce the hazard. Most states have also enacted similar laws.

Is Your Property Exempt From Federal Lead Regulations?

Certain rental properties are exempt from the federal lead paint disclosure and renovation regulations, including:

- Housing for which a construction permit was obtained, or on which construction was started, after January 1, 1978. Older buildings that have been completely renovated since 1978 are not exempt, even if every painted surface was removed or replaced.
- Housing certified as lead-free by a state-accredited lead inspector. Lead-free means the absence of any lead paint, even paint that has been completely painted over and encapsulated.
- Lofts, efficiencies, studios, and other "zero-bedroom" units, including dormitory housing and rentals in sorority and fraternity houses. University-owned apartments and married student housing are not exempt.
- Short-term vacation rentals of 100 days or less.
- A single room rented in a residential home.
- Housing designed for persons with disabilities (as explained in HUD's Fair Housing Accessibility Guidelines, 24 CFR, Ch. I, Subchapter A, App. II), unless any child less than six years old resides there or is expected to reside there.
- Retirement communities (housing designed for seniors, where one or more tenant is at least 62 years old), unless children under the age of six are present or expected to live there.

State law may still apply, even if the property isn't subject to federal rules.

Must You Have an Inspection?

Inspections are not required by federal or state law, but local law may require them. In New York City, for example, landlords must perform annual visual inspections of rental units where a child under age six resides and of any apartment that becomes vacant before it may be reoccupied. Landlords must inspect for lead-based paint hazards, defined as peeling paint or deteriorated subsurfaces such as exposed, painted wood beneath a newer coat of paint.

Even though it's not required, you might want to have an inspection done so that you can tell tenants that the property is lead-free and exempt from federal regulations. (See list of exemptions, above.) Also, if you take out a loan or buy insurance, your bank or insurance company may require a lead inspection.

Professional lead inspectors don't always inspect every unit in large, multifamily properties. Instead, they inspect a sample of the units and apply their conclusions to the property as a whole. Giving your tenants the results and conclusions of a building-wide evaluation satisfies the law, even if a particular unit was not tested. If, however, you have specific information regarding a unit that is inconsistent with the building-wide evaluation, you must disclose it to the tenant.

Disclose Lead Paint Hazards to Tenants

To comply with Title X, you must give tenants, before they sign or renew a lease or rental agreement, any information you have on lead paint hazards on the property, including individual rental units, common areas and garages, tool sheds, other outbuildings, signs, fences, and play areas. If you have had your property tested (testing must be done by state-certified inspectors; see "Lead hazard resources," below), you must show a copy of the report, or a summary written by the inspector, to tenants.

With certain exceptions (listed below), every lease and rental agreement must include a disclosure page, even if you have not tested. You can use the EPA's form, "Disclosure of Information on Lead-Based Paint and/or Lead-Based Paint Hazards." The copies are included (both Spanish and English) on Nolo's website (see Appendix B for the link to the forms in this book).

As you'll see, the disclosure form has a place for the tenant to initial, indicating that the tenant has reviewed the form. Be sure to note the time you received it, too, if you and the tenant are also signing the lease or rental agreement on the same day (and on that document enter the time you signed it, too). If you're ever challenged, you'll be able to prove that the tenant received the disclosure form before signing the rental documents.

Make a copy of the signed form and give it to the tenant; keep the original for at least three years. If a federal or state agency questions whether you're complying with the lead disclosure law (such agencies periodically do random checking), you'll have a cabinet full of signed forms as evidence. And if a tenant claims to have developed symptoms of lead poisoning from living in your rental property, you'll have proof that you disclosed what you knew.

If you have tenants who've been renting since before December 6, 1996 (the effective date of the law)—must you fill out a disclosure form for them, too? It depends on whether the tenant has a lease or is renting month to month:

- **Tenants with leases.** You need not comply until the lease ends and the tenant renews or stays on as a month-to-month tenant.
- **Month-to-month tenants.** You should have given month-to-month tenants a disclosure statement when you collected your first rent check dated on or after December 6, 1996. Do so now if you haven't yet.

Give Tenants the EPA Booklet on Lead

You must give all tenants the lead hazard information booklet *Protect Your Family From Lead in Your Home,* written by the Environmental Protection Agency (EPA), see "Lead hazard resources," below. A copy of the pamphlet (in English and Spanish) that you can print out and attach to the lease can be downloaded from the Nolo website. See Appendix B for the link to the forms in this book. The cover of this pamphlet is shown below. The pamphlet is also available in Vietnamese, Russian, Arabic, and Somali. For copies, see www.epa.gov/lead. The graphics in the original pamphlet must be included.

Some state agencies, that want to give consumers additional information about lead, have their own pamphlets, but you may not use them in place of the EPA version unless the EPA has approved them. California's pamphlet, *Residential Environmental Hazards: A Guide for Homeowners, Homebuyers, Landlords, and Tenants*, has been approved. To find out if your state has published an approved alternative, go to your state's department or agency in charge of consumer affairs, and use the search function to look for lead disclosure forms.

Enforcement and Penalties

The federal Housing and Urban Development Department (HUD) and the EPA enforce renters' rights to know about the presence of lead-based paint by using "testers," as they do when looking for illegal discrimination. Posing as applicants, testers look to see whether landlords comply with federal law.

Disclosure of Information on Lead-Based Paint and/or Lead-Based Paint Hazards

Lead Warning Statement

Housing built before 1978 may contain lead-based paint. Lead from paint, paint chips, and dust can pose health hazards if not managed properly. Lead exposure is especially harmful to young children and pregnant women. Before renting pre-1978 housing, lessors must disclose the presence of known lead-based paint and/or lead-based paint hazards in the dwelling. Lessees must also receive a federally-approved pamphlet on lead poisoning prevention.

Lessor's Disclosure

(a) Presence of lead-based paint and/or lead-based paint hazards (check (i) or (ii) below):

(i) _____ Known lead-based paint and/or lead-based paint hazards are present in the housing (explain).

_____

_____

(ii) _✓_ Lessor has no knowledge of lead-based paint and/or lead-based paint hazards in the housing.

(b) Records and reports available to the lessor (check (i) or (ii) below):

(i) _____ Lessor has provided the lessee with all available records and reports pertaining to lead-based paint and/or lead-based paint hazards in the housing (list documents below).

_____

_____

(ii) _____ Lessor has no reports or records pertaining to lead-based paint and/or lead-based paint hazards in the housing.

Lessee's Acknowledgment (initial)

(c) _____ Lessee has received copies of all information listed above.

(d) _____ Lessee has received the pamphlet *Protect Your Family from Lead in Your Home.*

Agent's Acknowledgment (initial)

(e) _____ Agent has informed the lessor of the lessor's obligations under 42 U.S.C. 4852d and is aware of his/her responsibility to ensure compliance.

Certification of Accuracy

The following parties have reviewed the information above and certify, to the best of their knowledge, that the information they have provided is true and accurate.

Bill Perry	*May 9, 20xx*		
Lessor	Date	Lessor	Date
Paula Hart	*Mary 9, 20xx*		
Lessee	Date	Lessee	Date
Agent	Date	Agent	Date

Protect
Your
Family
From
Lead in
Your
Home

 EPA United States
Environmental
Protection Agency

United States
Consumer Product
Safety Commission

United States
Department of Housing
and Urban Development

September 2013

Landlords who fail to distribute the required booklet or do not give tenants the disclosure statement when the lease or rental agreement is signed can receive one or more of the following penalties:

- a notice of noncompliance—the mildest reprimand—typically, you'll be given a certain number of days in which to notify all tenants.
- a civil penalty, which can include fines of up to $16,000 per violation for willful and continuing noncompliance
- an order to pay an injured tenant up to three times his actual damages, or
- a criminal fine of up to $25,000 per violation. (42 U.S.C. § 4852d, 15 U.S.C. § 2615(b).)

Government testers are also on the lookout for property owners who falsely claim that they

don't know of lead-based paint hazards on their property. Here's how it often comes up: A tenant who becomes ill with lead poisoning complains to HUD that you said that you knew of no lead-based paint hazards on your premises. If HUD decides to investigate whether, in fact, you knew about the hazard and failed to tell tenants, their investigators get access to your records. They comb leasing, maintenance, and repair files—virtually all your business records. If HUD finds evidence that you knew or had reason to know of lead paint hazards, such as a contract from a painting firm that includes costs for lead paint removal or a loan document indicating the presence of lead paint, you will be hard-pressed to explain why you checked the box on the disclosure form stating that you had no reports or records regarding the presence of lead-based paint.

RESOURCE

The Residential Lead-Based Paint Hazard Reduction Act, or Title X [Ten] can be found at 42 U.S. Code § 4852d. The Environmental Protection Agency (EPA) has written regulations that explain how landlords should implement lead hazard reduction. (24 Code of Federal Regulations Part 35, and 40 Code of Federal Regulations Part 745.) For more information, see "Lead hazard resources," below.

Give Tenants Information When You Renovate

If you renovate occupied rental units or common areas in buildings built before 1978, you must give current tenants lead hazard information before the work begins. (40 CFR §§ 745.80–88.) Contractors must be certified and follow specific work practices to prevent lead dust contamination.

The obligation to distribute lead information rests with the renovator. If you hire an outside contractor to perform renovation work, the contractor is the renovator. But if you or your property manager, superintendent, or other employees perform the renovation work, you are the renovator and are obliged to give out the information.

The type of information depends on where the renovation is taking place. If an occupied rental unit is being worked on, you must give the tenant a copy of the EPA pamphlet *The Lead-Safe Certified Guide to Renovate Right* (or simply *Renovate Right*). If common areas will be affected, you must distribute the pamphlet to every unit.

> **TIP**
>
> **Put it in the contract.** When you hire a contractor to perform renovations, the contractor is responsible for giving out the required information. To avoid misunderstandings, make sure your renovation contract or work agreement specifically requires the contractor to provide all required lead hazard information to tenants as provided under federal law and regulations.

What Qualifies as a Renovation?

According to EPA regulations, a renovation is any change to an occupied rental unit or common area that disturbs painted surfaces. Here are some examples:

- removing or modifying a painted door, wall, baseboard, or ceiling
- scraping or sanding paint, or
- removing a large structure like a wall, partition, or window.

Repainting a rental unit in preparation for a new tenant doesn't qualify as a renovation unless it's accompanied by sanding, scraping, or other surface preparation activities that might generate paint dust.

Not every renovation triggers the federal law. There are four big exceptions.

Emergencies. If a sudden or unexpected event, such as a fire or flood, requires you to make emergency repairs to a rental unit or common area, there's no need to distribute lead hazard information to tenants before work begins.

Minor repairs or maintenance. Minor work that affects less than six square feet of a room's painted surface, or 20 square feet or less on the exterior, is also exempt. This includes routine electrical and plumbing work, so long as no more than two square feet of the wall, ceiling, or other painted surface gets disturbed by the work.

Renovations in lead-free properties. If the rental unit or building in which the renovation takes place has been certified as containing no lead paint, you're not required to give out information.

Common area renovations in buildings with three or fewer units.

Give the EPA Pamphlet When Renovating Occupied Units

Before starting a renovation to an occupied rental unit, the renovator must give the EPA pamphlet *Renovate Right* to at least one adult occupant of the unit. This requirement applies to all rental properties, including single-family homes and duplexes, unless the property has been certified lead-free by an inspector.

The renovator (whether you or an outside contractor) may mail or hand-deliver the pamphlet to the tenant. If the renovator mails it, he or she must get a "certificate of mailing" from the post office dated at least seven days before the renovation work begins. Make sure the tenant will receive the pamphlet no more than 60 days before work begins—in other words, delivering the pamphlet more than 60 days in advance won't do. The renovator should use the confirmation form at the end of the *Renovate Right* pamphlet to record the delivery method and outcomes.

Give Out Notice When Renovating Common Areas

If your building has four or more units, the renovator—you or your contractor—must notify tenants of all affected units about the renovation and tell them how to get a free copy of the EPA pamphlet *Renovate Right*. (40 CFR § 745.84(b)(2).)

In most cases, common area renovations affect all units, meaning that you must notify all tenants about the renovation. But if you're renovating a "limited use common area" in a large (at least 50 units) apartment building, such as the 16th-floor hallway, you need only notify those units serviced by, or in proximity to, the area.

To comply, the renovator must deliver a notice to every affected unit describing the nature and location of the renovation work, and the dates you expect to begin and finish work. (See a sample "Common Area Renovations Notice," below.) If you can't provide specific dates, you may use terms like "on or about," "early June," or "late July." The notices *must be delivered within 60 days before work begins*. You can slip the notices under apartment doors or give them to any adult occupant of the rental unit. You may not mail them. After the notices are delivered, keep a copy in your file, with a note describing the date and manner in which you delivered the notices.

Common Area Renovations Notice

March 1, 20xx

Dear Tenant,

Please be advised that we will begin renovating the hallways on or about March 15, 20xx. Specifically, we will be removing and replacing the baseboards, wallpaper, and trim in the 2nd, 3rd, and 4th floor corridors, and sanding and repainting the ceilings. We expect the work to be completed in early May 20xx.

You may obtain a free copy of the pamphlet *Renovate Right* from Paul Hogan, the building manager. Paul may be reached at 212-555-1212.

We will make every attempt to minimize inconvenience to tenants during the renovation process. If you have questions about the proposed renovation work, feel free to contact Mr. Hogan or me.

Very truly yours,

Lawrence Levy

Lawrence Levy, Manager

Penalties

Failing to give tenants the required information about renovation lead hazards can result in harsh penalties. Renovators who knowingly violate the regulations can get hit with a penalty of up to $25,000 per day for each violation, and can even face prison time. (40 CFR § 745.87; 15 U.S. Code § 2615.)

State and Local Laws on Lead

Most states also prohibit the use of lead-based paint in residences and require the careful maintenance of existing lead paint and lead-based building materials. If your state has its own lead hazard reduction law, you'll see that, like its federal cousin, it does not directly require you to test for lead. Does this mean that you need not conduct inspections? Not necessarily. In New York City, for example, landlords must perform annual visual inspections of rental units where a child under age six resides. Landlords must inspect for "lead-based paint hazards," defined as peeling paint or deteriorated subsurfaces. New York City landlords must also visually inspect any apartments that become vacant on or after November 12, 1999 before the unit may be reoccupied.

Check your state's consumer protection agency to find out if state laws contain additional requirements regarding lead.

Leaded Miniblinds

Some miniblinds imported from China, Taiwan, Indonesia, or Mexico are likely to contain lead, but are not banned by the Consumer Product Safety Commission. If your property has leaded miniblinds, you do not have to disclose this fact unless you know that the blinds have begun to deteriorate and produce lead dust. To avoid problems, don't use these potentially dangerous miniblinds.

Why You Should Test for Lead

If you suspect that there might be lead lurking in your rental property's paint or water, you face a difficult choice. If you have the property tested and learn that lead is present, you'll know that your property has a hidden and dangerous defect. As a result, you must tell tenants and deal with the possibility that they will refuse to live on your property. If they stay, there's the potential of an expensive lead problem or risk of liability for injuries. But if you don't test, you'll live with the nagging fear that your property might be making your tenants sick and damaging the development of their children.

It may be tempting to adopt an ostrich-like approach and hope that all will work out. The odds may be with you for a while, but eventually this will prove to be a short-sighted solution. Here are six reasons why:

- Lead hazard control is much less burdensome than going through a lawsuit, let alone living with the knowledge that a child's health has been damaged.
- Ignorance of the condition of your property may not shield you from liability. At some point, some court is bound to rule that the danger of lead paint in older housing is so well known that owners of older housing are presumed to know of the danger. If that happens to you, a jury will have a difficult time believing that you were truly ignorant. Moreover, an injured tenant may be able to show the court that it was likely that you, in fact, knew of the lead problem and chose to ignore it.
- Recognizing that children are the ones most at risk for lead poisoning, you cannot simply refuse to rent to tenants with children—this is illegal discrimination in all states.
- If you include a clause in your lease or rental agreement attempting to shift responsibility for lead-based injuries from you to the tenant to protect yourself, you could effectively establish that you were aware of the lead problem. (Why else would you include it?) Many courts won't uphold this type of clause anyway.
- If you refinance or sell the property, the lender will probably require lead testing before approving a loan.
- You can expect your own insurance company to soon require lead testing as well. Lead poisoning cases are incredibly expensive— injured tenants can recover millions of dollars. It is only a matter of time before the insurance industry realizes that it cannot continue to blindly insure all properties against lead poisoning.

In sum, there is no effective way to hide a serious lead problem over the long run. Your best bet is to tackle it directly on your own terms, before you are forced to do so. The next section explains how to go about getting information on testing and reducing one of the most serious lead hazard risks: lead-based paint.

Your Insurance Policy May Not Cover Lead-Paint Poisoning Lawsuits

If you are hit with a lead poisoning lawsuit, don't presume that your insurance company will be there to defend you or compensate the victim. Depending on the terms of your policy, your insurer may be able to deny coverage for lead exposure claims—even if the suit is without merit. If you know (or presume) that your property contains lead-based paint, review your liability coverage with your insurance broker.

Because lead liability lawsuits are so expensive, some insurance companies have simply stopped writing general liability insurance on older buildings. Others exclude coverage for lead-based paint liability claims. You can still get coverage, but it might be limited or come at a higher cost.

RESOURCE

Lead hazard resources. The National Lead Information Center has information on the evaluation and control of lead-based paint and other hazards, disclosure forms, copies of the *Protect Your Family From Lead in Your Home* and *Renovate Right* pamphlets, and lists of EPA-certified lead paint professionals. Call 800-424-LEAD or go to www.epa.gov/lead. The EPA also provides pamphlets, documents, forms, and information on all lead paint hazards and federal laws and regulations on its website, and offers useful advice on topics such as finding a contractor licensed to test for and remove lead. (Check out its guide for "small entities," called *Small Entity Compliance Guide to Renovate Right*.) The EPA website (www.epa.gov) also includes a map with links to state and local websites.

HUD, specifically its Office of Lead Hazard Control and Healthy Homes (see www.hud.gov/lead), has many useful resources, including guidelines for evaluating and controlling lead-based paint hazards in housing.

State housing departments have information on state laws and regulations. Start by calling your state consumer protection agency. For a list of state consumer protection agencies, go to www.usa.gov/stateconsumer.

If you'd like to search for your state's legislation on your own, go to the Centers for Disease Control and Protection website at www.cdc.gov/nceh/lead. Choose the "Policy Resources" link that will take you to the database of state legislation.

Call In Expert Help to Clean Up Lead-Based Paint

Lead is relatively easy to detect—you can buy home-use kits that contain a simple swab, which turns color when drawn over a lead-based surface. Knowing how much lead is present, and how to best clean it up, however, are subjects for the experts. An environmental engineer will be able to tell you how much lead is present at floor level and above, which will alert you as to whether your property exceeds the amounts allowable by law.

In most states, you cannot legally perform lead abatement work without a special license from the state. To be on the safe side, become licensed yourself or only hire certified people.

Why not do it yourself? Because a DIY job, no matter how well-intentioned, might actually make the problem much worse. Wholesale paint removal, or sanding and repainting, often releases tremendous amounts of lead dust, the deadliest vector for poisoning. You also need special equipment to do a safe cleanup. Regular household cleaners, even TSP, do not do a very effective job of capturing lead, nor can a standard vacuum cleaner filter out microscopic lead particles.

Theoretically, some lead dust problems might be containable by frequent, lead-specific, and thorough cleaning, rather than repainting, and some cleaning companies specialize in lead dust cleaning. But painting over lead paint, if possible, is a better solution, even if it appears more costly than dust maintenance. It will certainly cost less than a lawsuit.

Radon

Radon is a naturally occurring radioactive gas that is associated with lung cancer. It can enter and contaminate a house built on soil and rock containing uranium deposits or enter through water from private wells drilled in uranium-rich soil. Radon becomes a lethal health threat when it is trapped in tightly sealed homes that have been insulated to keep in heat or have poor ventilation, when it escapes from building materials that have incorporated uranium-filled rocks and soils (like certain types of composite tiles or bricks), or when it is released into the air from aerated household water that has passed through underground concentrations of uranium. Problems occur most frequently in areas where rocky soil is relatively rich in uranium and in climates where occupants keep their windows tightly shut.

The Environmental Protection Agency estimates that millions of American homes have unacceptably high levels of radon. Fortunately, there are usually simple, inexpensive ways to measure indoor radon levels, and good ventilation will effectively disperse the gas in most situations. These measures range from the obvious (open the windows and provide cross-ventilation) to the more complex (sealing cracks in the foundation, or sucking radon out of the soil before it enters the foundation and venting it into the air above the door through a pipe). According to the EPA, a typical household radon problem can be solved for $500 to $2,500.

If you own rental property in an area known to have radon problems but don't test, warn tenants, or take action, you could be sued for harm that tenants suffer as a result.

State Laws on Radon

New Jersey, Florida, and Illinois have been at the forefront in addressing the radon problem. New Jersey has an extensive program that includes an information and outreach program. (N.J. Stat. Ann. §§ 26:2d-61, 26:2d-70, and 26:2d-71.) Florida taxes new construction to raise funds for the development of a radon-resistant construction code, and it requires landlords to warn tenants about the known presence of radon. (Fla. Stat. Ann. § 404.056.) The Illinois Radon Awareness Act (420 Ill. Comp. Stat. §§ 46/15, 46/25) does not require landlords to test for radon, but requires landlords to disclose to prospective tenants known radon hazard risks.

Whether to test for radon depends on the circumstances of each rental property; you are not legally required to test. Your city planning department or your insurance broker may know about local geology and radon dangers. Certainly, if you know radon levels are dangerously high in your area, you should test rental property. For the most professional results, hire an inspector certified by the EPA. Testing takes at least three days, and sometimes months. Do-it-yourself radon testing kits are also available. If you use one, make sure it says "Meets EPA Requirements." Kansas State University's National Radon Program Services (www.sosradon.org/test-kits) is a good source of discounted kits.

If testing indicates high radon levels, warn tenants and correct the problem. Start by giving them the EPA booklet *A Radon Guide for Tenants* (see "Radon resources," below).

RESOURCE

Radon resources. For information on the detection and removal of radon, contact the U.S. Environmental Protection Agency Radon Hotline Line at 800-767-7236, or visit www.epa.gov/radon. The EPA site has links to state agencies that regulate radon, gives information on finding a qualified radon reduction provider, and includes a map of radon zones by state. You can also download a copy of the booklet *A Radon Guide for Tenants* and other publications, including *A Citizen's Guide to Radon*.

Carbon Monoxide

Carbon monoxide (CO) is a colorless, odorless, lethal gas that can build up and kill within a matter of hours. Unlike any of the environmental hazards discussed so far, CO cannot be covered up or managed.

When CO is inhaled, it enters the bloodstream and replaces oxygen. Dizziness, nausea, confusion, and tiredness can result; high concentrations bring on unconsciousness, brain damage, and death. It is possible for someone to be poisoned from CO while sleeping, without waking up. Needless to say, a CO problem must be dealt with immediately.

Sources of Carbon Monoxide

Carbon monoxide is a byproduct of fuel combustion; electric appliances cannot produce it. Common home appliances, such as gas dryers, refrigerators, ranges, water heaters or space heaters; oil furnaces; fireplaces; charcoal grills; and wood stoves all produce CO. Cars and gas gardening equipment also produce CO. If appliances or fireplaces are not vented properly, CO can build up within a home and poison the occupants. In tightly sealed apartments, indoor accumulations are especially dangerous.

Preventing Carbon Monoxide Problems

If you have a regular maintenance program, you should be able to spot and fix the common malfunctions that cause CO buildup.

Here's how to avoid problems:

- Check chimneys and appliance vents for blockages.
- In your rules and regulations, prohibit the indoor use of portable gas grills or charcoal grills.
- Warn tenants never to use a gas range, clothes dryer, or oven for heating.
- Prohibit nonelectric space heaters, or specify that they must be inspected annually.
- Check the pilot lights of gas appliances as part of your regular maintenance routine. They should show a clear blue flame; a yellow or orange flame may indicate a problem.

But even the most careful service program cannot rule out unexpected problems like the blocking of a chimney by a bird's nest or the sudden failure of a machine part. You'll need a CO detector, explained below.

Carbon Monoxide Detectors

To ensure that residents are alerted immediately to the buildup of CO, you'll need to install a monitoring device, or detector, which will emit a loud shriek when CO is present. Unlike smoke detectors, which are required in every state, CO detectors are not universally mandated. But that's changing as more and more legislators recognize the need for these safety devices.

Single-family dwellings, which are more likely to have fossil-fuel-burning appliances than multifamily properties, are targeted most frequently, with laws requiring CO detectors in new construction, at renovation, and upon sale or transfer. But many states, including California, also require detectors in rentals. The National Conference of State Legislatures maintains a list of state laws at www.ncsl.org (type "Carbon Monoxide Detectors State Statutes" into the search box on the home page).

Savvy landlords will skip the research and just install the detectors. Make sure the device is "UL approved." Battery-operated models work fine, but like smoke detectors, their batteries must be changed regularly. Models that are connected to the building's interior wiring, with batteries as a back-up, are a better choice.

Responsibility for Carbon Monoxide Buildup

Most CO hazards are caused by a malfunctioning appliance or a clogged vent, flue, or chimney. It follows that the responsibility for preventing a CO buildup depends on who is responsible for the upkeep of the appliance.

Appliances. Appliances that are part of the rental, especially built-in units, are typically your responsibility, although the tenant is responsible for intentional or unreasonably careless damage. For example, if the pilot light on the gas stove that came with the rental is improperly calibrated and emits high amounts of CO, you must fix it. On the other hand, if your tenant brings in a portable oil space heater that malfunctions, that is his responsibility.

Vents. Vents, chimneys, and flues are part of the structure, and their maintenance is typically your job. In single-family houses, however, it is not unusual for landlords and tenants to agree to shift maintenance responsibility to the tenant. As always, write down any maintenance jobs that you have delegated so that it's clear. Chapter 9 discusses the pros and cons of delegating repairs to tenants.

RESOURCE

Carbon monoxide resources. The EPA offers useful instructional material, including downloadable pamphlets, at www.epa.gov/iaq/co.html. Local natural gas utility companies often have consumer information brochures available to their customers. You can also contact the American Gas Association for consumer pamphlets on carbon monoxide, at 202-824-7000 or www.aga.org.

Mold

Across the country, tenants have won multimillion-dollar cases against landlords for significant health problems—such as rashes, chronic fatigue, nausea, cognitive losses, hemorrhaging, and asthma—allegedly caused by exposure to "toxic molds" in their building.

Mold is among the most controversial of environmental hazards. There is considerable debate within the scientific and medical community about which molds, and what situations, pose serious health risks to people in their homes. (You can't tell by looking; mold comes in all colors and shapes, and while some molds look and smell disgusting, others are barely seen, hidden in walls, under floors and ceilings, or in basements and attics.) But courts have increasingly found landlords legally liable for tenant health problems associated with exposure to mold. It is crucial to identify and avoid problems with mold in your rental property before you find yourself in court.

Unsightly as it may be, not all mold is harmful to human health—for example, the mold that grows on shower tiles is not dangerous. It takes an expert to know whether a particular mold is harmful or just annoying. Your first response to discovering mold shouldn't be to call in the folks with the white suits and ventilators. Most of the time, proper clean-up and maintenance will remove mold. Better yet, focus on early detection and prevention of mold, as discussed below. This will help limit health problems of tenants as well as physical damage to structural components of your property.

Laws on Mold

No federal law sets permissible exposure limits or building tolerance standards for mold in rental properties, and only a few states have taken steps toward establishing permissible mold standards. This is bound to change as state legislators and federal regulators begin to study mold more closely. California, Indiana, Maryland, New Jersey, Texas, and Virginia are among the few that have passed legislation aimed specifically at the development of guidelines and regulations for mold in indoor air. California's law also requires landlords to disclose to current and prospective tenants the presence of any known or suspected mold. (Cal. Health & Safety Code §§ 26100 and following.)

A few cities have enacted ordinances related to mold. For example, San Francisco has added mold to its list of public health nuisances, which means tenants can sue landlords under private and public nuisance laws if they fail to clean up serious outbreaks. (San Francisco Health Code § 581.)

Your Liability for Tenant Exposure to Mold

Because there's little law on mold, you must look to your general responsibility to maintain and repair rental property for guidance. Your legal duty to provide and maintain habitable premises naturally extends to fixing leaking pipes, windows, and roofs—the causes of most mold. If you don't take care of leaks and mold grows as a result, you may be held responsible for damage to your tenant's personal belongings, such as clothes and furniture. And depending on the severity of the mold problem and your negligence in screening for or fixing it, a tenant may successfully sue you for medical bills and lost wages due to mold-caused health problems.

The picture changes when mold grows as the result of your tenant's behavior, such as keeping the apartment tightly shut, creating high humidity, and failing to keep it reasonably clean. You cannot be expected to police your tenant's lifestyle (and in many states, privacy statutes prevent you from unannounced inspections, as explained in Chapter 13). When a tenant's own negligence is the sole cause of injury, you are not liable.

> CAUTION
> **Using a lease clause stating that you won't be liable for injuries due to mold may not do you any good.** Courts are likely to see this ploy as against public policy, and won't enforce it. (*Cole v. Wyndchase Aspen Grove Acquisition Corp.*, 2006 WL 2827452, M.D. Tenn. 2006.)

Preventing Mold Problems

As we've stressed many times, the point is not who will win in court, but how to avoid getting dragged into a lawsuit, even one that you would probably win. Your efforts should be directed squarely at preventing the conditions that lead to the growth of mold. This requires maintaining the structural integrity of your property (the roof, plumbing, and windows) and adopting a thorough and prompt system for detecting and handling problems.

Here's how to proceed:

Watch the moisture. Before new tenants move in, inspect the premises and look for moisture problems (use the Landlord-Tenant Checklist form in Chapter 7). Mold often grows on water-soaked materials, such as wall paneling, paint, fabric, ceiling tiles, newspapers, or cardboard boxes. Throw in a little warmth and molds grow very quickly, sometimes spreading within 24 hours. Buildings in warm humid climates experience the most mold problems. But mold can grow whenever moisture is present; floods, leaking pipes, windows, or roofs are the leading causes. Poor ventilation makes the problem worse.

1. **Make sure every tenant understands the factors that contribute to the growth of mold.** Use your lease or house rules to educate tenants about sensible practices to reduce the chances of mold—or to fix problems should they arise. Give tenants specific advice, such as how to:
   - ventilate the rental unit
   - avoid creating areas of standing water— for example, by emptying saucers under houseplants, and
   - clean vulnerable areas, such as bathrooms, with cleaning solutions that discourage mold growth.

   The mold section of the EPA website includes lots of practical tips.

2. **Require tenants to immediately report signs of mold,** or conditions that may lead to mold such as plumbing leaks and weatherproofing problems.

3. **Check for conditions, such as leaky pipes, which could cause mold.** Do this as part of your recommended maintenance inspections (discussed in Chapter 9).

4. **Make all necessary repairs and maintenance to clean up or reduce mold.** For example:
   - Consider installing exhaust fans in rooms with high humidity (bathrooms, kitchens, and service porches), especially if window ventilation is poor.
   - Provide dehumidifiers in chronically damp climates, or rental units with poor ventilation.
   - Reduce window condensation by using storm windows or double-glazed windows.
   - Quickly respond to tenant complaints and clean up mold as discussed below.

EXAMPLE: The shower tray in Jay's bathroom begins to leak, allowing water to penetrate walls, floors, and ceilings below. Sydney, Jay's landlord, has repeatedly stressed the need for ventilation and proper housekeeping and encouraged all his tenants, including Jay, to promptly report maintenance problems. Jay ignores Sydney's recommendations, and mold grows in the bathroom. Jay develops a bad rash that he claims is a direct result of his exposure to the bathroom mold. Jay will have a tough time holding Sydney legally responsible for his health problems, simply because he failed to take advantage of Sydney's proven readiness to address the problem, which would have avoided the harm.

For useful advice on diagnosing and preventing mold, see Nolo's *Mold and Your Rental Property: A Landlord's Prevention and Liability Guide* eBook (see details in "Mold Resources," below).

Testing for Mold Toxicity

If you or your tenants discover mold on the property, should you test it to determine its harmfulness? Most of the time, no. You're better off directing your efforts to speedy cleanup. Knowing what kind of mold you have will not, in most cases, affect what you do to clean it up.

Properly testing for mold is also extremely costly. Over-the-counter test kits, which cost around $30, provide questionable results. A professional's basic investigation for a single-family home can cost $1,000 or more. And to further complicate matters, there are few competent professionals in this new field—unlike lead and asbestos inspectors, who must meet state requirements for training and competence, there are no state or federal certification programs for mold busters.

This said, it will be necessary to call in the testers if you are sued. In that event, your insurance company will hire lawyers who will be in charge of arranging for experts.

How to Clean Up Mold

Most mold is harmless, *not a threat to health* and easily dealt with. Most of the time, a weak bleach solution (one cup of bleach per gallon of water) will remove mold from nonporous materials. You and your tenants should follow these commonsense steps to clean up mold. Use gloves and avoid exposing eyes and lungs to airborne mold dust (if you disturb mold and cause it to enter the air, use masks). Allow for frequent work breaks in areas with plenty of fresh air.

- Clean or remove all infested areas, such as a bathroom or closet wall. Begin work on a small patch and watch to see if workers develop adverse health reactions, such as nausea or headaches. If so, call in a construction professional who is familiar with working with hazardous substances.
- Don't try removing mold from fabrics such as towels, linens, drapes, carpets, or clothing— just dispose of them.
- Contain the work space by using plastic sheeting and enclosing debris in plastic bags.

If the mold is extensive, consider hiring an experienced mold remediation company with excellent references, and any state-required licenses or certification. For more information, check out the sites noted in "Mold resources," below.

! CAUTION

People with respiratory problems, fragile health, or compromised immune systems should not participate in clean-up activities. If your tenant raises health concerns and asks for clean-up assistance, provide it—it's a lot cheaper than responding to a lawsuit.

Insurance Coverage of Mold Problems

If structural aspects of your property have been ruined by mold and must be replaced, especially if there's a lawsuit on the horizon brought by ill tenants, contact your insurance broker immediately. Your property insurance may cover the cost of the cleanup and repairs, but only if the damage is from an unexpected and accidental event, such as a burst pipe, wind-driven rain, sewerage backup, or unanticipated roof leak. Damage due to mold in a chronically damp basement will probably not be covered under your policy. If mold grows as a result of a flood, you may also be out of luck—flooding is excluded from most insurance coverage.

Your liability policy may also cover you if you are sued by ill tenants. But watch for the insurers to try to wiggle out as the amount of claims grows. Carriers have claimed that mold falls within the "pollution exclusion" (most policies do not cover you if you commit or allow pollution—for example, if you deliberately dump solvents on the property). Unfortunately, many insurers are now simply exempting damage due to mold in new or renewed property insurance policies. Read your policy (and ask your broker) to see whether mold-related claims are allowable under your policies.

 RESOURCE

Mold resources. For detailed advice on the subject of mold in residential rental properties—from mold prevention to cleanup and relevant liability and insurance issues (such as flood insurance coverage of mold problems)—see *Mold and Your Rental Property: A Landlord's Prevention and Liability Guide*, by Ron Leshnower (Nolo). This eBook, available on the Nolo website as well as on Amazon and other online retailers, includes useful sample forms, such as a mold inspection checklist. For information on the detection, removal, and prevention of mold, see www.epa.gov/mold; be sure to check out "Mold Remediation in Schools and Commercial Buildings" (which includes multifamily properties) and "A Brief Guide to Mold, Moisture, and Your Home." Publications written with the homeowner in mind are available from the California Department of Public Health at www.cdph.ca.gov. To see whether your state has enacted or is considering mold legislation that might affect residential rentals, log onto the website of the National Conference of State Legislatures (www.ncsl.org) and type "mold" into the search box on the home page. Look for the link to the "Environmental Health Legislation Databases Guide," and once there, filter by "All States" and "Indoor Air Quality—Mold." To check local mold-related rules, see your city or county website (find yours at www.statelocalgov.net). For an excellent study on the health effects of mold (and one that landlords may use in defending tenants' claims that mold accounts for their health issues), see the study "Damp Indoor Spaces and Health," conducted by the Institute of Medicine. You can read it at the website of the National Academies Press at www.nap.edu (type the title into the search box).

Bedbugs

They come out at night to gorge on human blood, but can last a year between meals. A single female will lay 500 eggs in her lifetime. You'll find them in sleazy digs with slobby tenants, as well as upscale apartments with fastidious residents. They're expert hitchhikers who can catch a ride on your suitcase, furniture, or clothing. No one really knows how to kill them. What are they? They're 21st-century bedbugs, and if they show up at your rental property, you'll probably conclude that mold, asbestos, or even lead-based paint are benign by comparison. Here's how to protect your tenants and your business from this potentially devastating pest.

What's a Bedbug—And Where Does It Come From?

Bedbugs are wingless insects, about a quarter-inch in length, oval but flattened from top to bottom. They're nearly white (after molting) and range to tan or deep brown or burnt orange (after they've sipped some blood, a dark red mass appears within the insect's body). They seek crevices and dark cracks, commonly hiding during the day and finding hosts at night. Bedbugs nest in mattresses, bed frames, and adjacent furniture, though they can also infest an entire room or apartment. They easily spread from apartment to apartment via cracks in the walls, heating systems, and other openings.

Bedbug populations have resurged recently in Europe, North America, and Australia, possibly a result of the banning of effective but toxic pesticides such as DDT. Bedbugs do not carry disease-causing germs (perhaps their one saving feature). Their bites resemble those of a flea or mosquito. Secondhand furniture is a common source of infestation.

How to Deal With an Infestation

You'll learn that bedbugs have infested your property when a tenant complains of widespread, annoying bites that appear during the night. To minimize the outbreak and attempt to stop the spread of the pests to other rental units, take the following steps immediately. We can't emphasize this enough: Unless you move swiftly and aggressively, identifying infested areas and treating them thoroughly, you will be doomed to a larger and harder-to-beat infestation. You may even end up with an unrentable property.

Hiring an experienced exterminator is the only way to deal with a bedbug infestation. A can of Raid is not going to do the job and will end up costing you more money in the long run. Expect to pay from $100 to $750 for the initial service of a single infested unit, and $75 to $300 for follow-up treatments. If you find a company that offers to control bedbugs for $50 per unit, get another bid.

> **TIP**
>
> **Encourage tenants to promptly report pest problems.** The sooner you learn about a bedbug infestation, the better you'll be able to manage it. Follow our advice in Chapter 9 for setting up a system for tenants to report problems in their rental unit, whether it's a leaky faucet or bedbugs.

Confirm the Infestation

First, make sure that you're dealing with bedbugs and not some other pest, such as fleas. Because several kinds of insects resemble bedbugs, you'll need to capture a critter or two and study them. Go to the sites mentioned above for more pictures of bedbugs than you ever wanted to see, and compare your samples. If it looks like a bedbug, call an experienced pest control operator, pronto. If you're not sure, submit your catch to a competent entomologist (insect specialist) for evaluation. To find a good entomologist, consult a reputable pest control company, look for references on your state's department of agriculture website, or look at the website of a nearby university's department of entomology.

Map the Infestation, Using a Competent Exterminator

In a multiunit building, bedbugs can travel from one unit to another. But chances are that one unit is the source, and it will have the highest concentrations of bedbugs. Hire a competent exterminator to measure the concentration of bugs in the complaining tenant's unit, and to also inspect and measure all adjoining units (on both sides, above, and below). Be sure to give all tenants proper notice of the exterminator's inspection and explain what's involved—a competent exterminator will need to look closely into drawers, closets, and shelves. Mapping the infestation (particularly if your exterminator does it more than once, over a period of time) may also help you determine when a particular unit became infested, which can help you apportion financial responsibility for the extermination. (See "Who Pays for All This?" below.)

Declutter, Move Tenants Out, Exterminate, Vacuum—And Do It Again

Bedbugs thrive in clutter, which simply gives them more hiding places. Before you can effectively deal with the bugs, tenants in infested units must remove all items from closets, shelves, and drawers, wash all bedding and clothing, and put washed items in sealed plastic bags. Then, you need to move tenants out during treatment, and allow them to return when the exterminator gives the all-clear. Most of the time, they can return the same day.

What Kills Bedbugs?

Although bedbugs are hard to kill using today's approved materials, exterminators have three ways to go after bedbugs:

- Insecticidal dusts, such as finely ground glass or silica, will scrape off the insects' waxy exterior and dry them out.
- Contact insecticides (such as chlorfenapyr, available only to licensed pest control operators) kill the bugs when they come into contact with it. For more information, search "Chlorfenapyr" at www.epa.gov.
- Insect growth regulators (IGR) interfere with the bugs' development and reproduction, and though quite effective, take a long time.

Pest control operators often use IGR in combination with other treatments. Most controllers recommend multiple treatments over a period of weeks, interspersed with near-fanatical vacuuming to capture dead and weakened bugs. Anecdotal reports claim that even with repeated applications of pesticides, it's not possible to fully eradicate heavy infestations. Honest exterminators will not certify that a building is bedbug-free.

Bedbugs will always be found in an infested room's bed. The only way to rid a mattress of bedbugs is to enclose it in a bag that will prevent bugs from chewing their way out (they will eventually die inside, but because it can take a long time, it's advisable to keep the mattress permanently sealed). Ask that tenants buy a bag guaranteed to trap bedbugs (some bags simply deter allergens). These are expensive—and you may as well resign yourself to buying them if your tenants won't or can't (depending on the mattress size, $100 to $250).

Upon return, tenants must thoroughly vacuum. Experienced exterminators will recommend a second and even a third treatment, with exhaustive cleaning and clutter-removing in between. You must insist, to the extent you're able (see "Proper Cleaning and Housekeeping: Can You Insist on It?" below), that tenants take these steps. If they don't and the infestation reappears and spreads, you could quite possibly find yourself with a building that is empty but for a thriving population of bedbugs.

Infested items that can't be treated must be destroyed. Do not allow tenants to remove infested items and simply bring them back. And use extreme care when removing infested belongings and furniture. Bag them in plastic before carting them away—otherwise, you may inadvertently distribute the bugs to the rest of the building.

Proper Cleaning and Housekeeping: Can You Insist on It?

Running a rental business involves striking a delicate balance between insisting that tenants take proper care of your property, and respecting their privacy. You can require that rental units be kept in a sanitary condition, but you can't inspect your tenants' housekeeping efforts every week.

When it comes to effectively eliminating bedbugs, however, extreme housekeeping is needed. Hopefully, your tenants will be so grateful that you're taking steps to deal with the bugs that they will cooperate voluntarily. If necessary, however, you may need to perform the vacuuming yourself (or hire someone to do it). Don't balk over the expense—compared to a widespread infestation and the potential of an empty building, the cost of a cleaning service is minimal.

CAUTION
Talk to a lawyer before deciding to evict a tenant who refuses to participate in your bedbug eradication program, or who reintroduces infested items. You may be within your rights, but you may also be courting a retaliatory eviction lawsuit, especially if the tenant was not the source of the infestation.

Who Pays for All This?

In keeping with your obligation to provide fit and habitable housing, you must pay to exterminate pests that tenants have not introduced. In Florida, this duty is explicit: since 1973, bedbugs are specified as one of the many vermin that landlords are required to get rid of, in order to maintain a fit and habitable rental. (Fla. Stat. Ann. § 83.51.) Arizona also makes landlords responsible for eradication. (Ariz. Rev. Stat. § 33-1319.) Fortunately, as explained below, your insurance may defray some of the costs.

Eradicating infestations caused by the tenant, however, can rightly be put on the tenant's tab. But determining who introduced the bedbugs is often very difficult. Even if you identify the unit where the infestation started (or the rental is a single-family home), that doesn't mean the tenants caused the problem. If they're new tenants, expect them to argue that the former occupants are responsible. Unless you discover that the new tenant came from a building that was also infested, you'll have a hard time laying responsibility on your new resident.

Another potential loss is the cost of replacing belongings that can't be salvaged. In extreme cases, bedbugs infest every nook and cranny of a rental and its contents—books, clothes, furniture, appliances. One New York landlord reported getting a phone call from a tenant who discovered bedbugs and moved out with only the clothes on his back, leaving everything—*everything*—behind. This tenant sued the owner for the cost of replacing his belongings, claiming that the landlord's ineffective eradication methods left him no choice.

Should this claim get before a judge, your liability would probably depend on the judge's view of the reasonableness of your response and the tenant's reaction. The more you can show that you took immediate and effective steps to eliminate the problem, the better you would fare. As for the tenant's response, understand that the psychological effects of living with bugs that bite you while you sleep can be very strong.

Will Your Insurance Step Up?

If you're facing a bedbug problem, you might get at least some help from your insurance policy. Here's the scoop.

Eradication. Property insurance typically does not cover instances of vermin or insect infestation.

Tenants' damaged belongings, medical expenses, and moving and living expenses. Your commercial general liability policy will probably cover you here, up to the limits of the policy.

Loss of rents. If you must leave a rental vacant while you have it treated, and you have loss of rents/business interruption insurance, it may cover you for your loss of rental income during this period.

If your tenants have renters' insurance, it might help here. If you can confidently trace the infestation to particular tenant's actions, you could present the bills to these tenants, suggesting that they refer the matter to their insurance company. The liability portion of their renters' policy should cover them.

Disclosure to Future Tenants

The last thing you want to tell prospective tenants is that you had a bedbug problem. Knowing that a bedbug can remain alive and dormant for over a year, and that eradication attempts are often not 100%, many prospects will never consider living in a unit that has experienced a bedbug problem, even when you've done everything possible to deal with the bugs.

Whether to disclose, however, may not be an option for you. State and local legislators are beginning to address the issue of whether landlords should be required to disclose a property's bedbug history, as well as tenant and landlord duties when an infestation appears. Maine requires landlords to disclose the property's history. (14 M.R.S.A. § 6021-A). Maine's law also requires tenants to promptly report problems, and to vacate the premises if necessary. Arizona prohibits landlords from knowingly renting an infested unit (Ariz. Rev. Stat. § 33-1319, and New York City requires landlords to inform tenants of the building's and the rental unit's bedbug history for the past year

(New York City Administrative Code § 27-2018.1). Many other states have legislation; for a list, go to the National Conference of State Legislatures, www.ncsl.org and search "state bedbug laws."

The majority of tenants, however, will not have the benefit of explicit disclosure laws. But that doesn't mean that you shouldn't be forthright. First, if a prospect questions you directly about a bedbug problem, especially if it's clear that this issue is of critical importance, you must answer truthfully or risk the consequences:

- **Breaking the lease.** A tenant who learns after the fact that you didn't answer truthfully will have legal grounds for breaking the lease and leaving without responsibility for future rent.
- **Increased chances of damages.** If the bug problem reappears and this tenant sues over lost or damaged possessions, costs of moving and increased rent, and the psychological consequences of having lived with the bugs, his chances of recovering will be enhanced by your lack of candor. A lawyer will argue that your failure to disclose a dangerous situation set the tenant up for misery that could have been avoided had you been truthful.

Now, suppose you are not questioned about a rental's bedbug history, you remain silent, and a problem reappears. Will your new tenants have a strong case for breaking the lease without responsibility for future rent, or use your silence as a way to increase their chances of collecting damages from you? The answer will depend on the facts, such as how aggressively and thoroughly you attempted to rid the property of bugs.

RESOURCE

Bedbugs. The Bedbugs section of the EPA website (www.epa.gov/bedbugs) has extensive information about bedbugs, including details on relevant regulations. For the definitive guide to the eradication and prevention of bedbugs, check out www.techletter.com, maintained by a pest management consulting firm. Read their articles or order the comprehensive *Bed Bug Handbook: The Complete Guide to Bed Bugs and Their Control*.

Electromagnetic Fields

Power lines, electrical wiring, and appliances emit low-level electric and magnetic fields. The farther away you are from the source of these fields, the weaker their force.

The controversy surrounding electromagnetic fields (EMFs) concerns whether or not exposure to them increases the chances of getting certain cancers—specifically, childhood leukemia. Although some early research raised the possibility of a link, later scientific studies discounted it. The same conclusion was reached in 2001 by the U.K. National Radiation Protection Board. (Scientific inquiry on EMFs has now shifted to the effects of cell phones.) The World Health Organization has exhaustively canvassed the scientific literature and has similarly concluded that "… current evidence does not confirm the existence of any health consequences from exposure to low level electromagnetic fields." (See "About electromagnetic fields" at www.who.int/peh-emf/about/en.)

Because you cannot insist that power companies move their transmitters or block emissions, you are not responsible for EMFs or their effect—if any—on your tenants. But if a tenant complains, what should you do?

Practically speaking, a tenant's only option is to move. A tenant who has a month-to-month rental agreement or an expiring lease can simply move on. A tenant who wants to break a lease or rental agreement because of EMFs would be justified only if there were a significant threat to her health or safety. Given the debate regarding the danger from EMFs, it is unclear whether a court would decide that their presence made your property unlivable.

RESOURCE

Electromagnetic fields resources. The National Institute of Environmental Health Sciences has useful resources on EMFs. To find them, search its website, www.niehs.nih.gov.

Landlord's Liability for Criminal Activity

No one expects you to build a moat around your rental property and provide round-the-clock armed security. But in virtually every state, landlords are expected to take reasonable precautions to protect tenants from foreseeable harm. This means you must take reasonable steps to:

- protect tenants from would-be assailants, thieves, and other criminals
- protect tenants from the criminal acts of fellow tenants
- warn tenants about dangerous situations you are aware of but cannot eliminate, and
- protect the neighborhood from illegal and noxious activities, such as drug dealing, by any of your tenants.

If you don't live up to these responsibilities, you may be liable for any injuries or losses that occur as a result.

This chapter discusses your legal duties under building codes, ordinances, statutes, and, most frequently, court decisions to protect your tenants and the neighborhood. It also discusses special issues regarding terrorism that concern landlords and rental property. It is our goal to provide practical advice on how to protect your tenants and the neighborhood from crime, limit your liability, and avoid trouble before it finds you.

We can't overstate the importance of taking this subject seriously. Landlords are sued more than any other group of business owners in the country, and the legal subspecialty of "premises liability" for criminal acts (suing landlords for injuries suffered by tenants at the hands of third-party criminals) is one of the fastest-growing areas of law. Why are lawyers so eager to try to pin responsibility for the acts of criminals on landlords? The not-so-surprising answer is money: Horrific crimes such as rape and assault result in tremendous monetary awards and settlements, of which the plaintiffs' attorneys take a sizable chunk. Only liability for lead poisoning rivals premises liability for astronomical settlement and jury award costs.

If this book motivates you to do only two things, it should be to assess and address the security situation on your rental property and to make sure your insurance policy provides maximum protection against the acts of criminals.

To protect yourself, you need to:

- follow state and local laws that mandate security measures
- take reasonable steps to prevent crime
- keep promises you make to tenants about security, and
- buy enough insurance to protect yourself.

Troubled Property: Is It Time to Cut Your Losses?

If you own property in a high-crime area, you may find it impossible to raise rents enough to cover the costs of providing secure housing and purchasing comprehensive insurance. The truth is that you may be better off selling at a loss than courting an excessive risk that you will be sued for criminal acts beyond your control. If you do keep high-crime property, consider ways to legally separate it from your other assets—for example, by establishing a corporation or limited liability company.

 RELATED TOPIC

Related topics covered in this book include:

- How to choose the best tenants and avoid legal problems: Chapter 1
- Lease and rental agreement provisions prohibiting tenants' illegal activities and disturbances: Chapter 2
- How to avoid renting to convicted criminals without violating privacy and antidiscrimination laws: Chapter 5
- How to minimize danger to tenants from a manager by checking applicants' backgrounds and references: Chapter 6
- Highlighting security procedures in a move-in letter to new tenants: Chapter 7
- Responsibilities for repair and maintenance under state and local housing law: Chapter 9

- Landlord's liability for a tenant's injuries from defective housing conditions: Chapter 10
- Landlord's right of entry and tenant's privacy: Chapter 13
- Evicting a tenant for drug dealing and other illegal activity: Chapter 17.

Comply With All State and Local Laws on Security

You should find and comply with all security laws, state or local, that apply to you. For information on security regulations, contact your state or local housing agency or rental property owners' association. Here's an idea of what to expect.

Specific Rules

In many areas of the country, local building and housing codes are rich with specific rules designed to protect tenants. For example, some city ordinances require peepholes, intercom systems, deadbolt locks, and specific types of lighting on the rental property.

Only a few states have specific laws as to land-lords' responsibilities to provide secure premises. For example:

- Under Florida law, landlords must provide locks and keep common areas in a "safe condition." A Florida tenant who was assaulted by someone who entered because of a broken back door lock was allowed to argue to a jury that the landlord was partially responsible. (*Paterson v. Deeb*, 472 So.2d 1210 (Fla. Dist. Ct. 1985).)
- All Texas rental units must be equipped with keyless bolts and peepholes on all exterior doors and pin locks on sliding glass doors, as well as a handle latch or security bar. (Tex. Prop. Code § 92.151-170.)

If you violate a law designed to protect tenants' safety—like a local ordinance requiring deadbolts— your tenants can complain to the agency in charge of enforcing the codes, often a local building or housing authority. The violation may also make you automatically liable for losses that stem from the violation. (The legal term for this is "negligence per se"—see Chapter 10.) This is devastating if you're sued after a crime occurs, because you cannot argue that it was unreasonable to expect you to provide the security measure in question.

General Security Responsibilities

Even if your state and local laws offer little specific direction, you still likely have a duty to keep your premises "clean and safe" or "secure." How the courts in your state will interpret the tenant safety laws that apply to your rental property is difficult to predict. Some courts interpret tenant safety laws more strictly than others.

EXAMPLE 1: The housing code in Andrew's city sets minimum standards for apartment houses, including a requirement that all areas of rental property be kept "clean and safe." The garage in Andrew's apartment house is poorly lit and accessible from the street because the automatic door works excruciatingly slowly. Andrew adds a few lights, but the garage is still far from bright. Andrew would be wise to spend the money to do the lighting job right and fix the garage door, because conditions like these could violate the "clean and safe" housing code requirement. If someone came in through the substandard garage door and assaulted a tenant, Andrew would likely be sued and found partially liable for the tenant's injuries.

EXAMPLE 2: Martin is a tenant in a state that requires rental housing to be maintained in a "fit and habitable" condition. Courts in his state have interpreted this to mean, among other things, that dwellings should be reasonably secure from unwanted intrusions by strangers. One evening Martin is assaulted in the elevator by someone who got into the building through the unlocked front door. Martin sues his landlord, Jim, and is able to show that the front door lock had been broken for a long time and that Jim had failed to fix it. The jury decides that Jim's failure to provide a secure front door violated the requirement to keep the place habitable, that he was aware of the problem and had plenty of time to fix it, and that the unsecured front door played a significant role in the assault. The jury awards Martin several thousand dollars for his injuries, lost wages, and pain and suffering.

Keep Your Promises About Security

If you promise tenants specific security features—such as a doorman, security patrols, interior cameras, or an alarm system—you must either provide them or be liable (at least partially) for any criminal act that they would have prevented.

Don't Exaggerate in Ads or Oral Descriptions

Landlords know that the promise of a safe environment is often a powerful marketing tool. In ads or during discussions with interested renters, you will naturally be inclined to point out security locks, outdoor lighting, and burglar alarms, because these features may be as important to prospective tenants as a fine view or a swimming pool.

Take care, however, not to exaggerate your written or oral description of security measures. Not only will you have begun the landlord-tenant relationship on a note of insincerity, but your descriptions of security may legally obligate you to provide what you have portrayed. If you fail to do so, or fail to conscientiously maintain promised security measures in working order (such as outdoor lighting or an electronic gate on the parking garage), a court or jury may find this lack of security to be a material factor in a crime on the premises. In this case, you may well be held liable for a tenant's losses or injuries. This is true even though you might not have been liable if you hadn't promised the specific security measures in the first place.

You won't be liable for failing to provide what was promised, however, unless this failure caused or contributed to the crime. Burned-out lightbulbs in the parking lot won't mean anything if the burglar got in through an unlocked trap door on the roof.

EXAMPLE: The manager of Jeff's apartment building gave him a thorough tour of the building before he decided to move in. Jeff was particularly impressed with the security locks on the gates of the high fences at the front and rear of the property. Confident that the interior of the property was accessible only to tenants and their guests, Jeff didn't hesitate to take his kitchen garbage to the dumpsters at the rear of the building late one evening. There he was accosted by an intruder who got in through a rear gate that had a broken lock. Jeff's landlord was held liable, because he had failed to maintain the sophisticated, effective locks that had been promised.

Ads That Invite Lawsuits

Advertisements like the following will come back to haunt you if a crime occurs on your rental property:

- "No one gets past our mega-security systems. A highly-trained guard is on duty at all times."
- "We provide highly safe, highly secure buildings."
- "You can count on us. We maintain the highest apartment security standards in the business."

Be Careful With Your Lease or Rental Agreement

The simple rule of following through with what you promise is even more crucial when it comes to written provisions in your lease or accompanying documents. Why? Your lease is a contract, and if it includes a "24-hour security" promise or a commitment to have a doorman on duty at night, your tenants have a right to expect it. If you fail to follow through, you could be sued and found liable for criminal acts that injure your tenants or their property.

EXAMPLE: The information packet given to Mai when she moved into her apartment stressed the need to keep careful track of door keys: "If you lose your keys, call the management, and the lock will be changed immediately." When Mai lost her purse containing her keys, she immediately called the management company but couldn't reach them, because it was after 5 p.m. and there was no after-hours emergency procedure. That evening, Mai was assaulted by someone who got into her apartment by using her lost key.

Mai sued the owner and management company on the grounds that they had disregarded their promise to change the locks promptly and so were partially responsible (along with the criminal) for the assailant's entry. The jury agreed and awarded Mai a large sum.

! CAUTION

Don't go overboard by specifying in your lease or rental agreement all the security measures you don't provide. Some landlords think that if they provide no security and say that tenants are completely on their own, they can eliminate liability for the acts of criminals. True, making it clear that you provide little or no security probably can reduce your potential liability for tenant injuries that result from criminal activity, but you can't excuse yourself from providing what is required by law. For example, if a local ordinance provides that exterior doors must have locks, you will increase—not decrease—your potential liability by failing to provide a front door lock.

Maintain What You Already Provide

Sometimes your actions can obligate you as much as an oral or written statement. If you provide enhanced security measures, such as security locks or a nighttime guard, without mentioning them in the lease, in advertisements, or through oral promises, you may be bound to maintain these features, even though you never explicitly promised to do so. Many landlords react with understandable frustration when their well-meaning (and expensive) efforts to protect their tenants actually *increase* their liability. But the answer is not to cut back to the bare minimum for security. Instead, be practical and keep your eye on your goal: Over time, using proven security measures will yield contented, long-term tenants and fewer legal hassles.

Prevent Criminal Acts

The best way to avoid liability for losses from crime is to prevent criminal acts in the first place.

The good news is that most successful prevention techniques—proper lighting, good locks, criminal-unfriendly landscaping, and well-trained on-site personnel—are not very expensive. Sometimes you'll have to go further, but whatever you spend on effective crime-prevention measures will pale in comparison to the costs that could result from crime on the premises.

Your Crime Prevention Checklist

- Meet or exceed requirements for safety devices, such as deadbolt locks, lighting, and window locks imposed by state and local housing codes.
- Don't hype your security measures. Keep oral and written promises regarding security measures—such as an advertisement promising garage parking or security personnel—to a truthful minimum.
- Provide and maintain adequate security measures based on an analysis of the vulnerability of your property and neighborhood. If your tenants will pay more rent if you make the building safer, you are foolish not to do it.
- Tighten up management practices to make your tenants and property safer—for example, practice strict key control.
- Educate tenants about crime problems and prevention strategies. Make it clear that they, not you, are primarily responsible for their own protection.
- Inspect the premises regularly to spot security problems, and ask tenants for their suggestions.
- Quickly respond to tenants' suggestions and complaints. If an important component of your security systems breaks, fix it on an emergency basis and provide appropriate alternative security.
- Be aware of threats to tenants' security from the manager or other tenants and handle safety and security problems pronto, especially those involving drug dealing.
- Buy adequate liability insurance to protect you from lawsuits related to crime on the property.

These costs can include increased insurance premiums, jury verdicts in excess of your insurance coverage, expensive attorney fees, and lost income due to rapid turnover of tenants. And there is no way to measure the sorrow and guilt that will come with knowing that you, as the landlord, may share responsibility for a crime because you did not take reasonable steps to prevent it. Don't pinch pennies here.

Evaluate Your Situation

The security steps you need to take depend on your circumstances: duplex or high-rise? peaceful neighborhood or high-crime area? Assess your needs and come up with a plan before you dash off to buy a security system you may not need.

Start With Your Own Inspection

Walk around your property and ask yourself two questions:

- Would I, or a member of my family, feel reasonably safe here, at night or alone?
- If I were a thief or assailant, how difficult would it be to get into the building or individual rental unit?

Schedule more than one assessment walk, at different times of the day and night. You might see something at 11 p.m. that you wouldn't notice at 11 a.m.

Consider the Neighborhood

Keep up-to-date on crime in the area of your rental property. If there have been no incidents in the neighborhood, you have less reason to equip your property with extensive security devices. (On the other hand, you certainly do not want one of your tenants to be the first to be raped or robbed on your block.) Especially if there have been criminal incidents in the neighborhood, talk to the neighbors and the police department about what measures have proven to be effective.

Get Advice From Experts

Most police departments will work with you to develop a sound security approach and educate tenants. Some will send an officer out to assess the vulnerability of your property and recommend security measures. Many will train tenants in neighborhood watch techniques, such as how to recognize and report suspicious behavior.

Another professional resource that may not immediately come to mind is your own insurance company. Some companies, having figured out that it's cheaper to offer preventive consultation services than to pay out huge awards to injured clients, consult with their clients for free on ways to deter crime. For example, drawing on its experience with claims generated by security breaches, your insurance company might be able to tell you which equipment has (and has not!) proven to be effective in preventing break-ins and assaults.

Another resource for advice is the private security industry. Listed in the phone book or online under "Security Systems," these firms typically provide an analysis of your situation before recommending specific equipment—whether it be bars on windows or an internal electronic surveillance system. Even if you do not ultimately engage their services, a professional evaluation may prove quite valuable as you design your own approach. As with other professional services, be sure to get several estimates and check references before selecting any security firm.

Security companies have a vested interest in getting you to buy products and services that may not be needed. If you own lots of rental properties, it may be worth your while to hire an independent security consultant for a disinterested evaluation. Call the International Association of Professional Security Consultants at 415-536-0288, or check their website at www.iapsc.org.

Take Basic Security Steps

At the very least, we recommend the following security measures for every rental property, from a single-family house or duplex to a multiunit building.

- **Exterior lighting.** Exterior lighting at entranceways and walkways should be activated by motion or on a timer. Do not rely on managers or tenants to turn on exterior lights. Many security experts regard the absence or failure of exterior lights as the single most common facilitator of break-ins and crime.

- **Interior lighting.** Have good, strong interior lights in hallways, stairwells, doorways, and parking garages.
- **Locks.** Sturdy dead-bolt door locks on individual rental units and solid window and patio door locks are essential, as are peepholes (with a wide-angle lens for viewing) at the front door of each unit. Lobby doors should have dead-bolt locks.
- **Landscaping.** Keep plants neat and compact. Shrubs should be no higher than three feet and trees cleared to seven feet from the ground. Trees and shrubbery should not obscure entryways or provide easy hiding places near doorways or windows. If yard maintenance is the tenants' responsibility in a single-family house, you may need to supervise the job.

You may also want to explore other measures, depending on the circumstances.

- **Security alarm.** You may want to install an alarm, hooked up to a security service.
- **Window bars.** Solid metal window bars or grills over ground floor windows are often a good idea in higher-crime neighborhoods, but local fire codes may restrict their use. All grills or bars must have a release mechanism, allowing the tenant to open them from inside. Too many people have tragically died in fires because they could not open window bars or grills that had no release mechanism.

Multiunit buildings may require additional measures:

- **Buzzers.** Intercom and buzzer systems that allow tenants to unlock the front door from their apartments are also a good idea; the front door can stay locked, and you can stress to tenants to open it only for people they know.
- **Doorman.** In some areas, a 24-hour doorman is essential and may do more to reduce

---

Don't Rely on "Courtesy Officers"

Some rental property owners provide on-site security by renting to police officers who, in exchange for a reduced rent, agree to be the resident "courtesy officer." The idea is to provide a professional presence on the property without paying for a regular security service. It's a poor idea, for several reasons:

- Calling the officer/tenant a courtesy officer does not change the fact that your tenants will look to him to provide consistent security protection. (In fact, because you are paying the officer by the rent reduction, he is not working as a courtesy at all.) A court would hold the police officer (and you) to the same standard of conduct expected of professional guard services.
- Because your officer/tenant can provide security only when he is home, the protection will be unpredictable. Tenants won't know when they can count on security coverage, and may do things (like coming home late at night) under the mistaken impression that the officer/tenant is on the property.
- The value of your officer/tenant's services will be as good as his wakefulness and attention. You are essentially asking him to assume a second job. But if he wants to unwind after a hard day with a few beers, how good will his judgment and response time be?

Paying a tenant for intermittent security makes you his employer, meaning you'll have to pay Social Security taxes and meet other employer obligations. (see Chapter 6 on tax issues and resident managers). And if a court finds your officer/tenant partially responsible for crime on the premises (by failing in his duties and allowing unauthorized access, for example), you will be liable as his employer.

A security service, on the other hand, is an independent contractor and takes care of these bookkeeping details. Independent contractors are generally responsible for their own lapses and should be insured (be sure you check). Of course, you could still be sued, but the chances of your being held liable will be reduced if an independent contractor provided the security service.

Signs of a Meth Lab

Landlords are increasingly encountering signs of methamphetamine (crystal meth) labs on rental properties. Meth is easily made by cooking common products such as cold remedies, salt, lighter fluid, gas, drain cleaners, and iodine on a stove or hot plate. Explosions and fires are common, and the byproducts of production pose an extreme health hazard.

According to the U.S. DEA, signs of a meth operation are:

- a large amount of cold tablet containers that list ephedrine or pseudoephedrine as ingredients
- jars containing clear liquid with a white or red colored solid on the bottom
- jars labeled as containing iodine or dark shiny metallic purple crystals inside of jars
- jars labeled as containing red phosphorus or a fine dark-red or purple powder
- coffee filters containing a white pasty substance, a dark-red sludge, or shiny white crystals
- bottles labeled as containing sulfuric, muriatic, or hydrochloric acid
- bottles or jars with rubber tubing attached
- cookware containing a powdery residue
- an unusually large number of cans of Camp Fuel, paint thinner, acetone, starter fluid, lye, and drain cleaners containing sulfuric acid or bottles containing muriatic acid
- large amounts of lithium batteries, especially ones that have been stripped
- soft silver or gray metallic ribbon (in chunk form) stored in oil or kerosene
- propane tanks with fittings that have turned blue
- strong smell of urine, or unusual chemical smells like ether, ammonia, or acetone.

If you think there's a meth lab in an occupied apartment or house, contact law enforcement immediately.

If you're left with an abandoned meth lab, here's what to do next:

- **Lock up and stay out.** Turning on lights could cause an explosion, and inhaling the fumes is very dangerous. Leave everything to the experts (see below).
- **Notify your insurance company.** Your policy may cover the cleanup costs, but some don't.
- **In case they don't know already, notify the police and fire department.** They will send a hazardous materials team to deal with the mess.
- **Cleaning.** Hire a company that specializes in meth lab cleanups to deal with the carpeting, walls, fixtures—basically, everything in the unit. Hire a licensed company if your state issues such licenses (contact the local health department to find out). Many states (either under the department of health or an environmental protection agency) include advice on cleaning up meth labs; see, for example, the Oklahoma Department of Environmental Quality (www.deq.state.ok.us) and search "guidelines for cleaning up former meth labs."
- **Test the apartment and get the official okay.** Use a different company to perform the test, and comply with any state- or local-mandated clearance requirements.
- **Find out whether you must notify future tenants.** Some states require landlords to tell applicants that the unit was a meth lab. Your state health department or health inspectors can tell you what your disclosure duties are. The Centers for Disease Control and Prevention includes of list of state departments of health at www.cdc.gov/mmwr/international/relres. html. The rental property's address may also appear on the U.S. Drug Enforcement Agency's "National Clandestine Laboratory Register" (www.dea.gov/clan-lab/clan-lab.shtml), for an indefinite time.

crime outside your building than anything else. Spread over a large number of units, a doorman may cost less than you think. If you hire a firm, insist on letters of reference and proof of insurance. You can also hire your own guard, but that gets complicated very quickly, because you will be responsible for his or her training and weapons used (if any).

- **Common areas.** Driveways, garages, and underground parking need to be well-lit and as secure (inaccessible to unauthorized entrants) as possible. Fences and automatic gates may be a virtual necessity in some areas.

- **Elevators.** Limiting access to the elevators by requiring a passkey and installing closed-circuit monitoring reduce the chances that an assailant will choose this site.

- **Security cameras.** A 24-hour internal security system with cameras and someone monitoring them is an effective crime detector. Though these systems are expensive, many reasonably affluent tenants will bear the extra costs in exchange for the added protection.

Initiate Good Management Practices

Physical safety devices and improvements aren't the only way you can improve security and decrease liability. Your business practices, including personnel policies, are crucial. They include:

Keep tenant information locked up. Keep tenant files in a locked cabinet. As an added precaution, identify residences by your own code, so that no one but you and your manager can read a tenant's file and learn where he or she lives.

Insist that employees respect tenants' privacy. Impress upon your employees the need to preserve your tenants' privacy. A tenant who wants friends, family, or bill collectors to know where she lives will tell them—you shouldn't.

Train employees to avoid dangerous situations and correct worrisome ones. Teach managers and employees to rigorously abide by your safety rules and to report areas of concern. Consider sending

employees to management courses on security offered by many landlords' associations.

Protect yourself and your employees when showing a unit. Ask for a photo ID and make a photocopy, which you should store in the office in a secure place. At the end of the tour, return the copy to the applicant or destroy it in the applicant's presence. Apply this practice to all applicants, not just those you think might pose a problem; selective practices invite discrimination claims (for example, don't ask for ID from only men, or any other protected class).

Don't undermine security measures with poor practices. Once you install security equipment, you must use it intelligently. For example, suppose you install locking gates at the property's entrance, but leave a key for the postal carrier in an unlocked box nearby. If an assailant gains entry by using that key, a jury could determine that you should be held partially responsible for the harm that ensued, because you were careless with the key.

Safeguard keys. The security of your rental property depends in large part on the locks on rental unit doors and the keys to those doors.

- Keep all duplicate keys in a locked area, identified by a code that only you and your manager know. Several types of locking key drawers and sophisticated key safes are available. Check ads in magazines that cater to the residential rental industry, or contact local locksmiths and security firms.

- Don't label keys with the rental unit number or name and address of the apartment building, and advise your tenants to take the same precaution.

- Allow only you and your manager access to master keys.

- Keep track of all keys provided to tenants and, if necessary, to your employees. Be sure all loaned keys are returned.

- Require tenants to return all keys at move-out.

- Rekey every time a new tenant moves in or loses a key.

- Give careful thought to the security problem of the front door lock: If the lock opens by an easy-to-copy key, there is no way to prevent a tenant from copying the key and giving it to others or using it after he moves out. Consider using locks that have hard-to-copy keys, or (with rental houses or small properties) rekey the front door when a tenant moves. There are also easy-to-alter card systems that allow you to change front door access on a regular basis or when a tenant moves. Again, locksmiths and security firms can advise you on options available.

- Give keys only to people you know and trust. If you have hired a contractor whom you do not know personally, open the unit for him and return to close up when he is done. Keep in mind that often even known and trusted contractors hire others you don't know.

When a Tenant Wants to Supply Additional Security

The form lease and rental agreements (Chapter 2) forbid the tenant from rekeying or adding locks or a burglar alarm without your written consent. But think carefully before you refuse permission to install extra protection. If a crime occurs that would have been foiled had the security item been in place, and you get sued, you will obviously be at a disadvantage before a judge or jury.

If you let a tenant add additional security measures, make sure the tenant gives you duplicate keys or instructions on how to disarm the alarm system and the name and phone number of the alarm company, so that you can enter in case of emergency.

Educate Tenants About Crime Prevention

After you have identified the vulnerabilities of the neighborhood—for example, by talking to the police—don't keep this information to yourself. Share it with your tenants. It's best to do this when you first show the rental unit to prospective tenants. We recommend a two-step process:

- Alert tenants to the specific risks of your neighborhood (for example, "problems are worst Friday and Saturday night between 10 p.m. and 1 a.m.") and what they can do to minimize the chances of assault or theft (avoid being alone on the street or in outside parking lots late at night), and
- No matter how secure your building, warn tenants of the limitations of the security measures you have provided.

> **EXAMPLE:** Paul moves into his apartment and is told by the manager that doormen are on duty only from 6 p.m. to 6 a.m. One afternoon, someone knocks on Paul's door and identifies himself as a "building inspector" who needs to check the heating system. Realizing that the doorman is not on duty to screen visitors, Paul demands identification. When the alleged inspector refuses to show ID, Paul won't open the door. He later finds out that someone in the neighborhood has been robbed, falling for the same ruse.

This twofold approach allows you to cover your legal bases by both disclosing the risks and frankly informing tenants that you cannot ensure their safety in all possible situations. If, despite your best efforts, a crime does occur on your property, your candid disclosures regarding the safety problems of your neighborhood and the limitations of the existing security measures may help shield you from liability.

From the tenant's point of view, such disclosures highlight the need to be vigilant and assume some responsibility for safety. If you do not disclose the limitations of the security you provide (or if you exaggerate) and a crime does occur, one of the first things your tenant will say (to the police, his lawyer, and the jury) is that he was simply relying upon the protection you had assured him would be in place.

Identify Specific Concerns

Give tenants information specific to your rental property. Here are some ideas:

- If there have been incidents of crime in the area, especially in your building, inform your tenants but don't disclose the identity of the victim.

- Update your information on the security situation as necessary. For example, let tenants know if there has been an assault in or near the building by sending them a note and post a notice in the lobby, including the physical description of the assailant.
- If you hire a professional security firm to evaluate your rental property, share the results of their investigation with your tenants.
- Encourage tenants to set up a neighborhood watch program. Many local police departments will come out and meet with citizens attempting to organize such a program.
- Encourage tenants to report any suspicious activities or security problems to you, such as loitering, large numbers of late-night guests, or broken locks. (Chapter 9 recommends a system for handling tenant complaints.)

Terrorist Attacks

If you want information on preparing tenants for possible terrorist attacks, including issues for high-rise buildings, see the U.S. government website, www.ready.gov (search "terrorist hazards").

Explain the Limitations of Your Security Measures

An important component of your disclosures to tenants involves disabusing them of any notion that you are their guardian angel. Let them know where your security efforts end, and where their own good sense (and the local police force) must take over. Specifically:

- Point out each security measure—such as locking exterior gates, key locks on windows, and peepholes in every front door—and explain how each measure works. It's best to do this in writing, either as part of a move-in letter to new tenants or at the time a new security item is installed.
- Highlight particular aspects of the property that are, despite your efforts, vulnerable to

the presence of would-be assailants or thieves. Say, for example, your apartment parking garage has a self-closing door. When you explain how this door works, you might also point out that it's not instantaneous. For example, a fast-moving person could, in most situations, slip into the garage behind an entering car despite the self-closing door. Pointing this out to your tenant may result in more careful attention to the rearview mirror.
- Place signs in potentially dangerous places that will remind tenants of possible dangers and the need to be vigilant. For example, place a notice in the lobby asking tenants to securely lock the front door behind them.
- Suggest safety measures. For example, tenants arriving home after dark might call ahead and ask a neighbor to be an escort.

Giving your tenants information on how they, too, can take steps to protect themselves will also help if you are sued. If a tenant argues that you failed to inform him of a dangerous condition, you will be able to show that you have done all that could be expected of a reasonably conscientious landlord.

Inspect and Maintain Your Property

Landlords are most often found liable for crime on their property when a criminal gained access through broken doors or locks. Not only is the best security equipment in the world useless if it has deteriorated or is broken, but the very fact that it's not working can be enough to result in landlord liability. By contrast, a jury is far less likely to fault a landlord who can show that reasonable security measures were in place and working, but were unable to stop a determined criminal.

Inspect your property frequently, so that you discover and fix problems before an opportunistic criminal comes along. At the top of your list should be fixing burned-out exterior floodlights and broken locks and cutting back overgrown shrubbery that provides a lurking spot for criminals.

Protect Yourself, Too

Landlords and managers need to take precautions for their own safety as well as for that of tenants. Whether or not you live on the rental property:

- Promptly deposit rent checks and money orders. If possible, do not accept cash.
- When you show a vacant apartment, consider bringing someone with you. A would-be assailant may be deterred by the presence of another person. If you must show apartments by yourself, alert a family member or friend to the fact that you are showing a vacant unit, and when you expect to be done.
- Especially if your building is in a high-crime area, carry a small alarm device (such as beeper-sized box that emits a piercing alarm when its pin is removed), and carry a cell phone.
- Work on vacant units during the day and be alert to the fact that, although keeping the front door open (to the building or the unit) may be convenient as you go to and fro for materials and equipment, it is also an invitation to someone to walk right into the building.

Enlist your tenants to help you spot and correct security problems—both in their own rental unit and in common areas such as parking garages. The people who actually live in your rental property will generally know first about security hazards. One good approach is to post several notices in central locations, such as elevators and main lobbies, asking tenants to promptly report any security problems, such as broken locks or windows. If you rent a duplex or house, periodically meet with your tenants and discuss any changes in the neighborhood or the structure of the building.

Handle Security Complaints Immediately

Take care of complaints about a dangerous situation or a broken security item immediately, even if it's the middle of the night. A broken lock or disabled intercom system is an invitation to crime and needs to be addressed pronto.

Either fix the problem or, if that's impossible, alert tenants and take other measures. For example, you might hire a security officer and close off other entrances for a few days if your front door security system fails and a necessary part is not immediately available. Failing to do this may saddle you with a higher level of legal liability should a tenant be injured by a criminal act while the security system is out of service or a window lock broken. A few examples of quick and appropriate responses:

- The glass panel next to the front door is accidentally broken late one afternoon by a departing workman. Conscious that this creates a major security problem, you call a 24-hour glass replacement service to get it replaced immediately.
- The intercom system fails due to a power surge following an electrical storm. You hire a 24-hour guard for the two days it takes to repair the circuitry.
- Several exterior floodlights are knocked out by vandals throwing rocks at 6 p.m. A tenant, who has been encouraged by management to immediately report problems of this nature, calls you. You alert the police and ask for an extra drive-by during the night, post signs in the lobby and the elevator, close off the darkened entrance, and advise tenants to use an alternate, lighted entryway instead. The next day, you get the floodlights repaired and equipped with wire mesh protection.

TIP
Establish good complaint procedures.
Encouraging tenants to keep you informed will help you prevent crime on the property. Such procedures can also limit your liability, should you be sued, for example, by a tenant whose assailant gained access because of a broken window lock that the tenant never told you about. See Chapter 9.

Protect Tenants From Each Other

What if one of your tenants is responsible for criminal activity on the premises, or poses a danger? (Physical disputes between tenants in the same household—domestic violence—are discussed in Chapter 8.) You have a duty to take reasonable steps to protect tenants if another resident threatens harm or property damage. If you don't, and a tenant is injured or robbed by another tenant, you may be sued and pay a hefty judgment. As with your duty to protect tenants from crime at the hands of strangers, your duty to keep the peace among your tenants is limited to what is *reasonably* foreseeable and to what a *reasonable* person in your position would do.

Note that the scenarios and advice that follow assume that you are not dealing with a dangerous tenant who is also legally disabled. In that situation, you may need to work with your tenant if you can reasonably expect that the behavior will stop. See "Do You Need to Accommodate Tenants With Disabilities Who Are Dangerous" in Chapter 5.

> **TIP**
> **Encourage tenants to report other tenants' suspicious or illegal activity.** Establish a system to collect tenants' complaints and concerns about other tenants or the manager, just the way you handle repair complaints. This will let you respond quickly. It will serve an additional function: If you are sued for something a manager or tenant does, and if your business records show that there were no prior complaints regarding his behavior, that will bolster your claim that you acted reasonably under the circumstances (by continuing to rent to or employ the individual), because you had no inkling that trouble was likely.

When to Act

If you learn that a tenant has threatened or committed violence on your property, you may need to take action. Whether to act—by terminating the tenancy—depends on the seriousness of the behavior, and the likelihood that similar acts will occur again on your property. Unless there's a clear history of serious problems with the offending tenant, landlords often win these cases.

> **EXAMPLE 1:** Evelyn decides to rent an apartment to David, although she knows that he was convicted of spousal abuse years earlier. For several months David is a model tenant, until he hits another tenant, Chuck, in the laundry room over a disagreement as to who was next in line for the dryer. Chuck sues but is unable to convince a jury that Evelyn should bear some responsibility for his injuries, because he cannot show that the incident was foreseeable.

> **EXAMPLE 2:** Mary rents to Carl, who appears to be a nice young man with adequate references. On the rental application, Carl states that he has no criminal convictions. Several months later, Carl is arrested for burglary and assault of another tenant in the building. It comes out that Carl had recently been released from state prison for burglary and rape. Because Mary had no knowledge of his criminal past, she is not held liable for his actions.

On the other hand, tenants sometimes win if they can show that the landlord knew about a resident's tendency towards violence and failed to take reasonable precautions to safeguard the other tenants.

> **EXAMPLE:** Bill receives several complaints from tenants about Carol, a tenant who pushed another resident out of the elevator, slapped a child for making noise, and verbally abused a tenant's guest for parking in Carol's space. Despite these warning signs, Bill doesn't terminate Carol's tenancy or even speak with her about her behavior. When Carol picks a fight with a resident whom she accused of reading her newspaper and badly beats her up, Bill is held partly liable on the grounds that he knew of a dangerous situation but failed to address it.

What to Do

When you learn of the potential for danger from a tenant and decide to act, your response should be swift and appropriate.

Law enforcement. In an emergency—for example, one tenant brandishes a gun—of course you would just call police. Do the same if drugs are involved.

Eviction. In less dire circumstances, you'll probably want to evict the worrisome tenant, and possibly post a guard and warn other tenants until he's gone. Many states now make it relatively simple for landlords to evict troublemakers. These laws specify that harm or the threat of harm to other persons justifies a quick eviction.

Incentives. If you don't want to go through the hassle of eviction, and you want to get someone out quickly, consider offering a financial incentive to leave. Let the tenant break the lease without a penalty—it's a small price to pay to defuse a dangerous situation.

Warnings to other tenants. In some cases, you might not be able to evict a tenant you think might pose a danger. For example, if you learn from your state's "Megan's Law" database that a current tenant has a conviction for a sexual offense, you might not legally be able to terminate the tenancy. (The issue is explained in "Other Tenant Violations of the Lease or Rental Agreement" in Chapter 17.) If you have no legal grounds to evict, but you think that this tenant poses a danger to your tenants, you should warn them. Your warning should be as factual and noninflammatory as possible. The last thing you want is an angry mob outside a tenant's door, demanding that he leave town (unfortunately, such scenes have happened).

Negotiation. If the danger seems minor, you can try to talk to the troublemaker and head off future problems. For example, suppose a tenant complains about a neighbor who bangs on the walls and yells every time the tenant practices the violin during the afternoon, and the pounding is getting louder every day. The tenant can reasonably expect you to intervene and attempt to broker a solution—perhaps an adjustment of the violinist's practice schedule or some heavy-duty earplugs for the neighbor.

Protect Tenants From Your Employees

Your property manager occupies a critical position in your business. The manager interacts with every tenant and often has access to their personal files *and* their homes. If your manager commits a crime—especially if you had any warning that it might occur—you are likely to be held liable. The same goes for other employees, such as maintenance personnel. Your liability usually turns on whether or not you acted reasonably under the circumstances in hiring and supervising your employees. Let's take a closer look at what this means.

> **RELATED TOPIC**
> **Chapter 6 discusses managers in detail.**

Check Your Employees' Backgrounds

It is essential to thoroughly check the background of your potential manager and other on-site workers. If a manager or other worker commits a crime—for example, he robs or assaults a tenant—you are likely to be sued for negligent hiring. You may be found liable if all of the following are true:

- You failed to investigate your employee's background to the full extent allowed by the privacy laws in your state.
- A proper investigation would have revealed a past criminal conviction that would have rendered the applicant unsuitable for the job.
- The employee's offense against the tenant is reasonably related to the past conviction.

EXAMPLE: When his longtime manager suddenly leaves, Martin feels pressured to replace her fast. He hires Jack without checking his background or the information provided on the application. Martin takes Jack at his word when he says that he has no felony convictions. Several months later, Jack is arrested for stealing stereo equipment from a tenant's home that he had entered using the master key. Martin is successfully sued when the tenant learns that Jack had two prior felony convictions for burglary and grand theft.

Supervise Your Manager

As the manager's employer, you may also be held liable if your manager's negligence makes it possible for another person to commit a crime against a tenant. For example, if your manager's sloppy practices make it possible for a criminal to get a tenant's key, you will be held responsible on the grounds that you failed to properly supervise the manager.

Deal With Drug-Dealing Tenants

If you look the other way while tenants engage in illegal activity on your property—by dealing drugs, storing stolen property, engaging in prostitution, or participating in gang-related activity—you can end up paying huge fines or even losing your property altogether to government seizure. This discussion focuses on the most common problem, drug dealing, but it applies equally to other illegal activities.

It's your responsibility to know what's going on at your property. In some situations, fines are levied or property is seized even though the landlord knew almost nothing about the tenants' activities. So keep yourself well-informed, and if you even suspect that illegal drug dealing is taking place on the rental property, act quickly and decisively. If you do nothing—either out of inertia, fear of reprisals from drug dealers, or a mistaken belief that you're unlikely to get in trouble—you will almost surely regret it.

The Cost of Renting to Drug-Dealing Tenants

Increasingly, laws and court decisions have made landlords liable when a tenant engages in a continuing illegal activity such as drug dealing. If you don't quickly evict drug-dealing tenants, you'll run into some big problems:

- Good tenants may be difficult to find and keep, and the value of your property will plummet.
- Good tenants, trying to avoid drug-dealing ones, may be able to legally move out without notice and before a lease runs out. They will argue that the presence of the illegal activity has, for all practical purposes, evicted them, in that the problems associated with drug dealing prevent them from the "quiet enjoyment" of their home or violate the implied warranty of habitability. In many states, the tenant will have a very strong case to break their lease.
- Tenants injured or annoyed by drug dealers, both in the building and neighborhood, may sue you for violating nuisance laws and building codes.
- Local, state, or federal authorities may levy stiff fines against you and may even empty your building for allowing the illegal activity to continue.
- Law enforcement authorities may pursue criminal penalties against both the tenants *and* you for knowingly allowing the activity to continue.
- Your rental property might even be confiscated by the state or federal government.

Nice Properties Are Not Immune

You may think that drug crime is a problem only in seedy neighborhoods. Think again. Drug dealers often prefer smaller apartment complexes with some measure of security over large, unprotected housing units. A drug dealer, like a law-abiding tenant, wants a safe, controlled environment.

Lawsuits Against You for Harboring a Nuisance

In legal terms, a nuisance is a pervasive, continuing, and serious condition—like a pile of stinking garbage or a group of drug dealers—that threatens public health, safety, or morals. In some states, it also includes obnoxious activity that is simply offensive, like excessive noise or open sexual conduct. Property used as a drug house, which injures and interferes with the rights of neighbors to use and enjoy their property easily qualifies as a legal nuisance.

The government, and sometimes the neighbors, can sue to get a nuisance stopped (abated), often by court order and fines against the landlord. If you tolerate a nuisance on your property, you can be sued. Even though the tenant causes the nuisance, the punishment may be directed at you, as the landlord.

> **EXAMPLE:** Alma owned a duplex in Wisconsin, which defines drug houses as nuisances. (Wisc. Stat. Ann. § 823.113.) Despite repeated complaints from the neighbors that one of her tenants was conducting a drug operation in his home (and in spite of the tenant's two arrests for dealing from that address), Alma did nothing about the problem. Responding to pressure from fed-up neighbors, the local police finally sued Alma to evict the tenant and close the duplex. The property was padlocked.

Using public nuisance abatement laws against crime-tolerant landlords is increasingly common in cities with pervasive drug problems. In extreme cases, where the conduct giving rise to the nuisance complaint is illegal (drug dealing or prostitution, for example), landlords themselves face civil fines or jail time. See "Civil and Criminal Nuisance Laws," below.

Each state has different standards for determining when a landlord may be found responsible under nuisance law. In most states, however, the landlord must have had *some* knowledge of the illegal activity before property can be seized. Generally, landlords are given a short time in which to cure the problem before the ax falls and the property is seized.

In reality, because most landlords are acutely aware of their tenants' illegal behavior—having been informed by disgusted neighbors and overwhelmed law enforcement—even in states that require that you have clear actual knowledge of the situation, this knowledge standard is usually met. Put another way, it's a rare situation in which you can credibly claim that you didn't know about drug-dealing tenants.

Know the Law

It is important to know the nuisance laws in your state. At the very least, this will alert you to the standard by which your actions (or inaction) will be judged should there be proceedings brought against you or your property. Chapter 18 gives tips on how to unearth the laws that apply to you.

Civil and Criminal Nuisance Laws		
	Civil Nuisance Laws	**Criminal Nuisance Laws**
Activities the laws target	Unhealthy, immoral, or obnoxious behavior which may be, but is not necessarily, a violation of the criminal law as well	Criminal behavior
Examples of targeted activities	Excessive noise, piles of garbage and trash, and inordinate amounts of foot or car traffic	Drug dealing, prostitution, gambling, and gang activities
Who can sue	Public agencies such as city health departments, law enforcement agencies, and, in many states, affected neighbors, who may band together and sue for large sums in small claims court	Law enforcement agencies only
How landlord's liability is determined	"Preponderance of evidence" shows landlord intentionally tolerated the illegal activity, or was negligent or reckless in allowing it to occur.	Prosecutor must prove guilt "beyond a reasonable doubt" and usually must show landlord had some knowledge of illegal activity.
Possible consequences to the landlord	A court ordering the offending tenant, and sometimes the landlord, to compensate other tenants. If a health, fire, or other enforcement agency brings the nuisance action based on many violations, it can result in a court order closing down the entire building.	Liability for money damages plus fines and imprisonment. Government may also close the property.

Tenants and neighbors, not just the government, can sue you for knowing about the activity but failing to take steps to clean up the property. They can seek:

- Monetary compensation for each of them for having put up with the situation. Each neighbor generally sues for the maximum allowed in state small claims court ($3,000 to $10,000 in most states), and the landlord often pays the maximum to *each* one. See the discussion of small claims courts in Chapter 16.
- An order from the judge directing you to evict the troublemakers, install security, and repair the premises. (Such orders are not available in all states.)

Private use of nuisance abatement laws is not as common as governmental use, but the practice will probably grow as people learn of others' successes.

Small (But Sometimes Mighty) Claims Court

The private enforcement of public nuisance laws has been creatively and successfully pursued in small claims courts in California and several other states, where groups of affected neighbors have brought multiple lawsuits targeted at drug houses.

In Berkeley, California, after failing to get the police and city council to close down a crack house, neighbors sought damages stemming from the noxious activities associated with the house. Each of the 18 plaintiffs collected the maximum amount allowed in small claims court ($3,500 at the time), avoided the expense of hiring counsel, and sent the landlord a very clear and expensive message. The problem was solved within a few weeks.

Losing Your Property: Forfeiture Laws

Federal or state forfeiture proceedings—where the government *takes* your property because of the illegal activities of one or more tenants—are the most dramatic possible consequence of owning crime-ridden rental property. Forfeitures are rare and not something you are likely to encounter if you follow the suggestions in this book for choosing decent tenants and maintaining safe and secure rental property. But they happen.

Unlike the nuisance abatement laws, which depend upon a pervasive and continuing pattern of illegal activity, forfeitures may be accomplished on the basis of a single incident. Also, unlike nuisance abatement laws, which temporarily deprive you of the use of your property, the consequence of a forfeiture is the complete and final transfer of title to the government.

You Might Forfeit the Rent Money, Too

If you know, or have reason to know, that a tenant's rent was earned in the course of an illegal act, the rent money is itself forfeitable, no matter where the act was committed. A clever dealer may live in your nice, respectable building and conduct his trade elsewhere—but if he pays the rent with the money received in drug transactions, the rent money will be forfeited if the government can show that you knew (or had reason to know) of its source.

It is harder for the government to prove that you knew of the source of the rental payments than it is to show that you knew about illegal activity on the premises—but not impossible. To protect yourself, be able to point to a careful background check (regarding the tenant's job, credit, and bank account) performed before renting to the tenant. If you can show that there appeared to be a legitimate source of income to cover the rent, it will be harder for the government to argue that it should have been obvious that the rent constituted ill-gotten gain. Your refusal to accept cash rent may help protect you from an assertion that the money was the fruit of a drug transaction.

Federal laws. The government can seize property that has "facilitated" an illegal drug transaction or that has been bought or maintained with funds, such as rent payments, gained through illegal drug dealing. (Comprehensive Drug Abuse

Prevention and Control Act of 1970, 21 U.S. Code § 881.) The government's power under this law must give any landlord pause. To start forfeiture proceedings, the government need show only that it is *reasonably probable* that illegal activities are occurring on the premises, and may do so by relying on circumstantial evidence and hearsay. You must then prove either that the property did not facilitate the crime, or that the tenants' activities were done without your knowledge or consent. Your deliberate blindness will be of no avail. To prevail, you must show that you have done *all* that reasonably could be expected to prevent the illegal use of your property.

State laws. Every state has adopted the Uniform Controlled Substances Act, modifying it to suit their policy aims. The Act specifies that land involved in drug transactions is *not* forfeitable. Drug "containers," however, can be seized, and some states have interpreted that term to include property—for example, the rental property where drugs were kept. In many states, the Act has been changed to include rental or other property that "facilitated" the illegal act.

Under the Act, you must be shown to have knowledge of the illegal activity in order for forfeiture to occur, but that requirement is interpreted very differently in different states. In some states, the prosecutor need only show constructive knowledge of drug dealing—that is, what a reasonable person in the circumstances would conclude. In others, the state must prove that you actually knew of the drug problem. In a few states, landowners are accountable if they were negligent in not knowing of the drug-related activities of their tenants. In any case, it is difficult to successfully prove ignorance.

How to Prevent Drug Lawsuits and Seizures

If you follow these steps, it is unlikely that conditions will deteriorate to the point that neighbors or the government feel it is necessary to step in and take over:

- Carefully screen potential renters.
- Keep the results of your background checks that show that your tenants' rent appeared to come from legitimate sources (jobs and bank accounts).
- Don't accept cash rental payments.
- Include a clause in your lease or rental agreement prohibiting drug dealing and other illegal activity, and promptly evict tenants who violate it.
- Let tenants know you intend to keep drug dealing out of the building.
- Respond to tenant and neighbor complaints about drug dealing on the property.
- Be aware of heavy traffic in and out of the premises.
- Inspect the premises and improve lighting and security.
- Get advice from police and security professionals *immediately* if you learn of a problem.
- Consult security experts to determine whether you have done all that one could reasonably expect to discover and prevent illegal activity on your property.

If You Are Sued

If your efforts at crime prevention fail, and a tenant is injured, will you be responsible? As mentioned, if you violated a specific law requiring a safety measure, and that's what led directly to the injury or loss, you will probably be liable. But you also have a general duty to take reasonable precautions to protect tenants from foreseeable criminal assaults and property crimes. To get an idea of whether or not your precautions were reasonable under the circumstances, take a look at these six key questions. They're also discussed in Chapter 10, because they're also used if an insurance adjuster or court evaluates your negligence and assesses responsibility when a tenant suffers accidental injury.

1. Did you control the area where the crime occurred? You aren't expected to police the entire world. But a lobby, hallway, or other common area is an area of high landlord control, which heightens your responsibility. However, you exert much less control over the sidewalk outside the front door, so it may be more difficult for you to minimize the chances of a crime occurring there.

2. How likely was it that a crime would occur? You are duty-bound to respond to the foreseeable, not the improbable. Have there been prior criminal incidents at a particular spot in the building? Elsewhere in the neighborhood? If you know that an offense is likely (because of a rash of break-ins or prior crime on the property), you have a heightened legal responsibility in most states to take reasonable steps to guard against future crime.

3. How difficult or expensive would it have been to reduce the risk of crime? If cheap or simple measures could significantly lower the risk of crime, it is likely that a court would find that you had a duty to undertake them if their absence facilitated a crime, especially in an area where criminal activity is high. For instance, would inexpensive new locks and better lighting discourage thieves? How about better management practices, such as strict key control, locked tenant files, scrupulous employee screening, and trained, alert on-site personnel? However, if the only solution to the problem is costly, such as structural remodeling or hiring a full-time doorman, it is doubtful that a court would expect it of you.

4. How serious an injury was likely to result from the crime? The consequences of a criminal incident (break-in, robbery, rape, or murder) may be very serious.

5. Did you fail to take reasonable steps to prevent a crime? As ever, reasonableness is evaluated in the context of each situation. For example, if you let the bushes near a door grow high and don't replace outdoor lights, it's clearly unreasonable.

But suppose you cut the bushes back halfway and installed one light. Would that have been enough? It would be up to a jury to decide.

"Reasonable precautions" in a crime-free neighborhood are not the same as those called for when three apartments in your building have been burglarized within a month. The greater the danger, the more you must do.

6. Did your failure to take reasonable steps to keep tenants safe contribute to the crime? A tenant must be able to connect your failure to provide reasonable security with the criminal incident. It is often very difficult for tenants to convince a jury that the landlord's breach caused (or contributed to) the assault or burglary.

When an intruder enters through an unsecured front door, you are not responsible for the criminal's determination to break the law, and many juries simply won't place any responsibility on you, even if, for example, your failure to install a lock made the entry possible. To convince a jury otherwise, a tenant must emphasize that a crime of this nature was highly foreseeable and would probably have been prevented had you taken appropriate measures.

If a jury decides that you didn't meet the duty to keep tenants safe, and that this failure facilitated the crime, it will typically split the responsibility for the crime between you and the criminal. For example, jurors might decide that you were 60% at fault and the criminal 40%.

How Much Money a Tenant Is Entitled To

To get financial compensation, an injured tenant must show that he or she was harmed from the criminal incident. Tragically, this is often quite obvious, and the only issue that lawyers argue about is the worth, in dollars, of dreadful injuries. Compensation may also be awarded for mental anguish and continuing psychological effects of the encounter.

Now let's look at two realistic cases, applying the six questions.

EXAMPLE 1: Elaine was assaulted and robbed by an intruder who entered her apartment through a sliding window that was closed but could not be locked. To determine whether or not the landlord would be liable, Elaine asked herself the six questions and came up with these answers:

1. The landlord controlled the window and was responsible for its operation.
2. This burglary was foreseeable, because there had been other break-ins at the building.
3. Installing a window lock was a minor burden.
4. The seriousness of foreseeable injury was high.
5. The landlord had done nothing to secure the window or otherwise prevent an intrusion.
6. The intruder could not have entered so easily and silently had the window been locked.

Elaine concluded that the landlord owed her the duty to take reasonable steps to fix the problem. She filed a claim with the landlord's insurance company, but it didn't offer a fair settlement, and the case went to trial. The jury decided that the landlord should have installed a window lock and that because the burglar might not have entered at all through a properly secured window, the landlord was partially responsible for Elaine's injuries. The jury fixed the value of her injuries at $500,000 and decided that the landlord was 80% responsible.

EXAMPLE 2: Nick was assaulted in the underground garage of his apartment building by someone who hid in the shadows. The neighborhood had recently experienced several muggings. Nick couldn't identify the assailant, who was never caught. The automatic garage gate was broken and wouldn't close completely, allowing anyone to slip inside.

Nick decided that:

1. The landlord controlled the garage.
2. In view of the recent similar crimes in the neighborhood, an assault was foreseeable.
3. Fixing the broken gate wouldn't have been a great financial burden.
4. The likelihood of injury from an assault was high.

Nick concluded that the landlord owed him a duty of care in this situation. He then considered the last two questions. The garage door was broken, which constituted a breach of the landlord's duty. But the garage was also accessible from the interior of the building, making it possible that the assailant had been another tenant or a guest. Nick's case fell apart because the landlord's failure to provide a secure outside door hadn't necessarily contributed to the crime. If the assailant were another tenant or guest, the landlord's failure to fix the gate would have been completely unconnected to the crime. Nick probably would have had a winning case if he could have proved that the assailant got in through the broken gate.

CHAPTER

13

Landlord's Right of Entry and Tenants' Privacy

FORMS IN THIS CHAPTER

Chapter 13 includes instructions for and a sample of the following form:

- Notice of Intent to Enter Dwelling Unit

The Nolo website includes a downloadable copy of this form. See Appendix B for the link to the forms in this book.

Next to disputes over rent or security deposits, one of the most common—and emotion-filled—misunderstandings between landlords and tenants involves conflicts between your right to enter the rental property and a tenant's right to be left alone at home. Fortunately many of these problems can be avoided if you adopt fair—and, of course, legal—policies to enter the tenant's unit and then clearly explain these policies to the tenant from the first day of your relationship. (And, if you employ a manager or management company, make sure they also follow your guidelines.)

This chapter recommends a practical approach that should keep you out of legal hot water.

maintenance of the premises. This means that, of necessity, you have a legal responsibility to keep fairly close tabs on the condition of the property. For this reason, and because it makes good sense to allow landlords reasonable access to their property, nearly every state has, by judicial decision or statute, clearly recognized the right of a landlord to legally enter rented premises while a tenant is still in residence under certain broad circumstances, such as to deal with an emergency and when the tenant gives permission.

For details on state rules, including allowable reasons for entry and notice requirements, see "State Laws on Landlord's Access to Rental Property" in Appendix A.

RELATED TOPIC
Related topics covered in this book include:

- Recommended lease and rental agreement clause for landlord's access to rental property: Chapter 2
- How to make sure your manager doesn't violate tenants' right of privacy: Chapter 6
- How to highlight access procedures in a move-in letter to new tenants: Chapter 7
- Tenants' right of privacy and landlord's policy on guests: Chapter 8
- Procedures for respecting tenants' right of privacy while handling tenant complaints about safety and maintenance problems and conducting an annual safety inspection: Chapter 9
- How to protect the confidentiality of tenants' credit reports and notify tenants of any breach in your security: Chapter 9
- Tenants' right of privacy if drug dealing or terrorist activity is suspected: Chapter 12
- How to handle disputes with tenants through negotiation, mediation, and other means: Chapter 16
- State Laws on Landlord's Access to Rental Property: Appendix A.

General Rules of Entry

In most states, the tenant's duty to pay rent is conditioned on your proper repair and

---

How to Respect Tenants' Privacy Rights

Step 1: Know and comply with your state's law on landlord's access to rental property.

Step 2: Include a lease or rental agreement clause that complies with the law and gives you reasonable rights of entry.

Step 3: To avoid any uncertainty, highlight your policies on entry in a move-in letter to new tenants and other periodic communications.

Step 4: Notify tenants whenever you plan to enter their rental unit.

Step 5: Provide as much notice as possible before you enter, or, at a minimum, the amount of time required by state law.

Step 6: Keep written records of your requests to enter rental units.

Step 7: Protect yourself from a tenant's claim that you or your employee or independent contractor is a thief—for example, try to arrange repairs only when the tenant is home.

Step 8: Meet—and possibly mediate—with any tenants who object to your reasonable access policies to come up with a mutual agreement regarding your entry.

Step 9: Never force entry, short of a true emergency.

Step 10: Consider terminating the tenancy of any tenant who unreasonably restricts your right to enter the rental unit.

Allowable Reasons for Entry

About half the states have access laws specifying the circumstances under which landlords may legally enter rented premises. Most access laws allow landlords to enter rental units to make repairs and inspect the property and to show property to prospective tenants or buyers.

Notice Requirements

State access laws typically specify the amount of notice required for landlord entry—usually 24 hours or two days (unless it is impracticable to do so—for example, in cases of emergency). A few states simply require the landlord to provide "reasonable" notice, often presumed to be 24 hours.

Must Notice Be in Writing?

State access laws do not uniformly require that notice be in writing, but it's a good idea to give written notice. If the tenant later claims that you didn't follow legal procedures regarding right to entry, your copy of a written notice that you mailed, left in the tenant's mailbox, or posted on his door is proof that you notified him in advance of your intention to enter. It's also wise to document all oral or email requests for entry—but written notice is preferable (as explained in "Using Emails for Notices or Other Communications to Tenants" in Chapter 7). A sample letter requesting entry and a formal Notice of Intent to Enter Dwelling Unit form are included below.

Time of Day You May Enter

Most state access laws either do not specify the hours when a landlord may enter or simply allow entry at "reasonable" times, without setting specific hours and days. Weekdays between 9 a.m. and 6 p.m. would seem to be reasonable times, and perhaps Saturday mornings between 10 a.m. and 1 p.m. On the other hand, some statutes are more specific, such as Florida (between 7:30 a.m. and 8 p.m.) and Delaware (between 8 a.m. and 9 p.m.).

The Best Approach

If your state does not set specific rules regarding landlords' entry, this doesn't mean you can—or should—enter a tenant's home at any time for any reason. Once you rent residential property, you must respect it as your tenant's home. We recommend you provide as much notice as possible (in writing), try to arrange a mutually convenient time, and only enter for clearly legitimate business reasons, such as to make necessary repairs. If it's not an emergency or clearly impractical, try to give at least 24 hours' notice, especially when entering a rental unit when the tenant is likely to be home. In some circumstances, less notice (say, ten or 15 hours) might be fine—for example, if you find out Thursday evening that an electrician is available Friday morning to put extra outlets in the tenant's apartment. Except for an emergency, less than four hours' notice is not ordinarily considered reasonable. Common sense suggests that you be considerate of your tenants' privacy and do your best to accommodate their schedules. You'll go a long way toward keeping tenants and avoiding disputes and legal problems by doing so.

Entry in Case of Emergency

In all states, you can enter a rental unit without giving notice to respond to a true emergency—such as a fire or gas leak—that threatens life or property if not corrected immediately.

Here are some examples of emergency situations when it would be legal to enter without giving the tenant notice:

- Smoke is pouring out the tenant's window. You call the fire department and use your master key—or even break in if necessary—to try to deal with the fire.
- You see water coming out of the bottom of a tenant's back door. It's okay to enter and find the water leak.
- Your on-site manager hears screams coming from the apartment next door. He knocks

on the apartment door, but no one answers. After calling the police, he uses his pass key to enter and see what's wrong.

On the other hand, your urge to repair a problem that's important but doesn't threaten life or property —say, a stopped-up drain that is not causing any damage—isn't a true emergency that would allow entry without proper notice.

If you do have to enter a tenant's apartment in an emergency, be sure to leave a note or call the tenant explaining the circumstances and the date and time you entered. Here's an example:

**Sample Note to Tenant Regarding
Entry in Case of Emergency**

September 2, 20xx

Dear Tammy,

Due to your oven being left on, I had to enter your apartment this afternoon around 3 o'clock. Apparently, you left your apartment while bread was still in the oven, and didn't return in time to take it out. Joe, your upstairs neighbor, called me and reported smoke and a strong burning smell coming from your kitchen window, which is below his. I entered your apartment and turned the oven off and removed the bread. Please be more careful next time.

Sincerely,

Herb Layton

Herb Layton

To facilitate your right of entry in an emergency, make sure your lease or rental agreement forbids tenants from rekeying, adding additional locks, or installing a security system without your permission. (See Clause 12 of the form agreements in Chapter 2.) If you grant permission to change or add locks, make sure your tenant gives you duplicate keys. If you allow the tenant to install a security system, make sure you get the name and phone number of the alarm company or instructions on how to disarm the system in an emergency.

> **CAUTION**
> **Don't change locks.** If your tenant installs a lock without your permission, don't change the lock, even if you immediately give the tenant a key. This invites a lawsuit and false claims that you tried to lock the tenant out or stole the tenant's possessions.

Entry With the Permission of the Tenant

You can always enter rental property, even without notice, if the tenant agrees. If your need to enter is only occasional, you can probably rely on a friendly telephone call to the tenant asking for permission.

> **EXAMPLE:** Because of corrosion problems with the pipes leading to water heaters, you want to check out all apartments in your building. You call your tenants, explain the situation, and arrange a mutually convenient date and time to inspect the pipes.

If the tenant agrees to let you enter his apartment or rental unit but has been difficult and not always reliable in the past, you might even want to cover yourself by documenting the tenant's apparent cooperation. Send him a confirmatory thank-you note and keep a copy for yourself. If this note is met with unease or outright hostility, you should send the tenant a formal notice of your intent to enter.

If you have a maintenance problem that needs regular attention—for example, a fussy heater or temperamental plumbing—you might want to work out a detailed agreement with the tenant covering entry.

> **CAUTION**
> **Don't be too insistent on entry.** If you pressure a tenant for permission to enter, perhaps implying or even threatening eviction if the tenant doesn't allow immediate or virtually unrestricted access, you may face a lawsuit for invasion of privacy.

Entry to Make Repairs or Inspect the Property

Many states, either by statute or court decision, allow you and your repairperson to enter the tenant's home to make necessary or agreed-upon repairs, alterations, or improvements or to inspect the rental property.

Entry to Make Repairs

If you need to make a repair—for example, to fix a broken oven, replace the carpet, or check the point of entry of a persistent ant infestation—you generally must enter only at reasonable times, and you must give at least the required amount of notice, usually 24 hours. However, if this is impracticable—for example, a repairperson is available on a few hours' notice—you will probably be on solid ground if you explain the situation to your tenant and then give shorter notice. Of course, if your tenant agrees to a shorter notice period, you have no problem.

> **EXAMPLE:** Amy told her landlord Tom that her bathroom sink was stopped up and draining very slowly. Tom called the plumber, who said that he had several large jobs in progress but would be able to squeeze in Amy's repair at some point within the next few days. The plumber promised to call Tom before he came over. Tom relayed this information to Amy, telling her he would give her at least four hours' notice before the plumber came.

How to Give Tenants Notice of Entry

In many situations, the notice period will not be a problem, since your tenant will be delighted that you are making needed repairs and will cooperate with your entry requirements. However, as every experienced landlord knows, some tenants are uncooperative when it comes to providing reasonable access to make repairs, while at the same time demanding that repairs be made immediately. (Of course, if the time is really inconvenient for the tenant—you want to make a nonemergency repair the day your tenant is preparing dinner for her new in-laws—try to be accommodating and reschedule a more convenient appointment.)

Here's how to avoid having a tenant claim that you violated his legal right of privacy:

- Meet your state notice requirements; or, if there's no specified amount of notice, provide at least 24 hours' notice.
- Try to reach the tenant at home or at work to give the required amount of notice. Make sure you know how to reach the tenant during the day to give required notice.
- Provide written notice as much as possible— either a brief letter or a formal Notice of Intent to Enter Dwelling Unit (see samples below). A downloadable copy of the formal notice is on the Nolo website. See Appendix B for the link to the forms in this book.
- If you give notice orally or by email, document this fact by keeping a log of your requests for entry.
- If you can't reach the tenant personally or by phone, and if your intended date of entry is too soon to enable you to send a letter, it's a good idea to post a note detailing your plan on the tenant's front door. If, despite all of these efforts, your tenant does not receive notice, you are probably on solid ground, in most states, to enter and do the repair, since you have done all that could reasonably be expected to comply with the notice requirements.
- Keep a copy of all requests for entry (written and oral) in your tenant's file, along with other communications, such as Resident's Maintenance/Repair Request forms (discussed in Chapter 9).

> **TIP**
> **Let the tenant know if your plans change.** A tenant may be justifiably annoyed if you or your repair person show up late or not at all—for example, if you're supposed to come at 2 p.m. and don't show up until 8 a.m. the next morning. If it isn't possible to come on time in the first place, call the tenant and explain the problem, and ask permission to enter later on. If the tenant denies permission, you'll have to give a second notice.

Notice of Intent to Enter Dwelling Unit

To: _Anna Rivera_
Tenant

123 East Avenue, Apt. #4
Street Address

Rochester, New York 14610
City and State

THIS NOTICE is to inform you that on _____ January 7, 20xx _____ ,

at approximately ___ 1:00 ___ A̶M̶/PM, the landlord, or the landlord's agent, will enter the premises

for the following reason: _____

_____

☑ To make or arrange for the following repairs or improvements:

fix garbage disposal

_____

_____

_____

_____ .

☐ To show the premises to:

☐ a prospective tenant or purchaser.

☐ workers or contractors regarding the above repair or improvement.

☐ Other: _____

_____

_____ .

You are, of course, welcome to be present. If you have any questions or if the date or time is inconvenient,

please notify me promptly at ___ 716-555-7899 ___ .
Phone Number

Marlene Morgan _____ _January 5, 20xx_
Landlord/Manager Date

Sample Informal Letter Requesting Entry

January 5, 20xx

Anna Rivera
123 East Avenue, Apartment 4
Rochester, New York 14610

Dear Ms. Rivera:

In response to your complaint regarding the garbage disposal in your apartment, I have arranged to have it repaired tomorrow, on Tuesday, January 6, at 2:00 p.m. I attempted to reach you today (at both your home and work phone numbers) and notify you of this repair appointment. Because I was unable to reach you by phone, I am leaving this note on your door.

Sincerely,

Marlene Morgan

Marlene Morgan

Entry to Inspect for Needed Repairs

It's an excellent idea to inspect your rental properties at least once or twice a year. That way you can find small problems before they become big ones, and tenants can't claim that they didn't have an opportunity to report complaints to you.

The lease and rental agreements in this book (see Clause 17 in Chapter 2) give you the right to enter a tenant's unit—after giving reasonable notice—to make this kind of regular inspection.

If you don't have a clause on access in your lease or rental agreement, state law may give you the right, anyway. All states with privacy statutes, except Utah, grant this right to inspect rental property. In other states, you must determine whether or not the courts in your state have addressed the issue of landlord inspections.

> **CAUTION**
> **Don't use the right to inspect improperly.** Don't use your right to access to harass or annoy the tenant. Repeated inspections absent a specific reason, even when proper notice is given, are an invitation to a lawsuit.

How to Avoid Tenant Theft Claims

By planning ahead, you can minimize the chances that you or your repairpersons will be accused of theft. Give plenty of notice of your entry—this gives the tenant the chance to hide valuables. Try to arrange repairs or visit the rental unit only when the tenant is home. If that's not possible, you or your manager should be present. Carefully check references of plumbers and other repair people, and only allow people whom you trust to enter alone.

Entry During Tenant's Extended Absence

Several states with privacy statutes give landlords the specific legal right to enter the rental unit during a tenant's extended absence, often defined as seven days or more. You are allowed entry to maintain the property as necessary and to inspect for damage and needed repairs. For example, if you live in a cold-weather place such as Connecticut, it makes sense to check the pipes in rental units to make sure they haven't burst when the tenant is away for winter vacation.

While many states do not address this issue either by way of statute or court decision, you should be on safe legal ground to enter rental property during a tenant's extended absence, as long as there is a genuine need to protect the property from damage. You should enter only if something really needs to be done—that is, something that the tenant would do if he were home, as part of his obligation to keep the property clean, safe, and in good repair. For example, if the tenant leaves the windows wide open just before a driving rainstorm, you would be justified in entering to close them.

> **TIP**
> **Require tenants to report extended absences.** To protect yourself and make sure your tenant knows what to expect, be sure your lease or rental agreement requires the tenant to inform you when he will be gone for an extended time, such as two weeks, and alerts him of your

intent to enter the premises during these times if necessary. See Clause 16 of the form agreements in Chapter 2.

Entry to Show Property to Prospective Tenants or Buyers

Most states with access laws allow landlords to enter rented property to show it to prospective tenants toward the end of a tenancy or to prospective purchasers if you wish to sell the property. Follow the same notice procedures for entry to make repairs, discussed above. As always, be sure your lease or rental agreement authorizes this type of entry. See Clause 15 of the form agreements in Chapter 2.

You can use the same Notice of Intent to Enter Dwelling Unit as the one used for entry to make repairs.

Showing Property to Prospective New Tenants

If you don't plan to renew a tenant's about-to-expire lease, or have given or received a notice terminating a month-to-month tenancy, you may show the premises to prospective new tenants during the last few weeks (or even months) of the outgoing tenant's stay. It is not a good idea, however, to show property if the current tenant is under the impression that his lease or rental agreement will be renewed, or if a dispute exists over whether the current tenant has a right to stay. If there's a chance the dispute will end up in court as an eviction lawsuit, the current tenant may be able to hang on for several weeks or even months. Insisting on showing the property in this situation only causes unnecessary friction at the same time that it's of little value, since you will be unable to tell the new tenants when they can move in.

The form lease and rental agreements in this book include a clause that may limit your liability if, for reasons beyond your control, you must delay a new tenant's move-in date after you've signed a lease or rental agreement. See Clause 17 in Chapter 2.

Showing Property to Prospective Buyers

You may also show your property—whether apartments in a multiple-unit building, a rented single-family house, or a condominium unit—to potential buyers or mortgage companies. Remember to give the required amount of notice to your tenant. It's also a good idea to tell the tenant the name and phone number of the realty company handling the property sale and the particular real estate agent or broker involved.

Problems usually occur when an overeager real estate salesperson shows up on the tenant's doorstep without warning, or calls on very short notice and asks to be let in to show the place to a possible buyer. In this situation, the tenant is within his right to say, "I'm busy right now—try again in a few days after we've set a time convenient for all of us." Naturally, this type of misunderstanding is not conducive to good landlord-tenant relations, not to mention a sale of the property. Make sure the real estate salespeople you deal with understand the law and respect your tenants' rights to advance notice.

Putting For Sale or For Rent Signs on the Property

Occasionally, friction is caused by landlords who put signs on tenants' homes, such as "For Sale" or "For Rent" signs in front of an apartment building or a rented single-family house. Even if the sign says "Don't Disturb Occupants" and you are conscientious about giving notice before showing property, prospective buyers or renters may nonetheless disturb the tenant with unwelcome inquiries.

A tenant who likes where he is living will often feel threatened and insecure about a potential sale. A new owner may mean a rent increase or eviction notice if the new owner wants to move in herself. In this situation, if your tenant's privacy is ruined by repeated inquiries the tenant may even resort to suing you for invasion of privacy, just as if you personally had made repeated illegal entries.

To head off this possibility, consider not putting a "For Sale" sign on the property. With online multiple-listing services and video house listings, signs aren't always necessary. Indeed, many real estate agents sell houses and other real estate without ever placing a "For Sale" sign on the property, except when an open house is in progress. If you or your real estate agent must put up a sign advertising sale or rental of the property, make sure it clearly warns against disturbing the occupant and includes a telephone number to call—for example, "Shown by Appointment Only" or "Inquire at 555-1357—Do Not Disturb Occupants Under Any Circumstances." If your real estate agent refuses to accommodate you, find a new one who will respect your tenants' privacy and keep you out of a lawsuit.

> **CAUTION**
>
> **Don't use a lockbox.** Under no circumstances should an owner of occupied rental property that is listed for sale allow the placing of a key-holding "lockbox" on the door. This is a metal box that attaches to the front door and contains the key to that door. It can be opened by a master key held by area real estate salespeople. Since a lockbox allows a salesperson to enter in disregard of notice requirements, it should not be used—period. A lockbox will leave you wide open to a tenant's lawsuit for invasion of privacy, and possibly liable for any property the tenant claims to have lost.

Getting the Tenant's Cooperation

Showing a house or apartment building occupied by a tenant isn't easy on anyone. At times, you will want to show the property on short notice. And, you may even want to have an occasional open house on weekends. From your tenant's point of view, any actions you take to show the property to strangers may seem like an intolerable intrusion. Also, if you're selling the property, your tenant may feel threatened by the change in ownership.

Obviously, the best way to achieve your ends is with the cooperation of the tenant. One good plan is to meet with the tenant in advance and offer a reasonable rent reduction in exchange for cooperation—for example, two open houses a month and showing the unit on two hour's notice, as long as it doesn't occur more than five times a week. Depending on how much the tenant will be inconvenienced, a 10% to 20% rent reduction might be reasonable. However, you should realize that this type of agreement is in force only so long as the tenant continues to go along with it. Technically, any written agreement changing the rent is really an amendment to the rental agreement, and rental agreement clauses under which tenants give up their privacy rights are typically void and unenforceable if it comes to a court fight. This may be one situation when an informal understanding that the rent be lowered so long as the tenant agrees to the frequent showings may be better than a written agreement.

Entry After the Tenant Has Moved Out

To state the obvious, you may enter the premises at any time after the tenant has completely moved out. It doesn't matter whether the tenant left voluntarily after giving back the key, or involuntarily following a successful eviction lawsuit.

In addition, if you believe a tenant has abandoned the property—that is, skipped out without giving any notice or returning the key—you may legally enter.

Entry by Others

This section describes situations when other people, such as municipal inspectors, may want entry to your rental property.

Health, Safety, or Building Inspections

While your state may set guidelines for your entry to rental property, the rules are different for entry by state or local health, safety, or building inspectors.

Neighbor's Complaints

If inspectors have credible reasons to suspect that a tenant's rental unit violates housing codes or local standards—for example, a neighbor has complained about noxious smells coming from the tenant's home or about his 20 cats—they will usually knock on the tenant's door and ask permission to enter. Except in the case of genuine emergency, your tenant has the right to say no.

Inspectors have ways to get around tenant refusals. A logical first step (maybe even before they stop by the rental unit) is to ask you to let them in. Since you can usually enter on 24 hours' notice, this is probably the simplest approach. We recommend that you cooperate with all such requests for entry.

If inspectors can't reach you (or you don't cooperate), their next step will probably be to get a search warrant based on the information from the tenant's neighbor. The inspectors must first convince a judge that the source of their information—the neighbor—is reliable, and that there is a strong likelihood that public health or safety is at risk. Inspectors who believe that a tenant will refuse entry often bring along police officers who, armed with a search warrant, have the right to do whatever it takes to overcome the tenant's objections.

Routine Inspections

Fire, health, and other municipal inspectors sometimes inspect apartment buildings even if they don't suspect noncompliance. These inspections may be allowed under state law or local ordinance. (Most ordinances exempt single-family homes and condominiums.) Your tenant has the right to say no. Then, the inspector will have to secure a warrant. A warrant will enable the inspector to enter to confirm fire or safety violations. Again, if there is any expectation that your tenant may resist, a police officer will usually accompany the inspector.

An inspector who arrives when the tenant is not home may ask you to open the door on the spot, in violation of your state's privacy laws. If the inspectors come with a warrant, you can give consent, since even the tenant couldn't prevent entry. But if the inspector is there without a warrant, you cannot speak for the tenant and say, "Come on in." Again, the inspector most show you a warrant before you can let him in.

To find out whether your city has a municipal inspection program, call your city manager's or mayor's office.

Inspection Fees

Many cities impose fees for inspections, on a per unit or building basis or a sliding scale based on the number of your holdings. Some fees are imposed only if violations are found. If your ordinance imposes fees regardless of violations, you may pass the inspection cost on to the tenant in the form of a rent hike. It's not illegal to do this, and, even in rent-controlled cities, the cost of an inspection might justify a rent increase.

If your ordinance imposes a fee only when violations are found, you should not pass the cost on to the tenant if the noncompliance is not his fault. For example, if inspectors find that you failed to install state-mandated smoke alarms, you should pay for the inspection; but if the tenant has allowed garbage to pile up in violation of city health laws, the tenant should pay the inspector's bill.

Police and Law Enforcement

Even the police may not enter a tenant's rental unit unless they can show you or your tenant a recently issued search or arrest warrant, signed by a judge. Put another way, even though you own the property, you do not have the legal right to give police permission to enter your tenant's home unless you've been shown a warrant. (*Chapman v. United States*, 365 U.S. 610 (1961).)

The police do not need a search warrant, however, if they need to enter to prevent a catastrophe such as an explosion, to retrieve or preserve evidence of a serious crime, which may otherwise be lost or destroyed, or if they are in hot pursuit of a fleeing criminal.

Also, different rules apply if law enforcement suspects terrorist activity by one of your tenants. See "Cooperating With Law Enforcement in Terrorism Investigations," just below.

Cooperating With Law Enforcement in Terrorism Investigations

The U.S.A. PATRIOT Act (PL 107-56) authorizes the FBI to obtain "tangible things," including books, records, or other documents, for use in terrorism investigations. The FBI must, however, have an order issued by a U.S. magistrate. You may not be sued if you cooperate in good faith pursuant to this section. However, you may not disclose to anyone else that the FBI has gathered this information.

Landlords have even broader immunity against suits by tenants when they cooperate with law enforcement's antiterrorism efforts. You may not be sued by tenants if you "[furnish] any information, facilities, or technical assistance in accordance with a court order or request for emergency assistance under this Act." (U.S.A. PATRIOT Act, Title II, § 225.) You can ask for a subpoena or warrant before you turn over tenant records or otherwise make your rental property or tenant belongings available to law enforcement, but you need not do so if your only fear is a lawsuit from the affected tenants.

For more information on terrorism and rental properties, contact the local office of the FBI; a list is at www.fbi.gov.

Your Right to Let Others In

You should not give others permission to enter a tenant's home. (Municipal inspections, however, may pose an exception.)

Occasionally, you or your resident manager will be faced with a very convincing stranger who will tell a heart-rending story:

- "I'm Nancy's boyfriend, and I need to get my clothes out of her closet now that I'm moving to New York."
- "If I don't get my heart medicine that I left in this apartment, I'll die on the spot."

- "I'm John's father, and I just got in from the North Pole, where a polar bear ate my wallet, and I have no other place to stay."

The problem arises when you can't contact the tenant at work or elsewhere to ask whether it's okay to let the desperate individual in. This is one reason why you should always know how to reach your tenants during the day.

The story the desperate person tells you may be the truth, and chances are that if your tenant could be contacted, she would say, "Yes, let Uncle Harry in immediately." But you can't know this, and it doesn't make sense to expose yourself to the potential liability involved should you get taken in by a clever con artist. There is always the chance that the person is really a smooth talker whom your tenant has a dozen good reasons to want kept out. You risk being legally responsible should your tenant's property be stolen or damaged. If you do let a stranger in without your tenant's permission, you may be sued for invasion of privacy for any loss your tenant suffers as a result.

In short, never let a stranger into your tenant's home without your tenant's permission. Even if you have been authorized to allow a certain person to enter, it is wise to ask for identification. Although this no-entry-without-authorization policy may sometimes be difficult to adhere to in the face of a convincing story, stick to it. You have much more to lose in admitting the wrong person to the tenant's home than you would have to gain by letting in someone who's "probably okay."

Other Types of Invasions of Privacy

Entering a tenant's home without his knowledge or consent isn't the only way you can interfere with the tenant's privacy. Here are a few other common situations, with advice on how to handle them.

Giving Information About the Tenant to Strangers

As a landlord, you may be asked by strangers, including creditors, banks, and prospective landlords, to provide credit or other information about your tenant. Did she pay the rent on time? Did she maintain the rental property? Cause any problems?

Basically, you have a legal right to give out normal business information about your tenant to people and businesses who ask and have a legitimate reason to know—for example, the tenant's bank when she applies for a loan or a prospective landlord who wants a reference. Resist your natural urge to be helpful, unless the tenant has given you written permission to release this sort of information. (We discuss release forms in Chapter 1.) You have nothing to gain, and possibly a lot to lose, if you give out information that your tenant feels constitutes a serious violation of her privacy.

And if you give out incorrect information—even if you believe it to be accurate—you can really be in a legal mess if the person to whom you disclose it relies on it to take some action that negatively affects your tenant.

> **EXAMPLE:** If you tell others that a tenant has filed for bankruptcy (and this isn't true), the tenant has grounds to sue you for defamation (libel or slander) if he is damaged as a result—for example, if he doesn't get a job.

Some landlords feel that they should communicate information to prospective landlords, especially if the tenant has failed to pay rent or maintain the premises or has created other serious problems. If you do give out this information, make sure you are absolutely factual and that the information you provide has been requested. If you go out of your way to give out negative information—for example, you try to blackball the tenant with other landlords in your area—you definitely risk legal liability for libeling your tenant.

Posting Information About Tenants Online

Online sites such as Yelp enable consumers to post reviews of everything from restaurants to car repair shops to doctors. Naturally, reviews of residential rentals are right up there in popularity, and many landlords have squirmed when encountering reviews of their buildings and management practices. It wasn't long before landlords got their own online outlets, using public and free sites designed to warn other property owners about problem tenants.

We urge you to think twice before posting information to one of these sites. In a recent case, a California court ruled that such Internet postings are not immune from libel suits, and that if the posting contains provably false statements, the poster could end up liable for damages. (*Bently Reserve L.P. v. Andreas G. Papaliolios*, 218 Cal. App.4th 418 (2013).) The same reasoning would apply to negative remarks about a tenant posted by a landlord. While you may ultimately prevail if you are challenged by a tenant who is the subject of your review, this is a headache you do not need.

> CAUTION
>
> **Beware of gossipy managers.** Many landlords have had serious problems with on-site managers who have gossiped about tenants who, for example, paid rent late, were served with an eviction notice, had overnight visitors, or drank too much. This sort of gossip may seem innocent but, if flagrant and damaging, can be an invasion of privacy for which you can be liable. Impress on your managers their duty to keep confidential all sensitive information about tenants.

Calling or Visiting Tenants at Work

Should you need to call your tenant at work (say, to schedule a time to make repairs), try to be sensitive to whether it's permissible for him to receive personal calls. While some people work at desks with telephones and have bosses who don't get upset about occasional personal calls, others have jobs that are greatly disrupted by any phone call.

Under no circumstances should you continue to call a tenant at work who asks you not to do so. This is especially true when calling about late rent payments or other problems.

Never leave specific messages with your tenant's employer, especially those that could reflect negatively on her. A landlord who leaves a message like "Tell your deadbeat employee I'll evict her if she doesn't pay the rent" can expect at least a lot of bad feeling on the part of the tenant and, at worst, a lawsuit, especially if your conduct results in the tenant losing her job or a promotion.

As for visiting the tenant at work—say, to collect late rent—this is something you should avoid unless invited. What it boils down to is that no matter what you think of your tenant, you should respect the sensitive nature of the tenant's relationship with her employer.

There may, however, be times you'll need to contact the tenant at work if you can't find the tenant at home after repeated tries—for example, to serve notice of a rent increase or an eviction notice.

Undue Restrictions on Guests

A few landlords, overly concerned about tenants moving new occupants into the property, go a little overboard in keeping tabs on the tenants' legitimate guests who stay overnight or for a few days. Often their leases, rental agreements, or rules and regulations require a tenant to "register" any overnight guest.

Clause 3 of the form agreements (Chapter 2) limits guests' visits to no more than ten days in any six-month period, to avoid having a guest turn into an illegal subtenant. While you should be concerned about persons who begin as guests becoming permanent unauthorized residents, it is overkill to require a tenant to inform you of a guest whose stay is only for a day or two. Keep in mind that just because you rent your tenant her home, you don't have the right to restrict her social life or pass judgment upon the propriety of her visitors' stays. Extreme behavior in this area—whether by you or a management employee—can be considered an invasion of privacy for which you may be held liable.

Send Only Business-Related Faxes and Texts to Residents

Since 1991, the Telephone Consumer Protection Act has prohibited businesses from sending "unsolicited" faxes (texts are also covered). Businesses that have an "established business relationship" with the recipient are exempted from this ban (Junk Fax Prevention Act of 2005). You may send faxes and texts to current, prospective, and prior tenants without worry, as long as the message concerns some aspect of the tenancy. You can also contact vendors and suppliers with faxes and texts that concern your contracts or business dealings with them. But be aware of the following requirements:

- The first page of a fax must have a conspicuous notice telling the recipient how to opt out of future faxes, giving the sender's phone number and fax number.
- The opt-out step must be free and available seven days a week, 24 hours a day.
- You may use only those fax numbers that you get from the recipients themselves or that they gave to a website or public directory for publication.

Sometime in the future, the Federal Communications Commission may issue regulations that will spell out the rules in more detail. These hopefully will guide landlords in how closely related the fax's or text's subject matter must be to landlord/ tenant matters to fit within the "established business relationship" exemption. In the meantime, play it safe and do not send faxes that are unrelated to your business. For example, resist the temptation to invite residents by fax to participate in your son's baseball team fundraiser.

Spying on a Tenant

As a result of worrying too much about a tenant's visitors, a few landlords have attempted to interrogate tenants' visitors, knock on their tenants' doors at odd hours or too frequently in order to see who answers, or even peek through windows.

Needless to say, this sort of conduct can render you liable for punitive damages in an invasion of privacy lawsuit. As far as talking to tenants' guests is concerned, keep your conversations to pleasant hellos or nonthreatening small talk.

Watch Out for Drug Dealing on Your Property

It's crucial that you keep a careful eye on your tenants if you suspect they're engaging in drug dealing or other illegal behavior. Landlords have a responsibility to keep their properties safe—that includes keeping dealers out by carefully screening prospective tenants (see Chapter 1) and kicking them out pronto when they are discovered. Other tenants and neighbors, as well as government agencies, may bring costly lawsuits against landlords who allow drug dealing on their properties. Chapter 12 discusses your liability for drug-dealing tenants and how to avoid problems, while at the same time respecting your tenants' legitimate expectations of privacy.

"Self-Help" Evictions

It is generally illegal for you to come on the rental property and do such things as take off windows and doors, turn off the utilities, or change the locks. For details, see "Illegal 'Self-Help' Evictions" in Chapter 17.

What to Do When Tenants Unreasonably Deny Entry

Occasionally, even if you give a generous amount of notice and have a legitimate reason, a tenant may refuse to let you in. If you repeatedly encounter unreasonable refusals to let you or your employees enter the premise, you can probably legally enter anyway, provided you do so in a peaceful manner.

Never push or force your way in. Even if you have the right to be there, you can face liability for anything that goes wrong.

For practical reasons, don't enter alone. If you really need entry and the tenant isn't home, it's just common sense to bring someone along who can later act as a witness in case the tenant claims some of her property is missing.

Another problem landlords face is that some tenants have their locks changed. This is probably illegal, because it restricts your right of access in a true emergency or when you have given proper notice. Your lease or rental agreement should require landlord key access, as well as notice of any change of locks or the installation of any burglar alarms. See Clause 12, Chapter 2.

If you have a serious conflict over access with an otherwise satisfactory tenant, a sensible first step is to meet with the tenant to see if the problem can be resolved. If you come to an understanding, follow up with a note to confirm your agreement. Here's an example:

Sample Note Confirming Agreement Regarding Entry

January 5, 20xx

Dear Anna,

This will confirm our conversation of January 5, 20xx regarding access to your apartment at 123 East Avenue, Apt. 4, for the purpose of making repairs. The management will give you 24 hours' advance written notice, and will enter only during business hours or weekdays. The person inspecting will knock first, then enter with a pass key if no one answers.

Thank you,

Marlene Morgan

If this doesn't work, you may wish to try mediation by a neutral third party. It's an especially good way to resolve disputes when you want the tenant to stay.

If attempts at compromise fail, you can terminate the tenancy. Unless your tenant has a long-term lease or lives in a rent control city that requires just cause for eviction, you can simply give the tenant a 30-day notice and terminate the tenancy, rather than put up with a problem tenant.

And, in every state, you can usually evict the tenant, including those with long-term leases, for violating a term of the lease or rental agreement. To do this, you must comply with your state law as to reasons for entry and notice periods. And your lease or rental agreement must contain an appropriate right-of-entry provision. The cause justifying eviction is the tenant's breach of that provision (see Clause 15 in the form lease and rental agreements, Chapter 2). Keep copies of any correspondence and notes of your conversations with the tenant.

If you're heading for court, you may need to consult a lawyer or do some legal research on your state's laws on evictions. If you do end up in court, be prepared to prove your entry was legal—as to purpose and amount of notice required. A good record-keeping system is crucial in this regard.

Tenants' Remedies If a Landlord Acts Illegally

Conscientious landlords should be receptive to a tenant's complaint that her privacy is being violated and work out an acceptable compromise. If you violate a tenant's right to privacy and you can't work out a compromise, the tenant may bring a lawsuit and ask for money damages. You may be held liable for your property manager's disrespect of the tenant's right of privacy, even if you never knew about the manager's conduct. A tenant who can show a repeated pattern of illegal activity, or even one clear example of outrageous conduct, may be able to get a substantial recovery.

In most states, it's easy for a tenant to press her claim in small claims court without a lawyer. For details on small claims court procedures and the maximum amount for which someone can sue, see Chapter 16.

Depending on the circumstances, the tenant may be able sue you for:

- trespass: entry without consent or proper authority
- invasion of privacy: interfering with a tenant's right to be left alone
- breach of the implied covenant of quiet enjoyment: interfering with a tenant's right to undisturbed use of his home, or
- infliction of emotional distress: doing any illegal act that you intend to cause serious emotional consequences to the tenant.

These types of lawsuits are beyond the scope of this book and require expert legal advice.

Finally, you should know that repeated abuses by a landlord of a tenant's right of privacy may give a tenant under a lease a legal excuse to break it by moving out, without liability for further rent.

Ending a Tenancy

 FORMS IN THIS CHAPTER

Chapter 14 includes instructions for and samples of the following forms:

- Amendment to Lease or Rental Agreement
- Tenant's Notice of Intent to Move Out

The Nolo website includes downloadable copies of these forms. See Appendix B for the link to the forms in this book.

Most tenancies end because the tenant leaves voluntarily. But little else is so uniform. Some tenants give proper legal notice and leave at the end of a lease term; others aren't so thoughtful and give inadequate notice, break the lease, or just move out in the middle of the night. And, of course, some tenants fail to live up to their obligations for reasons they can't control—for example, a tenant dies during the tenancy.

Whether your rentals turn over a lot or your tenants tend to stay put for years, you should understand the important legal issues that arise at the end of a tenancy, including:

- the type of notice a landlord or tenant must provide to end a month-to-month tenancy
- your legal options if a tenant doesn't leave after receiving (or giving) a termination notice or after the lease has expired
- what happens if a tenant leaves without giving required notice, and
- the effect of a condominium conversion on a tenant's lease.

This chapter starts with a brief discussion of a related topic—how you may change a lease or rental agreement during a tenancy.

RELATED TOPIC

Related topics covered in this book include:

- How to advertise and rent property before a current tenant leaves: Chapter 1
- Writing clear lease and rental agreement provisions on notice required to end a tenancy: Chapter 2
- Raising the rent: Chapter 3
- Highlighting notice requirements in a move-in letter to the tenant: Chapter 7
- Handling tenant requests to sublet or assign the lease, and what to do when one cotenant leaves: Chapter 8
- Tenant's right to move out if the rental unit is damaged or destroyed: Chapter 9
- Preparing a move-out letter and returning security deposits when a tenant leaves, and how to deal with any abandoned property: Chapter 15
- How and when to prepare a warning letter before terminating a tenancy: Chapter 16

- Terminating a tenancy when a tenant fails to leave after receiving a 30-day notice or violates the lease or rental agreement—for example, by not paying rent: Chapter 17
- State Rules on Notice Required to Change or End a Tenancy: Appendix A.

Changing Lease or Rental Agreement Terms

Once you sign a lease or rental agreement, it's a legal contract between you and your tenant. All changes should be in writing and signed by both of you.

If you use a lease, you cannot unilaterally change the terms of the tenancy for the length of the lease. For example, you can't raise the rent unless the lease allows it or the tenant agrees. If the tenant agrees to changes, however, simply follow the directions below for amending a rental agreement.

Amending a Month-to-Month Rental Agreement

You don't need a tenant's consent to change something in a month-to-month rental agreement. Legally, you need simply send the tenant a notice of the change. The most common reason landlords amend a rental agreement is to increase the rent.

To change a month-to-month tenancy, most states require 30 days' notice, subject to any local rent control ordinances (see "State Rules on Notice Required to Change or Terminate a Month-to-Month Tenancy" in Appendix A for a list of each state's notice requirements). You'll need to consult your state statutes for the specific information on how you must deliver a 30-day notice to the tenant. Most states allow you to deliver the notice by first-class mail.

TIP

Contact the tenant and explain the changes. It makes good personal and business sense for you or your manager to contact the tenant personally and tell him about a rent increase or other changes before you follow up with a written notice. If the tenant is opposed to your plan, your personal efforts will allow you to explain your reasons.

You don't generally need to redo the entire rental agreement in order to make a change or two. It's just as legal and effective to attach a copy of the notice making the change to the rental agreement. However, you may want the change to appear on the written rental agreement itself.

If the change is small and simply alters part of an existing clause—such as increasing the rent or making the rent payable every 14 days instead of every 30 days—you can cross out the old language in the rental agreement, write in the new, and sign in the margin next to the new words. Make sure the tenant also signs next to the change. Be sure to add the date, in case there is a dispute later as to when the change became effective.

If the changes are lengthy, you may either add an amendment page to the original document or prepare a new rental agreement, as discussed below. If an amendment is used, it should clearly refer to the agreement it's changing and be signed by the same people who signed the original agreement. A sample Amendment to Lease or Rental Agreement form is shown below and the Nolo website includes a downloadable copy. See Appendix B for the link to the forms in this book.

Preparing a New Rental Agreement

If you want to add a new clause or make several changes to your rental agreement, you will probably find it easiest to substitute a whole new agreement for the old one. This is simple to do if you use the lease or rental agreement shown in this book (Chapter 2) and included on this book's companion page on Nolo's website. If you prepare an entire new agreement, be sure that you and the tenant both write "Canceled by mutual consent, effective _(date)_ " on the old one, and sign it. All tenants (and any cosigner or guarantors) should sign the new agreement. The new agreement should take effect on the date the old one is canceled. To avoid problems, be sure there is no time overlap between the old and new agreements, and do not allow any gap between the cancellation date of the old agreement and the effective date of the new one.

> **TIP**
> **A new tenant should mean a new agreement.** Even if a new tenant is filling out the rest of a former tenant's lease term under the same conditions, it is never wise to allow her to operate under the same lease or rental agreement. Start over and prepare a new agreement in the new tenant's name. See Chapter 8 for details on signing a new agreement when a new tenant moves in.

How Month-to-Month Tenancies End

This section discusses how you or the tenant can end a month-to-month tenancy.

Giving Notice to the Tenant

If you want a tenant to move out, you can end a month-to-month tenancy simply by giving the proper amount of notice. No reasons are required in most states. (New Hampshire and New Jersey are exceptions, because landlords in these states must have a just or legally recognized reason to end a tenancy.) In most places, all you need to do is give the tenant a simple written notice to move, allowing the tenant the minimum number of days required by state law (typically 30) and stating the date on which the tenancy will end (see "State Rules on Notice Required to Change or Terminate a Month-to-Month Tenancy" in Appendix A). After that date, the tenant no longer has the legal right to occupy the premises.

In most states, a landlord who wants to terminate a month-to-month tenancy must provide the same amount of notice as a tenant—typically 30 days. But this is not true everywhere. For example, in Georgia, landlords must give 60 days' notice to terminate a month-to-month tenancy, while tenants need only give 30 days' notice. State and local rent control laws can also impose notice

Amendment to Lease or Rental Agreement

This is an Amendment to the lease or rental agreement dated _____March 1, 20xx_____ [the Agreement]
between _____Olivia Matthew_____ [Landlord]
and _____Steve Phillips_____ [Tenant]
regarding property located at _____1578 Maple St., Seattle, WA_____ [the premises].
Landlord and Tenant agree to the following changes and/or additions to the Agreement:

1. Beginning on June 1, 20xx, Tenant shall rent a one-car garage, adjacent to the main premises, from Landlord for the sum of $75 per month.

2. Tenant may keep one German shepherd dog on the premises. The dog shall be kept in the backyard and not in the side yard. Tenant shall clean up all animal waste from the yard on a daily basis. Tenant agrees to repair any damages to the yard or premises caused by his dog, at Tenant's expense.

_____Olivia Matthew_____   _____May 20, 20xx_____
Landlord/Manager   Date

_____Steve Phillips_____   _____May 20, 20xx_____
Tenant   Date

_____   _____
Tenant   Date

_____   _____
Tenant   Date

requirements on landlords. Things are different if you want a tenant to move because he or she has violated a term of the rental agreement—for example, by failing to pay rent. If so, notice requirements are commonly greatly shortened, sometimes to as little as three days.

Each state, and even some cities, has its own very detailed rules and procedures for preparing and serving termination notices. For example, some states specify that the notice be printed in a certain size or style of typeface. If you don't follow these procedures, the notice terminating the tenancy may be invalid. It is impossible for this book to provide all specific forms and instructions. Consult a landlords' association or local rent control board and your state statutes for more information and sample forms (Chapter 18 shows how to do your own legal research). Your state consumer protection agency may also have useful advice. Once you understand how much notice you must give, how the notice must be delivered, and any other requirements, you'll be in good shape to handle this work yourself—usually with no lawyer needed.

RESOURCE

California resource for terminating tenancies. If you are a California landlord, see *The California Landlord's Law Book: Evictions*, by David Brown. It covers rules and procedures and contains forms for serving termination notices in California. This book is available at bookstores and public libraries. You may also order it directly from Nolo's website (www.nolo.com), or by phone (800-728-3555).

How Much Notice the Tenant Must Give You

In most states, the tenant who decides to move out must give you at least 30 days' notice. Some states allow less than 30 days' notice in certain situations— for example, because a tenant must leave early because of military orders. And, in some states, tenants who pay rent more frequently than once a month can give notice to terminate that matches their rent payment interval—for example, tenants

who pay rent every two weeks would have to give 14 days' notice. If your tenant joins the military and wants to terminate a rental agreement, federal law specifies the maximum amount of notice you may require (but if state law requires less notice, you must follow state rules). See "Special Rules for Tenants Who Enter Military Service," below.

Must Tenants Give Notice on the First of the Month?

In most states, a tenant can give notice at any time—in other words, they don't have to give notice so that the tenancy will end on the last day of the month or the last day of the rental cycle. For example, a tenant who pays rent on the first of the month, but gives notice on the tenth, will be obliged to pay for ten days' rent for the next month, even if the tenant moves out earlier.

Some landlords insist that tenants give notice only on the day rent is due, possibly to avoid having to prorate the rent as described above. But a rule like this may violate your state's law on the proper use of security deposits, and may not be legal. Here's how: Suppose a tenant pays rent on the first, but gives you his 30-day notice on the tenth, because he intends to move out on the tenth day of the following month. If you stick to your rule, you'll expect him to pay for an additional 20 days (the balance of the next month), and if he doesn't, you'll probably use the security deposit to cover that debt. But that may not be a proper use of the deposit in your state, especially if your statute does not allow you or the tenant to modify the conditions under which the landlord may retain the deposit. If the rule applies to tenants only (that is, *you* remain free to deliver a 30-day notice at any time, and the 30 days begins as of the day of delivery), the chances that your rule will hold up will be even slimmer.

As tempting as it may be to deal with tenant turnover on the day rent is due and avoid having to prorate rent (and though the prospect of requiring that rent be paid over an extended period is attractive), we urge you to resist this ploy and accept notice at any time during the rent term.

To educate your tenants as to what they can expect, make sure your rental agreement includes your state's notice requirements for ending a tenancy (see Clause 4 of the form agreements in Chapter 2). It is also wise to list termination notice requirements in the move-in letter you send to new tenants.

For details on your state's rules, see "State Rules on Notice Required to Change or Terminate a Month-to-Month Tenancy" in Appendix A.

Restrictions to Ending a Tenancy

The general rules for terminating a tenancy described in this chapter don't apply in all situations:

- **Rent control ordinances.** Many rent control cities require "just cause" (a good reason) to end a tenancy, such as moving in a close relative. You will likely have to state your reason in the termination notice you give the tenant.
- **Discrimination.** It is illegal to end a tenancy because of a tenant's race, religion, or other reason constituting illegal discrimination.
- **Retaliation.** You cannot legally terminate a tenancy to retaliate against a tenant for exercising any right under the law, such as the tenant's right to complain to governmental authorities about defective housing conditions.

Insist on a Tenant's Written Notice of Intent to Move

In many states, a tenant's notice must be in writing and give the exact date the tenant plans to move out. Even if it is not required by law, it's a good idea to insist that the tenant give you notice in writing (as does Clause 4 of the form agreements in Chapter 2). Why bother?

Insisting on written notice will prove useful should the tenant not move as planned after you have signed a lease or rental agreement with a new tenant. The new tenant may sue you to recover the costs of temporary housing or storage fees for her belongings because you could not deliver possession of the unit. In turn, you will want to sue the old (holdover) tenant for causing the problem by failing to move out. You will have a much stronger case against the holdover tenant if you can produce a written promise to move on a specific date instead of your version of a conversation (which will undoubtedly be disputed by the tenant).

A sample Tenant's Notice of Intent to Move Out form is shown below and the Nolo website includes a downloadable copy (see Appendix B for the link to the forms in this book). Give a copy of this form to any tenant who tells you he or she plans to move.

Accepting Rent After a 30-Day Notice Is Given

If you accept rent for any period beyond the date the tenant told you he is moving out, this cancels the termination notice and creates a new month-to-month tenancy. This means you must give the tenant another 30-day notice to start the termination process again.

> **EXAMPLE:** On April 15, George sends his landlord Yuri a 30-day notice of his intent to move out. A few weeks later, however, George changes his mind and decides to stay. He simply pays the usual $800 monthly rent on May 1. Without thinking, Yuri cashes the $800 check. Even though she's already rerented to a new tenant who plans to move in on May 16th, Yuri is powerless to evict George unless she first gives him a legal (usually 30-day) notice to move. Unless the lease Yuri signed with the new tenant limits her liability, she will be liable to the new tenant for failing to put her in possession of the property as promised.

CAUTION
If you collected "last month's rent" when the tenant moved in, do not accept rent for the last month of the tenancy. You are legally obligated to use this money for the last month's rent. Accepting an additional month's rent may extend the tenant's tenancy.

Tenant's Notice of Intent to Move Out

April 3, 20xx
_____
Date

Anne Sakamoto
_____
Landlord

888 Mill Avenue
_____
Street Address

Nashville, Tennessee 37126
_____
City and State

Dear ____ Ms. Sakamoto _____ ,
                Landlord

This is to notify you that the undersigned tenants, ____ Patti and Joe Ellis _____

_____ , will be moving from

____ 999 Brook Lane, Apartment Number 11 _____ ,

on ____ May 3, 20xx _____ , ____ 30 days _____ from today.

This provides at least ____ 30 days' _____ written notice as required in our rental agreement.

Sincerely,

Patti Ellis
_____
Tenant

Joe Ellis
_____
Tenant

_____
Tenant

If the tenant asks for more time but you don't want to continue the tenancy as before, you may want to give the tenant a few days or weeks more, at prorated rent. Prepare a written agreement to that effect and have the tenant sign it. See the sample letter extending the tenant's move-out date.

Sample Letter Extending Tenant's Move-Out Date

Hannah Lewis
777 Broadway Terrace, Apartment #3
Richmond, Virginia 23233

Dear Hannah:

On June 1, you gave me a 30-day notice of your intent to move out on July 1. You have since requested to extend your move-out to July 18 because of last-minute problems with closing escrow on your new house. This letter is to verify our understanding that you will move out on July 18, instead of July 1, and that you will pay prorated rent for 18 days (July 1 through July 18). Prorated rent for 18 days, based on your monthly rent of $900 or $30 per day, is $540.

Please sign below to indicate your agreement to these terms.

Sincerely,

Fran Moore

Fran Moore, Landlord

Agreed to by Hannah Lewis, Tenant:
Signature *Hannah Lewis*
Date *June 20, 20xx*

When the Tenant Doesn't Give the Required Notice

All too often, a tenant will send or give you a "too short" notice of intent to move. And it's not unheard of for a tenant to move out with no notice or with a wave as he hands you the keys.

A tenant who leaves without giving enough notice has lost the right to occupy the premises, but is still obligated to pay rent through the end of the required notice period. For example, if the notice period is 30 days, but the tenant moves out after telling you 20 days ago that he intended to move, he still owes you for the remaining ten days.

In most states, you have a legal duty to try to rerent the property before you can charge the tenant for giving you too little notice, but few courts expect a landlord to accomplish this in less than a month. This rule, called the landlord's duty to mitigate damages, is discussed in "If the Tenant Breaks the Lease," below.

When You or Your Tenant Violates the Rental Agreement

If you seriously violate the rental agreement and fail to fulfill your legal responsibilities—for example, by not correcting serious health or safety problems—a tenant may be able to legally move out with no written notice or by giving less notice than is otherwise required. Called a "constructive eviction," this doctrine typically applies only when living conditions are intolerable—for example, if the tenant has had no heat for an extended period in the winter, or if a tenant's use and enjoyment of the property has been substantially impaired because of drug dealing in the building.

What exactly constitutes a constructive eviction varies slightly under the laws of different states. Generally, if a rental unit has serious habitability problems for anything but a very short time, the tenant may be entitled to move out without giving notice.

Along the same lines, a landlord may terminate a tenancy (and evict, if necessary) if the tenant violates a lease or rental agreement—for example, by failing to pay rent or seriously damaging the property—by giving less notice than is otherwise required to end a tenancy. Chapter 17 explains the situations in which landlords can quickly terminate for tenant misbehavior, and gives an overview of evictions.

Special Rules for Tenants Who Enter Military Service

Tenants who enter active military service after signing a lease or rental agreement have a federally legislated right to get out of their rental obligations. (War and National Defense Servicemembers Civil Relief Act, 50 U.S.C. §§ 3901 and following.) The Act protects tenants who are part of the "uniformed services," which includes the armed forces, commissioned corps of the National Oceanic and Atmospheric Administration (NOAA), commissioned corps of the Public Health Service, and the activated National Guard.

Tenants must mail written notice of their intent to terminate their tenancy for military reasons to the landlord or manager. The notice terminates the tenancy of the servicemember and any dependents listed on the lease or rental agreement.

The term "dependent" is defined more broadly than under the U.S. tax code (as explained in Table 5, "Overview of the Rules for Claiming an Exemption for a Dependent," in IRS Publication 501, *Exemptions, Standard Deduction, and Filing Information*). A dependent for purposes of the Servicemembers Act includes a child, spouse, or anyone whom the servicemember has supported within the preceding 180 days, by paying for more than half that person's living expenses. (50 U.S.C.A. § 3911(4).)

Rental agreements. Once the notice is mailed or delivered, the tenancy will terminate 30 days after the day that rent is next due. For example, if rent is due on the first of June and the tenant mails a notice on May 28, the tenancy will terminate on July 1. This rule takes precedence over any longer notice periods that might be specified in your rental agreement or by state law. If state law or your agreement provides for shorter notice periods, however, the shorter notice will control. Recently, many states have passed laws that offer the same or greater protections to members of the state militia or National Guard.

Leases. A tenant who enters military service after signing a lease may terminate the lease by following the procedure for rental agreements, above. For example, suppose a tenant signs a one-year lease in April, agreeing to pay rent on the first of the month. The tenant enlists October 10 and mails you a termination notice on October 11. In this case, you must terminate the tenancy on December 1, 30 days after the first time that rent is due (November 1) following the mailing of the notice. This tenant will have no continuing obligation for rent past December 1, even though this is several months before the lease expires. Removing a prior owner involves different procedures however.

How Leases End

A lease lasts for a fixed term, typically one year. As a general rule, neither you nor the tenant may unilaterally end the tenancy, unless the other party has violated the terms of the lease. There's an exception for tenants who join the military and want to terminate a lease, as explained in "Special Rules for Tenants Who Enter Military Service," above.

If you and the tenant both live up to your promises, however, the lease simply ends of its own accord at the end of the lease term. At this point, the tenant must either:

- move
- sign a new lease (with the same or different terms), or
- stay on as a month-to-month tenant with your approval.

As every landlord knows, however, life is not always so simple. Sooner or later, a tenant will stay beyond the end of the term or leave before it without any legal right to do so.

Giving Notice to the Tenant

Because a lease clearly states when it will expire, you may not think it's necessary to notify tenants before the expiration date. But doing so is a very good practice. And some states or cities (especially those with rent control) actually require reasonable notice before the lease expiration date if you want the tenant to leave.

We suggest giving the tenant at least 60 days' written notice that the lease is going to expire. This reminder has several advantages:

- **Getting the tenant out on time.** Two months' notice allows plenty of time for the tenant to look for another place if he doesn't—or you don't—want to renew the lease.
- **Giving you time to renegotiate the lease.** If you would like to continue renting to your present tenant but also change some lease terms or increase the rent, your notice reminds the tenant that the terms of the old lease will not automatically continue. Encourage the tenant to stay, but mention that you need to make some changes to the lease.
- **Getting a new tenant in quickly.** If you know a tenant is going to move, you can show the unit to prospective tenants ahead of time and minimize the time the space is vacant.

RENT CONTROL
Your options may be limited in a rent control area. If your property is subject to rent control, you may be required to renew a tenant's lease unless there is a legally approved reason (just cause) not to. Reasons such as your tenant's failure to pay rent or your desire to move in a close relative commonly justify nonrenewal. If you do not have a reason for nonrenewal that meets the city's test, you may be stuck with a perpetual month-to-month tenant. Check your city's rent control ordinance carefully.

If the Tenant Continues to Pay Rent After the Lease Expires

It's fairly common for landlords and tenants not to care, or not even to notice, that a lease has expired. The tenant keeps paying the rent, and the landlord keeps cashing the checks. Is everything just the same as it was before the lease expired? The answer depends on where you live.

Creating a month-to-month tenancy. In most states, you will have created a new, oral month-to-month tenancy on the terms that appeared in the old lease. In other words, you'll be stuck with the terms and

rent in the old lease, at least for the first 30 days. If you want to change the terms in a new lease, you must abide by the law regarding giving notice for a month-to-month tenancy (discussed above). It will usually take you at least a month, while you go about giving notice to your now month-to-month tenant.

EXAMPLE 1: Zev had a one-year lease and paid rent on the first of every month. When the lease expired, Zev stayed on and his landlord, Maria, accepted another month's rent check from him. Under the laws of their state, this made Zev a month-to-month tenant, subject to the terms and conditions in his now-expired lease.

Maria wanted to institute a "no pets" rule and to raise the rent. But since Zev was now a month-to-month tenant, she had to give him 30 days' notice (as required by her state's law) to change the terms of the tenancy. She lost a full month of the higher rent while she complied with the 30-day requirement.

EXAMPLE 2: Learning from her experience with Zev, Maria gave her tenant Alice a 60-day notice before Alice's lease expired. In that notice, Maria also told Alice about the new "no pets" rule and the rent increase. Alice, who wanted to get a cat, decided to move when the lease expired. Meanwhile, Maria was able to show Alice's apartment to prospective tenants and chose one who moved in—and started paying the higher rent—shortly after Alice's lease expired.

Of course, you can belatedly present the tenant with a new lease. If your tenant decides not to sign it, she can stay on as a month-to-month tenant, under the terms of the old lease, until you give her proper written notice to move on. As discussed above, this is usually 30 days.

Automatically renewing the lease. However, in a few states, the rule is quite different. If your lease expires and you continue to accept rent, the two of you have created a new lease for the same length (such as one year) and terms (such as the amount of rent) as in the old lease. In other words, you have automatically renewed the lease. The effects are dramatic: You and the tenant are now legally obligated for a new lease with the same term as the old one.

To avoid problems of tenants staying longer than you want, be sure to notify the tenant well before the lease expiration date, and don't accept rent after this date. If a tenant just wants to stay an extra few days after a lease expires, and you agree, it is wise to put your understanding on this arrangement in a letter. See the sample letter extending the tenant's move-out date above.

Retaliation and Other Illegal Tenancy Terminations

You can terminate a tenancy for a variety of reasons, such as nonpayment of rent, serious violations of the lease, and illegal activity such as drug dealing on the rental property. And, unless state or local laws require a reason, you can, with proper notice, terminate a month-to-month rental agreement or decline to renew a lease without giving any reason at all. But you can't terminate a tenancy for the *wrong* reason—in retaliation against a tenant for exercising her legal rights or in a way that discriminates illegally.

Just as you can't engage in illegal discrimination when you rent a unit in the first place, you can't unlawfully discriminate when it comes to terminating a month-to-month tenancy or deciding not to renew a lease—for example, by deciding not to continue to rent to persons of a certain ethnicity because of your political beliefs.

The second major landlord "no-no" when it comes to tenancy nonrenewals is retaliation. In most states, you may not end a tenancy in retaliation for a tenant's legally protected activities, such as complaining to a building inspector that a rental unit is uninhabitable. If you do, and the tenant stays on despite your wishes, the tenant can defend herself against a lawsuit to evict her by proving retaliation. Chapter 16 discusses laws prohibiting retaliation.

When a Lease Ends and You Want the Tenant Out

Once the lease expires, you don't have to keep renting to the tenant. If the tenant stays on after the lease ends and offers rent that you *do not accept*,

the tenant is a "holdover" tenant. In some states, you must still give notice, telling the tenant to leave within a few days; if the tenant doesn't leave at the end of this period, you can start an eviction lawsuit. A few states allow landlords to file for eviction immediately, as soon as the lease expires.

CAUTION
Avoid lease and rental agreement clauses that make holdover tenants pay a higher rent. Some landlords attempt to discourage tenants from staying past the end of their tenancy by making the tenant agree, in advance, to pay as much as three times the rent if they do. Clauses like this may not be legal—they are a form of "liquidated damages" (damages that are set in advance, without regard to the actual harm suffered by the landlord), which are illegal in residential rentals in many states, including California. (However, they have been upheld in Texas.) The clause would probably not hold up in a rent control city, nor would it survive a challenge if the clause describes the rent hike as a "penalty."

Evicting Tenants in Properties Purchased Following Foreclosure

The federal "Protecting Tenants at Foreclosure Act of 2009" (PTAFA) provided that when a "federally related" mortgage loan was foreclosed upon (almost every loan), and when the bank bought at the sale and took over as owner, most residential leases would survive a foreclosure—meaning the tenants could stay until the end of the lease. Under the PTAFA, month-to-month tenants (with some important qualifications) were also entitled to 90 days' notice before having to move out. Effective on December 31, 2014, the PTAFA expired. Even without this federal law, most states (and some cities) give tenants some protection from eviction in default and foreclosure situations (although the new owner of the property must still follow state eviction procedures in order to remove a tenant from the rental unit). For details on state and local protections for tenants in property purchased at foreclosure, check the website of the National Housing Law Project (www.nhlp.org).

If the Tenant Breaks the Lease

A tenant who leaves (with or without notifying you beforehand) before a lease expires and refuses to pay the remainder of the rent due under the lease is said to have "broken the lease."

Once the tenant leaves for good, you have the legal right to retake possession of the premises and rerent to another tenant. A key question that arises is, how much does a tenant with a lease owe if she walks out early? Let's start with the general legal rule. A tenant who signs a lease agrees at the outset to pay a fixed amount of rent: the monthly rent multiplied by the number of months of the lease. The tenant pays this amount in monthly installments over the term of the lease. In short, the tenant has obligated himself for the entire rent for the entire lease term. The fact that payments are made monthly doesn't change the tenant's responsibility to pay rent for the entire lease term. As discussed below, depending on the situation, you may use the tenant's security deposit to cover part of the shortfall, or sue the tenant for the rent owed.

Is the Tenant Really Gone?

Sometimes, it's hard to tell whether or not a tenant has left permanently. People do sometimes disappear for weeks at a time, for a vacation or family emergency. And, even a tenant who doesn't intend to come back may leave behind enough discarded clothing or furniture to make it unclear.

Often, your first hint that a tenant has abandoned the premises will be the fact that you haven't received the rent. Or you may simply walk by a window and notice the lack of furniture. Ordinarily, the mere appearance that the rental unit is no longer occupied doesn't give you the legal right to immediately retake possession. It does, however, often give you legal justification to inspect the place for signs of abandonment.

Here are some tips for inspecting property you suspect has been abandoned:

- Is the refrigerator empty, or is most of the food spoiled?
- Have electricity and telephone service been canceled?
- Are closets and kitchen cupboards empty?

If you conclude, under your state's rules, that the property is abandoned, you have the right to retake possession of it. Each state has its own definition of abandonment and its own rules for regaining possession of rental property. In Colorado, for example, property is considered abandoned if the tenant fails to pay rent or otherwise contact the landlord for at least 30 days and the landlord has no evidence to indicate that the tenant has not abandoned the property. See the Chapter 15 discussion of abandoned property.

Rather than trying to figure out if the situation satisfies your state's legal rules for abandonment, it may be easier to find the tenant and ask her whether or not she's coming back. If the tenant indicates that she's gone for good, get it in writing. You can write up a simple statement, along these lines: "I, Terri Tenant, have permanently moved out of my rental unit at [address] and have no intention of resuming my tenancy"—and ask the tenant to sign and date it. Or, use our Tenant's Notice of Intent to Move Out form (shown above), modified as needed. The Nolo website includes a downloadable copy of the form. See Appendix B for the link to the forms in this book.

(Also, if you try unsuccessfully to locate the tenant and then the original tenant shows up after you have rerented the unit, evidence of your efforts will be some protection if the original tenant complains.) Start by phoning each personal and business reference on the tenant's rental application. If that doesn't work, ask neighbors and, finally, check with the police.

Another way to find a tenant who has left a forwarding address with the Post Office but not with you is to send the tenant a "return receipt requested" letter, and check the box on the form that asks the postal service to note the address where the letter was delivered. You'll get the tenant's new address when you receive the return receipt.

Consider a Buyout Agreement With a Tenant Who Wants to Leave Early

A tenant who wants to get out of a lease may offer to sweeten the deal by paying a little bit extra. In the world of big business, this is known as a "buyout." For example, a tenant who wants to leave three months early might offer to pay half a month's extra rent and promise to be extra accommodating when you want to show the unit to prospective tenants. A sample Buyout Agreement is shown below.

Sample Buyout Agreement Between Landlord and Tenant

This Agreement is entered into on January 3, 20xx between Colin Crest, Tenant, who leases the premises at 123 Shady Lane, Capitol City, California, and Marie Peterson, Landlord.

1. Under the attached lease, Tenant agreed to pay Landlord monthly rent of $1,000. Tenant has paid rent for the month of January 20xx.

2. Tenant's lease expires on June 30, 20xx, but Tenant needs to break the lease and move out on January 15, 20xx.

3. Landlord agrees to release Tenant on January 15, 20xx from any further obligation to pay rent in exchange for Tenant's promise to pay January's rent plus one and one-half months' rent ($1,500) by January 15, 20xx.

4. Tenant agrees to allow Landlord to show his apartment to prospective new tenants on two hours' notice, seven days a week. If Tenant cannot be reached after Landlord has made a good-faith effort to do so, Landlord may enter and show the apartment.

5. If Tenant does not fulfill his promises as described in paragraphs 3 and 4 above, the attached lease, entered into on January 3, 20xx, will remain in effect.

Colin Crest _____   _January 3, 20xx_ _____
Colin Crest, Tenant   Date

Marie Peterson _____   _January 3, 20xx_ _____
Marie Peterson, Landlord   Date

> **TIP**
>
> **Require tenants to notify you of extended absences.** Clause 16 of the form lease and rental agreements (Chapter 2) requires tenants to inform you when they will be gone for an extended time, such as two or more weeks.

By requiring tenants to notify you of long absences, you'll know whether property has been abandoned or the tenant is simply on vacation. In addition, if you have such a clause and, under its authority, enter an apparently abandoned unit only to be confronted later by an indignant tenant, you can defend yourself by pointing out that the tenant violated the lease.

When Breaking a Lease Is Justified

There are some important exceptions to the blanket rule that a tenant who breaks a lease owes the rent for the entire lease term. A tenant may be able to legally move out without providing the proper notice in the following situations:

- **You violated an important lease provision.** If you don't live up to your obligations under the lease—for example, if you fail to maintain the unit in accordance with health and safety codes—a court will conclude that you have "constructively evicted" the tenant. That releases the tenant from further obligations under the lease.
- **State law allows the tenant to leave early.** A few states' laws list reasons that allow a tenant to break a lease.
  - **Job relocation or need to move because of health or age.** In Delaware, a tenant need only give 30 days' notice to end a long-term lease if he needs to move because his present employer relocated or because health problems (of the tenant or a family member) require a permanent move. In New Jersey, a tenant who has suffered a disabling illness or accident can break a lease and leave after 40 days' notice upon presenting proper proof of disability. In Rhode Island, a tenant who is 65 years of age or older (or who will turn 65 during the term of a rental agreement) may terminate the rental agreement in order to enter a residential care and assisted living facility, a nursing facility, or a unit in a private or public housing complex designated by the federal government as housing for the elderly. (R.I. Gen. Laws § 34-18-15.)
  - **Domestic violence.** In Oregon, a victim of domestic violence, sexual assault, or stalking may terminate the lease with 14 days' notice; Washington allows no-notice termination. (Ore. Rev. Stat. Ann. §§ 90.453 and following; Wash. Rev. Code Ann. §§ 59.18.575 and following.) For other states that give domestic violence victims early termination rights, see "State Laws in Domestic Violence Situations," in Appendix A.
  - **Military Service.** In all states, tenants who enter active military duty after signing a lease must be released after delivering proper notice. (See "Special Rules for Tenants Who Enter Military Service," above.) If your tenant has a good reason for a sudden move, you may want to research your state's law to see whether or not he's still on the hook for rent.
- **The rental unit is damaged or destroyed.** If the rental is significantly damaged—either by natural disaster or any other reason beyond the tenant's control—the tenant may consider the lease terminated and move out.
- **You seriously interfere with the tenant's ability to enjoy his or her tenancy**—for example, by sexually harassing the tenant or violating the tenant's privacy rights.

Your Duty to Mitigate Your Loss If the Tenant Leaves Early

If a tenant breaks the lease and moves out without legal justification, you normally can't just sit back and wait until the end of the term of the lease, and then sue the departed tenant for the total lost rent. In most states, you must try to rerent the property reasonably quickly and keep your losses to a minimum—in legalese, to "mitigate damages." Each state's rule is listed in "Landlord's Duty to Rerent" in Appendix A.

Even if this isn't the legal rule in your state, trying to rerent is obviously a sound business strategy. It's much better to have rent coming in every month than to wait, leaving a rental unit vacant for months, and then try to sue (and collect from) a tenant who's long gone.

If your state requires you to mitigate damages but you don't make an attempt (or make an inadequate one) to rerent, and instead sue the former tenant for the whole rent, you will collect only what the judge thinks is the difference between the fair rental value of the property and the original tenant's promised rent. This can depend on how easy it is to rerent in your area. Also, a judge is sure to give you some time (probably at least 30 days) to find a new tenant.

> CAUTION
>
> **No double-dipping is allowed.** Even if your state doesn't strictly enforce the mitigation-of-damages rules, if you rerent the property, you cannot also collect from the former tenant. Courts do not allow you to unjustly enrich yourself this way.

How to Mitigate Your Damages

When you're sure that a tenant has left permanently, then you can turn your attention to rerenting the unit.

You do not need to relax your standards for acceptable tenants—for example, you are entitled to reject applicants with poor credit or rental histories. Also, you need not give the suddenly available property priority over other rental units that you would normally attend to first.

You are not required to rent the premises at a rate below its fair market value. Keep in mind, however, that refusing to rent at less than the original rate may be foolish. If you are unable to ultimately collect from the former tenant, you will get *no* income from the property instead of less. You will have ended up hurting no one but yourself.

Keep Good Records

If you end up suing a former tenant, you will want to be able to show the judge that you acted reasonably in your attempts to rerent the property. Don't rely on your memory and powers of persuasion to convince the judge. Keep detailed records, including:

- the original lease
- receipts for cleaning and painting, with photos of the unit showing the need for repairs, if any
- your expenses for storing or properly disposing of any belongings the tenant left
- receipts for advertising the property and bills from credit reporting agencies investigating potential renters
- a log of the time you spent showing the property, and a value for that time
- a log of any people who offered to rent and, if you rejected them, documentation as to why, and
- if the current rent is less than the original tenant paid, a copy of the new lease.

EXAMPLE: When the mail began to pile up and the rent went unpaid, Jack suspected that Lorna, his tenant, had broken the lease and moved out. When his suspicions were confirmed, he added her apartment to the list of vacant units that needed his attention. In the same way that he prepared every unit, Jack cleaned the apartment and advertised it. Three months after Lorna left, Jack succeeded in rerenting the apartment.

Jack sued Lorna in small claims court and won a judgment that included the costs of advertising and cleaning and the three months' rent that he lost before the unit was rerented.

The Tenant's Right to Find a Replacement Tenant

A tenant who wishes to leave before the lease expires may offer to find a suitable new tenant, so that the flow of rent will remain uninterrupted. Unless you have a new tenant waiting, you have nothing to lose by cooperating. Refusing to cooperate could even hurt you. If you refuse to accept an excellent new tenant and then withhold the lease-breaking tenant's deposit or sue for unpaid rent, you may wind up losing in court, because you turned down the chance to reduce your losses (mitigate your damages).

Of course, if the rental market is really tight in your area, you may be able to lease the unit easily at a higher rent, or you may already have an even better prospective tenant on your waiting list. In that case, you won't care if a tenant breaks the lease, and you may not be interested in any new tenant he provides.

If you and the outgoing tenant agree on a replacement tenant, you and the new tenant should sign a new lease, and the outgoing tenant should sign a termination of lease form (discussed in Chapter 8). Since this is a new lease—not a sublease or assignment of the existing lease—you can raise the rent if you wish, unless local rent control ordinances prohibit it.

When You Can Sue

If a tenant leaves prematurely, you may need to go to court and sue for rerental costs and the difference between the original and the replacement rent. Obviously, you should first use the tenant's security deposit to cover these costs.

Deciding *where* to sue is usually easy: Small claims court (discussed in Chapter 16) is usually the court of choice because it's fast, is affordable, and doesn't require a lawyer. If you're seeking an amount that's substantially above your state's limit, you may file in regular court—but if the excess is small, you may wisely decide to forgo it and use the fast, cheap small claims court. If your lease contains an attorney fees clause (as does the form agreement in Chapter 2), you may be able to recover your attorney fees.

> **EXAMPLE:** Cree has a year's lease at $800 per month. She moves out with six months ($4,800 of rent) left on the lease. Cree's landlord, Robin, cannot find a new tenant for six weeks, and when she finally does, the new tenant will pay only $600 per month.

Unless Cree can show Robin acted unreasonably, Cree would be liable for the $200 per month difference between what she paid and what the new tenant pays, multiplied by the number of months left in the lease at the time she moved out. Cree would also be responsible for $1,200 for the time the unit was vacant, plus Robin's costs to find a new tenant. Cree would thus owe Robin $2,400 plus advertising and applicant screening costs. If Robin sues Cree for this money and uses a lawyer, and if there is an attorney fees clause in her lease, Cree will also owe Robin these costs, which can be upwards of a few thousand dollars.

Knowing *when* to sue is trickier. You may be eager to start legal proceedings as soon as the original tenant leaves, but, if you do, you won't know the extent of your losses, because you might find another tenant who will make up part of the lost rent. Must you wait until the end of the original tenant's lease? Or can you bring suit when you rerent the property?

The standard approach, and one that all states allow, is to go to court after you rerent the property. At this point, your losses—your expenses and the rent differential, if any—are known and final. The disadvantage is that you have had no income from that property since the original tenant left, and the original tenant may be long gone and not, practically speaking, worth chasing down.

CAUTION

Give accurate and updated information to credit bureaus about former tenants. The Fair Debt Collection Practices Act [FDCPA] (15 U.S. Code §§ 1692 and following) also applies when you give information to a credit reporting agency about a current or former tenant. The Act makes it illegal to give false information, and, if the tenant disputes the debt, you must mention the fact that the sum is disputed when you report it. You must notify the credit bureau if the tenant pays all or part of the debt.

The FDCPA even makes it illegal to give falsely *positive* information which you know to be untrue. When a credit bureau calls to ask about your least-favorite tenant who's applied for a home loan, don't describe him in falsely glowing terms, no matter how much you'd like to see him leave!

Termination Fees

A termination fee is a preset fee that landlords impose when tenants break a lease. They're often called cancellation fees, reletting fees, rerenting fees, or decorating fees. They're intended to compensate the landlord for the inconvenience and extra work caused by a broken lease, which include costs of cleaning, readying the unit for rerental, rekeying, advertising, showing the unit, and so on. Landlords who have to mitigate damages often add this fee to whatever loss of rent the landlord suffered before rerenting the unit. Landlords who do not have to mitigate damages may define the fee to cover both the inconvenience of the broken lease plus any lost rents.

If you've followed us through this section, you already know what the problem is with termination fees: They are preset damage amounts and, as such, are liquidated damages, which ought to run smack up against the ban on such damages in states that disallow them for lost rents. Quite so, but even in states that don't ban liquidated damages, they are ripe for attack under consumer protection statutes, which offer other ways to go after liquidated damages. Recently, they've appeared on plaintiffs' attorneys' radar, and have been disallowed in several states. The advice given to landlords by their attorneys and trade associations is uniform: Don't use them.

In response to aggressive legal challenges from tenants, one state has passed legislation that allows termination fees, as long as specific steps are followed. In Florida, before the lease is signed, landlords may offer the applicant the option of agreeing to a preset two-month's fee for breaking the lease, as long as the tenant gives the landlord two months' notice. If the applicant decides to take the offer, the lease must contain an addendum that further explains the fee. Tenants cannot be turned down if they refuse this option. (Fla. Stat. Ann. § 83.595.)

If you're determined to use a termination fee, understand that it must accurately reflect the financial losses you suffer when a tenant takes off unexpectedly, such as staff time spent securing the apartment or trying to locate the departed tenant.

To accurately and fairly charge lease-breaking tenants for the cost of rerenting, do a "time and motion" analysis of your actual costs to rerent, and add in how much your advertising costs, too. Since you'll be spending that money earlier than you'd planned, thanks to the tenant's early departure, figure out how much interest you'll be losing when you remove that money from your interest-bearing bank account. For example, if you typically spend $1,500 every time you rerent, and your tenant left six months early, your damages would be six months' of interest on $1,500.

> **CAUTION**
> **Don't ask for the return of "rent concessions."** If you've offered a free month's rent as a concession for new tenants, demanding its return when that tenant breaks a lease is risky. A court is likely to see your concession as simply a roundabout way to charge a lower, market rent spread over the period of the lease, and will not allow you to recoup it.

When a Tenant Dies

Occasionally, you may be faced with the death of a tenant who lives alone.

Whenever you or someone else first suspects or learns of a death of a tenant, immediately call the police or fire department. Next, try to reach the tenant's emergency contact listed on the rental application.

Preserving the Deceased Tenant's Property

You must take reasonable precautions to preserve the deceased tenant's property. Lock the door and keep everyone out of the premises. If you know or suspect that others have keys, you may even want to padlock the door or change the locks.

You can allow the tenant's next of kin to remove personal effects needed for the funeral, such as the deceased's clothing.

Otherwise, open the rental unit only for a person with legal authority to dispose of the deceased tenant's property. This may involve you in some unpleasant confrontations with pushy relatives or friends, but you are far better off to endure some uncomfortable moments than to risk being sued because you allowed unauthorized persons to plunder the estate.

> **CAUTION**
>
> **Protect yourself from charges of appropriation.** It is not unusual for an appreciable amount of time to go by before someone shows up with the proper authority to claim the tenant's belongings and clear out the unit. Generally, you may store the belongings and rerent the premises. Indeed, if the tenant had a fixed-term lease, you must take reasonably prompt steps to rerent, in order to minimize your losses (discussed above). Be careful, however, to carefully inventory the possessions. As an added precaution, have a disinterested helper with you who can testify to your honesty and thoroughness.

Who Gets the Tenant's Property?

You should and must release the tenant's personal belongings only to someone with legal authority. Depending on how the deceased left his affairs and the size of his estate, the authorized person will be:

- **The executor.** If the tenant left a will, it probably names an executor (called the personal representative in some states). This person is entitled to the property. If the tenant left enough valuable property, the executor will have a probate court order showing his authority. Ask to see the original court order, which will have a file stamp from the court on the first page and the original signature of the judge.
- **The inheritors.** If there is no probate proceeding, there is no court-authorized executor. You may release property to the persons entitled (under the terms of a will or state law) to inherit it. Usually, the inheritors must give you a signed, sworn statement (affidavit or declaration signed under penalty of perjury) stating that they are entitled to the property; the particulars depend on state law.

- **The administrator.** If the tenant died without a will and left more than a certain amount of property (each state has its own rules), the probate court will appoint an administrator to wind up his affairs. The administrator will have a court order to show you.
- **The successor trustee.** If the tenant created a probate-avoiding living trust and transferred his personal property to it, the person in authority will be called the successor trustee. Ask to see the original trust document, signed and notarized.

If someone shows up and claims to have the right to the tenant's belongings, how can you make sure that this person is, in fact, entitled to the items? Ask for a current picture ID and a legal document (one of those listed above) conferring authority.

> **CAUTION**
>
> **Don't get caught in the middle of a family fight.** If you are not sure of the authority of someone who wants to take the tenant's property, or if relatives are squabbling about who gets what, protect yourself. Insist that the claimants either show you convincing documents or show up with a probate court order.
>
> Disputes are especially common between the surviving member of an unmarried couple and the relatives of the deceased member of the couple. Don't get caught in a nasty crossfire.

Making a Claim on the Estate

After the deceased tenant's property is removed, you may be left with losses not covered by the deposit:

- repair costs
- if the deceased rented month to month, unpaid rent from before the tenant's death and beyond (the estate's responsibility for rent after the date of death varies according to state law)
- if the tenant died before the expiration of a fixed-term lease, unpaid rent for the balance of the lease term, less income you have as a consequence of rerenting, and
- storage costs.

To pay these bills, consider making a claim on the deceased tenant's estate (the assets he or she left). If a probate court proceeding has been initiated, you can fill out and submit a creditor's claim form (available from the court clerk) to the probate court. You will have a certain amount of time—a few months, in most states—in which to file your claim.

If the deceased tenant's assets were passed through a probate-avoiding trust, and there are no probate court proceedings, you will need to ask the successor trustee for payment. If there is neither a trust nor probate (because the tenant did not leave property of enough value to require probate), the best you can do is to bill the executor. If there is no will and no probate proceeding because the estate is too small, try billing the next of kin, who will be responsible only up to the value of the property that this person inherited.

Condominium Conversions

Converting a rental property into condominiums usually means the end of a tenant's tenancy. But condo conversions are not always simple.

Many states, such as California, Connecticut, and New York, regulate the conversion of rental property into condominiums—that is, they limit the number of conversions and give existing tenants considerable rights. Here are some of the basic issues that your state's condo conversion law may address:

- **Government approval.** Converting rental property to condos usually requires plan approval (often called a "subdivision map approval") from a local planning agency. If the property is subject to rent control, there are probably additional requirements.

- **Public input.** In most situations, the public—including current tenants—can speak out at planning agency hearings regarding the proposed condominium conversion and its impact on the rental housing market. You are usually required to give tenants notice of the time and place of these hearings.

- **Tenants' right of first refusal.** Most condominium conversion laws demand that you offer the units for sale first to the existing tenants, at prices that are the same as or lower than the intended public offering. To keep tenant opposition to a minimum, you may decide to voluntarily offer existing tenants a chance to buy at a significantly lower price.

- **Tenancy terminations.** Month-to-month tenants who don't buy their units should receive notice to move at some point during the sales process. Tenants with leases usually have a right to remain through the end of the lease. The entire condo conversion approval process typically takes many months—time enough for current leases to expire before the final okay has been given.

- **Renting after the conversion has been approved.** If you offer a lease or rental agreement *after* the condo conversion has been approved, many states require you to give the tenant plenty of clear written warnings (in large, bold-faced type) that the unit may be sold and the tenancy terminated on short notice. But, if you continue to rent units after you've gotten subdivision approval, you'll usually do so on a month-to-month basis, so the short notice really won't be any different from what any month-to-month tenant would receive.

- **Relocation assistance and special protections.** Some statutes require owners to pay current tenants a flat fee to help with relocation. Some also require owners to provide more notice or additional relocation assistance for elderly tenants or those with small children.

 RELATED TOPIC
For advice on researching your state's statutes and court cases on condominium conversions, see the discussion of legal research in Chapter 18.

Returning Security Deposits and Other Move-Out Issues

FORMS IN THIS CHAPTER

Chapter 15 includes instructions for and samples of the following forms:

- Move-Out Letter
- Letter for Returning Entire Security Deposit
- Security Deposit Itemization (Deductions for Repairs and Cleaning)
- Security Deposit Itemization (Deductions for Repairs, Cleaning, and Unpaid Rent)

The Nolo website includes downloadable copies of these forms. See Appendix B for the link to the forms in this book.

s any small claims court judge will tell you, fights over security deposits account for a large percentage of the landlord-tenant disputes. Failure to return security deposits as legally required can result in substantial financial penalties if a tenant files suit.

Fortunately, you can take some simple steps to minimize the possibility that you'll spend hours haggling in court over back rent, cleaning costs, and damage to your property. First, of course, you must follow the law scrupulously when you return security deposits. But it's also wise to send the tenant, before he or she moves out, a letter setting out your expectations for how the unit should be left.

This chapter shows you how to itemize deductions and refund security deposits as state laws require, and how to protect yourself both at the time of move-in and at termination. It describes the penalties you face for violating security deposit laws. This chapter also covers how to defend yourself against a tenant's lawsuit as well as the occasional necessity of taking a tenant to small claims court if the deposit doesn't cover unpaid rent, damage, or cleaning bills. Finally, it discusses what to do when a tenant moves out and leaves personal property behind.

We cover key aspects of state deposit law in this chapter and in Chapter 4. In addition, be sure to check local ordinances in all areas where you own property. Cities, particularly those with rent control, may add their own rules on security deposits.

RELATED TOPIC

Related topics covered in this book include:

- How to avoid deposit disputes by using clear lease and rental agreement provisions: Chapter 2
- Deposit limits; requirements for keeping deposits in a separate account or paying interest; last month's rent and deposits: Chapter 4
- Highlighting security deposit rules in a move-in letter to new tenants; taking photographs and using a Landlord-Tenant Checklist to keep track of the condition of the premises before and after the tenant moves in: Chapter 7

- Notice requirements for terminating a tenancy: Chapter 14
- State Security Deposit Rules: Appendix A.

Preparing a Move-Out Letter

Chapter 7 explains how a move-in letter can help get a tenancy off to a good start. Similarly, a move-out letter can also help reduce the possibility of disputes, especially over the return of security deposits.

Your move-out letter should tell the tenant how you expect the unit to be left, explain your inspection procedures, list the kinds of deposit deductions you may legally make, and tell the tenant when and how you will send any refund that is due.

A sample Move-Out Letter is shown below and the Nolo website includes a downloadable copy. See Appendix B for the link to the forms in this book. You may want to add or delete items depending on your own needs and how specific you wish to be.

Here are a few points you may want to include in a move-out letter:

- specific cleaning requirements, such as what to do about stained draperies that need special cleaning, or how to fix holes left from picture hooks or clean dirty walls
- instructions regarding recycling and disposing of paint and household hazardous wastes
- a reminder that fixtures (items that the tenant attaches more or less permanently to the wall, such as built-in bookshelves) must be left in place (see the discussion of fixtures in Chapter 9 and Clause 12 of the form agreements in Chapter 2)
- details of how and when the final inspection will be conducted
- a request for a forwarding address where you can mail the tenant's deposits
- information on state laws (if any) that allow a landlord to keep a tenant's security deposit if the tenant's forwarding address is not provided within a certain amount of time

Move-Out Letter

July 5, 20xx
Date

Jane Wasserman
Tenant

123 North Street, Apartment #23
Street Address

Atlanta, Georgia 30360
City and State

Dear _____Jane_____,
                    Tenant

We hope you have enjoyed living here. In order that we may mutually end our relationship on a positive note, this move-out letter describes how we expect your unit to be left and what our procedures are for returning your security deposit.

Basically, we expect you to leave your rental unit in the same condition it was when you moved in, except for normal wear and tear. To refresh your memory on the condition of the unit when you moved in, I've attached a copy of the Landlord-Tenant Checklist you signed at the beginning of your tenancy. I'll be using this same form to inspect your unit when you leave.

Specifically, here's a list of items you should thoroughly clean before vacating:

- ☑ Floors
    - ☑ sweep wood floors
    - ☑ vacuum carpets and rugs (shampoo if necessary)
    - ☑ mop kitchen and bathroom floors
- ☑ Walls, baseboards, ceilings, and built-in shelves
- ☑ Kitchen cabinets, countertops and sink, stove and oven—inside and out
- ☑ Refrigerator—clean inside and out, empty it of food, and turn it off, with the door left open
- ☑ Bathtubs, showers, toilets, and plumbing fixtures
- ☑ Doors, windows, and window coverings
- ☑ Other
    Microwave oven-clean inside and out

_____

_____

_____

_____

_____

_____

If you have any questions as to the type of cleaning we expect, please let me know.

Please don't leave anything behind—that includes bags of garbage, clothes, food, newspapers, furniture, appliances, dishes, plants, cleaning supplies, or other items that belong to you.

Please be sure you have disconnected phone and utility services, canceled all newspaper subscriptions, and sent the post office a change of address form.

Once you have cleaned your unit and removed all your belongings, please call me at _____555-1234_____ to arrange for a walk-through inspection and to return all keys. Please be prepared to give me your forwarding address where we may mail your security deposit.

It's our policy to return all deposits either in person or at an address you provide within _____one month_____ _____ after you move out. If any deductions are made—for past-due rent or because the unit is damaged or not sufficiently clean—they will be explained in writing.

If you have any questions, please contact me at _____555-1234_____ .

Sincerely,

Denise Parsons
Landlord/Manager

("Mailing the Security Deposit Itemization," below), and

- information on state laws regarding abandoned property (discussed at the end of this chapter).

Inspecting the Unit When a Tenant Leaves

After the tenant leaves, you will need to inspect the unit to assess what cleaning and damage repair is necessary. At the final inspection, check each item—for example, refrigerator or bathroom walls—on the Landlord-Tenant Checklist you and the tenant signed when the tenant moved in. (An excerpt is shown below. See Chapter 7 for a complete Checklist.) Note any item that needs cleaning, repair, or replacement in the middle column, *Condition on Departure*. Where possible, note the estimated cost of repair or replacement in the third column; you can subtract those costs from the security deposit.

RESOURCE

California has special rules and procedures for move-out inspections. California tenants are entitled to

a pre-move-out inspection, when you tell the tenant what defects, if any, need to be corrected in order for the tenant to optimize the security deposit refund. California landlords must notify the tenant in writing of the right to request an initial inspection, at which the tenant has a right to be present. (Cal. Civ. Code § 1950.5(f).) For details, see *The California Landlord's Law Book: Rights & Responsibilities*, by David Brown, Janet Portman, and Ralph Warner (Nolo). This book is available at bookstores and public libraries, or may be ordered directly from Nolo (online at www.nolo.com or by phone, 800-728-3555).

Many landlords do this final inspection on their own and simply send the tenant an itemized statement with any remaining balance of the deposit. If at all possible, we recommend that you make the inspection with the tenant who's moving out, rather than by yourself. A few states actually require this. Laws in Arizona, Maryland, and Virginia, for example, specifically give tenants the right to be present when you conduct the final inspection. Doing the final inspection with the tenant present (in a conciliatory, nonthreatening way) should alleviate any of the tenant's uncertainty concerning what deductions (if any) you propose to make from the deposit. It also gives the tenant a chance to present her point of view. But, best of all,

Landlord-Tenant Checklist

GENERAL CONDITION OF RENTAL UNIT AND PREMISES

572 Fourth St.   Apt. 11   Washington, D.C
Street Address   Unit No.   City

	Condition on Arrival	Condition on Departure	Estimated Cost of Repair/ Replacement
Living Room			
Floors & Floor Coverings	OK	OK	Ø
Drapes & Window Coverings	Miniblinds discolored	Miniblinds missing	$75
Walls & Ceilings	OK	Several holes in wall	$100
Light Fixtures	OK	OK	Ø
Windows, Screens, & Doors	Window rattles		Ø
& Locks	OK		

this approach avoids the risk that a tenant who feels unpleasantly surprised by the amount you withhold from the deposit will promptly take the matter to small claims court.

If you have any reason to expect a tenant to take you to court over deductions you plan to make from a security deposit, have the unit examined by another, more neutral person, such as another tenant in the same building. This person should be available to testify in court on your behalf, if necessary, should you end up in small claims court.

> **TIP**
>
> **Photograph "before" and "after."** In Chapter 7, we recommend that you take photos or videos of the unit before the tenant moves in. You should do the same when the tenant leaves, so that you can make comparisons and have visual proof in case you are challenged later in court.

Should You Let the Tenant Clean or Fix the Damage?

Many tenants, faced with losing a large chunk of their security deposit, may want the chance to do some more cleaning or repair any damage you've identified in the final inspection. A few states require you to offer the tenant a second chance at cleaning before you deduct cleaning charges from the security deposit. Even if your state does not require it, you may wish to offer a second chance anyway if the tenant seems sincere and capable of doing the work. This may help avoid arguments and maybe even a small claims action. But, if you need to get the apartment ready quickly for another tenant or doubt the tenant's ability to do the work, just say no. And think twice if repairs are required, not just cleaning. If a tenant does a repair poorly—for example, improperly tacking down a carpet that later causes another tenant to trip and injure herself—you will be liable for the injury.

To be on the safe side, keep your inspection notes, photos, videos, and related records for at least two years. Technically speaking, in most states tenants have up to four years to sue you over security deposit agreements, but few will do so after a year or so.

Applying the Security Deposit to the Last Month's Rent

If no portion of the tenant's deposit was called last month's rent, you are not legally obliged to apply it in this way. When giving notice, a tenant may ask you to apply the security deposit toward the last month's rent.

Why should you object if a tenant asks to use a deposit you are already holding as payment for the last month's rent? The problem is that you can't know in advance what the property will look like when the tenant leaves. If the tenant leaves the property a mess, but the whole security deposit has gone to pay the last month's rent, obviously you will have nothing left to use to repair or clean the property. You will have to absorb the loss or sue the tenant.

You have two choices if you are faced with a tenant who wants to use a security deposit for last month's rent. The first alternative is to grant the tenant's request. Tell the tenant that you'll need to make a quick inspection first, and then, if you have good reason to believe that the tenant will leave the property clean and undamaged, don't worry about the last month's rent. But don't forget to send the tenant a written statement setting out what happened to the deposit. You can prepare a brief letter, similar to the one we show in "Preparing an Itemized Statement of Deductions," below, for returning the tenant's entire security deposit.

Your second choice is to treat the tenant's nonpayment (or partial payment) of the last month's rent as an ordinary case of rent nonpayment. This means preparing and serving the notice necessary to terminate the tenancy, and, if the tenant doesn't pay, following up with an eviction lawsuit. But because it typically takes at least several weeks to evict a tenant, this probably won't get the tenant out much sooner than he would leave anyway. However, it will provide you with a court judgment for the unpaid last month's rent. This means that you may use the security deposit to pay for cleaning and repair costs, and apply any remainder to the judgment for nonpayment of rent. You then take your judgment and attempt to enforce it, as discussed below ("If the Deposit Doesn't Cover Damage and Unpaid Rent").

> **EXAMPLE:** Ari paid his landlord Jack a $1,000 deposit when he rented his $900-per-month apartment on a month-to-month basis. The rental agreement required Ari to give 30 days' notice before terminating the tenancy.
>
> Ari told Jack on November 1 that he would be leaving at the end of the month, but he did not pay his rent for November. When he left on December 1, he also left $500 worth of damages. Jack followed his state's procedures for itemizing and returning security deposits, and applied the $1,000 deposit to cover the damage. This left Jack with $900 for the $900 rent due, so he sued in small claims court for the $400 still owing. Jack was awarded a judgment for $400 plus the filing fee.

Basic Rules for Returning Deposits

You are generally entitled to deduct from a tenant's security deposit whatever amount you need to fix damaged or dirty property (outside of "ordinary wear and tear") or to make up unpaid rent (see "Purpose and Use of Security Deposits" in Chapter 4). But you must do it correctly, following your state's procedures. While the specific rules vary from state to state, you usually have between 14 and 30 days after the tenant leaves to return the tenant's deposit. See the column "Deadline for Landlord to Itemize and Return Deposit" in the "State Security Deposit Rules" chart in Appendix A. A few states require landlords to give tenants advance notice of intended deductions; see "Advance notice of deduction" in the same chart.

State security deposit statutes typically require you to mail, within the time limit, the following to the tenant's last known address (or forwarding address if you have one):

- The tenant's entire deposit, with interest if required, or

- A written, itemized accounting as to how the deposit has been applied toward back rent and costs of cleaning and damage repair, together with payment for any deposit balance, including any interest that is required. We show you below how to prepare an itemized statement, including how to handle situations when you're not sure of the exact deductions.

Even if there is no specific time limit in your state or law requiring itemization, promptly presenting the tenant with a written itemization of all deductions and a clear reason why each was made is an essential part of a savvy landlord's overall plan to avoid disputes with tenants. In general, we recommend 30 days as a reasonable time to return deposits.

> **TIP**
> **Send an itemization even if you don't send money.** Quite a few landlords mistakenly believe that they don't have to account for the deposit to a tenant who's been evicted by court order or who breaks the lease. But a tenant's misconduct does not entitle a landlord to pocket the entire deposit without further formality. In general, even if the tenant leaves owing several months' rent—more than the amount of the deposit—you still must notify the tenant in writing, within the time limit, as to how the deposit has been applied toward cleaning or repair charges and unpaid rent. You may then need to sue the tenant if the deposit doesn't cover damage and unpaid rent.

Deductions for Cleaning and Damage

As you can imagine, many disputes over security deposits revolve around whether or not it was reasonable for the landlord to deduct the cost of cleaning or repairing the premises after the tenant moved. Unfortunately, standards in this area are often vague. Typically, you may charge for any cleaning or repairs necessary to restore the rental unit to its condition at the beginning the tenancy, but not deduct for the cost of ordinary wear and tear.

Reasonable Deductions

In general, you may charge only for cleaning and repairs that are actually necessary. Items for which cleaning is often necessary—and costly—include replacing stained or ripped carpets or drapes (particularly smoke-contaminated ones) fixing damaged furniture, and cleaning dirty stoves, refrigerators, and kitchen and bathroom fixtures. You may also need to take care of such things as flea infestations left behind by the tenant's dog or mildew in the bathroom caused by the tenant's failure to clean properly. That's why we recommend highlighting these types of trouble spots in a move-out letter. See "Preparing a Move-Out Letter," above, for a sample move-out letter.

That said, every move-out is different in its details, and there are simply no hard and fast rules on what is wear and tear and what is your tenant's responsibility. But here are some basic guidelines:

- You should not charge the tenant for filth or damage that was present when the tenant moved in.
- You should not charge the tenant for replacing an item when a repair would be sufficient. For example, a tenant who damaged the kitchen counter by placing a hot pan on it shouldn't be charged for replacing the entire counter if an expertly done patch will do the job. Of course, you have to evaluate the overall condition of the unit—if it is a luxury property that looks like an ad in *Architectural Digest*, you don't need to make do with a patch.
- The longer a tenant has lived in a place, the more wear and tear can be expected. In practical terms, this means that you can't always charge a tenant for cleaning carpets, drapes, or walls, or repainting.
- You should not charge for cleaning if the tenant paid a nonrefundable cleaning fee. Landlords in some states are allowed to charge a cleaning fee, which is separate from the security deposit and is specifically labeled as nonrefundable.

- You should charge a fair price for repairs and replacements.

You can deduct a reasonable hourly charge if you or your employees do any necessary cleaning. If you have cleaning done by an outside service, be sure to keep your canceled checks or credit card receipts, and have the service itemize the work. It's wise to patronize only those cleaning services whose employees are willing to testify for you, or at least send a letter describing what they did in detail, if the tenant sues you in small claims court contesting your deposit deductions. See "If a Tenant Sues You," below.

TIP

Don't overdo deductions from security deposits. When you make deductions for cleaning or damage, it's often a mistake to be too aggressive. Tenants who believe they've been wronged (even if it isn't true) are likely to go to small claims court. The result will be that you or an employee will spend hours preparing your defense, waiting around the courthouse, and presenting your side of the case. Even if you prevail (or, as is most likely, the judge makes a compromise ruling), the value of the time involved will have been considerable. In the long run, it may be wiser to withhold a smaller portion of the deposit in the first place.

See "What Can You Charge For?" below, for some examples of what a court will consider to be ordinary wear and tear, and what crosses the line and is considered damage that the tenant must pay for.

Common Disagreements

Common areas of disagreement between landlords and tenants concern repainting, carpets, and fixtures.

Painting

Although most state and local laws (with the exception of New York City) provide no firm guidelines as to who is responsible for repainting when a rental unit needs it, courts usually rule that

What Can You Charge For?	
Ordinary Wear and Tear: Landlord's Responsibility	**Damage or Excessive Filth: Tenant's Responsibility**
Curtains faded by the sun	Cigarette burns in curtains or carpets
Water-stained linoleum by shower	Broken tiles in bathroom
Minor marks on or nicks in wall	Large marks on or holes in wall
Dents in the wall where a door handle bumped it	Door off its hinges
Moderate dirt or spotting on carpet	Rips in carpet or urine stains from pets
A few small tack or nail holes in wall	Lots of picture holes or gouges in walls that require patching as well as repainting
A rug worn thin by normal use	Stains in rug caused by leaking fish tank
Worn gaskets on refrigerator doors	Broken refrigerator shelf
Faded paint on bedroom wall	Water damage on wall from hanging plants
Dark patches of ingrained soil on hardwood floors that have lost their finish and have been worn down to bare wood	Water stains on wood floors and windowsills caused by windows being left open during rainstorms
Warped cabinet doors that won't close	Sticky cabinets and interiors
Stains on old porcelain fixtures that have lost their protective coating	Grime-coated bathtub and toilet
Moderately dirty miniblinds	Missing miniblinds
Bathroom mirror beginning to "de-silver" (black spots)	Mirrors caked with lipstick and makeup
Clothes dryer that delivers cold air because the thermostat has given out	Dryer that won't turn at all because it's been overloaded
Toilet flushes inadequately because mineral deposits have clogged the jets	Toilet won't flush properly because it's stopped up with a diaper

if a tenant has lived in your unit for many years, repainting should be done at your expense, not the tenant's. On the other hand, if a tenant has lived in a unit for less than a year, and the walls were freshly painted when she moved in but are now a mess, you are entitled to charge the tenant for all costs of cleaning the walls. If repainting badly smudged walls is cheaper and more effective than cleaning, however, you can charge for repainting.

When to Charge the Tenant for Repainting

One landlord we know uses the following approach, with excellent success, when a tenant moves out and repainting is necessary:

- If the tenant has occupied the premises for six months or less, the full cost of repainting (labor and materials) is subtracted from the deposit.
- If the tenant lived in the unit between six months and a year, and the walls are dirty, two-thirds of the painting cost is subtracted from the deposit.
- Tenants who occupy a unit for between one and two years and leave dirty walls are charged one-third of the repainting cost.
- No one who stays for two years or more is ever charged a painting fee. No matter how dirty the walls become, the landlord would always repaint as a matter of course if more than two years had passed since the previous painting.

Obviously, these general rules must be modified occasionally to fit particular circumstances.

Rugs and Carpets

If the living room rug was already threadbare when the tenant moved in a few months ago and looks even worse now, it's pretty obvious that the tenant's footsteps have simply contributed to the inevitable, and that this wear and tear is not the tenant's responsibility. On the other hand, a brand-new, good quality rug that becomes stained and full of bare spots within months has probably been subjected to the type of abuse the tenant will have to pay for. In between, it's anyone's guess. But clearly, the longer a tenant has lived in a unit, and the cheaper or older the carpet was when the tenant moved in, the less likely the tenant is to be held responsible for its deterioration.

> **EXAMPLE:** A tenant has ruined an eight-year-old rug that had a life expectancy of ten years. If a replacement rug would cost $1,000, you would charge the tenant $200 for the two years of life that would have remained in the rug had their dog not ruined it.

Fixtures

The law generally considers pieces of furniture or equipment that are physically attached to the rental property, such as bolted-on bookshelves, to be your property, even if the tenant (not you) paid for them. Disputes often arise when tenants, unaware of this rule, install a fixture and then attempt to remove it and take it with them when they leave. To avoid this kind of dispute, the lease and rental agreements in this book forbid tenants from altering the premises without your consent. That includes the installation of fixtures. See Clause 12 of the form agreements in Chapter 2.

If the tenant leaves behind built-in bookshelves, you can remove the shelves, restore the property to the same condition as before they were installed, and subtract the cost from the tenant's security deposit. Unless your lease or rental agreement says otherwise, you do not have to return the bookshelves to the tenant. Legally, you've only removed something that has become part of the premises and, hence, your property. Chapter 9 offers suggestions on how to avoid disputes with tenants over fixtures.

Deductions for Unpaid Rent

In most states you can deduct any unpaid rent from a tenant's security deposit, including any unpaid utility charges or other financial obligations required under your lease or rental agreement.

> **CAUTION**
> **Even if the tenant's debt far exceeds the amount of the security deposit, do not ignore your statutory duties to itemize and notify the former tenant of your use of the security deposit.** It may seem like a waste of time, but some courts will penalize you for ignoring the statute, even if you later obtain a judgment that puts the stamp of approval on your use of the deposit.

Month-to-Month Tenancies

If you rent on a month-to-month basis, ideally your tenant will give the right amount of notice and pay for the last month's rent. Usually, the notice period is the same as the rental period: 30 days. Then, when the tenant leaves as planned, the only issue with respect to the security deposit is whether the tenant has caused any damage or left the place dirty. But there are three common variations on this ideal scenario, and they all allow you to deduct from the tenant's security deposit for unpaid rent:

- The tenant leaves as announced, but with unpaid rent behind.
- The tenant leaves later than planned, and hasn't paid for the extra days.
- The tenant leaves as announced, but hasn't given you the right amount of notice.

Let's look at each situation.

The Tenant Leaves With Rent Unpaid

If the tenant has been behind on the rent for months, you are entitled to deduct what is owed from the security deposit—either during the tenancy or when the tenant leaves. If you deduct during the tenancy, be sure to follow your state's law on itemization.

The Tenant Stays After the Announced Departure Date

A tenant who fails to leave when planned (or when requested, if you have terminated the rental agreement) obviously isn't entitled to stay on rent-free. When the tenant eventually does leave, you can figure the exact amount owed by prorating the monthly rent for the number of days the tenant has failed to pay.

> **EXAMPLE:** Your tenant Erin gives notice on March 1 of her intent to move out. She pays you the rent of $1,200 for March. But because she can't get into her new place on time, Erin stays until April 5 without paying anything more for the extra five days. You are entitled to deduct $5/30$ (one-sixth) of the total month's rent, or $200, from Erin's security deposit.

The Tenant Gives Inadequate Notice

A tenant who gives less than the legally required amount of notice before leaving (typically 30 days) must pay rent for that entire period. If the tenant gave less than the legally required amount of notice and moved out, you are entitled to rent money for the balance of the notice period unless the place is rerented within the 30 days.

> **EXAMPLE 1:** Your tenant Tom moves out on the fifth day of the month, without giving you any notice or paying any rent for the month. The rental market is flooded, and you are unable to rerent the property for two months. You are entitled to deduct an entire month's rent (for the missing 30 days' notice) plus one-sixth of one month (for the five holdover days for which Tom failed to pay rent).

> **EXAMPLE 2:** Sheila pays her $900 monthly rent on October 1. State law requires 30 days' notice to terminate a tenancy. On October 15, Sheila informs you that she's leaving on the 25th. This gives you only ten days' notice, when you're entitled to 30. You're entitled to rent through the 30th day, counting from October 15, or November 14, unless you find a new tenant in the meantime. Because the rent is paid through October 31, Sheila owes you the prorated rent for 14 days in November. At $900 per month or $30 a day, this works out to $420, which you can deduct from Sheila's security deposit.

Fixed-Term Leases

If a tenant leaves before a fixed-term lease expires, you are usually entitled to the balance of the rent due under the lease, less any rent you receive from new tenants or could have received if you had made a diligent effort to rerent the property.

If a tenant leaves less than a month before the lease is scheduled to end, you can be almost positive that, if the case goes to court, a judge will conclude that the tenant owes rent for the entire lease term. It would be unreasonable to expect you to immediately find a new tenant to take over the few days left of the lease. But if the tenant leaves more than 30 days before the end of a lease, your duty to look for a new tenant will be taken more seriously by the courts. See Chapter 14 for more on your duty to try to rerent the property promptly.

> **EXAMPLE:** On January 1, Anthony rents a house from Will for $1,200 a month and signs a one-year lease. Anthony moves out on June 30, even though six months remain on the lease, making him responsible for a total rent of $7,200. Will rerents the property on July 10, this time for $1,250 a month (the new tenants pay $833 for the last 20 days in July), which means that he'll receive a total rent of $7,083 through December 31. That's $117 less than the $7,200 he would have received from Anthony had he lived up to the lease, so Will may deduct $117 from Anthony's deposit. In addition, if Will has spent a reasonable amount of money to find a new tenant (for newspaper ads, rental agency commissions, and credit checks), he may also deduct this sum from the deposit.

Deducting Rent After You've Evicted a Tenant

In most states, if you successfully sue to evict a holdover tenant, you will obtain a court order telling the tenant to leave (which you give to a law enforcement agency to enforce) and a money judgment ordering the tenant to pay you rent through the date of the judgment. Armed with these court orders, you can subtract from the security deposit:

- the amount of the judgment, and
- prorated rent for the period between the date of the judgment and the date the tenant actually leaves.

EXAMPLE: Marilyn sues to evict a tenant who fails to pay May's rent of $900. She gets an eviction judgment from the court on June 10 for rent prorated through that date. The tenant doesn't leave until the 17th, when the sheriff comes and puts him out. Marilyn can deduct the following items from the deposit:

- costs of necessary cleaning and repair, as allowed by state law
- the amount of the judgment (for rent through June 10)
- rent for the week between judgment and eviction (seven days at $30/day, or $210).

Before you subtract the amount of a court judgment for unpaid rent from a deposit, deduct any cleaning and repair costs and any unpaid rent not included in the judgment. The reason is simple: A judgment can be collected in all sorts of ways—for example, you can go after the former tenant's wages or bank account—if the security deposit is not large enough to cover everything owed you. However, you are much more limited when it comes to collecting money the tenant owes you for damage and cleaning if you don't have a judgment for the amount. If you don't subtract these items from the deposit, you'll have to file suit in small claims court as discussed below. But if you subtract the amount for cleaning, damage, and any unpaid rent not covered in the judgment first, you will still have the judgment if the deposit isn't large enough to cover everything.

EXAMPLE 1: Amelia collected a security deposit of $1,200 from Timothy, whom she ultimately had to sue to evict for failure to pay rent. Amelia got a judgment for $160 court costs plus $1,000 unpaid rent through the date of the judgment. Timothy didn't leave until the sheriff came, about five days later, thus running up an additional prorated rent of $100. Timothy also left dirt and damage that cost $1,000 to clean and repair.

Amelia (who hadn't read this book) first applied the $1,200 security deposit to the $1,160 judgment, leaving only $40 to apply toward the rent of $100 which was not reflected in the judgment, as well as the cleaning and repair charges, all of which totaled $1,100. Amelia must now sue Timothy for the $1,060 he still owes her.

EXAMPLE 2: Now, assume that Monique was Timothy's landlord in the same situation. But Monique applied Timothy's $1,200 deposit first to the cleaning and damage charges of $1,000, and then to the $100 rent not reflected in the judgment. This left $100 to apply to the $1,160 judgment, the balance of which she can collect by garnishing Timothy's wages or bank account.

Preparing an Itemized Statement of Deductions

Once you've inspected the premises and decided what you need to deduct for cleaning, repair, back rent, or other purposes allowed by your state statute, you're ready to prepare a statement for the tenant. The statement should simply list each deduction and briefly explain what it's for.

This section includes samples of three security deposit itemization forms, which you can use for different types of deductions. Copies of all three forms can be downloaded from the Nolo website. (See Appendix B for the link to the forms in this book.) Whatever form you use, be sure to keep a copy in your tenant records and receipts for repairs or cleaning in case the tenant ends up suing you at a later date. See "If a Tenant Sues You," below.

> **CAUTION**
> **If your city or state requires you to pay interest on a tenant's entire deposit, you must also refund this amount.** For details, see Chapter 4.

Returning the Entire Deposit

If you are returning a tenant's entire security deposit (including interest, if required), simply send a brief letter like the one below.

Itemizing Deductions for Repairs, Cleaning, and Related Losses

If you are making deductions from the tenant's security deposit only for cleaning and repair, use the Security Deposit Itemization (Deductions for Repairs and Cleaning). A sample is shown below.

Letter for Returning Entire Security Deposit

October 11, 20xx
Date

Gerry Fraser
Tenant

976 Park Place
Street Address

Sacramento, CA 95840
City and State

Dear Gerry   ,
                    Tenant

Here is an itemization of your $ __$1,500__ security deposit on the property at __976 Park Place__ ,

which you rented from me on a __month-to-month__ basis on __March 1, 20xx__ and vacated on __September 30, 20xx__ .

As you left the rental property in satisfactory condition, I am returning the entire amount of the security deposit of __$1,500, plus $150 in interest, for a total of $1,650__ .

Sincerely,

Tom Stein

Landlord/Manager

Security Deposit Itemization
(Deductions for Repairs and Cleaning)

Date _November 8, 20xx_

From: _Rachel Tolan_

123 Larchmont Lane

St. Louis, Missouri 63119

To: _Lena Coleman_

456 Penny Lane, #101

St. Louis, Missouri 63119

Property Address: _789 Cora Court, St. Louis, Missouri_

Rental Period: _January 1, 20xx to October 31, 20xx_

1. Security Deposit Received: $ _1,000_

2. Interest on Deposit (if required by lease or law): $ _N/A_

3. Total Credit (sum of lines 1 and 2): $ _1,000_

4. Itemized Repairs and Related Losses:

   Repainting of living room walls, required

   by crayon and chalk marks

   _____ $ _300_

5. Necessary Cleaning:

   Sum paid to resident manager for 5 hours

   cleaning at $20/hour: debris-filled

   garage, dirty stove, and refrigerator $ _100_

6. Total Cleaning & Repair (sum of lines 4 and 5): $ _400_

7. Amount Owed (line 3 minus line 6):

   ☐ Total Amount Tenant Owes Landlord: $ _____

   ☑ Total Amount Landlord Owes Tenant: $ _600_

Comments: _A check for $600 is enclosed._

For each deduction, list the item and the dollar amount. If you've already had the work done, attach receipts to the itemization. If your receipts are not very detailed, add more information on labor and supplies, for example:

- "Carpet cleaning by ABC Carpet Cleaners, $160, required because of several large grease stains and candle wax embedded in living room rug."
- "Plaster repair, $400, of several fist-sized holes in bedroom wall."
- "$250 to replace drapes in living room, damaged by cigarette smoke and holes."

"Deductions for Cleaning and Damage," above, will help you determine proper amounts to deduct for repairs and cleaning.

If you can't get necessary repairs made or cleaning done within the time required to return the security deposit, make a reasonable estimate of the cost. But keep in mind that if the tenant subsequently sues you, you will need to produce receipts for at least as much as the amount you deducted.

When you're trying to put a dollar amount on damages, the basic approach is to determine whether the tenant has damaged or substantially shortened the useful life of an item that does wear out. If the answer is yes, you may charge the tenant the prorated cost of the item, based on the age of the item, how long it might have lasted otherwise, and the cost of replacement.

Itemizing Deductions for Repairs, Cleaning, and Unpaid Rent

If you have to deduct for unpaid rent as well as cleaning and repairs, use the form Security Deposit Itemization (Deductions for Repairs, Cleaning, and Unpaid Rent). A sample is shown below.

Handling Deposits When a Tenant Files for Bankruptcy

Landlords often see a tenant's bankruptcy filing as the ultimate monkey wrench in what may already be a less-than-perfect landlord-tenant relationship.

Indeed, unless you've completed your eviction case and have received a judgment for possession before the tenant files for bankruptcy, you'll have to go to the bankruptcy court and ask for permission to begin (or continue) your eviction case. (Evictions and bankruptcy are explained in Chapter 17.) Fortunately, the effect of the bankruptcy on your use of the security deposit is not so drastic.

Your course of action all depends on timing: When did the tenant file his petition, and when did you use the deposit to cover unpaid rent or damage? Here are three common scenarios and the rules for each:

- **Tenant hasn't paid the rent and/or has caused damage. You assess your total losses and deduct from (or use up) the deposit, and then tenant files for bankruptcy.** No problem here, since you used the money before the tenant filed. You're also on solid ground if you've gone to court and obtained a money judgment that can be satisfied fully, or at least partially, by the security deposit. The key is to use the funds, or get the judgment, before the tenant files. (See *In re Johnson,* 215 B.R. 381 (Bkrtcy. N.D. Ill. 1997).)

TIP

Take care of business quickly. You probably won't know about your tenant's plans to file for bankruptcy. It's wise to assess your losses soon after the tenant vacates and to leave a paper trail that will establish that the deposit was used before the filing date. If you keep deposits in a separate bank account and move these funds to another account as you use them, you'll have good proof.

- **Tenant causes damage that would normally be covered by the security deposit, or fails to pay the rent.** Before you have the chance to use the money to pay for the damage or rent, you receive a notice from the bankruptcy court stating that the tenant has filed. Once you receive this notice, you are prohibited from taking any action against the tenant, including using the security deposit, without

Security Deposit Itemization
(Deductions for Repairs, Cleaning, and Unpaid Rent)

Date ___December 19, 20xx___

From: ___Timothy Gottman___

___8910 Pine Avenue___

___Philadelphia, Pennsylvania 19106___

To: ___Monique Todd___

___999 Laurel Drive___

___Philadelphia, Pennsylvania 19106___

Property Address: ___456 Pine Avenue #7, Philadelphia, Pennsylvania 19106___

Rental Period: ___January 1, 20xx to October 31, 20xx___

1. Security Deposit Received: $ _____1,200_____

2. Interest on Deposit (if required by lease or law): $ _____N/A_____

3. Total Credit (sum of lines 1 and 2): $ _____1,200_____

4. Itemized Repairs and Related Losses:

    ___Carpet repair $160, drapery cleaning $140, plaster___

    ___repair $200, painting of living room $300___

    ___(receipts attached)___ $ _____800_____

5. Necessary Cleaning:

    ___Sum paid to resident manager for 10 hours___

    ___cleaning at $20/hour: debris-filled garage,___

    ___dirty stove and refrigerator___ $ _____200_____

6. Defaults in Rent Not Covered by Any Court Judgment
    (list dates and rates):

    ___5 days at $20/day from November 6 to___

    ___November 11 (date of court judgment or___

    ___date of physical eviction)___ $ _____100_____

7. Amount of Court Judgment for Rent, Costs, Attorney Fees: $ _____1,160_____

8. Other Deductions:

Specify: _____

_____

_____ $ _____

9. Total Amount Owed Landlord (sum of lines 3 through 8): $ ____2,260____

10. Amount Owed (line 3 minus line 9):

☑ Total Amount Tenant Owes Landlord: $ ____1,060____

☐ Total Amount Landlord Owes Tenant: $ _____

Comments: _The security deposit has been applied as follows: $1,000 for damage and_
cleaning charges, $100 for defaults in rent (not covered by any court judgment),
and the remaining $100 toward payment of the $1,160 court judgment. This leaves
$1,060 still owed on the judgment. Please send that amount to me at once or I shall
take appropriate legal action to collect it.

an okay from the court (this is called a "Relief from Stay"). Instead of going to court, you can just sit tight and wait until the bankruptcy proceeding is over. Then, you can use the money to cover the tenant's debt.

- **Tenant files for bankruptcy, then causes damage that would normally be covered by the security deposit.** Follow the same advice as above.

> **! CAUTION**
> **Use "last month's rent" and "security deposit" correctly.** Some states do not allow you to use a deposit you have labeled "last month's rent" to cover damage or cleaning. If you live in a state that has adopted this approach, make sure that your security deposit itemization form complies with the law and that you use the available deposits correctly.

This Security Deposit Itemization (Deductions for Repairs, Cleaning, and Unpaid Rent) form includes spaces for you to include unpaid rent not covered by a court judgment (line 6) and, if you have won an eviction lawsuit against the tenant, the amount of the court judgment you won (line 7). ("Deductions for Unpaid Rent," above, shows you how to figure these amounts, and explains why it's better to deduct cleaning and damage costs from the security deposit before deducting any of a court judgment.) If the tenant has left without paying utility charges or another financial obligation required under your lease or rental agreement, provide details on line 6 (Defaults in Rent Not Covered by Any Court Judgment).

If there's a court judgment involved, explain how you applied the deposit in the Comments section at the bottom of the itemization form. This makes it clear that you are demanding the balance owed and that you can still collect any part of the judgment not covered by the security deposit.

Mailing the Security Deposit Itemization

Some tenants will want to personally pick up any deposit as soon as possible. If that isn't feasible, mail your security deposit itemization to the tenant's last known address or forwarding address as soon as is reasonably possible, along with payment for any balance you owe. Don't wait until the end of the legally specified period if you have all the information necessary to act sooner, as it almost guarantees that a large number of anxious tenants will contact you. And, if you miss the deadline, you may be liable for hefty financial penalties, as discussed in "If a Tenant Sues You," below. Some states require landlords to use certified mail; check your state's statutes for any special mailing requirements. If the tenant hasn't left you a forwarding address, mail the itemization and any balance to the address of the rental property itself. That, after all, is the tenant's last address known to you. If your former tenant has left a forwarding address with the Post Office, it will forward the mail.

It will be useful for you to know the tenant's new address if the tenant's deposit doesn't cover all proper deductions and you want to sue in small claims court. (See the discussion below.) It will also help you collect any judgment you have against the tenant.

There are two ways that you can learn the new address:

- **Set up an account with the Postal Service.** You can pay the Post Office in advance to tell you whenever one of your letters is forwarded. Because of the cost involved, this procedure makes sense for landlords with many rental units.
- **Use "Return Receipt Requested."** For smaller landlords or people who rarely face this situation, it may not be worth your while to prepay. Instead, you can send the letter "Return Receipt Requested" and, on the Postal Service form, check the box that tells the carrier to note the address where the letter was delivered. This address will be on the receipt that is sent back to you.

If the tenant has left no forwarding address, the letter will come back to you. The postmarked envelope is your proof of your good-faith attempt to notify the tenant, in case the tenant ever accuses you of not returning the money properly. Some states specifically allow the landlord to retain the deposit if he cannot locate the tenant after a reasonable effort or a certain amount of time has passed, such as 60 or 90 days. If your state laws do not specify what happens to the deposit if you cannot locate the tenant, you'll need to seek legal advice on what to do with the deposit.

Security Deposits From Cotenants

When you rent to two or more cotenants (they all sign the same written lease or rental agreement), you do not usually have to return or account for any of the deposit until they all leave. In other words, you're entitled to the benefit of the entire deposit until the entire tenancy ends. Legally, any question as to whether a departing cotenant is entitled to any share of the deposit should be worked out among the cotenants.

From a practical point of view, however, you may want to work out an agreement with a departing cotenant who wants part of the deposit back. For instance, you may be willing to refund his share of the deposit if the new cotenant gives you a check for that amount. The drawback of this approach is that the new cotenant will not want to get stuck paying for damage that was caused by the departing tenant. If you accommodate this request, too, you may have to do an extra inspection in the middle of the lease term. (On the other hand, you may welcome an opportunity to discover and correct problems before they grow.)

> **EXAMPLE:** Bill and Mark were cotenants who had each contributed $500 toward the $1,000 security deposit. Bill needed to move before the lease was up and asked Len, their landlord, if he would accept Tom as a new cotenant. Len agreed.
>
> Bill wanted his $500 back, and, although Tom was willing to contribute his share of the deposit, he did not want to end up paying for damage that had been caused before he moved in. To take care of this, Len agreed to inspect if Tom would first give him a check for $500. When he got the check, Len inspected and found $200 worth of damage. He deducted this amount from Bill's share of the deposit and wrote Bill a check for $300. Len left it up to Bill and Mark to fairly

apportion the responsibility for the damage. With Tom's $500 check, the security deposit was once again topped off.

If a Tenant Sues You

No matter how meticulous you are about properly accounting to your tenants for their deposits, sooner or later you may be sued by a tenant who disagrees with your assessment of the cost of cleaning or repairs. Tenants may also sue if you fail to return the deposit when and how required or violate other provisions of state or local law, such as a requirement that you pay interest on deposits.

Tenants usually sue in small claims court, where it's cheap to file, lawyers aren't necessary, and disputes typically go before a judge (there are no juries) within 30 to 60 days, without formal rules of evidence. (We use the term small claims court here, but the exact name may vary depending upon the state. The courts are called "Justice of the Peace," "Conciliation," "District," "Justice," "City," or "County" in different places.)

The maximum amount for which someone can sue in small claims court varies among the states, but in most states it's about $3,000 to $10,000. For details, see "State Small Claims Court Limits" in Appendix A.

> CAUTION
> **Penalties for violating security deposit statutes can turn a minor squabble into an expensive affair.** While it is rarely worth your while to go to court over a matter of $50 or even a couple of hundred dollars, the same is not true for the tenant. Why? Because many statutes allow a victorious tenant to collect not only actual damages (the amount improperly deducted from the deposit), but penalties as well. Small claims courts are empowered to award these penalties.

This section suggests several strategies for dealing with small claims suits over security deposits, including how to prepare and present a case in small claims court.

RESOURCE

For more information on small claims court procedures, see *Everybody's Guide to Small Claims Court* (National Edition), by Ralph Warner (Nolo).

When a Tenant May Sue

Before going to court, the tenant will most likely express dissatisfaction by way of a letter or phone call demanding that you refund more than you did or fix some other problem involving the deposit. In some states, this sort of demand must be made before the tenant can begin a small claims suit. After making a demand, the tenant can bring suit immediately.

A tenant who is going to sue will probably do it fairly promptly but may have up to a few years to do so, depending on the state. Don't throw out cleaning bills, receipts for repairs, or photographs showing dirt and damages after only a few months, lest you be caught defenseless.

Who Goes to Small Claims Court?

If your business is incorporated, you can send an employee such as a property manager, as long as the person is authorized to represent you in legal proceedings. If you are not incorporated, you'll probably have to go yourself, but a few states allow managers to go in your place. In most states you can be represented by a lawyer in small claims court, but it's rarely worth the cost. Procedures are simple and designed for nonlawyers.

Settling a Potential Lawsuit

If you receive a demand letter or phone call from a tenant, your best bet is almost always to try to work out a reasonable compromise. Be open to the idea of returning more of the deposit to the tenant, even if you believe your original assessment of the cost of repairs and cleaning was more than fair and you feel you will surely win in court. For practical reasons, it usually doesn't make sense for you or an employee to prepare a small claims case and spend time in court to argue over $50, $100, or even $200. This is especially true because, fair or not, some judges are prone to split the difference between the landlord's and the tenant's claims.

If you and the tenant can't reach a reasonable compromise, you may wish to get help from a local landlord-tenant mediation service.

Sample Settlement Agreement Regarding Return of Security Deposit

Lionel Washington, "Landlord," and LaToya Jones, "Tenant," agree as follows:

1. Landlord rented the premises at 1234 State Avenue, Apartment 5, Santa Fe, New Mexico, to Tenant on July 1, 20xx, pursuant to a written rental agreement for a tenancy from month to month.

2. Under the Agreement, Tenant paid Landlord $1,000 as a security deposit.

3. On October 31, 20xx Tenant vacated the premises.

4. Within 30 days (the time required by New Mexico law) after Tenant vacated the premises, Landlord itemized various deductions from the security deposit totaling $380 and refunded the balance of $620 to Tenant.

5. Tenant asserts that she is entitled to the additional sum of $300, only $80 of the deductions being proper. Landlord asserts that all the deductions were proper and that he owes Tenant nothing.

6. To settle the parties' entire dispute, and to compromise on Tenant's claim for return of her security deposit, Landlord pays to Tenant the sum of $150, receipt of which is hereby acknowledged by Tenant as full satisfaction of her claim.

Lionel Washington	12/1/xx
Lionel Washington, Landlord	Date
LaToya Jones	12/1/xx
LaToya Jones, Tenant	Date

If you arrive at a compromise settlement with your former tenant, you should insist that your payment be accepted as full and final satisfaction of your obligation to return the deposit. The best way to do this is to prepare and have the tenant sign a brief settlement agreement, like the sample shown above.

Splitting the Difference With Tenants

One landlord we know with thousands of units experiences about 250 move-outs each month. In about one-third, he receives a complaint from a tenant who claims too much of the deposit was withheld.

This landlord's general policy is to offer to settle for 70% of the disputed amount. Since the average amount withheld is $175, this means the landlord is willing to reduce this amount by $52.50. If a tenant refuses to accept this compromise, the landlord will often make a second offer of a 50% reduction.

He does this not because he thinks his original assessment was wrong, but because he finds that coming to a settlement with a tenant costs a lot less than fighting in court. However, if the settlement offer isn't accepted promptly by the tenant, he fights to win—and almost always does.

Preparing for a Small Claims Court Hearing

If no compromise is possible and the tenant sues you, the court will officially notify you of the date, time, and place of the small claims court hearing.

It's still not too late at this stage to try to work out a settlement by paying part of what the tenant's suing for. However, if you compromise at this stage, make sure the tenant has correctly dismissed the small claims courts suit. Be sure your settlement is in writing.

Before your court hearing, gather tangible evidence showing the premises needed cleaning or were damaged when the tenant left. It is essential to take to court as many of the following items of evidence as you can:

- Copies of the lease or rental agreement, signed by both you and the tenant.
- Copies of move-in and move-out letters clarifying rules and policies on cleaning, damage repair, and security deposits.
- A copy of the Landlord-Tenant Checklist that you should have filled out with the tenant when the tenant moved in and when she moved out, signed by both you and the tenant. This is particularly important if the tenant admitted, on the Checklist, to damaged or dirty conditions when she moved out.
- Photos or a video of the premises before the tenant moved in that show how clean and undamaged the place was.
- Photos or a video after the tenant left that show a mess or damage.
- An itemization of hours spent by you or your repair or cleaning people on the unit, complete with the hourly costs for the work, plus copies of receipts for cleaning materials or credit card itemizations or canceled checks.
- Damaged items small enough to bring into the courtroom (a curtain with a cigarette hole would be effective).
- Receipts or a canceled check for professional cleaning (particularly of carpets and drapes) and repair.
- One, or preferably two, witnesses who were familiar with the property, who saw it just after the tenant left, and who will testify that the place was a mess or that certain items were damaged. People who helped in the cleaning or repair are particularly effective witnesses. There is no rule that says you can't have a close friend or relative testify for you, but, given a choice, it's better to have a witness who's neither a friend nor kin.
- If it's difficult for a witness to come to court, a written statement (a signed letter) or a declaration under penalty of perjury can be used in most states. Documents, however, usually aren't as effective as live testimony. If you do present a written statement from a

Sample Declaration of Cleaning Service

I, Paul Stallone, declare:

1. I am employed at A & B Maintenance Company, a contract cleaning and maintenance service located at 123 Abrego Street, Central City, Iowa. Gina Cabarga, the owner of an apartment complex at 456 Seventh Street, Central City, Iowa, is one of our accounts.

2. On May 1, 20xx I was requested to go to the premises at 456 Seventh Street, Apartment 8, Central City, Iowa, to shampoo the carpets. When I entered the premises, I noticed a strong odor, part of what seemed like stale cigarette smoke. An odor also seemed to come from the carpet.

3. When I began using a steam carpet cleaner on the living room carpet, I noticed a strong smell of urine. I stopped the steam cleaner, moved to a dry corner of the carpet and pulled it from the floor. I then saw a yellow color on the normally white foam-rubber pad beneath the carpet, as well as smelled a strong urine odor, apparently caused by a pet (probably a cat) having urinated on the carpet. On further examination of the parts of the carpet, I noticed similar stains and odors throughout the carpet and pad.

4. In my opinion, the living room carpet and foam-rubber pad underneath need to be removed and replaced, and the floor should be sanded and sealed.

I declare under penalty of perjury under the laws of the State of Iowa that the foregoing is true and correct.

Paul Stallone   6/15/xx

Paul Stallone, Cleaner   Date

witness, make sure the statement includes the date of the event, exactly what the witness saw in terms of damage, any credentials that make the person qualified to testify on the subject, and any other facts that have a bearing on the dispute. A sample statement is shown above.

Small Claims Suits Don't Affect Other Lawsuits

Nothing that happens in small claims court affects the validity of any judgment you already have—for example, from an earlier eviction suit—against the tenant. So, if you got a judgment against a tenant for $1,200 for unpaid rent as part of an eviction action, this judgment is still good, even though a tenant wins $200 against you in small claims court based on your failure to return the deposit.

Penalties for Violating Security Deposit Laws

If you don't follow state security deposit laws to the letter, you may pay a heavy price if a tenant sues you and wins. In addition to whatever amount you wrongfully withheld, you may have to pay the tenant extra or punitive damages (penalties imposed when the judge feels that the defendant has acted especially outrageously) and court costs. In many states, if you "willfully" (deliberately and not through inadvertence) violate the security deposit statute, you may forfeit your right to retain any part of the deposit and may be liable for two or three times the amount wrongfully withheld, plus attorney fees and costs.

If the Deposit Doesn't Cover Damage and Unpaid Rent

Tenants aren't the only ones who can use small claims court. If the security deposit doesn't cover what a tenant owes you for back rent, cleaning, or repairs (or if your state prohibits the use of the security deposit for unpaid rent), you may wish to file a small claims lawsuit against the former tenant.

Be sure your claim doesn't exceed your state's small claims court limit or, if it does, decide whether it make sense to scale it back to the limit. Given the costs of going to formal court, this can sometimes make sense.

RESOURCE

For detailed advice, see *Everybody's Guide to Small Claims Court* **(National Edition), by Ralph Warner (Nolo).**

The Demand Letter

If you decide that it is worthwhile to go after your tenant for money owed, your first step is to write a letter asking for the amount of your claim. Although this may seem like an exercise in futility, the law in many states requires that you make a demand for the amount sued for before filing in small claims court. But, even if there is no such requirement, it is almost essential that you send some sort of demand letter. It is not only useful in trying to settle your dispute, it's also an excellent opportunity to carefully organize the case you will present in court.

Your demand can consist of a brief cover letter along with a copy of your earlier written itemization of how you applied the tenant's security deposit to the charges (in which you also requested payment of the balance). The tone of your cover letter should be polite, yet firm. Ask for exactly what you want, and be sure to set a deadline. Conclude by stating that you will promptly file a lawsuit in small claims court if you don't reach an understanding by the deadline.

Should You Sue?

If your demand letter does not produce results, think carefully before you rush off to your local small claims court. Ask yourself three questions:
- Do I have a strong case?
- Can I locate the former tenant?
- Can I collect a judgment if I win?

If the answer to any of these questions is no, think twice about initiating a suit.

Do You Have a Strong Case?

Review the items of evidence listed above in "Preparing an Itemized Statement of Deductions." If you lack a substantial number of these pieces of ammunition you may end up losing, even if you are in the right. Small claims court is rarely about justice, but always about preparation and skill.

Can You Locate the Former Tenant?

To begin your small claims court case, legal papers must be sent to the tenant. So, you'll need an address where the tenant lives or works. If the tenant left a forwarding address, locating the tenant won't be an issue. But if you don't have a home or work address for the tenant, you'll need to do a little detective work if you want to sue.

Start by filing a "skip-trace" form at the Post Office using the tenant's name and last known address. If the tenant asked the Post Office to forward mail to a new address, you'll be supplied with the forwarding address. Or, use an Internet search engine's "people finder" to check for a new address or phone number.

Can You Collect a Judgment If You Win?

Winning a small claims court case won't do you any good if you can't collect a judgment. Suing a person you know to be bankrupt, insolvent, or just plain broke may not be worth the effort, since you'll have little chance of transforming your court judgment into cash. When you evaluate the solvency of the tenant, keep in mind that small claims judgments are good for ten years in many states. So, if you have a spat with a student or someone who may get a job soon, it might be worthwhile to get a judgment with the hope of collecting later.

Using Collection Agencies

If you don't want to sue in small claims court, consider hiring a licensed local collection agency to try to collect from the tenant. The agency will probably want to keep as its fee anywhere from one-third to one-half of what it collects for you. (The older the debt or the more difficult it is to locate the tenant, the more the agency will want.) If the agency can't collect, you can authorize it to hire a lawyer to sue the ex-tenant, usually in a formal (non-small-claims) court. Many collection agencies pay all court costs, hoping to recover them if and when they collect the resulting judgment. In exchange for taking the risk of paying costs and losing the case, however, collection agency commissions often rise an additional 15%–20% when they hire a lawyer to sue.

Of course, turning a matter over to a collection agency doesn't necessarily mean you wash your hands of the matter. The collection agency still takes direction from you. If the tenant defends against a lawsuit filed by a collection agency's lawyer, you must be involved in the litigation. The only way to walk away from it completely is to sell the debt to the collection agency, which may pay you only a fraction of the amount owed.

Pay particular attention to the issue of how you will collect a judgment. The best way to collect any judgment against your ex-tenant is to garnish wages. If she's working, there is an excellent chance of collecting if payment is not made voluntarily. Another way is to find out the name and address of the defendant's employer. If you sued an employed person, you may be able to collect your judgment out of his or her salary. You can't, however, garnish a welfare, Social Security, unemployment, pension, or disability check. So, if the person sued gets income from one of these sources, you may be wasting your time unless you can identify some other asset that you can efficiently get your hands on.

Bank accounts, motor vehicles, and real estate are other common collection sources. But people who run out on their debts don't always have much in a bank account (or they may have moved the account to make it difficult to locate), and much of their personal property may be exempt under state debt protection laws.

> ⚠ CAUTION
> **Take care of your reputation.** If you are a landlord with many rental units and regularly use a local small claims court, make particularly sure that every case you bring is a good one. You do not want to lose your credibility with the court in future cases by ever appearing to be unfair or poorly prepared.

What to Do With Property Abandoned by a Tenant

Whether a tenant moves out voluntarily or with the aid of a sheriff or marshal after you win an eviction lawsuit, you may find yourself not only cleaning up and repairing damage, but also dealing with personal property left behind. Usually, this will just be trash that the tenant obviously doesn't want, such as old wine bottles, food, and newspapers. When it's clear that you're dealing with garbage, you're perfectly within your rights to dispose of it.

Getting rid of things clearly of some value—such as a bicycle, jewelry, clothes, or furniture—is another story. In some states, you can face serious liability for disposing of the tenant's personal property (other than obvious trash) unless you follow specific state rules. Typically, the more valuable the property left behind by a tenant, the more formalities you must comply with when disposing of it. Not surprisingly, states that heavily regulate other aspects of landlords' dealings with tenants also impose complicated requirements on how you handle abandoned property. States with fewer laws governing the landlord-tenant relationship tend to pay scant attention to this subject.

This section provides an overview of how to handle abandoned property. It covers the general legal issues that should be understood by all landlords: whether your state allows you to deal with the property as you see fit or requires you to follow detailed (and often onerous) procedures. Because state laws vary so much, we cannot give you detailed state-by-state instructions on how to comply. For this reason, it is critical that you read your own state statute for details on issues such as how to notify tenants and how much time you must give them to reclaim property before you may dispose of or sell it. In addition, you would be wise to check with your local landlords' association or state consumer protection agency to make sure that the process set out in your statute is all you need to know. In some states, courts have modified the procedures in the statutes, often imposing additional requirements—and, unfortunately, legislatures don't always revisit their statutes to bring them into line with court-ordered changes. "State Laws on Handling Abandoned Property" in Appendix A gives you citations to your state's statutes.

> **SEE AN EXPERT**
> **If you're dealing with property of obvious significant value or have good reason to suspect that a tenant may cause problems later, consult a lawyer before you dispose of, donate, or sell the tenant's possessions.** Obviously, you want to protect yourself from claims by the departing tenant that you have destroyed or stolen her property. In legal jargon, this is known as "unlawful conversion." Conversion occurs when you take someone else's property and convert it to your own use or benefit, either by selling it or otherwise disposing of it or using it yourself.

Why Has the Tenant Left?

In many states, your options when dealing with tenants' property will differ depending on the circumstances of the tenant's departure. To understand the issue, let's look at the reasons tenants leave. Here are typical scenarios, covered at length below:

- The tenant decides to move at the end of a lease or after giving you a termination notice. In this situation, many states give you maximum flexibility to dispose of leftover belongings.
- The tenant decides to move after receiving a termination notice (even one for cause, such as nonpayment of rent) from you. Many states give you maximum flexibility to dispose of leftover belongings in this situation.
- The tenant is physically evicted, along with his or her personal belongings that may be dumped on the street or sidewalk by the sheriff. Some states require landlords to take more pains with the property of a tenant who has been evicted—though some require less efforts.
- The tenant simply disappears. In a few states, property belonging to tenants who simply move out unexpectedly must be treated differently from property that's left after a clearly deliberate move.

When you read your state's law, be on the lookout for different rules based on the reason for the tenant's departure.

Planned Moves

Often, if the tenant has left voluntarily but has inconsiderately left you with a pile of stuff, you will have more latitude when it comes to discarding abandoned property than you will if the tenant has been evicted. The reasoning here is that tenants who decide upon and plan their own departure—even the ones who leave after receiving a three-day notice—have time to pack or dispose of their belongings themselves. Tenants who fail to take care of business are in no position to demand that you, the landlord, handle their property with kid gloves—and many state laws don't require that you do so.

Evicted Tenants

Law enforcement officials who physically evict tenants will also remove property from the rental unit. In these situations, tenants arguably have less opportunity to arrange for proper packing, storing, or moving than they would if they were moving voluntarily (even though most states give tenants a few days' warning of the sheriff's impending visit). For this reason, landlords in some states must make more of an effort to preserve the property, locate the tenant, and wait before selling or disposing of items left behind. Typically, law enforcement officials are permitted to place the tenant's possessions on the sidewalk or street; then the landlord may be required to step in and store the possessions.

Paradoxically, some states take the opposite approach, reasoning that a tenant who has lost an eviction lawsuit isn't entitled to special treatment when it comes to reclaiming items left in the rental unit.

Unannounced Departures

Odd as it seems, it's not unusual for tenants to simply disappear with no notice, leaving considerable belongings behind. Sometimes, the tenant is behind on the rent and figures that abandoning his possessions will be cheaper, in the long run, than paying the rent. Here again, your state may impose special procedures, which may require you to store the property for a significant time or make extra efforts to locate the tenant. One reason for this extra concern is to protect tenants who have *not* abandoned the tenancy or their possessions, but have gone on a trip or vacation and simply didn't bother to tell you. The idea is that by taking special pains to determine that the tenant is gone for good and giving tenants ample time to claim their things, landlords can avoid problems down the road. State rules requiring landlords to store property and locate tenants reduce a tenant's ability to sue you for prematurely disposing of property—that is, before the tenant reappears and demands his belongings. "If the Tenant Breaks the Lease" in Chapter 14 discusses how to tell whether tenants have really abandoned the premises, and how to locate them.

When the Tenant Owes You Money

It's annoying enough to have to deal with a tenant's abandoned belongings—but worse yet is when that tenant also owes you money. When a tenant who has moved voluntarily, been evicted, or simply disappeared also owes you back rent or money for damages, you may be inclined to first take or sell whatever property of value that's left behind, and worry about finding the tenant later. As tempting as this course appears, it's a risky one in many states—even if you have a court judgment for money damages.

Some states do allow you to keep or sell abandoned property if the tenant owes you money, even if there is no court judgment directing the tenant to pay. In legal parlance, you have an "automatic lien" on your tenants' belongings. This differs from the normal lien process—which involves formally recording your claim (your lien) against the tenant's property, then "getting in line" in case others have filed ahead of you.

Distress and Distraint: What Are They?

A few states still have statutes on the books that provide for "distress" or "distraint." These were medieval procedures that allowed a landlord who was owed money, after or even during the tenancy, to simply grab his tenant's possessions. In the words of one judge, it "allowed a man to be his own avenger." In America, the practice of requiring security deposits was developed in states that did not allow a landlord to use distress and distraint.

This crude, quick, and drastic remedy was the ultimate in self-help. It won't surprise you to learn that in states that still have laws providing for distress or distraint, courts have stepped in and ruled it unconstitutional, or have added so many safeguards (notice, a hearing, and so on) that the original process is unrecognizable. If you encounter a distress or distraint statute when reading your state's laws, resist the temptation to follow it without first learning—through legal research or talking to your landlords' association or lawyer—how modern landlords comply.

If your state statute gives you a lien on your tenant's property, we advise you to use it very carefully. In particular:

- **Use restraint when seizing consumer or other goods that may not be paid for.** If your tenant has financed his TV, sofa, or computer and is paying in installments, the merchant has a lien that's ahead of yours. This is called a "superior" lien—meaning that the merchant, not you, has first claim to the item when the tenant stops paying. (Not surprisingly, the tenant will typically stop payments after abandoning the item.) You cannot simply seize and sell an abandoned item, such as a computer, that is not paid off. Instead, you will have to turn the item over if the merchant comes to collect it. If you have already sold the item, you may have to pay the merchant the balance due or the value of the item. You can try to avoid this eventuality by publicizing your intent to seize and sell the item, as explained below.

- **Follow your state's rules for publicizing your lien.** Many states require a landlord to post notices in newspapers announcing your intent to sell an item abandoned by a tenant. This is to make sure that others—like the merchants mentioned above—who have superior liens on a tenant's property don't lose out when you jump ahead of them and take or sell the item. Merchants are presumed to read the legal notices; failure to do so may result in the merchants' losing their right to assert the superiority of their lien. It's a good idea to publicize the sale of a tenant's valuable abandoned property even if your statute doesn't require it.

- **Don't seize items that are necessary for basic living.** Many states that give landlords an automatic lien will exempt certain items, such as season-appropriate clothing, blankets, tools, and things needed for a minor child's education, from your grasp. If you're not sure whether an item is a tool of your ex-tenant's trade or simply supports his hobby, don't take it.

CAUTION

Check out court cases—don't rely on your lien statutes alone. In most states with lien statutes on the books, courts have stepped in with additional requirements, such as providing for notice and an opportunity for the tenant (and other creditors) to be heard. Read any cases that have interpreted your lien law (see Chapter 18 for help in doing legal research), or ask your landlords' association or lawyer for assistance.

Legal Notice Requirements

Many states require landlords to provide tenants written notice that they are dealing with abandoned property. California requires landlords to provide specific information regarding abandoned property on a variety of termination forms (Cal. Civ. Code §§ 1946, 1946.1). A few states even provide a form, which you'll see printed right in the statute. The notice must typically give the tenant a set amount of time to reclaim the property, after which the landlord can take specific steps. Some state rules require specific information in the notice, such as:

- **A detailed description of the property left behind.** It's a good idea to have an objective person (such as another tenant in the building or a neighbor) witness your inventory of the abandoned property to protect yourself against charges that you have taken or destroyed any of the tenant's property. Don't open locked trunks or suitcases; just list the unopened containers. You might consider photographing or videotaping the property.

- **The estimated value of the abandoned property.** Here, you're asked to guess what you could get for it at a well-attended flea market or garage sale.

- **Where the property may be claimed.** Many states sensibly require you to provide the address of the rental premises or an outside storage place.

- **The deadline for the tenant to reclaim property, such as seven or ten days.** This is usually set by state law.

- **What will happen if property is not reclaimed.** This also may be set by state law.

Even if your state law doesn't explicitly require it, it's a good idea to send tenants this kind of detailed notice and allow a reasonable amount of time for the tenant to pick up his belongings. Mail your notice "return receipt requested" so that you will have proof that the tenant received it—this will be useful should an ex-tenant show up months later looking for belongings left behind.

How to Handle Abandoned Property if the Tenant Doesn't Respond

If the ex-tenant doesn't contact you within the time specified in the notice, follow your state rules regarding what to do with property. In some states, landlords are pretty much free to do what they want if the tenant does not respond within the specified amount of time, such as 30 days— that is, you may throw the property out, sell it, or donate it to a nonprofit organization that operates secondhand stores. In some states, as explained above, landlords can use the property to satisfy unpaid rent or damages, or may even be allowed to keep it when there's no debt. Other states require you to give the property to the state. Depending on how thoroughly your state has legislated in this area, you'll encounter rules on the following issues:

- **Procedures based on the value of the property.** Several states allow landlords to keep or dispose of property only if the expense of storing or selling it exceeds a specified figure (such as a few hundred dollars) or the property's value.
- **Sale of abandoned property.** Some states require landlords to inventory, store, and sell tenants' property. A few require landlords to sell the property at a public sale (supervised by a licensed and bonded public auctioneer) after first publishing a notice in the newspaper.
- **Proceeds of sale of property.** States that require you to store and sell the property on behalf of the tenant also allow you to use any money

you make from the sale to cover the costs of advertising and holding the sale and storing the property. For example, you may be able to charge the tenant the prorated daily rental value for keeping the property on your premises or any out-of-pocket costs you incur for renting storage space (including moving the property to the storage space). As explained above, some states allow you to use the proceeds to pay for any money owed to you by the tenant—for example, for unpaid rent or damage to the premises. In many states, the excess proceeds of selling the tenant's property belong to the tenant, or you may be required to pay the balance to a government agency, such as the State Treasurer. State rules are often very specific on this issue, so don't just keep sale proceeds without a clear understanding of your state law.

Exceptions to State Rules on Abandoned Property

Your state's rules on abandoned property don't apply to obvious garbage—nor do they apply in the following situations:

Fixtures. If a tenant attaches something more or less permanently to the wall, such as built-in bookshelves, it is called a "fixture." As described in "Tenants' Alterations and Improvements" in Chapter 9, absent a specific written agreement such as a lease provision, fixtures installed by the tenant become a part of the premises. Fixtures belong to the landlord and do not have to be returned to the tenant.

Motor vehicles. Occasionally, a departing tenant will leave an inoperable or "junker" automobile in the parking lot or garage. Motor vehicles are often a special category of personal property to which state rules on abandoned property don't apply. If the tenant has left a car or other vehicle behind, call the local police, giving the vehicle's license plate number, make, and model, and indicate where it's parked. The police will probably arrange to have it towed after determining that it is abandoned after tagging it.

TIP

Don't hassle the tenant over a little amount of money. In most situations, where there is not a lot of property involved, you're probably better off giving the tenant his belongings and forgetting about any storage charges, particularly if you didn't incur any out-of-pocket expenses. It's just not worth it to get into fights over $100 worth of old dishes, books, and clothes.

Landlord Liability for Damage to Tenant's Property

A landlord will not generally be held liable for damage to property, unless this occurs through his or her willful destruction or negligent care of the tenant's property. To avoid problems, be sure you take care in moving and storing the tenant's belongings until they are returned to the tenant, disposed of, or sold.

Problems With Tenants: How to Resolve Disputes Without a Lawyer

FORMS IN THIS CHAPTER

Chapter 16 includes instructions for and a sample of the following form:

- Warning Letter for Lease or Rental Agreement Violation

The Nolo website includes a downloadable copy of this form. See Appendix B for the link to the forms in this book.

Legal disputes—actual and potential—come in all shapes and sizes when you're a landlord. Here are some of the more common ones:

- **Rent.** You and your tenant disagree about the validity, timing, or methods of a rent increase.

- **Habitability.** Your tenant threatens to withhold rent because he claims a leaky roof or some other defect has made the living room unusable.

- **Access to the premises.** Your tenant won't let you show her apartment to prospective new tenants or enter for some other good reason. You feel it's your legal right to do so, and your tenant claims that your legal reason for invading her privacy is bogus.

- **Security deposits.** You and a departing tenant disagree about how much security deposit you owe the tenant based on your claim that the unit is dirty or damaged or both.

- **Lease or rental agreement violation.** Your tenant (or former tenant) has failed to pay rent, moved in a new roommate (or a pet) without your permission, hosted a series of loud parties, or in some other way violated your lease or rental agreement.

How you handle such disputes can have a profound effect on your bottom line, not to mention your mental health. In some cases, such as a tenant's nonpayment of rent, your only option may be to terminate the tenancy. Rarely should lawyers and litigation be your first choice. Instead, you will usually want to consider alternatives that can give you better control over the time, energy, and money you spend.

This chapter discusses four commonly available options to resolve a legal dispute without a lawyer:

- negotiation
- mediation
- arbitration, and
- small claims court.

While we focus here on disputes with tenants, you should also find much of the advice useful for resolving all types of business disputes—for example, with your manager, insurance company, or repairperson.

This chapter also explains how to avoid charges of retaliation in your dealings with tenants.

RELATED TOPIC

How to terminate a tenancy based on non-payment of rent and other illegal acts is discussed in Chapter 17.

Put It in Writing

To help avoid legal problems in the first place, and minimize those that can't be avoided, it makes sense to adopt efficient, easy-to-follow systems to document important facts of your relationship with your tenants. Throughout this book, we recommend many forms and record-keeping systems that will help you do this, including move-in and move-out letters, a landlord-tenant checklist, and a maintenance/repair request form. The key is to establish a good paper trail for each tenancy, beginning with the rental application and lease or rental agreement through a termination notice and security deposit itemization. Such documentation will be extremely valuable if attempts at resolving your dispute fail and you end up evicting or suing a tenant, or being sued by a tenant. Also, you'll obviously want to keep copies of any correspondence and notes of your conversations with tenants. Chapter 7 recommends a system for organizing tenant information, including records of repair requests.

Negotiating a Settlement: Start by Talking

If you have a conflict with your tenant over rent, repairs, your access to the rental unit, noise, or some other issue that doesn't immediately warrant an eviction, a sensible first step is to meet with the tenant—even one you consider to be a hopeless troublemaker—to see if the problem can be resolved. This advice is based on the simple premise that unless you have the legal grounds (and the determination) to evict a tenant, it's almost always better to try and negotiate a settlement rather than let the dispute escalate into a court fight. This is doubly true if you are convinced your case is just. Given the cost and delays built into the arthritic American legal system, the more you rely on it, the more you are likely to regret going to court.

So forget about suing, except possibly in small claims court (discussed below), and try to evaluate the legal and financial realities objectively. Your goal should be to achieve the best result at the lowest cost. If instead you act on the conviction (whether it's right or wrong makes no difference) that your rights are being trampled by the other side, chances are you'll end up spending far too much time and money fighting for "the principle" involved. Over time, a landlord who allows himself to be controlled by this sort of emotional reaction is almost sure to fare emotionally and financially poorer than a person who keeps an eye on the overall objective: to make a good living and enjoy doing it.

Your first step in working toward a compromise with an unhappy or problem tenant is to call the tenant and arrange a time to meet. Dropping over unannounced to talk may work in some circumstances but is generally not a good idea, since it may emotionally threaten the tenant and put him in a defensive position. It may be appropriate to write a letter first, offering to meet with the tenant to work something out. (See, for example, the sample letter in Chapter 9 in which the landlord suggests a compromise with a tenant who withholds rent because of defective conditions in his apartment.)

Here are some helpful pointers for negotiating with tenants:

- **Solicit the tenant's point of view.** Once the tenant starts talking, listen closely and don't interrupt, even if some of his points are not true or some of his opinions are inflammatory.
- **When the tenant has wound down, acknowledge that you have heard his key points, even if you** disagree with them. Sometimes it's even a good idea to repeat the tenant's concerns so he will realize you know what they are and will stop repeating them.
- **Avoid personal attacks.** This only raises the level of hostility and makes settlement more difficult. Equally important, don't react impulsively to the emotional outbursts of the tenant.
- **Be courteous, but don't be weak.** If you have a good case, let the tenant know you have the resources and evidence to fight and win if you can't reach a reasonable settlement.
- **Before the negotiation goes too far, try and determine if the tenant is a truly an unbearable jerk whom you really want to be rid of or just another slightly annoying person.** If a tenant falls into the first category, your strategy should be to terminate the tenancy as soon as legally and practically possible.
- **If possible, try to structure the negotiation as a mutual attempt to solve a problem.** For example, if a tenant's guests have been disturbing the neighbors, jointly seek solutions that recognize the interests of both parties.
- **Try to figure out the tenant's priorities.** Maybe dollars are less important than pride, in which case a formula for future relations that meets the needs of a thin-skinned tenant to be treated with respect might solve the problem.
- **Put yourself in the tenant's shoes.** What would you want to settle? Sometimes your answer may be something like "a sense that I've won." Fine—the best settlements are often those in which both sides feel they've won (or at least not given up anything fundamental). So, your job is to let the tenant have at least a partial sense of victory on one or more of the issues in dispute.
- **When you propose a specific settlement, make it clear that you're attempting to compromise.** Offers of settlement (clearly labeled as such) can't be introduced against you if you ever end up in court.

- **Money is a powerful incentive to settlement.** If you are going to have to pay something eventually, or spend a lot of time and money on a costly eviction lawsuit or preparing a small claims case, it makes overall financial sense to come to the negotiating table willing to pay—perhaps by reducing rent for a short period of time, cutting in half the money owed for damages to the premises, or offering an outright cash settlement for the tenant to leave (with payment made only as the tenant leaves and hands you the keys). Savvy landlords know that many financially strapped tenants may settle at a surprisingly low figure if they can walk away from the bargaining table with payment in hand. If this saves the costs and delays inherent in a long eviction battle, and allows you to rerent the unit to a paying tenant, it can be well worth the money.

- **If you reach an understanding with your tenant, promptly write it down and have all parties sign it.** You or your lawyer should volunteer to prepare the first draft. If you're paying the tenant some money as part of your agreement, make sure the tenant acknowledges in writing that your payment fully satisfies her claim. Chapter 15 includes an example of a settlement agreement for a security deposit dispute that you can use as a model for settling disputes.

- **If the negotiation process indicates a larger problem with tenant dissatisfaction, think carefully how to avoid similar disputes in the future—**for example, you may need to revise your systems for handling repair complaints or returning security deposits.

RESOURCE

Recommended reading on negotiation.
Getting to Yes: Negotiating Agreement Without Giving In, by Roger Fisher, William Ury, and Bruce M. Patton (Penguin Books). This classic offers a strategy for coming to mutually acceptable agreements in all kinds of situations, including landlord-tenant disputes.

The Power of a Positive No: Save the Deal, Save the Relationship and Still Say No, by William Ury (Bantam Books). This sequel to *Getting to Yes* discusses techniques for negotiating with obnoxious, stubborn, and otherwise difficult people.

When Warning Notices Are Appropriate

In some situations, it may be appropriate to give a tenant a written notice to cease the problem or disruptive activity, particularly if the tenant has not created other problems and you feel that he's apt to respond to your polite but firm reproof. You may also want to send a warning notice if your oral warning or attempts to negotiate have been unsuccessful.

A sample Warning Letter for Lease or Rental Agreement Violation is shown below, and the Nolo website includes a downloadable copy (see Appendix B for the link to the forms in this book). You can use this warning letter for many purposes, such as warning the tenant to stop having loud parties, repair damage to your property, or get rid of a long-term guest.

Be sure your letter includes the following information:

- Details of the problem behavior, including dates and times of the occurrence.
- What exactly you want the tenant to do (such as stop having noisy parties, pay for damage to the rental unit, or get rid of a long-term guest).
- The specific lease or rental agreement provision that prohibits this behavior, such as a clause on tenant's right to quiet enjoyment (Clause 13 of our form lease and rental agreements in Chapter 2), a clause requiring tenants to repair damaged property (Clause 11 of our form agreements), or a lease restriction on guests (Clause 3 of our form agreements).
- The consequences for the tenant's failure to comply (such as termination or eviction proceedings).

Warning Letter for Lease or Rental Agreement Violation

November 4, 20xx
Date

Jerry Brooks
Tenant

179 Lynwood Drive
Street Address

Tampa, Florida 33611
City and State

Dear Jerry   ,
                            Tenant

This is a reminder that your lease prohibits annoying, disturbing, or interfering with the quiet
enjoyment and peace and quiet of any other tenant or nearby resident (Clause 13)
[violation]. It has come to my attention that, starting on November 2, 20xx   , [date
of violation] and continuing to the present, you have broken this condition of your tenancy by _____
holding several noisy parties that lasted until 2 a.m., disturbing other tenants

_____

_____ .

It is our desire that you and all other tenants enjoy living in your rental unit. To make sure this occurs, we
enforce all terms and conditions of our leases. So please immediately keep noise within reasonable
limits and no loud parties after midnight on weekends or 10 p.m. on weekdays

_____

_____ .

If it proves impossible to promptly resolve this matter, we will exercise our legal right to begin eviction
proceedings.

Please contact me if you would like to discuss this matter further and clear up any possible misunderstandings.

Yours truly,

Clark Johnson
Landlord/Manager

Belle Epoque, 387 Golf Road
Street Address

Tampa, Florida 33611
City and State

813-555-1234
Phone

> **CAUTION**
> **Don't waste your time sending a warning letter to someone unlikely to respond**—for example, a tenant who is always late in paying rent or whose behavior (such as drug dealing or violence) justifies immediate action. Instead, start termination proceedings right away.

What happens if the tenant does not reform, despite your reminder? If the misbehavior is grounds for terminating the tenancy and you want him out, in a sense you'll have to start over: You'll have to give him a formal termination notice that meets your state's requirements. (Termination notices are explained in Chapter 17.)

> **CAUTION**
> **Your warning note will not qualify as a termination notice.** For example, if your tenant has kept a dog in violation of the lease, and he keeps the pet despite your polite note asking him to remove the dog, in most states you'll have to give him a formal notice telling him to get rid of the dog within a certain number of days or move. (If he does neither, you can file for eviction.) In short, an informal warning may simply allow a wrongdoing tenant to delay the inevitable.

Understanding Mediation

If you're unsuccessful negotiating a settlement, but still want to work something out with the tenant, you may wish to try mediation by a neutral third party, often available at little or no cost from a publicly funded program. (See "How to Find a Mediation Group," below.)

Mediation can make good sense, especially if any of the following are true:

- You are dealing with someone who has proven to be a good tenant in the past and you think the tenant is worth dealing with in the future.
- The tenant agrees to split the cost (if any) of mediation.
- The tenant is as receptive as you are to some method of avoiding the expense and delay of litigation, or the possibility of being evicted.

- The tenant is up to date on rent (or the rent money is put in some type of escrow account).
- You are trying to avoid the risk of one influential tenant poisoning your relationship with others.

If mediation doesn't make sense, make clear your intention (and legal right) to sue or evict the tenant. See "Representing Yourself in Small Claims Court," below, and Chapter 17.

Many people confuse mediation with arbitration. While both are nonjudicial ways to resolve disputes, there's a huge difference: Arbitration results in a binding decision, while mediation doesn't, since the mediator has no power to impose a decision but is there simply to help the parties work out a mutually acceptable solution to their dispute.

Mediation in landlord-tenant disputes is usually fairly informal. More likely than not, the mediator will have everyone sit down together from the very beginning and allow both parties to express all their issues—even emotional ones. This often cools people off considerably and frequently results in a fairly quick compromise. If the dispute is not resolved easily, however, the mediator may suggest ways to resolve the problem, or may even keep everyone talking long enough to realize that the real problem goes deeper than the one being mediated. Typically this is done through a caucus process—each side is put in a separate room. The mediator talks to each person sequentially to try and determine his or her bottom line. Then, shuttling back and forth, the mediator helps the parties structure an acceptable solution. At some point, everyone has to get back together to sign off.

For example, if a tenant has threatened rent withholding because of a defect in the premises, the mediator may discover that the tenant's real grievance is that your manager is slow to make repairs. This may lead to the further finding that the manager is angry at the tenant for letting her kids pull up his tulips. So, the final solution may fall into place only when the tenant agrees to provide better supervision for the kids in exchange for the manager getting the repairs done pronto.

How to Deal With Noisy Tenants

Tenants often cite noise as one of their biggest complaints about apartment living. Many types of noise, including street traffic, garbage trucks, or rowdy bars, are out of the landlord's control. If tenants complain about noises outside the building, your best bet is to steer them to the city manager or mayor's office for help. Most cities have local ordinances that prohibit excessive, unnecessary, and unreasonable noise, and police enforce these laws. If the problem is a neighbor's barking dog, the local animal control agency is responsible. Most local noise ordinances designate certain "quiet hours"—for example, from 10 p.m. to 7 a.m. on weekdays. Some universally disturbing noises, such as honking car horns, are commonly banned or restricted. Many communities also prohibit sustained noise that exceeds a certain decibel level (set according to the time of day and the neighborhood zoning).

Noise caused by other tenants, however, is your responsibility. Anyone who lives in an apartment building must expect to hear the sounds of their neighbor's daily lives. But when the occasional annoying sound turns into an ongoing din—whether a blasting stereo, loud TV, or barking dog—expect to hear complaints from other residents in your property. You should take these complaints seriously. As discussed in Chapter 9, tenants are entitled to quiet enjoyment of the premises, the right to occupy their apartments in peace, free of excessive noise. You may face legal problems if you fail to stop disturbances that are of a regular and ongoing nature— for example, techno dance music blaring from a tenant's apartment each and every weekend. Landlords who tolerate excessive and unreasonable noise that interferes with other tenants' normal activities (such as sleeping at night) despite repeated tenant complaints may get hit with code violations or a small claims lawsuit (for tolerating a nuisance) or court-ordered rent reductions. Good tenants may move out.

Here are some specific tips to avoid problems with noisy tenants:

- Include a clause in your lease or rental agreement prohibiting tenants from causing disturbances or creating a nuisance that interferes with other tenants' peace and quiet and prevents neighbors from enjoying the use of their own homes. (See Clause 13 of the form agreements in Chapter 2.)

- Include specific noise guidelines in your tenant rules and regulations, such as the hours that loud music, dance parties, and barking dogs will not be tolerated. Look at your local noise ordinance for guidance and remind tenants of noise laws that may apply in your community, such as prohibitions against honking car alarms, firecrackers, or disorderly conduct. You might make the same points in a move-in letter to new tenants.

- Consider requiring rugs or carpets on wood floors to muffle the noise heard by tenants downstairs.

- Check out inexpensive ideas to soundproof paper-thin walls.

- Respond quickly to noise complaints. Start with an oral request to keep the noise down. Then, move on to a warning letter (such as the sample shown above) if necessary. Terminate the tenancy if necessary.

- Keep records of all tenant complaints about a neighbor's noise (with details on the date, time, and location of the noise), so that you have solid documentation to back up a termination or eviction case. If the noise is really bad, make a tape recording as additional evidence.

- If violence is involved, such as a domestic disturbance, call the police immediately.

RESOURCE

The Noise Pollution Clearinghouse (www.nonoise.org) is an excellent source of information on state and local noise laws. If you can't find your local ordinance there, do some online legal research (Chapter 18 explains how).

For a general overview of noise involving neighbors, see *Neighbor Law*, by Emily Doskow and Lina Guillen. If barking dogs is the problem, see *Every Dog's Legal Guide*, by Mary Randolph. Both books are published by Nolo and available online at www.nolo.com or by phone at 800-728-3555.

For free general information on noise problems, see Nolo's articles on noise and neighbors at www.nolo.com.

Does mediation really work? Surprisingly, yes, given the fact that there's no one to impose a solution. One reason is the basic cooperative spirit that goes into mediation. By agreeing to mediate a dispute in the first place, you and the tenant must jointly establish the rules, which, in turn, sets the stage for cooperating to solve your dispute. Also, the fact that no judge or arbitrator has the power to impose what may be an unacceptable solution reduces the fear factor on both sides. This, in turn, often means both landlord and tenant take less extreme—and more conciliatory—positions.

 RESOURCE
Recommended reading on mediation. *Mediate, Don't Litigate*, by Peter Lovenheim and Lisa Guerin (Nolo), available as a downloadable electronic book at www.nolo. com. This book explains the mediation process from start to finish, including how to prepare for mediation and draft a legally enforceable agreement.

How to Find a Mediation Group

For information on local mediation programs, call your mayor's or city manager's office, and ask for the staff member who handles "landlord-tenant mediation matters" or "housing disputes." That person should refer you to the public office or business or community group that attempts to informally—and at little or no cost—resolve landlord-tenant disputes before they reach the court stage. Most local courts also provide referrals to community mediation services. For lists of professional mediators and extensive information on mediation, see www.mediate.com.

Using Arbitration

Many organizations that offer mediation also conduct arbitration if the parties can't reach an agreement. Almost any dispute with a tenant or other party that can be litigated can be arbitrated. With arbitration, you get a relatively quick, relatively inexpensive

solution to a dispute without going to court. Like a judge, the arbitrator—a neutral third party—has power to hear the dispute and make a final, binding decision. Where does this power come from? From you and the other party. In binding arbitration, you agree in advance in writing to submit to arbitration and to be bound by the arbitrator's decision.

You can include a clause in your lease or rental agreement that requires that arbitration be used for any contractual dispute, although this usually makes sense more for longer-term leases of expensive properties. Otherwise, you and the tenant can also decide to use arbitration after a dispute arises. If you and the tenant agree to binding arbitration, an informal hearing is held. Each person tells his or her side of the story, and an arbitrator reaches a decision, which is enforceable in court.

If the losing party doesn't pay the money required by an arbitration award, the winner can easily convert the award to a court judgment, which can be enforced like any other court judgment. Unlike a judgment based on litigation, however, you generally can't take an appeal from an arbitration-based judgment. (An exception is when there was some element of fraud in the procedures leading to the arbitration award.)

How to Find an Arbitrator

To find an arbitrator or learn more about arbitration, contact the American Arbitration Association, the oldest and largest organization of its kind, with offices throughout the country. For more information, check your local phone book or see www.adr.org.

Keep in mind that you are not required to use an organization for arbitration. You and the other party are free to choose your own arbitrator or arbitration panel and to set your own procedural rules. Just remember that for arbitration to be binding and legally enforceable, you need to follow the simple guidelines set down in your state's arbitration statute. You can usually find the statute by looking in the statutory index under "Arbitration" or checking the table of contents for the civil procedure sections. See Chapter 18 for advice on doing this kind of legal research.

Representing Yourself in Small Claims Court

If your attempts at settling a dispute involving money fail, you may end up in a lawsuit. Fortunately, there are many instances when you can competently and cost-efficiently represent yourself in court. This is almost always true when your case is at the small claims level.

A few states use names other than small claims court, but traditionally the purpose has been the same: to provide a speedy, inexpensive resolution of disputes that involve relatively small amounts of money (generally less than $10,000). "State Small Claims Court Limits," in Appendix A, lists each state's small claims court limit.

Most people who go to small claims court handle their own cases. In fact, in some states, lawyers aren't allowed to represent clients in small claims court. In any event, representing yourself is almost always the best choice—after all, the main reason to use the small claims court is because the size of the case doesn't justify the cost of hiring a lawyer.

A landlord can use small claims court for many purposes—for example, to collect unpaid rent or to seek money for property damage after a tenant moves out and her deposit is exhausted. Small claims court offers a great opportunity to collect money that would otherwise be lost because it would be too expensive to sue in regular court. And, in a few states, eviction suits can be filed in small claims court.

Landlords can also be sued in small claims court—for example, by a tenant who claims that you failed to return a security deposit. Chapter 15 discusses small claims suits over security deposits.

TIP

Don't waste your time suing total deadbeats. As a general rule, if you suspect you cannot collect the money—from a paycheck, bank account, or other financial resource—don't waste your time in small claims court. A judgment you can't collect is worthless.

RESOURCE

Recommended reading on small claims court. *Everybody's Guide to Small Claims Court* (National Edition), by Ralph Warner (Nolo), provides detailed advice on bringing or defending a small claims court case, preparing evidence and witnesses for court, and collecting your money judgment when you win. *Everybody's Guide to Small Claims Court* will also be useful in defending yourself against a tenant who sues you in small claims court—for example, claiming that you failed to return a cleaning or security deposit. Your state's small claims court website (listed in the chart in Appendix A) will also have useful information on specific state rules and procedures.

Learning the Rules

Small claims court procedures are relatively simple and easy to master. Basically, you pay a small fee, file your lawsuit with the court clerk, see to it that the papers are served on your opponent, show up on the appointed day, tell the judge your story, and present any witnesses and other evidence. The key to winning is usually to present evidence to back up your story. For example, a photograph of a dirty or damaged apartment and the convincing testimony of someone who helped you clean up are usually all you need to prevail if you are trying to recover money over and above the tenant's deposit or defending against a tenant's suit for the return of a deposit.

Court rules—dealing with such things as where you file your lawsuit, how papers can be served on your opponent (service of process), and the deadline (statute of limitations) for filing a small claims suit—are usually published on small claims court websites. In addition, clerks in small claims court are expected to explain procedures to you. In some states, they may even help you fill out the necessary forms, which are quite simple, anyhow. If necessary, be persistent: If you ask enough questions, you'll get the answers you need to handle your own case comfortably. Also, in some states such as California, you can consult a small claims court adviser for free.

Meeting the Jurisdictional Limits

How much can you sue for in small claims court? The maximum amount varies from state to state. Generally, the limit is $3,000 to $10,000. But, more recently, recognizing that formal courts have become prohibitively expensive for all but large disputes, many states have begun to increase the monetary size of the cases their small claims courts can consider. Check your state's small claims court limit on the chart in Appendix A, but also ask the court clerk for the most current limit; state legislatures regularly increase these limits.

TIP

You can scale your case down to fit small claims court limits. Don't assume that your case can't be brought in small claims court if it's for slightly more than the limit. Rather than hiring a lawyer or trying to go it alone in formal court, your most cost-effective option may be to sue for the small claims maximum and forget the rest.

How to Avoid Charges of Retaliation

As we've discussed throughout this book, residential tenants have a number of legal rights and remedies. While the specifics vary by state, here are a few rights tenants typically have:

- the right to complain to governmental authorities about health or safety problems, and, in many states, the right to withhold rent from, or even to file a lawsuit against, a landlord who fails to keep the premises in proper repair
- the right to be free from discriminatory conduct based on factors such as race, religion, children, sex, and disability, and to complain to administrative agencies, or even courts, when she (the tenant) feels her rights are being violated
- privacy rights limiting landlord's access, and
- the right to engage in political activity; for example, a tenant who actively campaigns for local candidates whom you find obnoxious, organizes a tenant union, or campaigns for a rent control ordinance, has an absolute right to do so without fear of intimidation.

Because tenant protection laws would be meaningless if you could legally retaliate against a tenant who asserts her legal rights, the laws or court decisions in most states forbid such retaliation. For example, the right of a tenant to complain to the local fire department about a defective heater would be worth little if you, angry about the complaint, could retaliate against her with an immediate termination notice or by doing anything else that works to the tenant's disadvantage, such as increasing rent. The general idea is that tenants should not be punished by landlords just because they are invoking their legal rights or remedies.

Unfortunately, tenants sometimes unfairly accuse landlords of retaliatory misconduct—for example, a tenant who can't or won't pay a legitimate rent increase may claim you are guilty of retaliation. The same sort of unreasonable reliance on tenant protection laws can occur when you seek to terminate the tenancy for a perfectly legitimate reason and the tenant doesn't want to move. How do you cope with this sort of cynical misuse of the law? As with most things legal, there is no single answer. However, if you plan ahead and consider how one tenant might misuse the law and how you can counter this misuse, you should be able to minimize any legal problems.

You start with one great advantage when faced with a tenant who attempts to defeat your legitimate rent increase or tenancy termination with phony retaliation claims. As a businessperson, you have the organizational ability and mind-set to plan ahead—anticipate that some tenants will adopt these tactics, and prepare to meet them. The tenant, on the other hand, will probably be dealing with the situation on a first-time, ad hoc basis, and often will have a superficial, or just plain wrong, knowledge of the law.

Here are some tips on how to anticipate what tenants might do, so you're prepared to avoid or counter false retaliation claims.

Establish a good paper trail to document important facts of your relationship with your tenants. For example, set up clear, easy-to-follow procedures for tenants to ask for repairs, and respond quickly when complaints are made, coupled with annual safety inspections. (We show you how in Chapter 9.) This sort of policy will go a long way toward demonstrating that a complaint is phony—for example, if a tenant faced with a rent increase or tenancy termination suddenly complains to an outside agency about some defect in the premises they rent, without talking to you first. Also, if your periodic inquiries result in complaints from several tenants, but you only end one tenancy, you can show you don't have a policy of retaliating against tenants who do complain.

Be prepared to demonstrate that you have a good reason to end the tenancy—even though the law in your area may say that a landlord doesn't need a reason to terminate a tenancy. In other words, in anticipation of the possibility that a tenant may claim that you are terminating her tenancy for retaliatory reasons, you should be prepared to prove that your reasons were valid and not retaliatory. When you think of it, this burden isn't as onerous as it might first appear. From a business point of view, few landlords will ever want to evict an excellent tenant. And, assuming there is a good reason why you want the tenant out—for example, the tenant repeatedly pays his rent late in violation of the rental agreement—you only need document it.

Have legitimate business reasons for any rent increase or other change in the conditions of the tenancy, and make the changes reasonable. The best answer to a charge of retaliation is proof that your act was based on legitimate business reasons and was wholly independent of any exercise by tenants of their rights.

If a tenant makes a complaint for even an arguably legitimate reason at about the time you were going to raise the rent or give the month-to-month tenant a termination notice anyway, wait. First take care of the complaint. Next, let some time pass. Then, do what you planned to do anyway (assuming you can document a legitimate reason for your action). Be sure to check

"State Laws Prohibiting Landlord Retaliation" in Appendix A to see whether your state has any law as to the time period when retaliation is presumed. For example, the laws of Iowa and Kentucky presume retaliation if the landlord's action—such as ending the tenancy—occurred within one year of the tenant's exercise of a legal right such as a complaint about defective conditions. In other states, this time period is shorter: Delaware (90 days); Arizona and the District of Columbia (six months), and California (180 days). In these circumstances, the landlord must prove that retaliation has not occurred.

The delay may cost you a few bucks, or result in some inconvenience, or even cause you to lose some sleep while you gnash your teeth, but all of these are preferable to being involved in litigation over whether or not your conduct was in retaliation for the tenant's complaint.

> **EXAMPLE:** A tenant, Fanny, makes a legitimate complaint to the health department about a defective heater in an apartment she rents from Abe. Even though Fanny does so without having had the courtesy to tell her landlord Abe first, Fanny is still within her legal rights to make the complaint. About the same time Fanny files the complaint, neighboring tenants complain to Abe, not for the first time, about Fanny's loud parties that last into the wee hours of the morning. Other tenants threaten to move out if Fanny doesn't. In response to the neighboring tenants' complaints, Abe gives Fanny a 30-day notice. She refuses to move, and Abe must file an eviction lawsuit. Fanny responds that the eviction was in retaliation for her complaint to the health department. A contested trial results. Perhaps Abe will win in court, but, in this situation, there is a good chance he won't.

Now, let's look at how you might better handle this problem:

Step 1. Fix the heater.

Step 2. Write the tenant, reminding her of your established complaint procedures. Tell her very politely that you consider this sort of repair a routine matter which, in the future, can be handled more quickly and easily by telling you instead of the public agency. A sample letter is shown below.

**Sample Letter Reminding Tenant
of Complaint Procedure**

February 1, 20xx

Fanny Hayes
Sunny Dell Apartments
123 State Street, Apt. 15
Newark, NJ 07114

Dear Ms. Hayes:

As you know, Ms. Sharon Donovan, my resident manager at Sunny Dell Apartments, repaired the heater in your unit yesterday, on January 31.

Ms. Donovan informs me that you never complained about the heater or requested its repair. In fact, she learned about the problem for the first time when she received a telephone call to that effect from Cal Mifune of the County Health Department. Apparently, you notified the Health Department of the problem without first attempting to resolve it with Ms. Donovan.

While you certainly do have a legal right to complain to a governmental agency about any problem, you should be aware that the management of Sunny Dell Apartments takes pride in its quick and efficient response to residents' complaints and requests for repairs.

In the future, we hope that you'll follow our complaint procedure and contact the manager if you have a problem with any aspect of your apartment.

Sincerely,

Abe Horowitz
Abe Horowitz, Owner

Step 3. Carefully document the noise complaints of the neighbors. If possible, get them in writing. Feel out the neighbors about whether they would testify in court if necessary. Also, consider whether an informal meeting between all affected parties or a formal mediation procedure might solve the problem.

Step 4. Write the tenant about the neighbors' complaints. The first letter should be conciliatory. Offer to meet with the tenant to resolve the problem, but also remind the tenant of the rental agreement (or lease) provision prohibiting nuisances (such as excessive noise) that disturb the quiet enjoyment of other tenants (see Clause 13 of the form lease and rental agreements in Chapter 2). If the first letter doesn't work, follow up with another letter, even if you don't think this will do any good, either. These letters will help you greatly should a court fight develop later.

Step 5. If possible, wait a few months, during which you should carefully document any more complaints before giving the tenant a 30-day notice. As a general rule, the longer you can reasonably delay court action, the less likely a claim of retaliation by the tenant will stick.

This sort of preparatory work may influence the tenant not to claim you are guilty of retaliatory conduct. However, even if it does not, and you do end up in court, you should win easily.

Defending yourself against charges of retaliation is well beyond the scope of this book, and a lawyer is strongly advisable. A good insurance policy which protects you from so-called "illegal acts" may cover you if your act is not deliberate and intentional and you can turn your legal defense over to the insurance company.

Late Rent, Terminations, and Evictions

Unfortunately, even the most sincere and professional attempts at conscientious landlording sometimes fail, and you need to get rid of a troublesome tenant—someone who pays the rent late, keeps a dog in violation of a no-pets clause in the lease, repeatedly disturbs other tenants and neighbors by throwing loud parties or selling drugs, or otherwise violates your agreement or the law.

Termination is the first step toward an eventual eviction. You'll need to send the tenant a notice announcing that the tenancy is over, and that, if he doesn't leave, you'll file an eviction lawsuit. Or the notice may give the tenant a few days to clean up his act (pay the rent, find a new home for the dog). If the tenant leaves (or reforms) as directed, no one goes to court.

Eviction itself—that is, physically removing the tenant and his possessions from your property—generally can't be done until you have gone to court and proved that the tenant did something wrong that justifies ending the tenancy. If you win the eviction lawsuit, you can't just move the tenant and his things out onto the sidewalk. In most states, you must hire the sheriff or marshal to perform that task.

This chapter explains when and how you can terminate a tenancy based on nonpayment of rent and other illegal acts. It also provides an overview of the eviction procedure that follows a termination notice, and tells you what you can—and cannot—do under the law.

 RELATED TOPIC
Related topics covered in this book include:
- Rent control laws that require a legally recognized reason, or "just cause," to evict: Chapter 3
- Evicting a resident manager: Chapter 6
- Substantially failing to maintain rental property so that tenants cannot use it (constructive eviction): Chapter 9
- Ending a month-to-month tenancy with a 30-day notice: Chapter 14
- How to end a tenancy at a property that you have purchased at foreclosure: Chapter 14

- Using a security deposit to cover unpaid rent after you've evicted a tenant: Chapter 15
- How to use a warning letter, negotiation, or mediation to resolve a dispute with a tenant: Chapter 16
- How to get legal help for an eviction lawsuit: Chapter 18.

 CAUTION
Watch out for charges of retaliation. Landlords in most states may not end a tenancy in response to a tenant's legitimate exercise of a legal right, such as rent withholding, or in response to a complaint to a housing inspector or after a tenant has organized other tenants. What if your tenant has exercised a legal right (such as using a repair and deduct option) but is also late with the rent? Naturally, the tenant will claim that the real motive behind your eviction is retaliation.

In some states, the burden will be on you to prove that your motive is legitimate if you evict within a certain time (typically six months) of a tenant's use of a legal remedy or right. In others, it's up to the tenant to prove your motive. Chapter 16 includes advice on how to avoid charges of retaliation, and Appendix A gives details on state laws prohibiting landlord retaliation.

RESOURCE
California landlords should consult *The California Landlord's Law Book: Evictions*, by David Brown (Nolo). It contains eviction information and tear-out court forms.

The Landlord's Role in Evictions

The linchpin of an eviction lawsuit (sometimes called an unlawful detainer, or UD, lawsuit) is properly terminating the tenancy before you go to court. You can't proceed with your lawsuit, let alone get a judgment for possession of your property or for unpaid rent, without terminating the tenancy first. This usually means giving your tenant adequate written notice, in a specified way and form. If the tenant doesn't move (or reform), you can file a lawsuit to evict.

State laws set out very detailed requirements for landlords who want to end a tenancy. Each state has its own procedures as to how termination notices and eviction papers must be written and delivered ("served"). Different types of notices are often required for different types of situations. You must follow state rules and procedures exactly. Otherwise, you will experience delays in evicting a tenant—and maybe even lose your lawsuit—even if your tenant has bounced rent checks from here to Mandalay.

Because an eviction judgment means the tenant won't have a roof over his head (and his children's heads), state laws are usually very demanding of landlords. In addition, many rent control cities go beyond state laws (which typically allow the termination of a month-to-month tenant at the will of the landlord) and require the landlord to prove a legally recognized reason, or just cause, for eviction.

Alternatives to Eviction

Before you proceed with an eviction lawsuit, consider whether it might be cheaper in the long run to pay the tenant a few hundred dollars to leave right away. A potentially lengthy lawsuit—during which you can't accept rent that you may be unable to collect even after winning a judgment—may be more expensive and frustrating than buying out the tenant and quickly starting over with a better one. Especially if there's a possibility that your tenant might win the lawsuit (as well as a judgment against you for court costs and attorney fees), you may well be better off compromising—perhaps letting the tenant stay a few more weeks at reduced or no rent.

Chapter 16 provides tips on avoiding an eviction lawsuit by negotiating a settlement with a tenant.

Even if you properly bring and conduct an eviction lawsuit for a valid reason, you are not assured of winning and having the tenant evicted if the tenant decides to mount a defense. You always run the risk of encountering a judge who, despite the merits of your position, will hold you to every technicality and bend over backwards to sustain the tenant's position. The way that you have conducted business with the tenant may also affect the outcome: A tenant can point to behavior on your part, such as retaliation, that will shift attention away from the tenant's wrongdoing and sour your chances of victory. Simply put, unless you thoroughly know your legal rights and duties as a landlord before you go to court, and unless you dot every "i" and cross every "t," you may end up on the losing side. Our advice, especially if your action is contested, is to be meticulous in your business practices and lawsuit preparation.

It is beyond the scope of this book to provide all the step-by-step instructions and forms necessary to terminate a tenancy or evict a tenant. This chapter will get you started, and Chapter 18 shows how to research termination and eviction rules and procedures in your state. Many are clearly set out in state statutes. Other useful resources for eviction procedures and forms include:

- the website of the court that handles evictions in your area (see, for example, the Michigan Courts' Self-Help Center at www.courts.mi.gov/self-help/center)
- your state consumer protection or attorney general's office (find yours at www.usa.gov/stateconsumer)
- your state bar association (for example, the Florida State Bar website, www.floridabar.org, includes sample eviction forms), and
- your state or local apartment association.

California landlords should use the Nolo book described above.

Termination Notices

You may terminate a month-to-month tenancy simply by giving the proper amount of notice (30 days in most states). Reasons are usually not required. Leases expire on their own at the end of their term, and you generally aren't required to renew them.

If your tenant has done something wrong, you'll usually want him out sooner. State laws allow you to do this by serving the tenant with one of three different types of termination notices, depending on the reason why you want the tenant to leave. Although terminology varies somewhat from state to state, the substance of the three types of notices is remarkably the same.

- **Pay Rent or Quit** notices are typically used when the tenant has not paid the rent. They give the tenant a few days (three to five in most states) to pay or move out ("quit").
- **Cure or Quit** notices are typically given after a violation of a term or condition of the lease or rental agreement, such as a no-pets clause or the promise to refrain from making excessive noise. Typically, the tenant has a set amount of time in which to correct, or "cure," the violation; a tenant who fails to do so must move or face an eviction lawsuit.
- **Unconditional Quit** notices are the harshest of all. They order the tenant to vacate the premises with no chance to pay the rent or correct the lease or rental agreement violation. In most states, Unconditional Quit notices are allowed only when the tenant has repeatedly:
  - violated a lease or rental agreement clause
  - been late with the rent
  - seriously damaged the premises, or
  - engaged in illegal activity.

Many states have all three types of notices on the books. But, in some states, Unconditional Quit notices are the *only* notice statutes, as noted below. Landlords in these states may extend second chances if they wish, but no law requires them to do so.

Many states have standards for the content and look of a termination notice, requiring certain language and specifying size and appearance of type (consult your state's statute, as noted in Appendix A, before writing your notice). When you're sure that the notice complies with state law, resist any temptation to add threatening graphics or language. The Fair Debt Collection Practices Act, cited below, and its counterparts written by many states, forbids you from threatening unlawful actions or implying that you are affiliated with the government. Threats (or implications) that you will resort to a self-help eviction (covered below) or even using a picture of a policeman may constitute a deceptive collection practice.

You may have a choice among these three notices, depending on the situation. For example, a Wisconsin landlord may give month-to-month tenants an Unconditional Quit *or* a Pay Rent or Quit notice for late payment of rent. The tenant cannot insist on the more lenient notice.

For the details and citations to your state's statutes on termination notices, see the following charts in Appendix A:

- "State Rules on Notice Required to Change or Terminate a Month-to-Month Tenancy"
- "State Laws on Termination for Nonpayment of Rent"
- "State Laws on Termination for Violation of Lease," and
- "State Laws on Unconditional Quit Terminations."

Late Rent

Not surprisingly, the number one reason landlords terminate a tenancy is nonpayment of rent. If a tenant is late with the rent, in most states you can immediately send a termination notice, giving the tenant a few days—usually three to five—in which to pay up. The exact number of days varies from state to state. But not every state requires you to give a tenant a second chance to pay the rent; in a few states, if the tenant fails to pay rent on time, you can simply demand that he leave by sending an Unconditional Quit notice.

Legal Late Periods

In most states, you can send a Pay Rent or Quit notice as soon as the tenant is even one day late with the rent. A handful of states will not let you send a

Involving Your Lawyer May Trigger the Fair Debt Collection Practices Act

The Fair Debt Collection Practices Act (15 U.S. Code §§ 1692 and following) governs debt collectors and requires, among other things, that debtors be given 30 days in which to respond to a demand for payment (even if your pay-or-quit notice specifies fewer days). If you prepare and send your own pay-or-quit notices, you aren't a "debt collector," and you won't have to comply with this Act. However, if your lawyer sends the notice, the Act may apply. This can result if your lawyer regularly handles your termination work and genuinely gets involved in each case; ironically, you may also be subject to the Act if you're simply using the lawyer's name or stationery and he has no real connection with the case.

When your lawyer regularly sends notices for you and is genuinely involved in each case. Odd as it may sound, a lawyer who regularly handles rent demand notices on behalf of landlord-clients is considered a "debt collector" under the law in some cases—at least in Connecticut, New York, and Vermont (states covered by the federal Second Court of Appeals; *Romea v. Heiberger & Associates*, 163 F.3d 111 (2d Cir. 1998)). Consequently, the tenant must have 30 days to pay or quit, no matter what your statute says. However, if your lawyer does not regularly engage in debt collection, it's likely that the lawyer will not be considered a regular debt collector. (*Goldstein v. Hutton*, 374 F.3d 56 (2004).) A pay-or-quit rent demand notice that's signed or sent by a manager in these states, however, won't violate federal law, so long as it was the manager's job to collect rent before the tenant defaulted in the payment of rent. (*Franceschi v. Mautner-Glick Corp.*, 22 F.Supp.2d 250 (S.D. N.Y. 1998).)

When your lawyer rubber-stamps your notices. Under the Fair Debt Collection Practices Act, it's illegal for someone to lend his name to a creditor for its intimidation value. (15 U.S. Code § 1692j(a).) If your attorney simply sends out termination notices at your bidding (or lends you stationery or a signature stamp), and if the lawyer does not consider the facts of each case, it's likely that you'll come under this stricture. The consequence is that *you* will be held to the letter of the Act—and your pay-or-quit notice will, among other things, become a 30-day notice. (*Nielsen v. Dickerson*, 307 F.3d 623 (7th Cir. 2002).)

The lesson to be learned here is to handle your notices yourself!

---

termination notice (either a Pay Rent or Quit notice or an Unconditional Quit notice) until the rent is a certain number of days late. In these states, tenants enjoy a statutory "grace period," plus the time specified in the Pay Rent or Quit notice, in which to come up with the rent. See "State Rent Rules," in Appendix A, for states that impose a grace period.

> **EXAMPLE:** Lara, a Maine tenant, couldn't pay her rent on time. State law required her landlord Luke to wait until the rent was seven days late before he could send a termination notice. Luke did so on the eighth, giving Lara notice that she must pay or move within seven days. In all, Lara had fourteen days in which to pay the rent before Luke could file for eviction.

TIP

Late rent fees are unaffected by Pay Rent or Quit time periods or legal late periods. If your lease or rental agreement specifies late fees, they'll kick in as soon as your lease or rental agreement (or in some states, state law) says they can. The number of days specified in your Pay Rent or Quit notice will not affect them, nor will a legally required grace period.

Accepting Rent After You Deliver a Termination Notice

If the tenant is late with the rent and you deliver a termination notice—whether or not it gives the tenant a few days to pay the rent—you can expect a phone call, email, or a visit from your tenant, hoping to work something out. Chapter 16 offers some pointers on negotiating and dealing with these requests. Here are the legal rules.

If the Tenant Pays the Whole Rent

If you have sent a Pay Rent or Quit notice but then accept rent for the entire rental term, you have canceled the termination notice for that period. In most states, it's as if the tenant had paid on time in the first place.

> **EXAMPLE:** Zoe's rent was due on the first of the month. She didn't pay on time, and her landlord sent her a Three-Day Pay Rent or Quit notice. Zoe borrowed money from her parents and paid on the third day, saving her tenancy and avoiding an eviction lawsuit.

If the Tenant Is Chronically Late Paying Rent

In several states, you don't have to give tenants a second chance to pay the rent if they are habitually late. Typically, you're legally required to give the tenant a chance to pay and stay only once or twice within a certain period. In Georgia, for example, if your tenant has been late with the rent more than once in the past 12 months, the next time he doesn't pay on time you don't have to give him the option of paying the rent or leaving. Instead, you can send him an Unconditional Quit notice that simply tells him to leave within three days. If your state gives you a "no second chances" option for repeated late rent episodes, you'll see the rule reflected on the chart, "State Laws on Unconditional Quit Terminations" in Appendix A.

Some states insist that you give the tenant a *written* Pay Rent or Quit notice for the first late payment, so that there is proof that rent was late. Other statutes allow you to use the Unconditional Quit notice merely for "repeated lateness." In that case, you need not have given the tenant a notice to pay or quit for the first tardiness, but it's good business practice to do

---

Special Rules for Tenants in Military Service

If your tenant is in the military or the activated reserves, your ability to evict for nonpayment of rent is subject to the War and National Defense Servicemembers Civil Relief Act, 50 U.S.C. §§ 3951. The Act does not prevent you from serving a termination notice for nonpayment of rent. Instead, it requires the court to stay (postpone) an eviction for up to three months unless the judge decides that military service does not materially affect the tenant's ability to pay the rent.

The Act only applies to evictions for nonpayment of rent. It does not apply to evictions for other reasons, such as keeping pets in violation of the lease or failing to move when a lease is up. Nor does it apply if you've terminated a rental agreement with a 30-day notice.

- **Tenants affected.** The War and National Defense Servicemembers Civil Relief Act applies if your tenant's spouse, children, or other dependents occupy the rental unit. Courts give a broader meaning to the term "dependent" than the one used by the IRS.
- **Rental amount.** The Act's protections apply when the rent is $2,400 per month or less (adjusted annually for inflation). To learn the current rent ceiling, go to www.federalregister.gov and type "housing price inflation adjustment" in the query box. At press time, the available figure was for 2015 ($3,329.84).
- **The effect on an eviction lawsuit.** Once you have filed your lawsuit, you must tell the court that the tenant is an active service person. The judge will decide whether the service person's status in the military affects his or her ability to pay the rent. If the judge decides that it does, the case may be stayed for up to three months.
- **Requisitioned pay.** The Secretary of Defense or the Secretary of Transportation may order that part of the service person's pay be allotted to pay the rent. Ask the judge in your case to write a letter to the service branch, asking that a reasonable amount be sent to you to pay the rent. Be advised, however, that current Defense Finance and Accounting Service regulations make no provision for such allotments.

so, anyway. If your tenant claims that he has always paid the rent on time, you'll have prior Pay Rent or Quit notices to show otherwise.

TIP

You can always use a 30-day notice for month-to-month tenants who are chronically late. You need not worry about the complexities of your state's Unconditional Quit procedure for month-to-month tenants who repeatedly pay late. Simply terminate the tenancy with a 30-day notice, which may be quicker, in the long run, if the tenant challenges your use of the Unconditional Quit notice. Even if you live in a rent control area that requires landlords to have good reason to evict, repeatedly paying late is ample legal reason to end a tenancy.

If You Accept a Partial Rent Payment

By accepting even a partial amount of rent a tenant owes—whether for past months or even just the current month—you will, in most states, cancel the effect of a Pay Rent or Quit notice. But you can still go ahead with your attempts to get the tenant out—just pocket your tenant's payment with one hand and simultaneously hand him a new termination notice with the other, demanding that he pay the new balance or leave.

> **EXAMPLE:** Danny's rent of $900 was due on the first of the month. Danny didn't pay January's rent and didn't have enough for February, either. On February 2, Danny's landlord, Ali, sent him a three-day notice to pay $1,800 or leave. Danny paid $900 on February 3 and thought that he'd saved his tenancy. He was amazed when, later that day, Ali handed him a new notice to pay $900 or leave. Ali properly filed for eviction on February 7 when Danny failed to pay.

CAUTION

If you sign a written agreement with the tenant setting up a payment schedule for delayed or partial rent, you must comply with this agreement. If the tenant does not end up honoring this agreement, you may then take steps to terminate the tenancy.

Other Tenant Violations of the Lease or Rental Agreement

In addition to nonpayment of rent, you may terminate a tenancy if a tenant violates other terms of the lease or rental agreement, such as:

- keeping a pet in violation of a no-pets rule
- bringing in an unauthorized tenant
- subleasing or assigning without your permission
- repeatedly violating "house rules" that are part of the lease or rental agreement, such as using common areas improperly, making too much noise, having unruly guests, or abusing recreation facilities, or
- giving false information concerning an important matter on the rental application or lease.

Giving Tenants Another Chance

The laws in most states insist that you give the tenant a few days (anywhere from three to 30 days, depending on the state) to correct, or "cure," the violation before the tenancy can end. However, there are two important "but ifs" that allow you to use an Unconditional Quit notice instead of the more generous Cure or Quit notice:

- **Repeated violations.** If the tenant has violated the same lease clause two or more times within a certain period of time, he may lose the right to a second chance. You may give him an Unconditional Quit notice instead.
- **The violation cannot be corrected.** Some lease violations cannot be corrected because the effect of the violation is permanent. For instance, suppose your lease prohibits tenant alterations or improvements without your consent (see Clause 12 of the form agreements in Chapter 2). If, without asking, your tenant removes and discards the living room wallpaper, you can hardly demand that the tenant cease violating the lease clause, because it is simply too late to save the wallpaper. If a lease violation cannot be cured, you may use an Unconditional Quit notice.

Criminal Convictions

You are generally free to reject prospective tenants with criminal records. Sometimes, however, you won't know about these convictions until you have already rented the unit. Maybe you never checked the applicant's background, or you didn't have access to reliable information. Regardless of why you didn't know beforehand, if you learn that a tenant has a record—and particularly if he is a convicted sex offender—your first impulse will probably be to look for a way to get him out of your building. Here's what to do:

- **Month-to-month tenants.** You may terminate any month-to-month tenancy with a 30-day notice, and you need not give a reason, as long as you do not have discriminatory or retaliatory motives. Note, however, that tenants in rent control cities with "just cause" eviction protection, and all tenants in New Hampshire and New Jersey (where there are statewide just cause protections) may be able to resist a termination on this basis.
- **Tenants with leases.** You will not be able to terminate an otherwise law- and rule-abiding tenant purely because you now know that he has a criminal past, no matter how unsavory or alarming. However, if your lease or rental agreement states that false and material information on the rental application will be grounds for termination (as does the one in this book), you can terminate and evict on this basis.

Violations of a Tenant's Legal Responsibilities

Virtually every state allows you to terminate the tenancy of a tenant who has violated basic responsibilities imposed by law, including:

- grossly deficient housekeeping practices that cause an unhealthy situation, such as allowing garbage to pile up
- seriously misusing appliances, like damaging the freezer while attempting to defrost it with an icepick

- repeatedly interfering with other tenants' ability to peacefully enjoy their homes, such as hosting late parties, playing incessant loud music, or running a noisy small business (repairing cars in the driveway of a rental duplex, for example)
- substantially damaging the property—for instance, knocking holes in the walls or doors, and
- allowing or participating in illegal activities on or near the premises, such as drug dealing or gambling.

Many careful landlords incorporate these obligations into their leases or rental agreements—(something we recommend in Chapter 2, Clause 13, "Violating Laws and Causing Disturbances"). But, even if these obligations are not mentioned in your rental documents, tenants are still legally bound to observe them.

If a tenant or guest substantially damages the premises, you'll be within your rights to use an Unconditional Quit notice. The law does not require you to give tenants accused of serious misbehavior a second chance. Tenants who have earned this type of termination notice generally get only five to ten days to move out.

Tips on Dealing With a Tenant During an Eviction

- Avoid all unnecessary one-on-one personal contact with the tenant during the eviction process unless it occurs in a structured setting—for example, at a neighborhood dispute resolution center or in the presence of a neutral third party.
- Keep your written communications to the point and as neutral as you can, even if you are boiling inside. Remember, any manifestations of anger on your part can come back to legally haunt you somewhere down the line.
- Treat the tenant like she has a right to remain on the premises, even though it is your position that she doesn't. Until the day the sheriff or marshal shows up to evict the tenant, the tenant's home is legally her castle, and you may come to regret any actions on your part that don't recognize that fact.

Tenant's Illegal Activity on the Premises

In recent years, many states have responded aggressively to widespread drug dealing in residential neighborhoods by making it easier for landlords to evict based on these activities. Indeed, in some states you must evict known drug dealers or risk having authorities close down or even confiscate your entire property. To say the least, the threat of losing rental property is strong motivation to quickly evict tenants suspected of engaging in illegal acts.

You don't always have to wait until the tenant is convicted of a crime or even arrested. In North Carolina, for example, a judge will order a tenant's eviction if "a preponderance of the evidence" shows that criminal activity has taken place, committed by the tenant or with the tenant's knowledge and consent. (That burden of proof is easier to establish than "beyond a reasonable doubt.") (N.C. Stat. § 42-61.) By contrast, in New Jersey, you may not begin an eviction for illegal activity unless there's been a criminal conviction for criminal acts on the rented premises.

Evictions based on criminal activity are often called "expedited evictions," because they take less time than a normal eviction. Expedited evictions are preceded by an Unconditional Quit notice that tells the tenant to move out (and do it quickly). If the tenant stays, you can go to court and file for eviction. The court hearing on the eviction is typically held within a few days, and, if you win, the tenant is given very little time to move. For example, in Oregon, the tenant has 24 hours to vacate after a landlord wins in court.

How Eviction Lawsuits Work

When the deadline in the termination notice passes, your tenant will not be automatically evicted. In almost every state, you must file and win an eviction lawsuit before the sheriff or marshal can physically evict a tenant who refuses to leave after receiving the termination notice. The whole process may take weeks—or months—depending on whether or not the tenant contests the eviction in court.

What Court Hears Evictions?

Eviction lawsuits are filed in a formal trial court (called "municipal," "county," or "justice") or in small claims court. A few states, including Illinois, Massachusetts, and New York, have separate landlord-tenant courts in larger cities, similar to a small claims courts, specifically set up to handle evictions. Some states give landlords the choice; others confine eviction lawsuits to one court or the other. Call the clerk of your local small claims court to find out whether it handles evictions.

If you have a choice between regular trial court and small claims court, you'll want to consider:

- **Amount of unpaid rent.** If you're also suing for unpaid rent that is higher than the small claims court's jurisdictional amount, you must use a higher court. States' small claims court limits are listed on the chart in Appendix A.
- **Attorney fees clause.** If your lease or rental agreement contains an attorney fees clause, and you have a strong case and a reasonable chance of collecting from your tenant, you may want to hire an attorney and go to formal court, figuring that the fee will come from the tenant's pocket when you win. On the other hand, if the tenant has little or no funds, your chances of collection are dim, and you may realistically choose small claims instead.

There are important differences between regular trial courts and small claims (or landlord-tenant) court:

- In small claims court, the regular rules of evidence are greatly relaxed, and you can show or tell the court your side of the story without adhering to the "foundation" requirements that apply in higher courts. ("Laying a foundation" is explained in "Rules of Evidence in Formal Court," below.)

- In regular court, you and the tenant may engage in a pretrial process called "discovery," in which you ask each other about the evidence that supports your positions. Information gathered during discovery can be used at trial. Discovery includes depositions (where witnesses are questioned under oath), interrogatories (sets of preprinted questions that cover information normally involved in a landlord-tenant dispute), and "requests for admissions," (specific statements of fact that the other side is asked, under oath, to admit or deny). The discovery process is normally available in formal court, but not in small claims or landlord-tenant courts.

- In regular court, you and the tenant may each attempt to wash the case out of court quickly by filing pretrial requests to the court to dismiss or limit the case. In small claims and landlord-tenant court, the idea is to decide the entire case after one efficient court hearing, and these motions are not used.

RESOURCE

***Everybody's Guide to Small Claims Court*, by Ralph Warner (Nolo),** describes the workings of your small claims court in detail.

Represent Yourself in Court: How to Prepare & Try a Winning Case, by Paul Bergman and Sara J. Berman (Nolo), explains how to present evidence and arguments in formal court.

First Steps: The Complaint and Summons

An eviction lawsuit begins when you file a legal document called a "Complaint" or a similar term. The Complaint lists the facts that you think justify the eviction. It also asks the court to order the tenant to leave and pay back rent, damages directly caused by his unlawfully remaining on the property, court costs, and sometimes attorney fees.

Fortunately, your Complaint need not be a lengthy or complicated legal document. In some states, landlords use a preprinted Complaint form, prepared by the court, that allows you to simply check an appropriate box, depending on what you intend to argue. Courts are increasingly putting official forms online; typically, you can download the PDF file and complete it by hand, or complete it online and then print it (but not save it). To learn whether your court offers these downloads, type the court's name in your browser, then look for links to forms.

Even in states that still follow an old-fashioned approach of requiring that documents be typed up on numbered legal paper, you can find the information you need from legal form books available at law libraries. These books contain "canned" forms that fit many different situations. When you sign your Complaint, be sure to note under your typed name that you are appearing "Pro per" or "Pro se" if you have not hired a lawyer.

Attorneys and Eviction Services

Depending on your location, your particular situation, and the availability of self-help eviction guides, you may be able to handle all, or most of, an eviction lawsuit yourself. Many landlords hire "legal typing services" or "independent paralegals" (discussed in Chapter 18) to help with evictions. But there are some circumstances when you should definitely consult an attorney who specializes in landlord-tenant law:

- Your tenant is already represented by a lawyer, even before you proceed with an eviction.
- Your property is subject to rent control rules governing eviction.
- The tenant you are evicting is an ex-manager whom you have fired.
- Your tenant contests the eviction in court.
- Your tenant files for bankruptcy.
- The property you own is too far from where you live. Since you must file an eviction lawsuit where the property is located, the time and travel involved in representing yourself may be too great.

Rules of Evidence in Formal Court

It's important to back up your eviction lawsuit with as much hard evidence as possible. For example, if the basis of the termination is that the tenant has violated a rental rule (by keeping a pet), be sure that you have a copy of the lease and rules that your tenant signed when he moved in.

In small claims court, you can present practically any evidence you want to the judge. But, if you are in a formal court, the judge will not examine documentary evidence until you have established that it is likely to be trustworthy. Presenting the legal background of evidence is called "laying a foundation." Here are a few hints on how to prepare evidence for formal court:

- **Photographs.** If your termination notice is based on your tenant knocking a hole in the kitchen wall, show the judge a photograph of the gaping hole. To get the picture into evidence, someone will have to testify that the picture is an accurate depiction of how the wall looked. Ask a neutral witness to look at the wall and come to court ready to testify that the photo is an accurate portrayal. Your witness need not have taken the photo.
- **Letters.** You may have sent a termination notice for nonpayment of rent because your tenant

improperly used the repair and deduct remedy by failing to give you a reasonable amount of time to fix the problem yourself. You'll want to show the judge a copy of the letter you sent to the tenant promising to fix the defect within the week (the tenant didn't wait). In court, this means you'll need to introduce your letter into evidence. To do this, you can simply testify that the letter is a true copy, that the signature is your own, and that you mailed or handed it to your tenant.

- **Government documents.** If your tenant has withheld rent because of what she claims are uninhabitable conditions, you may decide to evict for nonpayment of rent. If the tenant filed a complaint with a local health department and they issued a report giving your property a clean bill of health, you'll want the report considered by the court (admitted into evidence). Ask the health department inspector to testify that he wrote the report as part of his normal duties when investigating possible health violations. To get the inspector to court, you'll need to ask the judge for an order, called a "subpoena," that you can serve on the inspector.

Normally, you cannot sue a tenant for anything but back rent and damages. Because an eviction procedure is so quick, most states do not allow you to add other legal beefs to an eviction Complaint. For example, if you claim that the tenants have damaged the sofa, and their security deposit won't cover the cost of replacement, you must sue the tenants in small claims court in a separate lawsuit.

When you file a Complaint, the clerk will assign a date on which the case will be heard by the court. That date is entered on the Summons, a piece of paper that tells the tenant he's been sued and must answer your charges in writing and appear in court within a specified number of days or lose the lawsuit. You must then arrange for the tenant to be given the Complaint and the Summons. In legal jargon, this is called "service of process."

State laws are quite detailed as to the proper way to deliver, or "serve," court papers. Most critically, neither you (including anyone who has an ownership interest in your business) nor your employees can serve these papers. (In some states, any adult not involved in the lawsuit can serve papers.) The method of delivery is specified, as well: Typically, the preferred way is "personal" service, which means that a law enforcement officer or professional process server personally hands the tenant the papers.

If, despite repeated attempts, the process server cannot locate the tenant, most states allow something called "substituted service." This means the process server leaves a copy of the papers with a competent adult at the tenant's home, or mails the papers first-class and also leaves a copy in a place where the tenant will likely see it, such as posted on his front door.

Failure to properly serve the tenant is one of the most common errors landlords make, and may result in court dismissal of your lawsuit even before trial. Even a seemingly minor mistake—such as forgetting to check a box, checking one you shouldn't, or filling in contradictory information—will increase the chances that your tenant can successfully contest the lawsuit. Again, it is vital that you pay close attention to your state rules and procedures on evictions.

The Tenant's Answer to the Complaint

The next step in a typical eviction lawsuit involves the tenant's response to your claims that something he's done (or not done) justifies his eviction. At this point, the lawsuit has gone beyond the technicalities of the way you filed the lawsuit, and you and the tenant are meeting the reasons for the eviction head-on.

The tenant must file a document called an Answer on or before the date printed on the Summons. Like your Complaint, it need not be a complex document. Your tenant will probably consult the same set of legal form books that you used in writing your Complaint.

In general, the Answer may contain two kinds of responses:

- **Denials.** The tenant may dispute that what you say is true. For example, if you are evicting for nonpayment of rent and your tenant claims that he paid his rent to the manager, he will simply deny that the rent is unpaid. Or, if you've filed an eviction lawsuit because the tenant has a dog, but the tenant claims that the animal actually belongs to the tenants in the next unit, he'll also simply check the "denials" box. If there is no Answer form, you'll see a typed paragraph that looks something like this: "Defendant denies the allegations in Paragraph X of Plaintiff's Complaint." (You are the plaintiff in the lawsuit; the tenant is the defendant.)
- **Affirmative defenses.** The Answer is also the place where your tenant can state what

the law calls "affirmative defenses"—good legal reasons (such as discrimination or retaliation) that he hopes will excuse what would otherwise be grounds for eviction. For example, a tenant who's being evicted for not paying the rent might use a habitability defense to justify his actions—in this case, the tenant would claim that he used some of the rent money to pay for repairing a serious problem you had ignored.

Complete Your Lawsuit, Even If You Think You've Won Already

It's very common for tenants to move out after receiving a Summons and Complaint. Especially if the security deposit will cover your losses, or you know that attempting to collect any excess won't be worth your time and trouble, you might be tempted to forget about the lawsuit and turn your attentions to rerenting quickly.

Never walk away from a lawsuit without formally ending it. Usually, this will involve appearing in court and asking the judge to dismiss the case. Doing so preserves your reputation as someone who uses the courts with respect—if you are simply a no-show, expect a chilly reception the next time you appear in court. In addition, if you don't appear for trial but the tenant does, *the tenant* may win and be entitled to move back in and collect court costs and attorney fees.

If you and the tenant have reached a settlement that involves the tenant paying you money but the tenant hasn't paid you yet, it's a good idea to take that written settlement with you to court and ask the judge to make it part of his ruling while dismissing the case. Depending on the rules in your state, you will then have a court order (sometimes called a "stipulated settlement") that you can immediately use if the tenant fails to pay voluntarily. (You can take it to a collection agency or use it to garnish wages.) Otherwise, you'll have to take the written agreement to small claims court to get a judgment.

Finally, don't overlook the possibility that the tenant may not have actually moved out (or may move back in). You'll be on safe ground if you get a judgment before retaking possession.

When Tenants Ignore the Summons and Complaint

If you properly terminate a tenancy and the tenant doesn't respond to the Summons and Complaint—he doesn't file an Answer or show up in court—you will usually automatically win the lawsuit. The court will grant what's called a "default judgment" against the tenant, ordering him to pay unpaid rent and, if your lease or rental agreement has an attorney fees and costs clause, those expenses as well. Of course, you will still have to hire the local law enforcement personnel to carry out the actual eviction, and you'll have to look to your security deposit to cover the monetary judgment. If the deposit is insufficient, you can always sue for the balance in small claims court.

The Trial

Many eviction cases never end up in trial—for example, because the tenant moves out or negotiates a settlement with the landlord. But each case that does go to trial will have its own unpredictable twists and turns that can greatly affect trial preparation and tactics. For this reason, you will probably need to hire a lawyer, if you haven't done so already, to help you prepare for and conduct the trial.

What you must prove at trial obviously depends on the issues raised in your Complaint and the tenant's Answer. For example, the testimony in a case based on nonpayment of rent where the tenant's defense is that you failed to keep the premises habitable will be very different from that in a case based on termination of a month-to-month tenancy by 30-day notice where the tenant denies receiving the notice.

All contested evictions are similar, however, in that you have to establish the basic elements of your case through solid evidence that proves your case (and refutes your tenant's defense). In formal court, you'll have to abide by your state's rules of evidence. But in an informal court, you may be able to introduce letters and secondhand testimony ("I heard her say that … "). Also, you can introduce evidence without elaborate "foundations." (See "Rules of Evidence in Formal Court," above.)

The Judgment

Eviction lawsuits are typically decided on the spot or very soon thereafter, after the judge has heard the witnesses and consulted any relevant statutes, ordinances, and higher court opinions.

If You Win

If you win the eviction case, you get an order from the judge declaring that you are entitled to possession of the property (you may get a money judgment for back rent and court costs and attorney fees, too). You'll need to take the order, called a judgment, to the local law enforcement official who will carry out the eviction.

Unfortunately, having a judgment for the payment of money is not the same as having the money itself. Your tenant may be unable (or unwilling) to pay you—despite the fact that you have converted your legal right to be paid into a formal court order. Unless the tenant voluntarily pays up, you will have to collect the debt—for example, by using the tenant's security deposit or hiring a collection agency.

If You Lose

If you lose the eviction case, your tenant can stay, and you'll likely end up paying for your tenant's court costs and fees. You may also be hit with money damages if the judge decides you acted illegally, as in the case of discrimination or retaliation.

If your tenant wins by asserting a habitability defense, the court may hold on to the case even after the trial is over. That's because the court doesn't want to simply return the tenant to an unfit dwelling. In some states, a judge may order you to make repairs while the rent is paid into a court account; when an inspector certifies that the dwelling is habitable, the judge will release the funds.

How Tenants May Stop or Postpone an Eviction

If you win the eviction lawsuit, you'll want to move quickly to physically remove the tenant from the property. In rare instances, a tenant may be able to get the trial judge to stop the eviction, but only if he can convince the court of two things:

- Eviction would cause a severe hardship for the tenant or his family. For example, the tenant may be able to persuade the judge that alternate housing is unavailable and his job will be in jeopardy if he is forced to move.
- The tenant is willing and able to pay any back rent owed (and your costs to bring the lawsuit) and future rent, as well.

It's very unusual for a judge to stop an eviction, for the simple reason that if the tenant's sympathetic predicament (and sufficient monetary reserves) weren't persuasive enough to win the case for him in the first place, it's unlikely that these arguments can prevail after the trial.

The tenant may, however, ask for a postponement of the eviction. Typically, evictions are postponed in three situations:

- **Pending an appeal.** If the tenant files an appeal, he may ask the trial judge to postpone ("stay") the eviction until a higher court decides the case. A tenant who has been evicted in small claims court may, in a few states, enjoy an automatic postponement during the appeal. Of course, this is one reason why smart landlords in these states never use small claims court.
- **Until the tenant's circumstances improve.** A tenant may be able to persuade a judge to give him a little more time to find a new home.
- **Until the weather improves.** Contrary to popular belief, judges in many cold-climate states (including Alaska, Minnesota, and North Dakota) are not required to postpone an eviction on frigid days. But there's nothing to stop tenants from asking the judge, anyway. In the District of Columbia, however, a

landlord may not evict on a day when the National Weather Service predicts at 8:00 a.m. that the temperature at the National Airport will fall below freezing within the next 24 hours. (D.C. Code § 42-3505.01(k).)

Eviction

In most states, you cannot move a tenant's belongings out on the street, even after winning an eviction lawsuit. Typically, you must give the judgment to a local law enforcement officer, along with a fee which the tenant has been charged as part of your costs. The sheriff or marshal gives the tenant a notice telling him that he'll be back, sometimes within just a few days, to physically remove him if the tenant isn't gone.

Illegal "Self-Help" Evictions

As any experienced landlord will attest, there are occasional tenants who do things so outrageous that the landlord is tempted to bypass normal legal protections and take direct and immediate action to protect his property. For example, after a tenant's numerous promises to pay rent, a landlord may consider changing the locks and putting the tenant's property out in the street. Or, a landlord who is responsible for paying the utility charges may be tempted to simply not pay the bill in the hopes that the resulting lack of water, gas, or electricity will hasten a particularly outrageous tenant's departure. When you realize how long a legal eviction can sometimes take, these actions can almost seem sensible.

If you are tempted to take the law into your own hands to force or scare a troublesome tenant out of your property, heed the following advice: *Don't do it!* Shortcuts such as threats, intimidation, utility shutoffs, or attempts to physically remove a tenant are illegal and dangerous, and if you resort to them you may well find yourself on the wrong end of a lawsuit for trespass, assault, battery, slander and libel, intentional infliction of emotional distress, and wrongful eviction. So, although the eviction process can often entail some trouble, expense, and delay, it's important to understand that it is the only game in town.

If you are sued by a tenant whom you forcibly evicted or tried to evict, the fact that the tenant didn't pay rent, left your property a mess, verbally abused you, or otherwise acted outrageously will not be a valid defense. You will very likely lose the lawsuit, and it will cost you far more than evicting the tenant using normal court procedures.

Today, virtually every state forbids "self-help" evictions—their eviction statutes warn landlords that their procedures are the *only* way to retake possession of rental property. And, in many states the penalties for violating these laws are steep. Tenants who have been locked out, frozen out by having the heat cut off, or denied electricity or water can sue not only for their actual money losses (such as the need for temporary housing, the value of food that spoiled when the refrigerator stopped running, or the cost of an electric heater when the gas was shut off), but also for penalties, as well. For example, in Arizona, a landlord can be forced to pay the tenant up to two months' rent or the tenant's actual damages, whatever is higher. And in Connecticut, the landlord may even be prosecuted for a misdemeanor. In some states, the tenant can collect and still remain in the premises; in others, he is entitled to monetary compensation only. See "Consequences of Self-Help Evictions" in Appendix A.

Even if your state has not legislated against self-help evictions, throwing your tenant out on your own is highly risky and likely to land you in more legal entanglements than had you gone to court for an eviction judgment in the first place. The potential for nastiness and violence is great; the last thing you want is a patrol car at the curb while you and your tenant wrestle over the sofa on the lawn. And you can almost count on a lawsuit over the "disappearance" of your tenant's valuable possessions, which she'll claim were lost or taken when you removed her belongings. Using a neutral law enforcement officer to enforce a judge's eviction order will avoid these unpleasantries.

> **CAUTION**
>
> **Don't seize tenants' property under the guise of handling "abandoned" property.** A few states allow you to freely dispose of a tenant's leftover property when he has moved out. Do so only if it is quite clear that the tenant has left permanently, intending to turn the place over to you. Seizing property under a bogus claim that the tenant had abandoned it will expose you to significant monetary penalties.

Stopping Eviction by Filing for Bankruptcy

Tenants with significant financial burdens may decide to declare bankruptcy. There are several kinds of bankruptcy; the most common are "Chapter 7," in which most debts are wiped out after as many creditors as possible have been paid; or "Chapter 13," in which the debts remain but are paid off over time according to a court-approved plan.

If your tenant has filed for either Chapter 7 or 13 bankruptcy and is behind in the rent, becomes unable to pay the rent, or violates another term of his tenancy (such as keeping a pet in violation of a no-pets clause), you can't deliver a termination notice or proceed with an eviction. This prohibition is known as the "automatic stay," and it means that you need to go to the federal bankruptcy court and ask the judge to "lift," or remove the stay. (11 U.S. Code § 365(e).) In most cases, you'll get the stay lifted within a matter of days and can proceed with your termination and eviction. (You won't have to go to court if your tenant is using illegal drugs or endangering the property, as explained below in "Bankrupt Tenants, Drugs, and Damage.")

The automatic stay does not apply, however if you completed your eviction proceeding and got a judgment for possession *before* the tenant filed for bankruptcy. Under the Bankruptcy Abuse Prevention and Consumer Protection Act of 2005, landlords can proceed with the eviction without having to go to court and ask for the stay to be lifted.

In very narrow circumstances, and only for evictions based on rent nonpayment, a tenant can stop the eviction even if you got a judgment before the tenant filed for bankruptcy. Here are the specifics:

- Along with his or her bankruptcy petition, the tenant must go to court and file a paper certifying that state law allows the tenant to avoid eviction by paying the unpaid rent, even after the landlord has won a judgment for possession. Very few states extend this option to tenants. The certification must be served on the landlord.
- At the same time, the tenant must deposit with the clerk of the bankruptcy court any rent that would be due 30 days from the date the petition was filed.
- The tenant then has 30 days after filing the petition to actually pay the back rent. He or she must file another certification with the bankruptcy court (and serve it on the landlord), stating that he or she has paid the amount due.

At any point during these 30 days, you can file an objection to the tenant's certification, and you'll get a hearing in the bankruptcy court within ten days. If you convince the judge that the tenant's certifications are not true, the court will lift the stay and you can proceed to recover possession of the property.

A Tenant's Lease After Bankruptcy

Filing for bankruptcy affects a tenancy even if the tenant is not behind in the rent or otherwise in violation of his lease. After the tenant files, the "bankruptcy trustee" (a person appointed by the bankruptcy court to oversee the case) must decide whether to carry on with or terminate the lease or rental agreement. In most situations, the trustee will let the tenant keep the lease, since it wouldn't be of any benefit to his creditors to force him to incur the expense of finding a new home and moving. First, however, he must pay any unpaid back rent.

If the trustee keeps the lease, you have the right to ask the bankruptcy court to demand that the tenant show proof of his ability to pay future rent. (11 U.S. Code §§ 365(b)(1)(A), (B), & (C).) Of course, if he becomes unable to pay the rent after the lease is assumed, you can ask the bankruptcy court to lift the stay so that you can terminate and, if necessary, evict.

Bankrupt Tenants, Drugs, and Damage

You may find yourself needing to evict a tenant who is using illegal drugs on the property or endangering your property. If the tenant files for bankruptcy before you win a judgment for possession, you'll be able to proceed with the eviction without asking the bankruptcy judge to lift the stay. Here are the steps to take:

- **When you've begun an eviction case but don't have a judgment.** Prepare a certification, or sworn statement, that you have begun an unlawful detainer case based on the tenant's endangerment of the property or use of illegal drugs on the property (or such use by the tenant's guests).
- **When you haven't yet filed your eviction lawsuit.** Prepare a certification, or sworn statement, that the activity described above has happened within the past 30 days.

- **File the certification with the bankruptcy court and serve the tenant as you would serve any legal notice.**

If your tenant does not file an objection within 15 days of being served, you can proceed with the eviction without asking the court for relief from the stay.

A tenant who objects must file with the court, and serve on you, a certification challenging the truth of your certification. The bankruptcy court will hold a hearing within ten days, at which the tenant must convince the court that the situation you describe did not exist or has been remedied. If the court rules for you, you may proceed with the eviction without asking that the stay be lifted; but if the tenant wins, you may not proceed.

Lawyers and Legal Research

Landlords should be prepared to deal with most routine legal questions and problems without a lawyer. If you bought all the needed information at the rates lawyers charge—$150 to $250 an hour—it should go without saying that you'd quickly empty your bank account. Just the same, there are times when good advice from a specialist in landlord-tenant law will be helpful, if not essential—for example, in lawsuits by tenants alleging housing discrimination or claiming that dangerous conditions or wrongful acts caused injury, or in complicated eviction lawsuits. Throughout this book, we point out specific instances when an attorney's advice or services may be useful.

Fortunately, for an intelligent landlord there are a number of other ways to acquire a good working knowledge of the legal principles and procedures necessary to handle problems with tenants and managers. Of course, that's the main purpose of this book. But in addition to the information we provide, this chapter specifically recommends a strategy to most efficiently and effectively use legal services and keep up to date on landlord-tenant law, so that you can anticipate and avoid many legal problems.

As a sensible landlord, it doesn't make sense to try and run your business without ever consulting a lawyer. When legal problems are potentially serious and expensive, it makes sense to get expert help. But since you almost surely can't afford all the services a lawyer might offer, you obviously need to set priorities. When thinking about a legal problem, ask yourself: "Can I do this myself?"; "Can I do this myself with some help from a lawyer?"; "Should I simply put this in my lawyer's hands?"

Or, put another way, your challenge isn't to avoid lawyers altogether, but rather to use them on a cost-effective basis. Ideally, this means finding a lawyer who's willing to serve as a kind of self-help law coach, to help you educate yourself. Then, you can often do routine or preliminary legal work on your own, turning to your lawyer only occasionally for advice and fine-tuning.

How Lawyers Can Help Landlords

Here are some important things lawyers can do to help landlords:

- prepare (or review your drafts of) key documents, such as your lease or manager agreement
- confirm that you have a good claim or defense vis-à-vis an individual tenant—whether it's a dispute over how much security deposit you must return or your right to raise the rent
- make a quick phone call or write a letter to the tenant and get a problem resolved quickly
- summarize and point you to the law that applies in a given situation
- provide any needed assistance with evictions, including preparing notices and forms
- answer questions along the way if you're representing yourself in court or in a mediation proceeding, and
- handle legal problems that are—or are threatening to become—serious, such as a tenant's personal injury lawsuit or discrimination charge.

Finding a Lawyer

How frequently you'll need a lawyer's help will depend on many factors, including the type, number, and location of rental units you own; the kinds of problems you run into with tenants; the number of property managers and other employees you hire; and your willingness to do some of the legal work yourself.

In looking for a lawyer you can work with, and to manage your subsequent relationship with that person, always remember one key thing: You're the boss. Just because your lawyer has specialized training, knowledge, skills, and experience in dealing with legal matters is no reason for you to abdicate control over legal decision making and how much time and money should be spent on a particular legal problem. We say this because, despite the fact that you have an intimate knowledge of your business and are in the best position to call the shots, some lawyers will be willing or even eager to try and run your business for you while overcharging you for the privilege. The key is to find a lawyer who can provide the amount and type of legal services you need.

How Not to Find a Lawyer

The worst lawyer referral sources are:

- Heavily advertised legal clinics, which are less likely to offer competitive rates for competent representation in this specialized area. While they may offer low flat rates for routine services such as drafting a will, it's less common to see legal clinics charge reasonable flat fees for other specific services.
- Referral panels set up by local bar associations. While bar association panels sometimes do minimal screening before qualifying the expertise of lawyers in landlord-tenant law, usually the emphasis is on the word "minimal." You may get a good referral from these panels, but they often refer people to inexperienced practitioners who don't have enough clients and who use the panel as a way of generating needed business.

Compile a List of Prospects

Finding a good, reasonably priced lawyer expert in landlord-tenant legal issues is not always an easy task. If you just pick a name out of the telephone book or you find one online—even someone who advertises as a landlord law expert—you may get an unsympathetic lawyer, or one who will charge too much, or one who's not qualified to deal with your particular problem. If you use an attorney you or a friend or relative has relied on for other legal needs, you will very likely end up with someone who doesn't know enough about landlord-tenant law.

This sorry result is not inevitable—there are competent landlords' lawyers who charge fairly for their services. As a general rule, deep experience in landlord-tenant law is most important. As with so many other areas of the law, the information needed to practice effectively in this field has become increasingly specialized in the past two decades—so much so that a general practitioner simply won't do.

The best way to find a suitable attorney is through some trusted person who has had a satisfactory experience with one. Your best referral sources are other landlords in your area. Ask the names of their lawyers and a little bit about their experiences. Also ask rental property owners about other lawyers they've worked with, and what led them to make a change. If you talk to a few landlords, chances are you'll come away with several leads on good lawyers experienced in landlord-tenant law.

Your local landlords' association will also likely know of lawyers who have experience in landlord-tenant law.

RESOURCE
Nolo's Lawyer Directory is an easy-to-use online directory of lawyers, organized by location and area of expertise (including landlord-tenant); you can find the directory and its comprehensive profiles at www.nolo.com/lawyers. Two other useful online resources are Lawyers.com and Martindale.com. You can search on these sites by practice area and location, and find detailed information, including ratings, on individual lawyers.

Shop Around

Once you have the names of hopefully top-notch prospects, your job has just begun. You need to meet with each attorney and make your own evaluation. If you explain that, as a local landlord, you have a continuing need for legal help, many lawyers will be willing to speak to you for a half-hour or so at no charge or at a reduced rate so that you can size them up and make an informed selection. Briefly explain your business and legal needs and how much work you plan to do yourself.

Look for experience, personal rapport, and accessibility. Some of these traits will be apparent almost immediately; others may take longer to discover. In addition to the person making the original recommendation, you may want to talk with some of the lawyer's other landlord clients about their satisfaction with the lawyer's work. A lawyer should be able to provide you with such a list.

Here are some things to look for in your first meeting.

Will the lawyer answer all your questions about fees, his experience in landlord-tenant matters, and your specific legal problems? Stay away from lawyers who make you feel uncomfortable asking questions. Pay particular attention to the rapport between you and your lawyer. No matter how experienced and well-recommended a lawyer is, if you feel uncomfortable with that person during your first meeting or two, you may never achieve an ideal lawyer-client relationship. Trust your instincts and seek a lawyer whose personality is compatible with your own. Be sure you understand how the lawyer charges for services.

Will the lawyer provide the kind of legal help you want? If you plan to be actively involved in dealing with your legal business, look for a lawyer who doesn't resent your participation and control. By reading this book all the way through and consulting other resources, such as those available online or at a nearby law library, you can answer many of your questions on your own. For example, you might do the initial legal work in evictions and similar procedures yourself, but turn over to a lawyer cases which become hotly contested or complicated.

Unfortunately, some lawyers are uncomfortable with the very idea of helping people help themselves. They see themselves as all-knowing experts and expect their clients to accept and follow their advice without question. Obviously, this is not the type of lawyer a self-helper will want.

Is the lawyer willing to assist you when you have specific questions, billing you on an hourly basis when you handle your own legal work—such as evictions? One key to figuring out if a lawyer is really willing to help you

help yourself is to ask: Is he willing to answer your questions over the phone and charge only for the brief amount of time the conversation lasted? If, instead, he indicates that he prefers to provide advice in more time-consuming (and therefore profitable) office appointments, you'll want to keep looking. There are plenty of lawyers who will be very happy to bill you hourly to help you help yourself. By providing helpful consultations on problems that are routine or involve small dollar amounts, a lawyer can generate referrals for full-service representation on bigger, more complex matters that you (or your friends or family) face in the future. And if, despite his initial assurances, the lawyer later tries to dissuade you from representing yourself or won't give any advice over the phone despite your invitation to bill you for it, find someone else.

Will the lawyer clearly lay out all your options for handling a particular legal problem, including alternate dispute resolution methods such as mediation?

Will the lawyer be accessible when you need legal services? Unfortunately, the complaint logs of all law regulatory groups indicate that many lawyers are not reasonably available to their clients in times of need. If every time you have a problem there's a delay of several days before you can talk to your lawyer on the phone or get an appointment, you'll lose precious time, not to mention sleep. And almost nothing is more aggravating than to leave a legal question or project in a lawyer's hands and then have weeks or even months go by without anything happening. So be sure to discuss with any lawyer whether she will really commit herself to returning your phone calls promptly, work hard on your behalf, and follow through on all assignments.

If your property is in a rent-controlled city, does the lawyer practice in or near that city and know its rent control laws and practices?

Does the lawyer represent tenants, too? Chances are that a lawyer who represents both landlords and tenants can advise you well on how to avoid many legal pitfalls of being a landlord. On the other hand, you'll want to steer clear of lawyers who represent mostly tenants, since their sympathies (world view) are likely to be different from yours.

Types of Fee Arrangements With Lawyers

How you pay your lawyer depends on the type of legal services you need and the amount of legal work you have. Once an agreement is reached, it's a good idea to ask for a written fee agreement—basically an explanation of how the fees and costs will be billed and paid. As part of this, negotiate an overall cap on what you can be billed absent your specific agreement.

If a lawyer will be delegating some of the work on your case to a less-experienced associate, paralegal, or secretary, that work should be billed at a lower hourly rate. Be sure to get this information recorded in your initial written fee agreement.

There are four basic ways that lawyers charge for their services.

Hourly fees. In most parts of the United States, you can get competent services for your rental business for $150 to $350 an hour, with most lawyers billing in ten- or 15-minute increments. Comparison shopping among lawyers will help you avoid overpaying. But the cheapest hourly rate isn't necessarily the best. You can often benefit by hiring a more experienced landlord's attorney, even if her hourly rates are high, since she will be further along the learning curve than a general practitioner and should take less time to review and advise you on the particulars of your job.

Flat fees. Sometimes, a lawyer will quote you a flat fee for a specific job. For example, a lawyer may offer to represent you in court for routine eviction cases (such as for nonpayment of rent) that present little trouble, even when they are contested by the tenant (which is actually fairly rare). In a flat fee agreement, you pay the same amount regardless of how much time the lawyer spends on a particular job. If you own many rental units and anticipate providing a fair amount of business over the years, you have a golden opportunity to negotiate flat fees that are substantially below the lawyer's normal hourly rate. After all, the lawyer will see you as a very desirable client, since you'll generate continuing business for many years to come.

Retainer fees. In some circumstances, it can also make sense to hire a lawyer for a flat annual fee, or retainer, to handle all of your routine legal questions and business, such as noncontested eviction cases. You'll usually pay in equal monthly installments and, normally, the lawyer will bill you an additional amount for extraordinary services—such as representing you in a complicated eviction lawsuit. Since the lawyer can count on a reliable source of income, you can expect lower overall fees. Obviously, the key to making a retainer fee arrangement work is to have a written agreement clearly defining what's routine and what's extraordinary. This type of fee arrangement is more economically feasible for larger landlords (a dozen or more rental units) with regular legal needs. Also, retainer fee agreements are usually best negotiated after you and your lawyer have worked together long enough to have established a pattern—you know and trust each other well enough to work out a mutually beneficial arrangement.

Contingency fees. This is a percentage (such as one-third) of the amount the lawyer obtains for you in a negotiated settlement or through a trial. If the lawyer recovers nothing for you, there's no fee. Contingency fees are common in personal injury cases, but relatively unusual for the kinds of legal advice and representation landlords need.

Saving on Legal Fees

There are many ways to hold down the cost of legal services. Here is a short list of some of the key ways to save on legal fees.

Be organized. Especially when you are paying by the hour, it's important to gather important documents, write a short chronology of events, and concisely explain a problem to your lawyer. Since papers can get lost in a lawyer's office, keep a copy of everything that's important, such as your lease or rental agreement, move-in letter to new tenants, correspondence with tenants, repair logs, and other records.

Be prepared before you meet. Whenever possible, put your questions in writing and email, fax, or deliver them to your lawyer before meetings, even phone meetings. That way, the lawyer can find answers if he doesn't know them off the top of his head without having to call you back and charge for a separate phone conference. Early preparation also helps focus the meeting, so there is less of a chance of digressing into (and having to pay to discuss) unrelated topics.

Read trade journals in your field, such as publications of your local or state apartment association. Law changes continuously, so you'll want to keep up with specific legal developments affecting your business. Send pertinent clippings to your lawyer—and encourage your lawyer to do the same for you. This can dramatically reduce legal research time.

Show that you're an important client. Mutual respect is key in an attorney-client relationship. The single most important way to show your lawyer how much you value the relationship is to pay your bills on time. Beyond that, let your lawyer know about plans for expansion and your business's possible future legal needs. And drop your lawyer a line when you've recommended him or her to your landlord colleagues.

Bundle your legal matters. You'll save money if you consult with your lawyer on several matters at one time. For example, in a one-hour conference, you may be able to review with your lawyer several items—such as a new lease or rental agreement clause, anti-age-discrimination policy, or advertisement for your apartment complex. Significant savings are possible, because lawyers commonly divide their billable hours into parts of an hour. For example, if your lawyer bills in 15-minute intervals and you only talk for five minutes, you are likely to be charged for the whole 15. So it usually pays to gather your questions and ask them all at once, rather than calling every time you have a question.

> **TIP**
>
> **Carefully review lawyer bills.** Always read your bill. Like everyone else, lawyers make mistakes, and your charges may be wrong. For example, a "0.1" of an hour (six minutes) may be transposed into a "1.0" (one hour) when the data are entered into the billing system. That's $200 instead of $20 if your lawyer charges $200 per hour. If you have any questions about your bill, feel free to ask your lawyer. You hired him to provide a service, and you have the right to expect a clear explanation of your bill.

Use nonlawyer professionals for evictions. Look to "unlawful detainer assistants," "legal typing services," or "independent paralegals" for help with evictions in large metropolitan areas. For a flat fee that is usually much lower than what lawyers charge, and often at a faster pace, nonlawyer eviction services take the basic information from you, provide the appropriate eviction forms, and fill them out according to your instructions. This normally involves typing your eviction papers so they'll be accepted by the court, arranging for filing, and then serving the papers on the tenant.

Unlawful detainer assistants, paralegals, and typing services aren't lawyers, and most handle only routine cases. They can't give legal advice about the requirements of your specific case and can't represent you in court if the tenant contests the eviction suit. You must decide what steps to take in your case, and the information to put in the needed forms.

To find a nonlawyer eviction service, check with a landlords' association, or look online or in the telephone book under "Eviction Services," "Paralegals," or "Unlawful Detainer Assistant." Be sure the eviction service or typing service is reputable and experienced, as well as reasonably priced. (The cost should not exceed a few hundred dollars for the service and fees.) Ask for references and check them. As a general matter, the longer a nonlawyer eviction service has been in business, the better.

RESOURCE

Recommended reading on lawsuits. California landlords can handle eviction lawsuits themselves by using *The California Landlord's Law Book: Evictions*, by David Brown (Nolo). Contact your state or local apartment association for information on any step-by-step guides to evictions in your state.

Represent Yourself in Court: How to Prepare & Try a Winning Case, by Paul Bergman and Sara J. Berman (Nolo), offers more general advice on handling any civil lawsuit on your own or with a lawyer-coach's help.

Costs Can Mount Up

In addition to the fees they charge for their time, lawyers often bill for some costs as well—and these costs can add up quickly. When you receive a lawyer's bill, you may be surprised at both the amount of the costs and the variety of the services for which the lawyer expects reimbursement. These can include charges for:

- overnight mail
- messenger service
- expert witness fees
- court filing fees
- process servers
- work by investigators
- work by legal assistants or paralegals
- deposition transcripts
- online legal research, and
- travel.

Many sensible lawyers absorb the cost of photocopying, faxes, phone calls, and the like as normal office overhead—part of the cost of doing business—but that's not always the case. So in working out the fee arrangements, discuss the costs you'll be expected to pay. If a lawyer is intent on nickel-and-diming you to death, look elsewhere. For example, if you learn the law office charges $3 or more for each page it faxes, red flags should go up. On the other hand, it is reasonable for a lawyer to pass along costs of things like court costs, process server fees, and any work by investigators.

TIP

Lawyer fees are a tax-deductible business expense. If you visit your lawyer on a personal legal matter (such as reviewing a contract for the purchase of a house) and you also discuss a business problem (such as a new policy for hiring managers), ask your lawyer to allocate the time spent and send you separate bills. At tax time, you can easily list the business portion as a tax-deductible business expense.

Resolving Problems With Your Lawyer

If you see a problem emerging with your lawyer, nip it in the bud. Don't just sit back and fume; call or write your lawyer. Whatever it is that rankles, have an honest discussion about your feelings. Maybe you're upset because your lawyer hasn't kept you informed about what's going on in your lawsuit against your tenant for property damage, or maybe your lawyer has missed a promised deadline for reviewing your new system for handling maintenance and repair problems. Or maybe last month's bill was shockingly high or you question the breakdown of how your lawyer's time was spent.

Your Rights as a Client

As a client, you have the following rights:

- courteous treatment by your lawyer and staff members
- an itemized statement of services rendered and a full advance explanation of billing practices
- charges for agreed-upon fees and no more
- prompt responses to phone calls and letters
- confidential legal conferences, free from unwarranted interruptions
- up-to-date information on the status of your case
- diligent and competent legal representation, and
- clear answers to all questions.

Here's one way to test whether a lawyer-client relationship is a good one: Ask yourself if you feel able to talk freely with your lawyer about your degree of participation in any legal matter and your control over how the lawyer carries out a legal assignment. If you can't frankly discuss these sometimes-sensitive matters with your lawyer, fire that lawyer and hire another one. If you don't, you'll surely waste money on unnecessary legal fees and risk having legal matters turn out badly.

Remember that you're always free to change lawyers. If you do, be sure to fire your old lawyer before you hire a new one. Otherwise, you could find yourself being billed by both lawyers at the same time. Also, be sure to get all important legal documents back from a lawyer you no longer employ. Tell your new lawyer what your old one has done to date and pass on the file.

But firing a lawyer may not be enough. Here are some tips on resolving specific problems:

- If you have a dispute over fees, the local bar association may be able to mediate it for you.
- If a lawyer has violated legal ethics—for example, conflict of interest, overbilling, or not representing you zealously—the state agency that licenses lawyers may discipline or even disbar the lawyer. Although lawyer oversight groups are typically biased in favor of the legal profession, they will often take action if your lawyer has done something seriously wrong.
- Where a major mistake has been made—for example, a lawyer has missed the deadline for filing a case—you can sue for malpractice. Many lawyers carry malpractice insurance, and your dispute may be settled out of court.

Attorney Fees in a Lawsuit

If your lease or written rental agreement has an attorney fees provision (see Clause 19 of the form agreements in Chapter 2), you are entitled to recover your attorney fees if you win a lawsuit concerning the meaning and implementation of that agreement. There's no guarantee, however, that a judge will award attorney fees equal to your attorney's actual bill, or that you will ultimately be able to collect the money from the tenant or former tenant. Also, as discussed in Chapter 2, an attorney fees clause in your lease or rental agreement usually works both ways. Even if the clause doesn't say so, you're liable for the tenant's attorney fees if you lose. (Landlord's insurance does not cover such liability where the lawsuit is unrelated to items covered by the policy, such as eviction lawsuits by the landlord and security deposit refund suits by the tenant.)

Doing Your Own Legal Research

Using this book is a good way to educate yourself about the laws that affect your business—but one book is not enough by itself. Some landlord associations publish legal updates in their newsletters and on their websites to keep members abreast of new laws and regulations that affect their property.

While we recommend that you get copies of state, local, and federal laws that affect your landlording business (see the section just below), at one time or another you'll probably need to do some further research. For example, you may want to read a specific court case or research a more open-ended question about landlord-tenant law—for instance, your liability for an assault that took place on your rental property.

Lawyers aren't the only source for legal help. There's a lot you can do on your own. Every state has placed its statutes online (go to your state's main page, which will be at www.[postal code abbreviation].gov, and look for links to laws or statutes). Rules put out by federal and state regulatory agencies are often available, too, and the Internet's legal resources grow every day.

In addition to the Internet, law libraries are full of valuable information, such as state statutes that regulate the landlord-tenant relationship. Your first step is to find a law library that's open to the public. You may find such a library in your county courthouse or at your state capitol. Publicly funded law schools generally permit the public to use their libraries, and some private law schools grant access to their libraries—sometimes for a modest fee.

Don't overlook the reference department of the public library if you're in a large city. Many large public libraries have a fairly decent legal research collection. Also, ask about using the law library in your own lawyer's office. Some lawyers, on request, will share their books with their clients.

RESOURCE

Recommended reading on legal research. We don't have space here to show you how to do your own legal research in anything approaching a comprehensive fashion. To get started, see Nolo's Laws and Legal Research page at www.nolo.com/legal-research. Here you can find links to state and federal laws, learn about researching and understanding statutes, and get advice on finding local ordinances and court cases. To go further, we recommend *Legal Research: How to Find & Understand the Law*, by Stephen Elias and the Editors of Nolo (Nolo). This nontechnical book gives easy-to-use, step-by-step instructions on how find legal information.

Where to Find State, Local, and Federal Laws

Every landlord is governed by state, local, and federal law. In some areas, like antidiscrimination standards, laws overlap. When they do overlap, the stricter laws will apply. In practical terms, this usually means that the laws that give tenants the most protection (rights and remedies) will prevail over less-protective laws.

State Laws

If you're a typical landlord, you'll be primarily concerned with state law. State statutes regulate many aspects of the landlord-tenant relationship, including deposits, landlord's right of entry, discrimination, housing standards, rent rules, repair and maintenance responsibilities, and eviction procedures.

The website of your state consumer protection agency or attorney general's office may provide a guide to state laws that affect landlords, and copies of the state statutes themselves. Also, representatives of state agencies can often help explain how the landlord-tenant laws they administer are interpreted. For a list of state consumer protection agencies, go to www.usa.gov/state-consumer.

We refer to many of the state laws affecting landlords throughout this book and include citations so that you can do additional research. State laws or codes are collected in volumes and are available online (discussed below) in many public libraries and in most law libraries. Depending on the state, statutes may be organized by subject matter or by title number ("chapter"), with each title covering a particular subject matter, or simply numbered sequentially, without regard to subject matter.

"Annotated codes" contain not only all the text of the laws (as do the regular codes), but also a brief summary of some of the court decisions (discussed below) interpreting each law and often references to treatises and articles that discuss the law. Annotated codes have comprehensive indexes by topic, and are kept up to date with paperback supplements ("pocket parts") stuck in a pocket inside the back cover of each volume.

Most states have made their statutes available online. You can find these by going to Nolo's State Law Resources page at www.nolo.com/legal-research/state-law.html.

If you know the statute's number or citation (available in the charts in Appendix A of this book), you can go directly there. If you don't know the statute number, you can enter a keyword that is likely to be in it, such as "deposit" or "security deposit." If you just want to browse through the statutes, you can search the table of contents for your state's laws. With a little trial and error, you should have no trouble finding a particular landlord-tenant statute.

RESOURCE

For a complete discussion of landlord-tenant laws in California, see *The California Landlord's Law Book: Rights & Responsibilities,* by David Brown, Janet Portman, and Ralph Warner; and *The California Landlord's Law Book: Evictions,* by David Brown. These books are published by Nolo and are available at bookstores and public libraries. They may also be ordered directly from Nolo's website at www.nolo.com or by calling 800-728-3555.

Local Ordinances

Local ordinances, such as rent control rules, health and safety standards, and requirements that you pay interest on tenants' security deposits, will also affect your business. Many municipalities have websites—just search for the name of a particular city. Sometimes the site is nothing more than a not-so-slick public relations page, but sometimes it includes a large body of information, including local ordinances available for searching and downloading. Check out State & Local Government on the Net (www.statelocalgov.net) and Municode. com, good sources for finding local governments online.

Finally, your local public library or office of the city attorney, mayor, or city manager can provide information on local ordinances that affect landlords. If you own rental property in a city with rent control, be sure to get a copy of the ordinance, as well as all rules issued by the rent board covering rent increases and hearings.

Federal Statutes and Regulations

Congress has enacted laws, and federal agencies such as the U.S. Department of Housing and Urban Development (HUD) have adopted regulations, covering discrimination, wage and hour laws affecting employment of managers, and landlord responsibilities to disclose environmental health hazards. We refer to relevant federal agencies throughout this book and suggest you contact them for publications that explain federal laws

affecting landlords, or copies of the federal statutes and regulations themselves.

We include citations for many of the federal laws affecting landlords throughout this book. The U.S. Code is the starting place for most federal statutory research. It consists of 50 separate numbered titles. Each title covers a specific subject matter.

Most federal regulations are published in the Code of Federal Regulations ("CFR"), organized by subject into 50 separate titles.

To access the U.S. Code online, see the Federal Law Resources page on Nolo's website at www.nolo .com/legal-research/federal-law.html. Also, visit the Cornell Legal Information Institute (www.law. cornell.edu). This site provides the entire U.S. Code as well as the Code of Federal Regulations. Finally, check www.usa.gov, the official U.S. website for government information.

How to Research Court Decisions

Sometimes the answer to a legal question cannot be found in a statute. This happens when:

- Court cases and opinions have greatly expanded or explained the statute, taking it beyond its obvious or literal meaning.
- The law that applies to your question has been made by judges, not legislators.

Court Decisions That Explain Statutes

Statutes and ordinances do not explain themselves. For example, a state law may require you to offer housing that is weatherproofed, but it may not tell you whether you must provide both storm windows and window screens. But others before you have had the same questions, and they may have come up in the context of a lawsuit. If a judge interpreted the statute and wrote an opinion on the matter, that written opinion, once published, will become "the law" as much as the statute itself. If a higher court (an appellate court) has also examined the question, then its opinion will rule.

To find out if there are written court decisions that interpret a particular statute or ordinance, look in an "annotated code" (discussed in "Where to Find State, Local, and Federal Laws," above). If you find a case that seems to answer your question, it's crucial to make sure that the decision you're reading is still "good law"—that a more recent opinion from a higher court has not reached a different conclusion. To make sure that you are relying on the latest and highest judicial pronouncement, you must use the library research tool known as *Shepard's*. Nolo's *Legal Research: How to Find & Understand the Law,* by Stephen Elias and the Editors of Nolo, has a good, easy-to-follow explanation of how to use the *Shepard's* system to expand and update your research.

Court Decisions That Make Law

Many laws that govern the way you must conduct your business do not even have an initial starting point in a statute or ordinance. These laws are entirely court-made, and are known as "common" law. An example is the implied warranty of habitability, which is court-made in many states.

Researching common law is more difficult than statutory law, because you do not have the launching pad of a statute or ordinance. With a little perseverance, however, you can certainly find your way to the cases that have developed and explained the legal concept you wish to understand. A good beginning is to ask the librarian for any "practice guides" written in the field of landlord-tenant law. These are outlines of the law, written for lawyers, that are kept up to date and are designed to get you quickly to key information. Because they are

so popular and easy to use, they are usually kept behind the reference counter and cannot be checked out. More sophisticated research techniques, such as using a set of books called "Words and Phrases" (which sends you to cases based on key words), are explained in the book *Legal Research,* mentioned above.

How to Read a Case Citation

If a case you have found in an annotated code (or through a practice guide or key word search) looks important, you may want to read the opinion. You'll need the title of the case and its "citation," which is like an address for the set of books, volume, and page where the case can be found. Ask the law librarian for help.

Although it may look about as decipherable as hieroglyphics, once understood, a case citation gives lots of useful information in a small space. It tells you the names of the people or companies involved, the volume of the reporter (series of books) in which the case is published, the page number on which it begins, and the year in which the case was decided.

> **EXAMPLE:** *Smith Realty Co. v. Jones,* 123 N.Y.S.2d 456 (1994). Smith and Jones are the names of the parties having the legal dispute. The case is reported in volume 123 of the New York Supplement, Second Series, beginning on page 456; the court issued the decision in 1994.

Most states publish their own official state reports. All published state court decisions are also included in seven regional reporters. There are also special reports for U.S. Supreme Court and other federal court decisions.

State Landlord-Tenant Law Charts

How to Use the State Landlord-Tenant Law Charts

The State Landlord-Tenant Law Charts are comprehensive, 50-state charts that give you two kinds of information:

- citations for key statutes and cases, which you can use if you want to read the law yourself or look for more information (see the legal research discussion in Chapter 18), and
- the state rules themselves, such as notice periods and deposit limits—in other words, what the statutes and cases say.

When you're looking for information for your state, simply find your state along the left-hand list on the chart, and read to the right—you'll see the statute or case, and the rule.

A few subjects, such as the legality of nonrefundable fees, are addressed by only a handful of states. For these issues, we've put minicharts in chapters throughout the book. These charts, which list only the states that address the issue, include the following:

- States That Allow Nonrefundable Fees (Chapter 4)
- States That Require a Landlord-Tenant Checklist (Chapter 7)

State Landlord-Tenant Statutes

Here are some of the key statutes pertaining to landlord-tenant law in each state. In some states, important legal principles are contained in court opinions, not codes or statutes. Court-made law and rent stabilization—rent control—laws and regulations are not reflected in this chart.

State	Statute	State	Statute
Alabama	Ala. Code §§ 35-9-1 to 35-9-100; 35-9A-101 to 35-9A-603	Missouri	Mo. Rev. Stat. §§ 441.005 to 441.880; §§ 535.010 to 535.300
Alaska	Alaska Stat. §§ 34.03.010 to 34.03.380	Montana	Mont. Code Ann. §§ 70-24-101 to 70-27-117
Arizona	Ariz. Rev. Stat. Ann. §§ 12-1171 to 12-1183; 33-1301 to 33-1381; 33-301 to 33-381	Nebraska	Neb. Rev. Stat. §§ 76-1401 to 76-1449
Arkansas	Ark. Code Ann. §§ 18-16-102 to 18-16-306; 18-16-501 to 18-16-509; 18-17-101 to 18-17-913	Nevada	Nev. Rev. Stat. Ann. §§ 118A.010 to 118A.530; 40.215 to 40.425
California	Cal. Civ. Code §§ 1925 to 1954.1; 1961 to 1995.340	New Hampshire	N.H. Rev. Stat. Ann. §§ 540:1 to 540:29; 540-A:1 to 540-A:8; 540-B:1 to 540-B:10
Colorado	Colo. Rev. Stat. §§ 38-12-101 to 38-12-104; 38-12-301 to 38-12-302; 38-12-501 to 38-12-511; 13-40-101 to 13-40-123	New Jersey	N.J. Stat. Ann. §§ 46:8-1 to 46:8-50; 2A:42-1 to 42-96
		New Mexico	N.M. Stat. Ann. §§ 47-8-1 to 47-8-51
Connecticut	Conn. Gen. Stat. Ann. §§ 47a-1 to 47a-74	New York	N.Y. Real Prop. Law §§ 220 to 238; Real Prop. Acts §§ 701 to 853; Mult. Dwell. Law (all); Mult. Res. Law (all); Gen. Oblig. Law §§ 7-101 to 7-109
Delaware	Del. Code Ann. tit. 25, §§ 5101 to 5907		
Dist. of Columbia	D.C. Code Ann. §§ 42-3201 to 42-3610; D.C. Mun. Regs., tit. 14, §§ 300 to 311	North Carolina	N.C. Gen. Stat. §§ 42-1 to 42-14.2; 42-25.6 to 42-76
Florida	Fla. Stat. Ann. §§ 83.40 to 83.682	North Dakota	N.D. Cent. Code §§ 47-16-01 to 47-16-41
Georgia	Ga. Code Ann. §§ 44-7-1 to 44-7-81	Ohio	Ohio Rev. Code Ann. §§ 5321.01 to 5321.19
Hawaii	Haw. Rev. Stat. §§ 521-1 to 521-82	Oklahoma	Okla. Stat. Ann. tit. 41, §§ 101 to 136
Idaho	Idaho Code §§ 6-301 to 6-324; §§ 55-208 to 55-308	Oregon	Ore. Rev. Stat. §§ 90.100 to 91.225
Illinois	735 Ill. Comp. Stat. §§ 5/9-201 to 321 & 765 Ill. Comp. Stat. §§ 705/0.01 to 742/30	Pennsylvania	68 Pa. Cons. Stat. Ann. §§ 250.101 to 399.18
		Rhode Island	R.I. Gen. Laws §§ 34-18-1 to 34-18-57
Indiana	Ind. Code Ann. §§ 32-31-1-1 to 32-31-9-15	South Carolina	S.C. Code Ann. §§ 27-40-10 to 27-40-940
Iowa	Iowa Code Ann. §§ 562A.1 to 562A.37	South Dakota	S.D. Codified Laws Ann. §§ 43-32-1 to 43-32-32
Kansas	Kan. Stat. Ann. §§ 58-2501 to 58-2573	Tennessee	Tenn. Code Ann. §§ 66-28-101 to 66-28-521
Kentucky	Ky. Rev. Stat. Ann. §§ 383.010 to 383.715	Texas	Tex. Prop. Code Ann. §§ 91.001 to 92.355
Louisiana	La. Rev. Stat. Ann. §§ 9:3251 to 9:3261; La. Civ. Code Ann. art. 2668 to 2729	Utah	Utah Code Ann. §§ 57-17-1 to 57-17-5, 57-22-1 to 57-22-7
Maine	Me. Rev. Stat. Ann. tit. 14, §§ 6000 to 6046	Vermont	Vt. Stat. Ann. tit. 9, §§ 4451 to 4469a
Maryland	Md. Code Ann. [Real Prop.] §§ 8-101 to 8-604	Virginia	Va. Code Ann. §§ 55-217 to 55-248.40
Massachusetts	Mass. Gen. Laws Ann. ch. 186, §§ 1A to 29; ch. 186a, §§ 1 to 6	Washington	Wash. Rev. Code Ann. §§ 59.04.010 to 59.18.912
		West Virginia	W.Va. Code §§ 37-6-1 to 37-6A-6
Michigan	Mich. Comp. Laws §§ 554.131 to 554.201; 554.601 to 554.641	Wisconsin	Wis. Stat. Ann. §§ 704.01 to 704.95; Wis. Admin. Code ATCP §§ 134.01 to 134.10
Minnesota	Minn. Stat. Ann. §§ 504B.001 to 504B.471	Wyoming	Wyo. Stat. §§ 1-21-1201 to 1-21-1211; 34-2-128 to 34-2-129
Mississippi	Miss. Code Ann. §§ 89-7-1 to 89-8-29		

State Rent Rules

Here are citations for statutes that set out rent rules in each state. When a state has no statute, the space is left blank. See the "Notice Required to Change or Terminate a Month-to-Month Tenancy" chart in this appendix for citations to raising rent.

State	When Rent Is Due	Grace Period	Where Rent Is Due	Late Fees
Alabama	Ala. Code § 35-9A-161 (c)		Ala. Code § 35-9A-161 (c)	
Alaska	Alaska Stat. § 34.03.020(c)		Alaska Stat. § 34.03.020(c)	
Arizona	Ariz. Rev. Stat. Ann. §§ 33-1314(C), 33-1368(B)		Ariz. Rev. Stat. Ann. § 33-1314(C)	Ariz. Rev. Stat. Ann. § 33-1368(B)[1]
Arkansas	Ark. Code Ann. § 18-17-401	Ark. Code Ann. §§ 18-17-701 & 18-17-901	Ark. Code Ann. § 18-17-401	
California	Cal. Civil Code § 1947		Cal. Civil Code § 1962	*Orozco v. Casimiro*, 121 Cal. App.4th Supp. 7 (2004) [2]
Colorado				
Connecticut	Conn. Gen. Stat. Ann. § 47a-3a	Conn. Gen. Stat. Ann. § 47a-15a	Conn. Gen. Stat. Ann. § 47a-3a	Conn. Gen. Stat. Ann. §§ 47a-4(a)(8), 47a-15a [3]
Delaware	Del. Code Ann. tit. 25, § 5501(b)		Del. Code Ann. tit. 25, § 5501(b)	Del. Code Ann. tit. 25, § 5501(d) [4]
D.C.				
Florida	Fla. Stat. Ann. § 83.46(1)			
Georgia				
Hawaii	Haw. Rev. Stat. § 521-21(b)		Haw. Rev. Stat. § 521-21(b)	
Idaho				
Illinois	735 Ill. Comp. Stat. Ann. § 5/9-218		735 Ill. Comp. Stat. Ann. § 5/9-218	
Indiana	*Watson v. Penn*, 108 Ind. 21 (1886), 8 N.E. 636 (1886)			
Iowa	Iowa Code Ann. § 562A.9(3)		Iowa Code Ann. § 562A.9(3)	Iowa Code Ann. § 562A.9 [5]
Kansas	Kan. Stat. Ann. § 58-2545(c)		Kan. Stat. Ann. § 58-2545(c)	
Kentucky	Ky. Rev. Stat. Ann. § 383.565(2)		Ky. Rev. Stat. Ann. § 383.565(2)	
Louisiana	La. Civ. Code Ann. art. 2703		La. Civ. Code Ann. art. 2703	
Maine		Me. Rev. Stat. Ann. tit. 14, § 6028		Me. Rev. Stat. Ann. tit. 14, § 6028 [6]
Maryland				Md. Code Ann. [Real Prop.] § 8-208(d)(3) [7]
Massachusetts		Mass. Gen. Laws Ann. ch. 186, § 15B(1)(c); ch. 239, § 8A		Mass. Gen. Laws Ann. ch. 186, § 15B(1)(c) [8]
Michigan	*Hilsendegen v. Scheich*, 21 N.W. 894 (1885)			
Minnesota				Minn. Stat. Ann. § 504B.177 [9]
Mississippi				

[1] Late fees must be set forth in a written rental agreement and be reasonable. (Arizona)

[2] Late fees will be enforced only if specified language is included in a written lease or rental agreement. (California)

[3] Landlords may not charge a late fee until 9 days after rent is due. (Connecticut)

[4] To charge a late fee, landlord must maintain an office in the county where the rental unit is located at which tenants can pay rent. If a landlord doesn't have a local office for this purpose, tenant has 3 extra days (beyond the due date) to pay rent before the landlord can charge a late fee. Late fee cannot exceed 5% of rent and cannot be imposed until the rent is more than 5 days late. (Delaware)

[5] When rent is $700 per month or less, late fees cannot exceed $12 per day, or a total amount of $60 per month; when rent is more than $700 per month, fees cannot exceed $20 per day or a total amount of $100 per month. (Iowa)

[6] Late fees cannot exceed 4% of the amount due for 30 days. Landlord must notify tenants, in writing, of any late fee at the start of the tenancy, and cannot impose it until rent is 15 days late. (Maine)

[7] Late fees cannot exceed 5% of the rent due. (Maryland)

[8] Late fees, including interest on late rent, may not be imposed until the rent is 30 days late. (Massachusetts)

[9] Late fee policy must be agreed to in writing, and may not exceed 8% of the overdue rent payment. The "due date" for late fee purposes does not include a date earlier than the usual rent due date, by which date a tenant earns a discount. (Minnesota)

State Rent Rules (continued)

State	When Rent Is Due	Grace Period	Where Rent Is Due	Late Fees
Missouri	Mo. Rev. Stat. § 535.060			
Montana	Mont. Code Ann. § 70-24-201(2)(c)		Mont. Code Ann. § 70-24-201(2)(b)	
Nebraska	Neb. Rev. Stat. § 76-1414(3)		Neb. Rev. Stat. § 76-1414(3)	
Nevada	Nev. Rev. Stat. Ann. § 118A.210		Nev. Rev. Stat. Ann. § 118A.210	Nev. Rev. Stat. Ann. § 118A.200(3)(g), (4)(c) [10]
New Hampshire				
New Jersey		N.J. Stat. Ann. § 2A:42-6.1	N.J. Stat. Ann. § 2A:42-6.1	N.J. Stat. Ann. § 2A:42-6.1 [11]
New Mexico	N.M. Stat. Ann. § 47-8-15(B)		N.M. Stat. Ann. § 47-8-15(B)	N.M. Stat. Ann. § 47-8-15(D) [12]
New York				
North Carolina		N.C. Gen Stat. § 42-46		N.C. Gen. Stat. § 42-46 [13]
North Dakota	N.D. Cent. Code § 47-16-20			
Ohio				
Oklahoma	Okla. Stat. Ann. tit. 41, § 109	Okla. Stat. Ann. tit. 41, § 132(B)	Okla. Stat. Ann. tit. 41, § 109	*Sun Ridge Investors, Ltd. v. Parker*, 956 P.2d 876 (1998) [14]
Oregon	Ore. Rev. Stat. § 90.220	Ore. Rev. Stat. § 90.260	Ore. Rev. Stat. § 90.220	Ore. Rev. Stat. § 90.260 [15]
Pennsylvania				
Rhode Island	R.I. Gen. Laws § 34-18-15(c)	R.I. Gen. Laws § 34-18-35	R.I. Gen. Laws § 34-18-15(c)	
South Carolina	S.C. Code Ann. § 27-40-310(c)		S.C. Code Ann. § 27-40-310(c)	
South Dakota	S.D. Codified Laws Ann. § 43-32-12			
Tennessee	Tenn. Code Ann. § 66-28-201(c)	Tenn. Code Ann. § 66-28-201(d)	Tenn. Code Ann. § 66-28-201(c)	Tenn. Code Ann. § 66-28-201(d) [16]
Texas		Tex. Prop. Code Ann. § 92.019		Tex. Prop. Code Ann. § 92.019 [17]
Utah				
Vermont	Vt. Stat. Ann. tit. 9, § 4455			
Virginia	Va. Code Ann. § 55-248.7(C)		Va. Code Ann. § 55-248.7(C)	
Washington				
West Virginia				
Wisconsin				
Wyoming				

[10] A court will presume that there is no late fee provision unless it is included in a written rental agreement, but the landlord can offer evidence to overcome that presumption. (Nevada)

[11] Landlord must wait 5 days before charging a late fee, but only when the premises are rented or leased by senior citizens receiving Social Security Old Age Pensions, Railroad Retirement Pensions, or other governmental pensions in lieu of Social Security Old Age Pensions; or when rented by recipients of Social Security Disability Benefits, Supplemental Security Income, or benefits under Work First New Jersey. (New Jersey)

[12] Late fee policy must be in the lease or rental agreement and may not exceed 10% of the rent specified per rental period. Landlord must notify the tenant of the landlord's intent to impose the charge no later than the last day of the next rental period immediately following the period in which the default occurred. (New Mexico)

[13] Late fee when rent is due monthly cannot be higher than $15 or 5% of the rental payment, whichever is greater (when rent is due weekly, may not be higher than $4.00 or 5% of the rent, whichever is greater); and may not be imposed until the rent is 5 days late. A late fee may be imposed only one time for each late rental payment. A late fee for a specific late rental payment may not be deducted from a subsequent rental payment so as to cause the subsequent rental payment to be in default. (North Carolina)

[14] Preset late fees are invalid. (Oklahoma)

[15] Landlord must wait 4 days after the rent due date before imposing a late fee, and must disclose the late fee policy in the rental agreement. A flat fee must be "reasonable." A daily late fee may not be more than 6% of a reasonable flat fee, and cannot add up to more than 5% of the monthly rent. (Oregon)

[16] Landlord can't charge a late fee until the rent is 5 days late (the day rent is due is counted as the first day). If day five is a Sunday or legal holiday, landlord cannot impose a fee if the rent is paid on the next business day. Fee can't exceed 10% of the amount past due. (Tennessee)

[17] Late fee provision must be included in a written lease and cannot be imposed until the rent remains unpaid one full day after the date it is due. The fee is valid only if it is a reasonable estimate of uncertain damages to the landlord that are incapable of precise calculation. Landlord may charge an initial fee and a daily fee for each day the rent is late. (Texas)

State Rules on Notice Required to Change or Terminate a Month-to-Month Tenancy

Except where noted, the amount of notice a landlord must give to increase rent or change another term of the rental agreement in a month-to-month tenancy is the same as that required to end a month-to-month tenancy. Be sure to check state and local rent control laws, which may have different notice requirements.

State	Tenant	Landlord	Statute	Comments
Alabama	30 days	30 days	Ala. Code § 35-9A-441	No state statute on the amount of notice required to change rent or other terms
Alaska	30 days	30 days	Alaska Stat. § 34.03.290(b)	
Arizona	30 days	30 days	Ariz. Rev. Stat. Ann. § 33-1375	
Arkansas	30 days	30 days	Ark. Code Ann. § 18-17-104	No state statute on the amount of notice required to change rent or other terms
California	30 days	30 or 60 days	Cal. Civ. Code § 1946; Cal. Civ. Code § 827a	30 days to change rental terms, but if landlord is raising the rent, tenant gets 60 days' notice if the sum of this and all prior rent increases during the previous 12 months is more than 10% of the lowest rent charged during that time. 60 days to terminate (landlord), 30 days (tenant).
Colorado	7 days	7 days	Colo. Rev. Stat. § 13-40-107	
Connecticut		3 days	Conn. Gen. Stat. Ann. § 47a-23	Landlord must provide 3 days' notice to terminate tenancy. Landlord is not required to give a particular amount of notice of a proposed rent increase unless prior notice was previously agreed upon.
Delaware	60 days	60 days	Del. Code Ann. tit. 25, §§ 5106, 5107	After receiving notice of landlord's proposed change of terms, tenant has 15 days to terminate tenancy. Otherwise, changes will take effect as announced.
District of Columbia	30 days	30 days	D.C. Code Ann. § 42-3202	No state statute on the amount of notice required to change rent or other terms
Florida	15 days	15 days	Fla. Stat. Ann. § 83.57	No state statute on the amount of notice required to change rent or other terms
Georgia	30 days	60 days	Ga. Code Ann. §§ 44-7-6 & 44-7-7	No state statute on the amount of notice required to change rent or other terms
Hawaii	28 days	45 days	Haw. Rev. Stat. §§ 521-71, 521-21(d)	
Idaho	One month	One month	Idaho Code §§ 55-208, 55-307	Landlords must provide 15 days' notice to increase rent or change tenancy.
Illinois	30 days	30 days	735 Ill. Comp. Stat. § 5/9-207	
Indiana	One month	One month	Ind. Code Ann. §§ 32-31-1-1, 32-31-5-4	Unless agreement states otherwise, landlord must give 30 days' written notice to modify written rental agreement.
Iowa	30 days	30 days	Iowa Code Ann. §§ 562A.34, 562A.13(5)	To end or change a month-to-month agreement, landlord must give written notice at least 30 days before the next time rent is due (not including any grace period).
Kansas	30 days	30 days	Kan. Stat. Ann. § 58-2570	No state statute on the amount of notice required to change rent or other terms
Kentucky	30 days	30 days	Ky. Rev. Stat. Ann. § 383.695	

State Rules on Notice Required to Change or Terminate a Month-to-Month Tenancy (continued)

State	Tenant	Landlord	Statute	Comments
Louisiana	10 days	10 days	La. Civ. Code Art. 2728	No state statute on the amount of notice required to change rent or other terms
Maine	30 days	30 days	Me. Rev. Stat. Ann. tit. 14 §§ 6002, 6015	Landlord must provide 45 days' notice to increase rent.
Maryland	One month	One month	Md. Code Ann. [Real Prop.] § 8-402(b)(3), (b)(4)	Two months' notice required in Montgomery County (single-family rentals excepted) and Baltimore City.
Massachusetts	See comments	See comments	Mass. Gen. Laws Ann. ch. 186, § 12	Interval between days of payment or 30 days, whichever is longer
Michigan	One month	One month	Mich. Comp. Laws § 554.134	
Minnesota	See comments	See comments	Minn. Stat. Ann. § 504B.135	For terminations, interval between time rent is due or three months, whichever is less; no state statute on the amount of notice required to change rent or other terms
Mississippi	30 days	30 days	Miss. Code Ann. § 89-8-19	No state statute on the amount of notice required to change rent or other terms
Missouri	One month	One month	Mo. Rev. Stat. § 441.060	No state statute on the amount of notice required to change rent or other terms
Montana	30 days	30 days	Mont. Code Ann. §§ 70-24-441, 70-26-109	Landlord may change terms of tenancy with 15 days' notice.
Nebraska	30 days	30 days	Neb. Rev. Stat. § 76-1437	No state statute on the amount of notice required to change rent or other terms
Nevada	30 days	30 days	Nev. Rev. Stat. Ann. §§ 40.251, 118A.300	Landlords must provide 45 days' notice to increase rent. Tenants 60 years old or older, or physically or mentally disabled, may request an additional 30 days' possession, but only if they have complied with basic tenant obligations as set forth in Nev. Rev. Stat. § 118A (termination notices must include this information).
New Hampshire	30 days	30 days	N.H. Rev. Stat. Ann. §§ 540:2, 540:3	Landlord may terminate only for just cause.
New Jersey	One month	One month	N.J. Stat. Ann. § 2A:18-56	Landlord may terminate only for just cause.
New Mexico	30 days	30 days	N.M. Stat. Ann. §§ 47-8-37, 47-8-15(F)	Landlord must deliver rent increase notice at least 30 days before rent due date.
New York	One month	One month	N.Y. Real Prop. Law § 232-b	No state statute on the amount of notice required to change rent or other terms
North Carolina	7 days	7 days	N.C. Gen. Stat. § 42-14	No state statute on the amount of notice required to change rent or other terms
North Dakota	30 days	30 days	N.D. Cent. Code §§ 47-16-15, 47-16-07	Tenant may terminate with 25 days' notice if landlord has changed the terms of the lease.
Ohio	30 days	30 days	Ohio Rev. Code Ann. § 5321.17	No state statute on the amount of notice required to change rent or other terms
Oklahoma	30 days	30 days	Okla. Stat. Ann. tit. 41, § 111	No state statute on the amount of notice required to change rent or other terms

State Rules on Notice Required to Change or Terminate a Month-to-Month Tenancy (continued)

State	Tenant	Landlord	Statute	Comments
Oregon	30 days or 72 hours (lack of bedroom exit only)	30 or 60 days	Ore. Rev. Stat. §§ 91.070; 90.427	No state statute on the amount of notice required to change rent or other terms. To terminate, 30 days for occupancies of one year or less; 60 days for occupancies of more than one year (but only 30 days if the property is sold and other conditions are met). Tenant may terminate on 72 hours' notice if landlord's failure to provide proper bedroom emergency exit, properly noticed, has not been corrected. Temporary occupants are not entitled to notice (Ore. Rev. Stat. § 90.275).
Pennsylvania			No statute	
Rhode Island	30 days	30 days	R.I. Gen. Laws §§ 34-18-16.1, 34-18-37	Landlord must provide 30 days' notice to increase rent.
South Carolina	30 days	30 days	S.C. Code Ann. § 27-40-770	No state statute on the amount of notice required to change rent or other terms
South Dakota	One month	One month	S.D. Codified Laws Ann. §§ 43-32-13, 43-8-8	If tenant (or spouse or minor child) is on active duty in the military, landlord must give two months' notice, in the absence of tenant misconduct, sale of the property, or passing of the property into the landlord's estate.
Tennessee	30 days	30 days	Tenn. Code Ann. § 66-28-512	No state statute on the amount of notice required to change rent or other terms
Texas	One month	One month	Tex. Prop. Code Ann. § 91.001	Landlord and tenant may agree in writing to different notice periods, or none at all. No state statute on the amount of notice required to change rent or other terms
Utah		15 days	Utah Code Ann. § 78B-6-802	No state statute on the amount of notice required to change rent or other terms
Vermont	One rental period, unless written lease says otherwise	30 days	Vt. Code Ann. tit. 9, §§ 4467, 4456(d)	If there is no written rental agreement, for tenants who have continuously resided in the unit for two years or less, 60 days' notice to terminate; for those who have resided longer than two years, 90 days. If there is a written rental agreement, for tenants who have lived continuously in the unit for two years or less, 30 days; for those who have lived there longer than two years, 60 days.
Virginia	30 days	30 days	Va. Code Ann. §§ 55-248.37, 55-248.7	Rental agreement may provide for a different notice period. No state statute on the amount of notice required to change rent or other terms, but landlord must abide by notice provisions in the rental agreement, if any, and tenant must consent in writing to any change.
Washington	20 days	20 days	Wash. Rev. Code Ann. §§ 59.18.200, 59.18.140	Landlord must give 30 days' notice to change rent or other lease terms.
West Virginia	One month	One month	W.Va. Code § 37-6-5	No state statute on the amount of notice required to change rent or other terms
Wisconsin	28 days	28 days	Wis. Stat. Ann. § 704.19	No state statute on the amount of notice required to change rent or other terms
Wyoming			No statute	

State Security Deposit Rules

Here are the statutes and rules that govern a landlord's collection and retention of security deposits. Many states require landlords to disclose, at or near the time they collect the deposit, information about how deposits may be used, as noted in the Disclosure or Requirement section. Required disclosures of other issues, such as a property's history of flooding, are in the chart, "Required Landlord Disclosures."

Alabama

Ala. Code § 35-9A-201

Exemption: Security deposit rules do not apply to a resident purchaser under a contract of sale (but do apply to a resident who has an option to buy), nor to the continuation of occupancy by the seller or a member of the seller's family for a period of not more than 36 months after the sale of a dwelling unit or the property of which it is a part.

Limit: One month's rent, except for pet deposits, deposits to cover undoing tenant's alterations, deposits to cover tenant activities that pose increased liability risks.

Deadline for Landlord to Itemize and Return Deposit: 60 days after termination of tenancy and delivery of possession.

Alaska

Alaska Stat. § 34.03.070

Limit: Two months' rent, unless rent exceeds $2,000 per month. Landlord may ask for an additional month's rent as deposit for a pet that is not a service animal, but may use it only to remedy pet damage.

Disclosure or Requirement: Orally or in writing, landlord must disclose the conditions under which landlord may withhold all or part of the deposit.

Separate Account: Required.

Advance notice of deduction: Not required.

Deadline for Landlord to Itemize and Return Deposit: 14 days if the tenant gives proper notice to terminate tenancy; 30 days if the tenant does not give proper notice or if landlord has deducted amounts needed to remedy damage caused by tenant's failure to maintain the property (Alaska Stat. § 34.03.120).

Arizona

Ariz. Rev. Stat. Ann. § 33-1321

Exemption: Excludes, among others, occupancy under a contract of sale of a dwelling unit or the property of which it is a part, if the occupant is the purchaser or a person who succeeds to his interest; occupancy by an employee of a landlord as a manager or custodian whose right to occupancy is conditional upon employment in and about the premises.

Limit: One and one-half months' rent.

Disclosure or Requirement: If landlord collects a nonrefundable fee, its purpose must be stated in writing. All fees not designated as nonrefundable are refundable.

Advance notice of deduction: Not required.

Deadline for Landlord to Itemize and Return Deposit: 14 days, tenant has the right to be present at final inspection.

Arkansas

Ark. Code Ann. §§ 18-16-303 to 18-16-305

Exemption: Excludes, among others, occupancy under a contract of sale of a dwelling unit or the property of which it is a part, if the occupant is the purchaser or a person who succeeds to his or her interest; occupancy by an employee of a landlord whose right to occupancy is conditional upon employment in and about the premises; and landlord who owns five or fewer rental units, unless these units are managed by a third party for a fee.

Limit: Two months' rent.

Advance notice of deduction: Not required.

Deadline for Landlord to Itemize and Return Deposit: 60 days.

California

Cal. Civ. Code §§ 1950.5, 1940.5(g)

Limit: Two months' rent (unfurnished); 3 months' rent (furnished). Add extra one-half month's rent for waterbed.

Advance notice of deduction: Required.

Deadline for Landlord to Itemize and Return Deposit: 21 days.

State Security Deposit Rules (continued)

Colorado

Colo. Rev. Stat. §§ 38-12-102 to 38-12-104

Limit: No statutory limit.

Advance notice of deduction: Not required.

Deadline for Landlord to Itemize and Return Deposit:
One month, unless lease agreement specifies longer period of time (which may be no more than 60 days); 72 hours (not counting weekends or holidays) if a hazardous condition involving gas equipment requires tenant to vacate.

Connecticut

Conn. Gen. Stat. Ann. § 47a-21

Exemption: Excludes, among others, occupancy under a contract of sale of a dwelling unit or the property of which the unit is a part, if the occupant is the purchaser or a person who succeeds to his interest; and occupancy by a personal care assistant or other person who is employed by a person with a disability to assist and support such disabled person with daily living activities or housekeeping chores and is provided dwelling space in the personal residence of such disabled person as a benefit or condition of employment.

Limit: Two months' rent (tenant under 62 years of age); one month's rent (tenant 62 years of age or older).

Separate Account: Required.

Interest Payment: Interest payments must be made annually (or credited toward rent, at the landlord's option) and no later than 30 days after termination of tenancy. The interest rate must be equal to the average rate paid on savings deposits by insured commercial banks, rounded to the nearest 0.1%, as published by the Federal Reserve Board Bulletin.

Advance notice of deduction: Not required.

Deadline for Landlord to Itemize and Return Deposit:
30 days, or within 15 days of receiving tenant's forwarding address, whichever is later.

Delaware

Del. Code Ann. tit. 25, §§ 5514, 5311

Limit: One month's rent on leases for one year or more; no limit for month-to-month rental agreements (may require additional pet deposit of up to one month's rent). No limit for rental of furnished units. Tenant may

offer to supply a surety bond in lieu of or in conjunction with a deposit, which landlord may elect to receive.

Separate Account: Required. Orally or in writing, the landlord must disclose to the tenant the location of the security deposit account.

Advance notice of deduction: Not required.

Deadline for Landlord to Itemize and Return Deposit:
20 days.

District of Columbia

D.C. Code Ann. § 42-3502.17; D.C. Mun. Regs. tit. 14, §§ 308 to 310

Exemption: Tenants in rent-stabilized units as of July 17, 1985 cannot be asked to pay a deposit.

Limit: One month's rent.

Disclosure or Requirement: In the lease, rental agreement, or receipt, landlord must state the terms and conditions under which the security deposit was collected (to secure tenant's obligations under the lease or rental agreement).

Separate Account: Required.

Interest Payment: Interest payments at the prevailing statement savings rate must be made at termination of tenancy.

Advance notice of deduction: Not required.

Deadline for Landlord to Itemize and Return Deposit:
45 days.

Florida

Fla. Stat. Ann. §§ 83.49, 83.43 (12)

Exemption: Occupancy under a contract of sale of a dwelling unit or the property of which it is a part in which the buyer has paid at least 12 months' rent or in which the buyer has paid at least 1 month's rent and a deposit of at least 5% of the purchase price of the property; cooperative properties, condominiums, and transient residencies.

Limit: No statutory limit.

Disclosure or Requirement: Within 30 days of receiving the security deposit, the landlord must disclose in writing whether it will be held in an interest- or non-interest-bearing account; the name of the account depository; and the rate and time of interest payments. Landlord who collects a deposit must include in the

State Security Deposit Rules (continued)

lease the disclosure statement contained in Florida Statutes § 83.49.

Separate Account: Landlord may post a security bond securing all tenants' deposits instead.

Interest Payment: Interest payments, if any (account need not be interest-bearing) must be made annually and at termination of tenancy. However, no interest is due a tenant who wrongfully terminates the tenancy before the end of the rental term.

Advance notice of deduction: Required.

Deadline for Landlord to Itemize and Return Deposit: 15 to 60 days depending on whether tenant disputes deductions.

Georgia

Ga. Code Ann. §§ 44-7-30 to 44-7-37

Exemption: Landlord who owns ten or fewer rental units, unless these units are managed by an outside party, need not supply written list of preexisting damage, or place deposit in an escrow account. Rules for returning the deposit still apply.

Limit: No statutory limit.

Disclosure or Requirement: Landlord must give tenant a written list of preexisting damage to the rental before collecting a security deposit.

Separate Account: Required. Landlord must place the deposit in an escrow account in a state or federally regulated depository, and must inform the tenant of the location of this account. Landlord may post a security bond securing all tenants' deposits instead.

Advance notice of deduction: Required.

Deadline for Landlord to Itemize and Return Deposit: One month.

Hawaii

Haw. Rev. Stat. § 521-44

Limit: One month's rent. Landlord may require an additional one month's rent as security deposit for tenants who keep a pet.

Advance notice of deduction: Not required.

Deadline for Landlord to Itemize and Return Deposit: 14 days.

Idaho

Idaho Code § 6-321

Limit: No statutory limit.

Advance notice of deduction: Not required.

Deadline for Landlord to Itemize and Return Deposit: 21 days, or up to 30 days if landlord and tenant agree.

Illinois

765 Ill. Comp. Stat. §§ 710/1, 715/2, & 715/3

Limit: No statutory limit.

Interest Payment: Landlords who rent 25 or more units in either a single building or a complex located on contiguous properties must pay interest on deposits held for more than six months. The interest rate is the rate paid for minimum deposit savings accounts by the largest commercial bank in the state, as of December 31 of the calendar year immediately preceding the start of the tenancy. Within 30 days after the end of each 12-month rental period, landlord must pay any interest that has accumulated to an amount of $5 or more, by cash or credit applied to rent due, except when the tenant is in default under the terms of the lease. Landlord must pay all interest that has accumulated and remains unpaid, regardless of the amount, upon termination of the tenancy.

Advance notice of deduction: Not required.

Deadline for Landlord to Itemize and Return Deposit: For properties with 5 or more units, 30 to 45 days, depending on whether tenant disputes deductions or if statement and receipts are furnished.

Indiana

Ind. Code Ann. §§ 32-31-3-9 to 32-31-3-19

Exemption: Does not apply to, among others, occupancy under a contract of sale of a rental unit or the property of which the rental unit is a part if the occupant is the purchaser or a person who succeeds to the purchaser's interest; and occupancy by an employee of a landlord whose right to occupancy is conditional upon employment in or about the premises. Does apply to leases signed after July 1, 2008, that contain an option to purchase.

Limit: No statutory limit.

State Security Deposit Rules (continued)

Advance notice of deduction: Not required.

Deadline for Landlord to Itemize and Return Deposit: 45 days.

Iowa

Iowa Code Ann. § 562A.12

Limit: Two months' rent.

Separate Account: Required.

Interest Payment: Interest payment, if any (account need not be interest-bearing) must be made at termination of tenancy. Interest earned during first five years of tenancy belongs to landlord.

Advance notice of deduction: Not required.

Deadline for Landlord to Itemize and Return Deposit: 30 days.

Kansas

Kan. Stat. Ann. §§ 58-2550, 58-2548

Exemption: Excludes, among others, occupancy under a contract of sale of a dwelling unit or the property of which it is a part, if the occupant is the purchaser or a person who succeeds to the purchaser's interest; and occupancy by an employee of a landlord whose right to occupancy is conditional upon employment in and about the premises.

Limit: One month's rent (unfurnished); one and one-half months' rent (furnished); for pets, add extra one-half month's rent.

Advance notice of deduction: Not required.

Deadline for Landlord to Itemize and Return Deposit: 30 days.

Kentucky

Ky. Rev. Stat. Ann. § 383.580

Limit: No statutory limit.

Disclosure or Requirement: Orally or in writing, landlord must disclose where the security deposit is being held and the account number.

Separate Account: Required.

Advance notice of deduction: Required.

Deadline for Landlord to Itemize and Return Deposit: 30 to 60 days depending on whether tenant disputes deductions.

Louisiana

La. Rev. Stat. Ann. § 9:3251

Limit: No statutory limit.

Advance notice of deduction: Not required.

Deadline for Landlord to Itemize and Return Deposit: One month.

Maine

Me. Rev. Stat. Ann. tit. 14, §§ 6031 to 6038

Exemption: Entire security deposit law does not apply to rental unit that is part of structure with five or fewer units, one of which is occupied by landlord.

Limit: Two months' rent.

Disclosure or Requirement: Upon request by the tenant, landlord must disclose orally or in writing the account number and the name of the institution where the security deposit is being held.

Separate Account: Required.

Advance notice of deduction: Not required.

Deadline for Landlord to Itemize and Return Deposit: 30 days (if written rental agreement) or 21 days (if tenancy at will).

Maryland

Md. Code Ann. [Real Prop.] § 8-203, § 8-203.1

Limit: Two months' rent.

Disclosure or Requirement: Landlord must provide a receipt that describes tenant's rights to move-in and move-out inspections (and to be present at each), and right to receive itemization of deposit deductions and balance, if any; and penalties for landlord's failure to comply. Landlord may include this information in the lease.

Separate Account: Required. Landlord may hold all tenants' deposits in secured certificates of deposit, or in securities issued by the federal government or the State of Maryland.

Interest Payment: For security deposits of $50 or more, when landlord has held the deposit for at least six months: Within 45 days of termination of tenancy, interest must be paid at the daily U.S. Treasury yield curve rate for 1 year, as of the first business day of each year, or 1.5% a year, whichever is greater, less any damages rightfully withheld. Interest accrues monthly but is not compounded, and no interest is due for any

State Security Deposit Rules (continued)

period less than one month. (See the Department of Housing and Community Development website for a calculator.) Deposit must be held in a Maryland banking institution.

Advance notice of deduction: Required.

Deadline for Landlord to Itemize and Return Deposit: 45 days.

Massachusetts

Mass. Gen. Laws Ann. ch. 186, § 15B

Limit: One month's rent.

Disclosure or Requirement: At the time of receiving a security deposit, landlord must furnish a receipt indicating the amount of the deposit; the name of the person receiving it, and, if received by a property manager, the name of the lessor for whom the security deposit is received; the date on which it is received; and a description of the premises leased or rented. The receipt must be signed by the person receiving the security deposit.

Separate Account: Required. Within 30 days of receiving security deposit, landlord must disclose the name and location of the bank in which the security deposit has been deposited, and the amount and account number of the deposit.

Interest Payment: Landlord must pay tenant 5% interest per year or the amount received from the bank (which must be in Massachusetts) that holds the deposit. Interest should be paid yearly, and within 30 days of termination date. Interest will not accrue for the last month for which rent was paid in advance.

Advance notice of deduction: Not required.

Deadline for Landlord to Itemize and Return Deposit: 30 days.

Michigan

Mich. Comp. Laws §§ 554.602 to 554.616

Limit: One and one-half months' rent.

Disclosure or Requirement: Within 14 days of tenant's taking possession of the rental, landlord must furnish in writing the landlord's name and address for receipt of communications, the name and address of the financial institution or surety where the deposit will be held, and the tenant's obligation to provide in writing a forwarding mailing address to the landlord within 4 days after termination of occupancy. The notice shall include the following statement in 12-point boldface type that is at least 4 points larger than the body of the notice or lease agreement: "You must notify your landlord in writing within 4 days after you move of a forwarding address where you can be reached and where you will receive mail; otherwise your landlord shall be relieved of sending you an itemized list of damages and the penalties adherent to that failure."

Separate Account: Required. Landlord must place deposits in a regulated financial institution, and may use the deposits as long as the landlord deposits with the secretary of state a cash or surety bond.

Advance notice of deduction: Required. Not a typical advance notice provision: Tenants must dispute the landlord's stated deductions within 7 days of receiving the itemized list and balance, if any, or give up any right to dispute them.

Deadline for Landlord to Itemize and Return Deposit: 30 days.

Minnesota

Minn. Stat. Ann. §§ 504B.175, 504B.178, & 504B.195

Limit: No statutory limit.

Disclosure or Requirement: Before collecting rent or a security deposit, landlord must provide a copy of all outstanding inspection orders for which a citation has been issued, pertaining to a rental unit or common area, specifying code violations that threaten the health or safety of the tenant, and all outstanding condemnation orders and declarations that the premises are unfit for human habitation. Citations for violations that do not involve threats to tenant health or safety must be summarized and posted in an obvious place. With some exceptions, landlord who has received notice of a contract for deed cancellation or notice of a mortgage foreclosure sale must so disclose before entering into a lease, accepting rent, or accepting a security deposit; and must furnish the date on which the contract cancellation period or the mortgagor's redemption period ends.

Interest Payment: Landlord must pay 1% simple, noncompounded interest per year. (Deposits collected before 8/1/03 earn interest at 3%, up to 8/1/03, then begin earning at 1%.) Any interest amount less than $1 is excluded.

State Security Deposit Rules (continued)

Advance notice of deduction: Not required.

Deadline for Landlord to Itemize and Return Deposit: Three weeks after tenant leaves and landlord receives forwarding address; five days if tenant must leave due to building condemnation.

Prelease Deposit: If landlord collects a "prelease deposit" and subsequently rents to tenant, landlord must apply the prelease deposit to the security deposit.

Mississippi

Miss. Code Ann. § 89-8-21

Limit: No statutory limit.

Advance notice of deduction: Not required.

Deadline for Landlord to Itemize and Return Deposit: 45 days.

Missouri

Mo. Ann. Stat. § 535.300

Limit: Two months' rent.

Advance notice of deduction: Not required.

Deadline for Landlord to Itemize and Return Deposit: 30 days**.**

Montana

Mont. Code Ann. §§ 70-25-101 to 70-25-206

Limit: No statutory limit**.**

Advance notice of deduction: Required. Tenant is entitled to advance notice of cleaning charges, but only if such cleaning is required as a result of tenant's negligence and is not part of the landlord's cyclical cleaning program.

Deadline for Landlord to Itemize and Return Deposit: 30 days; 10 days if no deductions.

Nebraska

Neb. Rev. Stat. § 76-1416

Limit: One month's rent (no pets); one and one-quarter months' rent (pets).

Advance notice of deduction: Not required.

Deadline for Landlord to Itemize and Return Deposit: 14 days.

Nevada

Nev. Rev. Stat. Ann. §§ 118A.240 to 118A.250

Limit: Three months' rent; if both landlord and tenant agree, tenant may use a surety bond for all or part of the deposit.

Disclosure or Requirement: Lease or rental agreement must explain the conditions under which the landlord will refund the deposit.

Advance notice of deduction: Not required.

Deadline for Landlord to Itemize and Return Deposit: 30 days.

New Hampshire

N.H. Rev. Stat. Ann. §§ 540-A:5 to 540-A:8; 540-B:10

Exemption: Entire security deposit law does not apply to landlord who leases a single-family residence and owns no other rental property, or landlord who leases rental units in an owner-occupied building of five units or fewer (exemption does not apply to any individual unit in owner-occupied building that is occupied by a person 60 years of age or older).

Limit: One month's rent or $100, whichever is greater; when landlord and tenant share facilities, no statutory limit.

Disclosure or Requirement: Unless tenant has paid the deposit by personal or bank check, or by a check issued by a government agency, landlord must provide a receipt stating the amount of the deposit and the institution where it will be held. Regardless of whether a receipt is required, landlord must inform tenant that if tenant finds any conditions in the rental in need of repair, tenant may note them on the receipt or other written instrument, and return either within five days.

Separate Account: Required. Upon request, landlord must disclose the account number, the amount on deposit, and the interest rate. Landlord may post a bond covering all deposits instead of putting deposits in a separate account.

Interest Payment: Landlord who holds a security deposit for a year or longer must pay interest at a rate equal to the rate paid on regular savings accounts in the New Hampshire bank, savings & loan, or credit union where it's deposited. If a landlord mingles security deposits in a single account, the landlord must pay the actual interest earned proportionately to each tenant. A tenant may request the interest accrued every three years, 30 days before that year's tenancy expires. The landlord must comply with the request within 15 days of the expiration of that year's tenancy.

State Security Deposit Rules (continued)

Advance notice of deduction: Not required.

Deadline for Landlord to Itemize and Return Deposit: 30 days; for shared facilities, if the deposit is more than 30 days' rent, landlord must provide written agreement acknowledging receipt and specifying when deposit will be returned—if no written agreement, 20 days after tenant vacates.

New Jersey

N.J. Stat. Ann. §§ 46:8-19, 44:8-21, 44:8-26

Exemption: Security deposit law does not apply to owner-occupied buildings with three or fewer units unless tenant gives 30 days' written notice to the landlord of the tenant's wish to invoke the law.

Limit: One and one-half months' rent. Any additional security deposit, collected annually, may be no greater than 10% of the current security deposit.

Separate Account: Required. Within 30 days of receiving the deposit and every time the landlord pays the tenant interest, landlord must disclose the name and address of the banking organization where the deposit is being held, the type of account, current rate of interest, and the amount of the deposit.

Interest Payment: Landlord with 10 or more units must invest deposits as specified by statute or place deposit in an insured money market fund account, or in another account that pays quarterly interest at a rate comparable to the money market fund. Landlords with fewer than 10 units may place deposit in an interest-bearing account in any New Jersey financial institution insured by the FDIC. All landlords may pay tenants interest earned on account annually or credit toward payment of rent due.

Advance notice of deduction: Not required.

Deadline for Landlord to Itemize and Return Deposit: 30 days; five days in case of fire, flood, condemnation, or evacuation.

New Mexico

N.M. Stat. Ann. § 47-8-18

Limit: One month's rent (for rental agreement of less than one year); no limit for leases of one year or more.

Interest Payment: Landlord who collects a deposit larger than than one month's rent on a year's lease must pay interest, on an annual basis, equal to the passbook interest.

Advance notice of deduction: Not required.

Deadline for Landlord to Itemize and Return Deposit: 30 days.

New York

N.Y. Gen. Oblig. Law §§ 7-103 to 7-108

Limit: No statutory limit for nonregulated units.

Disclosure or Requirement: If deposit is placed in a bank, landlord must disclose the name and address of the banking organization where the deposit is being held, and the amount of such deposit.

Separate Account: Statute requires that deposits not be commingled with landlord's personal assets, but does not explicitly require placement in a banking institution (however, deposits collected in buildings of six or more units must be placed in New York bank accounts).

Interest Payment: Landlord who rents out nonregulated units in buildings with five or fewer units need not pay interest. Interest must be paid at the "prevailing rate" on deposits received from tenants who rent units in buildings containing six or more units. The landlord in every rental situation may retain an administrative fee of 1% per year on the sum deposited. Interest can be subtracted from the rent, paid at the end of the year, or paid at the end of the tenancy according to the tenant's choice.

Advance notice of deduction: Not required.

Deadline for Landlord to Itemize and Return Deposit: A "reasonable time."

North Carolina

N.C. Gen. Stat. §§ 42-50 to 42-56

Exemption: Not applicable to single rooms rented on a weekly, monthly, or annual basis.

Limit: One and one-half months' rent for month-to-month rental agreements; two months' rent if term is longer than two months; may add an additional "reasonable" nonrefundable pet deposit.

Disclosure or Requirement: Within 30 days of the beginning of the lease term, landlord must disclose the name and address of the banking institution where the deposit is located.

Separate Account: Required. The landlord may, at his option, furnish a bond from an insurance company licensed to do business in the state.

State Security Deposit Rules (continued)

Advance notice of deduction: Not required.

Deadline for Landlord to Itemize and Return Deposit: 30 days; if landlord's claim against the deposit cannot be finalized within that time, landlord may send an interim accounting and a final accounting within 60 days of the tenancy's termination.

North Dakota

N.D. Cent. Code § 47-16-07.1

Limit: One month's rent. If tenant has a pet that is not a service or companion animal that tenant keeps as a reasonable accommodation under fair housing laws, an additional pet deposit of up to $2,500 or two months' rent, whichever is greater.

Separate Account: Required.

Interest Payment: Landlord must pay interest if the period of occupancy is at least nine months. Money must be held in a federally insured interest-bearing savings or checking account for benefit of the tenant. Interest must be paid upon termination of the lease.

Advance notice of deduction: Not required.

Deadline for Landlord to Itemize and Return Deposit: 30 days.

Ohio

Ohio Rev. Code Ann. § 5321.16

Limit: No statutory limit.

Interest Payment: Any deposit in excess of $50 or one month's rent, whichever is greater, must bear interest on the excess at the rate of 5% per annum if the tenant stays for six months or more. Interest must be paid annually and upon termination of tenancy.

Advance notice of deduction: Not required.

Deadline for Landlord to Itemize and Return Deposit: 30 days.

Oklahoma

Okla. Stat. Ann. tit. 41, § 115

Limit: No statutory limit.

Separate Account: Required.

Advance notice of deduction: Not required.

Deadline for Landlord to Itemize and Return Deposit: 30 days.

Oregon

Ore. Rev. Stat. § 90.300

Limit: No statutory limit. Landlord may not impose or increase deposit within first year unless parties agree to modify the rental agreement to allow for a pet or other cause, and the imposition or increase relates to that modification.

Advance notice of deduction: Not required.

Deadline for Landlord to Itemize and Return Deposit: 31 days.

Pennsylvania

68 Pa. Cons. Stat. Ann. §§ 250.511a to 250.512

Limit: Two months' rent for first year of renting; one month's rent during second and subsequent years of renting.

Disclosure or Requirement: For deposits over $100, landlord must deposit them in a federally or state-regulated institution, and give tenant the name and address of the banking institution and the amount of the deposit.

Separate Account: Required. Instead of placing deposits in a separate account, landlord may purchase a bond issued by a bonding company authorized to do business in the state.

Interest Payment: Tenant who occupies rental unit for two or more years is entitled to interest beginning with the 25th month of occupancy. Landlord must pay tenant interest (minus 1% fee) at the end of the third and subsequent years of the tenancy.

Advance notice of deduction: Not required.

Deadline for Landlord to Itemize and Return Deposit: 30 days.

Rhode Island

R.I. Gen. Laws § 34-18-19

Limit: One month's rent.

Advance notice of deduction: Not required.

Deadline for Landlord to Itemize and Return Deposit: 20 days.

South Carolina

S.C. Code Ann. § 27-40-410

Limit: No statutory limit.

State Security Deposit Rules (continued)

Advance notice of deduction: Not required.

Deadline for Landlord to Itemize and Return Deposit: 30 days.

South Dakota

S.D. Codified Laws Ann. § 43.32-6.1, § 43-32-24

Limit: One month's rent (higher deposit may be charged if special conditions pose a danger to maintenance of the premises).

Advance notice of deduction: Not required.

Deadline for Landlord to Itemize and Return Deposit: Two weeks, and must supply reasons if withholding any portion; 45 days for a written, itemized accounting, if tenant requests it.

Tennessee

Tenn. Code Ann. § 66-28-301

Exemption: Does not apply in counties having a population of less than 75,000, according to the 2010 federal census or any subsequent federal census.

Limit: No statutory limit.

Separate Account: Required. Orally or in writing, landlord must disclose the location of the separate account (but not the account number) used by landlord for the deposit.

Advance notice of deduction: Required.

Texas

Tex. Prop. Code Ann. §§ 92.101 to 92.109

Limit: No statutory limit.

Advance notice of deduction: Not required.

Deadline for Landlord to Itemize and Return Deposit: 30 days. Landlord need not refund deposit if lease requires tenant to give written notice of tenant's intention to surrender the premises.

Utah

Utah Code Ann. §§ 57-17-1 to 57-17-5

Limit: No statutory limit.

Disclosure or Requirement: For written leases or rental agreements only, if part of the deposit is nonrefundable, landlord must disclose this feature.

Advance notice of deduction: Not required.

Deadline for Landlord to Itemize and Return Deposit: 30 days.

Vermont

Vt. Stat. Ann. tit. 9, § 4461

Limit: No statutory limit.

Advance notice of deduction: Not required.

Deadline for Landlord to Itemize and Return Deposit: 14 days; 60 days if the rental is seasonal and not intended as the tenant's primary residence.

Virginia

Va. Code Ann. § 55-248.15:1

Exemption: Single-family residences are exempt where the owner(s) are natural persons or their estates who own in their own name no more than two single-family residences subject to a rental agreement. Exemption applies to the entire Virginia Residential Landlord and Tenant Act.

Limit: Two months' rent.

Deadline for Landlord to Itemize and Return Deposit: 45 days; tenant has right to be present at final inspection.

Washington

Wash. Rev. Code Ann. §§ 59.18.260 to 59.18.285

Exemption: Security deposit rules do not apply to a lease of a single-family dwelling for a year or more, or to any lease of a single-family dwelling containing a bona fide option to purchase by the tenant, provided that an attorney for the tenant has approved on the face of the agreement any lease so exempted. Rules also do not apply to occupancy by an employee of a landlord whose right to occupy is conditioned upon employment in or about the premises; or the lease of single-family rental in connection with a lease of land to be used primarily for agricultural purposes; or rental agreements for seasonal agricultural employees.

Limit: No statutory limit.

Disclosure or Requirement: In the lease, landlord must disclose the circumstances under which all or part of the deposit may be withheld, and must provide a receipt with the name and location of the banking institution where the deposit is being held. No deposit may be collected unless the rental agreement is in writing and a written checklist or statement specifically describing the condition and cleanliness of or existing damages to the premises and furnishings is provided to the tenant at the start of the tenancy.

State Security Deposit Rules (continued)

Separate Account: Not required.

Advance notice of deduction: Not required.

Deadline for Landlord to Itemize and Return Deposit: 14 days.

West Virginia

W.Va. Code § 37-6A-1 et seq.

Deadline for Landlord to Itemize and Return Deposit: 60 days from the date the tenancy has terminated, or within 45 days of the occupancy of a subsequent tenant, whichever is shorter. If the damage exceeds the amount of the security deposit and the landlord has to hire a contractor to fix it, the notice period is extended 15 days.

Limit: No statutory limit.

Wisconsin

Wis. Admin. Code ATCP 134.06, Wis. Stat. § 704.28

Exemption: Security deposit rules do not apply to a dwelling unit occupied, under a contract of sale, by the purchaser of the dwelling unit or the purchaser's successor in interest; or to a dwelling unit that the landlord provides free to any person, or that the landlord provides as consideration to a person whom the landlord currently employs to operate or maintain the premises.

Limit: No statutory limit.

Disclosure or Requirement: Before accepting the deposit, landlord must inform tenant of tenant's inspection rights, disclose all habitability defects, and show tenant any outstanding building and housing code violations, inform tenant of the means by which shared utilities will be billed, and inform tenant if utilities are not paid for by landlord.

Advance notice of deduction: Not required.

Deadline for Landlord to Itemize and Return Deposit: 21 days.

Wyoming

Wyo. Stat. §§ 1-21-1207, 1-21-1208

Limit: No statutory limit.

Disclosure or Requirement: Lease or rental agreement must state whether any portion of a deposit is non-refundable, and landlord must give tenant written notice of this fact when collecting the deposit.

Advance notice of deduction: Not required.

Deadline for Landlord to Itemize and Return Deposit: 30 days, when applying it to unpaid rent (or within 15 days of receiving tenant's forwarding address, whichever is later); additional 30 days allowed for deductions due to damage.

Required Landlord Disclosures

Many states require landlords to inform tenants of important state laws or individual landlord policies, either in the lease or rental agreement or in another writing. Common disclosures include a landlord's imposition of nonrefundable fees (where permitted), tenants' rights to move-in checklists, and the identity of the landlord or landlord's agent or manager. Disclosures concerning the security deposit are in the chart, "State Security Deposit Rules."

Alabama

Owner or agent identity: Landlord must disclose to the tenant in writing at or before the commencement of the tenancy the name and address of the person authorized to manage the premises, and an owner of the premises or a person authorized to act for and on behalf of the owner for the purpose of service of process and for the purpose of receiving notices and demands. (Exception: does not apply to resident purchaser under a contract of sale (but does apply to a resident who has an option to buy), nor to the continuation of occupancy by the seller or a member of the seller's family for a period of not more than 36 months after the sale of a dwelling unit or the property of which it is a part.) (Ala. Code § 35-9A-202)

Alaska

Owner or agent identity: Landlord must disclose to the tenant in writing at or before the commencement of the tenancy the name and address of the person authorized to manage the premises, and an owner of the premises or a person authorized to act for and on behalf of the owner for the purpose of service of process and for the purpose of receiving notices and demands. (Alaska Stat. § 34.03.080)

Extended absence: The rental agreement must require that the tenant notify the landlord of an anticipated extended absence from the premises in excess of seven days; however, the notice may be given as soon as reasonably possible after the tenant knows the absence will exceed seven days. (Alaska Stat. § 34.03.150)

Arizona

Nonrefundable fees permitted? Yes. The purpose of all nonrefundable fees or deposits must be stated in writing. Any fee or deposit not designated as nonrefundable is refundable. (Ariz. Rev. Stat. § 33-1321)

Move-in checklist required? Yes. Tenants also have the right to be present at a move-out inspection. (Ariz. Rev. Stat. § 33-1321)

Separate utility charges: If landlord charges separately for gas, water, wastewater, solid waste removal, or electricity by installing a submetering system, landlord may recover the charges imposed on the landlord by the utility provider, plus an administrative fee for the landlord for actual administrative costs only, and must disclose separate billing and fee in the rental agreement. If landlord uses a ratio utility billing system, the rental agreement must contain a specific description of the ratio utility billing method used to allocate utility costs. (Ariz. Rev. Stat. § 33-1314.01)

Owner or agent identity: Landlord must disclose to the tenant in writing at or before the commencement of the tenancy the name and address of the person authorized to manage the premises, and an owner of the premises or a person authorized to act for and on behalf of the owner for the purpose of service of process and for the purpose of receiving notices and demands. (Ariz. Rev. Stat. § 33-1322)

Business tax pass-through: If the landlord pays a local tax based on rent and that tax increases, landlord may pass through the increase by increasing the rent upon 30 days' notice (but not before the new tax is effective), but only if the landlord's right to adjust the rent is disclosed in the rental agreement. (Ariz. Rev. Stat. § 33-1314)

Availability of Landlord and Tenant Act: Landlord must inform tenant in writing that the Residential Landlord and Tenant Act is available on the Arizona department of housing's website. (Ariz. Rev. Stat. § 33-1322)

Bedbug information: Landlords must provide existing and new tenants with educational materials on bedbugs, including information and physical descriptions, prevention and control measures, behavioral attraction risk factors, information from federal, state, and local centers for disease control and prevention, health or housing agencies, nonprofit housing organizations, or information developed by the landlord. (Ariz. Rev. Stat. § 33-1319)

Arkansas

No disclosure statutes.

Required Landlord Disclosures (continued)

California

Nonrefundable fees permitted? No. (Cal. Civ. Code § 1950.5(m))

Move-in checklist required? No

Registered sexual offender database: Landlords must include the following language in their rental agreements: "Notice: Pursuant to Section 290.46 of the Penal Code, information about specified registered sex offenders is made available to the public via an Internet Web site maintained by the Department of Justice at www.meganslaw.ca.gov. Depending on an offender's criminal history, this information will include either the address at which the offender resides or the community of residence and ZIP Code in which he or she resides." (Cal. Civ. Code § 2079.10a)

Tenant paying for others' utilities: Prior to signing a rental agreement, landlord must disclose whether gas or electric service to tenant's unit also serves other areas, and must disclose the manner by which costs will be fairly allocated. (Cal. Civ. Code § 1940.9)

Ordnance locations: Prior to signing a lease, landlord must disclose known locations of former federal or state ordnance in the neighborhood (within one mile of rental). (Cal. Civ. Code § 1940.7)

Toxic mold: Prior to signing a rental agreement, landlord must provide written disclosure when landlord knows, or has reason to know, that mold exceeds permissible exposure limits or poses a health threat. Landlords must distribute a consumer handbook, developed by the State Department of Health Services, describing the potential health risks from mold. (Cal. Health & Safety Code §§ 26147, 26148)

Pest control service: When the rental agreement is signed, landlord must provide tenant with any pest control company disclosure landlord has received, which describes the pest to be controlled, pesticides used and their active ingredients, a warning that pesticides are toxic, and the frequency of treatment under any contract for periodic service. (Cal. Civ. Code § 1940.8, Cal. Bus. & Prof. Code § 8538)

Intention to demolish rental unit: Landlords or their agents who have applied for a permit to demolish a rental unit must give written notice of this fact to prospective tenants, before accepting any deposits or screening fees. (Cal. Civ. Code § 1940.6)

No-smoking policy: For leases and rental agreements signed after January 1, 2012: If the landlord prohibits or limits the smoking of tobacco products on the rental property, the lease or rental agreement must include a clause describing the areas where smoking is limited or prohibited (does not apply if the tenant has previously occupied the dwelling unit). For leases and rental agreements signed before January 1, 2012: A newly adopted policy limiting or prohibiting smoking is a change in the terms of the tenancy (will not apply to lease-holding tenants until they renew their leases; tenants renting month-to-month must be given 30 days' written notice). Does not preempt any local ordinances prohibiting smoking in effect on January 1, 2012. (Cal. Civ. Code § 1947.5)

Notice of default: Lessors of single-family homes and multifamily properties of four units or less, who have received a notice of default for the rental property that has not been rescinded, must disclose this fact to potential renters before they sign a lease. The notice must be in English or in Spanish, Chinese, Tagalog, Vietnamese, or Korean (if the lease was negotiated in one of these languages), and must follow the language specified in Cal. Civil Code § 2924.85(d).

Colorado

No disclosure statutes.

Connecticut

Common interest community: When rental is in a common interest community, landlord must give tenant written notice before signing a lease. (Conn. Gen. Stat. Ann. § 47a-3e)

Owner or agent identity: Before the beginning of the tenancy, landlord must disclose the name and address of the person authorized to manage the premises and the person who is authorized to receive all notices, demands and service of process. (Conn. Gen. Stat. Ann. § 47a-6)

Summary of Landlord-Tenant Code: A summary of the code, as prepared by the Consumer Protection Unit of the Attorney General's office, must be given to tenants at the beginning of the rental term. Failure to do so enables the tenant to plead ignorance of the law as a defense.

Required Landlord Disclosures (continued)

Delaware

Nonrefundable fees permitted? No, except for an optional service for actual services rendered, such as a pool fee or tennis court fee. Tenant may elect, subject to the landlord's acceptance, to purchase an optional surety bond instead of or in combination with a security deposit. Del. Code Ann. tit. 25, § 5311, *Stoltz Management Co. v. Phillip*, 593 A 2d 583 (1990).

Owner or agent identity: On each written rental agreement, the landlord must prominently disclose the names and usual business addresses of all persons who are owners of the rental unit or the property of which the rental unit is a part, or the names and business addresses of their appointed resident agents. (25 Del. Code Ann. § 5105)

Summary of Landlord-Tenant Law: A summary of the Landlord-Tenant Code, as prepared by the Consumer Protection Unit of the Attorney General's Office or its successor agency, must be given to the new tenant at the beginning of the rental term. If the landlord fails to provide the summary, the tenant may plead ignorance of the law as a defense. (25 Del. Code Ann. § 5118)

District of Columbia

Rental regulations: At the start of every new tenancy, landlord must give tenant a copy of the District of Columbia Municipal Regulations, CDCR Title 14, Housing, Chapter 3, Landlord and Tenant; and a copy of Title 14, Housing, Chapter 1, § 101 (Civil Enforcement Policy) and Chapter 1, § 106 (Notification of Tenants Concerning Violations).

Florida

Nonrefundable fees permitted? Yes. No statute directly on point, but by custom, nonrefundable fees are allowed.

Landlord identity: The landlord, or a person authorized to enter into a rental agreement on the landlord's behalf, must disclose in writing to the tenant, at or before the commencement of the tenancy, the name and address of the landlord or a person authorized to receive notices and demands on the landlord's behalf. (Fla. Stat. Ann. § 83.50)

Radon: In all leases, landlord must include this warning: "RADON GAS: Radon is a naturally occurring radioactive gas that, when it has accumulated in a building in sufficient quantities, may present health risks to persons who are exposed to it over time. Levels of radon that exceed federal and state guidelines have been found in buildings in Florida. Additional information regarding radon and radon testing may be obtained from your county health department." (Fla. Stat. Ann. § 404.056)

Georgia

Nonrefundable fees permitted? Yes. No statute, but by custom, nonrefundable fees such as pet fees are permitted.

Move-in checklist required? Yes. Landlords cannot collect a security deposit unless they have given tenants a list of preexisting damages. (Ga. Code Ann. § 44-7-33)

Flooding: Before signing a lease, if the living space or attachments have been damaged by flooding three or more times within the past five years, landlord must so disclose in writing. (Ga. Code Ann. § 44-7-20)

Owner or agent identity: When or before a tenancy begins, landlord must disclose in writing the names and addresses of the owner of record or a person authorized to act for the owner for purposes of service of process and receiving and receipting demands and notices; and the person authorized to manage the premises. If such information changes during the tenancy, landlord must advise tenant within 30 days in writing or by posting a notice in a conspicuous place. (Ga. Code Ann. § 44-7-3)

Former residents, crimes: If asked by a prospective tenant, landlord must answer truthfully when questioned about whether the rental was the site of a homicide or other felony, or a suicide or a death by accidental or natural causes; or whether it was occupied by a person who was infected with a virus or any other disease that has been determined by medical evidence as being highly unlikely to be transmitted through the occupancy of a dwelling place presently or previously occupied by such an infected person. (Ga. Code Ann. § 44-1-16)

Hawaii

Nonrefundable fees permitted? No.

Other fees: The landlord may not require or receive from or on behalf of a tenant at the beginning of a rental agreement any money other than the money for the first month's rent and a security deposit as provided in this section. (Haw. Rev. Stat. § 521-43)

Required Landlord Disclosures (continued)

Owner or agent identity: Landlord must disclose name of owner or agent; if owner lives in another state or on another island, landlord must disclose name of agent on the island. (Haw. Rev. Stat. § 521-43)

Move-in checklist required? Yes. (Haw. Rev. Stat.§ 521-42)

Tax excise number: Landlord must furnish its tax excise number so that tenant can file for a low-income tax credit. (Haw. Rev. Stat. § 521-43)

Idaho

No disclosure statutes.

Illinois

Utilities: Where tenant pays a portion of a master metered utility, landlord must give tenant a copy in writing either as part of the lease or another written agreement of the formula used by the landlord for allocating the public utility payments among the tenants. (765 Ill. Comp. Stat. § 740/5)

Rent concessions: Any rent concessions must be described in the lease, in letters not less than one-half inch in height consisting of the words "Concession Granted," including a memorandum on the margin or across the face of the lease stating the amount or extent and nature of each such concession. Failure to comply is a misdemeanor. (765 Ill. Comp. Stat. §§ 730/0 to 730/6.)

Radon: Landlords are not required to test for radon, but if the landlord tests and learns that a radon hazard is present in the dwelling unit, landlord must disclose this information to current and prospective tenants. If a tenant notifies a landlord that a radon test indicates the existence of a radon hazard in the rental unit, landlord must disclose that risk to any prospective tenant of that unit, unless a subsequent test by the landlord shows that a radon hazard does not exist. Requirements do not apply if the dwelling unit is on the third or higher story above ground level, or when the landlord has undertaken mitigation work and a subsequent test shows that a radon hazard does not exist. (420 Ill. Comp. Stat. §§ 46/15, 46/25)

Indiana

Agent identity: Landlord's agent must disclose in writing the name and address of a person living in Indiana who is authorized to manage the property and to act as the owner's agent. (Ind. Code Ann. § 32-31-3-18)

Iowa

Owner or agent identity: Landlord must disclose to the tenant in writing at or before the commencement of the tenancy the name and address of the person authorized to manage the premises, and an owner of the premises or a person authorized to act for and on behalf of the owner for the purpose of service of process and for the purpose of receiving notices and demands. (Iowa Code § 562A.13)

Utilities: For shared utilities, landlord must fully explain utility rates, charges, and services to the prospective tenant before the rental agreement is signed. (Iowa Code § 562A.13)

Contamination: The landlord or a person authorized to enter into a rental agreement on behalf of the landlord must disclose to each tenant, in writing before the commencement of the tenancy, whether the property is listed in the comprehensive environmental response compensation and liability information system maintained by the federal Environmental Protection Agency. (Iowa Code § 562A.13)

Kansas

Move-in checklist required? Yes. Within 5 days of move-in, landlord and tenant must jointly inventory the rental. (Kan. Stat. Ann. § 58-2548)

Owner or agent identity: Landlord must disclose to the tenant in writing at or before the commencement of the tenancy the name and address of the person authorized to manage the premises, and an owner of the premises or a person authorized to act for and on behalf of the owner for the purpose of service of process and for the purpose of receiving notices and demands. (Kan. Stat. Ann. § 58-2551)

Kentucky

Move-in checklist required? Yes. Landlord and tenant must complete a checklist before landlord can collect a security deposit. (Ky. Rev. Stat. Ann. § 383.580)

Owner or agent identity: Landlord must disclose to the tenant in writing at or before the commencement of the tenancy the name and address of the person authorized to manage the premises, and an owner of the premises or a person authorized to act for and on behalf of the

Required Landlord Disclosures (continued)

owner for the purpose of service of process and for the purpose of receiving notices and demands. (Ky. Rev. Stat. Ann. § 383.585)

Louisiana

No disclosure statutes.

Maine

Utilities: No landlord may lease or offer to lease a dwelling unit in a multiunit residential building where the expense of furnishing electricity to the common areas or other area not within the unit is the sole responsibility of the tenant in that unit, unless both parties to the lease have agreed in writing that the tenant will pay for such costs in return for a stated reduction in rent or other specified fair consideration that approximates the actual cost of electricity to the common areas. (14 Me. Rev. Stat. Ann. § 6024)

Energy efficiency: Landlord must provide to potential tenants who will pay for energy costs (or upon request from others) a residential energy efficiency disclosure statement in accordance with Title 35-A, section 10006, subsection 1 that includes, but is not limited to, information about the energy efficiency of the property. Before a tenant enters into a contract or pays a deposit to rent or lease a property, the landlord must provide the statement to the tenant, obtain the tenant's signature on the statement, and sign the statement. The landlord must retain the signed statement for at least 3 years. Alternatively, the landlord may include in the application for the residential property the name of each supplier of energy that previously supplied the unit, if known, and the following statement: "You have the right to obtain a 12-month history of energy consumption and the cost of that consumption from the energy supplier." (14 Me. Rev. Stat. Ann. § 6030-C)

Radon: By 2012 and every ten years thereafter, landlord must test for radon and disclose to prospective and existing tenants the date and results of the test and the risks of radon, using a disclosure form prepared by the Department of Health and Human Services (tenant must sign acknowledgment of receipt). (14 Me. Rev. Stat. Ann. § 6030-D)

Bedbugs: Before renting a dwelling unit, landlord must disclose to a prospective tenant if an adjacent unit or

units are currently infested with or are being treated for bedbugs. Upon request from a tenant or prospective tenant, landlord must disclose the last date that the dwelling unit the landlord seeks to rent or an adjacent unit or units were inspected for a bedbug infestation and found to be free of a bedbug infestation. (Me. Rev. Stat. Ann. § 6021-A)

Smoking policy: Landlord must give tenant written disclosure stating whether smoking is prohibited on the premises, allowed on the entire premises, or allowed in limited areas of the premises. If the landlord allows smoking in limited areas on the premises, the notice must identify the areas on the premises where smoking is allowed. Disclosure must be in the lease or separate written notice, landlord must disclose before tenant signs a lease or pays a deposit, and must obtain a written acknowledgment of notification from the tenant. (14 Me. Rev. Stat. Ann. § 6030-E)

Maryland

Move-in checklist required? Yes. Before collecting a deposit, landlord must supply a receipt with details on move-in and move-out inspections, and the receipt may be part of the lease. (Md. Code Ann. [Real Prop.] § 8-203.1)

Habitation: A lease must include a statement that the premises will be made available in a condition permitting habitation, with reasonable safety, if that is the agreement, or if that is not the agreement, a statement of the agreement concerning the condition of the premises; and the landlord's and the tenant's specific obligations as to heat, gas, electricity, water, and repair of the premises. (Md. Code Ann. [Real Prop.] § 8-208)

Owner or agent identity: The landlord must include in a lease or post the name and address of the landlord; or the person, if any, authorized to accept notice or service of process on behalf of the landlord. (Md. Code Ann. [Real Prop.] § 8-210)

Massachusetts

Move-in checklist required? Yes, if landlord collects a security deposit. (186 Mass. Gen. Laws § 15B(2)(c))

Insurance: Upon tenant's request and within 15 days, landlord must furnish the name of the company insuring the property against loss or damage by fire and the amount of insurance provided by each such company

Required Landlord Disclosures (continued)

and the name of any person who would receive payment for a loss covered by such insurance. (186 Mass. Gen. Laws § 21)

Michigan

Nonrefundable fees permitted? Yes. *Stutelberg v. Practical Management Co*, 245 N.W. 2d 737 (1976)

Move-in checklist required? Yes. However, the requirement does not need to be included in the rental agreement. (Mich. Comp. Laws § 554.608)

Owner or agent identity: A rental agreement must include the name and address at which notice can be given to the landlord. (Mich. Comp. Laws § 554.634)

Truth in Renting Act: A rental agreement must also state in a prominent place in type not smaller than the size of 12-point type, or in legible print with letters not smaller than 1/8 inch, a notice in substantially the following form: "NOTICE: Michigan law establishes rights and obligations for parties to rental agreements. This agreement is required to comply with the Truth in Renting Act. If you have a question about the interpretation or legality of a provision of this agreement, you may want to seek assistance from a lawyer or other qualified person." (Mich. Comp. Laws § 554.634)

Rights of domestic violence victims: A rental agreement or lease may contain a provision stating, "A tenant who has a reasonable apprehension of present danger to him or her or his or her child from domestic violence, sexual assault, or stalking may have special statutory rights to seek a release of rental obligation under MCL 554.601b." If the rental agreement or lease does not contain such a provision, the landlord must post an identical written notice visible to a reasonable person in the landlord's property management office, or deliver written notice to the tenant when the lease or rental agreement is signed. (Mich. Comp. Laws § 554.601(b))

Minnesota

Owner or agent identity: Landlord must disclose to the tenant in writing at or before the commencement of the tenancy the name and address of the person authorized to manage the premises, and an owner of the premises or a person authorized to act for and on behalf of the owner for the purpose of service of process and for the purpose of receiving notices and demands. (Minn. Stat. Ann. § 504B.181)

Outstanding inspection orders, condemnation orders, or declarations that the property is unfit: The landlord must disclose the existence of any such orders or declarations before the tenant signs a lease or pays a security deposit. (Minn. Stat. Ann. §504B.195)

Buildings in financial distress: Once a landlord has received notice of a deed cancellation or notice of foreclosure, landlord may not enter into a periodic tenancy where the tenancy term is more than two months, or a lease where the lease extends beyond the redemption period (other restrictions may apply). (Minn. Stat. Ann. § 504B.151)

Landlord and Tenant Mutual Promises: This mutual promise must appear in every lease or rental agreement: "Landlord and tenant promise that neither will unlawfully allow within the premises, common areas, or curtilage of the premises (property boundaries): controlled substances, prostitution or prostitution-related activity; stolen property or property obtained by robbery; or an act of domestic violence, as defined by MN Statute Section 504B.206 (1)(e), against a tenant, licensee, or any authorized occupant. They further promise that the aforementioned areas will not be used by themselves or anyone acting under their control to manufacture, sell, give away, barter, deliver, exchange, distribute, purchase, or possess a controlled substance in violation of any criminal provision of chapter 152."

Mississippi

No disclosure statutes.

Missouri

No disclosure statutes.

Montana

Nonrefundable fees permitted? No. A fee or charge for cleaning and damages, no matter how designated, is presumed to be a security deposit. (Not a clear statement that such a fee isn't nonrefundable, but by implication it must be.) (Mont. Code Ann. § 70-25-101(4))

Move-in checklists required? Yes, checklists are required when landlords collect a security deposit. (Mont. Code Ann. § 70-25-206)

Required Landlord Disclosures (continued)

Owner or agent identity: A landlord or a person authorized to enter into a rental agreement on his behalf must disclose to the tenant in writing at or before the commencement of the tenancy the name and address of the person authorized to manage the premises; and the owner of the premises or a person authorized to act for the owner for the purpose of service of process and receiving notices and demands. (Mont. Code Ann. § 70-24-301)

Nebraska

Owner or agent identity: The landlord or any person authorized to enter into a rental agreement on his or her behalf must disclose to the tenant in writing at or before the commencement of the tenancy the name and address of the person authorized to manage the premises, and an owner of the premises or a person authorized to act for and on behalf of the owner for the purpose of service of process and receiving notices and demands. (Neb. Rev. Stat. § 76-1417)

Nevada

Nonrefundable fees permitted? Yes. Lease must explain fees that are required and the purposes for which they are required. (Nev. Rev. Stat. Ann. § 118A.200)

Move-in checklist required? Yes. Lease must include a signed record of the inventory and condition of the premises under the exclusive custody and control of the tenant. (Nev. Rev. Stat. Ann. § 118A.200)

Nuisance and flying the flag: Lease must include a summary of the provisions of NRS 202.470 (penalties for permitting or maintaining a nuisance); information regarding the procedure a tenant may use to report to the appropriate authorities a nuisance, a violation of a building, safety, or health code or regulation; and information regarding the right of the tenant to engage in the display of the flag of the United States, as set forth in NRS 118A.325. (Nev. Rev. Stat. Ann. § 118A.200)

Foreclosure proceedings: Landlord must disclose to any prospective tenant, in writing, whether the premises to be rented is the subject of a foreclosure proceeding (disclosure need not be in the lease). (Nev. Rev. Stat. Ann. § 118A.275)

New Hampshire

Move-in checklist required? Yes. Landlord must inform tenant that if tenant finds any conditions in the rental in need of repair, tenant may note them on the security deposit receipt or other writing (not a true checklist). (N.H. Rev. Stat. Ann. § 540-A:6)

New Jersey

Flood zone: Prior to move-in, landlord must inform tenant if rental is in a flood zone or area (does not apply to properties containing two or fewer dwelling units, or to owner-occupied properties of three or fewer units). (N.J. Stat. Ann. § 46:8-50)

Truth in Renting Act: Except in buildings of 2 or fewer units, and owner-occupied premises of 3 or fewer units, landlord must distribute to new tenants at or prior to move-in the Department of Community Affairs' statement of legal rights and responsibilities of tenants and landlords of rental dwelling units (Spanish also). (N.J.S.A. §§ 46:8-44, 46:8-45, 46:8-46)

Child protection windowguards: Landlords of multi-family properties must include information in the lease about tenants' rights to request windowguards. The Legislature's Model Lease and Notice clause reads as follows: "The owner (landlord) is required by law to provide, install and maintain window guards in the apartment if a child or children 10 years of age or younger is, or will be, living in the apartment or is, or will be, regularly present there for a substantial period of time if the tenant gives the owner (landlord) a written request that the window guards be installed. The owner (landlord) is also required, upon the written request of the tenant, to provide, install and maintain window guards in the hallways to which persons in the tenant's unit have access without having to go out of the building. If the building is a condominium, cooperative or mutual housing building, the owner (landlord) of the apartment is responsible for installing and maintaining window guards in the apartment and the association is responsible for installing and maintaining window guards in hallway windows. Window guards are only required to be provided in first floor windows where the window sill is more than six feet above grade or there are other hazardous conditions that make installation of window guards necessary to protect the safety of children." The notice must be conspicuous and in boldface type.

New Mexico

Owner or agent identity: Landlord must disclose to the tenant in writing at or before the commencement of the tenancy the name and address of the person authorized to manage the premises, and an owner of the premises or a person authorized to act for and on behalf of the owner for the purpose of service of process and for the purpose of receiving notices and demands. (N.M. Stat. Ann. § 47-8-19)

New York

Air Contamination. Landlord who receives a government report showing that air in the building has, or may have, concentrations of volitile organic compounds (VOCs) that exceed governmental guidelines must give written notice to prospective and current tenants. The notice must appear in 12-point boldface type on the first page of the lease or rental agreement. It must read as follows: "NOTIFICATION OF TEST RESULTS. The property has been tested for contamination of indoor air: test results and additional information are available upon request." (N.Y. ECL § 27-2405)

North Carolina

Nonrefundable fees permitted? Yes. (N.C. Stat. Ann. § 42-46)

Other fees: Landlord may collect only one of the following, when specific conditions are met: Complaint filing fee, court appearance fee, and second trial fee. Failure to pay the fees cannot support a termination notice. (N.C. Stat. Ann. § 42-46)

North Dakota

Move-in checklist required? Yes. Landlord must give tenant a statement describing the condition of the premises when tenant signs the rental agreement. Both parties must sign the statement. (N.D. Cent. Code § 47-16-07.2)

Ohio

Owner or agent identity: Every written rental agreement must contain the name and address of the owner and the name and address of the owner's agent, if any. If the owner or the owner's agent is a corporation, partnership, limited partnership, association, trust, or other entity, the address must be the principal place of business in the county in which the residential property is situated. If there is no place of business in such county, then its principal place of business in this state must be disclosed, and must include the name of the person in charge thereof. (Ohio Rev. Code Ann. § 5321.18)

Oklahoma

Flooding: If the premises to be rented has been flooded within the past five (5) years and such fact is known to the landlord, the landlord shall include such information prominently and in writing as part of any written rental agreements. (41 Okla. St. Ann. § 113a)

Owner information: As a part of any rental agreement the lessor shall prominently and in writing identify what person at what address is entitled to accept service or notice under this act. Landlord must disclose to the tenant in writing at or before the commencement of the tenancy the name and address of the person authorized to manage the premises, and an owner of the premises or a person authorized to act for and on behalf of the owner for the purpose of service of process and receiving notices and demands. (41 Okla. St. Ann. § 116)

Oregon

Nonrefundable fees permitted? No. (Ore. Rev. Stat. § 90.302)

Other fees? Landlords' written rules may not provide for tenant fees, except for specified events as they arise, including a late rent payment; tenant's late payment of a utility or service charge; a dishonored check, pursuant to Ore. Rev. Stat. § 30.701(5); failure to clean up pet waste in areas other than tenant's unit; failure to clean up garbage and rubbish (outside tenant's dwelling unit); failure to clean pet waste of a service or companion animal from areas other than the dwelling unit; parking violations and improper use of vehicles within the premises; smoking in a designated nonsmoking area; keeping an unauthorized pet capable of inflicting damage on persons or property; and tampering with or disabling a smoke detector.

Owner or agent identity: Landlord must disclose to the tenant in writing at or before the commencement of the tenancy the name and address of the person authorized to manage the premises, and an owner of the premises or a person authorized to act for and on behalf of the

Required Landlord Disclosures (continued)

owner for the purpose of service of process and for the purpose of receiving notices and demands. (Ore. Rev. Stat. § 90.305)

Legal proceedings: If at the time of the execution of a rental agreement for a dwelling unit in premises containing no more than four dwelling units the premises are subject to any of the following circumstances, the landlord must disclose that circumstance to the tenant in writing before the execution of the rental agreement:

(a) Any outstanding notice of default under a trust deed, mortgage or contract of sale, or notice of trustee's sale under a trust deed;

(b) Any pending suit to foreclose a mortgage, trust deed, or vendor's lien under a contract of sale;

(c) Any pending declaration of forfeiture or suit for specific performance of a contract of sale; or

(d) Any pending proceeding to foreclose a tax lien. (Ore. Rev. Stat. § 90.310)

Utilities: The landlord must disclose to the tenant in writing at or before the commencement of the tenancy any utility or service that the tenant pays directly to a utility or service provider that directly benefits the landlord or other tenants. A tenant's payment for a given utility or service benefits the landlord or other tenants if the utility or service is delivered to any area other than the tenant's dwelling unit.

A landlord may require a tenant to pay to the landlord a utility or service charge that has been billed by a utility or service provider to the landlord for utility or service provided directly to the tenant's dwelling unit or to a common area available to the tenant as part of the tenancy. A utility or service charge that shall be assessed to a tenant for a common area must be described in the written rental agreement separately and distinctly from such a charge for the tenant's dwelling unit. Unless the method of allocating the charges to the tenant is described in the tenant's written rental agreement, the tenant may require that the landlord give the tenant a copy of the provider's bill as a condition of paying the charges. (Ore. Rev. Stat. § 90.315)

Recycling: In a city or the county within the urban growth boundary of a city that has implemented multifamily recycling service, a landlord who has five or more residential dwelling units on a single premises must notify new tenants at the time of entering into a rental agreement of the opportunity to recycle. (Ore. Rev. Stat. § 90.318)

Smoking policy: Landlord must disclose the smoking policy for the premises, by stating whether smoking is prohibited on the premises, allowed on the entire premises, or allowed in limited areas. If landlord allows smoking in limited areas, the disclosure must identify those areas. (Or. Rev. Stat. § 90.220)

Carbon monoxide alarm instructions: If rental contains a CO source (a heater, fireplace, appliance, or cooking source that uses coal, kerosene, petroleum products, wood, or other fuels that emit carbon monoxide as a by product of combustion; or an attached garage with an opening that communicates directly with a living space), landlord must install one or more CO monitors and give tenant written instructions for testing the alarm(s), before tenant takes possession. (Ore. Rev. Stat. § 90.316, 90.317)

Flood zone: If a dwelling unit is located in a 100-year flood plain, the landlord must provide notice in the dwelling unit rental agreement that the dwelling unit is located within the flood plain. If a landlord fails to provide a notice as required under this section, and the tenant of the dwelling unit suffers an uninsured loss due to flooding, the tenant may recover from the landlord the lesser of the actual damages for the uninsured loss or two months' rent. (Ore. Rev. Stat. § 90.228)

Renters' Insurance: Landlord may require tenants to maintain liability insurance (certain low-income and subsidized tenancies excepted), but only if the landlord obtains and maintains comparable liability insurance and provides documentation to any tenant who requests the documentation, orally or in writing. The landlord may provide documentation to a tenant in person, by mail, or by posting in a common area or office. The documentation may consist of a current certificate of coverage. Any landlord who requires tenants to obtain renters' insurance must disclose the requirement and amount in writing prior to entering into a new tenancy, and may require the tenant to provide documentation before the tenancy begins. (Ore. Rev. Stat. § 90.367)

Required Landlord Disclosures (continued)

Homeowner Assessments: If landlord wants to pass on homeowner association assessments that are imposed on anyone moving into or out of the unit, the written rental agreement must include this requirement. Landlord must give tenants a copy of each assessment before charging the tenant. (Ore. Rev. Stat. § 90.302)

Pennsylvania

No disclosure statutes.

Rhode Island

Owner disclosure: Landlord must disclose to the tenant in writing at or before the commencement of the tenancy the name and address of the person authorized to manage the premises, and an owner of the premises or a person authorized to act for and on behalf of the owner for the purpose of service of process and for the purpose of receiving notices and demands. (R.I. Gen. Laws §34-18-20)

Code violations: Before entering into any residential rental agreement, landlord must inform a prospective tenant of any outstanding minimum housing code violations which exist on the building that is the subject of the rental agreement. (R.I. Gen. Laws § 34-18-22.1)

Notice of Foreclosure: A landlord who becomes delinquent on a mortgage securing real estate upon which the rental is located for a period of 120 days must notify the tenant that the property may be subject to foreclosure; and until the foreclosure occurs, the tenant must continue to pay rent to the landlord as provided under the rental agreement.

South Carolina

Owner or agent identity: Landlord must disclose to the tenant in writing at or before the commencement of the tenancy the name and address of the person authorized to manage the premises, and an owner of the premises or a person authorized to act for and on behalf of the owner for the purpose of service of process and for the purpose of receiving notices and demands. (S.C. Code Ann. § 27-40-420)

Unequal security deposits: If landlord rents five or more adjoining units on the premises, and imposes different standards for calculating deposits required of tenants, landlord must, before a tenancy begins, post in a conspicuous

place a statement explaining the standards by which the various deposits are calculated (or, landlord may give the tenant the written statement). (S.C. Code Ann. § 27-40-410)

South Dakota

Meth labs: Landlord who has actual knowledge of the existence of any prior manufacturing of methamphetamines on the premises must disclose that information to any lessee or any person who may become a lessee. If the residential premises consists of two or more housing units, the disclosure requirements apply only to the unit where there is knowledge of the existence of any prior manufacturing of methamphetamines.

Tennessee

Owner or agent identity: The landlord or any person authorized to enter into a rental agreement on the landlord's behalf must disclose to the tenant in writing at or before the commencement of the tenancy the name and address of the agent authorized to manage the premises, and an owner of the premises or a person or agent authorized to act for and on behalf of the owner for the acceptance of service of process and for receipt of notices and demands. (Tenn. Code Ann. § 66-28-302)

Showing rental to prospective tenants: Landlord may enter to show the premises to prospective renters during the final 30 days of a tenancy (with 24 hours' notice), but only if this right of access is set forth in the rental agreement or lease. (Tenn. Code Ann. § 66-28-403)

Texas

Nonrefundable fees permitted? Yes. *Holmes v. Canlen Management Corp.*, 542 S.W.2d 199 (1976).

Owner or agent identity: In the lease, other writing, or posted on the property, landlord must disclose the name and address of the property's owner and, if an entity located off-site from the dwelling is primarily responsible for managing the dwelling, the name and street address of the management company. (Tex. Prop. Code Ann. § 92.201)

Security device requests: If landlord wants tenant requests concerning security devices to be in writing, this requirement must be in the lease in boldface type or underlined. (Tex. Prop. Code Ann. § 92.159)

Required Landlord Disclosures (continued)

Return of security deposit: A requirement that a tenant give advance notice of moving out as a condition for refunding the security deposit is effective only if the requirement is in the lease, underlined or printed in conspicuous bold print. (Tex. Prop. Code Ann. § 92.103)

Domestic violence victim's rights: Victims of sexual abuse or assault on the premises may break a lease, after complying with specified procedures, without responsibility for future rent. Tenants will be responsible for any unpaid back rent, but only if the lease includes the following statement, or one substantially like it: "Tenants may have special statutory rights to terminate the lease early in certain situations involving family violence or a military deployment or transfer." (Tex. Prop. Code Ann. § 92.016)

Tenant's rights when landlord fails to repair: A lease must contain language in underlined or bold print that informs the tenant of the remedies available when the landlord fails to repair a problem that materially affects the physical health or safety of an ordinary tenant. These rights include the right to repair and deduct; terminate the lease; and obtain a judicial order that the landlord make the repair, reduce the rent, pay the tenant damages (including a civil penalty), and pay the tenant's court and attorney fees. (Tex. Prop. Code Ann. § 92.056)

Landlord's towing or parking rules and policies: For tenants in multiunit properties, if the landlord has vehicle towing or parking rules or policies that apply to the tenant, the landlord must give the tenant a copy of the rules or policies before the lease agreement is signed. The copy must be signed by the tenant, included in the lease or rental agreement, or be made an attachment to either. If included, the clause must be titled "Parking" or "Parking Rules" and be capitalized, underlined, or printed in bold print.) (Tex. Prop. Code Ann. § 92.0131.)

Electric service interruption: Landlord who submeters electric service, or who allocates master metered electricity according to a prorated system, may interrupt tenant's electricity service if tenant fails to pay the bill, but only after specific notice and according to a complex procedure. Exceptions for ill tenants and during extreme weather. (Tex. Prop. Code Ann. § 92008(h))

Utah

Nonrefundable fees permitted? Yes. By custom, if there is a written agreement and if any part of the deposit is nonrefundable, it must be so stated in writing to the renter at the time the deposit is taken.

Move-in checklist required? Yes. Landlords must give prospective renters a written inventory of the condition of the residential rental unit, excluding ordinary wear and tear; give the renter a form to document the condition of the residential rental and allow the resident a reasonable time after the renter's occupancy of the unit to complete and return the form; or provide the prospective renter an opportunity to conduct a walkthrough inspection of the rental. (Utah Code. Ann. § 57-22-4)

Vermont

No disclosure statutes.

Virginia

Move-in checklist required? Yes. Within 5 days of move-in, landlord or tenant or both together must prepare a written report detailing the condition of the premises. Landlord must disclose within this report the known presence of mold. (Va. Code Ann. § 55-248.11:1)

Owner or agent identity: Landlord must disclose to the tenant in writing at or before the commencement of the tenancy the name and address of the person authorized to manage the premises, and an owner of the premises or a person authorized to act for and on behalf of the owner for the purpose of service of process and for the purpose of receiving notices and demands. (Va. Code Ann. § 55-248.12)

Military zone: The landlord of property in any locality in which a military air installation is located, or any person authorized to enter into a rental agreement on his or her behalf, must provide to a prospective tenant a written disclosure that the property is located in a noise zone or accident potential zone, or both, as designated by the locality on its official zoning map. (Va. Code Ann. § 55-248.12:1)

Mold: Move-in inspection report must include whether there is any visible evidence of mold (deemed correct unless tenant objects within five days); if evidence is present, tenant may terminate or not move in. If tenant

Required Landlord Disclosures (continued)

stays, landlord must remediate the mold condition within five business days, reinspect, and issue a new report indicating that there is no evidence of mold. (Va. Code Ann. § 55-248.11:2) If evidence of mold appears during the tenancy, landlord must promptly remediate, reinspect, and make available to the tenant copies of any available written information on how to get rid of mold. (Va. Code Ann. § 55-248.16)

Ratio utility billing: Landlord who uses a ratio utility billing service, who intends to collect monthly billing and other administrative and late fees, must disclose these fees in a written rental agreement. (Va. Code Ann. § 55-226.2)

Condominium plans: If an application for registration as a condominium or cooperative has been filed with the Real Estate Board, or if there is within six months an existing plan for tenant displacement resulting from demolition or substantial rehabilitation of the property, or conversion of the rental property to office, hotel, or motel use or planned unit development, the landlord or any person authorized to enter into a rental agreement on his or her behalf must disclose that information in writing to any prospective tenant. (Va. Code Ann. § 55-248.12(C).)

Defective Drywall: Landlords who know of the presence of unrepaired defective drywall in the rental must disclose this before the tenant signs a lease or rental agreement. (Va. Code § 55-248.12:2.)

Washington

Move-in checklists required? Yes. Checklists are required when landlords collect a security deposit. If landlord fails to provide checklist, landlord is liable to the tenant for the amount of the deposit. (Wash. Rev. Code Ann. § 59.18.285)

Nonrefundable fees permitted? Yes. If landlord collects a nonrefundable fee, the rental document must clearly specify that it is nonrefundable. (Wash. Rev. Code Ann. § 59.18.260)

Fire protection: At the time the lease is signed, landlord must provide fire protection and safety information, including whether the building has a smoking policy, an emergency notification plan, or an evacuation plan. (Wash. Rev. Code Ann. § 59.18.060)

Owner or agent identity: In the rental document or posted conspicuously on the premises, landlord must designate to the tenant the name and address of the person who is the landlord by a statement on the rental agreement or by a notice conspicuously posted on the premises. If the person designated does not reside in Washington, landlord must also designate a person who resides in the county to act as an agent for the purposes of service of notices and process. (Wash. Rev. Code Ann. § 59.18.060)

Mold: At the time the lease is signed, landlord must provide tenant with information provided or approved by the department of health about the health hazards associated with exposure to indoor mold. (Wash. Rev. Code Ann. § 59.18.060)

Screening criteria: Before obtaining any information about an applicant, landlord must provide (in writing or by posting) the type of information to be accessed, criteria to be used to evaluate the application, and (for consumer reports) the name and address of the consumer reporting agency to be used, including the applicant's rights to obtain a free copy of the report and dispute its accuracy. (Wash. Rev. Code Ann. § 59.18.257.)

Tenant screening fee: Landlords who do their own screening may charge a fee for time and costs to obtain background information, but only if they provide the information explained in "Screening Criteria," above. (Wash. Rev. Code Ann. § 59.18.257.)

West Virginia

Nonrefundable fees permitted? Yes. Nonrefundable fee must be expressly agreed to in writing. (W.Va. Code § 37-6A-1(14))

Wisconsin

Move-in checklist required? Yes. Tenant has a right to inspect the rental and give landlord a list of defects, and to receive a list of damages charged to the prior tenant. Tenant has 7 days after start of the tenancy to return the list to the landlord. (Wis. Admin. Code § 134.06, Wis. Stat. Ann. § 704.08)

Owner or agent identity: Landlord must disclose to the tenant in writing, at or before the time a rental agreement is signed, the name and address of:

Required Landlord Disclosures (continued)

- the person or persons authorized to collect or receive rent and manage and maintain the premises, and who can readily be contacted by the tenant; and

- the owner of the premises or other person authorized to accept service of legal process and other notices and demands on behalf of the owner. The address must be an address within the state at which service of process can be made in person. (Wis. Admin. Code § 134.04)

Nonstandard rental provisions: If landlord wants to enter premises for reasons not specified by law, landlord must disclose the provision in a separate written document entitled "NONSTANDARD RENTAL PROVISIONS" before the rental agreement is signed. (Wis. Admin. Code § 134.09)

Habitability deficiencies: Landlord must disclose serious problems that affect the rental unit's habitability. (Wis. Admin. Code § 134.04)

Utility charges: If charges for water, heat, or electricity are not included in the rent, the landlord must disclose this fact to the tenant before entering into a rental agreement or accepting any earnest money or security deposit from the prospective tenant. If individual dwelling units and common areas are not separately metered, and if the charges are not included in the rent, the landlord must disclose the basis on which charges for utility services will be allocated among individual dwelling units. (Wis. Admin. Code § 134.04)

Uncorrected code violations: Before signing a rental contract or accepting a security deposit, the landlord must disclose to the tenant any uncorrected code violation of which the landlord is actually aware, which affects the dwelling unit or a common area and poses a significant threat to the tenant's health or safety. "Disclosure" consists of showing perspective tenants the portions of the building affected, as well as the notices themselves. (Wis. Stat. § 704.07(2)(bm)134.04.)

Disposing of abandoned property: If landlord intends to immediately dispose of any tenant property left behind after move-out, landlord must notify tenant at the time lease is signed. (But landlord must hold prescription medications and medical equipment for seven days, and must give notice before disposing of vehicles or manufactured homes to owner and any known secured party.) (Wis. Stat. § 704.05 (5))

Wyoming

Nonrefundable fees permitted? Yes. If any portion of the deposit is not refundable, rental agreement must include this information and tenant must be told before paying a deposit. (Wyo. Stat. § 1-21-1207)

State Laws in Domestic Violence Situations

Many states extend special protections, such as early termination rights, to victims of domestic violence or stalking. Here is a summary of state laws. For more information, check with local law enforcement or a battered women's shelter.

Alabama

No statute

Alaska

Alaska Stat. § 29.35.125(a)

Miscellaneous provisions: A city may impose a fee on the owner of residential property if the police go to the property an excessive number of times during a calendar year when called for assistance or to handle a complaint, an emergency, or a potential emergency. This fee may not be imposed for responses to calls that involve potential child neglect, domestic violence, or stalking.

Arizona

Ariz. Rev. Stat. §§ 33-1315, 33-1318, 33-1414

- Lease cannot include a waiver of some or all DV rights
- Landlord entitled to proof of DV status
- Early termination right for DV victim
- Lease cannot prohibit calling the police in a DV situation or otherwise penalize DV victim
- DV victim has the right to have the locks changed
- Penalty for falsely reporting domestic violence (including obtaining early termination)
- Perpetrator of DV liable to landlord for resulting damages

Arkansas

Ark. Code Ann. § 18-16-112

- Landlord entitled to proof of DV status
- Landlord cannot refuse to rent to victim of DV
- Landlord cannot terminate a victim of DV
- Lease cannot prohibit calling the police in a DV situation or otherwise penalize DV victim
- DV victim has the right to have the locks changed
- Perpetrator of DV liable to landlord for resulting damages
- Landlord or court may bifurcate the lease

California

Cal. Civ. Code §§ 1941.5, 1941.6, 1946.7; Cal. Code Civ. Proc. §§ 1161, 1161.3

- Landlord entitled to proof of DV status
- Landlord cannot refuse to rent to victim of DV
- Landlord cannot terminate a victim of DV
- Early termination right for DV victim
- DV is an affirmative defense to an eviction lawsuit
- DV victim has the right to have the locks changed
- Landlord or court may bifurcate the lease
- Landlord has limited right to evict the DV victim

Miscellaneous provisions: Protection against termination has been expanded to include elder or dependent adults.

Colorado

Colo. Rev. Stat. §§ 13-40-104(4), 13-40-107.5(5), 38-12-401, 38-12-402, 38-12-503

- Lease cannot include a waiver of some or all DV rights
- Landlord entitled to proof of DV status
- Landlord cannot terminate a victim of DV
- Early termination right for DV victim
- Lease cannot prohibit calling the police in a DV situation or otherwise penalize DV victim

Connecticut

Conn. Gen. Stat. Ann. § 47a-11e

- Landlord entitled to proof of DV status
- Early termination right for DV victim

Delaware

25 Del. Code Ann. tit. 25, §§ 5141(7), 5314(b), 5316

- Landlord entitled to proof of DV status
- Landlord cannot terminate a victim of DV
- Early termination right for DV victim

District of Columbia

D.C. Code Ann. §§ 2-1402.21, 42-3505.07, 42-3505.08

- Lease cannot include a waiver of some or all DV rights
- Landlord entitled to proof of DV status
- Landlord cannot refuse to rent to victim of DV
- Early termination right for DV victim
- DV is an affirmative defense to an eviction lawsuit
- Lease cannot prohibit calling the police in a DV situation or otherwise penalize DV victim
- DV victim has the right to have the locks changed
- Landlord or court may bifurcate the lease

State Laws in Domestic Violence Situations (continued)

Miscellaneous provisions: Landlord must make reasonable accommodation in restoring or improving security and safety measures that are beyond the landlord's duty of ordinary care and diligence, when such accommodation is necessary to ensure the tenant's security and safety (tenant may be billed for the cost).

Florida

No statute

Georgia

No statute

Hawaii

HI Rev. Stat. § 521–A

- Landlord entitled to proof of DV status
- Early termination right for DV victim
- DV victim has the right to have the locks changed
- Penalty for falsely reporting domestic violence (including obtaining early termination)
- Landlord or court may bifurcate the lease

Miscellaneous provisions: Landlord may not disclose information gathered with respect to tenant's exercise of rights under these laws, unless the tenant consents in writing, the information is required or relevant in a lawsuit, or the disclosure is required by law.

Idaho

No statute

Illinois

765 Ill. Comp. Stat. §§ 750/1 through 750/35

- Landlord entitled to proof of DV status
- Early termination right for DV victim
- DV is an affirmative defense to an eviction lawsuit
- DV victim has the right to have the locks changed
- Landlord or court may bifurcate the lease

Miscellaneous provisions: Landlord may not disclose to others that a tenant has exercised a right under the law; violations expose landlord to damages that result, or $2,000.

Indiana

Ind. Code Ann. §§ 32-31-9-1 through 32-31-9-15

- Landlord entitled to proof of DV status
- Landlord cannot refuse to rent to victim of DV
- Landlord cannot terminate a victim of DV

- Early termination right for DV victim
- Lease cannot prohibit calling the police in a DV situation or otherwise penalize DV victim
- DV victim has the right to have the locks changed

Iowa

Iowa Code §§ 562A.27A, 562B.25A(3)

- Landlord entitled to proof of DV status
- Landlord cannot terminate a victim of DV
- Landlord has limited right to evict the DV victim

Kansas

No statute

Kentucky

No statute

Louisiana

La. Rev. Stat. Ann. § 9:3261.1

- Lease cannot include a waiver of some or all DV rights
- Landlord entitled to proof of DV status
- Landlord cannot refuse to rent to victim of DV
- Landlord cannot terminate a victim of DV
- Early termination right for DV victim
- Lease cannot prohibit calling the police in a DV situation or otherwise penalize DV victim

Miscellaneous provisions: Statute applies only to multifamily housing of six or more units; does not apply if building has ten or fewer units and one is occupied by the owner.

Maine

Me. Rev. Stat. Ann. tit. 14, §§ 6000, 6001, 6002, 6025

- Landlord entitled to proof of DV status
- Landlord cannot terminate a victim of DV
- Early termination right for DV victim
- DV victim has the right to have the locks changed
- Perpetrator of DV liable to landlord for resulting damages
- Landlord or court may bifurcate the lease

Maryland

Md. Real Prop. Law §§ 8-5A-01 through 8-5A-06

- Landlord entitled to proof of DV status
- Early termination right for DV victim

State Laws in Domestic Violence Situations (continued)

Massachusetts

186 Mass Gen. Laws §§ 24, 25, 26, and 28

- Lease cannot include a waiver of some or all DV rights
- Landlord entitled to proof of DV status
- Landlord cannot refuse to rent to victim of DV
- Early termination right for DV victim
- DV victim has the right to have the locks changed

Michigan

Mich. Comp. Laws § 554.601b

- Landlord entitled to proof of DV status
- Early termination right for DV victim
- Landlord or court may bifurcate the lease

Minnesota

Minn. Stat. Ann. §§ 504B.205, 206

- Lease cannot include a waiver of some or all DV rights
- Landlord entitled to proof of DV status
- Landlord cannot terminate a victim of DV
- Early termination right for DV victim
- DV is an affirmative defense to an eviction lawsuit
- Lease cannot prohibit calling the police in a DV situation or otherwise penalize DV victim

Miscellaneous provisions: Landlord must keep information about the domestic violence confidential. In a multitenant situation, termination by one tenant terminates the lease of all, though other tenants may reappply to enter into a new lease. All security deposit is forfeited.

Mississippi

No statute

Missouri

No statute

Montana

No statute

Nebraska

No statute

Nevada

Nev. Rev. Stat. Ann. §§ 118A.345, 118A.347, 118A.510

- Lease cannot include a waiver of some or all DV rights
- Landlord entitled to proof of DV status

- Landlord cannot terminate a victim of DV
- Early termination right for DV victim
- DV victim has the right to have the locks changed
- Perpetrator of DV liable to landlord for resulting damages

Miscellaneous provisions: Landlord may not disclose the fact of a tenant's early termination to a prospective landlord; nor may a prospective landlord require an applicant to disclose any prior early terminations. Antiretaliation protection extended to tenants who are domestic violence victims or who have terminated a rental agreement pursuant to law.

New Hampshire

N.H. Rev. Stat. Ann. § 540:2.VII

- Landlord entitled to proof of DV status
- Landlord cannot terminate a victim of DV
- DV victim has the right to have the locks changed
- Landlord or court may bifurcate the lease

New Jersey

N.J. Stat. Ann. §§ 46:8-9.5 through 46:8-9.12

- Lease cannot include a waiver of some or all DV rights
- Landlord entitled to proof of DV status
- Early termination right for DV victim

New Mexico

N.M. Stat. Ann. § 47-8-33(J)

- DV is an affirmative defense to an eviction lawsuit
- Landlord or court may bifurcate the lease

New York

N.Y. Real Prop. Law §§ 227-c (2) and 227–d, N.Y. Crim. Proc. Law § 530.13(1), N.Y. Dom. Rel. Law § 240 (3)

- Landlord cannot refuse to rent to victim of DV
- Landlord cannot terminate a victim of DV
- Early termination right for DV victim
- Penalty for falsely reporting domestic violence (including obtaining early termination)
- Landlord or court may bifurcate the lease

North Carolina

N.C. Gen. Stat. §§ 42-40, 42-42.2, 42-42.3, 42-45.1

- Landlord entitled to proof of DV status
- Landlord cannot refuse to rent to victim of DV

State Laws in Domestic Violence Situations (continued)

- Early termination right for DV victim
- DV victim has the right to have the locks changed

North Dakota

N.D. Cent. Code § 47-16-17.1

- Landlord entitled to proof of DV status
- Landlord cannot refuse to rent to victim of DV
- Landlord cannot terminate a victim of DV
- Early termination right for DV victim

Miscellaneous provisions: Landlord may not disclose information provided by a tenant that documents domestic violence. Landlords who violate the provisions providing early termination are subject to damages including actual damages, $1,000, reasonable attorney fees, costs, and disbursements.

Ohio

No statute

Oklahoma

No statute

Oregon

Or. Rev. Stat. §§ 90.449, 90.453, 90.456, 90.459

- Landlord entitled to proof of DV status
- Landlord cannot refuse to rent to victim of DV
- Landlord cannot terminate a victim of DV
- Early termination right for DV victim
- Lease cannot prohibit calling the police in a DV situation or otherwise penalize DV victim
- DV victim has the right to have the locks changed
- Landlord or court may bifurcate the lease
- Landlord has limited right to evict the DV victim

Pennsylvania

No statute

Rhode Island

R.I. Gen. Laws §§ 34-37-1 through 34-37-4

- Landlord cannot refuse to rent to victim of DV
- Landlord cannot terminate a victim of DV
- Landlord or court may bifurcate the lease

South Carolina

No statute

South Dakota

No statute

Tennessee

No statute

Texas

Tex. Prop. Code Ann. §§ 92.015, 92.016, 92.0161

- Lease cannot include a waiver of some or all DV rights
- Landlord entitled to proof of DV status
- Early termination right for DV victim
- Lease cannot prohibit calling the police in a DV situation or otherwise penalize DV victim

Miscellaneous provisions: Tenant who exercises termination rights will be released from any delinquent rent unless the lease includes a clause that specifically describes tenants' rights in domestic violence situations.

Utah

Utah Code Ann. § 57-22-5.1

- Landlord entitled to proof of DV status
- Early termination right for DV victim
- Lease cannot prohibit calling the police in a DV situation or otherwise penalize DV victim
- DV victim has the right to have the locks changed

Vermont

15 Vt. Stat. Ann. § 1103(c)(2)(B)

- Landlord or court may bifurcate the lease

Virginia

Va. Code Ann. §§ 55-225.5, 55-225.16, 55-248.18:1, 55-248.21:2, 55-248.31(D)

- Landlord entitled to proof of DV status
- Landlord cannot terminate a victim of DV
- Early termination right for DV victim
- DV victim has the right to have the locks changed
- Landlord or court may bifurcate the lease

Washington

Wash. Rev. Code Ann. §§ 59.18.570, 59.18.575, 59.18.580, 59.18.585, 59.18.352, 59.18.130(8)(b)(ii)

- Landlord cannot terminate a victim of DV
- Early termination right for DV victim
- DV is an affirmative defense to an eviction lawsuit

State Laws in Domestic Violence Situations (continued)

West Virginia

No statute

Wisconsin

Wis. Stat. Ann. § 106.50(5m)(d)

- Landlord cannot refuse to rent to victim of DV
- Landlord cannot terminate a victim of DV
- DV is an affirmative defense to an eviction lawsuit
- Landlord has limited right to evict the DV victim

Wyoming

Wyo. Stat. §§ 1-21-1301 to 1-21-1304

- Lease cannot include a waiver of some or all DV rights
- Landlord entitled to proof of DV status
- Landlord cannot terminate a victim of DV
- Early termination right for DV victim
- DV is an affirmative defense to an eviction lawsuit

State Laws on Rent Withholding and Repair and Deduct Remedies

State	Statute or case on rent withholding	Statute or case on repair and deduct
Alabama	Ala. Code § 35-9A-405	No statute
Alaska	Alaska Stat. §§ 34.03.190, 34.03.100(b)	Alaska Stat. §§ 34.03.180, 34.03.100(b)
Arizona	Ariz. Rev. Stat. Ann. § 33-1365	Ariz. Rev. Stat. Ann. §§ 33-1363 to -1364
Arkansas	No statute	No statute
California	*Green v. Superior Court*, 10 Cal.3d 616 (1974)	Cal. Civ. Code § 1942
Colorado	Colo. Rev. Stat. § 38-12-507	No statute
Connecticut	Conn. Gen. Stat. Ann. §§ 47a-14a to -14h	Conn. Gen. Stat. Ann. § 47a-13
Delaware	Del. Code Ann. tit. 25, § 5308(b)(3)	Del. Code Ann. tit. 25, §§ 5307, 5308
District of Columbia	*Javins v. First Nat'l Realty Corp.*, 428 F.2d 1071 (D.C. Cir. 1970)	D.C. Code Ann § 6-751.10 (for installation of alarms only)
Florida	Fla. Stat. Ann. § 83.60	No statute
Georgia	No statute	Not addressed by statute, but Georgia courts recognize a tenant's right to this remedy. See *Georgia Landlord Tenant Handbook*, 2012, Georgia Department of Community Affairs (http://www.dca.state.ga.us/ housing/housingdevelopment/programs/downloads/ Georgia_Landlord_Tenant_Handbook.pdf)
Hawaii	Haw. Rev. Stat. § 521-78	Haw. Rev. Stat. § 521-64
Idaho	No statute	No statute
Illinois	765 Ill. Comp. Stat. §§ 735/2, 735 /2.2 (applies only when a court has appointed a receiver to collect rents, following landlord's failure to pay for utilities)	765 Ill. Comp. Stat. § 742/5
Indiana	No statute	No statute
Iowa	Iowa Code Ann. § 562A.24	Iowa Code Ann. § 562A.23
Kansas	Kan. Stat. Ann. § 58-2561	No statute
Kentucky	Ky. Rev. Stat. Ann. § 383.645	Ky. Rev. Stat. Ann. §§ 383.635, 383.640
Louisiana	No statute	La. Civ. Code Ann. art. 2694
Maine	Me. Rev. Stat. Ann. tit. 14, § 6021	Me. Rev. Stat. Ann. tit. 14, § 6026
Maryland	Md. Code Ann. [Real Prop.] §§ 8-211, 8-211.1	No statute
Massachusetts	Mass. Gen. Laws Ann. ch. 239, § 8A	Mass. Gen. Laws Ann. ch. 111, § 127L
Michigan	Mich. Comp. Laws § 125.530	*Rome v. Walker*, 198 N.W.2d 850 (1972); Mich. Comp. Laws § 554.139
Minnesota	Minn. Stat. Ann. §§ 504B.215(3)(d), 504B.385	Minn. Stat. Ann § 504B.425
Mississippi	No statute	Miss. Code Ann. § 89-8-15

State Laws on Rent Withholding and Repair and Deduct Remedies (continued)

State	Statute or case on rent withholding	Statute or case on repair and deduct
Missouri	Mo. Ann. Stat. §§ 441.570, 441.580	Mo. Ann. Stat. § 441.234
Montana	Mont. Code Ann. § 70-24-421	Mont. Code Ann. §§ 70-24-406 to -408
Nebraska	Neb. Rev. Stat. § 76-1428	Neb. Rev. Stat. § 76-1427
Nevada	Nev. Rev. Stat. Ann. § 118A.490	Nev. Rev. Stat. Ann. §§ 118A.360, 118A.380
New Hampshire	N.H. Rev. Stat. Ann. § 540:13-d	No statute
New Jersey	*Berzito v. Gambino*, 63 N.J. 460 (1973)	*Marini v. Ireland*, 265 A.2d 526 (1970)
New Mexico	N.M. Stat. Ann. § 47-8-27.2	No statute
New York	N.Y. Real Prop. Law § 235-b, *Semans Family Ltd. Partnership v. Kennedy*, 675 N.Y.S.2d 489 (N.Y. City Civ. Ct.,1998)	For emergency repairs (such as broken door lock) only: N.Y. Real Prop. Law § 235-b; *Jangla Realty Co. v. Gravagna*, 447 N.Y.S.2d 338 (Civ. Ct., Queens County, 1981)
North Carolina	No statute	No statute
North Dakota	No statute	N.D. Cent. Code § 47-16-13
Ohio	Ohio Rev. Code Ann. § 5321.07 (does not apply to student tenants; or when landlord owns three or fewer rental units, as long as landlord has given written notice to tenant)	No statute
Oklahoma	Okla. Stat. Ann. tit. 41, § 121	Okla. Stat. Ann. tit. 41, § 121
Oregon	Ore. Rev. Stat. § 90.365	Ore. Rev. Stat. § 90.365
Pennsylvania	68 Pa. Cons. Stat. Ann. § 250.206; 35 Pa. Cons. Stat. Ann. § 1700-1	*Pugh v. Holmes*, 405 A.2d 897 (1979)
Rhode Island	R.I. Gen. Laws § 34-18-32	R.I. Gen. Laws §§ 34-18-30 to -31
South Carolina	S.C. Code Ann. § 27-40-640	S.C. Code Ann. § 27-40-630
South Dakota	S.D. Codified Laws Ann. § 43-32-9	S.D. Codified Laws Ann. § 43-32-9
Tennessee	Tenn. Code Ann. § 68-111-104	Tenn. Code Ann. § 66-28-502
Texas	No statute	Tex. Prop. Code Ann. §§ 92.056, 92.0561
Utah	No statute	Utah Code Ann. § 57-22-6
Vermont	Vt. Stat. Ann. tit. 9, § 4458	Vt. Stat. Ann. tit. 9, § 4459
Virginia	Va. Code Ann. §§ 54-248.25, 54-248.25.1, 54-248.27	No statute
Washington	Wash. Rev. Code Ann. §§ 59.18.110, 59.18.115	Wash. Rev. Code Ann. §§ 59.18.100, .110
West Virginia	No statute	No statute
Wisconsin	Wis. Stat. Ann. § 704.07(4)	No statute
Wyoming	Wyo. Stat. § 1-21-1206	No statute

State Laws on Landlord's Access to Rental Property

This is a synopsis of state laws that specify circumstances when a landlord may enter rental premises and the amount of notice required for such entry.

State	State Law Citation	Amount of Notice Required in Nonemergency Situations	Reasons Landlord May Enter				
			To Deal With an Emergency	To Inspect the Premises	To Make Repairs, Alterations, or Improvements	To Show Property to Prospective Tenants or Purchasers	During Tenant's Extended Absence
Alabama	Ala. Code §§ 35-9A-303, 35-9A-423	Two days	✓	✓	✓	✓	✓
Alaska	Alaska Stat. §§ 34.03.140, 34.03.230	24 hours	✓	✓	✓	✓	✓
Arizona	Ariz. Rev. Stat. Ann. § 33-1343	Two days (written or oral notice); notice period does not apply, and tenant's consent is assumed, if entry is pursuant to tenant's request for maintenance as prescribed in Ariz. Rev. Stat. § 33-1341, paragraph 8	✓	✓	✓	✓	
Arkansas	Ark. Code Ann. § 18-17-602	No notice specified		✓	✓	✓	
California	Cal. Civ. Code § 1954	24 hours (48 hours for initial move-out inspection)	✓	✓	✓	✓	
Colorado	No statute						
Connecticut	Conn. Gen. Stat. Ann. §§ 47a-16 to 47a-16a	Reasonable notice	✓	✓	✓	✓	
Delaware	Del. Code Ann. tit. 25, §§ 5509, 5510	Two days	✓	✓	✓	✓	
D.C.	No statute						
Florida	Fla. Stat. Ann. § 83.53	12 hours	✓	✓	✓	✓	✓
Georgia	No statute						
Hawaii	Haw. Rev. Stat. §§ 521-53, 521-70(b)	Two days	✓	✓	✓	✓	✓
Idaho	No statute						
Illinois	No statute						
Indiana	Ind. Code Ann. § 32-31-5-6	Reasonable notice	✓	✓	✓	✓	
Iowa	Iowa Code Ann. §§ 562A.19, 562A.28, 562A.29	24 hours	✓	✓	✓	✓	✓
Kansas	Kan. Stat. Ann. §§ 58-2557, 58-2565	Reasonable notice	✓	✓	✓	✓	✓
Kentucky	Ky. Rev. Stat. Ann. §§ 383.615, 383.670	Two days	✓	✓	✓	✓	✓
Louisiana	La. Civ. Code art. 2693	No notice specified			✓		
Maine	Me. Rev. Stat. Ann. tit. 14, § 6025	24 hours	✓	✓	✓	✓	
Maryland	No statute						
Massachusetts	Mass. Gen. Laws Ann. ch. 186, § 15B(1)(a)	No notice specified	✓	✓	✓	✓	
Michigan	No statute						
Minnesota	Minn. Stat. Ann. § 504B.211	Reasonable notice	✓	✓	✓	✓	
Mississippi	No statute						
Missouri	No statute						
Montana	Mont. Code Ann. §§ 70-24-312, 70-24-426	24 hours	✓	✓	✓	✓	✓

State Laws on Landlord's Access to Rental Property (continued)

State	State Law Citation	Amount of Notice Required in Nonemergency Situations	To Deal With an Emergency	To Inspect the Premises	To Make Repairs, Alterations, or Improvements	To Show Property to Prospective Tenants or Purchasers	During Tenant's Extended Absence
Nebraska	Neb. Rev. Stat. §§ 76-1423, 76-1432	One day	✓	✓	✓	✓	✓
Nevada	Nev. Rev. Stat. Ann. § 118A.330	24 hours	✓	✓	✓	✓	
New Hampshire	N.H. Rev. Stat. Ann. § 540-A:3	Notice that is adequate under the circumstances	✓	✓	✓	✓	
New Jersey	N.J.A.C. 5:10-5.1	One day, by custom; in buildings with three or more units, one day (by regulation)	✓	✓	✓	✓	
New Mexico	N.M. Stat. Ann. §§ 47-8-24, 47-8-34	24 hours	✓	✓	✓	✓	✓
New York	No statute						
North Carolina	No statute						
North Dakota	N.D. Cent. Code § 47-16-07.3	Reasonable notice	✓	✓	✓	✓	
Ohio	Ohio Rev. Code Ann. §§ 5321.04(A)(8), 5321.05(B)	24 hours	✓	✓	✓	✓	
Oklahoma	Okla. Stat. Ann. tit. 41, § 128	One day	✓	✓	✓	✓	
Oregon	Or. Rev. Stat. §§ 90.322, 90.410	24 hours	✓	✓	✓	✓	✓
Pennsylvania	No statute						
Rhode Island	R.I. Gen. Laws § 34-18-26	Two days	✓	✓	✓	✓	✓
South Carolina	S.C. Code Ann. §§ 27-40-530, 27-40-730	24 hours	✓	✓	✓	✓	
South Dakota	No statute						
Tennessee	Tenn. Code Ann. §§ 66-28-403, 66-28-507	24 hours (applies only within the final thirty days of the rental agreement term, when landlord intends to show the premises to prospective renters and this right of access is set forth in the rental agreement)	✓	✓	✓	✓	✓
Texas	No statute						
Utah	Utah Code Ann. §§ 57-22-4, 57-22-5(2)(c)	24 hours, unless rental agreement specifies otherwise	✓		✓		
Vermont	Vt. Stat. Ann. tit. 9, § 4460	48 hours	✓	✓	✓	✓	
Virginia	Va. Code Ann. §§ 55-248.18, 55-248.33	For routine maintenance only: 24 hours, but no notice needed if entry follows tenant's request for maintenance	✓	✓	✓	✓	✓
Washington	Wash. Rev. Code Ann. § 59.18.150	Two days; one day to show property to actual or prospective tenants or buyers	✓	✓	✓	✓	
West Virginia	No statute						
Wisconsin	Wis. Stat. Ann. § 704.05(2)	Advance notice	✓	✓	✓	✓	✓
Wyoming	No statute						

State Laws on Handling Abandoned Property

Most states regulate the way landlords must handle property left behind by departed tenants. Many set notice requirements as to how landlords must contact tenants regarding abandoned property. States may also regulate how landlords must store abandoned property and dispose of it if the tenant doesn't claim his or her belongings. For details, check your state statute, listed in this chart. Keep in mind that court cases not mentioned here may further describe proper procedures in your state.

State	Statute	State	Statute
Alabama	Ala. Code 1975 § 35-9A-423	Missouri	Mo. Rev. Stat. § 441.065
Alaska	Alaska Stat. § 34.03.260	Montana	Mont. Code Ann. § 70-24-430
Arizona	Ariz. Rev. Stat. Ann. § 33-1370	Nebraska	Neb. Rev. Stat. §§ 69-2303 to 69-2314
Arkansas	Ark. Code Ann. § 18-16-108	Nevada	Nev. Rev. Stat. Ann. §§ 118A.450, 118A.460
California	Cal. Civ. Code §§ 1965, 1980 to 1991	New Hampshire	N.H. Rev. Stat. Ann. § 540-A:3(VII)
Colorado	Colo. Rev. Stat. §§ 13-40-122, 38-20-116	New Jersey	N.J. Stat. Ann. §§ 2A:18-72 to 2A:18-84
Connecticut	Conn. Gen. Stat. Ann. §§ 47a-11b, 47a-42	New Mexico	N.M. Stat. Ann. § 47-8-34.1
Delaware	Del. Code Ann. tit. 25, §§ 5507, 5715	New York	No statute
D.C.	No statute	North Carolina	N.C. Gen. Stat. §§ 42-25.9, 42-36.2
Florida	Fla. Stat. Ann. §§ 715.104 to 715.111	North Dakota	N.D. Cent. Code § 47-16-30.1
Georgia	Ga. Code Ann. § 44-7-55	Ohio	*Ringler v. Sias*, 428 NE. 2d 869 (Ohio Ct. App. 1980)
Hawaii	Haw. Rev. Stat. § 521-56	Oklahoma	Okla. Stat. Ann. tit. 41, § 130
Idaho	Idaho Code § 6-311C	Oregon	Ore. Rev. Stat. §§ 90.425, 105.165
Illinois	735 Ill. Comp. Stat. § 5/9-318	Pennsylvania	68 P.S. § 250.505a
Indiana	Ind. Code. Ann. §§ 32-31-4-1 to 32-31-4-5, 32-31-5-5	Rhode Island	R.I. Gen. Laws § 34-18-50
		South Carolina	S.C. Code Ann. §§ 27-40-710(D), 27-40-730
Iowa	*Khan v. Heritage Prop. Mgmt.*, 584 N.W. 2d 725, 730 (Iowa Ct. App. 1998)	South Dakota	S.D. Codified Laws Ann. §§ 43-32-25, 43-32-26
Kansas	Kan. Stat. Ann. § 58-2565	Tennessee	Tenn. Code Ann. § 66-28-405
Kentucky	No statute	Texas	Tex. Prop. Code § 92.014
Louisiana	La. Civ. Code § 2707, La. Civ. Proc. § 4705	Utah	Utah Code Ann. § 78B-6-816
Maine	Me. Rev. Stat. Ann. tit. 14, §§ 6005, 6013	Vermont	Vt. Stat. Ann. tit. 9, § 4462; Vt. Stat. Ann. tit. 12, § 4854a
Maryland	Md. Code, Real Property, § 8-208	Virginia	Va. Code Ann. §§ 55-248.38:1 to 55-248.38:2
Massachusetts	M.G.L.A. 239 § 4	Washington	Wash. Rev. Code Ann. § 59.18.310
Michigan	No statute	West Virginia	W.Va. Code §§ 37-6-6, 55-3A-3
Minnesota	Minn. Stat. Ann. § 504B.271	Wisconsin	Wis. Stat. Ann. § 704.05(5)
Mississippi	Miss. Code Ann. §§ 89-7-31, 89-7-35, 89-8-13	Wyoming	Wyo. Stat. § 1-21-1210

State Laws Prohibiting Landlord Retaliation

State	Statute	Tenant's Complaint to Landlord or Government Agency	Tenant's Involvement in Tenants' Organization	Tenant's Exercise of Legal Right	Retaliation Is Presumed If Negative Reaction by Landlord Within Specified Time of Tenant's Act
Alabama	Ala. Code § 35-9A-501	✓	✓		
Alaska	Alaska Stat. § 34.03.310	✓	✓	✓	
Arizona	Ariz. Rev. Stat. Ann. § 33-1381	✓	✓		6 months
Arkansas [1]	Ark. Code Ann. § 20-27-608	✓			
California [2]	Cal. Civ. Code § 1942.5	✓	✓	✓	180 days
Colorado [3]	Colo. Rev. Stat. § 38-12-509	✓			
Connecticut	Conn. Gen. Stat. §§ 47a-20, 47a-33	✓	✓	✓	6 months
Delaware	Del. Code Ann. tit. 25, § 5516	✓	✓	✓	90 days
D.C.	D.C. Code § 42-3505.02	✓	✓	✓	6 months
Florida [4]	Fla. Stat. Ann. § 83.64	✓	✓	✓	
Georgia	No statute				
Hawaii	Haw. Rev. Stat. § 521-74	✓		✓	
Idaho	No statute				
Illinois	765 Ill. Comp. Stat. § 720/1	✓			
Indiana	No statute				
Iowa	Iowa Code Ann. § 562A.36	✓	✓		1 year
Kansas	Kan. Stat. Ann. § 58-2572	✓	✓		
Kentucky	Ky. Rev. Stat. Ann. § 383.705	✓	✓		1 year
Louisiana	No statute				
Maine [5]	4 Me. Rev. Stat. Ann. tit. 14, §§ 6001(3), (4), 6021-A	✓	✓	✓	6 months
Maryland	Md. Code Ann. [Real Prop.] § 8-208.1	✓	✓	✓	
Massachusetts [2]	Mass. Ann. Laws ch. 239, § 2A; ch. 186, § 18	✓	✓	✓	6 months
Michigan	Mich. Comp. Laws § 600.5720	✓	✓	✓	90 days
Minnesota	Minn. Stat. Ann. §§ 504B.441, 504B.285	✓		✓	90 days
Mississippi	Miss. Code Ann. § 89-8-17			✓	
Missouri	No statute				

[1] Only prohibits retaliation by landlord who has received notice of lead hazards. (Arkansas)

[2] Applies when a retaliatory eviction follows a court case or administrative hearing concerning the tenant's underlying complaint, membership in a tenant organization, or exercise of a legal right. In this situation, a tenant may claim the benefit of the antiretaliation presumption only if the eviction falls within six months of the final determination of the court case or administrative hearing. (California and Massachusetts)

[3] Tenant is protected against retaliation only for complaints of violations of the warranty of habitability. Tenant must prove actual violation in order to prevail. Any termination, rent increase, or service decrease that follows a complaint is presumed to be not retaliatory (timing alone of such actions will not make them retaliatory). (Colorado)

[4] Statute lists retaliatory acts as illustrative, not exhaustive, and includes retaliation after the tenant has paid rent to a condominium, cooperative, or homeowners' association after demand from the association in order to pay the landlord's obligation to the association; and when the tenant has exercised his or her rights under state, local, or federal fair housing laws. (Florida)

[5] Allows tenant to raise his complaint to a fair housing agency as an affirmative defense to an eviction; retaliation presumed if tenant is served with an eviction notice within 6 months of tenant's exercise of rights regarding bedbug infestations (does not apply to eviction for nonpayment or for causing substantial damage). (Maine)

State Laws Prohibiting Landlord Retaliation (continued)

State	Statute	Tenant's Complaint to Landlord or Government Agency	Tenant's Involvement in Tenants' Organization	Tenant's Exercise of Legal Right	Retaliation Is Presumed If Negative Reaction by Landlord Within Specified Time of Tenant's Act
Montana	Mont. Code Ann. § 70-24-431	✓	✓		6 months
Nebraska	Neb. Rev. Stat. § 76-1439	✓	✓		
Nevada	Nev. Rev. Stat. Ann. § 118A.510	✓	✓	✓	
New Hampshire	N.H. Rev. Stat. Ann. §§ 540:13-a, 540:13-b	✓	✓	✓	6 months
New Jersey [6]	N.J. Stat. Ann. §§ 2A:42-10.10, 2A:42-10.12	✓	✓	✓	
New Mexico	N.M. Stat. Ann. § 47-8-39	✓	✓	✓	6 months
New York	N.Y. Real Prop. Law § 223-b	✓	✓	✓	6 months
North Carolina	N.C. Gen. Stat. § 42-37.1	✓	✓	✓	12 months
North Dakota	No statute				
Ohio	Ohio Rev. Code Ann. § 5321.02	✓	✓		
Oklahoma	No statute				
Oregon	Ore. Rev. Stat. § 90.385	✓	✓		
Pennsylvania	68 Pa. Cons. Stat. Ann. §§ 250.205, 399.11		✓	✓	6 months (for exercise of legal rights connected with utility service)
Rhode Island	R.I. Gen. Laws Ann. §§ 34-20-10, 34-20-11	✓		✓	
South Carolina	S.C. Code Ann. § 27-40-910	✓			
South Dakota	S.D. Cod. Laws Ann. §§ 43-32-27, 43-32-28	✓	✓		180 days
Tennessee	Tenn. Code Ann. §§ 66-28-514, 68-111-105	✓		✓	
Texas	Tex. Prop. Code § 92.331	✓	✓	✓	6 months
Utah	*Building Monitoring Sys. v. Paxton*, 905 P.2d 1215 (Utah 1995)	✓			
Vermont [7]	Vt. Stat. Ann. tit. 9, § 4465	✓	✓	✓	90 days
Virginia	Va. Code Ann. §§ 55-225.18, 55-248.39	✓	✓	✓	
Washington	Wash. Rev. Code §§ 59.18.240, 59.18.250	✓		✓	90 days
West Virginia	*Imperial Colliery Co. v. Fout*, 373 S.E.2d 489 (1988)	✓		✓	
Wisconsin	Wis. Stat. § 704.45	✓		✓	
Wyoming	No statute				

[6] If a tenant fails to request a renewal of a lease or tenancy within 90 days of the tenancy's expiration (or by the renewal date specified in the lease if longer than 90 days), a landlord may terminate or not renew without a presumption of retaliation. (New Jersey)

[7] Retaliation presumed only when landlord terminates for reasons other than rent nonpayment, after tenant has filed complaint with a governmental entity alleging noncompliance with health or safety regulations. (Vermont)

State Laws on Termination for Nonpayment of Rent

If the tenant is late with the rent, in most states the landlord cannot immediately file for eviction. Instead, the landlord must give the tenant written notice that the tenant has a specified number of days in which to pay up or move. If the tenant does neither, the landlord can file for eviction. In some states, the landlord must wait a few days after the rent is due before giving the tenant the notice; other states allow the landlord to file for eviction immediately. The following rules may be tempered in domestic violence situations, depending on state law (see "State Laws in Domestic Violence Situations" in this appendix).

State	Statute	Time Tenant Has to Pay Rent or Move Before Landlord Can File for Eviction	Legal Late Period: How Long Landlord Must Wait Before Giving Notice to Pay or Quit
Alabama	Ala. Code § 35-9A-421	7 days	
Alaska	Alaska Stat. §§ 09.45.090, 34.03.220	7 days	
Arizona	Ariz. Rev. Stat. § 33-1368	5 days	
Arkansas	Ark. Stat. §§ 18-60-304, 18-16-101	Landlord may terminate with an Unconditional Quit notice.	
California	Cal. Civ. Proc. Code § 1161(2)	3 days	
Colorado	Colo. Rev. Stat. § 13-40-104(1)(d)	3 days	
Connecticut	Conn. Gen. Stat. §§ 47a-23, 47a-15a	9 days	Unconditional Quit notice cannot be delivered until the rent is 9 days late.
Delaware	Del. Code Ann. tit. 25, §§ 5501(d), 5502	5 days	If rental agreement provides for a late charge, but landlord does not maintain an office in the county in which the rental unit is located, due date for the rent is extended 3 days; thereafter, landlord can serve a 5-day notice.
District of Columbia	D.C. Code § 42-3505.01	30 days	
Florida	Fla. Stat. Ann. § 83.56(3)	3 days	
Georgia	Ga. Code Ann. §§ 44-7-50, 44-7-52	Landlord can demand the rent as soon as it is due and, if not paid, can file for eviction. Tenant then has 7 days to pay to avoid eviction.	
Hawaii	Haw. Rev. Stat. § 521-68	5 days	
Idaho	Idaho Code § 6-303(2)	3 days	
Illinois	735 Ill. Comp. Stat. § 5/9-209	5 days	
Indiana	Ind. Code Ann. § 32-31-1-6	10 days	
Iowa	Iowa Code § 562A.27(2)	3 days	
Kansas	Kan. Rev. Stat. §§ 58-2507, 58-2508, 58-2564(b)	10 days (tenancies over 3 months) 3 days (tenancies less than 3 months)	
Kentucky	Ky. Rev. Stat. Ann. § 383.660(2)	7 days	
Louisiana	La. Civ. Proc. art. 4701	Landlord can terminate with an Unconditional Quit notice.	
Maine	Me. Rev. Stat. tit. 14, § 6002	7 days	Notice cannot be delivered until the rent is 7 days late, and must tell tenant that tenant can contest the termination in court (failure to so advise prohibits entry of a default judgment).

State Laws on Termination for Nonpayment of Rent (continued)

State	Statute	Time Tenant Has to Pay Rent or Move Before Landlord Can File for Eviction	Legal Late Period: How Long Landlord Must Wait Before Giving Notice to Pay or Quit
Maryland	Md. Code Ann. [Real Prop.] § 8-401	Can file immediately; must give 5 days' notice to appear in court; if tenant doesn't pay and landlord wins, tenant has 4 days to vacate. If tenant pays all back rent and court costs before end of trial, tenant can stay.	
Massachusetts[1]	Mass. Ann. Laws ch. 186, §§ 11 to 12	Tenants with rental agreements or leases, in accordance with agreement, or if not addressed in the agreement, 14 days' notice (but tenant can avoid by paying rent and costs before answer); holdover tenants: landlord can file for eviction immediately.	
Michigan	Mich. Comp. Laws § 554.134(2)	Landlord may terminate immediately with 7-day notice.	
Minnesota	Minn. Stat. Ann. §§ 504B.135, 504B.291	14 days' notice required if tenancy at will (no lease); 30 days or more notice for a lease with a term of more than 20 years.	
Mississippi	Miss. Code Ann. §§ 89-7-27, 89-7-45	3 days. Tenant may stay if rent and costs are paid prior to removal.	
Missouri	Mo. Rev. Stat. § 535.010	Landlord can terminate with an Unconditional Quit notice.	
Montana	Mont. Code Ann. § 70-24-422(2)	3 days	
Nebraska	Neb. Rev. Stat. § 76-1431(2)	3 days	
Nevada	Nev. Rev. Stat. Ann. § 40.251	5 days	
New Hampshire	N.H. Rev. Stat. Ann. §§ 540:2, 540:3, 540:9	7 days. Tenant also owes $15 in liquidated damages, but use of this remedy is limited to three times within twelve months.	
New Jersey	N.J. Stat. Ann. §§ 2A:18-53, 2A:18-61.1, 2A:18-61.2, 2A:42-9	30 days. Landlord must accept rent and costs any time up to the day of trial.	
New Mexico	N.M. Stat. Ann. § 47-8-33(D)	3 days	
New York State	N.Y. Real Prop. Acts Law § 711(2)	3 days	
North Carolina	N.C. Gen. Stat. § 42-3	10 days	
North Dakota	N.D. Cent. Code § 47-32-01	Landlord can file for eviction when rent is 3 days overdue and can terminate with an Unconditional Quit notice.	
Ohio	Ohio Rev. Code Ann. § 1923.02(A)(9)	Landlord can terminate with an Unconditional Quit notice.	
Oklahoma	Okla. Stat. Ann. tit. 41, § 131	5 days	
Oregon[2]	Ore. Rev. Stat. § 90.394(2)(a)	72 hours (3 days)	Notice cannot be delivered until the rent is 8 days late.
	Ore. Rev. Stat. § 90.394(2)(b)	144 hours (6 days)	Notice cannot be delivered until the rent is 5 days late.

[1] For tenants at will who have not received notices in the preceding 12 months, 10 days to pay, 4 more to quit (unless notice is insufficient, then 14 days to pay). (Massachusetts)

[2] Landlord has a choice: Serve pay or quit notice after rent is 8 days late (tenant has 72 hours to pay or quit), or serve the notice earlier, after rent is overdue 5 days (tenant has longer, 144 hours, to pay or quit). (Oregon)

State Laws on Termination for Nonpayment of Rent (continued)

State	Statute	Time Tenant Has to Pay Rent or Move Before Landlord Can File for Eviction	Legal Late Period: How Long Landlord Must Wait Before Giving Notice to Pay or Quit
Pennsylvania	68 Pa. Cons. Stat. Ann. § 250.501(b)	10 days	
Rhode Island	R.I. Gen. Laws § 34-18-35	5 days. Tenant can stay if rent paid back prior to commencement of suit. If tenant has not received a pay or quit notice for nonpayment of rent within past 6 months, tenant can stay if rent and costs paid back prior to eviction hearing.	15 days.
South Carolina	S.C. Code Ann. § 27-40-710(B), § 27-37-10(B)	5 days. If there is a written lease or rental agreement that specifies in bold, conspicuous type that landlord may file for eviction as soon as tenant is 5 days late (or if there is a month-to-month tenancy following such an agreement), landlord may do so without further notice to tenant. If there is no such written agreement, landlord must give tenant 5 days' written notice before filing for eviction.	
South Dakota	S.D. Codified Laws Ann. §§ 21-16-1(4), 21-16-2	3 days, and landlord can terminate with an Unconditional Quit notice.	
Tennessee	Tenn. Code Ann. § 66-28-505	14 days to pay; additional 16 days to vacate.	
Texas	Tex. Prop. Code Ann. § 24.005	3 days' notice to move (lease may specify a shorter or longer time).	
Utah	Utah Code Ann. § 78B-6-802	3 days	
Vermont	Vt. Stat. Ann. tit. 9, § 4467(a)	14 days	
Virginia	Va. Code Ann. §§ 55-225, 55-243, 55-248.31	5 days. Tenant who pays rent, costs, interest, and reasonable attorney fees can stay, but may invoke this right only once in any 12-month period.	
Washington	Wash. Rev. Code Ann. § 59.12.030(3)	3 days	
West Virginia	W.Va. Code § 55-3A-1	Landlord can file for eviction immediately, no notice required, no opportunity to cure.	
Wisconsin	Wis. Stat. Ann. § 704.17	Month-to-month tenants: 5 days; landlord can use an Unconditional Quit notice with 14 days' notice. Tenants with a lease less than one year, and year-to-year tenants: 5 days (cannot use Unconditional Quit notice). Tenants with a lease longer than one year: 30 days (cannot use Unconditional Quit notice).	
Wyoming	Wyo. Stat. §§ 1-21-1002 to 1-21-1003	Landlord can file for eviction when rent is 3 days or more late and tenant has been given at least 3 days' notice. Landlord can also terminate with an Unconditional Quit notice.	

State Laws on Termination for Violation of Lease

Many states give the tenant a specified amount of time to cure or cease the lease or rental agreement violation or move before the landlord can file for eviction. In some states, if the tenant has not ceased or cured the violation at the end of that period, the tenant gets additional time to move before the landlord can file; in others, the tenant must move as soon as the cure period expires. And some states allow the landlord to terminate with an Unconditional Quit notice, without giving the tenant a chance to cure or cease the violation. The following rules may be tempered in domestic violence situations, depending on state law (see "State Laws in Domestic Violence Situations" in this appendix).

State	Statute	Time Tenant Has to Cure the Violation or Move Before Landlord Can File for Eviction
Alabama	Ala. Code § 35-9A-421	14 calendar days
Alaska	Alaska Stat. §§ 09.45.090, 34.03.220	10 days for violators of agreement materially affecting health and safety; 3 days to cure for failing to pay utility bills, resulting in shut-off, additional 2 to vacate.
Arizona	Ariz. Rev. Stat. § 33-1368	5 days for violations materially affecting health and safety; 10 days for other violations of the lease terms.
Arkansas	No statute	Landlord can terminate with an Unconditional Quit notice.
California	Cal. Civ. Proc. Code § 1161(3)	3 days
Colorado	Colo. Rev. Stat. § 13-40-104(1)(d.5), (e)	3 days (no cure for certain substantial violations).
Connecticut	Conn. Gen. Stat. Ann. § 47a-15	15 days; no right to cure for nonpayment of rent or serious nuisance.
Delaware	Del. Code Ann. tit. 25, § 5513(a)	7 days
District of Columbia	D.C. Code § 42-3505.01	30 days
Florida	Fla. Stat. Ann. § 83.56(2)	7 days (no cure for certain substantial violations).
Georgia	No statute	Landlord can terminate with an Unconditional Quit notice.
Hawaii	Haw. Rev. Stat. §§ 521-72, 666-3	10 days' notice to cure: if it has not ceased, must wait another 20 to file for eviction; 24 hours to cease a nuisance: if it has not ceased in 24 hours, 5 days to cure before filing for eviction.
Idaho	Idaho Code § 6-303	3 days
Illinois	735 Ill. Comp. Stat. § 5/9-210	10 days
Indiana	No statute	Landlord can terminate with an Unconditional Quit notice.
Iowa	Iowa Code § 562A.27(1)	7 days
Kansas	Kan. Stat. Ann. § 58-2564(a)	14 days to cure and an additional 16 to vacate.
Kentucky	Ky. Rev. Stat. Ann. § 383.660(1)	15 days
Louisiana	La. Civ. Proc. art. 4701	5 days
Maine	Me. Rev. Stat. Ann. tit. 14 § 6002	7 days
Maryland	Md. Real Prop. Code Ann. § 8-402.1	30 days unless breach poses clear and imminent danger, then 14 days (no cure).
Massachusetts	No statute	Landlord can terminate with an Unconditional Quit notice.
Michigan	Mich. Comp. Laws § 600.5714	For causing serious, continuous health hazards or damage to the premises: 7 days after receiving notice to restore or repair or quit (domestic violence victims excepted).
Minnesota	Minn. Stat. Ann. § 504B.285 (Subd.4)	Landlord can immediately file for eviction.
Mississippi	Miss. Code Ann. § 89-8-13	30 days
Missouri	No statute	Landlord can terminate with an Unconditional Quit notice.

State Laws on Termination for Violation of Lease (continued)

State	Statute	Time Tenant Has to Cure the Violation or Move Before Landlord Can File for Eviction
Montana	Mont. Code Ann. § 70-24-422	14 days; 3 days if unauthorized pet or person on premises.
Nebraska	Neb. Rev. Stat. § 76-1431	14 days to cure, 16 additional days to vacate.
Nevada	Nev. Rev. Stat. Ann. § 40.2516	5 days to cure
New Hampshire	N.H. Rev. Stat. Ann. § 540:3	30 days
New Jersey	N.J. Stat. Ann. §§ 2A:18-53(c), 2A:18-61.1(e)(1)	3 days; lease must specify which violations will result in eviction. (Some courts have ruled that the tenant be given an opportunity to cure the violation or condition any time up to the entry of judgment in favor of the landlord.)
New Mexico	N.M. Stat. Ann. § 47-8-33(A)	7 days
New York	N.Y. Real Prop. Acts Law §§ 711, 753(4)[NYC]	Regulated units: 10 days or as set by applicable rent regulation. Nonregulated units: No statute. Lease sets applicable cure and/or termination notice periods.
North Carolina	No statute	Landlord can terminate with an Unconditional Quit notice if lease specifies termination for violation.
North Dakota	No statute	Landlord can terminate with an Unconditional Quit notice if term is material.
Ohio	Ohio Revised Code §§ 1923.02(A)(9) and 1923.04	3 days
Oklahoma	Okla. Stat. Ann. tit. 41, § 132(A), (B)	10 days to cure, additional 5 days to vacate.
Oregon	Ore. Rev. Stat. §§ 90.392, 90.405	14 days to cure, additional 16 days to vacate; 10 days to remove an illegal pet.
Pennsylvania	No statute	Landlord can terminate with an Unconditional Quit notice.
Rhode Island	R.I. Gen. Laws § 34-18-36	20 days for material noncompliance.
South Carolina	S.C. Code Ann. § 27-40-710(A)	14 days
South Dakota	S.D. Codified Laws Ann. §§ 21-16-1(7), 21-16-2	Landlord must give tenant 3 days' notice to quit (no opportunity to cure) before filing for eviction, in specified situations. Other situations require no notice.
Tennessee	Tenn. Code Ann. § 66-28-505(d)	14 days
Texas	Tex. Prop. Code § 24.005	3 days
Utah	Utah Code Ann. § 78B-6-802	3 days
Vermont	Vt. Stat. Ann. tit. 9 § 4467(b)(1)	30 days
Virginia	Va. Code Ann. § 55-248.31	21 days to cure, additional 9 to quit.
Washington	Wash. Rev. Code Ann. § 59.12.030(4)	10 days
West Virginia	W.Va. Code § 55-3A-1	Landlord can immediately file for eviction; no notice is required.
Wisconsin	Wis. Stat. Ann. § 704.17	5 days, no opportunity to cure for public housing tenants who have committed drug-related violations
Wyoming	Wyo. Stat. §§ 1-21-1002, 1-21-1003	3 days

State Laws on Unconditional Quit Terminations

Here are state rules that allow landlords to terminate a tenancy within a short period of time, such as for a tenant's repeated violation of a lease term. These rules may be tempered in domestic violence situations, depending on state law (see "State Laws in Domestic Violence Situations" in this appendix).

State	Statute	Time to Move Out Before Landlord Can File for Eviction	When Unconditional Quit Notice Can Be Used
Alabama	Ala. Code § 35-9A-421	7 days	Intentional misrepresentation of a material fact in a rental application or rental agreement, possession or use of illegal drugs in the rental or common areas, discharge of a firearm (some exceptions), criminal assault of a tenant or guest on the premises (some exceptions)
Alaska	Alaska Stat. § 34.03.220(a)(1)	24 hours	Tenant or guest intentionally causing more than $400 of damage to landlord's property or same violation of lease within 6 months
	§ 9.45.090(a)(2)(G)	24 hours to 5 days	Tenant or guest intentionally causing more than $400 of damage to landlord's property and specified illegal activity on the premises, including allowing prostitution
	§ 34.03.220(e)	3 days	Failure to pay utility bills twice within six months
	§ 34.03.300(a)	10 days	Refusal to allow the landlord to enter
Arizona	Ariz. Rev. Stat. Ann. § 33-1368	10 days	Material misrepresentation of criminal record, current criminal activity, or prior eviction record
		Immediately	Discharging a weapon; homicide, prostitution, criminal street gang activity; use or sale of illegal drugs, assaults, acts constituting a nuisance or breach of the rental agreement that threaten harm to others
Arkansas	Ark. Stat. Ann. §§ 18-60-304, 18-16-101	3 days	Nonpayment of rent. Engaging in (or allowing others to engage in) illegal gambling, prostitution, or the unlawful sale of alcohol (tenant has five days to file an answer in court, and may defend at a court hearing).
California	Cal. Civ. Proc. Code § 1161(4)	3 days	Assigning or subletting without permission, committing waste or a nuisance, illegal activity on the premises
Colorado	Colo. Rev. Stat. § 13-40-104(1)(e.5)	3 days	Any repeated violation of a lease clause
Connecticut	Conn. Gen. Stat. Ann. §§ 47a-23, 47a-15, 47a-15a	3 days	Nonpayment of rent, serious nuisance, violation of the rental agreement, same violation within 6 months relating to health and safety or materially affecting physical premises, rental agreement has terminated (by lapse of time, stipulation, violation of lease, nonpayment of rent after grace period, serious nuisance, occupancy by someone who never had the right to occupy), when summary eviction is justified (refusal to a fair and equitable increase, intent of the landlord to use as a principal residence, removal of the unit from the housing market), domestic or farmworker who does not vacate upon cessation of employment and tenancy
	Conn. Gen. Stat. Ann. § 47a-31	Immediately	Conviction for prostitution or gambling

State Laws on Unconditional Quit Terminations (continued)

State	Statute	Time to Move Out Before Landlord Can File for Eviction	When Unconditional Quit Notice Can Be Used
Delaware	Del. Code Ann. tit. 25, §§ 5513, 5514	7 days	Violation of a lease provision that also constitutes violation of municipal, county, or state code or statute, or same violation of a material lease provision repeated within 12 months
		Immediately	Violation of law or breach of the rental agreement that causes or threatens to cause irreparable harm to the landlord's property or to other tenants
District of Columbia	D.C. Code § 42-3505.01(c)	30 days	Court determination that an illegal act was performed within the rental unit
Florida	Fla. Stat. Ann. § 83.56(2)(a)	7 days	Intentional destruction of the rental property or other tenants' property or unreasonable disturbances; for destruction, damage, or misuse of the landlord's or other tenants' property by intentional act or a subsequent or continued unreasonable disturbance (after written warning within previous 12 months); a subsequent or continuing noncompliance within 12 months of a written warning by the landlord of a similar violation
Georgia	Ga. Code Ann. §§ 44-7-50, 44-7-52	Immediately	Nonpayment of rent more than once within 12 months, holding over
Hawaii	Haw. Rev. Stat. §§ 521-70(c), 521-69, 666-3	Immediately	Causing or threatening to cause irremediable damage to any person or property
		5 days	Second failure to abate a nuisance within 24 hours of receiving notice
Idaho	Idaho Code § 6-303	Immediately	Using, delivering, or producing a controlled substance on the property at any time during the lease term
		3 days	Assigning or subletting without the consent of the landlord or causing serious damage to the property
Illinois	735 Ill. Comp. Stat. § 5/9-210	10 days	Failure to abide by any term of the lease
	740 Ill. Comp. Stat. § 40/11	5 days	Unlawful use or sale of any controlled substance
Indiana	Ind. Code Ann. § 32-31-1-8	Immediately	Tenants with lease: holding over. Tenants without lease: committing waste
Iowa	Iowa Code Ann. § 562A.27	7 days	Repeating same violation of lease within 6 months that affects health and safety
	Iowa Code Ann. § 562A.27A	3 days	Creating a clear and present danger to the health or safety of the landlord, tenants, or neighbors within 1,000 feet of the property boundaries
Kansas	Kan. Stat. Ann. § 58-2564(a)	30 days	Second similar material violation of the lease after first violation was corrected
Kentucky	Ky. Rev. Stat. Ann. § 383.660(1)	14 days	Repeating the same material violation of the lease within 6 months of being given a first cure or quit notice

State Laws on Unconditional Quit Terminations (continued)

State	Statute	Time to Move Out Before Landlord Can File for Eviction	When Unconditional Quit Notice Can Be Used
Louisiana	La. Civ. Code art. 2686, La. Code Civ. Proc. art. 4701	5 days	Failure to pay rent, using dwelling for purpose other than the intended purpose (lease may specify shorter or longer notice, or eliminate requirement of notice), or upon termination of the lease for any reason
Maine	Me. Rev. Stat. Ann. tit. 14, § 6002	7 days	Tenants at will: Violations of law relating to the tenancy, substantial and unrepaired damage to the premises; causing, permitting, or maintaining a nuisance; causing the dwelling to be unfit for human habitation; tenant is a perpetrator of domestic violence, sexual assault, or stalking and the victim is also a tenant
Maryland	Md. Code Ann. [Real Prop.] § 8-402.1(a)	14 days	Breaching lease by behaving in a manner that presents a clear and imminent danger to the tenant himself, other tenants, guests, the landlord, or the landlord's property, lease provides for termination for violation of lease clause, and landlord has given 14 days' notice
	Md. Code Ann. [Real Prop.] § 8-401 (e)(1)	30 days	Any lease violation if the lease states that tenancy can terminate for violation of the lease; and, when tenant is late with the rent three times within the past 12 months, but landlord must have won an eviction lawsuit for each prior nonpayment of rent episode (tenants may reinstate their tenancy by paying rent and court costs after the landlord has won an eviction lawsuit, but before physical eviction)
Massachusetts	Mass. Ann. Laws ch. 186, § 12	14 days	Tenant at will receiving second notice to pay rent or quit within 12 months
Michigan	Mich. Comp. Laws §§ 600.5714(d) and (e)	7 days	Failure to pay rent, causing or threatening physical injury to an individual (landlord must have filed a police report)
	Mich. Comp. Laws § 554.134	24 hours	Manufacture, dealing, or possession of illegal drugs on leased premises (landlord must first file a police report)
Minnesota	Minn. Stat. Ann. § 504B.135	14 days	Tenant at will who fails to pay rent when due
Mississippi	Miss. Code Ann. § 89-8-13	14 days	Repeating the same act, which constituted a lease violation and for which notice was given, within 6 months
		30 days	Nonremediable violation of lease or obligations imposed by statute
Missouri	Mo. Ann. Stat. §§ 441.020, 441.030, 441.040	10 days	Using the premises for gambling, prostitution, or possession, sale, or distribution of controlled substances; assigning or subletting without consent; seriously damaging the premises or violating the lease
Montana	Mont. Code Ann. § 70-24-422(1)(e)	5 days	Repeating the same act—that constituted a lease violation and for which notice was given—within 6 months
	Mont. Code Ann. § 70-24-422	3 days	Unauthorized pet or person living on premises; destroying or removing any part of the premises; creating a reasonable potential that the premises may be damaged or destroyed, or that neighboring tenants may be injured, due to tenant's drug, or gang-related, or other illegal activity
		14 days	Any other noncompliance with rental agreement that can't be remedied or repaired

State Laws on Unconditional Quit Terminations (continued)

State	Statute	Time to Move Out Before Landlord Can File for Eviction	When Unconditional Quit Notice Can Be Used
Nebraska	Neb. Rev. Stat. § 76-1431(1)	14 days	Repeating the same act—that constituted a lease violation and for which notice was given—within 6 months
Nevada	Nev. Rev. Stat. Ann. § 40.2514	3 days	Assigning or subletting in violation of the lease; substantial damage to the property; conducting an unlawful business; permitting or creating a nuisance; causing injury and damage to other tenants or occupants of the property or adjacent buildings or structures; unlawful possession for sale, manufacture, or distribution of illegal drugs
	§ 40.2516	Immediately	Violation of lease term that can't be cured
New Hampshire	N.H. Rev. Stat. Ann. § 540:1-a		Different rules apply depending on whether the property is "restricted" (most residential property) or "nonrestricted" (single-family houses, if the owner of such a house does not own more than 3 single-family houses at any one time; rental units in an owner-occupied building containing a total of 4 dwelling units or fewer; and single-family houses acquired by banks or other mortgagees through foreclosure).
	§§ 540:2, 540:3	7 days	Restricted property: Neglect or refusal to pay rent due and in arrears, upon demand; fourth instance within a 12-month period in which the rent has been in arrears; substantial damage to the premises; failure to comply with a material term of the lease; behavior of the tenant or members of his family that adversely affects the health or safety of the other tenants or the landlord or his representatives; failure of the tenant to accept suitable temporary relocation required by lead-based paint hazard abatement; other good cause. Nonrestricted: Neglect or refusal to pay rent due and in arrears, upon demand; substantial damage to the premises; behavior of the tenant or members of his family that adversely affects the health or safety of the other tenants or the landlord or his representatives; failure of the tenant to accept suitable temporary relocation required by lead-based paint hazard abatement; failure to prepare unit for insect (including bedbug) remediation
		30 days	Nonrestricted only: For any legal reason other than those specified just above (for which 7 days' notice is required)
New Jersey	N.J. Stat. Ann. §§ 2A:18-53(c), 2A:19-61.1, 2A:18-61.2(a)	3 days	Disorderly conduct; willful or grossly negligent destruction of landlord's property; assaults upon or threats against the landlord; termination of tenant's employment as a building manager, janitor, or other employee of the landlord; conviction for use, possession, or manufacture of an illegal drug either on the property or adjacent to it within the last two years, unless the tenant has entered a rehabilitation program (includes harboring anyone so convicted); conviction or civil liability for assault or terroristic threats against the landlord, landlord's family, or landlord's employee within the last two years (includes harboring); liability in a civil action for theft from landlord, landlord's family, landlord's employee, or another tenant; committing or harboring human trafficking
	N.J. Stat. Ann. §§ 2A:18-61.2(b), 2A:18-61.1	One month	Habitual failure to pay rent after written notice; continued violations, despite repeated warnings, of the landlord's reasonable rules and regulations; at the termination of a lease, refusal to accept reasonable changes of substance in the terms and conditions of the lease, including specifically any change in the term thereof

	State Laws on Unconditional Quit Terminations (continued)		
State	**Statute**	**Time to Move Out Before Landlord Can File for Eviction**	**When Unconditional Quit Notice Can Be Used**
New Mexico	N.M. Stat. Ann. § 47-8-33(I)	3 days	Substantial violation of the lease
	N.M. Stat. Ann. § 47-8-33(B) & (C)	7 days	Repeated violation of a term of the rental agreement within 6 months
New York	N.Y. Real Prop. Law § 232-a	30 days	In New York City, holdover of month-to-month tenancy
North Carolina	N.C. Gen. Stat. § 42-26(a)	Immediately	Violation of a lease term that specifies that eviction will result from noncompliance or holdover of tenancy
North Dakota	N.D. Cent. Code § 47-32-02	3 days	Failure to pay rent within 3 days of the due date; holding over after the lease has expired; holding over after a sale or any judicial process ending the tenancy; violating a material term of the lease; using the property in a manner contrary to the agreement of the parties
Ohio	Ohio Rev. Code Ann. §§ 1923.02 to 1923.04, 5321.17	3 days	Nonpayment of rent; violation of a written lease or rental agreement; when the landlord has "reasonable cause to believe" that the tenant has used, sold, or manufactured an illegal drug on the premises (conviction or arrest not required)
Oklahoma	Okla. Stat. Ann. tit. 41, § 132	Immediately	Criminal or drug-related activity or repeated violation of the lease
Oregon	Ore. Rev. Stat. §§ 90.396, 90.403	24 hours	Violence or threats of violence by tenant or a guest; intentionally causing substantial property damage; giving false information on an application within the past year regarding a criminal conviction (landlord must terminate within 30 days of discovering the falsity); committing any act "outrageous in the extreme" (see statute); intentionally or recklessly injuring someone (or placing them in fear of imminent danger) because of the tenant's perception of the person's race, color, religion, national origin, or sexual orientation; second failure to remove a pet that has caused substantial damage
Pennsylvania	68 Pa. Cons. Stat. Ann., § 250.501(b) and (d)	10 days	Nonpayment of rent
		15 days (lease 1 year or less or lease of unspecified time)	Violations of the terms of the lease
		30 days (lease more than 1 year)	Violations of the terms of the lease
	68 Pa. Cons. Stat. Ann., § 250.505-A	10 days (any tenancy)	First conviction for illegal sale, manufacture, or distribution of an illegal drug; repeated use of an illegal drug; seizure by law enforcement of an illegal drug within the leased premises
Rhode Island	R.I. Gen. Laws § 34-18-36(e)	20 days	Repeating an act that violates the lease or rental agreement or affects health or safety twice within 6 months (notice must have been given for the first violation)
	R.I. Gen. Laws §§ 34-18-24, 34-18-36(f)	Immediately	Any tenant who possesses, uses, or sells illegal drugs or who commits or attempts to commit any crime of violence on the premises or in any public space adjacent. "Seasonal tenant" whose lease runs from May 1 to October 15 or from September 1 to June 1 of the next year, with no right of extension or renewal, who has been charged with violating a local occupancy ordinance, making excessive noise, or disturbing the peace

State Laws on Unconditional Quit Terminations (continued)

State	Statute	Time to Move Out Before Landlord Can File for Eviction	When Unconditional Quit Notice Can Be Used
South Carolina	S.C. Code Ann. § 27-40-710	Immediately	Nonpayment of rent after receiving one notification during the tenancy or allowing illegal activities on the property
South Dakota	S.D. Cod. Laws §§ 21-16-1, 21-16-2	3 days	Nonpayment of rent, substantial damage to the property, or holdover
Tennessee	Tenn. Code Ann. §§ 66-28-505(a), 66-7-109	7 days (applies only in counties having a population of more than seventy-five thousand (75,000), according to the 2010 federal census or any subsequent federal census)	Repeating an act that violates the lease or rental agreement or affects health or safety twice within 6 months (notice must have been given for the first violation)
		3 days (applies only in counties of less than 75,000 residents, according to the 2010 federal census or any subsequent federal census; residential tenants in a housing authority; and tenants who are not mentally or physically disabled)	Committing a violent act; engaging in drug-related criminal activity; or behaving in a manner that constitutes or threatens to be a real and present danger to the health, safety, or welfare of the life or property of other tenants, the landlord, the landlord's representatives, or other persons on the premises
Texas	Tex. Prop. Code § 24.005	3 days (lease may specify a shorter or longer time)	Nonpayment of rent or holdover
Utah	Utah Code Ann. § 78B-6-802	3 days	Holdover, assigning or subletting without permission, substantial damage to the property, carrying on an unlawful business on the premises, maintaining a nuisance, committing a criminal act on the premises
Vermont	Vt. Stat. Ann. tit. 9, § 4467	30 days	Three notices for nonpayment or late rent within a 12-month period or any violation of the lease or landlord-tenant law
Virginia	Va. Stat. Ann. §§ 55-248.31, 55-248.32	30 days	Repeated violation of lease (after earlier violation was cured or nonremediable lease violation materially affecting health and safety)
		Immediately	A breach of the lease or rental agreement that is willful or a criminal act, is not remediable, and is a threat to the health or safety of others
Washington	Wash. Rev. Code Ann. § 59.12.030	3 days	Holdover, serious damage to the property, carrying on an unlawful business, maintaining a nuisance, or gang-related activity
West Virginia	W.Va. Code § 55-3A-1	Immediately	Failure to pay rent, violation of any lease provision, or damage to the property

State Laws on Unconditional Quit Terminations (continued)

State	Statute	Time to Move Out Before Landlord Can File for Eviction	When Unconditional Quit Notice Can Be Used
Wisconsin	Wis. Stat. Ann. § 704.17	14 days (month-to-month tenants)	Failure to pay rent, violation of the rental agreement, or substantial damage to the property
		14 days (tenants with a lease of less than one year, or year-to-year tenants)	Failing to pay the rent on time, causing substantial property damage, or violating any lease provision more than once within one year (must have received proper notice for the first violation)
		5 days (all tenants)	Causing a nuisance on the property (landlord must have written notice from a law enforcement agency regarding the nuisance)
Wyoming	Wyo. Stat. §§ 1-21-1002, 1003	3 days	Nonpayment of rent, holdover, damage to premises, interference with another's enjoyment, denying access to landlord, or violating duties defined by statute (such as maintaining unit, complying with lease, disposing of garbage, etc.)

State Small Claims Court Limits

Here are state dollar limits for small claims court and information on whether or not eviction lawsuits are heard in a state's small claims court.

State and Small Claims Website	Statutes	Dollar limit	Evictions
Alabama www.alabamalegalhelp.org (click "Consumer Issues/Small Claims Actions")	Ala. Code §§ 6-3-2; 6-3-7; 12-12-31; 12-12-70;12-12-71	$6,000	No.
Alaska www.courts.alaska.gov/forms/#sc (see "Small Claims" heading)	Alaska Stat. §§ 22.15.040; 22.15.050	$10,000	No. (See www. courtrecords.alaska. gov/webdocs/ forms/sc-100.pdf)
Arizona [1] www.azcourts.gov/selfservicecenter/Self-Service-Forms#SmallClaims http://legal.asua.arizona.edu/sc_ct.html	Ariz. Rev. Stat. Ann. §§ 22-501 to 22-524	$3,500	No. (www. mohavecourts. com/Justice/Jcss_ SmallClaims.html)
Arkansas https://courts.arkansas.gov/sites/default/ files/tree/small_claims_info_0.pdf www.arlegalservices.org/smallclaimspacket	Ark. Const. amend. 80, § 7	$5,000	No.
California www.courtinfo.ca.gov/selfhelp/smallclaims www.dca.ca.gov/publications/small_ claims/index.shtml	Cal. Civ. Proc. Code §§ 116.110 to 116.950	$10,00 for individuals, except that a plaintiff may not file a claim over $2,500 more than twice a year. Limit for local public entity or for businesses is $5,000. $6,500 is the limit in suits by an individual against a guarantor that charges for its guarantor or surety services.	No.
Colorado www.courts.state.co.us/userfiles/file/ Self_Help/smallclaimshandbook%20 finaltocourt%204-11.pdf www.courts.state.co.us/Forms/ SubCategory.cfm?Category=Small	Colo. Rev. Stat. §§ 13-6-401 to 13-6-417	$7,500	No.
Connecticut www.jud.state.ct.us/faq/smallclaims.html	Conn. Gen. Stat. Ann. §§ 47a-34 to 47a-42; 51-15; 51-345; 52-259	$5,000 (except in landlord-tenant security deposit claims).	No.
Delaware http://courts.delaware.gov/JPCourt/ http://courts.delaware.gov/help/ proceedings/jp_startcivil.stm	Del. Code Ann. tit. 10, §§ 9301 to 9640	$15,000	Yes.
District of Columbia www.dccourts.gov/internet/public/aud_ civil/smallclaims.jsf www.dccourts.gov/internet/documents/ SmallClaimsHandbook.pdf	D.C. Code Ann. §§ 11-1301 to 11-1323; 16-3901 to 16-3910; 17-301 to 17-307	$5,000	No.
Florida www.flcourts.org/resources-and-services/ family-courts/family-law-self-help-information/small-claims.stml www.flcourts.org/gen_public/family/ self_help/smallclaims.shtml		$5,000	Yes.

[1] Justice Courts, similar to small claims court but with more procedures, have a limit of $10,000. Rules can be found at Ariz. Rev. Stat. Ann. §§ 22-201 to 22-284. (Arizona)

State Small Claims Court Limits (continued)

State and Small Claims Website	Statutes	Dollar limit	Evictions
Georgia http://consumer.georgia.gov/consumer-topics/magistrate-court	Ga. Code Ann. §§ 15-10-1; 15-10-2; 15-10-40 to 15-10-53; 15-10-80; 15-10-87	$15,000 (no limit in eviction cases).	Yes.
Hawaii www.courts.state.hi.us/self-help/small_claims/small_claims.html	Haw. Rev. Stat. §§ 604-5; 633-27 to 633-36	$5,000; no limit in landlord-tenant residential security deposit cases. For return of leased or rented personal property, the property must not be worth more than $5,000.	No.
Idaho www.courtselfhelp.idaho.gov/small-claims	Idaho Code §§ 1-2301 to 1-2315	$5,000	No.
Illinois [2] www.ag.state.il.us/consumers/smlclaims.html	735 Ill. Comp. Stat. §§ 5/2-101 to 5/2-208; 705 Ill. Comp. Stat. § 205/11	$10,000	Yes.
Indiana www.in.gov/judiciary/2710.htm	Ind. Code Ann. §§ 33-28-3-2 to 33-28-3-10 (circuit court); 33-29-2-1 to 33-29-2-10 (superior court); 33-34-3-1 to 33-34-3-15 (Marion County Small Claims Court)	$6,000 ($8,000 in Marion County)	Yes, if total rent due does not exceed $6,000 ($8,000 in Marion County)
Iowa www.iowacourts.gov/Court_Rules__Forms/Small_Claims_Forms	Iowa Code §§ 631.1 to 631.17	$5,000	Yes.
Kansas www.kscourts.org/rules-procedures-forms/small-claims-information	Kan. Stat. Ann. §§ 61.2701 to 61.2714	$4,000	No.
Kentucky http://courts.ky.gov/courts/jefferson/smallclaims/Pages/default.aspx http://courts.ky.gov/resources/publicationsresources/Publications/P6SmallClaimsHandbookweb.pdf	Ky. Rev. Stat. Ann. §§ 24A.200 to 24A.360	$2,500	Yes.
Louisiana www.lsba.org/Public/CourtStructure.aspx http://brgov.com/dept/citycourt/civilfaqs.htm (Baton Rouge)	La. Rev. Stat. Ann. §§ 13:5200 to 13:5211 (city court); La. Code Civ. Proc., Art. 4831, 4832, 4845, 4901 to 4925, and Art. 42 (justice of the peace court)	$5,000 (city court); $5,000 (justice of the peace, but no limit in eviction case)	No.
Maine www.courts.state.me.us/maine_courts/small_claims/index.shtml	Me. Rev. Stat. Ann. tit. 14, §§ 7481 to 7487	$6,000	Yes.

2   An alternative procedure exists for claims of $1,500 or less in Cook County's Pro Se Court. Plaintiffs represent themselves, and lawyers are allowed for defendants. See www.cookcountyclerkofcourt.org/includes/pages/community_resources/pro_se_faqs.asp. (Illinois)

State Small Claims Court Limits (continued)

State and Small Claims Website	Statutes	Dollar limit	Evictions
Maryland www.courts.state.md.us/legalhelp/smallclaims.html	Md. Code Ann. [Cts. & Jud. Proc.] §§ 4-405; 6-403	$5,000	Yes, as long as the rent claimed does not exceed $5,000.
Massachusetts [3] www.mass.gov/ago/consumer-resources/consumer-assistance/small-claims-court.html	Mass. Gen. Laws ch. 218, §§ 21 to 25; ch. 223, § 6; ch. 93A, § 9 (consumer complaints)	$7,000; no limit for property damage caused by motor vehicle	No.
Michigan http://courts.mi.gov/administration/scao/forms/pages/small-claims.aspx www.michiganlegalaid.org/library_client/resource. 2006-03-07.5270199575	Mich. Comp. Laws §§ 600.8401 to 600.8427	$5,500	No.
Minnesota www.mncourts.gov/selfhelp/?page=313	Minn. Stat. Ann. §§ 491A.01 to 491A.03	$15,000 ($4,000 for claims involving consumer credit transactions, $15,000 for claims involving money or personal property subject to criminal forfeiture)	No.
Mississippi http://courts.ms.gov/trialcourts/justicecourt/justicecourt.html	Miss. Code Ann. §§ 9-11-9 to 9-11-33; 11-9-101 to 11-9-147; 11-25-1; 11-51-85	$3,500	Yes.
Missouri www.courts.mo.gov/page.jsp?id=704 www.mobar.org/uploadedFiles/Home/Publications/Legal_Resources/Brochures_and_Booklets/small%20claims.pdf	Mo. Rev. Stat. §§ 482.300 to 482.365	$5,000	No.
Montana http://doj.mt.gov/consumer/for-consumers/guide-to-small-claims-court	Mont. Code Ann. §§ 25-2-118; 3-12-101 to 3-12-107 (district court); 25-33-101 to 25-33-306 (appeals); 25-35-501 to 25-35-807; 3-10-1001 to 3-10-1004 (justice court)	$7,000	No.
Nebraska https://supremecourt.nebraska.gov/self-help/7223/small-claims-court	Neb. Rev. Stat. §§ 25-505.1; 25-2801 to 25-2807	$3,600 from July 1, 2015 through June 30, 2020 (adjusted every five years based on the Consumer Price Index)	No.
Nevada www.lasvegasjusticecourt.us/divisions/small_claims (Las Vegas) www.washoecounty.us/rjc/divisions/civil/small-claims-civil.php (Reno)	Nev. Rev. Stat. Ann. §§ 73.010 to 73.060	$10,000	No.

[3] Consumer complaint small claims: (1) plaintiff must make written demand for relief at least 30 days before filing suit; (2) attorney fees available; (3) triple damages available. (Massachusetts)

State Small Claims Court Limits (continued)

State and Small Claims Website	Statutes	Dollar limit	Evictions
New Hampshire www.courts.state.nh.us/district/eclaims/index.htm http://doj.nh.gov/consumer/complaints/small-claims.htm	N.H. Rev. Stat. Ann. §§ 503:1 to 503:11	$10,000	No.
New Jersey [4] www.judiciary.state.nj.us/civil/civ-01.htm	N.J. R LAW DIV CIV PT RULE 6:1-2	$3,000 ($5,000 for claims relating to security deposits); certain landlord-tenant suits cannot be brought	No.
New Mexico www.metrocourt.state.nm.us/xnet/pdf/pamphlets/SH101.pdf www.nmcourts.gov/newface/about/index.php www.nmcourts.gov/othercourts/magistrate_brochure.pdf	N.M. Stat. Ann. §§ 34-8A-1 to 34-8A-10 (metropolitan court); 35-3-3, 35-3-5, 35-8-1 and 35-8-2 (magistrate court); 35-11-2, 35-13-1 to 35-13-3 (appeals)	$10,000	Yes.
New York [5] www.courts.state.ny.us/courthelp/smallClaims/index.shtml	N.Y. Uniform City Ct. Act §§ 1801 to 1815, 1801-A to 1814-A (commercial claims); N.Y. Uniform Dist. Ct. Act §§ 1801 to 1815, 1801-A to 1814-A (commercial claims); N.Y. Uniform Just. Ct. Act §§ 1801 to 1815; N.Y. City. Civ. Ct. Act §§ 1801 to 1815; 1801-A to 1814-A (commercial claims)	$5,000 (town and village justice courts, $3,000)	No.
North Carolina www.nccourts.org/Courts/Trial/SClaims/ www.legalaidnc.org/public/learn/publications/small-claims/default.aspx	N. C. Gen. Stat. §§ 7A-210 to 7A-232; 42-29	$10,000	Yes.
North Dakota [6] www.ndcourts.gov/court/forms/small/form1.pdf www.ndcourts.gov/court/forms/Small/forms.htm	N. D. Cent. Code §§ 27-08.1-01 to 27-08.1-08	$15,000	No.

[4] The Special Civil Part, like the small claims court but with more procedures, has a limit of $15,000. See www.judiciary.state.nj.us/civil/civ-03.htm. (New Jersey)

[5] Corporations and partnerships cannot sue in small claims court, but may appear as defendants. (Does not apply to municipal and public benefit corporations and school districts). Instead, they can bring commercial claims, which have similar rules to small claims courts but are subject to these additional restrictions: (1) Same limits and procedures as regular small claims except claim is brought by corporation, partnership, or association; (2) Business must have principal office in N.Y. state; (3) Defendant must reside, be employed, or have a business office in the county where suit is brought. (New York)

[6] Plaintiff may not discontinue once small claims process is begun; if plaintiff seeks to discontinue, claim will be dismissed with prejudice (plaintiff cannot refile claim). (North Dakota)

State Small Claims Court Limits (continued)			
State and Small Claims Website	**Statutes**	**Dollar limit**	**Evictions**
Ohio www.supremecourt.ohio.gov/jcs/ interpretersvcs/forms/english/5.pdf www.ohiolegalservices.org/public/legal_ problem/courts-hearings/representing- yourself-in-court/small-claims/qandact_view	Ohio Rev. Code Ann. §§ 1925.01 to 1925.18	$3,000	No.
Oklahoma [7] www.oklahomacounty.org/courtclerk/ SmallClaims.aspx www.okbar.org/public/brochures/ smallclaimscourt.aspx	Okla. Stat. Ann. tit. 12, §§ 131 to 141; 1751 to 1773	$7,500	No.
Oregon www.osbar.org/public/legalinfo/1061_ SmallClaims.htm	Ore. Rev. Stat. §§ 46.405 to 46.570; 55.011 to 55.140	$10,000	No.
Pennsylvania http://fjd.phila.gov/municipal/civil/ [Philadelphia] www.pabar.org/clips/bringing suitBeforeDJ.pdf	42 Pa. Cons. Stat. Ann. §§ 1123; 1515	$12,000	Yes.
Rhode Island www.courts.ri.gov/Courts/districtcourt/ Pages/Small%20Claims%20Court.aspx] www.ribar.com/for%20the%20public/ findingandchoosingalawyer.aspx	R.I. Gen. Laws §§ 10-16-1 to 10-16-16; 9-4-3; 9-4-4; 9-12-10 (appeals)	$2,500	No.
South Carolina www.judicial.state.sc.us/selfhelp/ FAQMagistrate.pdf	S.C. Code Ann. §§ 22-3-10 to 22-3-320; 15-7-30;18-7-10 to 18-7-30	$7,500	Yes.
South Dakota http://ujs.sd.gov/Small_Claims	S.D. Codified Laws Ann. §§ 15-39-45 to 15-39-78; 16-12B-6; 16-12B-12; 16-12B-16; 16-12C-8; 16-12C-13 to 16-12C-15	$12,000	No.
Tennessee [8] http://tncourts.gov/programs/self-help- center http://gs4.shelbycountytn.gov/gscvinq/ gscv_civildivision (Shelby)	Tenn. Code Ann. §§ 16-15-501 to 16-15-505; 16-15-710 to 16-15-735; 16-15-901 to 16-15-905; 20-4-101; 20-4-103	$25,000. No limit in eviction suits or suits to recover personal property	Yes.

[7] Collection agencies may not sue in small claims court. (Oklahoma)

[8] Tennessee has no actual small claims system, but trials in general sessions court are normally conducted with informal rules. (Tennessee)

State Small Claims Court Limits (continued)

State and Small Claims Website	Statutes	Dollar limit	Evictions
Texas www.txcourts.gov/courts/overview/about-texas-courts/trial-courts.aspx www.tyla.org/tyla/assets/File/HowToSueInJusticeCourt-SB0119E-1013_Web.pdf	Tex. Gov't. Code Ann. § 27.060	$10,000	Separate small claims courts have been abolished as of August 2013; both small claims cases and evictions are heard in Justice Court. Evictions cases are governed by Rules 500-507 and 510 of Part V of the Rules of Civil Procedure.
Utah www.utcourts.gov/howto/smallclaims	Utah Code Ann. §§ 78A-8-101 to 78A-8-109	$10,000	No.
Vermont www.vermontjudiciary.org/SRL/small claims/default.aspx	Vt. Stat. Ann. tit. 12, §§ 5531 to 5541; 402	$5,000	No.
Virginia [9] www.courts.state.va.us/resources/small_claims_court_procedures.pdf www.courts.state.va.us/courts/gd/home.html	Va. Code Ann. §§ 8.01-262; 16.1-76; 16.1-77; 16.1-106; 16.1-113; 16.1-122.1 to 16.1-122.7	$5,000	No.
Washington www.courts.wa.gov/newsinfo/resources/?fa=newsinfo_jury.scc&altMenu=smal www.atg.wa.gov/small-claims-court-0	Wash. Rev. Code Ann. §§ 12.36.010 to 12.40.120; 3.66.040	$5,000	No.
West Virginia www.courtswv.gov/lower-courts	W.Va. Code §§ 50-2-1 to 50-6-3; 56-1-1	$5,000	Yes.
Wisconsin www.wicourts.gov/services/public/selfhelp/smallclaims.htm	Wis. Stat. §§ 799.01 to 799.445; 421.401; 801.50; 808.03	$10,000. No limit in eviction suits.	Yes.
Wyoming www.courts.state.wy.us/WSC/CourtRule?RuleNumber=14	Wyo. Stat. Ann. §§ 1-21-201 to 1-21-205; 5-9-128; 5-9-136	$6,000	No.

[9] General district courts, similar to small claims court but with more procedures, can hear claims up to $25,000. (See Va. Code Ann. §§ 16.1-77 to 16.1-80.) (Virginia)

Landlord's Duty to Rerent

State	Legal authority	Must make reasonable efforts to rerent	Has no duty to look for or rent to a new tenant	Law is unclear or courts are divided on the issue
Alabama	Ala. Code §§ 35-9A-105, 35-9A-423	✓		
Alaska	Alaska Stat. § 34.03.230(c)	✓		
Arizona	Ariz. Rev. Stat. § 33-1370	✓		
Arkansas	*Weingarten/Arkansas, Inc. v. ABC Interstate Theatres, Inc.,* 811 S.W.2d 295 (Ark. 1991)		✓	
California	Cal. Civ. Code § 1951.2	✓		
Colorado	*Schneiker v. Gordon,* 732 P.2d 603 (Colo. 1987)	✓ [1]	✓	
Connecticut	Conn. Gen. Stat. Ann. § 47a-11a	✓		
Delaware	25 Del. Code Ann. § 5507(d)(2)	✓		
District of Columbia	*Int'l Comm'n on English Liturgy v. Schwartz,* 573 A.2d 1303 (D.C. 1990)		✓ [2]	
Florida	Fla. Stat. Ann. § 83.595		✓ [3]	
Georgia	*Peterson v. Midas Realty Corp.,* 287 S.E.2d 61 (Ga. Ct. App. 1981)		✓	
Hawaii	Haw. Rev. Stat. § 521-70(d)	✓		
Idaho	*Consol. Ag v. Rangen, Inc.,* 128 Idaho 228 (Idaho 1996)	✓		
Illinois	735 Ill. Comp. Stat. § 5/9-213.1	✓		
Indiana	*Nylen v. Park Doral Apartments,* 535 N.E.2d 178 (Ind. Ct. App. 1989)	✓		
Iowa	Iowa Code § 562A.29(3)	✓		
Kansas	Kan. Stat. Ann. § 58-2565(c)	✓		
Kentucky	Ky. Rev. Stat. Ann. § 383.670	✓		
Louisiana	La. Civ. Code § 2002, *Gray v. Kanavel,* 508 So.2d 970 (La. Ct. App. 1987)			✓ [4]
Maine	14 Me. Rev. Stat. Ann. § 6010-A	✓		
Maryland	Md. Code Ann., [Real Prop.] § 8-207	✓		
Massachusetts	*Edmands v. Rust & Richardson Drug Co.,* 191 Mass. 123, 128 (1906) and assorted other cases	✓	✓	
Michigan	*Fox v. Roethlisberger,* 85 N.W.2d 73 (Mich. 1957)	✓		
Minnesota	*Control Data Corp. v. Metro Office Parks Co.,* 296 Minn. 302 (Minn. 1973)		✓	

[1] Case law is not dispositive, but state practice seems to require mitigation. See ColoradoLegalServices.org ("Breaking a Lease—What You Need to Know"). (Colorado)

[2] Despite this legal authority, D.C. attorneys report that judges take failure to mitigate into consideration when ascertaining the landlord's damages. (District of Columbia)

[3] Landlord has the option of rerenting, standing by and doing nothing (tenant remains liable for rent as it comes due), or invoking its right to a liquidated damages, or early termination provision. Latter remedy is available only if the lease includes a liquidated damages addendum, or addition, that provides for no more than two months' damages and requires tenant to give no more than 60 days' notice. Liquidated damages provision must substantially include specified language in Fla Stat. Ann. § 83.595. (Florida)

[4] Court decisions are not uniform although more recent decisions appear to require mitigation. (Louisiana)

Landlord's Duty to Rerent (continued)

State	Legal authority	Must make reasonable efforts to rerent	Has no duty to look for or rent to a new tenant	Law is unclear or courts are divided on the issue
Mississippi	*Alsup v. Banks*, 9 So. 895 (Miss. 1891)		✓ [5]	
Missouri	*Rhoden Inv. Co. v. Sears, Roebuck & Co.*, 499 S.W.2d 375 (Mo. 1973), Mo. Rev. Stat. § 535.300	✓ [6]		
Montana	Mont. Code Ann. § 70-24-426	✓		
Nebraska	Neb. Rev. Stat. § 76-1432	✓		
Nevada	Nev. Rev. Stat. Ann. § 118.175	✓		
New Hampshire	*Wen v. Arlen's, Inc.*, 103 A.2d 86 (N.H. 1954), *Modular Mfg., Inc. v. Dernham Co.*, 65 B.R. 856 (Bankr. D. N.H. 1986)			✓
New Jersey	*Sommer v. Kridel*, 378 A.2d 767 (N.J. 1977)	✓		
New Mexico	N.M. Stat. Ann. § 47-8-6	✓		
New York	*Rios v. Carrillo*, 53 AD3d 111, 115 (2nd Dept., 2008); *Gordon v. Raymond Eshaghoff*, 60 AD 3d 807, (2nd Dept., decided March 17, 2009,) and *Smith v. James*, 22 Misc. 3d 128 (A) Supreme Court, Appellate Term, 9th & 10th Dist., 2009)		✓	
North Carolina	*Isbey v. Crews*, 284 S.E.2d 534 (N.C. Ct. App. 1981)	✓		
North Dakota	N.D. Cent. Code § 47-16-13.5	✓		
Ohio	*Stern v. Taft*, 361 N.E.2d 279 (Ct. App. 1976)	✓ [7]		
Oklahoma	41 Okla. Stat. Ann. § 129	✓		
Oregon	Ore. Rev. Stat. § 90.410	✓		
Pennsylvania	*Stonehedge Square Ltd. P'ship v. Movie Merchs.*, 715 A.2d 1082 (Pa. 1998)		✓	
Rhode Island	R.I. Gen. Laws § 34-18-40	✓		
South Carolina	S.C. Code Ann. § 27-40-730 (c)	✓		
South Dakota	No cases or statutes in South Dakota discuss this issue.			✓
Tennessee	Tenn. Code Ann. § 66-28-507 (c)	✓ [8]		
Texas	Tex. Prop. Code Ann. § 91.006	✓		
Utah	Utah Code Ann. § 78B-6-816, *Reid v. Mutual of Omaha Ins. Co.*, 776 P.2d 896 (Utah 1989)	✓		
Vermont	9 Vt. Stat. Ann. § 4462		✓ [5]	
Virginia	Va. Code Ann. §§ 55-248.33, 55-248.35	✓		
Washington	Wash. Rev. Code Ann. § 59.18.310	✓ [9]		
West Virginia	W.Va. Code § 37-6-7, *Teller v. McCoy*, 253 S.E.2d 114 (W.Va. 1978)	✓		
Wisconsin	Wis. Stat. Ann. § 704.29	✓		
Wyoming	*Goodwin v. Upper Crust, Inc.*, 624 P.2d 1192 (Wyo. 1981)	✓		

[5] Many Mississippi attorneys believe this old case is not sound authority, and that a trial judge would find a duty to mitigate in spite of it. (Mississippi)

[6] Landlord must mitigate only if intending to use tenant's security deposit to cover future unpaid rent. (Missouri)

[7] Duty to mitigate applies in absence of any clause that purports to relieve the landlord of this duty (courts might enforce such a clause). (Ohio)

[8] Applies only in counties having a population of more than 75,000, according to the 2010 federal census or any subsequent federal census. (See Tenn. Code Ann. § 66-28-102.) (Tennessee)

[9] Detailed procedures must be followed when premises are vacant due to tenant's death. See Wash. Rev. Code Ann. § 59.18.595. (Washington)

Consequences of Self-Help Evictions

State	Amount Tenant Can Sue For	Statute Provides for Tenant's Court Costs & Attorney Fees	Statute Gives Tenant the Right to Stay	Statute or Legal Authority
Alabama	Self-help evictions are not allowed, but no specific penalties are provided (judge decides on consequences).	N/A	N/A	Ala. Code § 35-9A-427
Alaska	One and one-half times the actual damages. If tenant elects to terminate the lease, landlord must return entire security deposit.	No	Yes	Alaska Stat. § 34.03.210
Arizona	Two months' rent or twice the actual damages, whichever is greater. If tenant elects to terminate the lease, landlord must return entire security deposit.	No	Yes	Ariz. Rev. Stat. § 33-1367
Arkansas	Self-help evictions are not allowed, but it's up to the court to determine damages.	N/A	N/A	*Gorman v. Ratliff*, 712 S.W.2d 888 (1986)
California	Actual damages plus $100 per day of violation ($250 minimum). Tenant may ask for an injunction prohibiting any further violation during the court action.	Yes	Yes	Cal. Civ. Code § 789.3
Colorado	Tenant may sue for any damages.	N/A	N/A	Colo. Rev. Stat. § 38-12-510
Connecticut	Double actual damages. Landlord may also be prosecuted for a misdemeanor.	Yes	Yes	Conn. Gen. Stat. Ann. §§ 47a-43, 47a-46, 53a-214
Delaware	Triple damages or three times per diem rent for time excluded, whichever is greater. Tenant may recover court costs, but not attorney fees.	Yes	Yes	Del. Code Ann. tit. 25, § 5313
District of Columbia	Actual and punitive damages.	No	No	*Mendes v. Johnson*, 389 A.2d 781 (D.C. 1978)
Florida	Actual damages or three months' rent, whichever is greater.	Yes	No	Fla. Stat. Ann. § 83.67
Georgia	Landlord may not resort to self-help evictions. Damages are determined by the court.	N/A	N/A	*Forrest v. Peacock*, 363 S.E. 2d 581 (1987), reversed on other grounds, 368 S.E.2d 519 (1988)
Hawaii	Two months' rent or free occupancy for two months (tenant must have been excluded overnight). Court may order landlord to stop illegal conduct.	Yes	Yes	Haw. Rev. Stat. § 521-63(c)
Idaho				
Illinois				
Indiana	Statute doesn't specify damages.	N/A	N/A	Ind. Code Ann. § 32-31-5-6
Iowa	Actual damages, plus punitive damages up to twice the monthly rent and attorney's fees. If tenant elects to terminate the lease, landlord must return entire security deposit.	Yes	Yes	Iowa Code § 562A.26

Consequences of Self-Help Evictions (continued)

State	Amount Tenant Can Sue For	Statute Provides for Tenant's Court Costs & Attorney Fees	Statute Gives Tenant the Right to Stay	Statute or Legal Authority
Kansas	Actual damages or one and one-half months' rent, whichever is greater.	No	Yes	Kan. Stat. Ann. § 58-2563
Kentucky	Three months' rent.	Yes	Yes	Ky. Rev. Stat. Ann. § 383.655
Louisiana	Landlord may not resort to self-help evictions. Damages are determined by the court.	N/A	N/A	*Weber v. McMillan*, 285 So.2d 349 (1973)
Maine	Actual damages or $250, whichever is greater. The court may award costs and fees to landlord if it finds that the tenant brought a frivolous court lawsuit or one intended to harass.	Yes	No	Me. Rev. Stat. Ann. tit. 14, § 6014
Maryland	Landlord may not resort to self-help evictions. Damages are determined by the court.	N/A	N/A	*In re Promower, Inc., v. Scuderi, et al.*, 56 B.R. 619 (U.S. Bankruptcy Court, D. Maryland, 1986)
Massachusetts	Three months' rent or three times the actual damages.	Yes	Yes	Mass. Gen. Laws ch. 186, § 15F
Michigan	Up to three times actual damages or $200, whichever is greater.	No	Yes	Mich. Comp. Laws § 600.2918
Minnesota	Statute doesn't specify damages.	Yes	Yes	Minn. Stat. § 504B.375
Mississippi				
Missouri	Landlord may not resort to self-help evictions. Damages are determined by the court.	N/A	N/A	*Steinke v. Leight*, 235 S.W.2d 115 (1950)
Montana	Three months' rent or three times the actual damages, whichever is greater.	Yes	Yes	Mont. Code Ann. § 70-24-411
Nebraska	Up to three months' rent.	Yes	Yes	Neb. Rev. Stat. § 76-1430
Nevada	Up to $2,500 or actual damages, whichever is greater, or both. If tenant elects to terminate rental agreement or lease, landlord must return entire security deposit and any prepaid rent.	No	Yes	Nev. Rev. Stat. Ann. § 118A.390
New Hampshire	Actual damages or $1,000, whichever is greater; if court finds that landlord knowingly or willingly broke the law, two to three times this amount. Each day that a violation continues is a separate violation. Court may order a tenant who brings a frivolous suit or one intended to harass to pay landlord's costs and fees.	Yes	Yes	N.H. Rev. Stat. Ann. §§ 540-A:3, 540-A:4, 358-A:10
New Jersey	Self-help is prohibited, and landlord who engages in self-help is a "disorderly person," a criminal offense that subjects the landlord to up to six months in jail.	N/A	N/A	N.J. Stat. Ann. § 2C:43-8
New Mexico	A prorated share of the rent for each day of violation, actual damages, and civil penalty of twice the monthly rent.	Yes	Yes	N.M. Stat. Ann. § 47-8-36

	Consequences of Self-Help Evictions (continued)			
State	Amount Tenant Can Sue For	Statute Provides for Tenant's Court Costs & Attorney Fees	Statute Gives Tenant the Right to Stay	Statute or Legal Authority
New York	Three times the actual damages.	No	No	N.Y. Real Prop. Acts Law § 853
North Carolina	Actual damages.	No	Yes	N.C. Gen. Stat. § 42-25.9
North Dakota	Triple damages.	No	No	N.D. Cent. Code § 32-03-29
Ohio	Actual damages.	Yes	No	Ohio Rev. Code Ann. § 5321.15
Oklahoma	Twice the average monthly rental or twice the actual damages, whichever is greater.	No	Yes	Okla. Stat. tit. 41, § 123
Oregon	Two months' rent or twice the actual damages, whichever is greater.	No	Yes	Ore. Rev. Stat. § 90.375
Pennsylvania	Self-help evictions are not allowed, but no specific penalties are provided (it's up to the court to determine damages).	N/A	N/A	Wofford v. Vavreck, 22 Pa. D. & C.3d 444 (1981); Kuriger v. Cramer, 498 A.2d 1331 (1985)
Rhode Island	Three months' rent or three times the actual damages, whichever is greater.	Yes	Yes	R.I. Gen. Laws § 34-18-34
South Carolina	Three months' rent or twice the actual damages, whichever is greater.	Yes	Yes	S.C. Code Ann. § 27-40-660
South Dakota	Two months' rent. If tenant elects to terminate the lease, landlord must return entire security deposit.	No	Yes	S.D. Codified Laws Ann. § 43-32-6
Tennessee	Actual and punitive damages. If tenant elects to terminate the lease, landlord must return entire security deposit.	Yes	Yes	Tenn. Code Ann. § 66-28-504
Texas	A civil penalty of one month's rent plus $1,000, actual damages, court costs, and reasonable attorney's fees.	Yes	Yes	Tex. Prop. Code §§ 92.008, 92.0081, 92.009
Utah	Self-help evictions are not allowed, but no specific penalties are provided.	No	No	Utah Code Ann. § 78B-6-814
Vermont	Unspecified damages. Court may award costs and fees to landlord if the court finds that the tenant brought a frivolous lawsuit or one intended to harass.	Yes	Yes	Vt. Stat. Ann. tit. 9, §§ 4463, 4464
Virginia	Actual damages.	Yes	Yes	Va. Code Ann. §§ 55-248.26, 55-225.2
Washington	Actual damages. For utility shut-offs only, actual damages and up to $100 per day of no service. Court may award costs and fees to the prevailing party.	Yes	Yes	Wash. Rev. Code Ann. § 59.18.300
West Virginia				
Wisconsin	Self-help evictions are prohibited. The court will determine damages.	N/A	N/A	Wis. Adm. Code § ATCP 134.09 (7)
Wyoming				

How to Use the Interactive Forms on the Nolo Website

Throughis book comes with eForms that you can access online at **www.nolo.com/back-of-book/ELLI.html** To use the files, your computer must have specific software programs installed. Here is a list of types of files provided by this book, as well as the software programs you'll need to access them:

- **RTF.** You can open, edit, print, and save these form files with most word processing programs such as Microsoft *Word*, Windows *WordPad*, and recent versions of *WordPerfect*.
- **PDF.** You can view these files with Adobe *Reader*, free software from www.adobe.com. Government PDFs are sometimes fillable using your computer, but most PDFs are designed to be printed out and completed by hand.

Editing RTFs

Here are some general instructions about editing RTF forms in your word processing program. Refer to the book's instructions and sample agreements for help about what should go in each blank.

- **Underlines.** Underlines indicate where to enter information. After filling in the needed text, delete the underline. In most word processing programs you can do this by highlighting the underlined portion and typing CTRL-U.

- **Bracketed and italicized text.** Bracketed and italicized text indicates instructions. Be sure to remove all instructional text before you finalize your document.
- **Optional text.** Optional text gives you the choice to include or exclude text. Delete any optional text you don't want to use. Renumber numbered items, if necessary.
- **Alternative text.** Alternative text gives you the choice between two or more text options. Delete those options you don't want to use. Renumber numbered items, if necessary.
- **Signature lines.** Signature lines should appear on a page with at least some text from the document itself.

Every word processing program uses different commands to open, format, save, and print documents, so refer to your software's help documents for help using your program. Nolo cannot provide technical support for questions about how to use your computer or your software.

> **CAUTION**
> **In accordance with U.S. copyright laws, the forms provided by this book are for your personal use only.**

List of Forms Available on the Nolo Website

Go to: **www.nolo.com/back-of-book/ELLI.html**

Forms in RTF Format

File Title	File Name
Agreement for Delayed or Partial Rent Payments	Delay.rtf
Agreement Regarding Tenant Alterations to Rental Unit	Alteration.rtf
Amendment to Lease or Rental Agreement	Amendment.rtf
Consent to Assignment of Lease	AssignConsent.rtf
Consent to Contact References and Perform Credit Check	CheckConsent.rtf
Cosigner Agreement	Cosigner.rtf
Fixed-Term Residential Lease	FixedLease.rtf
Fixed-Term Residential Lease (Spanish Version)	PlazoFijo.rtf
Landlord/Tenant Checklist	Checklist.rtf
Landlord-Tenant Agreement to Terminate Lease	Terminate.rtf
Letter for Returning Entire Security Deposit	DepositReturn.rtf
Letter to Original Tenant and New Cotenant	TenantLetter.rtf
Month-to-Month Residential Rental Agreement	MonthToMonth.rtf
Month-to-Month Residential Rental Agreement (Spanish version)	Mensual.rtf
Move-In Letter	MoveIn.rtf
Move-Out Letter	MoveOut.rtf
Notice of Conditional Acceptance Based on Credit Report or Other Information	Acceptance.rtf
Notice of Denial Based on Credit Report or Other Information	Denial.rtf
Notice of Intent to Enter Dwelling Unit	EntryNotice.rtf
Property Manager Agreement	Manager.rtf

Forms in RTF Format

File Title	File Name
Receipt and Holding Deposit Agreement	Receipt.rtf
Rental Application	Application.rtf
Resident's Maintenance/Repair Request	RepairRequest.rtf
Security Deposit Itemization (Deductions for Repairs and Cleaning)	Itemization1.rtf
Security Deposit Itemization (Deductions for Repairs, Cleaning, and Unpaid Rent)	Itemization2.rtf
Semiannual Safety and Maintenance Update	SafetyUpdate.rtf
Tenant's Notice of Intent to Move Out	MoveNotice.rtf
Tenant References	References.rtf
Time Estimate for Repair	Repair.rtf
Verification of Disabled Status	StatusVerification.rtf
Warning Letter for Lease or Rental Agreement Violation	Warning.rtf

Forms in Adobe Acrobat PDF Format

File Title	File Name
Disclosure of Information on Lead-Based Paint or Lead-Based Paint Hazards (English version)	lesr_eng.pdf
Disclosure of Information on Lead-Based Paint or Lead-Based Paint Hazards (Spanish version)	spanless.pdf
Protect Your Family From Lead in Your Home	leadpdfe.pdf
Protect Your Family From Lead in Your Home (Spanish version)	leadpdfs.pdf
Rental Application	Application.pdf
Resident's Maintenance/Repair Request	RepairRequest.pdf
Tenant's Notice of Intent to Move Out	MoveNotice.pdf

Index

H

Habitability. *See* Implied warranty of habitability

Hawaii, 51, 72, 87, 110, 146, 202

Hazardous materials

　delegating repairs involving, 214

　See also Environmental health hazards

Health inspectors' right of entry, 294–295

High-crime areas, 266

Hold-harmless clauses of leases or rental agreements, 57

Holding deposits, 30, 31, 32

Holdover tenants, 53, 306, 311, 331–332

Home business of tenant, 40

Housesitters, 177

Housing codes

　changes to, 184

　compliance, 182, 184

　enforcement of, 183

　and minor repairs, 209, 210

　occupancy limits, 112–116

　overview, 181–182

　repairs required by, 151

　violations of, 183, 184, 206–207, 211–212, 236–237

　See also Implied warranty of habitability; Nuisances

HUD. *See* U.S. Department of Housing and Urban Development

I

Idaho, 182

Identity theft. *See* Security breaches

IGR (insect growth regulators), 260

Illegal activities. *See* Criminal activity prevention

Illegal "self-help" evictions, 372, 376–377

Illinois, 75, 86, 110, 159, 166, 254, 371

Immigration laws and employees, 136–137

Immigration Reform and Control Act (1986), 124

Immigration status of prospective tenants, 16, 99

Implied covenant of quiet enjoyment, 49–50, 182, 185, 212, 279

Implied promises, 187–188, 210–211

Implied warranty of habitability

　and bedbug eradication, 261

　compensation for living in substandard conditions, 200–201

　and drug-dealing tenants, 279

　"fit" and "habitable," 182–183

　illegal attempts to exempt your property, 199

　and maintenance updates, 197

　natural disasters causing damage, 208

　and nuisance of smoke, 185

　overview, 181–182, 237

　and repairs, 186, 201

　tenant moving out for habitability violations, 207–209

　as tenant's absolute right, 212

　tenant's right to move out, 207–209, 308

　See also Housing codes

Improvements and alterations by tenants, 48–49, 215–219, 331, 349, 369

Incentives

　deals, 76, 117

　financial incentive vs. eviction, 278

　for prospective tenants, 32

　for tenant of property you are selling, 294

　tenant subsequently breaks the lease, 317

Income, applicant's, 20, 92–93

Income taxes of employees, 130

Independent contractors

　emergency contact information, 142

　employees vs., 130

　exterminator for bedbugs, 259–260

　insurance policies of, 196

　and lead hazard removal, 249–251, 253

　management companies as, 137

　mold remediation companies, 258, 259

　and OSHA regulations, 243–244

　security consultants or services, 270, 271

　supervising work of, 229

　tenants hired for repairs or maintenance as, 214

Independent management companies, 116–117, 137–139

　See also Property managers

Indiana, 166, 256

Individual Taxpayer Identification Number (ITIN), 10, 16

Inheriting rental property, 37

Inheritors of a deceased tenant's estate, 318

Insect growth regulators (IGR), 260

Insecticides, 260

Inspections

　of apparently abandoned rental unit, 312

　before tenant moves in, 146–152

　by municipal inspectors, 294–295

　safety inspections, 197–198, 227, 292

NOLO | *Online Legal Forms*

Nolo offers a large library of legal solutions and forms, created by Nolo's in-house legal staff. These reliable documents can be prepared in minutes.

Create a Document

- **Incorporation.** Incorporate your business in any state.
- **LLC Formations.** Gain asset protection and pass-through tax status in any state.
- **Wills.** Nolo has helped people make over 2 million wills. Is it time to make or revise yours?
- **Living Trust (avoid probate).** Plan now to save your family the cost, delays, and hassle of probate.
- **Trademark.** Protect the name of your business or product.
- **Provisional Patent.** Preserve your rights under patent law and claim "patent pending" status.

Download a Legal Form

Nolo.com has hundreds of top quality legal forms available for download—bills of sale, promissory notes, nondisclosure agreements, LLC operating agreements, corporate minutes, commercial lease and sublease, motor vehicle bill of sale, consignment agreements and many, many more.

Review Your Documents

Many lawyers in Nolo's consumer-friendly lawyer directory will review Nolo documents for a very reasonable fee. Check their detailed profiles at **Nolo.com/lawyers**.

Nolo's Bestselling Books

NOLO

Save 15% *off your next order*

Register your Nolo purchase, and we'll send you a
coupon for 15% off your next Nolo.com order!

Nolo.com/customer-support/productregistration

On Nolo.com you'll also find:

Books & Software

Nolo publishes hundreds of great books and software programs for consumers and
business owners. Order a copy, or download an ebook version instantly, at Nolo.com.

Online Legal Documents

You can quickly and easily make a will or living trust, form an LLC or corporation, apply
for a trademark or provisional patent, or make hundreds of other forms—online.

Free Legal Information

Thousands of articles answer common questions about everyday legal issues
including wills, bankruptcy, small business formation, divorce, patents, employment,
and much more.

Plain-English Legal Dictionary

Stumped by jargon? Look it up in America's most up-to-date source for definitions
of legal terms, free at nolo.com.

Lawyer Directory

Nolo's consumer-friendly lawyer directory provides in-depth profiles of lawyers all
over America. You'll find all the information you need to choose the right lawyer.